# Representative Government in Modern Europe

Fifth Edition

**Fifth Edition**

# Representative Government in Modern Europe

Michael Gallagher
Michael Laver
Peter Mair

*The McGraw·Hill Companies*

London   Boston   Burr Ridge, IL   Dubuque, IA   Madison, WI   New York   San Francisco
St. Louis   Bangkok   Bogotá   Caracas   Kuala Lumpur   Lisbon   Madrid   Mexico City
Milan   Montreal   New Delhi   Santiago   Seoul   Singapore   Sydney   Taipei   Toronto

Representative Government in Modern Europe
© Michael Gallagher, Michael Laver, Peter Mair
ISBN-13 978-0-07-712967-5
ISBN-10 0-07-712967-9

**Mixed Sources**
Product group from well-managed
forests and other controlled sources
www.fsc.org  Cert no. TT-COC-002769
© 1996 Forest Stewardship Council

Published by McGraw-Hill Education
Shoppenhangers Road
Maidenhead
Berkshire
SL6 2QL
Telephone: 44 (0) 1628 502 500
Fax: 44 (0) 1628 770 224
Website: *www.mcgraw-hill.co.uk*

**British Library Cataloguing in Publication Data**
A catalogue record for this book is available from the British Library

**Library of Congress Cataloguing in Publication Data**
The Library of Congress data for this book has been applied for from the Library of Congress

Acquisitions Editor: Mark Kavanagh
Development Editor: Jackie Curthoys
Marketing Manager: Vanessa Boddington
Production Editor: Alison Davis

Text Design by Hard Lines
Cover design by Adam Renvoize
Printed and bound in the UK by Bell and Bain Ltd, Glasgow
Page Layout: SR Nova Pvt Ltd., Bangalore, India

ISBN-13 978-0-07-712967-5
ISBN-10 0-07-712967-9

The **McGraw·Hill** Companies

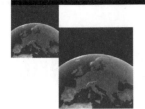

# Brief Table of Contents

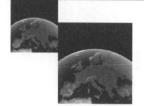

# Detailed Table of Contents

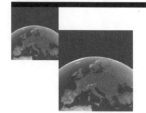

# List of Figures

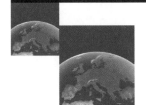

# List of Tables

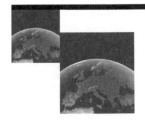

# Preface

This is the fifth edition of *Representative Government in Modern Europe*. The very fact that there is a fifth edition is evidence of continuing demand for a book that deals in a comprehensive way with the politics of representation in an area of the world that contains a goodly proportion of the world's democracies. Especially since the transitions to democracy in central and eastern Europe, which had not even begun when we wrote the first edition, but which have now for the most part put down strong roots, modern Europe is a rich field of study for anyone who is interested in representative government. Set in the context of the full range of political arrangements we find distributed over the entire planet, there are important ways in which the representative democracies of modern Europe all look quite similar, sharing many common cultural, economic and historical traditions. At the same time, they also differ from each other in systematic and important ways.

As before, our discussions of representative government in modern Europe cover countries that have joined the European Union (EU) plus Iceland, Norway and Switzerland. The latter three are unquestionably part of modern Europe but, for reasons that mostly have to do with domestic politics, they remain outside the EU. Since the last edition, however, the EU has expanded to comprise 27 member states, with the accession of Bulgaria and Romania. These countries are now included in this book. Taking the 30 countries we now study there are, more than ever, big variations in the types of electoral and party system we encounter, in the ways the administration of the state is organized, and in many other matters besides. We learn a lot from analysing the political impact of these variations, while holding constant the broad 'European' context. Homing in on the effects of particular causal factors, while holding as much as we can constant, is the essence of the comparative method. This makes modern Europe an extraordinarily good laboratory for anyone with a serious interest in representative government, and this is true whether or not Europe is the region they most want to know about. This, in short, is a book both for readers who are interested in modern Europe and for readers who are interested in comparative politics more generally, and see Europe as an excellent laboratory for exercising their ideas.

While expanding our country coverage we have been careful to retain the fundamental philosophy that has guided this book through its various editions and, to judge from the feedback we receive, is a major part of its appeal to readers. Our discussions are structured by what we see as the major substantive and intellectual themes in the study of representative government. We try as far as possible to discuss the full range of European countries, large and small, in the context of these themes, rather than organizing the book as a set of country studies. We have tried to keep the book as up to date as possible in its discussions of ongoing theoretical and empirical work on core features of representative government in modern Europe. Reviews of the book have stressed its value in introducing readers to current debates among those who analyse European politics, and this edition sets out to keep our discussion of these debates as up to the minute as possible. Naturally, we have also updated the data in most tables to make these as complete and current as possible.

The internet is increasingly the prime source of information for those looking to keep abreast of politics in Europe. In some chapters we have supplied a list of internet resources – sites that are particularly useful or, as specialist sites, possibly obscure – but in others we place our trust in the readers' own web navigation skills, not least because, in our experience, students are at least as likely to inform us about useful sites as we are to inform them.

We have been helped enormously while producing this fifth edition by advice and assistance from friends, colleagues and anonymous reviewers – far too many to list here. We are also grateful for the great help given to us in keeping things up to date by our researchers, many of whom also made significant intellectual contributions to the revised manuscript. These were: Fernando Casal Bertoa, Iulia Cioroianu, Drew Conway, Pablo Fernandez-Vazquez, Alex Herzog, Marko Klasnja, Didac Queralt Jimenez and David Willumsen.

What above all encouraged us to produce a fifth edition is that we remain every bit as intrigued by and enthused about the study of modern European politics as we were when we wrote the first edition over 20 years ago. Indeed, the events of recent decades have shown beyond all doubt why it is that developing a good understanding of political processes in general, and of representative government in particular, is such an important intellectual project.

Michael Gallagher
Michael Laver
Peter Mair

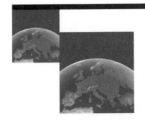

# About the Authors

**MICHAEL GALLAGHER** is Professor of Comparative Politics in the Department of Political Science, Trinity College, University of Dublin. He has also been a visiting professor at New York University, the City University of Hong Kong, and the University of Lille. He is co-editor of *Politics in the Republic of Ireland* (5th edition, Routledge, 2010), *The Politics of Electoral Systems* (Oxford, 2008), *How Ireland Voted 2007* (Palgrave Macmillan, 2008), *The Referendum Experience in Europe* (Palgrave Macmillan, 1996) and *Candidate Selection in Comparative Perspective* (Sage, 1988). His research interests include electoral systems and political parties.

**MICHAEL LAVER** is Professor of Politics at New York University. His current research interests are dynamic models of party competition, and methods for estimating the policy positions of important political actors. He is author of *Multiparty Government* (with Norman Schofield), *Making and Breaking Governments* (with Kenneth Shepsle), *Party Policy in Modern Democracies* (with Kenneth Benoit) and *Party Competition: An Agent-Based Model* (with Ernest Sergenti).

**PETER MAIR** is Professor of Comparative Politics at the European University Institute in Florence, Italy, and is co-editor of the journal *West European Politics*. He previously taught at the universities of Limerick, Strathclyde, Manchester and Leiden. He is a former winner of the Stein Rokkan Prize, and has recently co-edited *Political Representation and European Governance* (Routledge, 2010), *Accountability and European Governance* (Routledge, 2011) and *Party Government and Party Patronage in Contemporary European Democracies* (Oxford, 2011). He is co-director of the Observatory on Political Parties and Representation, based at the EUI in Florence, and is currently engaged in a wide-ranging study of political parties and contemporary democracy.

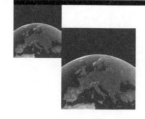

# Publisher's Acknowledgements

Our thanks go to the following reviewers for their comments at various stages in the text's development.

| | |
|---|---|
| Deniz Aksoy | Penn State University, US |
| Gerard Alexander | University of Virginia, US |
| Kai Arzheimer | University of Mainz, Germany |
| Michael Bruter | London School of Economics, UK |
| Clay Clemens | The College of William & Mary, US |
| Astrid Hedin | Uppsala University, Sweden |
| Derek Hutcheson | University College, Dublin, Ireland |
| Seth Jolly | Syracuse, US |
| Monique Leyenaar | Radboud University, The Netherlands |
| Ecaterina McDonagh | Dublin City University, Ireland |
| Peter Neidergaard | Copenhagen University, Denmark |
| Aneta Spendzharova | University of Maastricht, The Netherlands |
| Liam Weeks | University College, Cork, Ireland |

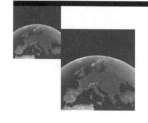

# Custom Publishing Solutions: Let us help make our content your solution

At McGraw-Hill Education our aim is to help lecturers to find the most suitable content for their needs delivered to their students in the most appropriate way. Our **custom publishing solutions** offer the ideal combination of content delivered in the way which best suits lecturer and students.

Our custom publishing programme offers lecturers the opportunity to select just the chapters or sections of material they wish to deliver to their students from a database called CREATE™ at **www.mcgrawhillcreate.com**

**CREATE**™ contains over two million pages of content from:

- textbooks
- professional books
- case books - Harvard Articles, Insead, Ivey, Darden, Thunderbird and BusinessWeek
- Taking Sides - debate materials

across the following imprints:
- McGraw-Hill Education
- Open University Press
- Harvard Business Publishing
- US and European material

There is also the option to include additional material authored by lecturers in the custom product – this does not necessarily have to be in English.

We will take care of everything from start to finish in the process of developing and delivering a custom product to ensure that lecturers and students receive exactly the material needed in the most suitable way.

With a Custom Publishing Solution, students enjoy the best selection of material deemed to be the most suitable for learning everything they need for their courses – something of real value to support their learning. Teachers are able to use exactly the material they want, in the way they want, to support their teaching on the course.

Please contact your local McGraw-Hill representative with any questions or alternatively contact Warren Eels **e:** warren_eels@mcgraw-hill.com.

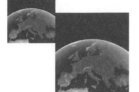

# CHAPTER 1

# Introduction

In this book we set out to discuss modern European politics. We do so from a distinctive point of view. First, we concentrate on the politics of representation, focusing especially on institutions, parties and governments. Second, our approach is wholeheartedly comparative. We organize our discussions around particular important themes in the politics of representation, not around particular important countries.

We are convinced that the benefits of our approach far exceed the costs. By restricting ourselves to the politics of representation, we give ourselves the space to take seriously the large body of comparative research and writing on this that can be found in the recent literature. By insisting on a comparative rather than a country by country approach, we give ourselves the opportunity to bring a much larger amount of evidence to bear on the problem at hand.

We feel strongly that many of the most important features of the politics of representation in modern Europe are overlooked by the still too common tendency to concentrate on only a few 'important' countries. The smaller European democracies are often the sources of the most suggestive evidence on matters as diverse as the nature of party systems, the patterns in voting behaviour, the importance of electoral laws, and the dynamics of coalition bargaining. If we want to find out how proportional representation electoral systems work, we do well to begin with the Netherlands. Comparing Ireland and Denmark is a good way to begin to understand what makes some minority governments stable and others not. If we wish to understand the recent successes of the far right, then we should certainly look at Austria, Hungary and Switzerland. The list could be extended indefinitely. Confining ourselves to a few big countries is not the way to come to grips with some of the most important and exciting features of the politics of representation in modern Europe.

Looking at the smaller countries as well as their bigger neighbours also reminds us of one of the great benefits of studying European politics, which is that it provides political scientists with one of the best laboratories for comparative political research. Within a shared general heritage, Europe offers a huge variety of practices in political behaviour and values, as well as an enormous array of institutional designs. Comparing European countries across space and across time offers researchers an almost endless capacity to explore the variety of conditions in which politics matters and through which politics can be explained.

Our way of doing things does have costs, of course, and it is as well to be aware of them. The most obvious has to do with depth. In a book of a certain size, when we broaden our coverage across a very wide range of countries, then our treatment of each is inevitably bound to be less detailed. In our view, the benefits of being comprehensive across Europe are much greater than the benefits of adding more detail on a small number of countries, but others may come to the opposite conclusion about this inevitable trade-off. There are plenty of other books and edited collections for these people to read, so we need not feel too sorry for them, but we should remember that they do have a point. In taking several steps back to expand our field of view, we may lose sight of important detail – but we may also gain a better sense of perspective.

Another potential cost has to do with consistency. We cannot, obviously, discuss every European country in relation to every theme that we select. But, if we pick and choose those countries to illustrate particular points, the reader may not get a clear sense of what is going on in any particular European country. We adopt a three-pronged approach to this problem, which we hope allows us to get the best of both worlds. First, we concentrate in the text on those examples best suited to help us explore particular themes. We do this to maximize the benefits of our broadly based approach. Second, although some of our information comes from authors who studied only a limited subset of European countries, we do our best in tables summarizing particular themes to include entries for every European country with which we are concerned. We do this to ensure consistency and completeness, at least at the level of basic information.

Finally, we have selected a group of eight countries on which we lavish somewhat greater attention. These are Denmark, France, Germany, Italy, the Netherlands, Poland, Spain and the United Kingdom. We selected these countries because between them they provide considerable variation on most of the important dimensions of politics that we wish to consider. They give us a wide geographic spread, from the north to the deep south. They include large and small countries; rural and urban countries; Protestant, Catholic and 'mixed religion' countries; richer and poorer countries; countries with stable and with unstable governments; new and old democracies; post-authoritarian and post-communist democracies; the countries with the most and the least proportional electoral systems; and so on. No matter which examples we have used in the main text, we pause in our discussion at key points to present a short box that summarizes key information for each of the eight countries in our core group. In this way we allow interested readers to follow this core group through our entire discussion, reaping many of the benefits of the more restricted country-based approach while paying none of its costs.

## 1.1 Modern Europe

In earlier editions of this book we had to make difficult decisions about how to incorporate the rapidly unfolding developments in post-communist Europe. Although politics in these systems was increasingly comparable to that in the west, the countries were still undergoing formative structuring processes of democratic development. Moreover, they obviously lacked the long history of post-war democratic experience that we frequently draw on in the western European examples to emphasize how some features of representative government remain the same and how other features change. By now, however, such contrasts are no longer problematic. Despite their different experiences and their different path to democracy, 10 of the post-communist polities are now full members of the European Union. For this reason, we now integrate these countries within our general thematic approach, even though we sometimes continue to make a distinction in the questions we address to the two groups of polities. Thus, for example, while we look for evidence of electoral dealignment and change within the long-established western democracies, we tend to look for evidence of alignment and stabilization in the post-communist world. And while we are usually concerned with how institutions adapt in the western countries, and whether political organizations survive, in the post-communist cases we are often more concerned with how institutions are established in the first place, and whether political organizations are being built. There is now one Europe, but within it there are distinct clusters of states, each with its own set of characteristics, path dependences and political processes.

We should also say a word about terminology and, to begin with, about our coverage of Europe's largest state, the Federal Republic of Germany. Before 1990 this state was familiarly referred to as West Germany, but after the absorption of the former communist East German state (the German Democratic Republic) this name ceased to be appropriate. In the following chapters, therefore, we have referred to 'Germany' when discussing features of the modern German state, but we also occasionally use the term 'West Germany' when referring to events or patterns prior to unification. Another country for which terminology is in some sense ambiguous is the United Kingdom. Formally, the United Kingdom of Great Britain and Northern Ireland includes England, Wales and Scotland (all three of which make up what is known as Britain or Great Britain), as well as Northern Ireland. In the tables and displays that follow, we always use the term United Kingdom, or UK, for the sake of consistency. In the text, for stylistic reasons, we refer sometimes to Britain and sometimes to the United Kingdom. Finally, throughout the book as a whole, we try to deal with patterns of representative government in a total of 30 countries – the 27 members of the European Union, plus Iceland, Norway and Switzerland. We call this world 'modern Europe', but of course the real Europe is more than this. The real Europe spreads further east and south, to include the states that were once part of the former Yugoslavia, as well as Albania and Moldova. In some versions it also includes Turkey, which in 2004 was invited to open negotiations with a view to possibly becoming a member of the European Union. In other versions it also includes Belarus and Ukraine, which currently border the Union, or even Georgia and Armenia, which border Turkey. Indeed, if and when Turkey does join the EU, the enlarged borders of the Union will extend to Syria, Iraq and Iran.

European politics is as fascinating and exciting at the beginning of the twenty-first century as at any time over the past 1000 years. The long-lasting post-war division of Europe into East and West is now part of that history, with formerly communist European states having established multiparty democracy, and, in the case of 10 of these countries, now joining their Western neighbours as part of a united Europe. As it now stands, the Union has 27 member states and a population of almost 500 million people. Although the area over which it is spread is only roughly half the size of the United States, it stretches from the Arctic Circle in the north to the shores of the Mediterranean in the south, and from the wild Atlantic coastline of Ireland in the west to the gentle and balmy coastline of the Greek islands in the east. As well as widening, the unique experiment of European integration continues to deepen, with European law superseding national law in increasingly many areas, with key decision-making in most policy areas occurring at the European level, and with a single currency – however threatened by the debt crises – creating a common means of exchange and a common monetary policy across many of the member states of the Union. In this book we introduce and interpret the politics of this distinctive and ever-changing continent.

## 1.2 Plan of campaign

In this book we describe representative government in our version of modern Europe in terms of an arena in which the hopes and fears of citizens are transformed by complex political interactions into the public policies that affect their everyday lives. At the end of this chapter we provide some basic information about modern European countries that should help set our subsequent discussions in context, often comparing the patterns in Europe with those in the United States in order to offer a more standardized perspective. In the remainder of the book we concentrate on two basic aspects of representative government. The first concerns the institutions and 'rules of the game' that create the arena for politics in modern Europe. The second concerns the political behaviour that actually takes place in that arena.

Although every European country is different, the institutions of politics in most modern European states share some fundamental similarities and are collectively quite distinct from those to be found in the United States – for example, something that makes politics in Washington a different business from politics in London, say, or in Berlin, Brussels, Stockholm, Rome, Madrid or Prague. This is because modern European states are almost all run according to the principles of *parliamentary government*, a set of institutions that gives a particularly important role to political parties and parliamentary elections. Constitutionally, these rules have to do with the relationship between legislature, executive and judiciary – that is, between parliament, government and the courts – and with the role of the head of state.

In the next five chapters, therefore, we look at five different features of the institutions of representative government in modern Europe. We look in Chapter 2 at the executive, and specifically at the head of state, the prime minister and the cabinet – in a constitutional setting where the head of state is typically far less important than in the United States of America. In Chapter 3 we examine the role of the legislature, which is typically responsible not only for legislating but also for generating and maintaining a government. In Chapter 4 we look at the role of constitutions, and at that of the courts in interpreting these constitutions. Here we also draw attention to the way in which the judiciary can have an important political role, despite popular notions that it is 'above' politics, and despite traditional European resistance to be governed by judges. Chapters 5 and 6 present the more general context of national politics in modern Europe. In Chapter 5 we look at supranational politics, and in particular at the European Union (EU), now such an important feature of the political landscape of modern Europe, and such an integral part of the domestic politics of most member states. In Chapter 6 we consider both the civil service and subnational systems of local and regional administration.

Every one of the institutional features discussed in Chapters 2 to 6 has a fundamental impact on the context of representative government in modern Europe, shaping the political behaviour that is the focus of the rest of the book. In Chapters 7 to 14 we move on to trace the behaviour that transforms individual interests into public policies through a number of stages. We begin in Chapter 7 by looking at the *party systems* that determine the choices offered to voters at election time. Here we introduce the party systems in the eight countries to which we pay special attention, and we puzzle over whether we can speak of a 'typical' European party system. In Chapter 8 we present the 'families' of parties that make up the cast of characters in most European elections, including communist parties, social democratic parties, liberal parties, Christian democratic parties, conservative parties, ecology parties, and the far right. We focus particular attention on the long-term patterns in the aggregate electoral development of these separate families across the past half-century, and we ask whether similar patterns can be seen in the emerging post-communist party systems. In Chapter 9 we consider the traditional cleavage structures that underpin party choice in the established democracies, as well as how these patterns might now be changing, and whether, at the end of a century of mass politics, national electorates and party systems themselves are in a state of flux. We also look to see whether electoral patterns in the post-communist states are finally beginning to settle down. In Chapter 10 we step inside parties to examine some of their workings – how they organize, how they choose their leaders and candidates, and how they raise money – and we look to see how organizations are developing in the new democracies in post-communist Europe.

Chapters 7 to 10 thus take into consideration the politics of representation from the bottom up, from the perspective of voters, elections and parties. Chapters 12 and 13 look at politics from the top down, from the perspective of legislatures and governments. Chapter 11 examines the key institution that links the two levels, the electoral system that turns votes cast by the electorate into seats won by legislators. Many different electoral systems are used throughout Europe, which is the world's premier laboratory for all who are interested in the workings of electoral law. Having examined how European legislatures are produced, we move on in Chapter 12 to look at what they do. The most important thing that they do, as we shall have seen in Chapters 2 and 3, is to produce and support a government. Because few European parties win a majority of seats in the legislature, forming a government typically involves forming a coalition. In Chapter 13 we acknowledge that the formal institutions of representative government are not the be all and end all of politics in modern Europe, and we look at politics outside the party system. Many political decisions – most of those to do with the vital area of economic policy, for example – are taken by governments without recourse to the legislature. These decisions may well be strongly influenced by those who set out to apply pressure to the government, whether as part of the political establishment in an alternative institutional setting or as political outsiders using the tried and tested techniques of pressure politics. Finally, in Chapter 14 we explore whether the formation of different governments with different party memberships actually makes a difference in the policies that eventually emerge. If governments do not make a difference, after all, it is difficult to see why we should take an interest in the parties, the elections, the coalition bargaining, and all of the other steps in the political process by which European governments are selected.

Notwithstanding the trend towards European integration, and the role model provided by western European states for the emerging democracies of the former eastern Europe, modern

Europe remains a collection of countries with intriguingly different cultures, traditions and political styles. There is no such thing as a 'typical' European country, which is why it is so important to look at the group of European countries taken as a whole, rather than at individual European countries one at a time. When we look at European politics in this way, distinct patterns do emerge. It is the search for such patterns that is the guiding purpose of this book. Before beginning the search, however, we devote the rest of this chapter to providing some basic information about the group of countries with which we are dealing. First we provide a brief overview of the past century of European history, and then we go on to outline some of the basic facts and figures about modern Europe.

## 1.3 A brief century of European history

This is a book about the contemporary politics of Europe, not about European history. Even so, every student of the present must be aware of the impact of the past, and there is no denying that history has played a part in shaping and constraining the options facing even the most powerful political leaders and governments in the early twenty-first century. We shall be making reference many times in this book to aspects of the history of particular states, but we shall take the opportunity here to provide a very brief overview of some of the main features of Europe's rich history during the last 100 years.

Anyone examining today a map of Europe as it stood in 1914 will be struck by the mixture of stability and change in the evolution of boundaries during the twentieth century. On the western half of the continent there has been hardly any change. The only exception is that whereas in 1914 the whole of Ireland was a part of the United Kingdom of Great Britain and Ireland (UK), in 1920 26 of the 32 counties on the island broke away to form an independent state. The other six counties were divided between *unionists*, who wanted to remain within the UK, and *nationalists*, who wanted to join the rest of the island in breaking the union with Britain. Since the unionists constituted a majority, these counties, now known as Northern Ireland, stayed in the UK. Northern Ireland has experienced many political difficulties, although these are now for the most part addressed through non-violent means, in contrast to the situation in the 1970s and the 1980s. Of the 30 countries that we write about in this book, nine of the ten that can be found in the south-western quadrant of the continent (Belgium, France, Ireland, Italy, Luxembourg, the Netherlands, Portugal, Spain, Switzerland and the United Kingdom) existed as independent states in 1914, with Ireland as the only subsequent addition to the list.

Scandinavia, in the north of the continent, also looks much the same. The main change here is that a century ago Finland was an autonomous Grand Duchy of the Russian empire, but it became fully independent in 1917. In addition, Iceland was governed by Denmark until achieving independence in 1944. Of today's five Nordic countries (Denmark, Finland, Iceland, Norway and Sweden), three were independent countries in 1914, and the other two were recognizable entities, even if not fully sovereign. Most of south-eastern Europe falls outside the ambit of this book, but we do cover the three states that are part of the EU: Greece, Cyprus and Malta. Of these three, Greece has a long history as an independent state, but a hundred years ago both Cyprus and Malta were ruled by Britain.

The relative stability in the borders within Scandinavia and south-western Europe over the past 100 years should not lead us to assume that all of the various nations have a timeless history as nation-states. Norway, for example, had become independent from Sweden only in 1905, while Belgium had come into being as an independent state in 1830 as a fusion of two linguistic groups – French speakers and Dutch speakers – the uneasy relations between whom still dominate Belgian politics. Italy, today one of Europe's largest states, had been divided into separate kingdoms and republics for many centuries, and only in 1870 was the Risorgimento (the movement for a united Italy) completed by Garibaldi, when his troops entered Rome. Still, even if some west European states were relatively new or even fragile a century ago, the configuration of 1914 has changed very little subsequently.

The same is not true of central and eastern Europe. In this book we cover 12 countries that belong geographically to this broad area: Austria, Bulgaria, the Czech Republic, Estonia, Germany, Hungary, Latvia, Lithuania, Poland, Romania, Slovakia and Slovenia. A hundred years ago, the territory now covered by these 12 states was ruled by just three: the German, Austro-Hungarian and Russian empires. Each of these empires bears the same name as one of today's states, but is by no means identical to it. Germany at that time consisted not just of present-day German territory but also of a large part of today's Poland, and indeed it extended right around the Baltic coast to include what is now the Kaliningrad enclave of Russia and part of Lithuania. Despite its size, and its industrial and military power, Germany, like Italy, was a relatively new creation: a unified Germany had not emerged until 1870, being forged by the Prussian leader Bismarck, who had brought together, in many cases by force, the plethora of separate kingdoms that had existed hitherto. The Russian empire covered Finland, the three states on the eastern shores of the Baltic Sea (Estonia, Latvia and Lithuania), and much of today's Poland. The Austro-Hungarian empire was a particularly unwieldy construction that included, besides the two countries after which it was named and which jointly ruled it, much of the Balkans. Today's countries of the Czech Republic, Slovakia and Slovenia all fell within its borders, as did parts of Romania. Bulgaria, ruled from Turkey, was formerly part of the Ottoman empire.

Borders of states, and indeed the existence of states, had proved anything but durable in central and eastern Europe over many centuries. This can be illustrated by the case of Poland, which had waxed and waned in dramatic fashion. A Polish state was established by around the year 1000, but by the middle of the thirteenth century it had largely fallen apart. A century later it had been unified once again, and at the start of the seventeenth century it was the largest country in Europe, with a territory that covered most of today's Lithuania, Belarus and Ukraine (almost as far as the Black Sea), along with parts of Latvia and Russia. However, its position between two powerful expansionist states, Prussia and Russia, made it permanently vulnerable to invasion, and in 1795 it simply disappeared from the map for more than 100 years as a result of the *Third Partition*, under which Prussia took its western half and Russia most of the east, with Austria–Hungary receiving a slice of its southern territories.

The First World War (1914–1918) led to a large-scale redrawing of the map of central and eastern Europe. The victors (Britain, France and Italy) imposed harsh terms on the losing allies, Germany and Austria-Hungary. As well as losing significant eastern territories to Poland, which now reappeared as a state, Germany was compelled to pay heavy financial reparations to the victorious countries. The Austro-Hungarian empire disintegrated. Austria and Hungary became separate states, and two new states emerged from within its former territory: Czechoslovakia and Yugoslavia. Neither of these 'successor states' was very cohesive: both Czechoslovakia and Yugoslavia contained distinct linguistic groups, some of whom wanted independence. Russia had been an initial member of the coalition that eventually won the war, but it had pulled out in

1917 because of its internal upheavals, which resulted, in October of that year, in its being taken over by the communists under the leadership of Lenin. After the war it was forced to relinquish a lot of territory to the reborn Polish state, and to grant independence to Finland, Estonia, Latvia and Lithuania. In 1922 the communists created the Union of Soviet Socialist Republics (USSR), widely known as the Soviet Union, which came to extend over much of the Transcaucasus and central Asia as well as Belarus and Ukraine, but ultimate power always rested in Moscow. The war was worldwide in two senses: first, in that fighting took place right across the globe in a number of the colonies of the European powers; and, second, in that troops from many other countries took part in the fighting in Europe. The entry of the USA in 1917 helped to bring the conflict to an end at a high cost in American lives, and many troops from Canada, Australia, New Zealand and Africa were also killed.

After the carnage of the First World War, during which at least seven million people were killed, many political leaders piously resolved that 'this must never happen again'. However, the settlement imposed on the losers has subsequently been seen by historians as having contained the seeds of the Second World War (1939–1945). In particular, many Germans perceived the Versailles Treaty, which set out the terms by which post-war Germany had to abide, as a 'diktat', and nationalistic German politicians found fertile ground for their arguments that German interests had been sold out at Versailles by political leaders who had been, at best, too accommodating to the demands of Germany's rivals, and, at worst, traitors. These political leaders represented the *Weimar Republic*, established in 1919 by liberal and left-wing political forces, and although its constitution provided for a model democratic state, many vested interests on the right wing of German politics never regarded it as fully legitimate. In addition, it suffered from government instability, and became further discredited by the perception that it was dominated by deal-making politicians with little interest in the people they nominally represented.

The inability of the Weimar regime to cope with the problems of economic depression in the late 1920s spelled its end. This provided the opportunity for the Nazi Party (the NSDAP, or National Socialist German Workers' Party), led by Adolf Hitler, to sweep to power. The Nazis had fought three elections in the 1920s with hardly any success, but now they began to grow dramatically. Business interests, along with the self-employed and farmers, saw them as an effective way to combat the perceived communist threat; the traditional nationalist right agreed with their invective against the Versailles Diktat and the liberal democracy of the Weimar regime; many workers were receptive to their arguments that only the Nazis could provide a return to full employment; and their overt anti-semitism also struck a chord with many Germans. As a result, the Nazis advanced from only 12 seats at the 1928 election to 107 in 1930 and 230 by July 1932. In the January 1933 election – by which time Hitler had already been appointed chancellor (prime minister) – they won 288 seats out of 647, twice as many as any other party. The institutions of liberal democracy were swiftly abolished or taken over, and by July 1933 the Nazis were the only party legally permitted to exist in Germany.

It was not just in Germany that democracy was replaced by authoritarianism. In Italy the fascist leader Benito Mussolini had come to power in 1922, and within a few years all parties except his own had been banned. In Spain an unstable post-war democracy was interrupted, first, by a military takeover in 1923, and then, after the restoration of a parliamentary regime in 1930, by a civil war launched in 1936 by General Francisco Franco. After three years of bitter struggle, in which at least half a million people were killed, Franco, who received military support from both Hitler and Mussolini, won unchallenged power, which he retained until his death in 1975, at which point a return to democracy began. In the adjoining country of Portugal functioning democracy had never got fully off the ground, and the limited democracy that existed was overthrown by the military in 1926. Portugal was dominated from 1928 until his incapacitation in the late 1960s by the conservative dictator António de Oliveira Salazar; it was not until 1974 that democratic government was established.

In eastern and central Europe, too, democracy did not flourish. In virtually all of the states established after the First World War, the initially archetypal liberal democratic regimes were either transformed into mere facade democracies or even overthrown. Leaders such as Admiral Miklós Horthy in Hungary, Marshal Josef Piłsudski in Poland, Tsar Boris III in Bulgaria, King Carol II in Romania, and Engelbert Dollfuss and Kurt von Schuschnigg in Austria ruled in an authoritarian manner, and were not accountable to their citizens through the mechanisms of representative government that we examine in this book. In Estonia the acting head of government, Konstantin Päts, became a *de facto* dictator from 1934 onwards. In Latvia the prime minister, Kärlis Ulmanis, staged a coup in 1934, abolishing parliament and banning parties. In the third Baltic state, Lithuania, the democratic experiment ended even earlier, as a military coup established an authoritarian regime under Antanas Smetona in 1926. In the whole region of eastern and central Europe, only Czechoslovakia remained a recognizable democracy, with regular free and fair elections, during the interwar period. The political cleavages that dominated politics in these countries in this period, and in some cases even the same parties, tended to re-emerge when competitive politics was restored in the 1990s after the end of communism. Regimes in western Europe and Scandinavia, in contrast, survived as liberal democracies in the interwar period; even though in many cases significant fascist or anti-democrat forces emerged, none of these was able to come close to gaining power.

By the late 1930s Hitler was behaving in an ever more aggressive manner towards his neighbours, making demands on those parts of their territories that were occupied by ethnic Germans, and implementing an extensive programme of rearming in violation of the Versailles Treaty. The main western powers, Britain and France, adopted a policy of appeasement, making concessions to him in the hope that if his immediate demands were met he would be content. Thus his troops were permitted to reoccupy the Rhineland (a part of Germany bordering France in which, under the terms of Versailles, Germany was not permitted to station troops) in 1936; Austria was allowed to merge with Germany (the so-called *Anschluss*) in March 1938; and in September 1938 the western powers pressed Czechoslovakia to hand over to Germany a region, known to Germans as the Sudetenland, demanded by Hitler. However, each concession simply led to further and greater demands. In August 1939 Hitler cleared the way for war by signing, to the amazement of the rest of the world, a non-aggression pact with the Soviet Union (known as the Nazi–Soviet pact, or the Hitler–Stalin pact), thereby securing his eastern flank. Under secret protocols of the pact, the two countries would each occupy half of Poland, while the USSR would take control of Estonia, Latvia and Lithuania.

The Nazis' invasion of Poland on 1 September 1939 marked the beginning of the Second World War. After quick successes in Poland, France, Belgium, the Netherlands, Denmark and Norway, Germany was unsuccessful in its attempts to mount an invasion of Britain. In 1941 Hitler broke the terms of the Nazi–Soviet pact by launching an unprovoked attack on the USSR. This was spectacularly successful initially, as German armies captured vast amounts of territory and reached the outskirts of Moscow, but the tide turned after their defeat at Stalingrad in the winter of 1942–43. From the summer of 1943 Soviet armies pushed German forces back across the ground they had earlier captured, and with the entry of the USA into the war as from December 1941, following Pearl Harbor, and the landings of Allied forces in occupied France in 1944, the complete defeat of Germany became inevitable. With Soviet troops just a few hundred yards from his bunker in Berlin, Hitler committed suicide in April 1945, and Germany surrendered a week later. The Second World War had been even more destructive of human life than the first, with non-combatants suffering greatly: perhaps 18 million non-combatants died, including approximately 6 million Jews killed by the Nazis in fulfilment of their genocidal policy.

After the war the map of central and eastern Europe was redrawn once again. Much of what had been eastern Poland prior to 1939 was now transferred into Belarus, one of the republics in the USSR, and much of what had been eastern Germany now became part of Poland. The reduced Germany was partitioned between the four main victorious powers. While the Americans, British and French merged their zones and established the liberal-democratic Federal Republic of Germany (often known as West Germany) as a functioning democracy in the west European mode, the Soviet zone became a communist state, titled the German Democratic Republic (often known as East Germany). The USSR retained the three small Baltic states that it had captured in 1940; these were now made Soviet republics, something that the rest of the world refused to recognize *de jure*, though it could do little about the annexation *de facto*. Indeed, virtually all those territories from which the Soviet Union's armies had driven out the German forces now remained firmly under Soviet control; the only exception was Austria, which was occupied by the USSR in 1945 but from which its troops withdrew in 1955. In most cases there was one fairly free post-war election but, whatever the result, by the end of the 1940s the country was firmly under complete communist control. The most blatant example of a communist takeover was in Czechoslovakia, where the local communist party and its supporters thwarted plans to hold an election in February 1948, and a few weeks later the non-communist foreign minister Jan Masaryk fell to his death (presumably pushed) from a window. A phrase used by Winston Churchill in 1946 gained wide currency: he declared that an *iron curtain* had descended across the continent.

From the late 1940s to the late 1980s, politics took very different forms on the two sides of this divide – which is why the first edition of this book did not cover the former communist countries at all, and the second and third editions dealt with them in a chapter of their own. In the western part of the continent, liberal democracy has not been seriously challenged since 1945. Learning the lessons of the Versailles Diktat, the victorious Allies did not impose 'victors' justice' upon the defeated Germany but, rather, sought to integrate it fully into the west European mainstream. This approach was formalized in the creation of what has become the European Union, which we discuss fully in Chapter 5. Italy, too, was reintegrated into the west European core. The other countries that had had autocratic regimes in 1939 took longer to join the democratic fold. Portugal and Spain, as we have said, did not emerge from dictatorship until the 1970s. Greece, which had had periods of military rule between the wars, returned to democracy in 1946; it again fell under military rule between 1967 and 1974, but then civilian rule was restored.

In central and eastern Europe, in contrast, the institutions of representative government had little meaning, because all power lay with the communist party. Even though 'elections' took place, voters had no power of choice, since there was only one candidate per constituency. Parliaments, governments and courts were all controlled by the party. Ultimate control, indeed, lay not with the national communist party but in Moscow; only in Yugoslavia, Albania and, in later years, Romania were communist regimes established that were not subject to the command of the USSR. There were occasional protests against communist rule. In October 1956 the Hungarian communist party leadership, responding to popular pressure, declared that the country would revert to a multiparty system and would leave the Warsaw Pact (the military alliance among the communist countries). A week later, Soviet forces invaded and restored orthodox communist rule. Czechoslovakia experienced a very similar 'Prague spring' in 1968; again, the experiment was promptly terminated by an invasion by Warsaw Pact armed forces. In the early 1980s the Solidarity trade union mounted a challenge to the regime in Poland, posing a threat to which the government responded by imposing martial law in 1981. There were also serious risings against the regimes in East Germany in 1953 and in Poland in 1956.

Although the communist parties justified their control of these states in terms of protecting the socio-economic rights of workers, rights that were not always well respected in the capitalist west, it was apparent that the regimes were accepted by their populations only under duress. The borders between the Warsaw Pact countries and the west were heavily guarded and lined with barbed wire, and the most striking symbol of the divide between east and west was created in 1961, when the East German regime built the Berlin Wall along the border between the two halves of the divided city. This reinforcement of the borders was explained as being necessary to protect against possible invasion by the west, but few doubted that the real reason was to prevent citizens of the Warsaw Pact countries moving, or 'escaping', to the west. There were some differences between the regimes, it is true. After 1956 the Hungarian regime gradually became the most liberal and least repressive in the communist world, allowing a degree of small-scale private enterprise and some space for civil society. Similarly, the Polish regime had to confront a strongly resistant civil society, and was unable ever to overcome completely the power that the Catholic church wielded. In contrast, the regimes in Czechoslovakia, the Baltic states and East Germany were seen as particularly hard-line and orthodox. Still, the differences between the various communist regimes were minor compared with the differences between these regimes and those in the west.

The communist regimes crumbled at the end of the 1980s. In their early years they had delivered a degree of economic growth, which was at least a trade-off against the lack of personal liberty, but by the 1980s it was obvious to their citizens that economically they were falling steadily further behind the west. Change in three countries precipitated the collapse of communism. First, in Poland, opposition forces, particularly the Solidarity movement and the Catholic church, were able to win ever more political space for themselves, and it was clear that the communist party's grip was weakening. In June 1989, following round-table talks between the regime and Solidarity, semi-competitive elections were held for parliament: although the communists were guaranteed control of a majority of the seats, Solidarity won virtually all the seats for which it was entitled to compete, thus removing all legitimacy from continued communist rule. Second, the Hungarian party leadership became convinced of the need for fundamental reform. By the spring of 1989 it had rebranded the 1956 uprising a 'popular uprising' rather than the 'counter-revolution' it had previously been labelled, and was moving towards a mixed economy and a multiparty system. Third, changes in Russia, with the arrival as leader of the reformist Mikhail Gorbachev, meant that reformists in other communist parties were encouraged, and that everyone knew there was no longer a danger of the USSR invading if any country tried to leave the fold.

The end came once Hungary opened its borders to the west in September 1989. Many East Germans travelled to Hungary and from there made their way to the west. Unable to stop the flow, in a highly symbolic gesture on 9 November the East German regime knocked a hole in the

Berlin Wall, allowing its citizens to travel to the west. There were mass protests against the communist regimes by huge crowds right across the Warsaw Pact area, and by the end of 1989 all these regimes had collapsed. Moreover, in all the countries that we cover in this book, with the partial exception of Romania, these regime changes were achieved without violence.

The map of Europe changed yet again as a result of these developments. First, the three Baltic states that had been taken over by the USSR in 1940 reclaimed their independence in 1990. Second, Germany was reunited in October 1990 when East Germany merged with the western state. Third, the multinational republic of Yugoslavia broke up into six new states. One of these, Slovenia – which declared independence in 1991, and had to fight a 10-day 'mini-war' against the Yugoslav army to secure this – is included in this book. Fourth, in 1992 Slovakia, which like Slovenia had never previously enjoyed independent statehood, broke away from Czechoslovakia in the so-called velvet divorce.

Throughout this book we refer repeatedly to 'post-communist' countries, by which we mean Bulgaria, the Czech Republic, Estonia, Hungary, Latvia, Lithuania, Poland, Romania, Slovakia and Slovenia. Of course, there are many differences between these countries: they have different levels of economic development and linguistic homogeneity, and they have different cultures. By referring to them all as post-communist countries we do not imply that they are all essentially the same. However, we do believe that their long experience of a common form of rule from which they all emerged at about the same time does make it sensible to look for common patterns in their contemporary politics – and indeed, as this book will show, those patterns emerge in several areas of political life.

## 1.4 The vital statistics

The modern Europe that we deal with in this book is divided into 30 independent states, with a total population of some 500 million – more than half as big again as that of the United States. As Table 1.1 shows, population density, on average about four times greater in the European Union area than in the United States, is – after the tiny island of Malta – highest in Belgium, the Netherlands, Germany and the UK. Indeed, the area around the Netherlands and northern Germany is a very heavily populated region, where the concentration of major cities and industrial infrastructure supports a population of more than 350 persons per square kilometre. In the more peripheral areas of modern Europe, by contrast, population density can be relatively low: there are only some 20 persons per square kilometre in the vast but unevenly populated country of Sweden, and 62 persons per square kilometre in the harsh and inhospitable landscape of Basilicata in southern Italy. In the peripheral Irish Republic, for example, a land area of some 70 000 square kilometres supports a population of some 4 million; in the more centrally located Netherlands, on the other hand, an area of some 41 000 square kilometres, little more than half that of Ireland, supports a population of more than 16 million, almost four times that of Ireland.

Modern Europe is an immensely diverse area, riven by many cultural, religious and linguistic boundaries. Despite an overwhelmingly Christian culture, for example, a marked source of traditional diversity is created by the balance between Roman Catholics and the various Protestant denominations. Table 1.1 shows that in some places Roman Catholics are an overwhelming majority – for example, in the southern and western parts of Europe, as well as in Poland. In Greece the vast majority formally adhere to the Greek Orthodox Church, which is quite close to Catholicism. In a second group of countries Roman Catholics tend to be very thin on the ground,

**TABLE 1.1** General and demographic data on European democracies

| Country | Capital | Total area (× 1000 km²) | Population 2010 total (× 1000) | Population per km² | Catholic (%) | Gender empowerment measure (GEM value), 2008[a] |
|---|---|---|---|---|---|---|
| Austria | Vienna | 84 | 8375 | 97 | 18.1 | 0.788 |
| Belgium | Brussels | 31 | 10827 | 355 | 17.8 | 0.850 |
| Bulgaria | Sofia | 111 | 7564 | 68 | 1 | 0.606 |
| Cyprus | Nicosia | 9 | 798 | 8 | 1.3 | 0.580 |
| Czech Republic | Prague | 79 | 10507 | 132 | 26.8 | 0.627 |
| Denmark | Copenhagen | 43 | 5535 | 128 | 2 | 0.875 |
| Estonia | Tallinn | 45 | 1340 | 30 | 0.4 | 0.637 |
| Finland | Helsinki | 338 | 5351 | 16 | 0.1 | 0.887 |
| France | Paris | 549 | 64714 | 115 | 86 | 0.718 |
| Germany | Berlin | 357 | 81800 | 229 | 34 | 0.831 |
| Greece | Athens | 132 | 11295 | 85 | 0.4 | 0.622 |
| Hungary | Budapest | 93 | 10013 | 108 | 51.9 | 0.569 |
| Iceland | Reykjavik | 103 | 318 | 3 | 2.5 | 0.862 |
| Ireland | Dublin | 70 | 4456 | 73.4 | 87.4 | 0.699 |
| Italy | Rome | 301 | 60340 | 199.8 | 90 | 0.693 |
| Latvia | Riga | 64 | 2248 | 34 | 17.1 | 0.619 |
| Lithuania | Vilnius | 65 | 3329 | 54 | 79 | 0.669 |
| Luxembourg | Luxembourg | 3 | 502 | 194 | 87 | – |
| Malta | Valletta | 0.3 | 413 | 1262 | 98 | 0.514 |
| Netherlands | Amsterdam | 41 | 16578 | 400 | 30 | 0.859 |
| Norway | Oslo | 324 | 4858 | 13 | 1 | 0.910 |
| Poland | Warsaw | 313 | 38167 | 122 | 89.8 | 0.614 |
| Portugal | Lisbon | 92 | 10638 | 115 | 84.5 | 0.692 |
| Romania | Bucharest | 238 | 21462 | 90 | 4.7 | 0.497 |
| Slovakia | Bratislava | 49 | 5425 | 111 | 68.9 | 0.630 |
| Slovenia | Ljublijana | 20 | 2047 | 100 | 57.8 | 0.611 |
| Spain | Madrid | 505 | 45989 | 91 | 94 | 0.794 |
| Sweden | Stockholm | 450 | 9341 | 21 | 1.6 | 0.906 |
| Switzerland | Berne | 41 | 7783 | 188 | 41.8 | 0.660 |
| United Kingdom | London | 245 | 62008 | 255 | 14 | 0.783 |
| United States | Washington, D.C. | 9372 | 310232 | 32 | 23.9 | 0.762 |
| EU-27 | Brussels | 4324 | 501062 | 116 | – | – |

[a] The higher the value of this index, the stronger the position of women in society and in politics.

*Sources*: United Nations, *Human Development Report*, 2009, 2010; CIA, *World Factbook*, 2010.

particularly in the Scandinavian countries – Denmark, Finland, Iceland, Norway and Sweden – where the overwhelming proportion of the population is at least nominally affiliated to one of a variety of Protestant denominations. Indeed, it is really only in the central spine of Europe – in Germany, the Netherlands and Switzerland, as well as in the former Czechoslovakia – that we find some sort of even balance between Catholics and Protestants, with Catholics forming a significant minority of the population. Even in these countries, Catholics often tend to cluster in areas where they constitute an overwhelming majority – in areas such as Limburg in the south of the Netherlands, or Bavaria in southern Germany. Catholics also constitute a substantial minority in Northern Ireland, which forms part of the United Kingdom, and where a virtual civil war between Catholics and Protestants persisted for more than 25 years. Note, however, that the nominal affiliations listed in Table 1.1 exaggerate the numbers of active adherents, with the proportion of non-practising Catholics being particularly pronounced in France and southern Europe, for example.

The balance between these Christian denominations has played a major role in framing the political alternatives of many European states. As we shall show in Chapter 8, for example, Christian democratic parties – one of the most important party families in Europe – have always been strongest in areas where Catholics constituted a substantial minority (e.g., the Netherlands, Germany, Switzerland), or where practising Catholics felt threatened by liberal, secular forces (e.g., Belgium, France, Italy). Non-Catholic countries, on the other hand, have tended to give rise to secular conservative rather than Christian democratic parties (e.g., Norway, Sweden, UK), although they are also often home to smaller, more fundamentalist Protestant political groupings. Historical divisions therefore often shape contemporary political alignments, with the alignments themselves surviving even after their original founding divisions have faded to irrelevance. But while traditional religious divides might still seem very important in modern Europe – though weakening, the Christian democrats still constitute one of the biggest party families – in practice they often count for less than those in the United States. According to data gathered by the World Values study in 2000 (http://www.worldvaluessurvey.org), for example, Europeans (75 per cent) are somewhat less likely than Americans (96 per cent) to believe in God, and substantially less likely (29 per cent versus 75 per cent) to believe in hell. And while close to half of all Americans attend a religious service at least once a week, only one in five Europeans does so. European culture is in this sense a much more secular culture, with only 16 per cent of Europeans claiming that God is important in their lives (as against 58 per cent of Americans), and with 12 per cent agreeing with the idea that politicians who don't believe in God are unfit for public office, as compared with 38 per cent of Americans. This is now one of the key differences between the two cultures, and it is increasing rather than diminishing in importance.

That said, religion is now re-emerging as an issue in European politics through its connection to immigration, with growing evidence of hostility between the indigenous European populations, on the one hand, and the minority Muslim community, on the others. The overall number of Muslim immigrants and their immediate descendants is still quite limited in Europe, of course. In Europe as a whole, according to recent figures compiled by the Pew Research Center, the Muslim population amounts to some 5 per cent of the total, a figure that includes countries from the former Yugoslavia, where Muslims constitute a very substantial minority. The percentage is lower in the European Union as such, but the numbers do vary from country to country. In Bulgaria, which was formerly part of the Ottoman empire, Muslims account for some 12 per cent of the population. In France and the Netherlands the figure is some 6 per cent, and it is 4 per cent in Austria and Belgium, although within some of these countries the immigrant population is particularly high in the city areas. In Madrid the Muslim population is estimated at some 14 per cent, while in the Netherlands it has been estimated that more than 50 per cent of school-going children in the four biggest cities – Amsterdam, Rotterdam, The Hague and Utrecht – are of non-western immigrant descent, and primarily Muslim. This in itself poses a major problem for integration and cohesion within Europe's modern urban cultures, and it has become even more acute since both 9/11 and the Madrid bombings of 3/11. The issue has also become widely politicized in recent years, initially by the new far-right populist parties – the National Front in France, the Danish People's Party, Flemish Interest, the Swiss People's Party, and the Pim Fortuyn List in the Netherlands – and then by other centre-right and sometimes even centre-left parties that followed in their wake. Late in 2009, for example, the Swiss voted in favour of a referendum that prohibited the future construction of minarets in Switzerland, and in 2010 the French parliament recommended a ban on the burqa, the full veil worn by small numbers of Muslim women. The issue has also led to violence and other forms of protest, such as in Sweden, where white racist gangs have become very active; in Denmark, where riots followed the publication of cartoons depicting Muhammad; and in the Netherlands, where a spate of incidents involving the burning of mosques and churches followed soon after the murder of film-maker and anti-Islam propagandist Theo van Gogh in November 2004. Two members of the Dutch parliament, who were also very critical of Islam, also received death threats at that time and were obliged to go into hiding.

One of the issues that had concerned the critics of Islamic practices in the Netherlands, and which had initially been voiced by the radical populist Pim Fortuyn, himself later assassinated, was the attitude to women's rights, on the one hand, and to gay rights, on the other. Fortuyn's argument was that those who had chosen to be immigrants within a liberal state were obliged to assimilate, and to respect the prevailing liberal culture – which meant, in this case, learning the indigenous language and respecting the rights of women, gays and other minorities. Fortuyn himself was gay, and very publicly so. Indeed, one of the ironies of this burgeoning conflict is that in some of the countries in which women have been most strongly empowered, and where women's rights and hence egalitarianism seem most firmly ensconced, new far-right parties have now made quite substantial headway (Denmark, Norway, the Netherlands, Belgium – see also Table 8.9 below). Though anti-immigrant, these parties nevertheless often couch their appeals in the form of a defence of traditional liberal values.

The position of women in politics and society is noted in the final column of Table 1.1, which reports values of the so-called Gender Empowerment Index, which has been devised by the United Nations *Human Development Reports* (http://hdr.undp.org). This index is a composite measure of the degree of women's representation in key areas of political and economic life, and takes account of the number of women in national parliaments (see also Chapter 11), their share of earned income, and their levels of occupancy in a range of professions. As can be seen from the table, women enjoy their strongest position in Europe in countries such as Denmark, Finland, Norway, Sweden, the Netherlands and Belgium, and are weakest in eastern and southern Europe. Two factors seem to be important here, and these factors recur in many of the topics relating to representative government that we discuss in this book. On the one hand, there is the evident difference between the newer and the older democracies, with, in this case, women tending to play a stronger public role in the latter group. On the other hand, there is the difference between Catholic and Protestant Europe, and again, in this case, it is in the latter group that women have tended to achieve the greater success.

Cultural diversity involves much more than religious or gender differences, of course. One of the major differences between the European Union and the United States is that virtually every modern European country has its own language. There are exceptions, of course. Austria is a German-speaking country; Ireland is an English-speaking country; in Belgium, some 57 per cent speak Dutch and some 42 per cent speak French; in Luxembourg, the native language coexists with both French and German; Cyprus, or at least the southern part that is now a member of the EU, is Greek-speaking, while in Switzerland some 74 per cent use a version of German, some 20 per cent use French, and some 5 per cent use Italian. In addition, a variety of countries have small linguistic minorities – including the Basque and Catalan minorities in Spain, the German-speaking minority in north-east Italy, the Swedish-speaking minority in Finland, the Hungarian minority in Slovakia, the Welsh in Britain, and a small number of Gaelic speakers in both Ireland and Scotland. Across modern Europe as a whole, German is the most widely used native language, being used as a mother tongue by roughly 95 million people, followed by French (64 million) and English (63 million), and then by Italian (57 million), and Polish and Spanish (both just less than 40 million). There is then a large drop to Dutch (just over 20 million). As a second language, English is increasingly popular in each of the other language groups.

Germany also enjoys the strongest economy in modern Europe. Even before unification in 1990, West Germany's gross domestic product (GDP) was more than one-quarter again as big as that of the UK, the next biggest; now the economy of the unified Germany is about a third bigger than that of the UK (see Table 1.2). In general, however, the individual European economies are dwarfed by that of the United States. The combined GDP of the four largest economies – Germany, France, Italy and the United Kingdom – actually totals only to some 70 per cent of that of the United States. Taking all the EU-27 countries together, however, including the poorer post-communist countries, yields a total GDP of some $14.8 billion at 2009 exchange rates, and this was then marginally greater than the US figure of $14.4 billion. In effect, and allowing for the fluctuating exchange rate in this period, the two economies were identical in size.

The highest European levels for GDP per head of population, when converted into the now standard purchasing power parities (PPPs) – this is a way of adjusting and standardizing GDP per capita so that a fixed sum buys the same bundle of goods and services in every country – can be found in Luxembourg, Norway, Ireland and Switzerland, with only Luxembourg and Norway exceeding the comparable US figure of $46 400. The average EU-27 figure was about two-thirds that of the US. There is enormous variation within Europe in this regard, with levels ranging from highs of $78 000 in Luxembourg and $58 600 in Norway to the west European low of just $21 800 in Portugal and the extreme post-communist lows of $12 600 in Bulgaria and $11 500 in Romania – the two most recent entrants to the EU. Not all post-communist countries rank at the bottom of this scale, however: both the Czech Republic and Slovenia – the latter being the real success story of the former Yugoslavia – have a higher per capita income than Portugal. Performances also vary over time, of course. When we prepared the original first edition of this volume, using data from 1988–89, Ireland ranked as the third poorest country in western Europe, with a GDP per capita (measured in PPPs) that was little more than 40 per cent of the US figure. In 2009, more than a decade after the beginning of the sustained growth rates associated with the Celtic Tiger, Ireland was the third richest country in Europe, with a GDP per capita that was almost 90 per cent of that in the US. By 2010, however, following the world financial crisis and

**TABLE 1.2**  Gross domestic product in European democracies

| Country | Total 2009, $ billion (current exchange rates) | Per capita, 2009 $ (current exchange rates) | $ per capita PPPs (purchasing power parities) |
|---|---|---|---|
| Austria | 378.8 | 46 100 | 39 400 |
| Belgium | 466.9 | 44 800 | 36 600 |
| Bulgaria | 45.2 | 6 300 | 12 600 |
| Cyprus | 23.5 | 21 700 | 21 200 |
| Czech Republic | 191.9 | 18 800 | 25 000 |
| Denmark | 311.9 | 56 700 | 36 000 |
| Estonia | 18.3 | 14 100 | 18 700 |
| Finland | 238.2 | 45 400 | 34 900 |
| France | 2 151 | 41 600 | 32 800 |
| Germany | 3 237 | 39 800 | 34 100 |
| Greece | 342.2 | 31 900 | 32 100 |
| Hungary | 125.7 | 12 700 | 18 600 |
| Iceland | 11.9 | 38 900 | 36 600 |
| Ireland | 229.4 | 54 600 | 42 200 |
| Italy | 2 114 | 36 400 | 30 300 |
| Latvia | 24.5 | 11 000 | 14 500 |
| Lithuania | 36.4 | 10 200 | 15 400 |
| Luxembourg | 47.1 | 95 700 | 78 000 |
| Malta | 7.8 | 19 300 | 23 800 |
| Netherlands | 799 | 47 800 | 39 200 |
| Norway | 373.3 | 80 100 | 58 600 |
| Poland | 427.9 | 11 100 | 17 900 |
| Portugal | 222.4 | 20 800 | 21 800 |
| Romania | 162.6 | 7 300 | 11 500 |
| Slovakia | 89.3 | 16 400 | 21 200 |
| Slovenia | 50.1 | 25 000 | 27 900 |
| Spain | 1 466 | 36 200 | 33 700 |
| Sweden | 402.4 | 44 400 | 36 800 |
| Switzerland | 489.8 | 64 400 | 41 700 |
| United Kingdom | 2 224 | 36 400 | 35 200 |
| United States | 14 430 | 47 000 | 46 400 |
| EU-27 | 14 793 | 32 900 | 32 600 |

*Sources*: OECD; Eurostat; CIA, *World Factbook*, 2010.

the bursting of the Celtic Tiger bubble, the Irish economy was particularly badly hit, and a combination of lower growth rates and rapidly increasing public debt is likely to pull it back down the ladder in the coming years.

Although Ireland has suffered particularly badly as a result of the global financial crisis in 2008–2010, none of the European economies escaped unharmed. The Eurozone, which refers to the countries in Europe that have adopted the euro as their currency, was hit by a particularly severe monetary crisis in early 2010. The European currency is not managed by the individual member states, but is controlled at the European level by the European Central Bank. But while the intention is to ensure strict control of monetary policy – including inflation, interest rates, and so on – the European level has no competence in the area of fiscal policy, which is a policy area that still belongs strictly to the individual member states. This means that the European level must attempt to manage a currency securely while at the same it lacks the means to control or even co-ordinate how national governments tax and spend. The tension involved in this unhappy division of competences became especially manifest in 2010, when, in the wake of the global financial crisis, the value and credibility of the euro were threatened by the overall debt levels and by the rising budget deficits of a number of the member states, including especially those of the so-called PIGS: Portugal, Ireland, Greece and Spain. Although the European Union has expanded its competences in terms of debt support and control in an effort to deal with the problems, the overall result of the monetary crisis has been to oblige the European polities, and the Eurozone countries in particular, to adopt a number of severe austerity measures. In 2010, governments committed themselves to major reductions in public spending, including cuts in welfare expenditures and public sector pay, and to a freeze on major infrastructural projects.

Perhaps surprisingly, however, the severe economic policies adopted by most of the governments have not always been strongly opposed or challenged by the opposition parties. Partisan opposition can be seen, of course, but this usually takes the form of the non-governing parties promising a more gradual reduction in budget deficits than those proposed by their cabinets. In other words, while there are disputes regarding the pace at which the countries should travel down the road of retrenchment, there tends to be a cross-party consensus on the direction itself. That said, there is some small variation from country to country. In those systems in which social democratic parties were in government and had to deal with the crisis, as in the UK until mid 2010 and in Spain, for example, the conservative opposition has tended to underline the need for cuts. In those countries where the conservatives were in government, however, as in Germany, Ireland and Hungary, for example, the social democratic opposition also tended to argue for tackling deficits by raising tax levels.

The most striking differences in the European economies remain those of wealth and structure, with the imbalances being related strongly to imbalances and differences in levels of economic modernization (within western Europe) as well as to the communist legacy (in eastern Europe). With some exceptions, these imbalances also tend to be organized in terms of geographic division between richer countries in northern and central western Europe and poorer countries in the Mediterranean south, and, of course, in the east. Indeed, this difference is strikingly evident in terms of regional disparities within the boundaries of a single country, Italy. The very prosperous northern part of the country enjoys one of the highest standards of living in modern Europe, contrasting sharply with the southern part of Italy, one of western Europe's poorest regions. This social and economic tension is now also being exacerbated by a regional political divide, with the Northern League mobilizing in favour of greater political autonomy for northern

Italy. Lower levels of prosperity also tend to be quite strongly associated with a continuing reliance on agriculture as a major source of employment, as in Bulgaria and Romania in particular, as well as with poorly developed industrial and service sectors.

Differences in sectoral development across modern Europe are less marked than was once the case. For example, as Table 1.3 shows, Bulgaria, Romania and Ireland are the only countries in the European Union where the contribution of agriculture to GDP reaches 5 per cent. This is despite the often relatively high levels of employment in this sector. Ireland and Romania are also the only two countries where the service sector contributes less than 60 per cent. In all 30 European states, however, without exception, it is this latter sector that contributes most to GDP, accounting for an average that now runs close to the balance in the United States. Perhaps surprisingly, in view of Ireland's conventional image as having one of the most traditional and unspoiled landscapes in Europe, in these figures it emerges as having the single biggest industrial sector (just ahead of Norway). Again, this is due largely to the enormous economic growth in the so-called Celtic Tiger period, which has led to a situation in which the only leprechauns that are still to be found are those that are made of resin and packaged up for export to gift shops around the world.

Ireland does less well when it comes to the degree of equality in the distribution of income. This is measured by the Gini index, and ranges from 0, when there is perfect equality, to 100, when there is perfect inequality. The west European countries that score low on this index, and hence which have more egalitarian income distributions, tend to be those that also figured highly on the Gender Empowerment Index (Table 1.1) – Denmark, Iceland and Sweden. The Czech Republic, Slovakia and particularly Slovenia also emerge as having a high level of equality, while Ireland scores towards the non-egalitarian end, ranking closely with Switzerland and the UK. Most of the European countries remain very distant from the inequality levels measured in the United States, however, and hence, despite internal variation, this is something that again marks Europe out as distinct. Through most of the post-war period, the large majority of western European countries shared a common commitment to progressive taxation, and to the strengthening of social citizenship. Despite variation in the programmes that were set in place to realize these goals, this commitment led most of the European polities to develop a large public sector, and to build an expensive and quite all-encompassing welfare state. This also meant generous unemployment benefits, comprehensive health care, and well-funded pension schemes, and it is precisely these programmes that are now under threat in the fallout from the monetary and fiscal crises. As these programmes were built up from the 1960s onwards, however, they led to less inequality, and to a levelling out of lifestyles rather than simply opportunities. Today we tend to see this as having been a product of social democracy, and social democratic parties have indeed been at the heart of European mass politics for most of the twentieth century. But it is important to recognize this approach as being also the product of that other powerful European party family, the Christian democrats, a group that was just as committed as the social democrats to the funding of the welfare state, and to the promotion of 'social capitalism'.

Table 1.3 highlights the different levels of government expenditure relative to GDP in the different European countries. These figures relate to spending and employment on public welfare programmes such as health, education, employment and housing, as well as the defence forces, police, administration, and publicly owned companies. The figures are not always easily comparable, however, since different state traditions use different definitions and categorizations for what are functionally equivalent activities. Moreover, the comparisons across the post-communist

**TABLE 1.3** Sector, labour force and public sector data

| Country | Sectoral contribution to GDP, 2009 (%) | | | Total general government expenditure, 2009 (% GDP) | Gini index (inequality index), 2008[a] | Population aged 65 or over, 2009 (%) |
|---|---|---|---|---|---|---|
| | **Agriculture** | **Industry** | **Services** | | | |
| Austria | 1.7 | 32.3 | 65.8 | 51.8 | 26 | 18.1 |
| Belgium | 0.8 | 24.5 | 74.7 | 54.2 | 28 | 17.8 |
| Bulgaria | 7.5 | 27.6 | 64.9 | 40.7 | 31.6 | 17.9 |
| Cyprus | 2.1 | 19 | 78.9 | 46.4 | 29 | 10.2 |
| Czech Republic | 2.8 | 35 | 62.3 | 46.1 | 26 | 15.9 |
| Denmark | 4.9 | 30.7 | 64.7 | 58.7 | 24 | 16.6 |
| Estonia | 3 | 24.4 | 72.6 | 45.4 | 34 | 17.6 |
| Finland | 3.4 | 30.9 | 65.8 | 55.6 | 29.5 | 17.2 |
| France | 2.1 | 19 | 78.9 | 55.6 | 28 | 16.5 |
| Germany | 0.9 | 27.1 | 72 | 47.6 | 28 | 20.4 |
| Greece | 3.4 | 20.8 | 75.8 | 50.4 | 33 | 19.4 |
| Hungary | 3.4 | 34.3 | 62.4 | 49.8 | 28 | 16 |
| Iceland | 5.2 | 24 | 70.8 | 51.5 | 25 | 12.4 |
| Ireland | 5 | 46 | 49 | 48.4 | 32 | 12.2 |
| Italy | 2.1 | 25 | 72.9 | 51.9 | 33 | 20.3 |
| Latvia | 3.6 | 24 | 72.4 | 42.9 | 37.7 | 17 |
| Lithuania | 4.4 | 27 | 68.6 | 43.0 | 36 | 16.3 |
| Luxembourg | 0.4 | 13.6 | 86 | 42.4 | 26 | 14.8 |
| Malta | 1.7 | 17.4 | 80.9 | 44.3 | 28 | 15.1 |
| Netherlands | 1.9 | 24.4 | 73.7 | 51.6 | 30.9 | 15.2 |
| Norway | 2.2 | 45.1 | 52.7 | 45.8 | 28 | 15.6 |
| Poland | 4.6 | 28.1 | 67.3 | 44.5 | 36 | 13.5 |
| Portugal | 2.9 | 24.4 | 72.8 | 51.0 | 38 | 17.8 |
| Romania | 12.4 | 35 | 52.6 | 40.4 | 31 | 14.7 |
| Slovakia | n/a | n/a | n/a | 40.8 | 26 | 12.6 |
| Slovenia | 2 | 37 | 61 | 49.9 | 24 | 16.6 |
| Spain | 3.4 | 26.9 | 69.6 | 45.9 | 32 | 18.4 |
| Sweden | 1.6 | 26.6 | 71.8 | 55.8 | 23 | 19.3 |
| Switzerland | 3.8 | 23.9 | 72.3 | 32.2[b] | 33.7 | 16.6 |
| United Kingdom | 1.2 | 23.8 | 75 | 51.7 | 34 | 16.4 |
| United States | 1.2 | 21.9 | 76.9 | 42.7 | 45 | 13 |

[a] The Gini index measures inequality in income distribution or in consumption: 0 represents perfect equality, and 100 represents perfect inequality.

[b] Data for 2007.

*Sources*: OECD; Eurostat; United Nations, *Human Development Report*, 2009; CIA, *World Factbook*, 2010.

countries may be particularly misleading, since in these particular cases the high expenditure levels can simply reflect lingering legacies of the pre-democratic period. According to the west European figures, governments in Denmark, Finland, France and Sweden spend more than 55 per cent of GDP, with Belgium, Germany, the Netherlands and Italy coming close behind. The lowest level of spending is reported by Switzerland, which approximates to the more limited American figure. In general, however, over-time analysis suggested that it is towards this Swiss-US level that most of the European polities were likely to point in the future – even before the constraints imposed by the economic crisis of 2008–2010 (see above). Within the budgetary guidelines set by the EU when establishing the single currency, European governments had already been divesting themselves of public spending commitments, and had been attempting to reduce the government share of national income. In some cases they had little choice. Health costs have been rising throughout Europe, and the population is ageing. The result is that even to maintain present welfare programmes at their existing levels would have cost the governments an ever-increasing share of revenue. The solution has been therefore to privatize and to divest responsibilities: to encourage more and more private health insurance, on the one hand, and to demand that citizens retire later and provide for the bulk of their own pension arrangements, on the other.

Table 1.3 also reports the percentage of the population aged 65 and above, 65 being still the most common age for compulsory retirement in Europe. The contrasts with the United States are often striking, as are the internal variations. Thus some 19–20 per cent of the population are now of retirement age in Germany, Greece, Italy and Sweden, and given the lower birth rates now being recorded in many of these countries, this proportion is expected to increase in the coming decade. This places a huge burden on the developed European welfare states, and has been one of the factors contributing to the problematic budget deficits of recent years, particularly since the overall dependency ratio (the ratio of those working to those either too young or too old to work, or who are sick or unemployed) is worsening every year. Cutting pension payments and forcing people to retire later is part of the solution to the budgetary crisis that is implied by this demographic shift, and which is now being pushed even harder by the European authorities. Getting more people into the labour market is another, which means getting more women and older people into the workforce, and probably also more immigrants, but this is difficult in a period of austerity, and, as we shall see in Chapters 8 and 9, the latter solution in particular can lead to other political problems, including fuelling the growth of xenophobic far-right parties.

Although policy problems such as these are common to most European countries, and are especially hard felt in the Eurozone, and although the legacy of generous social provisions that was built up during the peaceful post-war decades is now coming under strain throughout the long-established democracies, it is still evident that we cannot talk about modern Europe as though it were constituted by a homogeneous group of polities. Instead, we are talking about a collection of places with quite distinctive social, economic and political profiles. Whether these differences are large or small depends on your point of view. As we have suggested, to travel within Italy from prosperous north to poor south is to see quite a striking social contrast. To cross the border from the newly democratized and now financially troubled Hungary to the more established but politically divided Austria is to see another strong social and economic contrast. Yet even the poorer southern parts of Italy or the more impoverished parts of Hungary are in no sense whatsoever among the world's poor regions – their levels of prosperity are far above that of virtually every state in the developing world, whether we measure this in terms of money, life expectancy, literacy, or indeed any other aspect of the quality of life. Moreover, while the differences between regions and countries in Europe can be quite pronounced, these are less striking when viewed from within the increasingly cosmopolitan and internationalized world of the major cities and towns. To the average visitor, Catania may not seem that different from Turin, nor Budapest from Vienna.

For all their diversity and commonality, and for all the problems that now face their economies, the countries of Europe constitute the world's largest collection of successful capitalist democracies, as well as the most effective laboratory for comparative political research. Moreover, most of these European countries are tied together in an ever more powerful political union, the European Union, which we discuss in detail in Chapter 5. But the differences that we have highlighted must also be kept in mind in the comparative discussions that follow. We are, after all, talking about a collection of different countries, and that is one of the things that makes the study of modern European politics so interesting and so challenging: the systems are at once so similar and so different. At the same time, of course, the differences must not also be exaggerated. This is why it makes sense to analyse politics in the collection of European countries in terms of their underlying similarities as well as their distinctive features. This is the main purpose of the chapters that follow.

# CHAPTER 2

# The Executive

## Chapter contents

## 2.1  Introduction

Ultimately, democracy involves people choosing their own governments and holding members of these governments accountable. The system of government in any modern democracy has four constitutional building blocks: legislature, executive and judiciary and, presiding over all of this, head of state. In theory, each of these institutions has a different job to do. The legislature, or parliament, legislates – it enacts laws. The executive, or *government*, runs the country – subject to the laws and constitution currently in force. And, in light of the prevailing laws and constitution, the judiciary adjudicates disputes between individuals and other legal entities such as corporations, as well as disputes between these and the executive. There may be direct or indirect popular involvement in the selection and accountability of legislature, executive and head of state – where by indirect we mean that an elected legislature, for example, may choose a chief executive or head of state. Though there are notable exceptions in the United States, the *independence of the judiciary* is typically held to preclude popular involvement in the selection and accountability of judges.

Whatever theoretical distinctions there might be about the allocation of responsibilities between different branches of government, the practical realities can often be quite different. This can be seen by looking at the reactions of many governments to the global financial crisis that emerged in late 2008. Quick and decisive action was needed to avert potential financial disaster, often late at night over a weekend before the markets opened on a Monday morning. The official players in these late-night dramas were members of the executive, not the legislature. The action that was taken was executive action. Government guarantees were provided to prevent major financial institutions from collapsing with knock-on effects for the rest of the economy. Decisions were made about the government's willingness to lend huge sums of money at cheap rates to distressed businesses. Massive additional liquidity was injected into financial markets. A host of crucial decisions were made in settings where time was of the essence, and there was no prospect whatsoever of involving the entire democratic system of government. Clearly, these decisions could be neither illegal nor unconstitutional. However, the range of potential legal and constitutional responses to the urgent and vital policy decisions that were needed was enormous, and these decisions were made by just a few key members of the executive. These people were politically accountable *after the fact* for the decisions they made, and some of these decisions might well have required legislation before they could be fully implemented. No doubt this conditioned how their decisions were made. But, at the end of the day, it is a plain fact that these crucial decisions were *executive* decisions, so that who, precisely, occupied the relevant executive positions was an absolutely critical matter.

The global financial crisis is an extreme example of the realities of executive policymaking that makes our point very clearly, but it is not in the least exceptional. This is particularly obvious in the realm of foreign policy, which is typically subject to neither legislation nor judicial action, but it is also true in almost any policy area we can think of. Policies on education, environment, health or housing, for example, are clearly subject to both legislation and litigation. But many of the real-world decisions that, taken together, comprise *de facto* education, environment, health or housing policy are made by the relevant government departments, under the direction of key members of the executive. We see this in sharp relief when a new government first comes into power and can make important changes to education, environment, health or housing policy without needing to pass any new law. For this reason, and notwithstanding the finer points of democratic theory, it makes sense to treat the executive as the ultimate source of political power and decision-making capacity in modern democracies, and to see the other organs of government – legislature, judiciary and head of state – as creating a system of checks and balances on the executive.

## 2.2 Separation or fusion of powers?

Fundamental constitutional differences between modern democracies specify different checks and balances for interactions between legislature, executive, judiciary and head of state. These differences have major implications for the politics of first choosing governments and then holding these accountable. Perhaps the most important difference contrasts constitutions that specify a *separation of powers* between legislature and executive and those that specify an effective *fusion* of such powers. This is also commonly referred to as the distinction between *presidential* and *parliamentary* government systems, although as we shall see there are huge differences between the powers of the president in different parliamentary systems. We also need to make a distinction between presidents who are chief executives and those who are heads of state – perhaps with very few powers. Given this wide variation in the political role of people who may be called 'president', it is more helpful to see the key distinction as being between *separation-of-powers* and *fusion-of-powers* regimes.

## 2.2.1 Separation-of-powers regimes

In separation-of-powers regimes there is a clear constitutional separation between the legislature, elected by the people and given the job of making laws, and the executive, given the job of running the country under the constitution and laws of the land. The chief executive in a separation-of-powers regime is typically elected by the people and called *president*. He or she will typically name a *cabinet* of senior politicians (who need not be elected) who take political responsibility for particular policy areas and the associated government departments. This separation of powers is most obvious in the defining and binding constitutional stipulation that the *executive cannot dismiss the legislature and the legislature cannot dismiss the executive.* That is what is meant by separation of powers. Except in extreme circumstances, both branches of government, each democratically elected, must learn to live with each other. If the executive wants new legislation, it must persuade the legislature to enact this and, crucially, the legislature has the power to approve the executive's annual budget. Other than by threatening legislative or budgetary sanctions, however, the legislature has no direct power to force the executive to do anything and, crucially, cannot get rid of an executive of which it disapproves.

The classic example of a separation-of-powers regime is found in the United States of America. The US president is elected by the people every four years to be chief executive. The president nominates a partisan cabinet, some of whom have never fought an election in their lives, and some of whom are former state governors or members of the legislature. Following his election in November 2008, for example, President Barack Obama named a former elected senator, Hillary Clinton, as his Secretary of State (responsible for foreign affairs) and Timothy Geithner, a former president of the Federal Reserve Bank of New York, as Secretary of the Treasury. The cabinet serves at the pleasure of the president, but cabinet members must be approved by the Senate, the elected upper house of bicameral US legislature of which the lower house is the House of Representatives. Other than the power of the Senate to block presidential nominations to senior executive and judicial positions, and the requirement for the president to get the executive's budget approved by the legislature in the form of appropriations bills, the US legislature has no direct power over the executive. While, as became relevant in the wake of President Richard Nixon's involvement in the Watergate scandal, Congress has the power to impeach a president for 'high crimes and misdemeanours', it has no power whatsoever to dismiss a president with whom it has bitter and fundamental disagreements.

Discussions of the political consequences of the separation-of-powers regime in the United States can be found in Edwards (1990), Neustadt (1991), Jones (1999, 2005), Mayhew (2005) and Peterson (1993).

## 2.2.2 Fusion-of-powers regimes

Classic examples of fusion-of-powers, or 'parliamentary government', regimes are found in Europe. The formal distinction is very clear, and is expressed in plain language in the constitution. In a fusion-of-powers regime, *the executive is constitutionally responsible to the legislature.* This is typically achieved with an explicit and binding constitutional provision that the executive must *retain the confidence* of the legislature. In practice this means that, constitutionally, *the executive must resign, and is otherwise deemed to have been dismissed, if it loses a legislative motion of no confidence.* In a nutshell, the legislature can bring down the government in a parliamentary government system. Strikingly, notwithstanding that the French roots of the word 'parliament' imply a 'talking shop', the term 'parliamentary government' (as opposed to the potential 'legislative government') is typically applied when there is a fusion of powers between legislature and executive. When people talk about parliamentary systems they typically do not just mean political systems with parliaments; they mean systems with parliaments that have the constitutional authority to bring down the government.

Even though it is not a logical necessity, it is also invariably the case in parliamentary systems that the executive in general, and the chief executive in particular, are not directly elected by the people but are instead chosen 'indirectly' by an elected parliament. In some countries, for example Greece, Poland, Portugal and Spain, this is embedded in an institutional requirement that an incoming government can take office only following a formal investiture vote in parliament. For all practical purposes, however, the situation is the same in other countries, for example Austria, Britain, France, the Netherlands or Slovenia, that do not have a requirement for formal investiture of the executive by the legislature. This is because any incoming government is immediately exposed to the possibility of a legislative vote of no confidence, and must be able to win this if it is to remain in office. Either way in a parliamentary system, therefore, the incoming government must receive the explicit or tacit approval of the legislature.

Discussions of the political consequences of the fusion-of-powers regimes typically found in modern Europe can be found in Shugart and Carey (1992), Laver and Shepsle (1996), Lijphart (1999), Tsebelis (2002), Strøm *et al.* (2003) and Cheibub (2007).

Parliaments in fusion-of-powers systems not only choose the incoming prime minister and cabinet, but can also dismiss these at will using the no-confidence procedure. The government can be changed in this way without any recourse to voters. Despite superficial appearances, this arrangement is seen as democratic, because the prime minister, while not elected, is nonetheless responsible to an elected parliament, in which he or she must always be able to win majority support. The most striking consequence of all of this is that legislative elections in a parliamentary government system, in sharp distinction to elections in a separation-of-powers system, do two different jobs at the same time. Not only are legislative elections how voters choose their legislature they are also, indirectly, how voters choose their government – since the incoming legislature goes on to select a new prime minister and cabinet.

Balancing the defining constitutional power of the legislature to dismiss the executive, it is common in parliamentary democracies for the chief executive, the prime minister, to have the power to dissolve the legislature and effectively force new legislative elections, possibly doing this in consultation with the head of state. This is neither a logically necessary nor a defining feature of parliamentary democracies. Some parliamentary democracies, for example Norway, have fixed-term parliaments, and this was also part of a package of institutional reforms proposed in Britain by the Conservative–Liberal Democrat coalition that took office in May 2010.

While an important part of the definition of a *separation* of powers between legislature and executive includes a provision that the executive *cannot* dissolve the legislature and force new elections, the *possibility* that the prime minister can force new elections is a common feature of parliamentary government, European style. The rationale is that, in the event of a deep conflict between legislature and executive, the chief executive can in effect ask the people to decide, by calling an early election. The net effect, to which we return in Chapter 12 when discussing government durability, is that endogenous rather than fixed timing of elections is an important feature of most European parliamentary democracies. While these countries are democracies in the sense that their constitutions specify a *maximum* period between elections, typically of four or five years, they need not specify a *minimum* period. *Early* elections are typically on the political agenda in most European parliamentary democracies.

### 2.2.3  Splitting the difference? 'Semi-presidentialism'

We have thus far presented separation- and fusion-of-powers regimes as stark alternatives, but there are constitutional regimes that might appear to get the best of both worlds, the best known of which is the type of *semi-presidential* system found in France. This looks like a separation-of-powers system, in that there a president who is directly elected by the people; who has considerable powers, especially over foreign policy; and who has the exclusive right to nominate, though not to sack, the prime minister. The president may also select and dismiss other ministers with the agreement of the prime minister, and may dissolve the national assembly to – in effect – call new elections. But France is also like a parliamentary system in that there is a prime minister and a cabinet who have full responsibility for government policy, and who must, crucially, maintain majority support in a directly elected legislature. Thus, while only the president can nominate, only the legislature can dismiss, the prime minister. Nobody, however, can dismiss the president, who is unquestionably the most senior political figure in France.

France's semi-presidential constitution creates the potential for conflict between prime minister and president, particularly when these people come from different political parties. This was particularly true before a constitutional reform enacted in 2002 shortened the presidential term of office, with the effect that presidential and parliamentary elections are now held on the same cycle. Before this, the presidential term (seven years) was longer than the parliamentary term (five years), generating a constitutional requirement for a parliamentary election in the mid-term of the presidency. As a result there were several periods during which different parties controlled presidency and prime ministership – a situation known in France as *cohabitation* and closely analogous to *divided government* in the United States. It became clear during these periods that, when a president was forced to cohabit with a prime minister from a different party, the powers of the French president were less sweeping than had previously been supposed.

It is thus very significant that the French constitution was changed in 2002 to bring the presidential term down from seven to five years. Both president and parliament now have the same terms of office. It is also significant that the decision was made to hold legislative elections a few weeks *after* presidential elections, with the same party in practice likely to win both elections. This greatly reduces the probability of *cohabitation* between a president and prime minister of different parties, and for this reason increases the *de facto* power of a French president, creating a situation whereby the French semi-presidential system is coming to look more like a presidential than a parliamentary system of government.

France is not the only country considered by scholars to have a semi-presidential system of government, though it is the 'model generator' people have in mind when they talk about semi-presidentialism. As we shall see when we return below to the role of presidents in parliamentary democracies, both Finland and Poland have for periods had presidents who were powerful enough to cause these countries to be classified as semi-presidential. In each of these cases, however, constitutional reforms in the 1990s cut back the powers of the president, to the extent that these countries are now typically seen as parliamentary systems, with presidential powers that are at the strong end of the spectrum. While the semi-presidential model remains on the agenda when new constitutions are being discussed, real-world interest in this model is, if anything, on the wane.

For discussions of semi-presidentialism, see Elgie (1999, 2009), Grossman (2009) and Grossman and Sauger (2009).

## 2.3 Parliamentary government in modern Europe

Parliamentary government is the norm in modern Europe. It is also striking that, when politicians in former Soviet-bloc countries in eastern Europe had a once-in-a-lifetime opportunity to choose a new system of government as they moved away from their old constitutions, most opted for the constitutional regime of parliamentary government (Baylis, 1996; Lijphart and Waisman, 1996; Frye, 1997; Elster et al., 1998).

Figure 2.1 summarizes the core political dynamics of parliamentary government in modern Europe. This is of course a continuous process that never ends, but we start on the left of the figure with an incumbent government, noting that democratic constitutions are always extremely scrupulous about ensuring there is a legal incumbent government in any conceivable situation. Moving one step to the right of this in Figure 2.1, a key question concerns whether or not there is to be an election. The question that is always at the back of the mind of any incumbent

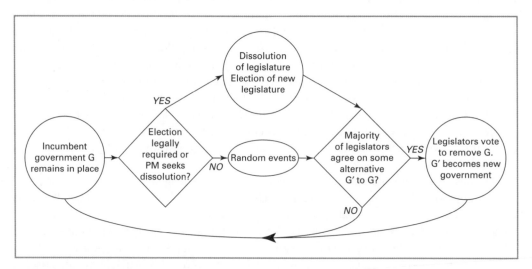

**FIGURE 2.1** Dynamics of parliamentary democracy
*Source:* Adapted from Laver *et al.* (2010)

prime minister, except in those rare parliamentary systems with fixed-term elections, is whether to dissolve the legislature and in effect call an early election. Either way, the upshot is that any incumbent government, even in the most favourable political climate, will ultimately face either a scheduled election or an election that has been sought by the prime minister.

If there is no election, and tracing the middle path through Figure 2.1, the incumbent government stays in place and must deal both with the expected and with the unexpected. The expected can be factored into whatever agreements are made when the government is formed. The unexpected, by definition, cannot be anticipated. The life and times of any incumbent government are thus characterized by the constant need to deal with a stream of 'random' events. As former British prime minister Harold Macmillan is famously credited with saying to a young journalist, it is 'events, dear boy, events' that tend to blow governments off course. Thus, while a majority of legislators might have preferred the incumbent government to any alternative at the moment this took office, subsequent events and the government's responses to these may well cause them to change their minds. It may therefore no longer be true that a majority of legislators now prefer the incumbent government to some specific alternative they might have in mind.

If a majority of legislators do indeed still prefer the incumbent government, then the path at the bottom of Figure 2.1 shows that the system loops back and the cycle is repeated. This loop is 'business as usual' – the normal state of affairs when an incumbent government stays in office in what is in effect a dynamic equilibrium. If on the other hand a majority of legislators, taking everything into consideration (and there is a lot to take into consideration), now prefer some alternative executive then, under the rules of parliamentary government, they have the constitutional authority to remove the incumbent and install their preferred alternative. This alternative becomes the new incumbent. The system then loops back to the beginning and the cycle is repeated.

The other possibility is that the legislature is dissolved and there is an election for a new legislature. This election may be either legally scheduled or sought by the incumbent prime minister. It may be sought from a position of strength, to capitalize on some short-term political advantage for the prime minister. It may also be sought from a position of weakness, because the incumbent government faces defeat or has already been defeated, and no alternative can be found, given the current political composition of the legislature. It is constitutionally unambiguous that the incumbent government remains in place, in what is sometimes referred to as a *caretaker* capacity, from the moment an election has been called until the eventual swearing-in of a new government. It is vital that the country has a legal government, even after a formal resignation of the prime minister, both during the course of an election and in the immediate aftermath while a new government is being formed. Once again, members of the new legislature have to decide whether there is some specific alternative that they prefer to the incumbent government. If there is not, the incumbent has in effect 'won' the election and stays in place. If the newly elected legislators do, however, prefer some specific alternative, they are now in a constitutional position to replace the incumbent with this alternative. The outgoing government has in effect 'lost' the election.

We go on to unpack various political consequences of this system of government in the rest of this chapter, beginning with the role of the chief executive, and moving on to consider the executive more broadly, before considering the often underestimated role of the head of state. We return to consider the role of parliaments in Chapter 3.

## 2.4 The prime minister: chief executive

The chief executive or head of government in modern European democracies is almost always referred to in English as *prime minister* – though Austrian and German chief executives are called *chancellors*. The prime minister is typically not only head of the government but also head of one of the main legislative parties, often the largest. The combination of these roles can create a position of considerable power – arguably greater in some cases than that of a US president. This power arises precisely because of the fusion of powers between legislature and executive under parliamentary government. Since an incoming prime minister must win a *legislative* majority in order to become chief *executive*, a successful incoming prime minister is demonstrably able to control both legislature and executive, at least at the moment of taking office.

In countries such as Britain or Greece, which have almost always experienced legislatures in which one single party wins an overall majority of seats, the prime minister is typically leader of the single party that controls the legislature and, at the same time, is also chief executive of the country. Three powerful roles – chief executive, ability to control a legislative majority, and party leader – are thereby concentrated on one single person. When this happens, the only real threat to prime ministerial power comes from inside the governing party itself. Even in the more typical European country with a proportional representation electoral system and a resulting tradition of coalition governments, a tradition we explore in depth in Chapter 12, the prime minister must still command a legislative majority in order to take office, although he or she now depends on leaders of some other party or parties in order to do this. The threat to the incumbent prime minister now comes from inside the majority legislative coalition that allows the government to win votes of confidence. Provided this coalition holds firm, the prime minister, by definition, is a chief executive who also controls a legislative majority. The considerable real power of prime ministers in most modern European democracies thus flows as much from the practical politics of a fusion-of-powers regime as from any explicit constitutional provisions that list the powers of the chief executive (Rose, 1991; Bergman *et al.*, 2003; Dowding and Dumont, 2009; King and Allen, 2010).

Perhaps the most important aspect of *de facto* prime ministerial power stems from the fact that choosing the prime minister is by far the most important job for any new legislature immediately after an election. If the election result means that the incumbent prime minister can muster sufficient parliamentary votes to stay in office then, for all practical purposes, he or she has 'won' the election – even if this election resulted in large losses for the prime minister's party. If in contrast the election result means that the incumbent prime minister *cannot* control enough parliamentary votes to remain in office, then the prime minister has 'lost' the election. This means that changes of *chief executive* are the most obvious and dramatic changes that result from most European *legislative* elections, which have become much more about choosing between alternative governments than about choosing a set of legislators to do what legislators are ostensibly meant to do, which is to legislate. In terms of practical politics this means that election campaigns tend to be fought out between alternative big-name candidates for the office of prime minister, who are typically the leaders of major parties. Crucially, *if citizens want to change their chief executive in a parliamentary government system, they do this by voting in legislative elections.*

A second aspect of the practical political power of a typical European prime minister arises from this person's twin roles as head of both the cabinet and a major political party. A prime minister typically has the *formal power to hire and fire cabinet ministers*. As we shall see in

Chapter 12, when governments are coalitions this power is constrained by the need to come to agreements with leaders of other parties. Even in coalition cabinets, however, the prime minister typically has immense power over ministers from his or her own party. This gives the prime minister effective control over the political careers of party colleagues, when deciding the distribution of the most coveted set of political prizes – seats at the cabinet table – that are sought by senior politicians. This makes his or her position as the head of the party, and thereby as chief executive, considerably more secure (Kam, 2009).

A third facet of prime ministerial power in modern Europe derives from the typical legal right to dissolve the legislature and call an early election. While other politicians can certainly make the PM's life difficult – by resigning from the government, for example – only the PM is in this constitutionally privileged position. Other coalition partners – and even party colleagues – may resign from the cabinet and desert the incumbent prime minister in moments of political crisis, and these are obviously very important *political* exigencies that could augur the end of the government. *Constitutionally*, however, while opponents may try to force the PM's hand in one way or another, they themselves cannot force dissolution of the legislature. This means that the incumbent prime minister is in a privileged position – able to choose between the legislature that is currently in place and the alternative legislature that, on best estimates, would result from an early election.

The incredible complexity and specialization of the job of running any modern democracy underpins a fourth facet of prime ministerial power. It might seem on the face of things that this would weaken the power of the prime minister: how can any one person be in control of all of this, or even know a fraction of what is actually happening? Of course, there is always much that goes on that the prime minister does not know about, but the important thing is that he or she sits at the very centre of the entire decision-making process. The prime minister has access to information about every branch of government, unlike any other senior politician, and this informational advantage is a tremendous source of power. Whereas other members of the cabinet are given specific tasks, the prime minister's job is to co-ordinate these and, crucially, to set the government's decision-making agenda – to decide which proposals are discussed by the government, in what order, and which proposals are buried. Political scientists have long known that an agenda-setting role such as this gives the prime minister huge, if often unobserved, power to affect the outcomes of political decision-making (Huber, 1996; Diermeier and Feddersen, 1998; Tsebelis, 2002; Döring and Hallerberg, 2004; Bräuninger and Debus, 2009).

There are other sources of prime ministerial power, but the bottom line is that European prime ministers are typically very powerful people in their own countries. Notwithstanding this, it is also clear that a prime minister is by no means a dictator. This is because an unwanted prime minister can be disposed of, sometimes ignominiously and at very short notice, by one of three basic methods.

The first method of disposal requires an election, whether scheduled or otherwise. The need for scheduled legislative elections obviously means that an unpopular chief executive must eventually face the music in a parliamentary system. Over and above this, while political opponents of the prime minister have no official right to seek an early election, they can certainly make the PM's position untenable, and effectively force an early election in this way. Before this can happen, of course, the prime minister must have alienated at least some former supporters. Once this has happened, an unpopular incumbent could try to hang on, awaiting defeat in the legislature, but he or she may well prefer to cut and run for an early election ahead of such a defeat. Indeed, many early elections arise for this reason – not because the PM has called an election from a position of strength, but because, for many reasons, the PM prefers seeking an early election to being explicitly dismissed by the legislature.

The second method of removing the prime minister does not require an election, but rather a change in the majority coalition of legislators that keeps the government in office. As soon as a group of politicians who between them control the votes of a majority of legislators come to prefer some specific alternative to the incumbent administration, they can replace the prime minister by forcing a vote of no confidence, if the prime minister does not resign first in anticipation of this. In several European countries – Belgium, Finland, France and Italy are examples – it has been common in the past for the prime minister to be changed as a result of this type of legislative politics, without an intervening election. Italy is best known for this phenomenon, but five governments formed and fell in Belgium between April 1979 and November 1981, without an intervening election. Three different prime ministers headed different French governments, again without an intervening election, between July 1988 and March 1993. Similarly, there was a rapid alternation of governments in Poland between 1997 and 2007, many of these forming without an intervening election. In one sense it might seem that, when the chief executive is changed by the legislature between elections, the new prime minister has a 'stale mandate' arising from voters' preferences expressed in a legislative election some time previously. However, this mandate is no more or less stale than that of a government that has already been in office for three or four years.

The third way of dismissing a prime minister comes from inside his or her own party. We have already noted that a prime minister is typically, though not inevitably, leader of a major political party. This means that a PM's practical political position can collapse quickly as a result of losing the party leadership. We return in Chapter 10 to discuss the internal politics of European political parties. For now, what is important is that parties can, and certainly do, get rid of their leaders on a periodic basis, whether or not formal procedures are in place to do this. Losing the party leadership implies no change in the formal *constitutional* status of the prime minister, whose constitutional seal of office as chief executive cannot legally be taken away by any political party. Nonetheless, the position of a PM who has been stripped of the party leadership is almost always politically untenable, forcing the person concerned to resign. For example, Leszek Miller, prime minister of Poland between 2001 and 2004, lost support within his own party, the Democratic Left Alliance, which was the leading party of the government coalition, and resigned the party leadership in February 2004. He continued as prime minister, however, but was forced to resign at the end of March. The government collapsed, and was replaced by a minority government led by an apolitical appointee, Marek Belka.

What is remarkable about all of this is that the prime minister of the country, the most powerful political figure in the land, can be thrown out of office on the basis of the decisions of a small number of people inside a particular political party. In 1990, for example, a few hundred members of the British Conservative parliamentary party removed Margaret Thatcher, one of post-war Europe's best-known, longest-serving and most powerful prime ministers, and replaced her with John Major. None of the 60 million or so other members of the British public was involved in this process, although it is fair to say that her increasing unpopularity in opinion polls was an important factor in her fall. The same fate befell Tony Blair, another famous and powerful British prime minister, who resigned as Labour Party leader and thus prime minister in

2007 when his personal opinion poll ratings were very low, following British involvement in the war in Iraq. He was replaced by Gordon Brown, who himself then narrowly survived a series of leadership challenges in 2008 and 2009, before losing an election in 2010. If successful, these challenges would have resulted in two changes of British prime minister between elections – each change involving no direct input from voters, though nonetheless made in the context of unpopularity as measured by opinion polls. Indeed, the huge volume and detail of opinion poll data now available in most European countries has had the important effect that the unpopularity of incumbent prime ministers is very easy to measure. While there has been no hard research on this matter of which we are aware, one logically plausible effect of an increased volume of opinion poll feedback is a greater vulnerability of incumbent PMs to challenges from within their own parties.

Putting all of this together, the fusion of powers between legislature and executive that we find in most modern European democracies means that, although prime ministers can be powerful chief executives while they remain in office, their positions can be snatched from them suddenly, and sometimes quite brutally, if they lose support either in the legislature as a whole or in their own party. Moreover, although some of the powers of, and constraints on, the prime minister are spelled out in the formal rules of the political game, the effective position of most European prime ministers, who sit at the very heart of the political system, to a large extent depends on their practical abilities to dominate the cut and thrust of day-to-day politics. Anyone who has won the office of prime minister, after all, has climbed to the top of a very greasy political pole, and typically has the ability to stay there – at least for a while.

## 2.5 The cabinet

If the prime minister is political chief executive in a typical modern European democracy, then the political executive as a whole – the country's board of directors – is the cabinet. For most practical political purposes we can think of the prime minister and the cabinet between them as being the *government* of the country. The cabinet comprises a set of ministers. Each minister plays two vital political roles. One is as *individual* head of a government department. The other is as member of a cabinet that makes or approves important political decisions as a *collective* entity.

The first role of a cabinet minister is as the political head of a major department of state. Crudely speaking, when cabinet ministers go to work in the morning, they typically go to work in a government department. From this vantage point they direct a team of senior civil servants, and have overall responsibility for policy initiation and administration in a key area of state activity such as foreign affairs, public finance, justice, health, environmental protection or education. Departments of state are politically accountable by virtue of the fact that they are each responsible to a designated cabinet minister, for example a minister of foreign affairs, finance or justice, who is directly responsible for the department to the cabinet as a whole, to the legislature, and thereby to voters. If there is a problem in the department, constitutional theory in most European states specifies a doctrine of *individual ministerial responsibility*, according to which the buck stops with the minister, whether he or she knew about the problem or not. Indeed, a minister may even be obliged to resign in response to a problem or scandal of which he or she had no personal knowledge. This constitutionally mandated accountability, at least in theory, gives ministers the incentives to make sure their departments are run properly.

## BOX 2.1: EXECUTIVES AND HEADS OF STATE

### Denmark

Despite the fact that the Danish constitution (1849) theoretically attributes full powers to the monarchy, the role of the Danish monarch is in practice ceremonial, and *de facto* executive authority resides with the prime minister. When a new government is to be formed, the monarch meets with party leaders to find out which government alternative is most likely to obtain the confidence of parliament. As a result of these consultations, he or she appoints the politician who is entitled to lead the cabinet formation talks as 'royal *informateur*'. Once an agreement on the composition of the government is reached, the monarch appoints the prime minister and the other ministers. Although it is the monarch who formally calls new elections, the decision is made by the prime minister.

### France

France has an unusual executive structure in the European context, having a president who is powerful, and directly elected. Executive power is vested jointly in the president and the cabinet (the Council of Ministers). Typically, the president asks a senior legislator in his own party to head a cabinet, which may be a single-party administration or a coalition. On several occasions since 1986, French presidents have been forced to 'cohabit' with prime ministers from a different party and, in these situations, the power of the French president was significantly undermined. Since 2002, however, constitutional reforms have reduced the French presidential term and aligned this with the parliamentary term, drastically reducing the prospect of *cohabitation* and in this way, somewhat paradoxically, enhancing the power of the French president.

### Germany

The powers of the German head of state, the federal president, are among the weakest in Europe. After a general election the president nominates a prime minister, the federal chancellor, but almost all other actions of the president must be countersigned by the chancellor. As a consequence, the role of president is largely ceremonial, although, as with the British monarch, the head of state could in theory refuse to call elections when asked to do so by the chief executive. This has never actually happened in either country. The ability of the legislature to remove the executive is constrained by the need for a constructive vote of no confidence, which requires that the legislature can bring down a government only if it can also agree on a replacement.

### Italy

The Italian president is indirectly elected by an electoral college comprising both houses of the legislature and 58 representatives of regional parliaments. He has some practical political power, arising from the right to dissolve the legislature and the fact that he remains in office for seven years. Given the chaotic state of the scandal-racked Italian party system during the 1990s, the stability provided by the presidency did much to enhance the role of the office, and Presidents Cossiga and Scalfaro were significant political figures. In government formation, the president may nominate any legislator as prime minister, and takes account of deals between parties when doing this, although he or she is very likely to nominate the candidate who emerges from bargaining between parties. Changes to the Italian electoral system since the 1990s, however, have encouraged the formation of pre-electoral coalitions, and have had the effect that Italian voters, rather than the president, have chosen the incoming prime minister.

### Netherlands

The Dutch constitution makes no reference whatsoever to parliamentary government, vesting all executive authority in the monarch, who appoints ministers and dismisses them at will (Art. 86.2). In practice the Netherlands has developed a parliamentary government system, although the queen still plays quite an active role in government formation. After an election or a government resignation, the queen consults all party leaders, and then typically appoints an elder statesperson as *informateur* to identify the person best placed politically to lead government formation negotiations. These negotiations can be very lengthy, involving the agreement of an extensive, detailed and technical government programme, a process that can take up to six months. Once a prime minister designate has agreed on a coalition deal with other parties, the queen appoints cabinet ministers on his or her advice, although there is a strong tradition that individual parties have control over who fills their portfolios.

### Poland

The powers of the Polish president have varied throughout the history of the Polish state: from presidentialism under the 1952 constitution, through semi-presidentialism under the 1992 interim constitution, to parliamentary government with some elements of semi-presidentialism under the 1997 constitution. In constitutional terms, the Polish president has lost a considerable amount of power, and the locus of power has shifted towards a prime minister accountable directly to parliament. As a result, Poland can be seen as moving away from the 'semi-presidential' model. However, the president still retains some significant powers, such as the right to initiate legislation, refer bills to the Constitutional Tribunal, and nominate various key state officials. Despite a weakened constitutional position, the president continues to impose some limitations on the government. The executive's decision-making capacity is constrained mainly by the presidential veto, which becomes very significant during periods of *cohabitation* between president and prime minister of different political persuasions.

### Spain

Spain's monarchy played a very important role in the country's transition to democracy, siding with those who favoured democratic development and thereby reducing the probability that, following the end of the authoritarian regime under General Franco, Spanish politics would continue down the authoritarian path. The role has given the monarchy high prestige. While the Spanish monarch is head of state, under Article 97 of the 1978 constitution executive authority is vested in a cabinet led by a prime minister. The king proposes a candidate for the office of prime minister, and the candidate is elected by an absolute majority of the legislature. Typically, however, the results of elections in Spain have been decisive enough to give the king no practical role in government formation.

### United Kingdom

The United Kingdom is the only state in modern Europe without a codified constitution, and so government formation is governed by custom and precedent, codified by a civil service handbook in 2010, with the intention of insulating the monarch from any perceived involvement in political decision-making. The leader of the largest party is typically asked by the monarch to become prime minister and form a government; on accepting this invitation, he or she immediately becomes prime minister. This process was delayed by five days in 2010, since no single party won a legislative majority in the 6 May parliamentary election and, unusually for Britain, negotiations between party leaders were needed to determine who could control a parliamentary majority. The PM then nominates a cabinet of senior party legislators, whose nominations are formally accepted by the monarch, and the incoming cabinet needs no formal investiture vote in the House of Commons.

Notwithstanding the formal constitutional doctrine of individual ministerial responsibility, the political reality is often quite different. There is an increasing reluctance on the part of cabinet ministers in almost every European country to resign in response to problems in their own department, particularly problems in which they do not see themselves as being directly involved. The real-world position is that ministers tend to be forced out of office only over major policy catastrophes or serious scandals for which they bear direct responsibility, and not even then if they continue to enjoy the steadfast support of their cabinet colleagues. Since these colleagues are only too well aware that they too may find themselves under a similar threat at some time in the future, they tend to be 'understanding' about the travails of ministerial colleagues. It is fair to say that, these days, departmental problems provide a convenient excuse to get rid of an unwanted minister, but popular or powerful ministers are rarely sacked when something bad happens on their departmental watch. In this sense, the doctrine of individual ministerial responsibility is more a convenient constitutional fiction than a hard fact of political life.

The second key role for a cabinet minister is as a member of the government, constitutionally defined in each European parliamentary democracy as a *collective* entity. This means that members of the cabinet must sink or swim together, bound by a doctrine of *collective cabinet responsibility*. This doctrine means that, while ministers may debate issues with great ferocity in cabinet meetings, the final cabinet decision, once taken, is collective cabinet policy, and by extension is also the official policy position of every cabinet minister. The rationale for the doctrine of collective cabinet responsibility is clear and simple. Citizens need to know where they stand, so there should be no ambiguity about the settled policy of the government on any matter. Every cabinet member is bound not only to *observe* each cabinet decision but also to *defend* this in public, even if he or she violently opposed it in private debate around the cabinet table, and even if defending the decision is politically damaging. If any minister cannot publicly stand over a cabinet decision in this way, then he or she must resign or face dismissal. The constitutional doctrine of collective cabinet responsibility goes hand in hand with a doctrine of *cabinet confidentiality*. Ministers are typically prohibited from revealing the substance of political discussions within the cabinet, since to do so would reveal internal divisions that would undermine the collective nature of the decision.

For reviews of the role of the cabinet in a number of European countries, see Blondel (1991), Laver and Shepsle (1994), Blondel and Müller-Rommel (1997, 2001), Bergman *et al.* (2003), Müller and Strøm (2003) and Strøm *et al.* (2003).

On balance, and with a few notable exceptions, the constitutional doctrine of collective cabinet responsibility is diligently observed as a matter of political practice in modern European democracies, unlike the doctrine of individual ministerial responsibility. Collective cabinet responsibility and confidentiality are usually in the long-term political interest of all ministers, despite short-term incentives that individual ministers might on occasion have to defect from them. Cabinets must often take politically unpopular decisions, and there is comfort for ministers in the knowledge that they can shelter from the political fallout of these decisions under the cloak of collective cabinet responsibility. No one minister can be singled out when the going gets tough; all ministers sink or swim together. In the same way, the practical political advantages of cabinet confidentiality are very much like those of the mafia code of *omertà*. While there might be short-term temptations to talk in public about disagreements around the cabinet table, ministers know they are far better off holding to the principle that such disagreements are never brought into the public domain. This gives opponents of the government fewer opportunities to exploit the inevitable internal divisions that periodically arise within any cabinet. Thus, regardless of formal or informal rules, one of the hard facts of political life is that members of a cabinet do indeed sink or swim together. Sometimes an individual minister may be thrown to the sharks as punishment for a major but self-contained blunder but, for the most part, when a cabinet runs into trouble, it runs *collectively* into trouble. It is this, more than any written rules or cabinet procedure guidelines, that forces collective responsibility upon the cabinet.

Collective cabinet responsibility does tend to hold firm in practice, and is indeed one of the main causes of ministerial resignation in modern Europe. A high-profile example was the resignation in 2003 of the British foreign affairs minister, the late Robin Cook, because he was unwilling to stay silent about his opposition to cabinet decisions on Iraq. Since such resignations typically put the government under pressure, and trigger something of a political storm, the doctrine of collective cabinet responsibility forces cabinet decision-making to be largely consensual. While no single minister can formally veto a cabinet decision, any minister can threaten to resign if a particular decision is made. This threat can be implemented only once. Nonetheless, if it is indeed implemented, it can have very serious consequences for the government. This creates strong informal pressure to keep all cabinet ministers 'on side' when important decisions are being made, leading to a situation that can sometimes look like an informal veto system in the cabinet, especially over issues that are not important enough for cabinet members to be prepared to risk potential bad fallout for the government.

The twin roles of a minister, as individually accountable head of a government department and as member of a collectively responsible cabinet, interact in a potent manner, given the vast volume and complexity of the business that any government must conduct. In Sweden, for example, it is estimated that the cabinet makes about 20 000 collective decisions every year. Not surprisingly, most of these are waved through, by the hundreds, in formal weekly half-hour cabinet meetings (Larsson, 1994). The 'real' business tends to be discussed in far more informal settings, including daily lunches at which all ministers who are in Stockholm tend to eat together. While details may differ, the bottom line is that there is a huge volume of formal government business to be nodded through by any modern cabinet, accompanied by a much smaller number of urgent and/or complex policy issues to be decided, either on pressing external developments to which the government must respond, or which represent important new policy initiatives for the government.

This vast volume of business means that the only realistic way in which a *fully specified and implementable* policy proposal can be put to the cabinet for decision is for this to be developed within one or more government departments. The cabinet does not and cannot sit around in a meeting and make policy in a vacuum. Real-world policymaking on complex issues involves the cabinet accepting, rejecting or amending specific and detailed proposals that are presented to it, based on extensive and often very technical documentation. Only the government department with responsibility for the policy area in question has the resources and expertise to generate such a proposal. Thus only the minister in charge of the relevant department is in a position to send this proposal to the cabinet, giving this minister a privileged position in the policy jurisdiction in question. An important consequence of this is that there is an intense *division of labour* in cabinet decision-making, with each minister responsible for bringing forward policy proposals in his or her own area of jurisdiction. Conversely, ministers are poorly placed to make substantial contributions to the formation of policy in areas over which they have no jurisdiction. The minister of foreign affairs does not have access to the departmental resources and expertise to develop detailed proposals on education policy, for example. The minister for education does not have the resources to develop detailed proposals on foreign affairs. The result is a norm that, in the Dutch case for example, is seen as a *tacit rule of non-intervention*, according to which ministers are discouraged from intervening in policy decisions that are not directly relevant to their own portfolios (Andeweg and Bakema, 1994). In part, this arises out of an understanding that it is unwise for a minister to give a hard time to a cabinet colleague whose future support on other matters might be critical. In part, it also arises from a situation in which ministers tend to be briefed for cabinet meetings by their senior civil servants, who may not know much, or may not tell the minister much, about the affairs of other departments.

This situation in the Netherlands is common in other cabinet systems, in which a huge volume of work creates strong incentives for a *de facto* division of labour that gives cabinet ministers near-monopolies on policy initiation in their own areas of jurisdiction. Cabinet decisions may appear to be made collectively, both constitutionally and on the face of things. Ultimately cabinet members do collectively sink or swim together, so they all have an interest in intervening to prevent colleagues running other departments from making errors or ill-judged policies However, most of the practical policy decisions that cabinets make involve choosing between the status quo and some specific alternative policy that has been developed by the minister and department with responsibility for the issue in question. The result is that the effective choice of policy outcomes by the cabinet is very much structured along departmental lines. Although all ministers do take collective *responsibility* for every cabinet decision, each minister does not, and indeed cannot, have equal input into the *formulation* of every decision that is taken. In this sense, cabinet ministers inevitably put themselves into one another's hands, and ministers are agenda setters in their own policy jurisdictions. The upshot of this, which we revisit in Chapter 12 when looking at government formation, is that one of the most effective ways to change cabinet policy is to change the minister with control over the agenda in the relevant policy jurisdiction.

## 2.6  Junior ministers

The power of cabinet ministers to set the policy agenda in their own areas of jurisdiction, often away from the public gaze, is something that might worry cabinet colleagues from other parties. One way to assuage these fears arises from the fact that, in all European states, the political executive extends well beyond the cabinet. It extends both to what are typically known as *junior ministers*, and to other crucial political offices such as that of attorney-general or equivalent. Junior ministers, sometimes known as undersecretaries or ministers of state, are not members of the cabinet; they are neither officially privy to its secrets nor subject to its disciplines. Junior ministers are typically appointed to head subsections of the major departments of state – a department of education might have a junior minister for higher education, for example – and thus rank unambiguously below cabinet ministers. However, junior ministers do not report in a strict sense to the cabinet minister in charge of their department – they too are appointed by the prime minister on behalf of the government as a whole.

In effect, parts of the cabinet minister's jurisdiction are often delegated to a junior minister, who does have a *de facto* independent role *vis-à-vis* the minister within his or her subjurisdiction. This delegation is part of the deal that sets up the cabinet, under which a cabinet minister is allocated particular junior ministers, and cannot sack these unilaterally if they turn out to be nothing but a nuisance. This has led Michael Thies to suggest that the junior ministers appointed to departments may tend in coalition cabinets to come from parties other than that of the departmental cabinet minister, giving these other parties the chance to monitor the behaviour of the cabinet minister and ensure that he or she does not stray too far from agreed government policy (Thies, 2001). Thies finds systematic empirical evidence that junior ministers in modern Europe do tend to come from parties other than that of the cabinet minister, a conclusion confirmed in more detailed analyses of the appointment of junior ministers in Italy (Mershon, 2001; Giannetti and Laver, 2005). Overall, therefore, while cabinet ministers can be very powerful people, there is some evidence that this power may be trimmed, when the cabinet is formed, by the appointment of junior ministers from other parties.

## 2.7 The head of state

Over and above the chief executive and cabinet in a typical European democracy we find the head of state – the country's first citizen. The president under a separation-of-powers system may well also be head of state, as with the president of the United States of America. This is almost unheard of under European-style parliamentary government, where the head of state is seen as 'above' politics, a lofty figurehead for the state and its citizens. There is typically a clear separation of powers between chief executive and head of state, although, as we have seen, the line between these roles may be blurred in semi-presidential systems such as France. This is a relic of the evolution of many European states from traditional autocratic monarchies into the parliamentary democracies we see today. Indeed, many modern European states retain monarchs at their head: the list of *constitutional monarchies* includes Belgium, Britain, Denmark, Luxembourg, the Netherlands, Norway, Spain and Sweden (see Table 2.1). While details vary from country to country, Europe's republics have also tended to evolve a role for the president, as head of state, that is like that of a constitutional monarch. Functions include the procedural (for example, presiding over the transfer of power from one chief executive to the next, or providing the final ratification of laws), the diplomatic (greeting other heads of state and visiting dignitaries, and going on official state visits to other countries), and the purely symbolic (as first citizen, and the personal embodiment of the state). Such presidents may be directly elected by the people or indirectly elected by parliament, though Margit Tavits found that the power of the president does not tend to be related to whether or not he or she is directly elected (Tavits, 2009).

Many European countries – for example Austria, Cyprus, Finland, Iceland, Ireland, Portugal – have directly elected presidents, though few have constitutional powers equivalent to those of the president of France. The number of such presidents swelled as a result of the democratization of eastern Europe, since many former communist states – for example Croatia, Lithuania, Poland, Slovakia and Slovenia – opted for a directly elected presidency, though not for full presidential government. Of these, Finland and, as we have seen, Poland have in the past come closest to being semi-presidential in nature.

For much of the post-war period the Finnish constitution gave the president a central role in foreign policy. The special circumstances of Finland's role in the Second World War and its long land border with the Soviet Union made this power very important throughout the Cold War. The long-serving President Kekkonen did more than anyone else to establish harmonious relations

**TABLE 2.1** Heads of state in Europe, 2011

| | Constitutional status of head of state | Head of state (January 2011) | When came to office | How came to office |
|---|---|---|---|---|
| Austria | President | Heinz Fischer | 2004 | Direct election |
| Belgium | Monarch | King Albert II | 1993 | Heredity |
| Bulgaria | President | Georgi S. Parvanov | 2002 | Direct election |
| Cyprus | President | Dimitris Christofias | 2008 | Direct election |
| Czech republic | President | Václav Klaus | 2003 | Election by legislature |
| Denmark | Monarch | Queen Margrethe II | 1972 | Heredity |
| Estonia | President | Toomas Hendrik Ilves | 2006 | Election by legislature |
| Finland | President | Tarja Halonen | 2000 | Direct election |
| France | President | Nicolas Sarkozy | 2007 | Direct election |
| Germany | President | Christian Wulff | 2010 | Election by legislature |
| Greece | President | Karolos Papoulias | 2005 | Election by legislature |
| Hungary | President | László Sólyom | 2005 | Election by legislature |
| Iceland | President | Ólafur Ragnar Grimsson | 1996 | Direct election |
| Ireland | President | Mary McAleese | 1997 | Direct election |
| Italy | President | Giorgio Napolitano | 2006 | Election by legislature |
| Latvia | President | Valdis Zatlers | 2007 | Election by legislature |
| Lithuania | President | Dalia Grybauskaitė | 2009 | Direct election |
| Luxembourg | Grand Duke | Grand Duke Henri | 2000 | Hereditary |
| Malta | President | George Abela | 2009 | Election by legislature |
| Netherlands | Monarch | Queen Beatrix | 1980 | Heredity |
| Norway | Monarch | King Harald V | 1991 | Heredity |
| Poland | President | Bronisław Komorowski | 2010 | Direct election |
| Portugal | President | Aníbal Cavaco Silva | 2006 | Direct election |
| Romania | President | Traian Băsescu | 2004 | Direct election |
| Slovakia | President | Ivan Gašparovič | 2004 | Direct election |
| Slovenia | President | Danilo Türk | 2007 | Direct election |
| Spain | Monarch[a] | King Juan Carlos | 1975 | Heredity |
| Sweden | Monarch | King Carl XVI Gustaf | 1973 | Heredity |
| Switzerland | President | Micheline Calmey-Rey | 2011 | Election by legislature |
| United Kingdom | Monarch | Queen Elizabeth II | 1952 | Heredity |

[a] Spain was a republic from 1931 to 1975. Juan Carlos, grandson of the king ousted in 1931, was nominated by the dictator General Franco to succeed him as head of state, and took over this position when Franco died in 1975.

with Finland's powerful and potentially dangerous neighbour. The Finnish president at that time also had considerable influence in domestic policy, though the initiative in policymaking lay with the government. Following disintegration of the former Soviet Union and the end of the

Cold War, a series of constitutional reforms in 1994 and 2000 significantly cut back the powers of the Finnish president. A two-term limit was imposed, and the president's independent powers to dismiss a government, dissolve parliament and call new elections were all removed. The Finnish presidency now has more or less the same powers as those found elsewhere in modern Europe (Nousiainen, 2002; Paloheimo, 2003; Raunio, 2004).

As in many other states in transition from the former Soviet bloc, Polish democracy initially operated under a set of amendments to the pre-existing communist constitution. In 1992 parliament adopted the so-called *Little Constitution*, intended to operate until a comprehensive new constitution could be agreed on. Under the terms of this, the Polish president was elected by popular vote for a five-year term, and had significant powers. These included the right to nominate the prime minister, subject to approval by a lower house that could reject the presidential nominee and appoint its own candidate without seeking presidential approval. Prior presidential consultation was required for appointment of ministers of defence, internal affairs and foreign affairs, while the president had to approve all other cabinet appointments. The president also could dissolve parliament, the Sejm, in special circumstances, and had the right to veto legislation passed by parliament, although this veto could be overturned by a two-thirds majority in the Sejm. A new constitution was adopted in 1997, which weakened the powers of the Polish president. The Sejm can now overrule a presidential veto with a three-fifths rather than a two-thirds majority, and this veto can no longer be applied to the budget. The president has no special role with regard to defence, security or foreign affairs, strengthening the prime minister's side of this dual executive. Overall, the effect of the new constitution was to strengthen the position of cabinet and prime minister *vis-à-vis* both parliament and the president, making constitutional arrangements in Poland much more like fusion-of-powers systems found elsewhere in modern Europe (Krouwel, 2003; Elgie 2009).

In Austria, Iceland, Ireland and Portugal a less powerful elected president exercises certain responsibilities in specified circumstances, but in practice tends not to get involved in day-to-day politics. In Ireland, for example, the role of the president is extensively and explicitly curtailed by the constitution. Even so, the Irish president does have two important powers that could be politically important in certain circumstances. The first is the power to refer bills passed by the legislature directly to the Supreme Court in order to test their constitutionality, a power used on quite a few occasions, some controversial. (We return to this in Chapter 4.) The second is the power, valid only if the prime minister has lost a vote of confidence, to refuse a request for dissolution of the legislature, and thereby block new elections. This power has never been used in Ireland – dissolutions have always been granted on request – but its existence is an important constraint on the freedom of Irish prime ministers to call elections whenever they feel like it.

A dramatic example of apparently 'weak' presidents activating seldom-used but nonetheless potentially significant formal powers arose in Iceland in January 2010, when President Ólafur Grimsson (formerly a political scientist) generated national and international turmoil by withholding formal approval for a bill authorizing the repayment of more than €3.8 billion to Britain and the Netherlands as compensation for losses arising from the collapse in those countries of an Icelandic bank in 2008. Citing the unpopularity of the bill with the Icelandic public, Grimsson's refusal had the effect of forcing a referendum on this matter. The resulting referendum defeated the bill, with a 93 per cent vote against, although other arrangements for addressing the problem were on the table by the time the referendum was held. This example illustrates the important general point that formal constitutional powers, even if rarely or never used, potentially have a significant impact on events. The very possibility that such powers might be used may cause politicians to trim their sails in anticipation of this.

า the other European republics the president is elected indirectly, usually by members ot parliament. In none of these countries is the constitutional role of the president particularly strong, although disputes between indirectly elected presidents and prime ministers were common in central and eastern European states during transitions to democracy, clearly illustrated by the situation that emerged in the Czech Republic shortly after its formation following the dissolution of the former federal state of Czechoslovakia. The new Czech constitution, approved in 1992, provided for a president elected by a majority vote in parliament. In 1993 the leading former dissident, Václav Havel, who had been elected first post-communist president of Czechoslovakia in 1990, was re-elected to office, this time as first president of the new Czech Republic. A proposal for the direct election of the Czech president by the people had been rejected, for fear this might lead to the accumulation of too much personal power by the incumbent. The president was given the right to dissolve parliament in certain limited circumstances (such as when the government had been defeated in a vote of no confidence); to suspend but not veto legislation; and to appoint the prime minister and ministers, subject to the approval of the House. Although the new constitution came down firmly in favour of a parliamentary system, sharp tensions quickly emerged between President Havel and the prime minister, Václav Klaus, who had been Havel's former ally in the pro-democracy Civic Forum. Such disputes between a constitutionally powerful head of government and an ostensibly ceremonial head of state are virtually unknown in most long-established parliamentary democracies, even those with a president rather than a monarch at their head. In post-communist Europe, on the other hand, including both the Czech and Slovak republics, they are not uncommon, reflecting continuing uncertainty about the division of executive authority in everyday politics (Baylis, 1996; Krouwel, 2003; Kysela and Kühn, 2007).

What we see in these examples is the other side of the French coin. The French president is undeniably strong, but is much stronger when formal constitutional powers are reinforced by a favourable political situation. Other presidents, such as those in Italy or the Czech Republic, are undeniably weak, but may become stronger in particular political circumstances. It is thus unwise to write off the *potential* political power of any European president in times of crisis, even if it is easy to underestimate that power when things are running smoothly (Protsyk, 2005; Amorim Neto and Strøm, 2006; Kang, 2009).

### 2.7.1 Monarchs

European countries that do not have presidents retain monarchs as heads of state, although no former monarch has been restored to the throne in ex-communist eastern Europe. Many European monarchies are very ancient institutions, and monarchs might be thought of as peculiar anachronisms in the twenty-first century. They still can have an important role to play, however, although this is even further removed from the cut and thrust of party politics than the role played by presidents. In the past, some monarchs have succumbed to the temptation to intervene politically, using their power and position to favour some parties over others. This has usually caused widespread resentment, and has rebounded on those who have tried it. It was the main factor behind referendums leading to the abolition of the monarchies in Greece and Italy, and the Belgian monarchy survived only narrowly in a vote in 1950. Royal houses that have remained aloof from partisan politics have managed to survive, and given the often high degree of public cynicism towards politicians, an unelected king or queen may even command more popular affection than an elected leader.

An interesting counter-example to the strong norm that monarchs in modern Europe steer well clear of party politics can be found in Bulgaria. The former Tsar of Bulgaria, Simeon Saxe-Coburg-Gotha, returned to Bulgaria in 2001, after 55 years in exile, and decided to enter Bulgarian politics. He formed the National Movement Simeon II (NMSII) barely three months before the election. The party was hugely successful, although the restoration of the monarchy was not mooted during the campaign, and finished just one seat short of an absolute majority. Simeon himself became the prime minister, and held this position until August 2005, an unprecedented example of a former monarch who went on to become an elected prime minister (Harper, 2001).

The classic example of a monarchy that plays an important role in society comes from Britain, where the Queen sits at the apex of the social system, and is even head of the established church, the Church of England. While a British monarch has never recently been involved in explicit party politics, one reason for this is that Britain's first-past-the-post electoral system typically delivers decisive election results (see Chapter 11). Even when this does not happen, and the identity of the next government is in some doubt, following an election result that has not generated a single majority party, as happened in May 2010, elaborate procedures are in place, involving the head of the permanent civil service, which avoid the need for any explicit political involvement by a head of state in government formation negotiations.

No other European monarchy wraps itself in as much pomp and ceremony as the British royal family, but a monarch's very existence as a symbol of the nation can be important. King Baudouin of Belgium used to describe himself as 'the only Belgian', a reference to the fact that virtually all others in the linguistically divided country think of themselves first and foremost as either Flemish (if they speak Dutch) or Walloon (if they speak French). The monarchy is one of the few symbols with which both language groups can identify. In Spain, the monarch exercised a vital political role in the years after the death of the dictator Franco in 1975. King Juan Carlos, designated successor to the dictator General Franco, was expected to perpetuate the authoritarian system. In fact, he quickly dismantled the Franco dictatorship and initiated Spain's return to democracy. His intervention was also decisive in thwarting an attempted military coup in 1981. While the Spanish monarch does also have formal powers to designate a prime minister, who then takes office subject to a majority vote in the legislature, these powers have not been significant in practice, given election results that have usually been decisive. However, the combination of moral authority and formal powers means that the Spanish monarch retains considerable potential to play an important political role in the event of serious failure in the mainstream political process (Heywood, 1995).

Overall, despite the parliamentary government system that designates the prime minister the chief executive and leaves the head of state a largely ceremonial role, monarchs and presidents in modern Europe cannot be dismissed as mere ciphers. Apart from explicit powers that some have in the area of government formation, which we return to in Chapter 12, they can play a significant part in legitimizing the entire political system. However, it is true to say that they generally keep out of the risky business of day-to-day politics, so that real executive power in today's European states is typically in the hands of the executive branch of government rather than those of the head of state.

## 2.8 Putting it all together

The institutional theory of parliamentary government concentrates political accountability of the entire governmental process on one key institution, the legislative vote of confidence in the executive. Parliamentary government can be said to be representative government, because the legislature is held to represent the population as a whole (a matter to which we return in Chapter 11) and because the government is responsible to, and can be dismissed by, the legislature (Chapter 12). The administration of government is conducted by a civil service, overseen by ministerial masters who are themselves responsible to the cabinet and thus to the legislature.

We move in the next chapter to consider the general political role of legislatures. In the present context what is important is that, while legislatures can of course legislate, passing laws that implement policy decisions, control by the government over both the legislative agenda and the civil service – vital in the planning and drafting of effective legislation – greatly undermines the practical political effect of this formal legislative role. What a legislature can do in theory – and what many legislatures actually do in practice – is to eject governments from office, using either an actual or a threatened vote of no confidence. This sweeping power can be used only in important political circumstances, giving the incumbent government considerable latitude to get its own way, even against the wishes of the majority, on many minor matters. Nonetheless, one of the core principles of modern European parliamentary democracy is that an 'unelected' government must be able to maintain the support of an elected legislature. When all is said and done, this is what ensures that representative government in modern Europe is also democratic government.

## References

**Amorim Neto, O. and K. Strøm** (2006) 'Breaking the parliamentary chain of delegation: presidents and non-partisan cabinet members in European democracies', *British Journal of Political Science*, 36 (4), 619–643.

**Andeweg, Rudy and Wilma Bakema** (1994) 'The Netherlands: ministers and cabinet policy', pp. 56–72 in M. Laver and K.A. Shepsle (eds), *Cabinet Ministers and Parliamentary Government*, Cambridge University Press, New York.

**Baylis, Thomas A.** (1996) 'Presidents versus prime ministers: shaping executive authority in Eastern Europe', *World Politics*, 46, 297–323.

**Bergman, Torbjörn, Wolfgang C. Müller, Kaare Strøm and Magnus Blomgren** (2003) 'Democratic delegation and accountability: cross-national patterns', pp. 109–221 in K. Strøm, W.C. Müller and T. Bergman (eds), *Delegation and Accountability in Parliamentary Democracies*, Oxford University Press, Oxford.

**Blondel, Jean** (1991) 'Cabinet government and cabinet ministers', pp. 5–18 in Jean Blondel and Jean-Louis Thiebault (eds), *The Profession of Government Minister in Western Europe*, Macmillan, London.

**Blondel, Jean and Ferdinand Müller-Rommel** (1997) *Cabinets in Western Europe*, 2nd edn, Macmillan, Basingstoke.

**Blondel, Jean and Ferdinand Müller-Rommel** (eds) (2001) *Cabinets in Eastern Europe*. Palgrave, London.

**Bräuninger, T. and M. Debus** (2009) 'Legislative agenda-setting in parliamentary democracies', *European Journal of Political Research*, 48 (6), 804–839.

**Cheibub, José Antonio** (2007) *Presidentialism, Parliamentarism, and Democracy*, Cambridge University Press, New York.

**Diermeier, D. and T.J. Feddersen** (1998) 'Cohesion in legislatures and the vote of confidence procedure', *American Political Science Review*, 92 (3), 611–621.

**Döring, H. and M. Hallerberg** (2004) *Patterns of Parliamentary Behaviour: Passage of Legislation Across Western Europe*, Ashgate, Aldershot.

**Dowding, Keith and Patrick Dumont** (2009) *The Selection of Ministers in Europe: Hiring and Firing*, Routledge, New York.

**Edwards, G.C.** (1990) *At the Margins: Presidential Leadership of Congress*, Yale University Press, New Haven, CT.

**Elgie, Robert** (1999) *Semi-Presidentialism in Europe*, Oxford University Press, Oxford.

**Elgie, Robert** (2009) 'Duverger, semi-presidentialism and the supposed French archetype', *West European Politics*, 32 (2), 248–267.

**Elster, John, Claus Offe and Ulrich Klaus Preuss** (1998) *Institutional Design in Post Communist Societies*, Cambridge University Press, Cambridge.

**Frye, Timothy** (1997) 'A politics of institutional choice: post-communist presidencies', *Comparative Political Studies*, 30 (5), 523–552.

**Giannetti, Daniela and Michael Laver** (2005) 'Policy positions and jobs in the government', *European Journal of Political Research*, 44 (1), 91–120.

**Grossman, E.** (2009) 'The president's choice? Government and cabinet turnover under the Fifth Republic', *West European Politics*, 32 (2), 268–286.

**Grossman, E. and N. Sauger** (2009) 'The end of ambiguity? Presidents versus parties or the four phases of the Fifth Republic', *West European Politics*, 32 (2), 423–437.

**Harper, Marcus A.G.** (2001) 'The 2001 parliamentary and presidential elections in Bulgaria', *Electoral Studies*, 22, 325–395.

**Heywood, Paul** (1995) *The Government and Politics of Spain*, Macmillan, London.

**Huber, J.D.** (1996) *Rationalizing Parliament: Legislative Institutions and Party Politics in France*, Cambridge University Press, Cambridge.

**Jones, Charles O.** (1999) *Separate but Equal Branches*, Chatham House, New York.

**Jones, Charles O.** (2005) *The Presidency in a Separated System*, Brookings Institution Press, New York.

**Kam, Christopher J.** (2009) *Party Discipline and Parliamentary Politics*, Cambridge University Press, Cambridge.

**Kang, S.G.** (2009) 'The influence of presidential heads of state on government formation in European democracies: empirical evidence', *European Journal of Political Research*, 48 (4), 543–572.

**King, Anthony and Nicholas Allen** (2010) '"Off with their heads": British prime ministers and the power to dismiss', *British Journal of Political Science*, 40, 249–278.

**Krouwel, A.** (2003) 'Measuring presidentialism and parliamentarism: an application to Central and East European countries', *Acta Politica*, 38 (4), 333–364.

**Kysela, J. and Z. Kühn** (2007) 'Presidential elements in government: the Czech Republic', *European Constitutional Law Review*, 3 (1), 91–113.

**Larsson, Torbjörn** (1994) 'Cabinet ministers and parliamentary government in Sweden', in M. Laver and K.A. Shepsle (eds), *Cabinet Ministers and Parliamentary Government*, Cambridge University Press, New York.

**Laver, Michael and Kenneth A. Shepsle** (1994) *Cabinet Ministers and Parliamentary Government*, Cambridge University Press, Cambridge.

**Laver, Michael and Kenneth A. Shepsle** (1996) *Making and Breaking Governments: Cabinets and Legislatures in Parliamentary Democracies*. Cambridge University Press, New York.

**Lijphart, Arend** (1999) *Patterns of Democracy: Government Forms and Performance in Thirty-Six Countries*. Yale University Press, New Haven, CT.

**Lijphart, Arend and Carlos H. Waisman** (1996) *Institutional Design in New Democracies: Eastern Europe and Latin America*, Westview Press, Boulder, CO.

**Mayhew, David R.** (2005) *Divided We Govern: Party Control, Lawmaking and Investigations, 1946–2002*, Yale University Press, New Haven, CT.

**Mershon, Carol** (2001) 'Party factions and coalition government: portfolio allocation in Italian Christian Democracy', *Electoral Studies*, 20, 555–580.

**Müller, W.C. and K. Strøm** (2003) *Coalition Governments in Western Europe*, Oxford University Press, New York.

**Neustadt, R.E.** (1991) *Presidential Power and the Modern Presidents: The Politics of Leadership from Roosevelt to Reagan.* The Free Press, New York.

**Nousiainen, J.** (2002) 'From semi-presidentialism to parliamentary government: political and constitutional developments in Finland', *Scandinavian Political Studies*, 24 (2), 95–109.

**Paloheimo, H.** (2003) 'The rising power of the prime minister in Finland', *Scandinavian Political Studies*, 26 (3), 219–243.

**Peterson, Mark A.** (1993) *Legislating Together: The White House and Capitol Hill from Eisenhower to Reagan.* Harvard University Press, Cambridge, MA.

**Protsyk, O.** (2005) 'Prime ministers' identity in semi-presidential regimes: constitutional norms and cabinet formation outcomes', *European Journal of Political Research*, 44 (5), 721–748.

**Raunio, T.** (2004) 'The changing Finnish democracy: stronger parliamentary accountability, coalescing political parties and weaker external constraints', *Scandinavian Political Studies*, 27 (2), 133–152.

**Rose, R.** (1991) 'Prime ministers in parliamentary democracies', *West European Politics*, 14 (2), 9–24.

**Shugart, Matthew S. and John M. Carey** (1992) *Presidents and Assemblies: Constitutional Design and Electoral Dynamics*, Cambridge University Press, Cambridge.

**Strøm, Kaare, Wolfgang C. Müller and Torbjörn Bergman** (2003) *Delegation and Accountability in Parliamentary Democracies*, Oxford University Press, Oxford.

**Tavits, Margit** (2009) *Presidents with Prime Ministers: Do Direct Elections Matter?* Oxford University Press, Oxford.

**Thies, Michael** (2001) 'Keeping tabs on partners: the logic of delegation in coalition governments', *American Journal of Political Science*, 45 (3), 580–598.

**Tsebelis, George** (2002) *Veto Players: How Political Institutions Work*, Princeton University Press, Princeton, NJ.

# Parliaments

## Chapter contents

## 3.1 Introduction

As we saw in Chapter 2, European states, with only a few exceptions, are run according to the principles of parliamentary government, a set of institutions and behaviour patterns that gives a particularly important role to political parties. Put simply, the decisive body in running the country is the government, but the government is installed by, is answerable to, and can be dismissed from office by the parliament elected by the voters at general elections. (In this chapter we use the terms 'parliament' and 'legislature' interchangeably.) In classical liberal democratic theory the government merely does the bidding of parliament; parliament makes the laws and lays down the policies, and the government, a mere 'agent' of parliament, dutifully carries these out. In reality this was never really the way things worked, and it certainly does not sum up the relationship between governments and parliaments today. In fact, many have suggested that the wheel has turned full circle, and that now it is a case of governments making all the decisions and parliaments merely rubber-stamping these. In reality the situation is more nuanced than this – so nuanced, indeed, that it can sometimes be difficult to be sure what the real relationship between government and parliament is.

There are many reasons why the initiative lies with governments rather than with parliaments, and the most important one concerns the central role played in European politics by cohesive, disciplined political parties that can ensure that all of their members in parliament vote the same way on all important issues. Before we examine the relevance of parliaments, though, we need to clarify just what we mean by 'parliament', which should not be looked upon either as a unitary actor or as a body that has an essentially competitive relationship with the government. Rather than ask about the extent to which parliament controls or is controlled by government, we need to examine the role of parliaments in a number of areas, including sustaining the government, law-making, and scrutiny of the government. After this, we consider in depth the crucial role played by political parties in determining the place of parliaments in European political systems, and then assess the significance of the representation that is provided to Europeans by the constituency role of members of parliament. Finally, given that a number of states have a second chamber, often termed an *upper house*, as well as a directly elected first chamber, often termed the *lower house*, we consider whether it makes a difference whether parliaments have one chamber or two.

## 3.2 Parliaments and governments

The question most frequently asked about parliaments is: how much power do they have *vis-à-vis* governments? But it is arguable that, in most of modern Europe, this is simply 'the wrong question', or, at best, 'more confusing than it is illuminating' (Andeweg and Nijzink, 1995: 152). When, as in virtually every European country (Cyprus and Switzerland are the exceptions), the government is elected by parliament and can be ousted from office by it, it makes little sense to envisage parliament and government as two distinct bodies vying for power. In a presidential system, when president and parliament are elected independently of each other, such a perspective does make sense, just as it used to in European countries in centuries past, when the monarch appointed a government without having to consult parliament. To ask, for example, about the power of the US Congress *vis-à-vis* the president is a perfectly reasonable question. In the parliamentary systems of government that characterize modern Europe, however, it is more realistic to see parliament as wielding power *through* the government that it has elected, than to see it as seeking to *check* a government that has somehow come into being independently of it. This is especially applicable when, as is the case in many countries, many or most members of the government are also members of parliament.

The reason why the 'governments versus parliaments' framework is not particularly fruitful for analysing European parliaments is that both of these institutions, like nearly every other aspect of political life, are dominated by political parties, as we elaborate in more detail later, and these parties are powerful and generally well disciplined (Bowler *et al.*, 1999; Cox, 2006). As early as 1867, the British political journalist Walter Bagehot wrote of the House of Commons that 'party is inherent in it, is bone of its bone, and breath of its breath' (Bagehot, 1993: 160). The behaviour of both MPs and ministers is likely to be conditioned more by their membership of a party than by their belonging to either parliament or government (Andeweg and Nijzink, 1995: 152). MPs do indeed feel that they are part of a continuous battle, but one that pitches the government against the opposition, not government against parliament. Virtually all parliamentarians in Europe belong to some political party or other, and their party expects them to support the party line on all important issues when it comes to voting in parliament. If the party is in government, its parliamentarians are expected to support the government on all issues. If the parties making up the government command between them a majority of seats in parliament, they can realistically expect all their proposals to be approved by parliament, unless they run into serious resistance from their own rank-and-file MPs. (Members of parliament have many different titles across Europe. In this chapter we use the terms 'deputy', 'member of parliament', 'MP' and 'parliamentarian' interchangeably.)

For the most part, then, when we talk about 'parliament' or 'the legislature' we are not really talking either about a monolithic body or about the interaction of a large number of independent legislators; in practice we are talking about the interaction of a small number of political party groups. The organization of parliament's work is usually built around the various party groups, known generically as *parliamentary party groups*, or PPGs (Heidar and Koole, 2000a). We can take Germany as a fairly typical example. Here the groups are termed *Fraktionen*, and the Bundestag has been described as a *Fraktionenparlament* – in other words, a parliament dominated by the party groups. The *Fraktionen* dominate the life of the Bundestag. The leaders of the *Fraktionen* form a 'council of elders', which pre-structures all debates, allocating speaking time in such a way that there is hardly any scope for spontaneous action by individual MPs. Each *Fraktion* decides which member goes onto which committee, and can recall members from a committee; the party MPs on each committee are there very much as agents of the PPG, and the PPG makes it clear to them in advance of every meeting what line they are expected to take on each issue due to come before the committee (Schüttemeyer, 1994: 35–39). Although the dominance of the *Fraktionen* and their leaders in Germany is perhaps more visible than in many other countries, this is only a matter of degree; everywhere, MPs are very strongly oriented to their party group. It is the norm for the overwhelming majority of a party's MPs to vote with the party group in parliament, and, moreover, many of the rights given by parliamentary rules to individual MPs can in practice be exercised only with the permission of the PPG, whose approval is needed even to put down questions to a minister in some countries, such as the Netherlands. Parliaments all over Europe are dominated by party blocs; every parliament is to a greater or lesser degree a *Fraktionenparlament*, even if it is only in Germany that this specific term is used. The emergence of (fairly) cohesive PPGs in post-communist Europe in the 1990s, even in the absence of significant extra-parliamentary party organizations, shows that they are indispensable to the functioning of the legislature in a modern parliamentary system of government (Bowler, 2000; Heidar and Koole, 2000b: 268).

Once we view the political world in this light, we can see that any constraints imposed by parliament on government come not from a monolithic body called 'parliament' but from one of four possible sources. One is that there may be rules, which are not easy to change, that allow the opposition to block or defeat government plans. There might, for example, be rules requiring certain legislative or other measures (especially constitutional changes, or the appointment of members of constitutional courts, as we discuss in the next chapter) to achieve the support of a qualified majority in parliament, perhaps three-fifths or two-thirds, which means that such measures need the support of at least some of the opposition parties. The second potential source is that there may be political cultural constraints that inhibit the government from railroading its proposals through in the face of strong objections from the opposition, even if the formal rules allow this. The third is that the government might not have majority support in parliament in the first place; at times of minority government there is obviously an increased likelihood that government proposals will be amended or even rejected by parliament. Though minority government is sometimes seen as exceptional, examination of the record shows that over a third of post-war European governments have fallen into this category (see Table 12.2 below). The role of the Norwegian Storting, for example, has become more meaningful since minority rather than majority government became the norm (Rommetvedt, 2003: 18–66). The fourth is that the government may receive only conditional support from its own MPs, who may refuse to support it in some circumstances, or at least may demand an input into proposals as the price of their support, and this factor is of growing significance in a number of countries. Thus, even if governments do not always get their way as a proposal proceeds through parliament, we might hesitate before ascribing power to 'parliament' rather than to government backbenchers and/or an opposition party, but it is true that it is the requirement for parliamentary support that gives these actors power.

Writing over 30 years ago, Anthony King (1976) suggested that parliaments could be better analysed not in terms of relations between 'parliament' and 'government' but in terms of a number of *modes* in which key players might interact. This typology has been refined by Andeweg and Nijzink (1995: 153–154), who identify

- an *inter-party mode*, in which relations between different actors in parliament and government are determined primarily by their respective party affiliations;
- a *cross-party mode*, in which ministers and MPs combine to interact on the basis of cross-party interests; and
- a *non-party mode*, in which government and parliament interact without regard to party.

The third, non-party, mode corresponds to the 'traditional' model that sees government and parliament as two separate bodies, and seeks to assess the relative power of each. In reality, given the centrality of parties to European politics, it is the inter-party mode that characterizes most of the behaviour of ministers and members of parliament. However, we can expect to find a degree of variation across Europe, brought about by different institutional rules, contingent circumstances and political cultures.

In discussing this, we can draw on Arend Lijphart's distinction between two categories of democratic regime. The first is the Westminster-type *majoritarian* model; the United Kingdom provides the clearest European example, with Greece, France and Malta also displaying many of the characteristics of political systems in this category (Lijphart, 1999: 248; Rhodes *et al.*, 2009). In the archetypal majoritarian system the government of the day has an assured majority among members of parliament (MPs), and can rely on getting all of its legislation through virtually unscathed, provided it does not embark on a course of action so far removed from traditional party policy (or so unpopular in the country at large) as to alienate a significant number of its own followers, in which case it is likely to make concessions to its dissidents. The majority party or coalition is prepared, if necessary, to railroad all of its legislation through, regardless of the feelings of the opposition. Effective constraints from any quarter of parliament are so low that the situation is virtually one of 'cabinet dictatorship'. Moreover, the opposition sees its role as criticizing the government rather than trying to influence it. The second of Lijphart's categories is the *consensus model*, exemplified by Germany, the Netherlands and Austria. (The European Union also belongs in this category; we discuss it in Chapter 5.) The emphasis here is, as the name suggests, on finding a broad consensus in parliament if possible, rather than on merely imposing the will of the parliamentary majority. In countries in this category, cabinets 'tend to have a genuine "give-and-take" relationship with parliament' (Lijphart, 1999: 36).

We should emphasize that the distinction between the two types of parliament is not simply a matter of their having different rules. There are two problems with using parliamentary rules to measure, or explain variations in, the power of parliaments. One is that on paper the rules may imply that a parliament wields much more power than it actually does. Even if it is the body that formally 'makes' every law, for example, a particular parliament may be doing no more than tamely approving all of a government's proposals. An exercise in calculating 'power scores' for a large number of parliaments across the world bases its calculations on the formal powers of legislatures rather than what actually happens (Fish and Kroenig, 2009: 756–757), and some of its findings would raise the eyebrows of students of legislative politics. The position of Germany and Italy at the top (0.84 on a scale running from 0 to 1) is in line with conventional judgements, as are the low scores for the presidential system of Cyprus (0.41) and the semi-presidential system of France (0.56). However, it is surprising to find the notoriously government-dominated parliament of Greece only slightly below Germany and Italy at 0.81, ahead of the Dutch Second Chamber (0.78). Likewise, the assessment of the UK House of Commons (0.78) as being well ahead of parliaments in Finland, Norway and Sweden (all 0.72) is contentious. While it is useful to have an index based on formal powers, it is obvious that the power actually wielded by a parliament will depend on other factors too, and is likely to vary over time even without any changes in the rules.

The second problem with using variations in parliamentary rules to explain variations in power is that it is questionable how far differences in rules can really explain anything. Of course, the rules by which any parliament operates, and the balance that these rules prescribe between the respective powers of the government and the legislature, do tell us something – and yet it would be misleading to assume that the explanation as to why any given parliament is 'weak' lies in the fact that the rules do not give it much leverage over government. After all, the rules were not engraved in stone and then imposed upon parliaments; they were adopted by each parliament, and could be changed if most MPs wanted to change them. As with the other institutions that we examine in this book, the rules outlining the respective powers of parliament and government have an impact upon political actors, yet those rules were chosen by political actors in the first place, and could be seen as an expression of those actors' preferences rather than as an external constraint upon the actors. Changing the rules will not have clearly identifiable effects if the old rules better reflected actors' preferences (Esaiasson and Heidar, 2000: 434). In all parliaments there are many more MPs than there are members of the government, and if MPs collectively wanted to change the rules so as to give parliament much more power, they could do this. The fact that they do not suggests strongly that most MPs do not want to do this, and the reason is that, first and foremost, MPs think and act along party lines.

Our expectation, then, would be to find that in Lijphart's majoritarian-model countries virtually all relationships between governments and parliaments take place in the inter-party mode, with MPs and ministers having a strong party orientation that transcends any sense of 'parliament' as an institution. In contrast, in consensus-model countries we would expect to encounter somewhat greater recourse to the cross-party or non-party mode. With this in mind, we shall examine the record of European parliaments with respect to a number of roles in which they interact with governments.

## 3.3 The roles of parliaments

Later in the chapter we shall look in detail at the upper houses of parliaments that exist in a number of countries, but it is true to say that in virtually every one of these countries, and in almost every respect, the lower house is the more significant. In most of our subsequent discussion, then, we shall concentrate on the activities and impact of the lower house. This can have a role to play in three areas. The first concerns the creation, sustaining and possible termination of governments; the second is legislating; the third involves scrutinizing the behaviour of governments. We shall examine the significance of European parliaments on each of these dimensions.

### 3.3.1 Appointing and dismissing governments

As we saw in Chapter 2 and will discuss in more detail in Chapter 12, the government in most European countries is responsible to the legislature – typically the lower house. It often needs the approval of parliament to take office in the first place, and in nearly all countries parliament can force the resignation of the government by passing a motion of no confidence in it (for full details see Table 12.1). This in itself shows that the familiar contrast between the 'powerful' US Congress and the 'weak' parliaments of Europe is simplistic; whatever else it can do, Congress cannot dismiss the administration, but even the humblest European parliament (with the exceptions of those in Cyprus and Switzerland) has it in its power to turn the country's government out of office. If a parliament does pass such a motion of no confidence in the government, the latter usually has two options: either to resign and allow parliament to elect a new government, or to dissolve parliament and call a general election. One exception to this is Norway, where the life of a parliament is fixed at four years, and 'premature' general elections are not allowed. In addition, several countries – such as Belgium, Germany, Poland and Spain – employ the *constructive vote of no confidence*, which means that parliament may dismiss a government only if it simultaneously specifies a new prime minister in whom it has confidence (again, see Table 12.1 for details).

It is true that European parliaments rarely use this power. For example, even in Finland and Italy, where the turnover of governments used to be extensive, government defeats in confidence motions have been rare; in Finland there have been only four since 1918, and no Italian government was ousted by such a vote until Romano Prodi's centre-left coalition lost a confidence motion by one vote in October 1998. However, parliaments use this power so rarely because usually they do not need to use it; when a government knows that it has lost the confidence of parliament, and that it faces certain defeat there, it will often bow to the inevitable and jump off the cliff rather than wait to be pushed. What is important is not how often parliament has used the power but the fact that it possesses it in the first place. Because governments know that they can be dismissed from office by parliament at any time, they must be sensitive to the feelings of the key actors in parliament – which is to say, their own MPs and, if the government controls only a minority of seats, some sections of the opposition. Moreover, because most European countries use proportional representation electoral systems, which rarely give 'artificial' parliamentary majorities to parties that win less than a majority of votes, most European governments depend for their existence on legislative coalitions composed of more than one party. This means that, if the legislative coalition backing the government should collapse for any reason, an executive can fall quite suddenly, without necessarily losing an actual confidence vote in parliament. Thus it is quite common in some countries – Finland and Italy used to be the classic cases, and Latvia is now a good example – to see changes in government between elections as a result of political developments, changes on which the electorate is not asked to pass judgement. This power of parliaments, of course, is balanced by the constitutional authority of governments in most European countries to dissolve the legislature and force an election whenever they choose, as we shall see (see Table 12.1 for details), although, as we discuss further in Chapter 11, in many countries governments do not really have a completely free hand as to when they call an election.

### 3.3.2 Parliaments and law-making

Parliaments, then, usually have the power to throw a government out of office, but this is rather a drastic measure. For the most part, MPs would be happy enough with some real degree of influence on the policymaking process. However, European governments are rarely keen to allow MPs a significant role in making laws. The very high levels of party discipline in parliament mean that a government that controls a majority of seats will usually expect to be able to rely on party discipline to push its programme through the legislature. In addition, the government controls the civil service, a key element in planning and implementing legislation (see Chapter 6).

This marks one of the key differences between parliamentary and presidential systems of governments: in the former, governments can expect to see the great majority of their proposals accepted by parliament. Moreover, not only do government proposals generally get adopted by European parliaments; the other side of the coin is that, in most countries, proposals not initiated by the government are usually unsuccessful. Members of parliament in Europe simply do not see themselves as American-style legislators with the role of initiating and piloting through pieces of legislation. Although most parliaments contain provision for a bill to be proposed by a deputy or a group of deputies (termed a *private member's bill* in the United Kingdom and some other countries), such a bill, unless it is trivial in content, rarely becomes law unless the government decides not to oppose it (Mattson and Strøm, 1995: 478–479). A common theme in studies of European politics has been the *decline of parliaments*, which have everywhere, according to some perceptions, lost to the grasping hands of governments the power they supposedly possessed late in the nineteenth century. By the middle of the twentieth century it was generally agreed that governments acted while parliaments just talked.

Measuring the impact of parliaments upon legislation is riddled with methodological difficulties. As we have said, the proportion of government bills that become law, and the proportion of laws that originated as government bills, are both generally very high, yet they vary around Europe, and at first glance it might seem that comparing these figures across countries would give a good indication of the respective strengths of parliaments and governments. Even simple statistics such as these, though, need to be interpreted with caution. For one thing, government bills that do not make it into law are very rarely defeated on the floor of the house; if we learn that in a particular parliament 'only' 65 per cent of government bills tend to make it into law, this certainly does not mean that the other 35 per cent are defeated by 'parliament'. The bills that do not make it onto the statute books may be withdrawn because of changing circumstances that render them unnecessary, or because of resistance from government MPs, or as a result of discussions with interest groups, or because a shortage of legislative time means that they had to make way for higher-priority bills, or because their main provisions were subsumed into other bills and thus incorporated into law that way (Pettai and Madise, 2006: 303). It is common, also, to count the number of bills that are amended during their passage through parliament, on the assumption that this is an indirect measure of how far governments get their way. Yet it may be that many or most amendments come from the government itself, amending its proposals in the light of discussions with stakeholders, or to rectify defects in rushed draft bills, and that the effect of most amendments is to strengthen the bill by taking on board suggestions for improvement that do not conflict with its main principle. Likewise, if bills emanate from sources other than the government, this does not prove that 'parliament' is a powerful independent legislator. Bills that are presented in the name of an MP, or several MPs, may *de facto* be government bills. There could be political benefits to the government – such as keeping its MPs loyal by giving them occasional rewards, or building a reputation as a government willing to allow initiative to ordinary MPs – from 'giving' its backbench MPs bills from whose passage they will be able to claim credit, as occurs in Britain and France. Alternatively, there may be procedural advantages in having a bill originate from some source other than the government, as in Germany, or bills promoted by individual government MPs may in fact represent behaviour supportive of the government rather than independent of it, as in a number of post-communist parliaments (Goetz and Zubek, 2007: 528; Kopecký and Spirova, 2008: 147; Miller and Stecker, 2008: 318).

With all the caveats, though, the amount of variation around Europe is such that we cannot dismiss all European parliaments as mere rubber stamps. As we would expect from our earlier discussion, the variation here is related to Lijphart's distinction between majoritarian and consensus systems of governments. Three institutional features of parliaments reflect this distinction and affect the significance of parliament's role in law-making. The first is that, in parliaments in majoritarian systems, the government tends to control the parliamentary agenda, whereas in consensual systems the agenda is decided either by agreement among the party groups, or by the president of parliament after consultation with the party groups (Döring, 1995). The second is that in consensual parliaments the most important work is done in committees, whereas in parliaments in majoritarian systems the floor of the chamber is the main arena. The third is that, in parliaments in consensual systems, bills typically go to committees before they are debated by the full parliament. This increases the likelihood that bills will be amended by cross-party consensus. In majoritarian systems, on the other hand, it is more common for bills to go to committees only after they have been approved by the whole house, by which stage the issues may have become highly politicized.

Although it may seem a trivial detail, one indicator of the nature of parliament may be found in the seating arrangements in the chamber (these are illustrated in Andeweg and Nijzink, 1995: 158). In some parliaments, government ministers and their opposition counterparts face each other across the chamber, each with their own backbench supporters ranged behind them. (We use the term 'backbencher' to denote any MP who does not hold a government position and who is not a leading opposition MP.) This format might seem almost designed to engender a confrontational attitude between government and opposition and to lead to an 'inter-party' mode of behaviour. Indeed, the parliaments that are organized like this, namely those of Britain and Ireland, tend to operate in just such a mode. At the other end of the scale, some governments (in Iceland, Switzerland, Italy, Austria, Portugal, Finland, Greece and the Netherlands, for example) sit together facing the entire chamber of MPs, an arrangement that may be more likely to lead to some kind of collective consciousness on the part of MPs that they constitute a body that is genuinely separate from government. MPs are usually seated by party, but in Norway and Sweden they are grouped by constituency, and in Iceland places are allocated annually by lot.

### Parliaments and law-making in majoritarian countries

As examples of government-dominated parliaments, we can look briefly at the parliaments in Greece, Britain, France and Ireland. The Greek parliament (the Vouli) takes the majoritarian model to perhaps its furthest extreme. The two main parties, New Democracy and PASOK, are bitter rivals, even though genuine policy differences between them are far fewer than in the past. Almost all Greek governments are single-party majority governments, and the opposition in parliament has been effectively powerless, with government taking no account of its views. Oppositions (both of PASOK and of New Democracy) have responded by being as obstructive as they could be within the rules of parliament, with their approach generally taking the form of 'endless lists of speakers who make repetitive speeches which add nothing to what has already been said' (Alivizatos, 1990: 145). Parliament operates according to 'a model of spectacular confrontation', and the chamber is merely a forum for 'vague, repetitive and usually outdated monologues' (Alivizatos, 1990: 144, 147). Virtually every bill passed by the Vouli is a government bill. Committees exist, but they are all chaired by government party members and have a majority of government supporters.

In the United Kingdom the main non-government party, unlike non-government parties elsewhere in Europe, receives a special status – that of 'Her Majesty's Opposition' – but it has less influence than non-government parties in most other countries. Governments routinely command overall majorities in the House of Commons; the opposition is reduced to making speeches against the government's proposals, not in the hope of bringing about a change in its plans but as part of an attempt to persuade the electorate that the opposition has alternative and better policies. For opposition MPs, speaking in the chamber, though ostensibly a contribution to the policymaking process, is no more fruitful than 'heckling a steamroller', in the words of Labour MP Austin Mitchell. Critics see the Commons chamber as a place of theatre rather than a serious working body, with debates dominated not by those with most expertise but by MPs who possess 'meretricious rhetorical skills' (Kingdom, 2003: 400). The Commons has developed a reasonably comprehensive system of committees since the early 1980s, but these play a role in overseeing the behaviour of government rather than in actually making laws or policies. Even though speeches by MPs have scarcely any effect on legislation, the House of Commons spends quite a lot of its time on debates – mainly, some believe, as part of a strategy by the party leaderships to keep their restive MPs out of mischief and focused instead on the main inter-party battle.

Deputies in France, when asked to rate their influence on laws on a five-point scale, where 1 is the lowest and 5 the highest score, gave an average response of 2.4, with their self-assessed influence on government bills even lower at 1.9. Not surprisingly, as we shall see later in the chapter, their limited chances of making a meaningful impact on legislation lead them to spend much of their time on the more satisfying activity of constituency work (Costa and Kerrouche, 2009a: 229–230). French governments may be genuinely stymied if the ruling party itself is divided (quite a common occurrence), with several heavyweights vying to be the party's candidate at the next presidential elections. If the party's leading figure in the Assembly is a rival of the prime minister, the former may do his best to thwart the plans of the government without ever expressing outright opposition (Lazardeux, 2009: 293–294). In Ireland, virtually all legislation consists of government bills – a private member's bill passed in 1989 was the first for over

40 years. As in Britain, parliament has been strengthening its committee system in recent years, and major reforms in the 1990s greatly expanded the scope of committees, both in examining legislation and in scrutinizing the work of governments, although the real power still lies firmly with the government (Gallagher, 2010). In Ireland, as in Britain, the government has virtually complete control of the parliamentary agenda (Döring, 1995: 225). Another similarity between Ireland and Britain is that, more than anywhere else in Europe, government and parliament are almost entirely 'fused' – that is, all or almost all government ministers are simultaneously members of parliament, and in such cases any idea of a clear distinction between government and parliament seems especially artificial. It is worth noting, indeed, that all over western Europe most ministers, even if they are not MPs while in office, will have been MPs at some stage in their political career (see chapters in Dowding and Dumont, 2009).

### Parliaments and law-making in consensus countries

Turning to more consensual systems, we shall look at the examples provided by Germany, Austria, the Netherlands, Scandinavia and Italy. In Germany, the highly developed committee system in the Bundestag is the main focus of parliamentarians' working week. Bundestag committees concentrate on technical details of bills rather than on general principles, which are more likely to be the subject of partisan debate in which the government prevails. As long as the opposition does not obstruct the passage of bills, the government of the day is usually prepared to be flexible on the details, and there is a good deal of negotiation and compromise between government and opposition. The result is that on average over half of all bills are amended in committee (admittedly, many of the changes are little more than technical), with the great majority of routine legislation then being passed unanimously by the full parliament. As a rule, the opposition does not criticize government proposals full-bloodedly; in return, the government allows the opposition meaningful input into the details of legislation, at least in areas that are not heavily politicized, or where the government knows that it will need the support of the opposition to get a piece of legislation through the second chamber, which we discuss later (Miller and Stecker, 2008: 308, 318). Thus, in the terms used by Andeweg and Nijzink, the Bundestag frequently adopts the *cross-party* mode, in contrast with the confrontational style of the British House of Commons, where the *inter-party* mode dominates.

Committees in the Austrian parliament, the Nationalrat, are also significant; they are sometimes charged with devising legislation in a particular area, with the full parliament virtually certain to accept their recommendations. In the Netherlands, too, committees of the lower house (the Tweede Kamer, or Second Chamber) play an important role in considering legislation. Although governments aim to ensure that their legislative proposals pass through parliament without too much trouble, parliament can set its own agenda and timetable, and is not dominated by government to the same extent as legislatures in more majoritarian systems. Nearly half of all bills passed are amended in the Second Chamber, not because the opposition is prevailing over the government but mainly as a result of assertiveness on the part of government backbenchers, or because the government accepts suggestions for incremental improvements to a bill from individual MPs (Andeweg and Irwin, 2009: 161). The relative separation of government and parliament in the Netherlands is markedly greater than in fused systems such as Germany or Britain. In the Netherlands, as in several other countries (including France, Norway, Portugal and Sweden), government ministers cannot – according to the constitution – simultaneously be MPs, although in practice most Dutch ministers are former MPs.

Scandinavian parliaments are generally thought of as relatively powerful, as *working parliaments* rather than debating societies. Scandinavian political culture emphasizes modesty and conscientious work rather than theatrical self-advertisement, and most Scandinavian MPs are oriented towards detailed consideration of the small print of legislation in committee work rather than towards making dramatic speeches in the parliament chamber (Arter, 1999: 215). The sight of a group of members of, say, the Finnish Eduskunta working their way section by section through a bill concerning the regulation of public transport may make for less exciting television viewing than a British opposition MP delivering a withering rhetorical attack on the government in the chamber of the House of Commons, accompanied by a Greek chorus of supporting or dissenting voices, with a bewigged Speaker in the chair trying to keep order, but there is no doubt about which makes more impact on the shape of legislation. In all the Scandinavian countries, committees have enabled parliament to maintain more control over and input into what governments do at EU level than in other member states (Bergman and Damgaard, 2000). In both Iceland and Sweden, MPs have an additional input by serving on government commissions, which are very important in formulating policies (Kristjánsson, 2004: 158; Arter, 2008: 125). In the Scandinavian countries as well as Italy and the Netherlands, furthermore, the government has relatively little power to determine parliament's agenda (Döring, 1995: 225).

If the Greek parliament is at one end of the scale, being totally dominated by government, then the Italian parliament, the Chamber of Deputies, is close to the other end. Until 1988 there was provision for secret ballots and, since nearly all votes were secret, party leaders were unable to ensure discipline. Before 1990, the government's agenda-setting power was exceptionally weak: the agenda was set entirely by agreement among the leaders of the various party groups. In an attempt to bring greater stability to Italian politics, the rules allowing for secret ballots in the legislature were changed and, moreover, the government was given at least some input into the parliamentary agenda. Italian legislative committees, again in contrast to the general European pattern, have explicit law-making powers: they can give final approval to some legislation without having to refer it to the full parliament, and they scrutinize all other legislation. Until the late 1980s most laws were so-called little laws (*leggine*), whose scope in many cases was minimal, and they were passed by committees rather than by the full parliament. It was a common diagnosis that the Italian parliament passed too many *leggine* and not enough substantive laws. Law-making is particularly central to the Italian parliament because matters that in other countries are typically dealt with through administrative action require a law in Italy (Newell, 2006: 389). This is one reason why the country possesses and makes far more laws than any other: between 1996 and 2006 around 22 500 bills were introduced, and although 'only' 6700 of these made it into law, that still represents an average of almost two bills passed on every day of the year over a 10-year period (Giuliani, 2008: 3). Even after being passed, bills might take years to reach the statute books. The unusual power of the Italian parliament relative to government has not done much for its status in the eyes of the public. Its image in the past has been of an ineffective, fractious legislature, whose members drag their feet over more important decisions, which in practice are more likely to be made by agreement among the various political parties than by discussion in parliament.

Most post-communist countries are difficult to place reliably on the majoritarian versus consensus democracy scale, and the significance of their parliaments varies (Kopecký, 2004, 2007). As a generalization we can say that, in the early years of the reborn democratic states, parliaments seemed quite strong, largely because governments – which under communism had been very much secondary to the communist party – were so weak. Thus much legislation was initiated by individual MPs, upon whom parliamentary parties found it difficult to impose discipline. Indeed, parliamentary parties themselves were not fixed entities, as 'party-hopping' by MPs was widespread. The result was that much legislation not backed by the government was passed – and in many cases it was ill-considered and of poor quality. Further into the 1990s things began to change. Under the urging of the EU, and in preparation for membership of that body, the core executive in most countries became stronger: fast-track procedures were used for this purpose, and were sometimes used for other legislation too. At the same time as the core executive has professionalized, observers are frequently unimpressed by the competence of MPs: one analysis of Poland's Sejm identified a trend in 'the growth of the category of poorly prepared deputies of mediocre abilities' (Nalewajko and Wesołowski, 2007: 78). Parliamentary parties imposed stronger discipline upon their members (for the Sejm see Gwiazda, 2009: 359), and MPs who persisted in independent behaviour found themselves expelled from the group. Slovakia provides a good example. Until 1994 it was virtually a case of *assembly government*, with parliament opposing cabinet proposals, deputies voting down ministers from their own parties, short-lived coalition cabinets and unclear accountability. The imposition of strong party discipline and a virtual end to party-hopping brought an end to this chaotic state of affairs (Malová, 2001: 357–358).

### 3.3.3  Parliaments and oversight of government

Only some parliaments, then, play a part in influencing or making the laws, but all parliaments see themselves as having the role of overseeing the work of government. This function of scrutiny or oversight is, not surprisingly, carried out with different degrees of effectiveness across Europe. Parliaments have a number of methods of carrying out the role (Döring, 1995; Bergman *et al.*, 2003: 146–177). Needless to say, opposition MPs are far more likely than are government MPs to want to scrutinize the government by means of parliamentary mechanisms.

Nearly all European parliaments have, as part of their weekly routine, some kind of 'question time'. This gives members of parliament the right to submit questions in writing to ministers, and these questions must be answered within a fixed time, varying from three working days in Ireland's Dáil to over a month in some other parliaments (Russo and Wiberg, 2010). In some countries there is a question time every day where questions are answered orally by ministers, other questions being answered in writing, and in others this happens less frequently. Parliamentary questions allow members of parliament to extract information from the government. In many countries they are used in practice more to try to embarrass the government by asking awkward questions than to find anything out, as the questioner already has a good idea what the answer is. In response, ministers often aim to produce answers that, although not untruthful, give away as little as possible. The pattern right across Europe is of an often dramatic increase in the number of questions that MPs are asking (Green-Pedersen, 2010: 354). To give a few examples, between 1989 and 2006 the number of written questions asked per annum rose in France from 15 000 to 32 000; in Ireland the number jumped from 4000 a year in the mid 1960s to 39 000 in the mid 2000s; and in Spain there was a sixfold increase in 20 years (Capo Giol, 2005: 126; Kerrouche, 2009: 74; Gallagher, 2010: 216). This upsurge in activity is sometimes seen as evidence that parliaments are wielding their oversight powers more effectively, and are thus making governments more accountable, though sceptics maintain that while the dogs may be barking more, they still cannot bite.

A similar but somewhat weightier weapon that most parliaments can employ is the interpellation, which differs from a simple question because the reply from the minister can be debated by parliament if a sufficient proportion of deputies request this. There are far fewer interpellations than questions, but the number of interpellations is also increasing in parliaments that make provision for them.

The most effective method through which parliaments keep an eye on the behaviour of governments is by means of a system of committees set up to monitor government departments. The strongest oversight committee systems have a number of characteristics. First, they reflect the structure of government, with each government department monitored by a committee. Second, each MP belongs to only one committee, which increases the likelihood that he or she will develop expertise in that area, and that 'small-group psychology' will foster a sense of cross-party identification with the committee, both of which are aided further if there is some continuity from one parliament to the next in committee membership. Third, committee chair positions are distributed proportionally among the PPGs rather than being monopolized by the government. Fourth, the members of each committee are able to elect, by secret ballot, their chair from among the members of the party whose right it is to chair that committee. Fifth, they have the power to summon individuals, including ministers, to appear before them. Sixth, they have a right to all the information in the possession of the government that they deem relevant. If the last two conditions are met, committees can call the relevant government minister before them to defend his or her performance in office, and civil servants can be asked to make available to the committee the information upon which ministers have based their decisions. Seventh, if committees meet behind closed doors they can be more effective, and are more likely to operate in a cross-party mode, though this comes at an obvious cost in terms of transparency.

The first requirement is met in most parliaments, although often there are other committees too, set up either to give MPs something to do or for the more persuasive reason that some policy areas cut across several government departments. The second is easier to meet in large parliaments, where the number of MPs may exceed the number of committee places, than in small ones, where many MPs pretty much have to be on several committees simultaneously. Of course, not all MPs are interested in building up an expertise. In France it is suggested that usually only a small proportion of members are present when a committee convenes, while in Portugal continuity even from one meeting to the next is disrupted by the unusual facility whereby MPs can stand aside for up to 18 months, during which time they are replaced by a substitute, and then resume the seat, an option of which on average over 100 MPs avail themselves each year (Leston-Bandeira, 2004: 92–94; Costa and Kerrouche, 2009a: 230). In contrast, in Norway it is much more common for MPs to retain membership of the same committee across several parliaments. The third, as we would expect, is met more in the consensus parliaments than in the majoritarian ones. Chairs are allocated proportionally in four of the five Nordic countries (Iceland is the exception) as well as in Austria, Belgium and the Netherlands (Hagevi, 2000: 246; Andeweg et al., 2008: 94). Whereas in some parliaments the great majority of committees are chaired by a government MP, overall the distribution of chairs is a good deal more proportional than the distribution of cabinet positions (Carroll et al., 2006). The fourth is rare: although there have been moves towards this in the UK, in most countries chairs are chosen by the relevant PPG or in effect the party leader, not by the committee members. The fifth and the sixth vary across parliaments, with Nordic committees typically in the vanguard here. Regarding privacy, in most countries committees have that option for some types of business but generally meet in open session, though in some, such as Italy and Norway, private meetings are the norm.

## Denmark

The Danish Folketing, like its Nordic counterparts, is seen as essentially a hard-working and outcome-oriented body, rather than an arena for MPs to indulge in rhetorical speeches. It has the potential to be effective, given the high frequency of minority government in Denmark, which reached its apogee during the 'four-leaf clover' minority government of 1982–1988, when on a number of occasions the government, having sustained a defeat in the Folketing on some measure, ended up implementing policies with which it disagreed. These days minority governments are more likely to reach a long-term agreement with one of the non-government parties rather than leave themselves at the mercy of a hostile opposition in the chamber. Under the 1915 constitution Denmark had an upper house, the Landsting, but the 1953 constitution made Denmark a unicameral country. The constraint on government formerly provided by the existence of the Landsting was now given expression in a provision entitling a third of MPs to call a referendum on any bill.

## France

The constitution of the Fifth French Republic marked a reaction against the experience of the Fourth Republic (1946–1958), in which parliament was thought to have too much power to thwart governments without being able to achieve anything very effectively itself. In consequence, the National Assembly is, by design, ineffective when it comes to overseeing the actions of the government or the president. The constitution specifies the areas in which parliament can legislate, and allows the government to act by decree in all other areas, and it contains many other devices to guarantee the dominance of the government over parliament. The opposition has resorted to desperate tactics, such as tabling thousands of computer-generated amendments to slow down the passage of a bill, compelling the government to resort to heavy artillery parliamentary weapons to get its legislation through. The Assembly has only six committees, two of which have over 100 members (more than some full parliaments) – this was prescribed by the 1958 constitution precisely in order to prevent the committees from becoming effective. Some governments allow the National Assembly some degree of influence when it comes to discussing and amending bills, but if there is a confrontation the government holds all the cards. Deputies, nearly all of whom hold a local elected office such as mayor along with their position in the National Assembly, are seen by their constituents primarily as emissaries from their district to central government, and spend a lot of time on constituency work. The Senate, with its inbuilt right-wing majority, is a minor irritant to right-wing governments and a major irritant to left-wing ones.

## Germany

The lower house of the German parliament, the Bundestag, is strongly organized, and its members (MdBs) have better resources to assist them in their work than parliamentarians anywhere else in Europe. The main emphasis of its work is not in grand debates on general principles of legislation in plenary session but in detailed scrutiny of legislation in committees, where there tends to be a good deal of co-operation between government and opposition parties. The work of each MdB is closely overseen by the parliamentary group (*Fraktion*), leaving little scope for spontaneous parliamentary action by individual MdBs. MdBs are quite active in constituency work, on which they spend around 40 per cent of their working time. The upper chamber, the Bundesrat, which represents the *Land* governments, acts as an important check on the government, since it has significant power, and moreover is often dominated by opposition parties.

## Italy

The Italian parliament, the Camera dei Deputati, is less dominated by the government than most European parliaments. It can set its own agenda, and it expects as of right that the government will consult it before introducing legislative proposals. Its committees are powerful, and can actually pass laws without reference to the full parliament. Much of its legislative output over the years, though, has consisted of 'little laws' (*leggine*) of benefit only to microsectional interests, which deputies have promoted in order to win favour with their constituents. When the Italian political system entered a state of crisis in the 1990s, the ability of parliament to block government action was widely seen as part of the problem rather than part of the solution, and there was agreement that steps should be taken to facilitate effective government, but in the event changes have been less significant than anyone would have expected back in the mid 1990s. The powers and (usually) the composition of the Senate are virtually identical to those of the Chamber. For critics, having two directly elected chambers of parliament with identical powers and functions, with no method of resolving disagreements between them, is an idea that comes straight out of the handbook on 'How Not to Design a Political System'.

## Netherlands

The lower house, the Tweede Kamer (Second Chamber), is by no means a rubber stamp for government. It can set its own agenda and timetable, and it plays an influential role in amending bills. Because government members cannot, under the constitution, simultaneously be members of parliament, there is, psychologically at least, a greater separation between executive and legislature than in most other European countries, where government ministers are often also members of parliament. Parliamentary activity has increased greatly since the 1960s, although opinions are divided as to whether parliament is any stronger as a result. The Tweede Kamer is dominated by the parliamentary groups, with individual MPs having very little freedom of action. The upper house (the Eerste Kamer, or First Chamber) cannot initiate legislation or amend bills, but it can veto bills, and its use of – or threat to use – this power means that governments cannot ignore it.

## Poland

After 1989 Poland seemed to be developing a parliamentary-dominant system with government instability and considerable legislative activity by individual MPs, but developments in the Polish political system, such as preparation for EU entry, led to a progressive strengthening of the core executive's position *vis-à-vis* parliament. Even though the Sejm's star waned somewhat during the 1990s, it retained more significance as an arena than most post-communist parliaments did. Poland's long parliamentary tradition, going back to the fifteenth century, gives the Sejm a status that not all parliaments enjoy – its committees made some impact behind the scenes even under communist rule. Polish governments have a harder job persuading MPs to pass their bills than most of their western counterparts do, and a significant proportion of legislation emanates from Sejm committees or from MPs, although an unknown proportion of this legislation is in reality government-inspired. Turnover in the Sejm is high, with a majority of MPs after each of the first four post-communist elections being first-timers. The second chamber of the parliament, the Senat, has some minor legislative and appointive powers, but for the most part it can simply delay policies and legislation rather than block or propose them.

▶ **BOX 3.1: CONTINUED**

**Spain**

The Spanish parliament, like other institutions of democracy, was suppressed during the Franco dictatorship (1939–1975). Under the majority socialist government of 1982–1993 it had a marginal position, with the prime minister, Felipe Gonzáles, rarely taking the trouble to visit it even to inform it of the government's activities, let alone to be questioned. His successors, José María Aznar and José Luis Rodríguez Zapatero, were scarcely more respectful. The Cortes is not seen as one of Europe's more significant parliaments, not helped by the fact that turnover is high, with almost half of the members of each parliament being first-term deputies. The upper house, the Senado, is very weak and of little political significance, and critics wonder, as they do of Poland's Senat, just what it is for.

**United Kingdom**

Ironically, although those who refer to a 'golden age' of parliaments usually have in mind the House of Commons at some times during the nineteenth century, today's British parliament is not regarded as being among the most effective of European parliaments. A combination of single-party majority governments (prior to the 2010 coalition) and a party system based on conflict between the two main parties has left the parliamentary opposition with very little influence on legislation, or on policy in general. The British tradition places great emphasis on plenary sessions in the main debating chamber – performance in debates and 'ability to command the chamber' are important, for instance, in deciding which MPs are promoted to leadership positions – even though there are few signs that those outside 'Westminster World' follow parliamentary debates with much interest, or that debates have any effect on government policies. Committees, the main forum for the work of most modern parliaments, have traditionally had a much less significant role in the House of Commons, although since the early 1980s they have been increasingly effective in scrutinizing the work of government. The upper house, the House of Lords, is often regarded as an irrelevant (or splendid) anachronism, but a majority of its members these days are 'working peers', and it has imposed effective constraints on governments, especially on civil liberties issues.

Overall, scrutiny of government by committees can be quite effective in Germany, Britain, Poland and Denmark, for example, but it is not a strong feature of parliament in Greece, France or Spain. Committees are usually most significant when they are small and moderately numerous, as opposed to large and few, as in France. Here the constitution stipulates that there can be only six committees (four of 72 members and two with 144 members each), each of which has at least 70 members, so they operate like 'mini-parliaments', and the largest have been described as 'dustbins' into which the least significant business is thrown (Knapp and Wright, 2006: 145). When committees become significant, interest groups seek to 'colonise' them, so there is a tendency for the agriculture committee to be dominated by farmers and the education committee by teachers, for example, with each committee seeking extra resources for the special interests that dominate it. This pattern has been noted in a variety of countries, including Germany and Belgium (De Winter, 1999: 95–97; Saalfeld, 1999: 57–61). In such cases, even in majoritarian-model countries, MPs are prepared to operate in cross-party mode. We should not forget that committees, as well as performing an oversight role, also offer an access point into the political system for interest groups and individual citizens, who may be given the opportunity to present their case on some issue to the relevant committee (Shaw, 1998: 792–793; Gellner and Robertson, 2001: 111–112). They might also have an impact if their recommendations are reported in the media, or influence parties' policies (Hindmoor *et al.*, 2009). We should also acknowledge the limitations of committees, which, certainly in majoritarian countries, can highlight government errors but cannot actually change anything. In Britain, for example, a few committee reports may generate some media coverage, but most are not debated by parliament, and they are unable to cause heads to roll, even on foot of mistakes identified (Budge *et al.*, 2007: 427).

## 3.4 Parliaments and parties

All relations between governments and members of parliament, as we have seen, take place within a context dominated by political parties. Greater power for parliament therefore would really mean more power not for a unitary body called 'parliament' but for the *Fraktionen* (the parliamentary party groups), or for specific actors within them. If the government controls only a minority of seats, then 'more power for parliament' is in practice likely to mean 'more power for the opposition'. During periods of majority government, the main constraints are imposed not by the opposition but by the backbench MPs of the governing party or parties, and it is particularly difficult to tell how much influence these members wield. If government MPs are unhappy about a government proposal, this is rarely expressed in votes, or even in complaints against the measure on the floor of parliament; instead, the matter will be raised behind closed doors at meetings of the *Fraktion*, and if backbench reservations are strong enough, the minister may have little choice but to amend or withdraw the proposal. What goes on at these meetings, though, is unknown both to the public and to all but the most assiduous researchers.

One problem with assessing arguments about the domination of parliament by political parties or by government is that it is notoriously difficult to try to measure the power of any parliament. If a parliament approves every government proposal without making any amendments, we cannot be sure whether this indicates a supine parliament or whether the government, obeying the law of anticipated reactions, is taking care not to put forward any proposals without first making sure that parliament will approve them. In the words of Schüttemeyer (2009: 7): 'the continuous acceptance of the government's superiority rests on its capacity to represent successfully, i.e. anticipate the political will of its majority and assess correctly what can be done with its parliamentary parties and what not.' Studies of European parliaments do not usually indulge in 'roll-call analysis' of the bill-by-bill voting records of individual legislators, an activity that 'has been viewed as the political science equivalent of stamp collecting or train spotting' (Cowley and Stuart, 2004: 301), because it seems pointless. Indeed, in a number of countries, including the Netherlands and Portugal, the official proceedings normally record the votes of parliamentary parties rather than of individual MPs. Researchers are generally unconvinced by hypotheses trying to link variation in the degree of PPG unity in votes to factors such as the electoral system, for example, for the simple reason that there is hardly any variation to explain. PPG unity is very high almost everywhere, and such small variations as can be identified are either not related, or at most weakly related, to the electoral system (Sieberer, 2006: 163; Depauw and Martin, 2009: 111–117). In Chapter 10 we shall look in greater detail at the internal politics of political parties, but we can see even at a cursory glance that PPG unity means that the leaders of these parties are far more important people, politically, than the typical rank-and-file member of parliament.

The high degree of solid party voting among parliamentarians might suggest to the uninitiated that members of parliament are mere 'dumb sheep' or 'lobby fodder', who must docilely vote in whatever manner the party leaders direct. That may, indeed, be the popular perception. German evidence suggests that most voters believe that MPs should be able to make up their own minds as to how to vote on each issue in parliament, and should be open to persuasion by speeches by other MPs. The reason why MPs do not behave like this, in the opinion of most Germans, is that 'party bosses' and whips compel them to vote along party lines (Patzelt, 2000: 45–46). Constitutions sometimes help to propagate this misconception by proclaiming that MPs are entirely autonomous, and that no one has the right to tell an MP which way to vote on an issue, thus disregarding the central role of political parties in modern politics. However, this perspective is, as Patzelt puts it, 'pure fiction', and shows 'little understanding of collective action as a result of rational adaptation to team-building strategic premises'. To put it simply, it makes sense for individual MPs to band together into parties that operate as cohesive entities, and it certainly makes for better policy outcomes compared with the chaotic policymaking that would ensue if all MPs acted as independent agents and took an ad hoc approach to each issue. When MPs in the Nordic countries (where PPG discipline is already very strong) were asked whether they felt the current levels of PPG discipline were satisfactory, 72 per cent said they were, and of the rest twice as many (19 per cent compared with 9 per cent) wanted it to be even stronger as wanted it to be looser (Jensen, 2000: 221). Besides, while people might claim to want MPs to behave in a more independent-minded fashion, in practice voters tend to punish parties that convey an image of disunity. From the voters' perspective, PPG unity helps 'reduce the risks of democratic delegation' (Strøm et al., 2003: 731). It better enables voters to hold their representatives accountable, as they know that parties are the actors that can be credited or blamed for past events, and they are offered a choice of programmes for the future.

Although it is true that unpleasant punishments await those deputies who are disloyal to the party, as we discuss further on, the relationship between parties and individual members of parliament is not fundamentally due to the imposition of discipline. Government backbenchers are not cowed by the government, as publics might think, but broadly supportive of it. For one thing, members of parliament belonging to the same party have a natural sense of identity; their instincts are always to vote with their party out of a sense of loyalty, solidarity and common purpose, and for the most part they are glad to keep in line, and do not need to be threatened. By definition, since they all joined the same party, they probably have similar views in the first place. Moreover, decision-making within each parliamentary party may be fairly democratic, so even those members who dislike a particular decision will go along with it if it represents a majority view. They are much more likely to do this, of course, if they know that other members of the group will do the same when the majority decision goes against *them*. The ad hoc 'log-rolling' (mutual support with anticipated reciprocation) that characterizes parliaments in which party solidarity is lower, such as the US Congress, is in Europe institutionalized in the form of cohesive and disciplined PPGs. For that reason, the success of virtually all government legislation in European parliaments may represent the outcome of a bargaining process in which the government takes into account the views of its own backbenchers, rather than implying that those backbenchers have no significant input into public policymaking. Thus, governments will not in general proceed with legislation that their backbenchers have already indicated they will not support. In Germany, it is common for the chairpersons of the government *Fraktionen* to attend cabinet meetings to ensure that government proposals are acceptable to the *Fraktion* (Schüttemeyer, 1994: 39). In Austria,

France and the Netherlands, too, there is evidence of close consultation between members of the government and their parliamentary parties (Heidar and Koole, 2000b: 258; Elgie, 2003: 172–173; Timmermans and Andeweg, 2003: 383). Rank-and-file government MPs cannot afford to be mere 'dumb sheep' or 'robots', because they know their own re-election prospects depend on the government's fortunes, giving them a strong incentive to keep a watchful eye on what the government does (Schüttemeyer, 2009: 6).

For example, in Britain the decisive political relationships are usually *within* parties rather than *between* parties (things became different after the formation of the UK's first two-party coalition in May 2010, of course). The rate of backbench rebellion in the 1997–2001 parliament, the Labour government's first term, was exceptionally low, and Labour MPs came to be spoken of dismissively as timid, gutless, sycophantic, cowardly, poodles, sheep, androids or Daleks. However, their loyalty in the division lobbies was not the result of intimidation by the party leadership, but came about partly because Labour MPs were often able to gain concessions behind the scenes from ministers on issues they felt strongly about, and also because, after 18 years in opposition, they were acutely aware of the electoral damage that an image of party disunity could do (Cowley and Stuart, 2003). Even so, there were limits to their loyalty, and after the 2001 election they rebelled against government attempts to install supposedly 'reliable', government-friendly MPs as committee chairs. In March 2003 139 Labour MPs voted against their government's Iraq policy, the largest revolt by government MPs for over a century. By the summer of 2003 there had been more rebellions by MPs than in any previous post-war parliament (Cowley and Stuart, 2004: 311). Nor was it only veto power that they were able to exercise. King affirms that it was backbench pressure that led the government to bring in legislation to ban fox-hunting in 2004; it did not really wish to do so, but it wanted even less to alienate its backbenchers by not doing so (King, 2007: 340).

However, even if governments in some countries have to work a little harder for the backing of their parliamentarians than they used to, the picture is still one of very strong party solidarity in parliament. The existence of large and disciplined voting blocs is central to the practice of European parliamentary democracy. The coherence of European parties when compared, for example, with their US counterparts depends on two basic and related behavioural phenomena. The first is that voters tend to vote for parties rather than for individual candidates. The second is that individual parliamentarians think of themselves first and foremost as members of their party's parliamentary group, rather than as individual members. We shall return to political parties several times in our subsequent discussions. However, we must explore these particular points now in order to be able to provide a comprehensive picture of European parliamentary democracy.

### 3.4.1 Voters vote for parties

Most Europeans, when they vote in a parliamentary election, are voting primarily for a party rather than for a person. Even in those few countries where the myth that voters choose people rather than parties is still cherished, prominent and colourful individuals who eschew parties and fight elections as independents usually come to a sticky end – often at the hands of unknown opponents wielding nothing but a party label. Most European parliamentarians have got where they are by being candidates of political parties rather than by being particularly outstanding individuals in their own right.

European voters tend to vote in legislative elections for parties rather than for people precisely because, when they vote, they feel that they are helping to choose a government. Because it is the government that has the initiative in shaping public policy, voters' main concern is with which party or parties will control the government, rather than with the personal qualities of individual candidates. They therefore have strong incentives to look for a clear-cut choice between alternative governments or, at the very least, between party blocs powerful enough to change the complexion of governments during the process of coalition bargaining. Except in very finely balanced situations, a legislator who is not a member of a political party is not likely to have much of an impact on government formation and maintenance, the single most important job of European legislatures.

The primacy of parties over individual candidates in Europe is made explicit in some countries where the electoral system is such that voters simply choose a party ticket without being able to express a view on specific candidates, something that we discuss in detail in Chapter 11. Even in countries where voters do have an opportunity to vote for an individual candidate, the fact that it is parties rather than individual candidates who are ultimately important in European elections means that European legislators usually get a far smaller *personal vote* (that is, the vote won by a candidate because of his or her perceived merits rather than because of the party he or she represents) than their American counterparts. This is a direct consequence of the system of parliamentary government, and has a number of political effects. Three are of direct relevance here.

First, because the size of a politician's personal vote is so much less in Europe than it is in the United States, the fate of European candidates is determined much more by national political forces than by what particular people have done for particular local constituencies. European politicians who want to advance their careers usually face incentives to concentrate on national politics rather than on the provision of goodies for their local constituents.

A second, related, matter is that incumbent candidates have much less of a built-in advantage in Europe than they do in the United States. In the United States the incumbent is the one who brings home the bacon, thereby building a personal vote that provides a strong insulation from winds of political change at the national level. Many local incumbents in the United States are able to survive what appear to be national landslides against their party, resulting in an average re-election rate of incumbents of over 90 per cent in House elections since the Second World War. In Europe, in contrast, being an incumbent gives less of an inherent advantage when it comes to the next election. In Britain, for example, individual MPs can do far less for their constituents than their American equivalents. As Cox puts it, 'the mainstays of the US Congressman's particularistic usefulness to his constituents' – civil service patronage and 'local improvement' bills securing public expenditure on rivers and harbours, railways, roads, dams, canals, and so on – were all largely shut off from the influence of the backbench MP from the middle of the nineteenth century onwards (Cox, 1987: 133–134). In nearly all European countries MPs simply cannot supply particularized benefits ('pork') to their localities through legislation. Parliamentary committees do not, as in the USA, have distributive power, and members tend to operate as agents of their PPG rather than as autonomous political entrepreneurs. In Germany, for example, 'consensus cannot be based on distributive log-rolls between individual members', because Bundestag committee members operate under tight party control (Miller and Stecker, 2008: 319). The main exception is Greece, where bills often end up with a whole raft of such amendments, often completely unconnected to the subject of the bill, although even here the practice has been somewhat curbed of late (Trantas *et al.*, 2003: 378). Generally, though, legislation in Europe is free of the 'earmarks' beloved of US Congress members, paragraphs inserted into appropriations bills that designate funding for spending on a specific project in some member's geographical constituency (Mezey, 2008: 93–117).

Because the personal vote in Europe is not large, when the political tide turns against a particular party its candidates tend to lose their seats, no matter who they are or what they have done for their constituency. It is true that under some list systems of proportional representation, parties can protect their senior politicians by placing them high on party lists (see Chapter 11), and that under other electoral systems, which pit candidates of the same party against each other, there is such a thing as a personal vote for individuals within the party fold. Even so, prominent politicians can disappear abruptly from parliament simply because their party is doing badly. Whereas in the USA incumbent re-election rates are not far below 100 per cent, as we have said, across Europe between 30 and 40 per cent of outgoing MPs are replaced at each election. In nearly all post-communist countries turnover at each election averages over 50 per cent, and in Spain on average almost half of Cortes members after each election are first-time deputies (Oñate, 2005: 133; Ilonszki and Edinger, 2007: 156). Such levels of turnover make it difficult for parliaments and their committees to build up high degrees of expertise.

The third, and probably the most important, consequence of the fact that European voters vote for parties rather than for people is that party labels are very valuable commodities in Europe. This makes party legislators unwilling to do anything – such as voting against the party line in parliament – that might cost them the label at the next election, for if they are not picked as party candidates in the next election (a subject to which we return in Chapter 10), their political careers may well be over. That would represent the loss of a sizeable investment, as most MPs have spent many years building their political career – and we use the word 'career' deliberately, as MPs these days are characteristically professional politicians. In Germany, for example, the average MP is elected to parliament at the age of 42, having spent nine years in local councils and another nine years before that working towards his or her first elective office. These three aspects of MPs' backgrounds, incidentally, are typical of European MPs generally: MPs tend to be middle-aged (few under 30 or over 65), to have been elected to local office before entering the national parliament, and to be professional politicians. (They differ most starkly from the population as a whole in their under-representation of women, a topic to which we return in Chapters 10 and 11.) Once individuals make it to the Bundestag, they are understandably loath to jeopardize their pension, and they know that career progression is through a set of steps: first on a PPG specialist committee, then on a Bundestag committee, and eventually as a member of their PPG's executive committee and perhaps of the government (Patzelt, 2000: 41; Schüttemeyer, 2009: 7–8). Behaving in a disloyal or maverick fashion in any of these roles is not the way to get promoted further. The battlefields of European politics are littered with the corpses of those who have defied the party line. In post-communist states, too, the job of a deputy is 'lucrative', making MPs reluctant to risk losing their position by excessive independence (Kopecky, 2007: 153). As a result of all these factors, European legislative parties are highly disciplined.

### 3.4.2 Parliamentarians and party discipline

As we have pointed out, parliamentarians usually follow the party line in parliament mainly because this is what their instincts tell them to do, not because they are being threatened with dire sanctions if they do not do so. If their instincts should happen to tell them to vote against the party line on some issue, however, they quickly discover that a range of punishments await those who stray from the fold (Heidar and Koole, 2000b: 256). To put it another way, there are powerful incentives to vote the party line, whatever an MP's private policy preferences. We have already seen that one such incentive is fear of losing the party label at the next election, given that voters choose parties rather than people, because it is parties rather than individual MPs that can influence the shape of governments. Party leaders have power over rank-and-file members of parliament because the latter know that if they become habitually disloyal to the party line in parliament, the candidate selectors (usually local party members) may well deny them access to the party label at the next election, and thereby cast all but the most resilient out into the political wilderness. The extreme case here is perhaps Ireland, where in July 1993 the parliamentary group of the country's then largest party, Fianna Fáil, decided that, in future, voting against the party line on any issue (or even abstaining) would automatically mean expulsion from the parliamentary party. In Britain, the parliamentary parties have what are termed *whips* (the term refers to the 'whipping in' of foxhounds in hunting, and as such is revealing of the strength of tradition in the House of Commons), whose job it is to ensure that all MPs follow the party line in votes. The whips control access to some of the perks of being a parliamentarian, such as the best-situated offices, in-demand committee assignments, or trips abroad, and every MP knows that such benefits will go to loyal MPs rather than to rebels. If need be, the whips will ensure the expulsion from the parliamentary group of persistent mavericks, although this is very rare.

A second source of power for party oligarchs is that if they are not already senior government members, then they are the people who will be senior government members when the party next gets into government. This means that European party leaders are the gatekeepers to political office; they can use this position to reward those who are loyal to the party and punish those who are not. In Britain's House of Commons, the most closely studied European parliament, there is clear evidence that the increase in party cohesion in parliamentary voting around the end of the nineteenth century was strongly linked to an increase in the number of MPs seeking ministerial posts and concluding that the best way of gaining preferment was to remain loyal at all times to the party leadership, and this in turn led to voters developing a strong party rather than personal orientation at elections (Cox, 1987: 75–79). This now applies to virtually every European parliament. Thus party discipline is made much stronger by the system of parliamentary government. Because the legislature is the main recruiting ground for members of the executive in most countries, those who aspire to executive office must behave themselves in the legislature. If they do not, they will displease those with the power to promote them. The implication is that it is 'dejected' MPs (consisting of the 'rejected', who see no prospect of promotion, and the 'ejected', those who were once ministers but are now on the downward slope of their careers) who are most likely to rebel, as they have little to lose, and British evidence backs this up (Benedetto and Hix, 2007).

## 3.5 Parliamentarians and constituency representation

The formal role of parliaments in the process of representation is clear enough, and to a greater or lesser degree may be stated in a country's constitution: the people elect their representatives, and these representatives, answerable to the people at the next election, sustain, monitor, and can ultimately oust the government. A more tangible form of representation provided by MPs to many Europeans is informal in the sense that it receives little or no constitutional recognition. This is constituency representation, whereby MPs promote and defend the interests of their geographical constituency, of particular sectors within their constituency, or of individual constituents. Whether an ordinary European feels 'represented' by his or her MP may depend less on the views that the MP expresses in the chamber of parliament or in a committee than on whether the MP will take up a matter of personal concern, or help secure some redress of a grievance. Because this kind of behaviour is not constitutionally prescribed, there is sometimes a tendency to neglect it. It is possible to read some works on certain European parliaments without realizing that, for many MPs, as much time is spent dealing with constituency work as on the formally assigned tasks of an MP, such as taking part in debates or sitting on committees.

In real life, however, constituency work looms large in the lives of many, probably most, MPs around Europe, and indeed the rest of the world. As Mezey (2008: 85) puts it:

> **"** Legislators around the world and at every level of government report that they devote substantial time to errand-running and pork-barrel activities on behalf of individuals or specific groups of constituents. Most representatives view these efforts as important to their re-election, but many also believe that responding to these individual requests for assistance is simply a part of their job. **"**

In France, where constituency representation has always been the main role of a *député*, research produced a diary of a typical rural French MP (reproduced in Safran, 1998: 223–224), which shows the MP arriving in Paris on Tuesday morning and returning to his or her constituency on Thursday evening. Friday, Saturday, Sunday and Monday are all spent in local political activity and, even while the deputy is in Paris, some of his or her time is spent in following up constituency business. On average, about two-thirds of the assistants that deputies can employ are deployed in their deputy's constituency rather than in the National Assembly building. The benches in the parliamentary chamber are usually virtually empty. Most French MPs were born in the *département* where their constituency is located, and around 90 per cent of them hold a local office, most often mayor, as well as being a deputy – the so-called *cumul des mandats*. This local implantation makes it difficult for parties to threaten credibly to deselect MPs (Lazardeux, 2005: 258; Dewoghélaëre *et al.*, 2006; Knapp and Wright, 2006: 155; Dogan, 2007; Costa and Kerrouche, 2009a). In Britain there has been a huge increase in the volume of constituency work since 1970, with MPs spending about half of their time on it (Rush, 2001: 210–211, 216). In Ireland, constituency service is central to deputies' role (Gallagher and Komito, 2010). In Nordic countries, too, MPs tend to be strongly locally oriented. Links between citizens and MPs can be especially close in small countries: in Malta MPs are very active constituency workers, while in Iceland over half of the voting population claims to know an MP personally (Arter, 1999: 211). In contrast, there are some countries, such as the Netherlands, Portugal and Spain, where performance of constituency duties is close to non-existent. In post-communist countries, too, MPs devote little time to such duties, although the increasing professionalism of MPs at least gives them the resources to begin performing such a function (Kopecký, 2007: 153).

The causes and consequences of this kind of representation are a matter of some dispute. When trying to explain variations in the amount of constituency work carried out by parliamentarians in different countries, some writers identify the electoral system as important (Gallagher, 2008: 557–562). For most MPs around Europe, as we have seen, constituency work offers one way through which they might build a personal vote, and electoral incentives might help to explain its incidence. Under certain electoral systems, as we shall discuss in more detail in Chapter 11, candidates of each party are competing with each other, as well as with candidates of other parties, and thus have a strong incentive to try to build up a personal vote. Some electoral systems provide individual MPs with a much greater incentive to cultivate a personal vote than others (Carey and Shugart, 1995; Mitchell, 2000: 340–344). This might help to explain why MPs operating under electoral systems giving voters a choice of candidates within parties, as in Ireland and Malta, do a great deal of constituency work, whereas those in countries where there is little or no incentive to cultivate a personal vote, such as Portugal, do relatively little.

The electoral system does not explain everything, though. In some countries, such as Britain and France, there is an expectation that MPs will perform these duties. MPs in Britain are not provided with any electoral incentive to undertake constituency work: they are at no risk of being ousted by a party running mate, and the large number of safe seats means that many do not need to fear losing to a rival from another party, and yet most of them are assiduous constituency workers, like their German counterparts (Saalfeld, 2002: 56). One explanation for this is that MPs derive psychological gratification from doing constituency work, which, moreover, they believe is one of their duties as an MP (Norris, 1997: 47). In addition, even under a list system where MPs have no incentive to cultivate a personal vote, such as in Belgium in the 1990s, MPs may well fear that they will fall out of favour with their party's candidate selectors unless they maintain a high local profile (De Winter, 2002: 96–97). Political culture, the hard-to-quantify set of expectations of political elites and ordinary voters, also plays a part: local roots and a record in local government are more important in Norway, where the voters cannot oust an MP in favour of a party running mate, than in Denmark, where they can (Pedersen *et al.*, 2004: 343, 350). New technology could conceivably make a difference. In Portugal, MPs who previously had no contact with voters now have greater communication with the public thanks to email (Leston-Bandeira, 2007: 412–413). Most MPs around Europe have their own websites, but the jury is still out as to whether these are likely to facilitate two-way communication between MPs and constituents, or merely allow MPs to promote themselves.

The consequences of constituency work for the political representation of Europeans are mixed. On the one hand, immersion in constituency duties, whether casework for individual constituents or activity on behalf of the constituency as a whole, may distract MPs from their purely parliamentary roles, leaving them with less time to play a part in formulating legislation and scrutinizing government activity. On the other hand, it keeps MPs in touch with people who live ordinary lives, and provides a form of representation that to many people is more meaningful than the representation of opinion. In that way it builds support for the political system as a whole, as well as reducing the alienation of those who would otherwise have no ready conduit to the state. Moreover, it helps MPs discharge their oversight role in parliament, in that hearing citizens' grievances alerts them to problems with the design or implementation of government policy.

## 3.6 European parliaments: one chamber or two?

The question of whether there should be one or two legislative chambers is one of the most venerable in debates over parliamentary design. The main arguments in favour of *bicameralism* – that is, having two chambers – are that a second chamber can act as a check on the possibility of an overbearing majority in the lower house, and that it may be able to discuss policy proposals in a more reflective manner than the highly politicized lower house, applying 'sober second thoughts' and drawing on non-party technical expertise (Russell, 2000: 21–22; on bicameralism generally see Tsebelis and Money, 1997; Heller, 2007). The main argument against bicameralism is summed up in the frequently quoted (if perhaps apocryphal) comment of the Abbé Sieyès, made more than 200 years ago, to the effect that 'if the second chamber agrees with the first it is superfluous, and if it does not it is pernicious'. Worldwide, bicameralism is in decline. Prior to the First World War a second chamber was virtually *de rigueur* for a sovereign state, but now only about a third of countries have one (Massicotte, 2000: 282).

Since upper houses are rarely in a position to block governments or lower houses, second chambers in Europe are often seen as unimportant. Tsebelis and Money (1997), however, argue that bicameralism can make a significant difference to a country's politics. They maintain that its impact is inherently conservative, as its effect is to protect the status quo, and they argue that the relationship between the two houses is determined not only by the formal rules about how much power each has but also by how much bargaining power each house possesses in some particular conflict. For example, if the upper house has the power to delay legislation for a year, then at times when an election is less than a year away the upper house will have greater power. The lower house (to be precise, the government) will then have to decide whether to press ahead with its preferred measure, knowing that it might well end up with nothing, or reach a compromise in order to get at least part of its proposals passed into law before the election. Of course, the upper house, knowing of the 'impatience' of the lower house in this situation, will be tempted to drive a particularly hard bargain. Lijphart, too, identifies 'strong bicameralism' as a key feature of his model of 'consensus democracy'. The conditions of strong bicameralism are, first, that the upper house is not elected on the same basis as the lower house (thus creating a likelihood that the government does not control the upper house) and, second, that it has real power (Lijphart, 1999: 39). In western Europe, he judges, only the Swiss and German systems amount to strong bicameralism (Lijphart, 1999: 212).

In this light, the impact of bicameralism depends primarily on the composition and the powers of a second chamber, if one exists. As Table 3.1 shows, in 2010 the position varied around Europe, with only 13 of the 30 states having a second chamber. The two factors that seem to have the strongest influence on whether a state is bicameral are size and centralization (Patterson and Mughan, 2001: 44–46); the 17 states without a second chamber are all small, unitary states. Of the 13 states with an upper house only three are both small and unitary (Czech Republic, Ireland and the Netherlands); the rest are federal (Austria, Belgium, Switzerland), large or at least medium-sized (France, Italy, Poland, Romania, Spain, the United Kingdom), or both (Germany). One of these anomalies may soon end, since by the end of 2010 all the main parties in Ireland were in agreement that the country's upper house should be abolished within a matter of months.

**TABLE 3.1** Second chambers of parliament in Europe

| Country | Name of second chamber | Size of second chamber | Comments |
|---|---|---|---|
| Austria | Bundesrat | 64 | Indirectly elected (by members of state parliaments) |
| Belgium | Sénat/Senaat | 71 | 40 directly elected; 21 indirectly elected; 10 co-opted |
| Bulgaria | – | – | |
| Cyprus | – | – | |
| Czech Republic | Senat | 81 | Directly elected; one-third of membership is renewed every two years |
| Denmark | – | – | Upper house abolished in 1953 |
| Estonia | – | – | |
| Finland | – | – | |
| France | Sénat | 321 | Indirectly elected (mainly by local councillors) |
| Germany | Bundesrat | 69 | Composed of members of state governments, or their designated substitutes |
| Greece | – | – | |
| Hungary | – | – | |
| Iceland | – | – | Upper chamber abolished in 1991 |
| Ireland | Seanad | 60 | 43 indirectly elected, mainly by local councillors; 11 appointed by prime minister; 6 elected by university graduates |
| Italy | Senato | 322 | 315 are directly elected |
| Latvia | – | – | |
| Lithuania | – | – | |
| Luxembourg | – | – | 21-member Council of State plays the same role as a second chamber |
| Malta | – | – | |
| Netherlands | Eerste Kamer (First Chamber) | 75 | Indirectly elected (by members of provincial legislatures) |
| Norway | – | – | |
| Poland | Senat | 100 | Directly elected |
| Portugal | – | – | Corporatist second chamber of Salazar regime abolished in 1974 |
| Romania | Senat | 137 | Directly elected |
| Slovakia | – | – | |
| Slovenia | – | – | Directly elected 40-member National Council has analogous role, but is essentially an advisory organ without full law-making powers |
| Spain | Senado | 257 | 208 directly elected; the other 49 indirectly elected |

**TABLE 3.1** (*continued*)

| Country | Name of second chamber | Size of second chamber | Comments |
|---|---|---|---|
| Sweden | – | – | Upper house abolished in 1970 |
| Switzerland | Ständerat/ Conseil des États (Council of States) | 46 | Nearly all directly elected |
| United Kingdom | House of Lords | 722 | Mainly appointed for life by government of the day, plus some remaining hereditary peers |

*Sources*: Inter-Parliamentary Union website (www.ipu.org), and parliamentary websites (to which the IPU site provides links); Tsebelis and Money (1997: 48–52).

In six of these 13 countries the most common route to the upper house is indirect election or appointment by local or provincial councils – and since these bodies tend to over-represent rural areas, where left-wing parties are relatively weak, right-wing parties are often stronger in upper chambers than in lower ones (Vatter, 2005: 196–197). In France, for example, the Senate has never had a left-wing majority (Elgie, 2003: 153–155). Since subnational government bodies may be under the control of the parties that are in opposition at the national level, there is an inherent potential for conflict between the two houses. The First Chamber in the Netherlands is elected by members of the 12 provincial councils; members of Austria's Bundesrat are appointed by the state parliaments; and local councillors dominate the election of 43 of the 60 members of Ireland's Seanad. French senators are elected for nine-year terms, with a third of them standing down every three years, by an electorate of whom 95 per cent are local councillors. This inbuilt right-wing majority can be almost as awkward for the right as for the left, as it is not very amenable to party discipline, and has 'a leisurely pace of deliberation' befitting its typically elderly membership; it is an independent-minded institution or, less politely, a 'conservative, curmudgeonly' one, which is unlikely to change its nature, since it has the power to veto bills to reform it (Knapp and Wright, 2006: 155–157).

In Germany, the Bundesrat (also known as the Federal Council) consists of the prime ministers and certain other members of the *Land* governments, and although these individuals often appoint substitutes to attend meetings, the substitutes are either people of their own political complexion or, very often, civil servants attending committee meetings under their direction. Bundesrat members from each *Land* must cast their votes en bloc, even if the *Land* government is a coalition. The allocation of seats to *Länder* follows the principle of *degressive proportionality* – in other words, the smaller *Länder* are generously over-represented in relation to their size. With, on average, four *Land* elections taking place every year, the Bundesrat's composition is constantly changing.

There may seem to be only a weak argument for a directly elected second chamber that is not designed to provide a different kind of political representation from that in the first chamber. In seven countries, however, direct election plays a significant role (Massicotte, 2000). In Poland and Romania all (and in Italy almost all) the senators are elected by the people at the same time

as the lower chamber. Election of the Czech Republic's senate follows the model of its US counterpart: senators serve six-year terms, with a third of the body standing down every two years. In
Belgium, Spain and Switzerland most members of the upper house are directly elected: in these
cases, the role of the upper house is to protect regional or cantonal interests.

The most distinctive upper house is Britain's House of Lords, where for many centuries the
majority of members held their positions simply by inheriting them. Even though many hereditary peers rarely or never attended parliament, their existence was widely seen by left-wing and
liberal forces in Britain as an anomaly in the democratic era. The Labour government elected in
1997 developed plans to reform the Lords fundamentally, so that the hereditary component
in the Lords would first be drastically reduced and then be eliminated altogether. Consequently,
in 1999 the number of hereditary peers with voting rights was reduced to 92. Of the remaining
members, 26 were bishops (including two archbishops) and the others were *life peers*: that is,
individuals appointed for life by the government of the day. The number in this last category (and
hence the total membership of the house) varies over time: in 2010 there were 605 life peers.
Many critics of the House of Lords argued that even these plans did not bring about a second
chamber that was particularly representative. The 1999 change was supposed to be the first step
in a programme entailing a complete overhaul, but reform plans stalled subsequently, as it was
impossible to secure agreement on exactly how a new upper house should be composed, and
upper house reform is a low priority given that 'the general public could not care less' (Kelso,
2006; King, 2007: 312; Bogdanor, 2009: 145–172; McLean, 2010: 223–250). The government
was wary of allowing a significant number of the chamber's members to be directly elected, and
preferred a system of appointment, which critics said would result in a house of the prime minister's loyalists. Also distinctive is Luxembourg's Council of State (which is not technically a
second chamber, although it plays the same role), whose 21 members, once appointed, hold
office until the age of 72. They are nominally appointed by the head of state, the Grand Duke,
although in practice the nominations are controlled by the three major parties.

Parliaments elsewhere have only one chamber. In some of these countries there are devices
that go some way towards creating a second chamber. For example, after each election Norway's
parliament, the Storting, used to divide into two chambers, though this ended in 2007. In
Denmark the abolition of the upper house coincided with the introduction of the right of a third
of MPs to call a referendum on any bill, giving the opposition a constraining power somewhat
analogous to that of a second chamber. In those states that have abolished their second chambers (Denmark, Iceland, Portugal and Sweden are the only post-war European examples), there
are no detectable signs of nostalgia (Massicotte, 2001). One analysis, though, argues that the
abolition of the upper houses in Denmark and Sweden has led to less predictable economic policies, and that while these countries were bicameral, policies were 'more faithful to the long-run
interests of the median voter' (Congleton, 2006: 184).

Whether upper houses matter depends largely upon how much power they have. Constitutional
rules usually prescribe that disputes between the two houses must be resolved by means of a
*navette* (shuttle), whereby bills on which the two chambers disagree pass back and forth between
them until some conflict resolution mechanism comes into play. This might be, for example, a
stipulation that the lower house prevails after the measure has shuttled back and forth a certain
number of times, or provision for a committee composed of members of both houses to meet and
attempt to resolve the deadlock (see Tsebelis and Money, 1997: 54–70). Almost invariably, the
upper house has less power than the lower house. Italy is an exception: the Senate has exactly

the same powers as the Chamber of Deputies, so every bill must pass both houses to become law, and the cabinet is answerable to both houses equally. There is no conflict resolution mechanism, and the *navette* can continue indefinitely (Zucchini, 2008). The Romanian Senat, too, has essentially the same powers and composition as the lower house, and the Belgian Sénat/Senaat is only a little less powerful than the lower house. The few post-communist second chambers are generally weak, although the Czech Senat has been able to exercise some of its amendment powers, given the frequency of minority government there (Olson and Norton, 2007: 187–188).

Typically, the upper house is able only to delay legislation passed by the lower house, but sometimes it can veto certain types of legislation (for example, legislation changing the constitution). The Dutch First Chamber vetoed 54 bills between 1945 and 2008, and around 80 others were withdrawn or amended by the government to avoid their meeting the same fate (Andeweg and Irwin, 2009: 149). In Germany, the Bundesrat has a veto over legislation that affects the power of the states (the *Länder*), and if it defeats a bill on any other subject by a two-thirds majority, only a two-thirds majority in the lower house, the Bundestag, can overrule it. In addition, since a 1992 amendment to the constitution, the Bundesrat has had a strong voice in the formulation of the line that German ministers are to take within the Council of the European Union (which we discuss in Chapter 5). Originally it was expected that only a small proportion of legislation would require the consent of the Bundesrat, but in practice most legislation turned out to fall into this category, until a constitutional reform in 2006 reduced the proportion to around 35–40 per cent (Green *et al.*, 2008: 59). Very few Bundestag bills are explicitly vetoed by the Bundesrat – only 1 per cent of bills approved by the Bundestag between 1949 and 2003 met this fate – but that is because the government anticipates the reception its proposals will get in the Bundesrat, and adjusts its law-making priorities accordingly (Manow and Burkhart, 2007; Brunner and Debus, 2008: 235; Green *et al.*, 2008). The Bundesrat is a particularly significant actor, given that it has usually been dominated by the parties that are in opposition at federal level: between 1970 and 2005 there were only nine years when the government parties held a majority of Bundesrat seats (Manow and Burkhart, 2007: 168). This gives the opposition parties a significant input into national policymaking. However, since the priorities of, say, an SPD *Land* government and the SPD's national leadership do not always coincide, opposition members of the Bundesrat, particularly those from *Länder* with pressing financial problems, are sometimes more willing to come to an agreement with the government than their counterparts in the lower house would wish. The Bundesrat is thus a particularly powerful body even though, technically, it is not actually a second chamber of parliament (von Beyme, 2000: 34).

In Britain, the House of Lords, which in the nineteenth century could veto bills, has had its power reduced in successive reforms, so by the start of the twenty-first century it could only delay bills by a year. It is not completely irrelevant, though, since by defeating a government bill when an election is less than a year away it effectively kills the bill. In the last analysis the Commons can overrule the Lords by invoking the Parliament Act, although this is very rarely done – when the Commons did this in November 2004 to insist on the passage of a bill to abolish fox-hunting, it was only the sixth time it had happened since the Commons acquired this power in 1911. On other occasions when the Lords defeat a bill, the government may simply decide to let the bill lapse, in effect handing the Lords a veto (King, 2007: 307). The Irish upper house, Seanad Éireann, can do no more than delay bills for 90 days. The French Senate has even less power than the already weak French lower house; it can refuse to pass bills coming from the lower house, and has sometimes been obstructive to government plans as a result, but if it pushes its obstruction too far the government can and does exercise its own power to call upon the lower house to deliver a decisive vote on the bill (Safran, 1998: 230–234).

## 3.7 The significance of parliaments: an assessment

In most discussions of parliaments in Europe, as we have noted, the phrase 'decline of parliaments' crops up somewhere along the line. It sums up a feeling, which seems to have been around since the early years of the twentieth century, that parliaments are not what they were. Once upon a time, so the feeling goes, they really ran countries and swept governments into and out of office as they pleased, whereas nowadays they have been reduced to mere rubber stamps, tamely approving whatever proposals governments place before them. Needless to say, both of these images are exaggerated. The 'golden age' of parliaments never really existed, certainly as far as most countries are concerned. And today's parliaments, although perhaps lacking in excitement, can do useful work in improving legislation through detailed examination in committees.

Certainly, it is clear that parliaments, considered as institutions, do not play an active role in the decision-making process. In many countries, members of parliament suffer from a sense of irrelevance, certainly as far as plenary sessions are concerned. There is genuine uncertainty as to whether anyone is listening when a deputy speaks, as chambers are virtually empty, and newspapers, television and radio devote very little time or space to reporting the speeches that parliamentarians make. In Denmark there is even a joke that an MP wishing to keep something secret should announce it in the Folketing, because then it is certain that nobody will hear it. No one really expects to see government MPs changing their minds – and their votes – as a consequence of a brilliant speech by an opposition MP. The reasons for this state of affairs are not difficult to identify. The whole business of making policy is now so complex that governments spend a lot of time consulting with experts in the civil service and with the major interest groups involved, such as business interests, trade unions and farmers' groups (see Chapters 6 and 13). If a package can be put together that satisfies all these groups, the government will be reluctant to allow parliament to tinker with it. In addition, a lot of policy is made at EU level (see Chapter 5), and the impact of the EU is generally seen as having strengthened governments at the expense of parliaments, which find it hard to cope with 'the volume and pace of EU legislative output' (Ladrech, 2010: 91). An assessment based on the pre-2004 EU suggested that only in one parliament (the Danish Folketing) could MPs really determine ministerial behaviour within the EU's Council of Ministers; in five other countries parliament exercised moderate influence, and in the other nine parliament was weak in this area (Raunio, 2008: 7–11). Governments have many more resources than parliaments: for example, in Denmark the 1750 graduates employed in ministerial *cabinets* contrasts with the fewer than 100 working for the parliament (Damgaard and Jensen, 2006: 437). Moreover, when it comes to getting straight answers from government ministers, the procedural devices that parliaments have at their disposal are often less effective than questioning by journalists in the mass media, which in many cases have become the main means by which governments are forced to give an account of themselves to the general public.

Nonetheless, some factors are working in favour of parliaments. For one thing, members of parliament are becoming more professional. In a number of countries, there has been a decline in the number of MPs who combine this role with another job; the trend is towards parliaments of full-time professional politicians. Moreover, parliaments are becoming better resourced, although in no country, not even Germany, do they have anything like the personal staffs that American Congress members enjoy. Parliaments are becoming more active, according to most quantifiable indicators; MPs are asking more questions, initiating more interpellations and, it seems, spending more time in committees. Most important of all, the government remains the government only for so long as it retains the confidence of parliament. It is true that, right across Europe, parliament very rarely votes a government out of office, but this should not obscure the importance of this relationship. Governments are well aware that parliament does have this ulti-mate power, and so they act with this consideration always in their minds, ensuring in particular that their own MPs do not become disaffected.

We have seen that the relevance of parliaments varies from country to country, but this vari-ation is not random. We can detect a clear pattern. In particular, as we would expect, the inter-party mode of behaviour dominates in those countries characterized by Lijphart as majori-tarian. Relations between MPs and government ministers, or among MPs, are determined by their respective party affiliations; there is at all times a keen sense that the government, and the MPs of the government party or parties, are on the government 'side', while the rest are on the opposition 'side'. If government MPs amount to a majority, governments need only retain the loy-alty of their own backbenchers to ensure that all their proposals are approved by parliament. This model applies to such countries as the United Kingdom, Greece, France, Malta and Ireland. In consensus systems, although the inter-party mode is still the most common, cross-party or non-party modes are also manifested. MPs of different parties may combine on some issues, and there may be a sense across party lines of 'parliament' as a body that can and should scrutinize government and perhaps formulate policies with or without the full agreement of government. This model fits such countries as Switzerland, the Netherlands, Belgium, Germany and Austria. It should also be borne in mind that the differences between varieties of parliamentarianism are, arguably, less than the difference between parliamentarianism *tout court* and presidentialism. Gerring *et al.* (2009) argue that parliamentary systems perform better than presidential ones on a whole range of indicators, especially those related to economic and human development.

Any overall assessment of parliaments, however, simply cannot ignore the central role of political parties. The power of a parliament at any given time will depend to a great extent on the balance of power between parties, and on the distribution of power within the government par-ties. It is difficult to overestimate the importance of party discipline in setting the whole tone of politics in a typical European country. The system of parliamentary government would not work without it, because the party oligarchs who constitute the political executive would never know when they would be able to retain the support of the legislature. Governments would thus be liable to fall unpredictably, and would have no guarantee of being able to implement their legis-lative programme. This scenario reads very much like a description of the problems that beset the European system in which party discipline was at its lowest – the French Fourth Republic (1946–1958). The consequence, in a parliamentary government system, was chronic political instability. Effective government was impossible, and the outcome was not, in any real sense, more power in decision-making for parliament, but, rather, political chaos and the discrediting of the political class generally. This situation was brought to an end in 1958, with the establish-ment of the Fifth Republic and the creation of a strong, separately elected executive president. The dismal history of the Fourth Republic illustrates the fact that parliamentary government cannot exist without party discipline. Above all, it explains why political parties feature so prominently in our account of representative government in modern Europe.

## Internet resources

By far the most useful is the site of the Inter-Parliamentary Union, which contains information on the parliament of every country in the world, plus a link to that parliament's site. Really, the IPU site is the only one needed, but we list also the sites of the parliaments in the eight countries we are covering in boxes in the chapters. These sites typically have onward links to the party groups, individual MPs, and often information on the country's political system.

www.ipu.org/english/home.htm
  Site of the Inter-Parliamentary Union.

www.ft.dk/
  Site of Denmark's Folketing (English-language version available).

www.assemblee-nationale.fr/
  Site of France's National Assembly (English-language version available).

www.bundestag.de/
  Site of Germany's Bundestag (English-language version available).

www.parlamento.it/
  Site of the Italian parliament. There are links to both houses (the Chamber of Deputies and the Senate of the Republic), but none has an English-language version.

www.tweedekamer.nl/
  Site of the Dutch lower house (English-language version available).

www.sejm.gov.pl/
  Site of Poland's Sejm (English-language version available).

www.congreso.es/portal/page/portal/Congreso/Congreso
  Site of Spain's Congress of Deputies (parts available in English).

www.parliament.uk/
  Site of the United Kingdom's parliament, covering both the House of Commons and the House of Lords. Contains information on how to 'contact a Lord' and even how to address one, but site is available only in English.

## References

**Alivizatos, Nikos** (1990) 'The difficulties of "rationalization" in a polarized political system: the Greek Chamber of Deputies', pp. 131–153 in Ulrike Liebert and Maurizio Cotta (eds), *Parliament and Democratic Consolidation in Southern Europe: Greece, Italy, Portugal, Spain and Turkey*, Pinter, London.

**Andeweg, Rudy B. and Galen A. Irwin** (2009) *Governance and Politics of the Netherlands*, 3rd edn, Palgrave Macmillan, Basingstoke.

**Andeweg, Rudy B. and Lia Nijzink** (1995) 'Beyond the two-body image: relations between ministers and MPs', pp. 152–178 in H. Döring (ed.), *Parliaments and Majority Rule in Western*

*Europe*, Campus Verlag, Frankfurt, and St Martin's Press, New York.

**Andeweg, Rudy B., Lieven De Winter and Wolfgang C. Müller** (2008) 'Parliamentary opposition in post-consociational democracies: Austria, Belgium and the Netherlands', *Journal of Legislative Studies*, 14 (1), 77–112.

**Arter, David** (1999) *Scandinavian Politics Today*, Manchester University Press, Manchester.

**Arter, David** (2008) 'From "parliamentary control" to "accountable government"? The role of public committee hearings in the Swedish Riksdag', *Parliamentary Affairs*, 61 (1), 122–143.

**Bagehot, Walter** (1993) *The English Constitution*, Fontana, London (first published 1867).

**Benedetto, Giacomo and Simon Hix** (2007) 'The rejected, the ejected, and the dejected: explaining government rebels in the 2001–2005 British House of Commons', *Comparative Political Studies*, 40 (7), 755–781.

**Bergman, Torbjörn and Erik Damgaard (eds)** (2000) *Delegation and Accountability in European Integration: The Nordic Parliamentary Democracies and the European Union*, Frank Cass, London.

**Bergman, Torbjörn, Wolfgang C. Müller and Kaare Strøm** (2003) 'Democratic delegation and accountability: cross-national patterns', pp. 109–220 in K. Strøm, W.C. Müller and T. Bergman (eds), *Delegation and Accountability in Parliamentary Democracies*, Oxford University Press, Oxford.

**Bogdanor, Vernon** (2009) *The New British Constitution*, Hart, Oxford.

**Bowler, Shaun** (2000) 'Parties in legislatures: two competing explanations', pp. 157–179 in R.J. Dalton and M.P. Wattenberg (eds), *Parties without Partisans: Political Change in Advanced Democracies*, Oxford University Press, Oxford.

**Bowler, Shaun, David M. Farrell and Richard S. Katz (eds)** (1999) *Party Discipline and Parliamentary Government*, Ohio State University Press, Columbus, OH.

**Brunner, Martin and Marc Debus** (2008) 'Between programmatic interests and party politics: the German Bundesrat in the legislative process', *German Politics*, 17 (3), 232–251.

**Budge, Ian, David McKay, Ken Newton and John Bartle** (2007) *The New British Politics*, 4th edn, Pearson Education, Harlow.

**Capo Giol, Jordi** (2005) 'The Spanish parliament in a triangular relationship, 1982–2000', pp. 107–129 in Cristina Leston-Bandeira (ed.), *Southern European Parliaments in Democracy*, Routledge, London.

**Carey, John M. and Matthew Soberg Shugart** (1995) 'Incentives to cultivate a personal vote: a rank ordering of electoral formulas', *Electoral Studies*, 14 (4), 417–439.

**Carroll, Royce, Gary W. Cox and Mónica Pachón** (2006) 'How parties create electoral democracy, chapter 2', *Legislative Studies Quarterly*, 31 (2), 153–174.

**Congleton, Roger D.** (2006) 'On the merits of bicameral legislatures: intragovernmental bargaining and policy stability', pp. 163–188 in Roger D. Congleton and Birgitta Swedenborg (eds), *Democratic Constitutional Design and Public Policy: Analysis and Evidence*, MIT Press, Cambridge, MA.

**Costa, Olivier and Eric Kerrouche** (2009a) 'Representative roles in the French National Assembly: the case for a dual typology', *French Politics*, 9 (3/4), 219–242.

**Costa, Olivier and Eric Kerrouche** (2009b) 'MPs under the Fifth Republic: professionalisation within a weak institution', *West European Politics*, 32 (2), 327–344.

**Cowley, Philip and Mark Stuart** (2003) 'In place of strife? The PLP in government, 1997–2001', *Political Studies*, 51 (2), 315–331.

**Cowley, Philip and Mark Stuart** (2004) 'Parliament: more Bleak House than Great Expectations', *Parliamentary Affairs*, 57 (2), 301–314.

**Cox, Gary W.** (1987) *The Efficient Secret: The Cabinet and the Development of Political Parties in Victorian England*, Cambridge University Press, Cambridge.

**Cox, Gary W.** (2006) 'The organization of democratic legislatures', pp. 141–161 in Barry R. Weingast and Donald A. Wittman (eds), *The Oxford Handbook of Political Economy*, Oxford University Press, Oxford.

**Damgaard, Erik and Henrik Jensen** (2006) 'Assessing strength and weakness in legislatures: the case of Denmark', *Journal of Legislative Studies*, 12 (3), 426–442.

**Depauw, Sam and Shane Martin** (2009) 'Legislative party discipline and cohesion in comparative perspective', pp. 103–120 in Daniella Giannetti and Kenneth Benoit (eds), *Intra-Party Politics and Coalition Governments*, Routledge, London.

**De Winter, Lieven** (1999) 'Belgium: insider pressure groups in an outsider parliament', pp. 88–109 in P. Norton (ed.), *Parliaments and Pressure Groups in Western Europe*, Frank Cass, London.

**De Winter, Lieven** (2002) 'Belgian MPs: between omnipotent parties and disenchanted citizen-clients', pp. 89–110 in Philip Norton (ed.), *Parliaments and Citizens in Western Europe*, Frank Cass, London.

**Dewoghélaëre, Julien, Raul Magni Berton and Julien Navarro** (2006) 'The *cumul des mandats* in contemporary French politics: an empirical study of the XIIe legislature of the Assemblée Nationale', *French Politics*, 4 (3), 312–332.

**Dogan, Mattei** (2007) 'Parliamentarians as errand-boys in France, Britain, and the United States', *Comparative Sociology*, 6 (4), 430–463.

**Döring, Herbert** (1995) 'Time as a scarce resource: government control of the agenda', pp. 223–246 in *Parliaments and Majority Rule in Western Europe*, Herbert Döring (ed.), Campus Verlag, Frankfurt and St Martin's Press, New York.

**Dowding, Keith and Patrick Dumont (eds)** (2009) *The Selection of Ministers in Europe: Hiring and Firing*, Routledge, Abingdon.

**Elgie, Robert** (2003) *Political Institutions in Contemporary France*, Oxford University Press, Oxford and New York.

**Esaiasson, Peter and Knut Heidar** (2000) 'Learning from the Nordic experience', pp. 409–438 in Peter Esaiasson and Knut Heidar (eds), *Beyond Westminster and Congress: The Nordic Experience*, Ohio State University Press, Columbus, OH.

**Fish, M. Steven and Matthew Kroenig** (2009) *The Handbook of National Legislatures: A Global Survey*, Cambridge University Press, Cambridge.

**Gallagher, Michael** (2008) 'Conclusion', pp. 535–578 in Michael Gallagher and Paul Mitchell (eds), *The Politics of Electoral Systems*, paperback edn, Oxford University Press, Oxford.

**Gallagher, Michael** (2010) 'The Oireachtas: president and parliament', pp. 198–229 in John Coakley and Michael Gallagher (eds), *Politics in the Republic of Ireland*, 5th edn, Routledge and PSAI Press, Abingdon.

**Gallagher, Michael and Lee Komito** (2010) 'The constituency role of Dáil deputies', pp. 230–262 in John Coakley and Michael Gallagher (eds), *Politics in the Republic of Ireland*, 5th edn, Routledge and PSAI Press, Abingdon.

**Gellner, Winand and John D. Robertson** (2001) 'Germany: the continuing dominance of neocorporatism', pp. 101–117 in Clive S. Thomas (ed.), *Political Parties and Interest Groups: Shaping Democratic Governance*, Lynne Rienner, Boulder, CO, and London.

**Gerring, John, Strom C. Thacker and Carola Moreno** 2009. 'Are parliamentary systems better?', *Comparative Political Studies*, 42 (3), 327–359.

**Giuliani, Marco** (2008) 'Brand new, somewhat new or rather old? The Italian legislative process in an age of alternation', *South European Society and Politics*, 13 (1), 1–10.

**Goetz, Klaus H. and Radoslaw Zubek** (2007) 'Government, parliament and law-making in Poland', *Journal of Legislative Studies*, 13 (4), 517–538.

**Green, Simon, Dan Hough, Alister Miskimmon and Graham Timmins** (2008) *The Politics of the New Germany*, Routledge, London.

**Green-Pedersen, Christoffer** (2010) 'Bringing parties into parliament: the development of parliamentary activities in western Europe', *Party Politics*, 16 (3), 347–369.

**Gwiazda, Anna** (2009) 'Poland's quasi-institutionalized party system: the importance of elites and institutions', *Perspectives on European Politics and Society*, 10 (3), 350–376.

**Hagevi, Magnus** (2000) 'Nordic light on committee assignments', pp. 237–261 in Peter Esaiasson and Knut Heidar (eds), *Beyond Westminster and Congress: the Nordic experience*, Ohio State University Press, Columbus, OH.

**Heidar, Knut and Ruud Koole (eds)** (2000a) *Parliamentary Party Groups in European Democracies: Political Parties behind Closed Doors*, Routledge, London.

**Heidar, Knut and Ruud Koole** (2000b) 'Parliamentary party groups compared', pp. 248–270 in Knut Heidar and Ruud Koole (eds), *Parliamentary Party Groups in European Democracies: Political Parties Behind Closed Doors*, Routledge, London.

**Heller, William B.** (2007) 'Divided politics: bicameralism, parties, and policy in democratic legislatures', *Annual Review of Political Science*, 10, 245–269.

**Hindmoor, Andrew, Phil Larkin and Andrew Kennon** (2009) 'Assessing the influence of select committees in the UK: the Education and Skills Committee, 1997–2005', *Journal of Legislative Studies*, 15 (1), 71–89.

**Ilonszki, Gabriella and Michael Edinger** (2007) 'MPs in post-communist and post-Soviet nations: a parliamentary elite in the making', *Journal of Legislative Studies*, 13 (1), 142–163.

**Jensen, Torben K.** (2000) 'Party cohesion', pp. 210–236 in Peter Esaiasson and Knut Heidar (eds), *Beyond Westminster and Congress: The Nordic Experience*, Ohio State University Press, Columbus, OH.

**Kelso, Alexandra** (2006) 'Reforming the House of Lords: navigating representation, democracy and legitimacy at Westminster', *Parliamentary Affairs*, 59 (4), 563–581.

**Kerrouche, Eric** (2009) 'Gone with the wind? The National Assembly under the Fifth Republic', pp. 59–78 in Sylvain Brouard, Andrew M. Appleton and Amy G. Mazur (eds), *The French Fifth Republic at Fifty: Beyond Stereotypes*, Palgrave Macmillan, Basingstoke.

**King, Anthony** (1976) 'Modes of executive–legislative relations: Great Britain, France, and West Germany', *Legislative Studies Quarterly*, 1 (1), 11–34.

**King, Anthony** (2007) *The British Constitution*, Oxford University Press, Oxford.

**Kingdom, John** (2003) *Government and Politics in Britain: An Introduction*, 3rd edn, Polity Press, Cambridge.

**Knapp, Andrew and Vincent Wright** (2006) *The Government and Politics of France*, 5th edn, Routledge, London.

**Kopecký, Petr** (2004) 'Power to the executive! The changing executive–legislative relations in Eastern Europe', *Journal of Legislative Studies*, 10 (2/3), 142–153.

**Kopecký, Petr** (2007) 'Structures of representation', pp. 145–160 in S. White, J. Batt and P.G. Lewis (eds), *Developments in Central and East European Politics 4*, Palgrave Macmillan, Basingstoke.

**Kopecký, Petr and Maria Spirova** (2008) 'Parliamentary opposition in post-communist democracies: power of the powerless', *Journal of Legislative Studies*, 14 (1), 133–159.

**Kristjánsson, Svanur** (2004) 'Iceland: searching for democracy along three dimensions of citizen control', *Scandinavian Political Studies*, 27 (2), 153–174.

**Ladrech, Robert** (2010) *Europeanization and National Politics*, Palgrave Macmillan, Basingstoke.

**Lazardeux, Sébastien** (2005) '"Une question écrite, pour quoi faire?" The causes of the production of written questions in the French Assemblée Nationale', *French Politics*, 3 (3), 258–281.

**Lazardeux, Sébastien G.** (2009) 'The French National Assembly's oversight of the executive: changing role, partisanship and intra-majority conflict', *West European Politics*, 32 (2), 287–309.

**Leston-Bandeira, Cristina** (2004) *From Legislation to Legitimation: The Role of the Portuguese Parliament*, Routledge, London.

**Leston-Bandeira, Cristina** (2007) 'Are ICTs changing parliamentary activity in the Portuguese parliament?', *Journal of Legislative Studies*, 13 (3), 403–421.

**Lijphart, Arend** (1999) *Patterns of Democracy: Government Forms and Performance in Thirty-Six Countries*, Yale University Press, New Haven, CT, and London.

**Malovà, Darina** (2001) 'Slovakia: from the ambiguous constitution to the dominance of informal rules', pp. 347–377 in Jan Zielonka (ed.), *Democratic Consolidation in Eastern Europe, vol. 1: Institutional Engineering*, Oxford University Press, Oxford.

**Manow, Philip and Simone Burkhart** (2007) 'Legislative self-restraint under divided government in Germany, 1976–2002', *Legislative Studies Quarterly*, 32 (2), 167–191.

**Massicotte, Louis** (2000) 'Second-chamber elections', pp. 282–287 in Richard Rose (ed.), *International Encyclopedia of Elections*, CQ Press, Washington, DC.

**Massicotte, Louis** (2001) 'Legislative unicameralism: a global survey and a few case studies', pp. 151–170 in Nicholas D.J. Baldwin and Donald Shell (eds), *Second Chambers*, Frank Cass, London.

**Mattson, I. and K. Strøm** (1995) 'Parliamentary committees', pp. 249–307 in H. Döring (ed.),

*Parliaments and Majority Rule in Western Europe*, Campus Verlag, Frankfurt and St Martin's Press, New York.

**McLean, Iain** (2010) *What's Wrong with the British Constitution?*, Oxford University Press, Oxford.

**Mezey, Michael L.** (2008) *Representative Democracy: Legislators and Their Constituents*, Rowman and Littlefield, Lanham, MD.

**Miller, Bernhard and Christian Stecker** (2008) 'Consensus by default? Interaction of government and opposition parties in the committees of the German Bundestag', *German Politics*, 17 (3), 305–322.

**Mitchell, Paul** (2000) 'Voters and their representatives: electoral institutions and delegation in parliamentary democracies', *European Journal of Political Research*, 37 (3), 335–351.

**Nalewajko, Ewa and Włodzimierz Wesołowski** (2007) 'Five terms of the Polish parliament, 1989–2005', *Journal of Legislative Studies*, 13 (1), 59–82.

**Newell, James L.** (2006) 'Characterising the Italian parliament: legislative change in longitudinal perspective', *Journal of Legislative Studies*, 12 (3), 386–403.

**Norris, Pippa** (1997) 'The puzzle of constituency service', *Journal of Legislative Studies*, 3 (2), 29–49.

**Olson, David M. and Philip Norton** (2007) 'Post-communist and post-Soviet parliaments: divergent paths from transition', *Journal of Legislative Studies*, 13 (1), 164–196.

**Oñate, Pablo** (2005) 'Parliament and citizenship in Spain: twenty-five years of a mismatch?', pp. 130–150 in Cristina Leston-Bandeira (ed.), *Southern European Parliaments in Democracy*, Routledge, London.

**Patterson, Samuel C. and Anthony Mughan** (2001) 'Fundamentals of institutional design: the functions and powers of second chambers', pp. 39–60 in Nicholas D.J. Baldwin and Donald Shell (eds), *Second Chambers*, Frank Cass, London.

**Patzelt, Werner J.** (2000) 'What can an individual MP do in German parliamentary politics?', pp. 23–52 in Lawrence D. Longley and Reuven Y. Hazan (eds), *The Uneasy*

*Relationships between Parliamentary Members and Leaders*, Frank Cass, London.

**Pedersen, Mogens N., Ulrik Kjaer and Kjell A. Eliassen** (2004) 'Institutions matter – even in the long run', pp. 335–353 in Hanne Marthe Narud and Anne Krogstad (eds), *Elections, Parties, and Political Representation*, Universitetsforlaget, Oslo.

**Pettai, Vello and Ülle Madise** (2006) 'The Baltic parliaments: legislative performance from independence to EU accession', *Journal of Legislative Studies*, 12 (3), 291–310.

**Raunio, Tapio** (2008) 'Ensuring democratic control over national governments in European affairs', pp. 3–27 in Gavin Barrett (ed.), *National Parliaments and the European Union: The Constitutional Challenge for the Oireachtas and other Member State Legislatures*, Clarus Press, Dublin.

**Rhodes, R.A.W., John Wanna and Patrick Weller** (2009) *Comparing Westminster*, Oxford University Press, Oxford.

**Rommetvedt, Hilmar** (2003) *The Rise of the Norwegian Parliament*, Frank Cass, London.

**Rush, Michael** (2001) *The Role of the Member of Parliament since 1868: From Gentlemen to Players*, Oxford University Press, Oxford.

**Russell, Meg** (2000) *Reforming the House of Lords*, Oxford University Press, Oxford.

**Russo, Federico and Matti Wiberg** (2010) 'Parliamentary questioning in 17 European parliaments: some steps towards comparison', *Journal of Legislative Studies*, 16 (2), 215–232.

**Saalfeld, Thomas** (1999) 'Germany: Bundestag and interest groups in a "party democracy"', pp. 43–66 in Philip Norton (ed.), *Parliaments and Pressure Groups in Western Europe*, Frank Cass, London.

**Saalfeld, Thomas** (2002) 'Parliament and citizens in Germany: reconciling conflicting pressures', pp. 43–65 in Philip Norton (ed.), *Parliaments and Citizens in Western Europe*, Frank Cass, London.

**Safran, William** (1998) *The French Polity*, 5th edn, Longman, New York and Harlow.

**Schüttemeyer, Suzanne S.** (1994) 'Hierarchy and efficiency in the Bundestag: the German answer for institutionalizing parliament', pp. 29–58 in Gary W. Copeland and Samuel C. Patterson (eds), *Parliaments in the Modern World:*

*Changing Institutions*, University of Michigan Press, Ann Arbor, MI.

**Schüttemeyer, Suzanne S.** (2009) 'Deparliamentarisation: how severely is the German Bundestag affected?', *German Politics*, 18 (1), 1–11.

**Shaw, Malcolm** (1998) 'Legislative committees', pp. 786–793 in G.T. Kurian (ed.), *World Encyclopedia of Parliaments and Legislatures*, Fitzroy Dearborn, Chicago and London.

**Sieberer, Ulrich** (2006) 'Party unity in parliamentary democracies: a comparative analysis', *Journal of Legislative Studies*, 12 (2), 150–178.

**Strøm, Kaare, Wolfgang C. Müller and Torbjörn Bergman** (2003) 'Challenges to parliamentary democracy', pp. 707–750 in Kaare Strøm, Wolfgang C. Müller and Torbjörn Bergman (eds), *Delegation and Accountability in Parliamentary Democracies*, Oxford University Press, Oxford.

**Timmermans, Arco and Rudy B. Andeweg** (2003) 'The Netherlands: rules and mores in delegation and accountability', pp. 498–522 in Kaare Strøm, Wolfgang C. Müller and Torbjörn Bergman (eds), *Delegation and Accountability*

*in Parliamentary Democracies*. Oxford University Press, Oxford.

**Trantas, Georgios, Paraskevi Zagoriti, Torbjörn Bergman, Wolfgang C. Müller and Kaare Strøm** (2003) 'Greece: "rationalizing" constitutional powers in a post-dictatorial country', pp. 376–398 in Kaare Strøm, Wolfgang C. Müller and Torbjörn Bergman (eds), *Delegation and Accountability in Parliamentary Democracies*, Oxford University Press, Oxford.

**Tsebelis, George and Jeanette Money** (1997) *Bicameralism*, Cambridge University Press, Cambridge.

**Vatter, Adrian** (2005) 'Bicameralism and policy performance: the effects of cameral structure in comparative perspective', *Journal of Legislative Studies*, 11 (2), 194–215.

**von Beyme, Klaus** (2000) 'The Bundestag – still the centre of decision-making?', pp. 32–47 in Ludger Helms (ed.), *Institutions and Institutional Change in the Federal Republic of Germany*, Macmillan, Basingstoke.

**Zucchini, Francesco** (2008) 'Dividing parliament? Italian bicameralism in the legislative process (1987–2006)', *South European Society and Politics*, 13 (1), 11–34.

# CHAPTER 4

# Constitutions, Judges and Politics

## 4.1 Introduction

As we have seen in the previous two chapters, the relationship between parliaments and governments plays an important part in the governance of Europe. But parliaments and governments together do not have anything like free rein when it comes to the policy choices they make, because judicial bodies may refuse to allow them to proceed with their plans, even ones for which they have received an electoral mandate. This is well known in the USA, where books on government and politics invariably stress the important role of the courts and the constitution. Books on European government and politics, in contrast, often say nothing about either. This might give students of the subject the impression that in the USA judges have both the will and the power to have a major impact on policy outputs, whereas in Europe judges have little power, and are, in any case, objective and non-political actors who simply implement the laws decided by elected representatives. Such an impression would be not so much simplistic as simply wrong (this chapter will of course focus on Europe; for just one of the innumerable studies of the role of the judiciary in the USA, see Epstein and Knight, 1998). The 'rules of the game' play a large part in determining a country's government and politics, and these are generally set down in a country's constitution and laws. These rules usually impose significant constraints on actors such as political parties, parliaments and governments. Although some of the rules may sometimes be inconvenient to politicians and political parties, and some of them may be sufficiently vague to allow politicians some leeway, in the last resort they are there to determine how things are done. European constitutions contain a number of common features, but also exhibit some significant variation. In the two previous chapters, and in subsequent ones, we look in detail at the *contents* of constitutions regarding such important matters as the powers of governments, presidents and parliaments, as well as electoral law and the decentralization of power, but in this chapter we concentrate on constitutions *per se*, along with the authorities who interpret and apply constitutions.

Constitutions and the judiciary together can act as a significant constraint upon elected representatives. If there is some doubt or dispute as to exactly what course of action the laws or constitution spell out (or rule out) in some specific situation, there is a need for someone to act as a referee or umpire. This is where the courts come in. Constitutions need the muscle of a judicial body to ensure that they are not just words on paper, and the judiciary has little power unless it is authorized to interpret and enforce a constitution or constitution-like rules.

Much of the recent writing on politics and the law concurs in seeing what is variously termed 'the global expansion of judicial power' (Tate and Vallinder, 1995) or the growing 'judicialization' or 'juridification' of politics. As Hirschl (2004: 1) puts it, 'Around the globe, in more than eighty countries and in several supranational entities, constitutional reform has transferred an unprecedented amount of power from representative institutions to judiciaries.' The transformation of popular democracies into juridical democracies is, says one writer, 'arguably the major political development of our time' (Kommers, 2006: 126). To some extent the growing assertiveness of the judiciary in many countries has primarily domestic roots, but it is more than just coincidence that the same trend can be observed across most of Europe, and indeed elsewhere. Worldwide judicial networks have grown up, facilitated by annual conferences and seminars, socializing their members 'as participants in a common global judicial enterprise' (Slaughter, 2004: 99). The growing role of the judiciary carries obvious advantages, yet there is also a fear of 'government by judges', and concern that increasing the power of unaccountable actors might undermine representative democracy.

In this chapter we consider the way in which judicial review has become a central fact of political life in many European countries. By judicial review we mean the process by which either the regular courts or, more commonly, a special constitutional court can constrain political actors, for example by striking down legislation that is not compatible with the constitution. Once again, there is significant variation across the continent. We look at the interaction between the judiciary and politics, examining the often politicized manner in which judges are appointed. The appointment of a set of judges to a country's constitutional court receives nothing like the public attention that a parliamentary election does, yet it may matter just as much for what the next government can do. Finally, we consider the implications of judicial power for representative government in Europe.

## 4.2 European constitutions

### 4.2.1 The origins of constitutions

A constitution has been defined as 'a body of rules that specifies how all other legal rules are to be produced, applied, and interpreted' (Stone Sweet, 2000: 20). Why have a constitution at all? A constitution regulates the relationship between political actors such as parliaments, governments, presidents and courts, ensuring that the powers of each are clearly defined, and are not the subject of free-form bargaining or confrontation each time an issue arises. Constitutions are sometimes seen as a device of 'precommitment' (Holmes, 1988; Sunstein, 2001: 96–101), whereby the people, in a state of reason, voluntarily place limits on their future freedom of action, just as the Greek hero Ulysses had his sailors bind him to the mast of his ship so that he would be unable to throw himself to his death when he heard the irresistible song of the Sirens.

The political turbulence in much of Europe in the nineteenth century and in the first half of the twentieth century means that most European countries have adopted more than one constitution during the past 200 years (Bogdanor, 1988; Johnson, 1993). There have been various 'waves' of constitution-making. One occurred in those countries regaining independence at the end of the Napoleonic wars, and there was a second following the 1848 revolutions. After the First World War a number of countries, especially the successor states to the Austro-Hungarian empire, drew up new constitutions. Most of the constitutions drawn up in these first three waves failed to survive – though Norway still operates under its constitution of 1814, the oldest in Europe, albeit one that has been amended over 200 times. (The line distinguishing amendment from replacement is 'sometimes fuzzy'; Elkins *et al.*, 2009: 55–59.) A more durable set of constitutions was promulgated in the aftermath of the Second World War, when those countries emerging from occupation adopted new constitutions, which in some cases were modified versions of their pre-war constitution. More recently, new constitutions have been adopted by countries moving from autocratic to democratic forms of government: Greece, Portugal and Spain in the 1970s, and the post-communist regimes of central and eastern Europe in the late 1980s and early 1990s.

Constitutions, then, are often adopted as part of a 'fresh start' – either a change of political regime or the achievement of national independence. Just as the USA drew up a new constitution in 1787, so Finland in 1919 and Ireland in 1922 had to devise a constitution when they embarked upon independent statehood. Dramatic changes of regime led to new constitutions in Italy in 1948, Germany in 1949, Portugal in 1976 and Spain in 1978, and in nearly all of the post-communist countries in the early 1990s. On other occasions, a new constitution may be adopted in order to adjust the nature of an existing liberal democratic system: examples here are Denmark in 1953, France in 1958, Sweden in 1974, Belgium in 1989 and Finland in 2000.

Sometimes, however, major political changes do not lead to a new constitution. In Italy, even though there was a widespread feeling that fundamental constitutional amendment was needed to recast the country's political system in the wake of the upheavals of the 1990s, agreement could not be reached on precisely what changes should be made. In the end the right went ahead unilaterally, and a set of major constitutional amendments it backed was put to, and rejected by, the people in a referendum in June 2006. The German constitution (known as the 'Basic Law') of 1949, which originally applied only to West Germany, envisages its own demise when the reunited German people choose a new constitution: Article 146 states that 'This Basic Law ... shall cease to be in force on the day in which a constitution adopted by a free decision of the German people comes into force.' In the event, the reunification of Germany in 1990 took place under the terms of Article 23 of the Basic Law, which allows new units to join the Federal Republic. The Basic Law, though originally seen as only an interim document pending reunification, is thus still in operation, with no great popular demand that it be replaced; the changes made to it following reunification proved to be minor indeed. Likewise, after the collapse of communism, Hungary extensively amended its communist-era constitution (dating from 1949) rather than adopt a new one (for post-communist constitutions see Albi, 2005: 18–35). When the Baltic states left the Soviet Union in 1990 they were keen to emphasize to the world that they were not mere sections of a country that were seceding; rather, they were independent countries, forcibly brought into the USSR in 1940 under the terms of the Hitler–Stalin pact, which were now regaining their independence. Consequently, two of them now resurrected their pre-1940 constitutions. Latvia resumed political life under the terms of its constitution of 1922, with some amendments, and in Lithuania the 1938 constitution was symbolically restored for an hour before it was superseded by a newly drawn up 'basic law' (Gelazis, 2001: 168).

If nothing dramatic happens in a country's history, there may seem to be no need for a new constitution. This is part of the reason why Britain does not have a document called 'The Constitution'. Britain has not been invaded for several centuries, and has not experienced a regime change since 1688; the emphasis since then has been on continuity and evolution, with no 'clean break' with the past. This is not to say that no changes have taken place (Bogdanor, 2009; McLean, 2009). On the contrary: as Anthony King puts it, 'although few people seem to have noticed the fact, the truth is that the United Kingdom's constitution changed more between 1970 and 2000, and especially between 1997 and 2000, than during any comparable period since at least the middle of the 18th century' (King, 2001: 53). Among these changes King lists membership of the EU, the introduction of referendums as a means of deciding major constitutional questions, the increase in judicial review, devolution for Scotland and Wales, and devolution for Northern Ireland. The reason why he suggests that 'few people … have noticed' the implications of these developments for the constitution is that none of the changes has required altering articles of a codified constitution, let alone the promulgation of a new codified constitution. Britain experienced no 'constitutional moment', and the changes were largely ad hoc and not part of any grand coherent plan for constitutional redesign (King, 2007: 349–351). Thus major changes can be made under the general impression of constitutional continuity.

Britain is unique among European democracies in having no formal codified constitution, so it is hard to be certain about what exactly makes up the British constitution, which has been seen as deriving from a number of sources (Norton, 1982: 5–9). The first is statute law: some very fundamental pieces of legislation, such as the 1707 Act of Union that brought Scotland into the United Kingdom while preserving a separate Scottish church and legal system, are part of the British constitution. The fact that statute law is part of the British constitution shows that the common view that Britain has an unwritten constitution is not entirely true; the constitution is, in significant measure, written, but it is not codified into a single text. Second, the EU treaties to which Britain has acceded, and the European Convention on Human Rights, which was incorporated into British law in 2000, also form written components of the constitution. The third source of the constitution is common law, including some customs such as the supremacy of parliament and major judicial decisions. The fourth source is convention, which dictates that certain things – such as the appointment of a prime minister who does not hold a seat in the House of Commons, or any refusal on the part of the monarch to consent to a measure passed by parliament – cannot now be done simply because it is generally accepted by the political elite that they cannot be done, even though they happened in the past.

Despite the stress usually laid by constitutions on popular sovereignty, most new constitutions are brought into being by representative organs, following the American precedent. In a minority of cases the people of a country have been given the opportunity to vote in a referendum on whether they wish to adopt a document as their country's constitution. In France, when the wartime leader of the Free French, Charles de Gaulle, was invited in 1958 to return to power, he had a constitution hastily drawn up, and this was put to and passed by the people in a referendum, thereby bringing into existence the Fifth Republic. Other examples of European constitutions being adopted by referendum are Switzerland in 1874, Ireland in 1937, Denmark in 1953, Spain in 1978, Romania in 1991, Estonia and Lithuania in 1992, and Poland in 1997. In the first three of these cases, and in Romania, the element of popular sovereignty is strengthened by the stipulation that any subsequent change to the constitution requires the consent of the people at a referendum.

Constitutions, of course, vary from country to country, but there are certain near-universal features (Murphy, 1993; Finer *et al.*, 1995). Constitutions regulate the organization of the government, stipulating, for example, whether government is parliamentary or presidential, what power the legislature has to constrain the executive, the role of the judiciary, and how power is divided between national organs of government and state or provincial bodies. In addition, they usually declare a number of rights, though sometimes what they say on this subject is primarily aspirational. The Polish constitution, for example, declares a whole range of socio-economic rights such as housing, child care, consumer protection and economic protection but, implicitly acknowledging that because of limited resources governments are unlikely to be able to guarantee all of these, allows governments to regulate the delivery of these 'rights' through appropriate legislation (Sanford 2002: 94–95).

### 4.2.2 Constitutional traditions

The fact that both the USA and most European countries possess a document called 'The Constitution' should not mislead us into assuming that all constitutions enjoy the same status in the eyes of the people who live under them. Ulrich Preuss contrasts the American pattern of constitutional authority with that in France. In the USA, he suggests, the constitution has priority not only over the government but also over the will of the people themselves. The constitution has a crucial place in history, in creating the United States of America: 'It is the sanctity of the founding act by which the polity has been created which imputes to the constitution the authority of the supreme law. The supremacy of its authority over all other laws flows from the inherent significance and uniqueness of the act of nation building' (Preuss, 1996: 20–22). Interpretation of the constitution is thus very important, leading to 'the almost obsessive passion' of Americans for questions of constitutional interpretation. Regarding rights, the constitution gives the impression that government and parliament are as likely to be a source of endangerment as a defender of these.

In France, in contrast, the genuine spirit of constitutionalism is encapsulated not in the constitution but in the constituent power of the nation: this constituent power cannot be bound by any constitution (Preuss, 1996: 22–24). The creation of the constitution was not the founding act for the French nation; the French nation is seen as having existed long before the first French constitution, let alone the current one. The constitution is one of the emanations of the nation, which is prior to every institution. The nation has power to 'constitute and reconstitute its sovereign power and give it its appropriate institutional shape at will'. This helps to account for the relatively large number of constitutions in France over the past 200 years, and the lack of veneration for any one that is comparable to the veneration accorded to its American counterpart

(Knapp and Wright, 2006: 390). Constitutions come and go, and – like the family car – can be replaced when their useful life is finished. Political actors are seen as more important than the constitution, and as the appropriate actors to rectify wrongs.

Most European countries might fall somewhere on the spectrum between France and the USA, while being much closer to the French position than to the American. It would be fair to say that no European constitution inspires the kind of reverence that many Americans feel for their own constitution. Many Europeans have never seen a copy of their country's constitution, and have only the most general notion of what it contains. Europeans tend to evaluate their constitutions in pragmatic and instrumental terms, with no compunction about amending or replacing an existing constitution if it prevents a favoured course of action from being followed. Partly for this reason, the relationship between constitutionalism and democracy, which has been so extensively explored in the American context, has generated far less agonizing in Europe. Even so, European constitutions, given vitality by constitutional courts, now impose significant constraints on governments and parliaments.

### 4.2.3 Amending a constitution

The extent to which a constitution, promulgated by people or parliament at one point in time, binds successive generations in a manner that can be seen as 'rule by the dead' depends partly upon how easy it is to change it. A constitution that is very difficult to amend or replace clearly constrains a nation in a way that a less rigid document does not. No one would advocate the imposition of a totally rigid, unchangeable document, but at the same time there would be little point in having a constitution that is as easy to change as any law. Such a constitution would not constrain short-term majorities, who would be able to change the rules of the game as they saw fit. Consequently, virtually all constitutions stipulate that amending them requires the support of more than a simple parliamentary majority (Rasch and Congleton, 2006: 326–328). Certain constitutions can be changed only by referendum; as we have already pointed out, the constitutions to which this constraint applies – those of Denmark, Ireland, Romania and Switzerland – were brought in by referendum in the first place. In some other countries, such as Austria, Estonia, Iceland, Latvia, Lithuania, Malta, Poland and Spain, minor changes can be made by parliament, but major changes may require the consent of the people in a referendum. In Germany proposals for change must be passed by votes of two-thirds in both the directly elected Bundestag and the Bundesrat, which represents state (*Land*) governments. Thus any change needs agreement between the government and the opposition in the national parliament, as well as the consent of most of the *Land* governments. Moreover, certain provisions are declared unamendable, such as the federal and democratic nature of the state. Another supermajoritarian amendment method requires that a change be approved in two separate parliamentary votes, with a general election in between; this is employed in several Scandinavian countries. Not surprisingly, the more rigid a constitution is, the less frequently it is amended (Lorenz, 2005).

The French constitution can be amended in one of two ways (Carcassonne, 1995; Morel, 1996). Article 89 outlines a procedure under which the agreement of both houses of parliament is needed for any proposed change. Unless a joint meeting of both houses then approves the proposal by a 60 per cent vote, it goes to a referendum. The French Senate is dominated by conservative rural members, which means that changes proposed by the left face an uphill struggle if they are to be passed by the parliamentarians, although several proposed by the right have been passed in this way without the need for a referendum. However, constitutional change in France has often followed a different route, by means of Article 11, under

## BOX 4.1: CONSTITUTIONS

### Denmark

Denmark's constitution dates from 1953, when 79 per cent of voters cast an affirmative ballot in a referendum to replace the 1915 constitution. One provision of the constitution is that any constitutional amendment itself requires a referendum, an uncommon feature among contemporary constitutions. Cross-European surveys asking about satisfaction with democracy at the national level usually find that Danes are right at the top when it comes to pride in one's political system, and there is virtually no pressure for fundamental constitutional reform.

### France

France has had a number of constitutions during the course of the last 200 years, including three different ones even before the end of the eighteenth century. The current constitution, the Constitution of the Fifth Republic, dates from 1958, when it was approved by the people in a referendum. Some subsequent changes have been made by parliament, but others have been made by referendum, including the most important, the 1962 amendment that introduced the direct election of the president. It has been argued that French political culture values the constituent power of the nation far more highly than it values any specific constitution.

### Germany

The German constitution, known as the Basic Law, dates from 1949. The constitution cannot be amended without the consent of two-thirds majorities in both houses of parliament, so in practice any change requires the consent of both the national opposition and most of the state governments. Although in 1949 it was assumed that the Basic Law would be replaced by a new constitution when German unity was achieved, in the event unification took place in 1990 within the framework of the Basic Law. The Basic Law stands high in the esteem of Germans, especially those living in the former West Germany.

### Italy

The Italian constitution was promulgated in 1948, and, in reaction to the dictatorship of Mussolini, it provided for checks and balances to a degree that critics say has hampered the achievement of effective government in post-war Italy. The political upheavals of the 1990s led to calls for a new constitution, or at least a fundamental revision of the existing one, but the political elite was unable to reach a consensus on the amendments that should be made, so not very much has been changed.

### Netherlands

The Dutch constitution dates from 1815, although it has been subjected to a number of major overhauls, most notably in 1848 and most recently in 1983. In most countries the constitution can be seen as a 'basic law', with a status superior to that of any ordinary law, but in the Netherlands

which the government may propose a change and the president can then refer it direct to the people in a referendum. (In practice, the president usually tells the government what to propose to him; de Gaulle sometimes announced the referendum before he had formally received the government's proposal.) This is not really the way the constitution seems to envisage the constitution scarcely has this position. It states explicitly that the courts cannot review the constitutionality of acts of parliament and, unlike most constitutions, does not provide any real constraint on the behaviour of parliament. Amendment of the constitution requires two parliamentary votes, separated by a general election, with a two-thirds majority required in the second vote.

### Poland

Poland's chequered constitutional history reflects its attempts to establish an independent state in the face of occupations and partitions, particularly by its neighbours Germany and Russia, along with experience of autocratic rule. It adopted new constitutions in 1791, 1921, 1935 and 1952, as well as temporary 'Little Constitutions' in 1947 and 1992. Its current constitution was drawn up in the mid 1990s after extensive discussion and bargaining, and in some respects is something of a political compromise between various conceptions of the state. It is very long and – containing elements inspired by socialism, Christian democracy, liberalism and agrarianism – occasionally inconsistent. It bestows on citizens many socio-economic 'rights' that, quite obviously, the state does not in practice have the resources to assure. It was endorsed by the people in a referendum in May 1997, by a 53 per cent majority on a 43 per cent turnout, and given the difficulty of securing agreement on its contents seems likely to remain the basic law of the country for the foreseeable future.

### Spain

Once the long Franco dictatorship ended, a new constitution was drawn up and was approved by the people, with a 92 per cent vote in favour, in a referendum in 1978. It provides for a constitutional monarchy and recognizes the multinational nature of Spain, while simultaneously asserting the indivisibility of the country. Although it has been criticized for vagueness or ambiguity in this and other areas, it provided the framework for a successful transition to democracy.

### United Kingdom

Unlike every other country in Europe, the United Kingdom does not have a document called 'The Constitution'. It is not the case, though, that its constitution is therefore unwritten; some central elements of it are contained in acts of parliament, some of them several centuries old. The principle of parliamentary sovereignty is strong, and although in recent years there have been calls for the adoption of a formal constitution setting out the limits on the powers of government and parliament, such attempts at reform have made little headway. Dramatic changes have been made to the constitutional framework of British government and politics in recent years and, with uncertainty still in the air, Anthony King has described the current state of affairs as 'a new constitutional unsettlement'.

amendment taking place, but it has become accepted that it is a valid way of doing this. The French public has shown little sign of objection, evidently feeling that it does have the right to change the constitution in this way, in line with the general attitude to the constitution identified by Preuss (see above).

In Italy constitutional change is in the control of parliament, but subject to a challenge by referendum. This was illustrated by the attempt by the right-wing government in Italy to make major constitutional changes in 2006, which, as we mentioned earlier, was the anti-climactic end product of 20 or more years of deliberation on the idea of a totally new constitution. Both chambers of parliament need to pass a law amending the constitution, not once but twice, with an interval of at least three months between the votes. In 2005 the Berlusconi government used its parliamentary majority to achieve this, over the opposition of the left, but the left then took the necessary measures to subject the package to a referendum (Bull and Newell, 2009: 53–61). When the referendum took place in June 2006, the proposed change was defeated by a margin of 62 to 38.

When it comes to amending the British constitution, there are no firm rules, as we would expect. There is nothing that says that those pieces of statute that are regarded as constitutional in nature cannot be changed, just like any other statute. After all, these statutes came into being in the first place simply by being passed by parliament. Yet there are powerful political cultural constraints in existence: for example, it is generally felt that the House of Commons could not simply repeal the laws that preserve Scotland's separate judicial system, something guaranteed under the 1707 Act of Union, against the wishes of the Scots. When the question of adopting a new electoral system was placed high on the political agenda after the 2010 election, there was general agreement that this would need the approval of the people through a referendum, even though there is no written rule to this effect. Similarly, given that the devolved institutions in Scotland and Wales were brought into existence by referendums in 1999, it is questionable whether they could be abolished except by fresh referendums. Other major aspects, though, certainly can be changed by parliament, such as reductions in the powers of the House of Lords; these occurred twice in the twentieth century, as we saw in Chapter 3.

## 4.3 The appointment of judges

Constitutions, and indeed laws, need to be enforced by judicial bodies if they are to mean anything. As we shall see, judges in most European countries have significant power to constrain political actors, and so in order to understand how much power they have, and how independent of political actors they really are, we need to know who appoints judges and controls their career advancement. The potential for interaction between the judiciary, the executive and the legislature is seen clearly in this area. Although practice varies from country to country, the appointment of judges is politically controlled in most countries. We shall look first at appointments to constitutional courts, which exist in most countries to enforce compliance on the part of government and parliament with the constitution, and then at the appointment of 'ordinary' judges.

### 4.3.1 Constitutional courts

Members of constitutional courts are appointed mainly by political authorities, but the spirit in which this power of appointment is exercised varies. The most common pattern is that parliament appoints some or all of the members, but such appointments need a supermajority (such as 60 per cent, or even two-thirds), which ensures that each of the main parties receives its proportionate share of appointments. In Germany, care is taken to balance the nominees not only among the parties but also among the *Länder*. In most countries members need strong legal credentials, such as those required to become a regular judge, and many appointees are legal academics.

One upshot of major party control of the nomination process is that the political views of the appointees will not be too far from the centre of the political spectrum. Characteristically, terms run for six, nine or even twelve years, and members can serve only one term, which removes any incentive to behave in such a way as to secure reappointment (though some judges may have their eye on other careers in the government's gift after their term is over, so this does not necessarily render them entirely indifferent to the preferences of political actors); in a few cases, such as Hungary and Portugal, judges may serve two terms. The appointment of a member of Portugal's constitutional court to the cabinet in 2007 led to predictable opposition questions about the independence of the judiciary.

The main exception to this is France, where the right to appoint individual members of the Constitutional Council is explicitly controlled by political actors. The Constitutional Council contains nine members, each of whom serves a nine-year term. The President of France, the president of the lower house of parliament (the National Assembly), and the president of the Senate each appoint one member every three years. Although there are no formal legal or other qualifications for membership of the Council, only about one in seven have no legal background, many combining this with a political record, as around two-thirds are former holders of elected positions (Brouard, 2009a: 105). A new government is thus liable to be faced with a council dominated by appointees of its political opponents, although the political dominance of the right, which has always had control of the Senate (see Chapter 3) and has usually controlled the National Assembly as well, means that the court has contained a majority of left-wing appointees for only nine years (1989–1998) of the life of the Fifth Republic (Brouard, 2009a: 114). While the appointment process thus looks very different from the superficially non-partisan approach used in most other countries, in reality it is distinctive mainly in that the partisan influences on appointments are highly visible.

## 4.3.2 The court system

Whereas the appointment of constitutional court judges pretty much marks the end of the matter, 'ordinary' judges are concerned not only about their initial appointment but also about their prospects of advancement up the judicial career ladder. In most countries the government of the day has a major role in deciding on the appointment and promotion of judges, and judges can be removed from office by a majority vote in parliament. However, this of itself does not necessarily lead to a politically biased judiciary. Even if governments do use their role in the appointment and promotion process to favour men and women of their own outlook, they are realistic enough to know that judges cannot be kept on a political leash. In some countries, notably in Scandinavia, the political culture militates strongly against any attempt to politicize the judiciary. In Britain, a 2005 law placed the appointment of members of the judiciary in the hands of an independent judicial appointments commission (Bevir, 2008: 572–573), although in any case party patronage in judicial appointments is felt to have died out by the end of the Second World War. In Ireland and Norway, though, the government has effective power over judicial appointments (Gallagher, 2010: 90–91), and while it is part of political discourse that, once judges are appointed, they sever their political connections and behave without regard to their former allegiance, this is more of an assumption than a demonstrated fact.

The option of dismissing a judge who has given decisions inconvenient to the government of the day, although legally possible, is usually politically unthinkable, as it would be regarded by the public as unjustified interference with the judicial process in most, if not all, European countries. For example, although the two houses of parliament in Britain (the House of Commons and the House of Lords) can dismiss a judge, no judge has been dismissed since early in the nineteenth century.

When it comes to career advancement, there are suggestions from several countries that ambitious judges know that the right political connections can help them to get ahead. This is perhaps taken furthest in Greece, where appointments of senior judges are usually the occasion of political wrangling. The government's control of both appointments and promotions ensures the 'political responsiveness' of the judiciary and 'the political control of the top echelons of the judiciary by the executive'. Whereas in most countries voters may blithely assume that the judiciary is independent of political actors, in Greece the overt jousting for political control over the judiciary reduces the prestige of the courts (Magalhães *et al.*, 2006: 167–168, 184–185). In Romania matters are alleged to be even worse: 'Romanian politicians are still able to influence the outcome of trials and to avoid prosecution by intimidating or buying out judges' (Stan, 2010: 395).

In most countries judges, whether in the regular court system or in a constitutional court, are low-profile individuals who would not be known to the public, but in some countries, especially Italy, Portugal and Spain, the last 20 years have seen the rise of the phenomenon of the 'celebrity judge', 'judicial entrepreneur' or 'assault judge', who attracts the limelight by presenting himself or (rarely) herself as the person who is trying to tackle a problem that political actors prefer to sweep under the carpet. One example came from Italy in the 1990s during the unearthing of the massive Tangentopoli (Bribesville) scandal, which entailed numerous links between politicians and organized crime. This operation was initiated by magistrates from Milan, who achieved nationwide prominence for their *mani pulite* (clean hands) investigation (see Chapter 7). Some identified a new relationship of shared interests between judges and the media, with the growth of a media-friendly 'judicial populism' (Guarnieri and Pederzoli, 2002: 190). It seemed that judges and elected politicians were competing for public support, and the judges were ahead in the competition until inquiries started to turn up corrupt links 'between certain judges and the political and entrepreneurial world', with several judges themselves being indicted for corruption (Della Porta and Vannucci, 2007: 835, 840). One judge involved in *mani pulite*, Antonio Di Pietro, went on to form a party and become an MP, while Baltazar Garzón in Spain and José Narciso da Cunha Rodrigues in Portugal also became well-known national figures, Garzón even becoming a government minister for a short time.

Italy is, in fact, a country whose judges have a reputation for being exceptionally politicized – although, ironically, its judges have a higher degree of formal independence from government than their counterparts anywhere else (Volcansek, 2006). Judges enter their positions in their mid-twenties with little experience of the world outside the law, and, since promotion is determined entirely on the basis of seniority rather than performance, they are certain to rise to the top. (As a result, the highest court of appeals has more than 400 judges, for example.) Judges choose to leverage their freedom from dependence on political actors not into a resolutely independent-minded approach to the delivery of justice but, rather, into a willingness to become allies of particular parties in exchange for promises of lucrative extra-judicial assignments, such as well-paid positions on commissions, or the promise of post-judicial careers. Some run for political office, and are always able to return to the judiciary without loss of seniority.

The Italian magistrature is divided into political tendencies – of left, centre and right – which run slates in the internal elections for leadership positions in the magistrates' union. Each party tries to build up a pool of sympathetic judges, and as a result many judges are perceived as being allied to one or another party. Magistrates may have their own political goals to achieve as well as, or rather than, purely financial ones. The political vacuum that followed the discrediting of the pre-1992 political class as a result of *mani pulite* was filled by politicians such as Silvio Berlusconi, who capitalized on the public's revulsion at the corruption of the established political class, but once in power was himself frequently indicted by the judiciary for alleged corruption, which he attributed to a 'political conspiracy' against him by 'red judges'. Given the willingness of judges to align themselves to parties, few Italians see the judiciary as 'above politics', and Berlusconi's supporters at least did not regard his accusation as implausible. The investigation of the political class under *mani pulite* resulted in 94 per cent of MPs being placed under investigation by magistrates in the early 1990s. While this would be a staggering figure in most countries, in Italy it differed only in degree from the usual pattern: in every parliament since 1948, at least 24 per cent of MPs have been served with notices of investigation (Volcansek, 2006: 162). As a result, relations between legislature and judiciary are fraught, and while the media may lionize certain judges, the judiciary as a whole, and individual judges, are the regular subject of invective in parliamentary speeches.

## 4.4  Judicial review

Constitutions regulate the power of political actors, in relation both to each other and to civil society. The referee or umpire whose role it is to decide whether the rules have been broken is usually the judiciary, and the power of a court to declare a law or regulation to be in conflict with the constitution of a country and hence to be invalid is one aspect of judicial review. We are focusing particularly on the power to strike down legislation on the grounds that it is incompatible with the constitution, and thus the term 'constitutional review' might seem to be more appropriate, especially given that in most countries it is not the ordinary courts but rather constitutional courts that wield this power. Constitutional courts are not part of the 'regular' judiciary, and indeed in some countries it has been a challenge for them to assert their authority over the regular courts. However, since 'judicial review' is the more widely used phrase we shall employ it here and, likewise, when we speak of 'judges' in this chapter, this term usually includes members of constitutional courts. By 'judicial review' we are referring to 'the authority of an institution to invalidate the acts of government – such as legislation, administrative decisions, and judicial rulings – on the grounds that these acts have violated constitutional rules' (Stone Sweet, 2000: 21). The importance of judicial review varies across Europe, according to the stipulations of different countries' constitutions and to legal traditions, and it is this variation that we now explore.

Before turning to the power of judges to pass judgment on the laws through judicial review, we should point out that there is also variation in judges' capacity to make law in the first place. This relates to the distinction, once very important but now of much reduced relevance, between common law and civil law countries. Common law systems are confined to Britain and English-speaking former British colonies. Within Europe, only Britain and Ireland are classifiable as common law countries. Outside Europe, examples of common law countries are most of the United States and Canada, as well as Australia and New Zealand. Most European countries belong instead to the civil law tradition, which originated within a continental tradition of 'Roman' law that has now been transformed into a comprehensive system of legal codes. Codified legal systems of one form or another prevail in all European states other than Britain and Ireland; more generally, this group includes many former continental European colonies, such as Louisiana, much of Latin America, and parts of Canada.

The main difference, on paper anyway, is that in common law countries a decision made by a judge in a case where the written law is indeterminate *becomes* the law, and will be cited as a binding precedent by subsequent judges faced with similar cases. The earlier judgment will have the same force as a statute passed by parliament. In civil law countries, in contrast, the ultimate foundation of the law is a comprehensive and authoritative legal code, and every legal decision, in principle, can be deduced from the legal code and subsequent enacted statutes. The first and most influential of the modern legal codes is the Napoleonic Code, the *Code Napoléon*, which emerged as a part of the new order after the French Revolution, and its influence can be clearly seen in the legal systems of Belgium, France, Luxembourg, the Netherlands, Italy, Spain and Portugal. The second major source of codified European law is the German Civil Code of 1900. Besides Germany, the five Nordic countries – Norway, Sweden, Denmark, Finland and Iceland – are usually identified, for historical and cultural reasons, with this tradition. Civil law judges are then mere legal technicians whose decisions could in theory be made equally well by a computer into which the appropriate rules and the facts of the specific case had been fed.

In practice, these differences have dwindled greatly in recent years. In the common law systems of Britain and Ireland, law is increasingly based on statute; the volume of legislation has expanded, and, in cases where precedent and statute point to different decisions, judges are obliged to give priority to statute. At the same time, in civil law countries, precedent has come to acquire increasing significance – or, perhaps, it would be better to say that the importance of precedent has become increasingly acknowledged. Although *stare decisis* ('let the decision stand' – in other words, the principle that judges consider themselves bound by judgments in previous essentially similar cases) is not officially recognized, hundreds of volumes of case reports are published, and lawyers in France and in other civil law countries cite precedents in their arguments in court just as British or American lawyers do (Shapiro, 1981: 147; de Cruz, 1995: 67). Analyses of judicial practice in a number of Europe's civil law jurisdictions are in agreement that 'as a practical matter, civil law constitutional judges are roughly as constrained as their common law counterparts,' being 'mindful not to contradict past decisions for reasons of institutional consistency and integrity' (Rosenfeld, 2005: 201). Judges in both common law and civil law countries, then, have some law-making power: in the former, not as much power as they used to have, and in the latter, rather more power than they used to have.

Although this is important, what we are mainly concerned with in this chapter is the power of judicial actors to pass judgment on the laws themselves, and in particular to block laws passed by the democratically elected legislature on the grounds that these laws conflict with deeper norms, usually expressed in a constitution. Review of legislation can take one or both of two forms. *Concrete* judicial review refers to a challenge to a law arising out of some specific case before a court, and *abstract* judicial review involves the consideration of a law without reference to any specific case. Whereas concrete judicial review can be initiated by any defendant in a court case who feels that the law under which he or she is being prosecuted is unconstitutional, or is otherwise null and void, abstract review can usually be initiated only by a designated set of political authorities (such as the head of state, the prime minister, or a specified number – typically around a quarter – of members of parliament). Abstract review itself can take two forms: in some countries it can be initiated only for a short period (typically up to three months) after a law has been passed (this is known as *a posteriori* abstract review); in Portugal, it can also be initiated *before* a bill has become law; in France and Ireland, abstract review can be initiated *only* before a bill becomes law (this is known as *a priori* abstract review).

In some European countries judicial review simply does not exist, and in countries where it does exist, it may be wielded either by the regular court system or by a special constitutional court. We need also to remember that, for the 27 countries of the European Union (EU), the Court of Justice of the European Communities, which is based in Luxembourg, can exercise the power of judicial review, because it can declare any law of a member state to be invalid if it conflicts either with the constitution of the EU or with an EU law (we discuss the Court of Justice, which many would see as Europe's most powerful constitutional court, in the next chapter). In countries where judicial review is strong, the political role of judges is widely analysed, and is acknowledged to be very significant. In countries where judicial review has traditionally been seen as weak, judges are becoming more assertive. We shall now explore these patterns in greater detail.

## 4.4.1 Strong judicial review

First, we shall look at countries where there is express provision for a judicial body to strike down legislation as unconstitutional; at the last count, 158 out of 191 constitutional systems included such provision (Ginsburg, 2008: 81).

There are two models here. One employs a dedicated constitutional court, separate from the regular court system, a model that was designed by the Austrian jurist Hans Kelsen (1881–1973) after the First World War (Öhlinger, 2003). In Kelsen's scheme the constitution was the highest order of norm (a *Grundnorm*) and legitimized lower-order norms, specifically laws. Moreover, all laws, to be valid, had to conform to the constitution, and the task of ensuring that they did so could not be left to governments or parliaments; instead, it properly belonged to a body that had this sole and specific purpose, a constitutional court. Prior to 1945, Austria, Czechoslovakia and Germany were the only countries that had such a body (and only in Austria was it significant), but today Kelsenian ideas dominate European constitutionalism. Such constitutional courts exist in virtually all the post-communist countries we are considering, along with Austria, Germany, Italy, Luxembourg, Malta, Portugal and Spain; a similar body, the Constitutional Council, fulfils this function in France. In nearly all of these countries the establishment of the constitutional court was part of a new constitutional settlement following the overthrow of an authoritarian regime; in countries that never had authoritarian regimes, judicial review takes different forms. In the three exceptions to this – countries that adopted a constitutional court without having experienced authoritarianism – the constitutional court is a little different from the European norm. In France, as we shall see, the Constitutional Council is not exactly a judicial body, and in Luxembourg and Malta the members of the constitutional court are judges from the higher realms of the ordinary court system, wearing, so to speak, a different hat. Constitutional courts are not quite part of the regular court system; indeed, in the text of constitutions they usually have a section to themselves, sometimes symbolically placed between the section on parliament and that on the courts. In that way the power they have does not amount to 'government by judges', which in a number of European countries has been seen as something to avoid at all costs.

In the second model, there is no dedicated constitutional court. Instead, the ordinary court system (in Ireland) or a body attached to it (in Estonia) exercises the power of constitutional review; this is also the situation in the United States. In the other countries examined in this book judicial review is weak, although in most cases growing stronger. When we examine the record of specific countries, we shall see how significant the role of the courts can be in a country's politics.

The nearest thing to an archetypal constitutional court, and one that other countries have taken as a model, is the German Federal Constitutional Court (FCC), based in Karlsruhe, which has been described as 'an institution of major policymaking importance' (Kommers, 1997: 1). The FCC can exercise both abstract review (bills can be referred to it by a third of the members of the Bundestag, or by a *Land* government) and concrete review (a law can be referred to it for a definitive verdict on its constitutionality by an ordinary court during the course of a case, and citizens themselves can write directly to the FCC, complaining that their constitutional rights have been violated). Ordinary courts cannot judge the constitutionality of laws; if a question of constitutionality arises, it must be referred to the FCC. The overwhelming majority of the cases reaching the FCC are constitutional complaints from individual citizens (although 99 per cent of these complaints are not substantial enough to warrant the court examining them in any detail), with about 2.5 per cent consisting of cases of concrete review and 0.1 per cent abstract review (von Beyme, 2002: 105).

Since 1951 the FCC has declared about 5 per cent of the bills passed by the Bundestag to be invalid (Helms, 2000: 90–94; Schmidt, 2003: 120). Some of its decisions have had major politi-cal overtones. In the 1950s it banned a communist and a neo-Nazi party, and in September 1990 it declared unconstitutional one aspect of the electoral system originally proposed for the first all-German elections in December of that year. In 1995 it made a controversial decision in a case where the parents of a child in Bavaria objected to a Bavarian school ordinance that made it compulsory for a crucifix to be displayed in elementary schools. The court ruled that the ordi-nance violated the constitutional right to religious freedom. This decision prompted widespread protests, especially in Bavaria, a strongly Catholic region of Germany. The state parliament responded by passing a new law that differed very little from the one struck down, and in practice the crucifixes remained in the schools – a warning that if even the most powerful court moves too far from public opinion, its decisions may in effect be ignored (Vanberg, 2005: 2–7).

Perhaps most controversial of all have been its decisions on the subject of abortion. In 1975 the court struck down legislation passed by the centre-left majority in parliament that had made abortion legal within the first three months of pregnancy. The FCC decided that this proposed law would not give adequate protection to life, so it gave the Bundestag instead a fairly detailed (and much more restrictive) prescription as to how abortion legislation should be framed, which the Bundestag duly incorporated in revised legislation. In doing so, it arguably moved beyond the Kelsenian role of *negative legislator* (a veto player able to limit the power of the legislature) to *positive legislator*, in effect writing the laws itself. In the early 1990s the court declared unconstitutional some key aspects of a new abortion law that parliament had passed to bridge the gap between the more restrictive West German law of 1976 and the more liberal East German law of the same year. The FCC rejected the new law, requested the Bundestag to enact a fresh one, and presented an interim regulation that would be valid until such a fresh law was passed (Kommers, 1997: 335–356). In addition, the FCC arbitrates in disputes over the jurisdiction of various organs of government, sometimes giving judgments that protect the rights of the *Land* governments and parliaments against threatened encroachment by their central (federal) coun-terparts, and on other occasions giving decisions that favour the federal government.

Generally speaking, Germans have a high regard for the FCC. Polls have found it to enjoy substantially more public trust than other major German institutions (Vanberg, 2005: 98). The court's ultimate legitimacy in the German system 'rests on its moral authority and the willingness of the political arms of government to follow its mandates' (Kommers, 1997: 54–55), and the

FCC has developed its own techniques to preserve this moral authority. Sometimes, when faced with a politically sensitive issue, it delays making a decision until the controversy has died or the matter is settled by political means. It also has the power to distinguish between laws that are null and void as a result of being in conflict with the constitution and laws that, although unconstitutional, are not actually void. In the latter case, parliament is allowed a period of grace to put matters right, and during this period the law remains in operation. Similarly, the court may uphold a statute while warning that it could soon become unconstitutional. This opens the door to a situation where, even though the legislature never explicitly defies the FCC, the court's approach allows parliament to procrastinate interminably (laws criticized by the FCC have remained in existence for over 20 years while parliament sets up committees to consider the implications of a judgment, for example), or to respond by passing a revised bill that, while different in some respects from the one censured by the court, still contains the key features to which the court objected (Vanberg, 2001). Its former supremacy is also under threat from the European Court of Justice (see next chapter), and from *Land* constitutional courts, which have become both more numerous and more active in the wake of unification (Helms, 2000: 98).

The fact that the FCC has struck down only about 5 per cent of laws passed by the Bundestag does not give an accurate reflection of its impact. For one thing, a number of laws have received conditional approval by the court; using the approach of *interpretation in conformity with the constitution*, the court can declare that a law is constitutional provided that it means what the court interprets it to mean. Of course, this interpretation may not always coincide with the original intentions of parliament. For another, parliament, when drafting legislation, goes to great lengths to try to ensure that laws will not be found to be unconstitutional, including seeking the advice of legal experts as to how the FCC will react to specific laws, and whose role has sometimes been compared to that of astrologers or soothsayers. The Bundestag has been seen as legislating 'in the shadow' of the court, and as being excessively cautious for fear of displeasing it (Kommers, 1997: 56).

Turning to the Constitutional Court of Italy, this too is also fairly highly regarded by that country's citizens, at least in comparison with most other Italian political institutions. In the 1970s the court showed itself willing to stand up to the power of the Catholic church at a time when most of the political parties were not. In 1971 it invalidated fascist-era laws prohibiting contraception, between 1970 and 1974 it gave six decisions affirming the constitutionality of laws that allowed divorce, and in 1975 it nullified the portion of the penal code that made a woman's consent to an abortion a criminal act (de Franciscis and Zannini, 1992: 74). In recent years it has become more cautious, and aware of the potential economic and political implications of its decisions: for example, it has created an office to estimate the financial burden that would be created were it to strike down a law (Rolla and Groppi, 2002: 157). Unfortunately, it is impossible to tell how many laws have been declared unconstitutional: no records are maintained on the matter 'because of the disorganization of the statute books'. Indeed, no one even knows how many laws there are in Italy, though there is agreement that the number is huge, perhaps between 100 000 and 150 000, compared with fewer than 10 000 in both France and Germany (Volcansek, 2000: 27, 29).

The court has been characterized as generally a defender of civil liberties, and has not slavishly followed the wishes of the government of the day, but it would be wrong to exaggerate its independence. The court collectively does not deviate too far from the sentiments of the mainstream political elite, and individual members may be receptive to the views of the party that secured their nomination, perhaps because many of them plan to enter or re-enter political life after the expiry of their term on the court. In the mid 1990s, when most of the established Italian parties collapsed, the Constitutional Court became more independent and interventionist, perhaps because the judges knew that their sponsoring parties could no longer offer them future patronage (Volcansek, 2000: 49). The court is not seen as completely independent of the political parties, but it is at least felt to be less controlled by them than are most other Italian institutions. It affirmed its independence in 2004 and 2009 when it struck down controversial laws passed by parliament that would have given senior politicians, especially prime minister Silvio Berlusconi, immunity from prosecution.

The virtually universal implementation in post-communist eastern and central Europe (Estonia is the only exception) of constitutional courts is striking evidence of the dominance of the Kelsenian model. There was little or no consideration of the American model of leaving judicial review to the regular courts, let alone of the idea of letting governments and parliaments make whatever laws they chose, and part of the 'training' for members of the new constitutional courts involved visits to their west European counterparts (Malovà and Haughton, 2002: 114–115; Piana, 2010: 113). These courts have been significant actors, given the frequency of rows between prime ministers and presidents, for example, that are common in new democracies. One of the most significant is the Polish constitutional tribunal (the TK) (for the TK see Garlicki, 2002; Sanford, 2002: 208–214). A wide range of actors can refer questions of constitutionality to it: not only the usual bodies (president, chairs of the two houses of parliament, 50 deputies or 30 senators, any court) but also a wide variety of religious, trade union and local government bodies, along with individual citizens. Initially parliament could, with a two-thirds majority, overturn its judgments, but since 1999 its decisions have been final. The TK has made controversial decisions on subjects such as abortion, a proposed national health fund, and the rents paid by private tenants (Rose-Ackerman, 2005: 64–66). It has made a number of decisions regarding lustration (the vetting of individuals who had collaborated with the security services during the communist period), and when, in 2007, it struck down as unconstitutional elements of a new and more sweeping lustration law brought in by the right-wing PiS government, leaders of the PiS accused it of being politically biased. It has wide public approval, although critics say that this is because it tends to make 'populist' decisions in defence of welfare and pension entitlements (Sájo, 2004: 47).

In other post-communist countries, too, constitutional courts have been important. In Hungary, for example, the court, which has exceptionally wide jurisdiction, was very active in the 1990s, in clarifying or determining the balance of power between the president and prime minister in particular, although it has become less active since then (Rose-Ackerman, 2005: 66–70). In 2008 the Romanian constitutional court was called on several times to resolve disputes between the president and prime minister, and thus became the *de facto* referee in the central power struggle in the country's politics. The Czech court has struck down laws on the funding of political parties and on electoral system reform, earning criticism from some parties and indeed threats of defiance from the parliamentary majority (Pribán, 2002). The Slovenian court has been very active, to the extent that it has been criticized for insufficient self-restraint, and its practice of basing its judgments on principles that are nowhere to be found in the constitution gives it great freedom of action (Cerar, 2001: 399–400). While we shall not discuss the work of all the post-communist bodies in detail, the picture is much the same everywhere: constitutional courts have made decisions with major political consequences (see Zielonka, 2001; Sadurski, 2002: Chapters 7–17).

Two countries where comparable bodies have been significant constraints on government, but where a rather different model was chosen, are France and Ireland. The French Constitutional Council, as its name suggests, is not formally a judicial body, and, compared with the constitutional courts we have just discussed, is much more likely to find its decisions interpreted in partisan political terms. It was established by the 1958 constitution, but made little public impact until a constitutional amendment in 1974. The right to refer bills to the Council, hitherto reserved for a few figures who were likely to be government supporters and thus unlikely to want to test the constitutionality of legislation, was extended: any group of 60 deputies (or 60 senators) was given the power to refer a bill to the Council. When the Socialist Party entered government for the first time, in 1981, it drew up wide-ranging plans for the nationalization of a number of private companies, which the right-wing opposition parties referred to the Council. To the government's dismay, the Council ruled that the compensation arrangements provided for were in conflict with the constitution, and it in effect elaborated a new compensation formula, which would raise the cost of the nationalization programme by about 25 per cent. The government duly drew up a new law incorporating this formula, and the Council pronounced this bill constitutional (Stone, 1992: 140–172). The Socialist government's plans fell foul of the Council on other issues, too – most important of all, surely, on the independence of university professors – to the satisfaction of the opposition parties.

After 1986, when the right won power in France, the boot was on the other foot. Now the Socialists began to refer many bills to the Council, and the right-wing parties complained about the power of the Council in terms even more bitter than those used by the Socialists between 1981 and 1986. Relations between the Council and politicians were relatively quiet during the next spell of Socialist government (1988–1993) – from 1989 onwards, a majority of Council members were Socialist nominees – but, when the right returned to power after the 1993 elections, conflicts began again. In August 1993 the Council struck down some of the new government's anti-immigration legislation, and in January 1994 it declared unconstitutional the central aspects of a bill that would have led to a great increase in the amount of public money being spent on private, church-run, schools. Between 1997 and 2002, once again, a left-wing government faced a Council dominated by the right, and some of its legislation – for example, concerning devolution of power to the Corsican Assembly – was struck down (Elgie, 2003: 189). Like its German counterpart, the Constitutional Court is prone, when striking down legislation, to offer an alternative wording that it says would be constitutional, and sometimes these passages are copied verbatim into the revised bill, making it seem like a quasi-legislature.

The important role played by the Constitutional Council exists despite a wariness about judicial review as such, which has existed since the French Revolution and owes its existence partly to the feeling that any check on parliament would be a check on the 'general will' of the people. The idea that the United States has 'government by judges', and that this is highly undesirable, is part of political discourse in France. The Council's power was confined to legislation in abstract form until recently; once a bill had become law, its constitutionality could not be challenged. A change to the constitution made in 2008 opens up the possibility of concrete review. A new Article 61-1 gives anyone the right to claim that a law is unconstitutional, in which case either of two other bodies (the Conseil d'État or the Cour de Cassation) may refer the law to the Constitutional Council. The Council's decisions are often interpreted in political rather than in purely constitutional terms, and it has not succeeded, unlike Kelsenian constitutional courts, in being widely regarded as an impartial, non-partisan institution. One reason for this is that bills go to the Council immediately after their passage through parliament: this means that the Council is invariably judging bills that have very recently been the subject of partisan political battles on the floor of the National Assembly, and so some claim it is akin to a decisive third chamber of parliament, an impression fostered by the partisan nature of appointments, which we discussed earlier. Even so, unlike a parliament but like a court, it must couch the justifications for its decisions in terms of legal rather than political discourse ('good law' rather than 'good policy').

Finally, we look at the case of Ireland, which differs from all other European countries in that judicial review is exercised not by a special constitutional court or council but by the regular court system, as in the United States. This may be because the constitution was adopted in 1937, before the merits of the Kelsenian model were widely appreciated. The High Court and the Supreme Court in Ireland – rather than every court, as in the USA – are empowered to pass judgment on the constitutionality of laws, and they can exercise not just concrete review, as in the United States, but also abstract review (the *a priori* form only). The right of referral of bills to the courts for abstract review is, though, much more restrictive than in the other countries we have looked at: only the president of Ireland may refer bills to the Supreme Court for this purpose. Between 1937 and 2010 only 15 bills were so referred (eight were found by the Supreme Court to be constitutional and the other seven to be wholly or in part unconstitutional). As in other countries, the number of actual referrals understates the significance of abstract review, for the very existence of this presidential power has no doubt made parliament particularly careful not to pass legislation that might prove to be in conflict with the constitution.

More significant in Ireland has been concrete review. Again as in other countries, the courts in Ireland became more active from the early 1960s in exercising the power of judicial review, and lawyers have been more inclined to challenge the constitutionality of statutes (Gallagher, 2010). The courts have moved from a literal approach to interpreting the constitution to what is termed a 'creative' approach, which implies that the judges do not feel limited by the actual words in the constitution but move beyond them to consider what they claim to be its overall spirit and tenor. The courts made a number of important decisions as a consequence. In 1973 they declared unconstitutional the existing law banning the sale or importation of contraceptives, and in 1992 the Supreme Court decided that the constitution conferred upon women, in certain circumstances, the right to have an abortion. Anti-abortionists were aggrieved by the latter decision, especially as it was based on a section of the constitution that had been added in 1983, at the behest of anti-abortionists, precisely in order to try to *prevent* any future Supreme Court finding that the constitution permitted abortion. One of their leaders criticized the very concept of judicial review, declaring that 'it is unacceptable and indeed a deep affront to the people of Ireland that four judges who are preserved by the constitution from accountability can radically alter the constitution and place in peril the most vulnerable section of our society' (quoted in Gallagher, 2010: 94). However, this criticism was unusual, for despite the fact that the government of the day appoints judges and has traditionally attached great importance when doing so to the political links of potential appointees, the courts are widely seen as 'above' politics, and no government has publicly attributed political motives to a judge who has delivered a decision that it did not like. In 1987 the Supreme Court made a decision that turned out to have ramifications across the continent, when it declared that, under the constitution, the Irish government cannot sign any EU treaty that would tie its own hands when it came to conducting Irish foreign policy. The government could sign the treaty only if the constitution was amended appropriately. As a result, given that the Irish constitution cannot be amended without a referendum, every subsequent EU treaty has required a referendum in Ireland, and since all EU treaties need to be ratified by every member state, this nearly sank the Lisbon Treaty when the people voted against it in 2008, only to change their mind when the treaty, slightly revised, was put to them again the following year (see next chapter).

Judicial review is very significant in Ireland: for example, the Irish courts have proved much readier to identify unenunciated rights than their American counterparts. The jurisprudence of the courts has been extensively analysed (see Hogan and Whyte, 2003, which runs to nearly 2200 pages). As in Germany, the courts in Ireland can exercise power not merely by striking down legislation but also by imposing their own interpretation on it. The courts approach each statute with the *presumption of constitutionality*: that is, 'if a statutory provision is open to differing constructions, one constitutional, the other not, the court must opt for the former' (Casey, 2000: 364–367). Although this might seem to strengthen the position of parliament – it means that less of its legislation will be struck down than if there were no presumption of constitutionality – it can work to limit the power of parliament, because it may mean that the court chooses the narrowest of a number of meanings that an act could have, and consequently reduces the scope of the act.

We have seen from this brief survey that courts that have the power to strike down legislation can be significant political actors. Clearly, this can be frustrating for political parties and governments, amounting to a veto by a small number of unelected individuals on policies that might have had widespread support. However, there may be times when political actors welcome the intervention of the courts. For example, the Lithuanian political class faced a dilemma in the early 1990s: it knew that the country would have to abolish the death penalty in order to gain admission to the EU, but it also knew that the people strongly favoured retaining capital punishment. The solution was to ask the constitutional court to state whether the laws allowing the death penalty were constitutional, and the court obligingly declared that they were not (Gelazis, 2002: 400–401). Some of those politicians who complain that the courts have prevented them from fulfilling election pledges may be secretly relieved not to have to try to implement policies in which they never really believed, or may be thankful to be able to pass political hot potatoes to the courts for resolution.

## 4.4.2 Weak judicial review

We now turn to those countries where the courts have limited or no power to strike down legislation on the ground of incompatibility with the constitution – although we need to emphasize at the outset that in many countries the judges are now starting to flex muscles that had been thought to be atrophied or even non-existent. In the United Kingdom, and in Scandinavia, courts can no longer be ignored by students of government.

In Britain, the absence of a formal codified constitution leads to a degree of vagueness as to what the constitution stipulates in any given situation, so the question of unconstitutionality simply has not arisen. The courts, of course, play a role in interpreting the laws, but they cannot strike down a law on grounds of non-conformity with the constitution. However, it certainly does not follow, as is sometimes assumed, that the courts are irrelevant in deciding what governments can and cannot do. From the early 1980s onwards, judges in Britain have proved increasingly troublesome for governments, possibly stepping in to fill a perceived 'constitutional vacuum' caused by the feebleness of the political opposition to Margaret Thatcher's rule in the 1980s (King, 2007: 119–121). They have the power to prevent ministers from exercising power beyond their legal authority (*ultra vires*), although parliament may then change the laws to confer the desired power on the minister. As judges have become more willing to exercise judicial review, so individuals and organizations have been more inclined to try this route: the annual number of non-criminal applications for judicial review rose from 356 in the early 1980s to over 5000 by 2005 (King, 2007: 126). Even if most of these applications fail, they have an impact on the way public administration works, and civil servants are now issued with a booklet entitled *The Judge over your Shoulder* to advise them how to make sure their actions do not fall foul of judicial review. In addition, judges have increasingly been used, with their agreement, by the government of the day to chair inquiries, investigations, commissions and committees, a further dimension of the increasing 'judicialization' of politics (King, 2007: 136).

The incorporation into British law of the European Convention on Human Rights (ECHR) as from 2000 has the potential to prove a significant development in this area, though the long-term impact is not yet clear (King, 2007: 133; Leyland, 2007: 172; Bogdanor, 2009: 53–88; McLean, 2010: 201–220). The courts can now refer a bill to a committee of parliament if they believe that it conflicts with the Convention – although the law can still be applied while a new bill is being drafted. The courts have found against the government in a number of cases in which they have held that a law conflicted with the provisions of the Convention, leading the then Home Secretary, David Blunkett, to declare on one occasion in 2003: 'Frankly, I'm personally fed up with having to deal with a situation where parliament debates issues and the judges then overturn them' (King, 2007: 141). This was not a problem that confronted most of his predecessors. Cases involving the treatment of refugees and asylum-seekers have been particularly prone to see a judicial check on the government of the day, and in 2006 the courts declared a central component of the government's anti-terror legislation to be incompatible with the ECHR (Bevir, 2008: 574).

There have been many calls for Britain to adopt a codified constitution, possibly including a supreme court that would have the power to declare acts of parliament unconstitutional (Bogdanor, 2009: 215–231). On the left of the British political spectrum, though, there has always been a reluctance to give the judiciary more power. Even though the courts have become increasingly willing to check governments of all persuasions, as we have seen, left-wing critics have often seen the judiciary as fundamentally conservative. Consequently, the Labour governments of 1997–2010 moved cautiously in this area. In 2009 parliament established a new Supreme Court, whose members no longer sit in the House of Lords as the highest-ranking judges in the land had done for centuries. This draws a clear line between the judiciary and the legislature, but the Supreme Court does not have the power to strike down acts of parliament.

The absence of provision for the courts to strike down laws also applies to a number of other countries. The courts of the Netherlands are expressly prohibited by Article 120 of the constitution from considering the constitutionality of laws, and until the 1960s there was little pressure for the introduction of judicial review. However, the courts can declare government measures to be *ultra vires*, and can annul acts of parliament that contravene European treaties to which the Netherlands is a party. As a result, perhaps, of a declining respect for politicians and an increased respect for the courts, the Dutch courts have become more assertive, and have fired a 'warning shot' regarding the constitutionality of laws (Andeweg and Irwin, 2009: 185–189). The question of explicitly enshrining judicial review in the constitution has been discussed in recent years, partly in response to trends in other European countries, but although this step was recommended by a national convention in 2006, no action was taken. In Switzerland the highest court – the Federal Tribunal – can strike down legislation passed by the cantons but not by the federal parliament. It is obliged to apply all federal laws, even those that it considers to be unconstitutional (Rothmayr, 2001; Kriesi and Trechsel, 2008: 67).

Judicial review has never been a strong feature of political life in the Scandinavian countries – indeed, none of these countries has a Kelsenian constitutional court – because of the political cultural feeling, similar to that in France, that since power emanates from the people, the decisions made by the parliament elected by the people should not be open to challenge (e.g. Smith, 2004: 185). Yet the judiciary is stirring, even in Scandinavia. In Norway the roots of judicial review go back to the nineteenth century, and signs of an increase in judicial activism have been apparent since the mid 1970s. Individual and groups are increasingly casting their claims in judiciable terms, and the courts have been empowered by the incorporation of human rights conventions into Norwegian law (Narud and Strøm, 2004: 194; Selle and Østerud, 2006: 563). In Denmark the Supreme Court started to throw off its habitual caution in the late 1990s, and in 1999, for the first time ever, it declared a law unconstitutional (Damgaard, 2004: 125). Similarly, in Iceland the Supreme Court has made some 'landmark' decisions that have had an 'explosive impact' on the political system, proclaiming a 'newly born constitutional authority' and in 2000 striking down an act of parliament that dealt with state financial support for the disabled (Kristjánsson, 2004: 168–169). In a rather unconventional step for a Supreme Court, its president then wrote to the speaker of parliament to make it clear just what the court's objection had been (Hardarson and Kristinsson, 2002: 977). In Sweden a body called the Lagrådet (Law Council), which is composed of judges from the Supreme Court and the Supreme Administrative Court, may give its advice on proposed legislation, and this is not lightly disregarded. Indeed, government departments when preparing legislation go to some lengths to anticipate the Law Council's views, and to ensure that legislation conforms with these (Holmström, 1994: 159). In 2000 the Supreme Court went so far as to strike down a law on the grounds of incompatibility with the constitution. Finland's 2000 constitution expressly provides for judicial review of legislation, and in any case a committee of the legislature pre-screens the contents of legislation to check their compatibility with the constitution (van den Brandhof 2004: 197).

### 4.4.3 Judicial review and representative government

Courts in many European countries, then, have an important voice in determining the policy choices that can be made by political actors. Is this a good thing or a bad thing, and how does it relate to the idea of 'representative government' that we are examining in this book?

For many people this is a welcome development. Parliaments, as we saw in Chapter 3, usually seem unable or unwilling to impose a meaningful check on governments, because they are dominated by the same political parties as control the government. If parliaments cannot constrain governments, perhaps courts can. Government ministers in most European countries are not kept awake at nights wondering whether or not parliament will approve a bill they have drawn up, but many ministers clearly do worry about whether the courts will approve their plans, and indeed they go to some lengths to ensure that their schemes will meet with the approval of the judicial authorities. This can be seen as a good thing, on the grounds that there are rights so fundamental that not even a majority should be allowed to ride roughshod over them, and the courts and the constitution provide a necessary check on the exercise of power by governments. A more pragmatic defence of judicial power is that the judiciary prevents government policy in certain areas from drifting too far from the middle of the road; this has been especially apparent in France since the early 1980s, where governments of both left and right have had their wings clipped by the Constitutional Council. It is also argued that judicial independence has positive economic effects (Feld and Voigt, 2006). Defenders point out that courts do not necessarily

## BOX 4.2: THE COURTS AND POLITICS

### Denmark

The political role of the courts used to be regarded as a subject with all the relevance to Denmark of, say, mountaineering or the exploration of coral reefs. However, Denmark has not been immune from worldwide trends towards a more assertive judiciary, and in 1999, for the first time, the Supreme Court struck down a law on the basis that it was not compatible with the constitution. The incorporation of the European Convention on Human Rights into Danish law has given the courts additional scope to exercise judicial review of the behaviour of political actors. Even so, the Danish judiciary, like its Scandinavian counterparts, would not be seen as among the most active in Europe when it comes to constraining government or parliament.

### France

Although judicial review as such does not exist, partly because of a fear of 'government by judges', a quasi-judicial body, the Constitutional Council, can consider the constitutionality of legislation after it has been passed by parliament and before it is signed into law by the president. The parliamentary opposition refers virtually all major pieces of legislation to the Council. Appointment to the Council takes place very much on political grounds, and conflict with the government is likely to arise when the two bodies are dominated by opposite sides. In the first half of the 1980s the Council, which then contained a majority of right-wing appointees, made a number of rulings restricting the Socialist government's freedom of action, and the same pattern emerged between 1997 and 2002. When the right-wing parties won power in 1986, and again in 1993, the Council continued its activist approach and caused as much annoyance to the right as it had to the Socialists. Unlike corresponding bodies in the rest of western Europe at least, the Constitutional Council has never been able to attain the status in the public's eyes of being an impartial agency, because many of its decisions are perceived as springing from political considerations rather than from purely legal ones. A constitutional change made in 2008 (although still requiring legislation to make it fully operational) opened up the possibility that the Council may in future be able to exercise the power of concrete judicial review – that is, to strike down existing laws.

### Germany

The Federal Constitutional Court, whose members are appointed on a cross-party basis, exerts a significant impact on policymaking. It has made major political decisions, curbing the extent to which the abortion laws could be liberalized in both 1975 and 1993, and banning two political parties in the 1950s. The non-partisan and serious manner in which it approaches its work has given it considerable national prestige, and parliament invariably defers to its judgments; indeed, parliament is sometimes criticized for being too ready to anticipate its reactions, and for restricting itself for fear of falling foul of the court. German jurists ask whether the FCC has become a 'parallel government' or 'counter-government' whose views count for just as much as the democratically elected one.

### Italy

The post-war Italian judiciary has been highly politicized, with factions of judges linked to the major political parties. Judges and magistrates can become well known nationally through taking the initiative in tackling what they identify as problems, and although some see them as all too often motivated by a desire for publicity, the role of judges in the fight against organized crime and the corruption of Italian politics in the mid 1990s earned them respect. The Italian Constitutional Court has also been highly regarded, and over the years it has generally worked to enhance the civil liberties of citizens, for example by declaring repressive legislation dating from the fascist era to be invalid.

## Netherlands

There is no tradition of judicial review in the Netherlands, with Article 120 of the Dutch constitution declaring that the courts cannot review the constitutionality of acts of parliament. The courts, then, have generally had relatively little impact on politics, although they are coming to play an increasing role by interpreting the meaning of laws when parliament passes rather vague legislation, by reserving the right to annul government measures that go beyond what legislation permits, and by striking down laws that they deem to conflict with international obligations or with EU law.

## Poland

The Polish Constitutional Tribunal (the Trybunał Konstytucyjny, or TK) was established, although it did not wield effective power, under the communist regime in 1985. Its members are appointed by parliament but, unusually for a constitutional court, this is not done on the basis of cross-party consensus; instead, the government parties virtually monopolize the appointments. Its main power is to review the constitutionality of acts of parliament. The president, before signing a bill, can refer it to the TK for a judgment on its validity. Moreover, after a bill has been signed into law, a wide range of actors – including 50 deputies, 30 senators, local government units, trade unions and religious organizations – may challenge its constitutionality. In addition, if an ordinary court hearing a case has any doubts about the constitutionality of a statute, it must refer the matter to the TK. For some time the TK struggled to assert its authority over the 'regular' court system, as courts sometimes refused to apply laws, declaring them unconstitutional without consulting the TK, but its status now seems more secure. Like its counterparts in other post-communist countries the TK has made its mark, for example by striking down a liberalizing abortion bill in 1996 on the grounds that it did not sufficiently protect the right to life of the unborn, and by a 2009 judgment in favour of the government rather than the president when it comes to Polish policy towards and representation within the EU.

## Spain

The Spanish Constitutional Court (the Tribunal Constitucional) has the power to exercise abstract review of a law if requested to do so by a group of 50 deputies or 50 senators. After the Socialist Party won power in 1982, the court was used by the right-wing opposition as a means of slowing the pace of radical legislation, but its decisions are not widely seen as politically motivated. Eight of its 12 members are appointed by the parliament by consensus among the parties, with two appointed by the government and two by the body representing Spanish judges. Like its counterparts in other countries, it has been dragged into controversy by some of its decisions regarding abortion legislation passed by parliament. Unlike its French counterpart, most of its cases do not arise from opposition referrals of government bills in the hope that these will be struck down; rather, they concern the relationship between the centre and the regions, with most cases being brought either by a regional government against a law or action of the national parliament or government that it believes trespasses on regional autonomy, or by the central government against an action by a regional government or parliament that it alleges constitutes a threat to Spain's indivisibility. In June 2010, after four years of deliberation, the court struck down several sections of the Statute of Catalunya, which referred to Catalunya as a 'nation' and had been approved by both the Catalan parliament and the Cortes in Madrid, declaring them incompatible with the 'indissoluble unity of the Spanish nation', a ruling that brought hundreds of thousands of people out onto the streets of Barcelona in protest.

> ### BOX 4.2: CONTINUED

### United Kingdom

Because there is no document called 'The British Constitution', the possibility of legislation being declared unconstitutional does not exist. The judges do, however, have the right to declare the behaviour of public authorities invalid if they deem it to go beyond those authorities' allotted powers, and their decisions in some such cases have brought them into the field of political controversy. Critics in the past accused the British judiciary of being implicitly sympathetic to the views of the Conservative Party, and of not showing sufficient concern for civil rights. However, the judiciary started to become more assertive under the reign of Margaret Thatcher, the Conservative prime minister of the 1980s, and has blocked initiatives of governments of different partisan complexions.

prevent the people's representatives from doing what the people elected them to do; they may instead prevent the political class from acting out of self-interest rather than the public interest, as when the German FCC insisted in 1976 that even very small parties should be able to benefit from state funding, or when in 2001 the Czech constitutional court prevented the two main parties colluding in the adoption of a new electoral system that would have adversely affected all the smaller parties (Kommers, 2006: 121; Kopecký and Spirova, 2008: 152–153).

On the other hand, opponents of the growing power of the judiciary make the point that judicial review contradicts the very notion of representative government. Judicial review, according to its critics, entails giving power to a handful of unelected, unaccountable and unrepresentative individuals to override the wishes of those who were elected by the people and upon whom the people will be able to pass judgement at the next election. Judges may be informally accountable to others – such as legal scholars, their peers, and to some extent the mass media, all of whom may call attention to unexpected or politically relevant behaviour – but they are not formally accountable in the way that elected politicians are. Commenting on the argument that constitutions are a valuable precommitment device, Elster (2000: 174) suggests that 'the dangers of a ... dogmatic constitutional court may be worse than the opportunistic behaviour [that it is] set up to prevent.' Similarly, for Bellamy, courts have many of the same vices that legal constitutionalists criticize in legislatures, though with fewer of the compensating virtues. The use of counter-majoritarian institutions such as courts, he argues, 'is usually bad for minorities and the under-privileged because it is biased towards the privileged and well-organized', and he is unconvinced that courts are necessary to prevent a dictatorship of the majority for the simple reason that it is only democratic pluralist societies, which respect minority rights, that would think of constraining political power through a judiciary in the first place (Bellamy, 2007: 7, 42, 51). Opponents are also unpersuaded by the argument that judicial review ensures that government policies do not drift too far from the centre of the political spectrum: if the people want a radical break with centrism, should a handful of unelected figures in the judiciary be able to prevent this?

The implications for representative government depend partly upon the basis on which judges make decisions. It is difficult to discover how courts in Europe decide in cases of judicial review – one reason why European research in this area focuses almost entirely on the effects of decisions, whereas the US research also examines courts' decision-making processes (Rehder, 2007). Researchers in Europe are greatly hampered because constitutional courts work entirely behind closed doors and do not make any aspect of their deliberations public, even retrospectively.

It seems that typically they reach decisions through verbal discussions rather than by the circulation of notes that might later become available to researchers. Most of them do not allow dissenting opinions – in other words, the court delivers just one judgment, in the name of all the judges, regardless of who argued what during the deliberations – and even when dissenting opinions are permitted, as in Germany and Spain, strong norms discourage these, and so they are rare.

Three models of the way in which courts reach decisions seem too simple. A naive model, perhaps subscribed to by many citizens, would assume that judges, when considering a challenge to a law, simply apply the constitution in an objective manner, using the principle of *fiat justitia, ruat caelum* ('let justice be done, though the heavens should fall'). This would pose no particular problem for representative government; indeed, giving practical effect to the constitution, the expression of the people's deepest values, is what judges are 'supposed to do' in this form of government. However, matters are not this simple, because many constitutional principles, and even laws themselves, may be somewhat indeterminate, and it is by definition the indeterminate areas that most require judicial resolution. People, including judges, might quite legitimately disagree as to whether a government wealth redistribution measure does or does not contravene a constitutional guarantee of a right to private property. A second simplistic model sees judges as brute preference maximizers, who decide every case according to their own political views. If judges did this, it would undoubtedly weaken and challenge representative government, enabling the views of the people to be swept aside at will by a tiny unrepresentative elite. However, even if constitutions and laws can be somewhat indeterminate, it is unrealistic to imagine that they do not constrain judges at all, especially as judges' decisions need to be expressed in terms of legal and constitutional justification rather than political argument (Dyevre, 2010: 311–312). A third model imagines that judges are pawns of the party responsible for their nomination (either because they hope for future benefits from the party, or because they share its worldview) and can be guaranteed to adopt the same position within the court as their party did when the legislation under consideration was discussed politically. This would in effect turn the court into another chamber of parliament, and in terms of the implications for representative government the arguments are similar to those for and against second chambers, which we discussed in Chapter 3. This model is more plausible than the others, especially as we know that in some countries (Italy, as we have seen, and also France and Spain) there are different groups within the judiciary linked to the main parties. However, the point about judicial actors being constrained by the words of constitutions and laws applies here too, and matters seem to be slightly more nuanced than it suggests, as we shall now discuss.

The way in which the French Constitutional Council is composed – staggered appointments by actors of identifiable political affiliations, as explained above – offers researchers the opportunity to see what effect its changing composition has on its behaviour. Brouard finds that there is indeed a relationship between the Council's propensity to strike down legislation and the political affiliations of its nominators. During periods of divergence (that is, when a majority of Council members were nominated by right-wing politicians and a left-wing government is in power, or vice versa) 57 per cent of laws referred to it have been vetoed, but during periods of convergence (when the background of the nominators of most Council members and of the current government are the same) the figure falls to 45 per cent (Brouard, 2009a: 115). This suggests strongly that the political background of Council members makes a difference – but it also shows that partisan affiliations are by no means the whole story, and that it would be mistaken to see the Council as a 'third chamber of parliament', because if that was the case we would expect the figures to be close to 100 per cent and 0 per cent respectively. After all, while the Council that struck down the left's nationalization proposals in

1981 was predominantly appointed by right-wing politicians, so was the Council that vetoed the right-wing government's privatizations in 1986. In Germany, too, there is a relationship between convergence or divergence between the court majority and the government on the one hand, and the likelihood of a government bill being vetoed on the other (Hönnige, 2009: 976–979).

Vanberg sees the relationship between the German FCC and the legislature as one of 'mutual strategic interplay'. As we have seen, the Bundestag is often accused of legislating in a self-limiting manner, trying to anticipate the opinion of the FCC and thus avoiding having its legislation vetoed. Vanberg suggests that the FCC, in turn, aims to avoid giving decisions that will be disobeyed by political actors, because if they are seen to get away with disobedience the FCC's prestige will suffer, and others will start thinking that they too can ignore its decisions. Some FCC members whom he interviewed felt with hindsight that the Bavarian crucifix decision (see p. 98 above) had been a mistake, because it flew in the face of public sentiment, or at least that such decisions should not be made too often (Vanberg, 2005: 125–126). Likewise, if the FCC feels compelled on constitutional grounds to give a decision that it believes the government and parliament will disregard, it may give a judgment that is sufficiently vague that defiance will not be apparent to most people (Staton and Vanberg, 2008). In countries where the constitutional court or equivalent is not so highly regarded as the FCC, mutual interplay may not arise, because governments may be less concerned about having their legislation struck down. In France, for example, the decisions of the Constitutional Council are widely perceived as being influenced by partisan factors. Consequently, oppositions can routinely refer legislation to the Council to show to their supporters that they are using every available weapon to stymie the government, while governments may promote legislation favoured by their supporters even if privately they expect it to be vetoed by the Council. The perception that the Council makes decisions at least partly on the basis of political considerations, rather than being 'above politics', means that neither side will feel at all humiliated by receiving an adverse decision there (Brouard, 2009b: 395–399).

Over and above the short-term manoeuvrings that may go on between courts and parliaments or governments, there are some long-term strategies that courts in many countries employ. One is the so-called *seed-planting* technique, whereby the judges pronounce that, in the name of a hitherto unheard-of constitutional principle, they could have vetoed a particular piece of legislation, but that for certain specific reasons the principle does not apply to the bill under consideration. They are 'past masters at awarding immediate victory in a particular case to one party while planting doctrinal seeds that will eventually favour the other'. The politicians whose bill received this judgment have horizons that are more short-term than those of the judges, so they do not try to tear up the seeds, because all that matters is that they have won the immediate victory – but in the long term the seeds sprout (Shapiro, 1999: 212). Another is simply to delay giving a judgment in the hope that the political heat will drain away from an issue: in December 2007 the Slovakian Constitutional Court delivered a judgment on abortion six years after being asked to rule on the issue, and delay is also one of the tactics in the FCC's repertoire, as we have mentioned.

## 4.5 Conclusions

The courts in many European countries have increasingly found themselves compelled, or presented with the opportunity, to make decisions on the legality or constitutionality of the actions of political authorities. Pressure groups and individuals perceiving a threat to their rights or interests have turned with growing frequency to the courts for redress. Dedicated constitutional courts such as those in Germany and Italy have the power to constrain and even direct government and parliament, as do the Constitutional Council in France and the Supreme Court of Ireland. Even where courts cannot or do not strike down legislation as unconstitutional, as in Britain and the Netherlands, close examination reveals that the judiciary is not as passive and irrelevant to decision-making as some used to assume.

Quite clearly, arguments about the wisdom or otherwise of judicial review, which have been animatedly discussed in the United States for the last two centuries, will never be definitively resolved (see Zurn, 2007). Courts and judges may be an essential check on the behaviour of governments and parliaments – but who judges the judges? Systematic data on the opinions of the European public on the issue of judicial power are lacking, although we may note that observers from a range of countries do not detect any popular resentment at the growing influence of the courts, and indeed in most countries the judicial authorities are more highly regarded than parliaments or political parties, the archetypal actors of representative government. Surveys across the EU in the autumn of 2009 found that courts seemed to be more highly trusted than these institutions: 43 per cent expressed trust in their country's legal system, compared with 30 per cent for the parliament, 29 per cent for the government, and only 16 per cent for political parties (Eurobarometer 72, annex 1: 40–43). The legal system had 10 percentage points less trust than parliament in both Bulgaria and Portugal, but had over 25 percentage points more trust than parliament in Hungary, Ireland and the UK, more because of below-average trust in parliament in those countries than because of above-average trust in the legal system.

The impact of the judiciary on politics in Europe has been growing steadily in recent years, and no account of European governance can neglect the role of courts and constitutions. To the extent that courts stand 'above' governments and parliaments, their power has certain implications for representative government, constituting a significant constraint on the power of elected actors. On the other hand, as we have seen, in most countries neither constitutional courts nor regular courts are in practice entirely separate from political actors, and judicial bodies may in that sense be seen as part of the representative governance of Europe. In 27 of our 30 countries governments are further constrained by the role of a body that, if not 'above politics', is certainly above purely domestic politics. Accordingly, we next turn our attention to the European Union.

## Internet resources

www.politicsresources.net/const.htm
Richard Kimber's politics resources site: links to constitutions, constitutional courts and other constitution-related material.

confinder.richmond.edu/index.html
Links to the constitutions of pretty much every country in the world.

www.comparativeconstitutionsproject.org/
Describes the project and has some data on constitutions plus news on recent constitutional events around the world.

www.confcoconsteu.org/
Site of the Conference of European Constitutional Courts, containing information about 33 such courts across Europe.

## References

**Albi, Anneli** (2005) *EU Enlargement and the Constitutions of Central and Eastern Europe*, Cambridge University Press, Cambridge.

**Andeweg, Rudy B. and Galen A. Irwin** (2009) *Governance and Politics of the Netherlands*, 3rd edn, Palgrave Macmillan, Basingstoke.

**Bellamy, Richard** (2007) *Political Constitutionalism: A Republican Defence of the Constitutionality of Democracy*, Cambridge University Press, Cambridge.

**Bevir, Mark** (2008) 'The Westminster model, governance and judicial reform', *Parliamentary Affairs*, 61 (4), 559–577.

**Bogdanor, Vernon** (1988) 'Conclusion', pp. 380–386 in Vernon Bogdanor (ed.), *Constitutions in Democratic Politics*, Gower, Aldershot.

**Bogdanor, Vernon** (2009) *The New British Constitution*, Hart, Oxford.

**Brouard, Sylvain** (2009a) 'The Constitutional Council: the rising regulator of French politics', pp. 99–117 in Sylvain Brouard, Andrew M. Appleton and Amy G. Mazur (eds), *The French Fifth Republic at Fifty: Beyond Stereotypes*, Palgrave Macmillan, Basingstoke.

**Brouard, Sylvain** (2009b) 'The politics of constitutional veto in France: Constitutional Council, legislative majority and electoral competition', *West European Politics*, 32 (2), 384–403.

**Bull, Martin J. and James L. Newell** (2009) 'Still the anomalous democracy? Politics and institutions in Italy', *Government and Opposition*, 44 (1), 42–67.

**Carcassonne, Guy** (1995) 'The constraints on constitutional change in France', pp. 152–177 in Joachim Jens Hesse and Nevil Johnson (eds), *Constitutional Policy and Change in Europe*, Oxford University Press, Oxford.

**Casey, James** (2000) *Constitutional Law in Ireland*, 3rd edn, Round Hall, Sweet and Maxwell, Dublin.

**Cerar, Miro** (2001) 'Slovenia: from elite consensus to democratic consolidation', pp. 378–405 in Jan Zielonka (ed.), *Democratic Consolidation in Eastern Europe: Volume 1, Institutional Engineering*, Oxford University Press, Oxford.

**Damgaard, Erik** (2004) 'Developments in Danish parliamentary democracy: accountability, parties and external constraints', *Scandinavian Political Studies*, 27 (2), 115–131.

**de Cruz, Peter** (1995) *Comparative Law in a Changing World*, Cavendish, London.

**de Franciscis, Maria Elisabetta, and Rosella Zannini** (1992) 'Judicial policy-making in Italy', pp. 68–79 in Mary L. Volcansek (ed.), *Judicial Politics and Policy-Making in Western Europe*, Frank Cass, London.

**Della Porta, Donatella and Alberto Vannucci** (2007) 'Corruption and anti-corruption: the political defeat of "Clean Hands" in Italy', *West European Politics*, 30 (4), 830–853.

**Dyevre, Arthur** (2010) 'Unifying the field of comparative judicial politics: towards a general theory of judicial behaviour', *European Political Science Review*, 2 (2), 297–327.

**Elgie, Robert** (2003) *Political Institutions in Contemporary France*, Oxford University Press, Oxford.

**Elkins, Zachary, Tom Ginsburg and James Melton** (2009) *The Endurance of National Constitutions*, Cambridge University Press, Cambridge.

**Elster, Jon** (2000) *Ulysses Unbound: Studies in Rationality, Precommitment, and Constraints*, Cambridge University Press, Cambridge.

**Epstein, Lee, Jack Knight and Olga Shvetsova** (1998) *The Choices Justices Make*, Congressional Quarterly Press, Washington, DC.

**Feld, Lars P. and Stefan Voigt** (2006) 'Judicial independence and economic growth: some proposals regarding the judiciary', pp. 251–288 in Roger D. Congleton and Birgitta Swedenborg (eds), *Democratic Constitutional Design and Public Policy: Analysis and Evidence*, MIT Press, Cambridge, MA.

**Finer, S.E., Vernon Bogdanor and Bernard Rudden (eds)** (1995) *Comparing Constitutions*, Clarendon Press, Oxford.

**Gallagher, Michael** (2010) 'The changing constitution', pp. 72–108 in John Coakley and Michael Gallagher (eds), *Politics in the Republic* of Ireland, 5th edn, Routledge and PSAI Press, Abingdon.

**Garlicki, Leszek Lech** (2002) 'The experience of the Polish constitutional court', pp. 265–282 in Wojciech Sadurski (ed.), *Constitutional Justice, East and West: Democratic Legitimacy and Constitutional Courts in Post-Communist Europe in a Comparative Perspective*, Kluwer Law International, The Hague.

**Gelazis, Nida** (2001) 'Institutional engineering in Lithuania: stability through compromise', pp. 165–185 in Jan Zielonka (ed.), *Democratic Consolidation in Eastern Europe: Volume 1, Institutional Engineering*, Oxford University Press, Oxford.

**Gelazis, Nida** (2002) 'Defending order and freedom: the Lithuanian Constitutional Court in its first decade', pp. 395–408 in Wojciech Sadurski (ed.), *Constitutional Justice, East and West: Democratic Legitimacy and Constitutional Courts in Post-Communist Europe in a Comparative Perspective*, Kluwer Law International, The Hague.

**Ginsburg, Tom** (2008) 'The global spread of constitutional review', pp. 81–98 in Keith E Whittington, R. Daniel Kelemen and Gregory A. Caldeira (eds), *The Oxford Handbook of Law and Politics*, Oxford University Press, Oxford.

**Guarnieri, Carlo and Patrizia Pederzoli** (2002) *The Power of Judges: A Comparative Study of Courts and Democracy*, Oxford University Press, Oxford.

**Hardarson, Ólafur Th. and Gunnar Helgi Kristinsson** (2002) 'Iceland', *European Journal of Political Research*, 41 (7/8), 975–977.

**Helms, Ludger** (2000) 'The Federal Constitutional Court: institutionalising judicial review in a semisovereign democracy', pp. 84–104 in Ludger Helms (ed.), *Institutions and Institutional Change in the Federal Republic of Germany*, Macmillan, Basingstoke.

**Hirschl, Ran** (2004) *Towards Juristocracy: The Origins and Consequences of the New Constitutionalism*, Harvard University Press, Cambridge, MA.

**Hogan, Gerard and Gerry Whyte** (2003) *J.M. Kelly: The Irish Constitution*, 4th edn, LexisNexis Butterworths, Dublin.

**Holmes, Stephen** (1988) 'Pre-commitment and the paradox of democracy', pp. 195–240 in Jon Elster and Rune Slagstad (eds), *Constitutionalism and Democracy*, Cambridge University Press, Cambridge.

**Holmström, Barry** (1994) 'The judicialisation of politics in Sweden', *International Political Science Review*, 15 (2), 153–164.

**Hönnige, Christoph** (2009) 'The electoral connection: how the pivotal judge affects oppositional success at European constitutional courts', *West European Politics*, 32 (5), 963–984.

**Johnson, Nevil** (1993) 'Constitutionalism in Europe since 1945: reconstruction and reappraisal', pp. 26–45 in Douglas Greenberg, Stanley N. Katz, Melanie Beth Oliviero and Steven C. Wheatley (eds), *Constitutionalism and Democracy: Transitions in the Contemporary World*, Oxford University Press, Oxford.

**King, Anthony** (2001) *Does the United Kingdom Still Have a Constitution?*, Sweet and Maxwell, London.

**King, Anthony** (2007) *The British Constitution*, Oxford University Press, Oxford.

**Knapp, Andrew and Vincent Wright** (2006) *The Government and Politics of France*, 5th edn, Routledge, London.

**Kommers, Donald P.** (1997) *The Constitutional Jurisprudence of the Federal Republic of Germany*, 2nd edn, Duke University Press, Durham, NC, and London.

**Kommers, Donald P.** (2006) 'The Federal Constitutional Court: guardian of German democracy', *Annals of the American Academy of Political and Social Science*, 603 (1), 111–128.

**Kopecký, Petr and Maria Spirova** (2008) 'Parliamentary opposition in post-communist democracies: power of the powerless', *Journal of Legislative Studies*, 14 (1), 133–159.

**Kriesi, Hanspeter and Alexander H. Trechsel** (2008) *The Politics of Switzerland: Continuity and Change in a Consensus Democracy*, Cambridge University Press, Cambridge.

**Kristjánsson, Svanur** (2004) 'Iceland: searching for democracy along three dimensions of citizen control', *Scandinavian Political Studies*, 27 (2), 153–174.

**Leyland, Peter** (2007) *The Constitution of the United Kingdom: A Contextual Analysis*, Hart Publishing, Oxford.

**Lorenz, Astrid** (2005) 'How to measure constitutional rigidity: four concepts and two alternatives', *Journal of Theoretical Politics*, 17 (3), 339–361.

**Magalhães, Pedro C., Carlo Guarnieri and Yorgos Kaminis** (2006) 'Democratic consolidation, judicial reform and the judicialization of politics in southern Europe', pp. 138–196 in Richard Gunther, P. Nikiforos Diamandouros and Dimitri A. Sotiropoulos (eds), *Democracy and the State in the New Southern Europe*, Oxford University Press, Oxford.

**Malová, Darina and Tim Haughton** (2002) 'Making institutions in Central and Eastern Europe, and the impact of Europe', *West European Politics*, 25 (2), 101–120.

**McLean, Iain** (2010) *What's Wrong with the British Constitution?*, Oxford University Press, Oxford.

**Morel, Laurence** (1996) 'France: towards a less controversial use of the referendum?', pp. 66–85 in Michael Gallagher and Pier Vincenzo Uleri (eds), *The Referendum Experience in Europe*, Macmillan, Basingstoke.

**Murphy, Walter** (1993) 'Constitutions, constitutionalism and democracy', pp. 3–25 in Douglas Greenberg, Stanley N. Katz, Melanie Beth Oliveira and Steven C. Wheatley (eds), *Constitutionalism and Democracy: Transitions in the Contemporary World*, Oxford University Press, Oxford.

**Narud, Hanne Marthe and Kaare Strøm** (2004) 'Norway: Madisonianism reborn', *Scandinavian Political Studies*, 27 (2), 175–201.

**Norton, Philip** (1982) *The Constitution in Flux*, Martin Robertson, Oxford.

**Öhlinger, Theo** (2003) 'The genesis of the Austrian model of constitutional review of legislation', *Ratio Juris*, 16 (2), 206–222.

**Piana, Daniela** (2010) *Judicial Accountabilities in New Europe: From Rule of Law to Quality of Justice*, Ashgate, Farnham.

**Preuss, Ulrich K.** (1996) 'The political meaning of constitutionalism', pp. 11–27 in Richard Bellamy (ed.), *Constitutionalism, Democracy and Sovereignty: American and European Perspectives*, Avebury, Aldershot.

**Pribán, Jiri** (2002) 'Judicial power vs. democratic representation: the culture of constitutionalism and human rights in the Czech legal system', pp. 373–394 in Wojciech Sadurski (ed.), *Constitutional Justice, East and West: Democratic Legitimacy and Constitutional Courts in Post-Communist Europe in a Comparative Perspective*, Kluwer Law International: The Hague.

**Rasch, Bjørn Erik and Roger D. Congleton** (2006) 'Amendment procedures and constitutional stability', pp. 319–342 in Roger D. Congleton and Birgitta Swedenborg (eds), *Democratic Constitutional Design and Public Policy: Analysis and Evidence*, MIT Press, Cambridge, MA.

**Rehder, Britta** (2007) *What Is Political about Jurisprudence? Courts, Politics and Political Science in Europe and the United States*, Discussion paper 07/5, Max Planck Institute for the Study of Societies, Cologne.

**Rolla, Giancarlo and Tania Groppi** (2002) 'Between politics and the law: the development of constitutional review in Italy', pp. 143–159 in Wojciech Sadurski (ed.), *Constitutional Justice, East and West: Democratic Legitimacy and Constitutional Courts in Post-Communist Europe in a Comparative Perspective*, Kluwer Law International, The Hague.

**Rose-Ackerman, Susan** (2005) *From Elections to Democracy: Building Accountable Government in Hungary and Poland*, Cambridge University Press, Cambridge.

**Rosenfeld, Michel** (2005) 'Constitutional adjudication in Europe and the United States: paradoxes and contrasts', pp. 197–238 in Georg Nolte (ed.), *European and US Constitutionalism*, Cambridge University Press, Cambridge.

**Rothmayr, Christine** (2001) 'Towards the judicialisation of Swiss politics?', *West European Politics*, 24 (2), 77–94.

**Sadurski, Wojciech (ed.)** (2002) *Constitutional Justice, East and West: Democratic Legitimacy and Constitutional Courts in Post-Communist Europe in a Comparative Perspective*, Kluwer Law International, The Hague.

**Sájo, András** (2004) 'National institutions: implications for government trustworthiness in east European democracies', pp. 29–51 in János Kornai and Susan Rose-Ackerman (eds), *Building a Trustworthy State in Post-Socialist Transition*, Palgrave Macmillan, Basingstoke.

**Sanford, George** (2002) *Democratic Government in Poland: Constitutional Politics since 1989*, Palgrave Macmillan, Basingstoke.

**Schmidt, Manfred G.** (2003) *Political Institutions in the Federal Republic of Germany*, Oxford University Press, Oxford.

**Selle Per and Øyvind Østerud** (2006) 'The eroding of representative democracy in Norway', *Journal of European Public Policy*, 13 (4), 551–568.

**Shapiro, Martin** (1981) *Courts: A Comparative and Political Analysis*, University of Chicago Press, Chicago and London.

**Shapiro, Martin** (1999) 'The success of judicial review', pp. 193–219 in Sally J. Kenney, William M. Reisinger and John C. Reitz (eds), *Constitutional Dialogues in Comparative Perspective*, Macmillan, Basingstoke.

**Slaughter, Anne-Marie** (2004) *A New World Order*, Princeton University Press, Princeton and Oxford.

**Smith, Eivind** (2004) 'Courts and parliament: the Norwegian system of judicial review of legislation', pp. 171–187 in Eivind Smith (ed.), *The Constitution as an Instrument of Change*, SNS Förlag, Stockholm.

**Stan, Lavinia** (2010) 'Romania: in the shadow of the past', pp. 379–400 in Sabrina P. Ramet (ed.), *Central and Southeast European Politics since 1989*, Cambridge University Press, Cambridge.

**Staton, Jeffrey K. and Georg Vanberg** (2008) 'The value of vagueness: delegation, defiance, and judicial opinions', *American Journal of Political Science*, 52 (3), 504–519.

**Stone, Alec** (1992) *The Birth of Judicial Politics in France: The Constitutional Council in Comparative Perspective*, Oxford University Press, Oxford.

**Stone Sweet, Alec** (2000) *Governing with Judges: Constitutional Politics in Europe*, Oxford University Press, Oxford.

**Sunstein, Cass R.** (2001) *Designing Democracy: What Constitutions Do*, Oxford University Press, Oxford.

**Tate, C. Neal and Torbjörn Vallinder (eds)** (1995) *The Global Expansion of Judicial Power*, New York University Press, New York.

**Vanberg, Georg** (2001) 'Legislative–judicial relations: a game-theoretic approach to constitutional review', *American Journal of Political Science*, 45 (2), 346–361.

**Vanberg, Georg** (2005) *The Politics of Constitutional Review in Germany*, Cambridge University Press, Cambridge.

**van den Brandhof, Hans** (2004) 'The Republic of Finland', pp. 181–235 in Lucas Prakke and Constantijn Kortmann (eds), *Constitutional Law of 15 EU Member States*, Kluwer, Deventer.

**Volcansek, Mary L.** (2000) *Constitutional Politics in Italy: The Constitutional Court*, Macmillan, Basingstoke.

**Volcansek, Mary L.** (2006) 'Judicial selection in Italy: a civil service model with partisan results', pp. 159–175 in Kate Malleson and Peter H. Russell (eds), *Appointing Judges in an Age of Judicial Power*, University of Toronto Press, Toronto.

**von Beyme, Klaus** (2002) 'The German Constitutional Court in an uneasy triangle between parliament, government and the federal Länder', pp. 101–118 in Wojciech Sadurski (ed.), *Constitutional Justice, East and West: Democratic Legitimacy and Constitutional Courts in Post-Communist Europe in a Comparative Perspective*, Kluwer Law International, The Hague.

**Zielonka, Jan (ed.)** (2001) *Democratic Consolidation in Eastern Europe: Volume 1, Institutional Engineering*, Oxford University Press, Oxford.

**Zurn, Christopher F.** (2007) *Deliberative Democracy and the Institutions of Judicial Review*, Cambridge University Press, Cambridge.

## CHAPTER 5

# The European Union and Representative Government

## Chapter contents

## 5.1  Introduction

In earlier chapters of this book, and in Chapters 7 to 14, we focus primarily on the politics of representation in the individual countries of Europe, identifying general patterns and broad trends as well as interesting variations. In this chapter and the next we turn our attention to other levels of government. In Chapter 6 we examine subnational government, looking at the division of powers within countries among central, regional and local governments. In this chapter we look at governance beyond the nation state, as we consider a new development, quite different from anything that has ever taken place in any other part of the world, which in recent years has made European politics even more intriguing than before. We are referring to the moves towards a pooling of sovereignty among most European states that is expressed in their membership of the European Union (the EU). Although some would like the EU to reach the point where it facilitates close and smooth co-operation between the governments of the member countries and then to stop, others hope that the Union is going down a road leading to a federal Europe. In this chapter we assess the significance of the emergence of the EU as a major factor in politics in contemporary Europe.

First of all, we shall outline the evolution of the European Union since the dream of European unity began to be taken seriously in the 1940s. We shall then look at how the EU works, and consider whether it has made national governments less important political actors. As in the other chapters of this book, we shall examine the process whereby interests and preferences are turned into policies, which entails asking who plays what role in the decision-making process, and to whom the various actors are accountable. Finally, we shall attempt to assess the direction of the Union, and the chances that a United States of Europe will one day parallel the United States of America.

Before we begin, we had better clear up one matter of terminology that is liable to confuse, namely the distinction between the European Community (EC) and the European Union. The EC evolved from the 1950s as an entity with political institutions, each with defined powers and responsibilities. The European Union, on the other hand, came into existence in November 1993, and was envisaged metaphorically as a kind of building resting on three 'pillars'. One of these pillars was the original EC; the other two were intergovernmental co-operation on foreign and security policy (the second pillar), and co-operation on judicial and home affairs (the third pillar). The EU, then, was a new body, not just another name for the EC, or a revamped EC. The 2009 Lisbon Treaty, which we discuss later, eliminated this pillar structure and created a single legal institution, the European Union. Consequently, for the sake of simplicity, throughout this chapter we shall refer to the body under discussion as the EU.

## 5.2  The development of European unity

Given the record of war between European countries during the first half of the twentieth century, and for many centuries before that, the prospects of a united continent might not have seemed bright in the 1940s. However, the very ruthlessness and destructiveness of modern warfare contributed to a conviction among the post-war political elites in a number of countries that such conflict must never again take place on European soil. The causes of the Second World War were, of course, many and varied, but, as we explained in Chapter 1, two of the more obvious were unbridled and sometimes rabid nationalism (manifesting itself both in xenophobia and in the persecution of internal national minorities) and the diktat imposed on the vanquished Germany after the First World War. However understandable the latter might have been from the viewpoint of the victorious Allies, it served merely to fuel German resentment, and was eventually seen to have contained the seeds of the 1939–45 war. For this reason, once the Second World War was over, the politicians of the wartime Allies – such as Jean Monnet, a prominent figure in the French Fourth Republic – looked for ways to integrate Germany into the post-war European framework rather than ostracize it. They also looked for structures that would promote co-operation rather than rivalry between the countries of western Europe. The emergence of the 'iron curtain' dividing Europe, following the imposition of communist regimes in the Stalinist mould on the reluctant populations of eastern and central European states, heightened a belief in the west that adherence to common democratic political values was something worth preserving.

Despite all of this, the road towards even a partial undermining of the traditional fetish of absolute national sovereignty was long and rocky (for details, see Burgess, 2000; Dinan, 2005, 2006; Cini and Pérez-Solórzano Borragán, 2010: 15–67). One of the first tangible steps was taken in April 1951 with the signing of the Treaty of Paris, which established the European Coal and Steel Community (ECSC). The treaty came into effect in July 1952. Many countries were invited to take part in the creation of this new body, but in the end only six did so: France, Germany, Italy, and the three Benelux countries (Belgium, the Netherlands and Luxembourg). By joining the ECSC, member states ceded some of their sovereignty to a supranational body, and this factor was enough to dissuade Britain from joining. Britain's economic significance at that time was such that a number of smaller countries that felt that their fortunes depended on the British market (particularly Ireland and the Scandinavian countries) also declined to join.

The European Coal and Steel Community worked very satisfactorily from the viewpoint of the member states, and this led to a discussion of the idea of extending the range of policy areas in which countries might agree to combine in similar organizations. In the summer of 1955 the foreign ministers of the six countries met in Messina, Sicily, and decided to work towards the establishment of a customs union that would involve the creation of a common, or single, market embracing all the countries. They invited Britain to join them in this enterprise, but the invitation was declined. The British, while keen on the idea of turning western Europe into a free trade area, were still suspicious of any supranational political authority with the right to constrain their own government, and they remained unconvinced that their destiny lay primarily with the rest of Europe. The ideas of the six ECSC countries were fleshed out over the next two years, and in March 1957 two Treaties of Rome were signed.

Each of these two treaties established a new Community. The more important and wide-ranging in scope was the Treaty of the European Economic Community (EEC), which laid down policy aims and guidelines concerning the establishment of a common market and the creation of a common policy in areas such as agriculture and transportation. Unlike the ECSC, which had a 50-year lifespan, this had no termination date. The other treaty was the Euratom Treaty, which dealt with atomic energy and covered matters such as the pooling of resources and research.

As a result, the six countries involved were now members of three different communities: the ECSC, the EEC and Euratom. Following the 1965 Merger Treaty, which came into effect in 1967, the body to which the member states belonged was generally known as the 'European Community' before the European Union was established in 1993. The two founding treaties from 1957, together with subsequent treaties and acts amending them, make up what is in effect the Union's written constitution.

Since 1958, the European Union (EU), as we shall henceforth call it, has grown to 27 countries (see Table 5.1). There have been four phases of enlargement: a northern enlargement in the 1970s, a southern one in the 1980s, a Nordic and Austrian one in the 1990s, and a predominantly eastern and central European one in the 2000s. The first expansion occurred in 1973, with the accession of Britain, Denmark and Ireland. Britain, having stood aloof from the integration process in the 1950s, changed its mind in the 1960s, but French president Charles de Gaulle vetoed its admission. Once de Gaulle retired in 1969, the way was open for the membership of Britain, and three smaller countries that were then highly reliant on the British market were also invited. Two of these, Denmark and Ireland, joined along with Britain, but the other, Norway, did not; the issue generated a deep division in Norwegian society, culminating in a referendum in which the people voted by a narrow majority against EU entry (Wyller, 1996). In the 1980s the Community expanded further to 12 members with the admission of Greece (in 1981) and Portugal and Spain (in 1986); all three countries were emerging from periods of dictatorship, and were keen to join both to consolidate their democracy and to reap economic benefits.

In the 1990s, three countries that had maintained a policy of neutrality during the Cold War – Austria, Finland and Sweden – joined. Norway successfully negotiated terms of entry, but, once more, a referendum of its people rejected membership. In contrast to the 1980s entrants, these three new members were all wealthy countries, and in each there was a significant bloc of people, both before and after EU entry, that was fundamentally opposed to EU membership. The largest expansion took place in 2004, when 10 countries joined. Eight of these were post-communist states whose levels of wealth were well below those of the existing members (see Table 1.2); the other two were small and relatively wealthy Mediterranean islands. The economic and environmental problems of many of the 2004 entrants led to some reservations about admitting them, but these feelings were overcome by enlightened self-interest. It was in the economic and security interests of the existing 15 members to facilitate the development of the post-communist countries into stable, prosperous democracies, and in addition the EU has always been sensitive to accusations that it is a 'rich persons' club', so it would be uncomfortable about turning away any European democracy that wanted to join. All of these countries but Cyprus made the decision by referendum: the size of the Yes vote ranged from 54 per cent in Malta up to 94 per cent in Slovakia (Szczerbiak and Taggart, 2004: 560). The post-communist enlargement

---

**TABLE 5.1** Member countries of the European Union

| Country | Year of joining EU | Year of joining Eurozone | Country | Year of joining EU | Year of joining Eurozone |
|---------|--------------------|--------------------------|---------|--------------------|--------------------------|
| Belgium | 1958 | 1999 | Sweden | 1995 | – |
| France | 1958 | 1999 | Cyprus | 2004 | 2008 |
| Germany | 1958 | 1999 | Czech Republic | 2004 | – |
| Italy | 1958 | 1999 | Estonia | 2004 | 2011 |
| Luxembourg | 1958 | 1999 | Hungary | 2004 | – |
| Netherlands | 1958 | 1999 | Latvia | 2004 | – |
| Denmark | 1973 | – | Lithuania | 2004 | – |
| Ireland | 1973 | 1999 | Malta | 2004 | 2008 |
| United Kingdom | 1973 | – | Poland | 2004 | – |
| Greece | 1981 | 2001 | Slovakia | 2004 | 2009 |
| Portugal | 1986 | 1999 | Slovenia | 2004 | 2007 |
| Spain | 1986 | 1999 | Bulgaria | 2007 | – |
| Austria | 1995 | 1999 | Romania | 2007 | – |
| Finland | 1995 | 1999 | | | |

*Note*: The first six countries were all founding members of the EEC and of Euratom in 1958, and were all already members of the ECSC. The next nine countries joined all three communities upon their respective accessions; the ECSC had ceased to exist by the time the last 12 joined. The European Union itself came into existence in November 1993.

was taken further in 2007, when Bulgaria and Romania were admitted, both without a referendum – although in a 2003 referendum 91 per cent of Romanian voters had approved the constitutional changes that made EU entry possible. These two countries were far poorer even than the 2004 entrants, and there was widespread concern that they had been admitted 'before they were ready' in terms of their administrative competence and the operation of the rule of law.

Enlargement has affected the nature of the EU considerably. The original six members were close to one another geographically and, with the exception of southern Italy, had very similar levels of wealth and economic development. Two languages (French and German) were enough for virtually all informal transactions between members of the political elite. Even if the EU did not always operate entirely harmoniously, in its original form it was much more of a cosy club than its expanded version proved to be. Now that it embraces nearly the whole of Europe, the EU's diversity mirrors that of the continent. The process of making decisions is more complex, and often more protracted, than was the case when there were only six member states, and if the Union still consisted of only these six, it is likely that the process of European integration would have advanced much further than it actually has. There has been a traditional tension between widening the membership of the EU and deepening the level of integration between the member states: the greater the range of members, the more difficult it becomes to press ahead with deeper integration.

The original treaties have been amended over time. The Single European Act of 1987 reformed the Union's decision-making process so as to facilitate the creation of a single market with no trade barriers between member states. In December 1991, in the Dutch city of Maastricht, the Treaty on European Union was agreed (it was formally signed two months later, and finally came into operation in November 1993). This treaty established the *European Union*, further amended decision-making procedures, laid the foundation for monetary union and the creation of the *euro*, and formalized member state co-operation in the areas of foreign policy and of justice and home affairs. The Amsterdam Treaty of 1997 brought about some streamlining of EU decision-making, and enhanced the position of the European Parliament. The Nice Treaty of 2000, which came into operation in 2003, established new voting weights for the member states, eliminated national vetoes in several policy areas, agreed to reduce the size of the Commission, and established a procedure whereby some member states would be allowed to integrate even more closely than the Union as a whole.

Up to that point, these agreements had simply amended the original set of treaties. Following the Nice Treaty, however, it was agreed that a root and branch review of the Union's legal and constitutional underpinnings was necessary, both to make the Union more effective and to make it more understandable to its own citizens. A Constitutional Convention was thus established, bringing together national parliamentarians, government representatives and members of the European Parliament under the chairmanship of former French president Valéry Giscard d'Estaing. Within 18 months this *Convention on the Future of Europe* drew up a draft constitutional treaty that was submitted to national governments and which – following some difficult negotiations – emerged as the draft treaty establishing a Constitution for Europe (Castiglione *et al.*, 2007). This treaty was signed by EU governments in Rome on 29 October 2004, and was submitted for ratification to the member states with a view to its coming into operation in late 2006. However, a number of countries chose to put it to their people for approval in a referendum. In the first half of 2005 four countries voted on it, and although it was approved in both Spain and Luxembourg, defeats in France in May 2005 and in the Netherlands a few days later put an end to the project, especially given the near certainty that it would also be defeated by referendum in the United Kingdom, and perhaps elsewhere too.

After a 'pause for reflection', the heads of government agreed a new treaty at Lisbon in December 2007 (Dinan, 2008; Sieberson, 2008). Whereas the abortive constitution would have been a stand-alone document replacing all the existing treaties, the Lisbon Treaty had no substance itself, but it significantly amended the two major treaties: the 1957 Treaty establishing the European Community (which, confusingly, it retrospectively renamed), and the 1993 Maastricht Treaty (the Treaty on European Union). Most of the content of the constitution was retained, but the provocative term 'constitution', with all that it implied about the nature of the EU, was dropped. Only one country, Ireland, held a referendum on the Lisbon Treaty, all the others ratifying it by parliament. The Irish people rejected it in the first referendum in June 2008, but once some changes had been made – notably, the dropping of the original provision that only 18 of the 27 member states would have a member of the Commission at any one time – they approved it in a second referendum in October 2009, and it came into operation on 1 December 2009. The fact that designing this treaty took, in effect, the whole of the first decade of the new century means that there is little stomach for more treaty-making in the near future.

## 5.3 How the European Union works

As is often said, the EU is a unique body and operates in a unique way. According to the Lisbon Treaty, 'The functioning of the Union shall be founded on representative democracy,' but it is not representative democracy as we understand it in the 30 states examined in this book. In Chapter 3 we outlined two models of democracy identified by Lijphart, which he terms the Westminster-type *majoritarian model* and the *consensus model*, and he cites the European Union as an archetypal example of the latter, because of the way in which, as we shall see in the course of this chapter, power is diffused among a number of institutions, with none being dominant (Lijphart, 1999: 42–47). The EU has five main institutions: the Commission, the European Parliament, the Council of Ministers, the European Council, and the Court of Justice. (There are also a number of others, such as the European Central Bank, which oversees the single currency and is both powerful and unaccountable, and the Court of Auditors, which has the role of checking whether the EU's money has been spent as it should have been: see Laffan, 2006; McNamara, 2006.)

We now look in more detail at the role played by each of these institutions (for accounts of how the EU works see Hix, 2005; Nugent, 2010; Wallace *et al.*, 2010). We follow the flow of policies through the EU's decision-making process, from Commission to Parliament to Council. As noted above, there has been extensive amendment of the treaties since the mid 1980s, particularly in the area of decision-making. Thus, as a general rule of thumb (and there are some exceptions), the cumulative effect of these amendments has been to create a system in which the Commission proposes legislation, and then the Council and Parliament jointly pass, amend or reject that legislation. Once a proposal has been passed, the Commission is responsible for its implementation – either on its own or in partnership with national and/or local government. The European Council, which is made up of the heads of government of the member states, has emerged as the most powerful body of all. It is this body that provides the overall political direction of the Union and within which final decisions are made.

### 5.3.1 The Commission

The Commission looks, at least at first sight, like the 'government' of the EU (for the Commission see Egeberg, 2010; Nugent, 2010: 105–137). In reality, it is more of a hybrid between a government and a civil service, as the Council also has a governmental role. The Commission, which is headed by a president, consists of 27 members, one from each country, each with a specific policy juris-diction (or *portfolio*). The formation of a Commission begins with the governments nominating a person as president; they can decide this by qualified majority vote (see details below), but in practice they operate on the basis of unanimity. The *de facto* need for the nominee to be accept-able to all the governments means that the desire to have a strong and effective leader will always be balanced by the requirement for inoffensiveness. The European Parliament (EP) can approve or reject this nominee. Assuming it gives approval, then the governments, in consultation with the president (who may be quite directive in signalling his or her preferences), nominate their com-missioners. Once a full team of commissioners has been put together, the entire proposed Commission requires the assent of the Parliament before it can take office.

The Commission president can make a big difference to the development of the EU. He or she is a significant actor, with the right to attend all meetings of the most powerful body in the EU, the European Council, which we discuss later. Under the former French finance minister Jacques Delors (president from 1985 to 1994), some major steps were taken towards integration, most notably the completion of the single market (Egan, 2010). His successor, Jacques Santer (1995–1999), a former Luxembourg prime minister, was not the first choice of most heads of government and proved rather ineffective. Romano Prodi (1999–2004) started with the advan-tage of being a political heavyweight, as a former Italian prime minister. Prodi was able to be more assertive than his predecessors about the composition of his Commission, strengthened by the additional powers conferred upon the president by the Amsterdam Treaty. In addition, he secured from each commissioner upon appointment an undertaking that should he ask them to resign, they would do so, whereas previous presidents were unable to dismiss individual com-missioners whose behaviour was tarnishing the entire Commission. However, his influence waned as his term proceeded, partly because of his growing (re-)involvement in domestic Italian politics. To succeed him, the heads of government chose José Manuel Barroso (2004–), the Portuguese prime minister, who was reappointed to a second term in 2009. Although not regarded as a decisive political figure, Barroso has provided steady leadership over a period of considerable political and economic turmoil. His dedication to consensus-building, however, somewhat lowered the Commission's profile in confronting member states over critical issues. Still, even if the president is not quite the 'prime minister of Europe', a phrase used by Walter Hallstein, who was Commission president in the 1960s, he is at least coming to look more like a prime minister of the EU.

The Commission has a five-year term in office, and is based in the Berlaymont building in the 'European quarter' in the eastern part of Brussels, the capital of Belgium. Most commissioners are former senior politicians in their home countries, and the weight of the domestic offices they previously held is rising over time, with the commissioners of small states especially likely to have held high domestic office (Döring, 2007). Most commissioners are associated with a party in the government that appointed them, so the members of any one Commission are likely to have different party-family backgrounds. Commissioners also vary in ability: some are chosen as the person who seems likely to be able to achieve most, whether for the government that appointed them, for the country, or for the EU as a whole, but the appointment of others results from side deals done among coalition government parties in the member states when dividing up the ministries, or the need to free up a key position in government in order to allow a govern-ment reshuffle to take place.

Once the commissioners have been nominated, the president decides which commissioner should be given which portfolio. This is a key power, one that gives the president considerable leverage over national governments when it comes to their choice of nominee. Member governments often lobby vigorously to get 'their' commissioner assigned to a significant position, but such lobbying is less effective than it once was. The portfolios, which more or less correspond to ministries in domestic government, include economic and financial affairs, agriculture, external economic affairs, industrial affairs, social affairs and employment, environment, regional policy, and so on, though given that there are 27 portfolios some look as if they have been created simply to give some countries' nominees a job title. Each commissioner-designate appears before a European Parliament committee to be questioned, and finally the Commission as a whole must receive a vote of approval from the European Parliament before it can enter office. The significance of this power was illustrated forcefully in October 2004 when it became clear that the EP would reject the proposed Commission put together by Barroso because he refused to reconsider his nomination to the justice portfolio of Rocco Buttiglione, an Italian politician whose conservative Catholic views (he described homosexuality as a sin, for example) made him unacceptable to a majority of members of the European Parliament (MEPs). Barroso had to withdraw his proposed Commission from the firing line and put together a new one, which did not contain either Buttiglione or several other members of the original team. This was finally approved by the EP in November 2004, nearly a month after the Commission was supposed to have taken office. Similarly, in 2009, negative signals from the EP induced some governments to change their nominees.

Although commissioners are nominated on national lines, they are emphatically not in the Commission to represent national interests – at least in theory. Upon taking office, each commissioner has to take an oath to the effect that he or she will serve the overall interest of the EU, and will not take instructions from a national government or from any other body. After all, another Union institution, the Council, exists expressly to safeguard national interests, as we shall see. In addition the Commission, like domestic governments (see Chapter 2), operates as a collective body, with each commissioner sharing responsibility for every decision. Despite this, it is tacitly accepted that commissioners do not suddenly slough off their national identities the moment they are appointed and become transformed into Euromen or Eurowomen. For one thing, the commissioner from, say, Slovakia might well receive representations from Slovakian interest groups, which are likely to see him or her as 'the Slovakian commissioner'. Moreover, any commissioner who hopes to be reappointed has an incentive not to alienate the government that has the nomination in its control. This is not to say that any commissioner acts as a government puppet, but undoubtedly governments do expect 'their' commissioner to give them advance warning of impending developments, and generally to advise them as to how to maximize benefits for the country. Commissioners may harbour ambitions for a return to national politics in one form or another, and so will wish to be seen as having 'done their bit' for the country or the government while working in Brussels. Analysis of Commission proposals shows a significant level of agreement between these and the policies of the home member states of the commissioners who had prime responsibility for drafting the proposal, especially when the proposal would need only majority, as opposed to unanimous, support from the Council (Thomson, 2008a). It matters, in policy terms, which country gets which Commission post – just as in domestic governments it matters which party gets which ministry, as we shall see in Chapter 12. One of the provisions of the original Lisbon Treaty that led to opposition in the Irish referendum of 2008 was a reduction in the number of commissioners from 27 to 18, with states taking it in turns to spend five years without a commissioner. In the revised version, as a result of pressure from Ireland and from other countries, each state retains its commissioner. While a body of 27 is too many to be an effective decision-making body, Thomson's research shows that countries without a commissioner at any given time would have risked losing out in policy terms.

The Commission has two main powers. First, it has the primary responsibility for initiating legislation, and it sends a steady stream of proposals and recommendations into the EU's policy-making process, although it usually tests the water first to ensure that its proposals have a realistic chance of being accepted by the other institutions, especially the Council. As a result, the Commission spends a lot of its time consulting and being lobbied by the 27 governments and major interest groups about its ideas. In addition, the Council as a whole, national governments individually, and the Parliament all attempt to use the Commission to push matters forward in areas that are important to them. Although it is true that only the Commission can actually initiate most legislation, in practice it is often heavily lobbied to table or amend draft proposals, and may often act more as a mediator and broker between various interests than as a real independent initiator (Bouwen, 2009). The question of whether the Commission should be a *principal* – an independent actor with its own agenda – or merely an *agent* of other actors, such as the Council or national governments, was left unspecified from the start, and the issue still divides senior Commission officials (Hooghe, 2001: 142–167; Pollack, 2003: 75–154).

The Commission's second main responsibility lies in trying to ensure that others in the Union are behaving as they should. When EU legislation is passed, this generally imposes obligations on the 27 national governments and/or parliaments to take action, either by introducing domestic legislation or by implementing a policy. If this is to mean anything, then clearly someone has to check that these obligations are being fulfilled, and the Commission has this role. However, the Commission is grossly understaffed, with only about 25 000 employees (many of whom are translators), making it roughly equal in size to Barcelona city council or the French Ministry of Culture (Bomberg and Stubb, 2008: 50). It is unable to monitor Union-wide policy implementation in anything like a comprehensive fashion, so it tends to concentrate on potential major breaches, or to respond to specific complaints. If it discovers a case where a national government has apparently failed to meet its obligations, it notifies the government and waits a specified period for a formal response. If the government in question is uncooperative, the Commission can ultimately refer the case to the Court of Justice. Partly because of the Commission's limited resources, implementation of Union law is always a major issue, as we shall see later in the chapter.

The Commission, then, plays a vital role in providing an overall Union viewpoint on important matters, however attenuated or diluted this may sometimes appear, and in negotiating with and mediating between the other actors in the decision-making process. In addition, the Commission represents the Union externally in important ways: it negotiates on trade issues with other international actors, and its president attends the gatherings of the heads of government of the wealthiest nations in the world, known as the G8. However, the Commission is a far cry from the engine of European integration that some would like it to be. It contains a mix both of nationalities and of political views – typically containing commissioners from most of the main political tendencies in the EU apart from the extremes of left and right. The fact that the Commission is appointed in a piecemeal fashion by governments of varying political persuasions, as opposed to being made up of party representatives pledged to implement an agreed election manifesto, has sometimes led to its having no clear overall goal or programme of the sort that national governments usually adopt, and Commissions can appear to lack a sense of purpose. However, a powerful and dynamic president may be able to avoid this problem by ensuring that the incoming

Commission sets out a clear programme and works to achieve it, and all Commissions now start with a five-year list of strategic objectives, and also issue annual work programmes.

## 5.3.2 The European Parliament

The European Parliament has been steadily growing in significance in recent years. It has three main powers, which concern appointment and dismissal of the Commission, legislation, and the budget (for the EP see Corbett *et al.*, 2007; Judge and Earnshaw, 2008).

The power of the Parliament in the appointment of the Commission has existed only since 1993. After each five-yearly EP election, the endorsement of the Parliament is needed for the appointment of the next Commission president, and then the new Commission as a whole requires approval by a vote in the EP before it can take office, as we have seen. The EP can also dismiss a Commission. Formally, a motion to do this needs to be passed by a two-thirds majority, with those voting for the motion amounting to more than half of the total number of MEPs; politically, though, it is questionable whether a Commission could survive a simple majority vote of no confidence from MEPs. Events in 1999, following evidence that there was mismanagement and corruption within the Commission bureaucracy for which commissioners were not taking appropriate responsibility, showed that this EP power has real substance. In January of that year a motion to dismiss the Commission was defeated by a margin of only 293 to 232 votes, and two months later, as EP dissatisfaction with the Commission continued to rise, the Commission pre-empted further steps against it by resigning en masse.

The EP's role in the legislative process, the second area where it plays a part, has been steadily expanding. Virtually all proposals are now decided under what used to be called the *co-decision* procedure, now designated the *ordinary legislative procedure*. Neither the Council of Ministers nor the European Parliament can overrule the other, and differences over legislative proposals must be resolved in a *conciliation committee* to the satisfaction of a majority of members in each institution. If such agreement cannot be reached, the proposal fails. In a few particularly important areas the *assent procedure* comes into play; in these areas, no change can be made by the EU without the EP's express approval. These areas include the admission of new member states, all major international agreements including association agreements between the EU and other countries, treaty change, and the role of the European Central Bank.

Finally, the EP has a significant role in deciding the EU's budget (for the budgetary procedure see Jones, 2001: 182–203; Laffan and Lindner, 2010). The EP is kept informed as the budget is being drafted, and the final outcome represents the result of negotiations between the EP and the Council on the basis of the Commission's proposals. At the final stage, the EP is entitled to make some changes in certain areas of spending. If these changes satisfy it, the president of the Parliament signs the budget into law. If the EP is still not satisfied – in other words, if it would like to make changes greater than those it is allowed to make under the terms of the treaties – then it can reject the entire budget. In order to do this, it needs a two-thirds majority, provided that those voting for rejection constitute a majority of all MEPs. Although this happened several times in the 1980s, since then the EU has committed itself to more medium-term financial planning (the current budgetary period runs from 2007 to 2013), so the parameters of the budget are broadly settled well in advance of the detailed preparation, and the scope for disagreement between the various EU institutions is much less than in the past.

Having outlined the Parliament's powers, we turn now to its composition and operation. At the time of the 2009 election the Parliament contained 736 members, who come from the member states in approximate proportion to their population, although the smaller states are generously over-represented in per capita terms – a principle that the EU, with its weakness for jargon, terms *degressive proportionality* (see Table 5.2). In terms of the measure for disproportionality that we employ in Chapter 11, the least squares index, disproportionality in the EP seat allocation among

**TABLE 5.2** Seats in the European Parliament at the 2009 election

| Country | Population Jan 2010 (thousands) | Seats | Population per MEP (thousands) | Seats entitlement if seats were strictly proportional to population |
|---------|-------------------------------|-------|-------------------------------|--------------------------------------------------------------------|
| Germany | 81 800 | 99 | 826 | 120 |
| France | 64 714 | 72 | 899 | 95 |
| United Kingdom | 62 008 | 72 | 861 | 91 |
| Italy | 60 340 | 72 | 838 | 89 |
| Spain | 45 989 | 50 | 920 | 67 |
| Poland | 38 167 | 50 | 763 | 56 |
| Romania | 21 462 | 33 | 650 | 31 |
| Netherlands | 16 578 | 25 | 663 | 24 |
| Greece | 11 295 | 22 | 513 | 17 |
| Belgium | 10 827 | 22 | 492 | 16 |
| Portugal | 10 638 | 22 | 484 | 16 |
| Czech Republic | 10 507 | 22 | 478 | 15 |
| Hungary | 10 013 | 22 | 455 | 15 |
| Sweden | 9 341 | 18 | 519 | 14 |
| Austria | 8 375 | 17 | 493 | 12 |
| Bulgaria | 7 564 | 17 | 445 | 11 |
| Denmark | 5 535 | 13 | 426 | 8 |
| Slovakia | 5 425 | 13 | 417 | 8 |
| Finland | 5 351 | 13 | 412 | 8 |
| Ireland | 4 456 | 12 | 371 | 7 |
| Lithuania | 3 329 | 12 | 277 | 5 |
| Latvia | 2 248 | 8 | 281 | 3 |
| Slovenia | 2 047 | 7 | 292 | 3 |
| Estonia | 1 340 | 6 | 223 | 2 |
| Cyprus | 798 | 6 | 133 | 1 |
| Luxembourg | 502 | 6 | 84 | 1 |
| Malta | 413 | 5 | 83 | 1 |
| EU-27 | 501 062 | 736 | 685 | 736 |

*Note*: Proportional allocation made by the Sainte-Laguë method, which is unbiased in that it does not favour either large or small countries.

*Source for population*: Eurostat news release 111/2010, p. 2.

countries is 4.8, comparable to the amount of disproportionality at an Italian or Spanish election, and below the European average (see Table 11.5). Under the Lisbon Treaty, from the 2014 elections the number of MEPs will be capped at 751, with no state having fewer than 6 MEPs or more than 96. Direct elections to the EP have taken place at five-yearly intervals every June since 1979. The elections take place in all countries within a few days of each other; the different dates reflect different national traditions as to the day of the week (usually Thursday or Sunday) on which elections are held. No results are supposed to be released from the early-voting countries until voting is completed in every country, because of a pious belief that voters might be influenced by news of results elsewhere, although there is no evidence that voters have any interest at all in EP results in other countries (or even much interest in their own country's, in many cases). Although the Treaty speaks of a uniform electoral system being used for European Parliament elections, this can happen only if all member governments acting in the Council agree on one, and the EP itself approves it. Every country uses some variant of proportional representation (PR) to elect its MEPs, although not necessarily the same one as it uses in domestic elections (Farrell and Scully, 2007: 79).

Elections to the European Parliament are, in some senses, rather curious affairs. They are impressive in their own way, as the people of 27 countries, with a total electorate of over 380 million, turn out at about the same time to elect a genuinely transnational parliament, the only one of its kind in the world. But they are a far cry from being the EU equivalent of national general elections. In general elections the question of the composition of the next government is uppermost in voters' minds, even if, as we shall see in Chapter 12, government formation is sometimes a complex process not directly brought about by the preferences expressed by voters. But in European Parliament elections it is often hard to say exactly what is at stake. Certainly, no government is accountable to the EP or will be put together from it, let alone be turfed out of office by it. Many voters undoubtedly conclude that in fact nothing much is at stake, and so only a minority actually turn out to vote (see Table 5.3). Turnout in 2009 was below 40 per cent in 12 countries and below 30 per cent in six of them; it was particularly low in the 10 post-communist countries, averaging only 32 per cent. Overall turnout is declining steadily at EP elections (it was 62 per cent at the first elections in 1979), to levels well below the comparable figures for domestic general elections. Comparative evidence suggests that wider adoption of electoral systems giving voters a choice of candidate, which would make MEPs individually accountable to voters, might increase turnout, although probably only marginally (Farrell and Scully, 2007: 205–206). EP elections are sometimes referred to as *second-order* elections, but this may overstate their importance. In Belgium, for instance, they are *fourth-order* or *last order*, ranking behind national elections, regional elections, and local elections (Rihoux *et al.*, 2007: 892). If EP elections are intended to provide popular democratic legitimacy for the EU's decision-making process, they must be adjudged a failure.

This lack of clarity about the real purpose of European Parliament elections arises partly because, despite the theory, they are not fought on the basis of European issues. Indeed, few could say if pressed just what 'European issues' really are. It is true that there are pan-EU political groups that correspond quite closely to the party families that we discuss in Chapter 8, the most important of which are the European People's Party (mainly representing Christian Democratic parties) and the Socialist group, but outside the EP itself these are essentially very loose umbrella bodies linking national parties, and the manifestos that they issue at EP elections are very bland and largely indistinguishable from each other (Irwin, 1995). EP elections are fought on the ground

**TABLE 5.3** Results of European Parliament elections, June 2009

| Country | Seats | Electorate (m) | Votes (m) | Turnout (%) | EPP-ED | S&D | ALDE | Greens/EFA | ECR | EUL/NGL | EFD | NA |
|---|---|---|---|---|---|---|---|---|---|---|---|---|
| Austria | 17 | 6.4 | 2.6 | 41.5 | 6 | 4 | | 2 | | | | 5 |
| Belgium | 22 | 7.8 | 6.6 | 84.7 | 5 | 5 | 5 | 4 | 1 | | | 2 |
| Bulgaria | 17 | 6.7 | 2.6 | 38.5 | 6 | 4 | 5 | | | | | 2 |
| Cyprus | 6 | 0.5 | 0.3 | 58.2 | 2 | 2 | | | | 2 | | |
| Czech Rep | 22 | 8.4 | 2.4 | 28.1 | 2 | 7 | | | 9 | 4 | | |
| Denmark | 13 | 4.1 | 2.3 | 57.7 | 1 | 4 | 3 | 2 | | 1 | 2 | |
| Estonia | 6 | 0.9 | 0.4 | 43.7 | 1 | 1 | 3 | 1 | | | | |
| Finland | 13 | 4.1 | 1.7 | 40.2 | 4 | 2 | 4 | 2 | | | 1 | |
| France | 72 | 44.3 | 17.2 | 38.9 | 29 | 14 | 6 | 14 | | 5 | 1 | 3 |
| Germany | 99 | 62.2 | 26.3 | 42.3 | 42 | 23 | 12 | 14 | | 8 | | |
| Greece | 22 | 10.0 | 5.1 | 51.3 | 8 | 8 | | 1 | | 3 | 2 | |
| Hungary | 22 | 8.0 | 2.9 | 36.0 | 14 | 4 | | | 1 | | | 3 |
| Ireland | 12 | 3.3 | 1.8 | 56.1 | 4 | 3 | 4 | | | 1 | | |
| Italy | 72 | 50.3 | 30.6 | 60.9 | 35 | 21 | 7 | | | | 9 | |
| Latvia | 8 | 1.5 | 0.8 | 52.1 | 3 | 1 | 1 | 1 | 1 | 1 | | |
| Lithuania | 12 | 2.7 | 0.5 | 20.4 | 4 | 3 | 2 | | 1 | | 2 | |
| Luxembourg | 6 | 0.2 | 0.2 | 82.4 | 3 | 1 | 1 | 1 | | | | |
| Malta | 5 | 0.3 | 0.2 | 77.0 | 2 | 3 | | | | | | |
| Netherlands | 25 | 12.4 | 4.6 | 36.8 | 5 | 3 | 6 | 3 | 1 | 2 | 1 | 4 |

**TABLE 5.3** (*continued*)

| Country | Seats | Electorate (m) | Votes (m) | Turnout (%) | EPP-ED | S&D | ALDE | Greens/EFA | ECR | EUL/NGL | EFD | NA |
|---------|-------|----------------|-----------|-------------|--------|-----|------|------------|-----|---------|-----|-----|
| Poland | 50 | 30.6 | 7.4 | 24.5 | 28 | 7 | | | 15 | | | |
| Portugal | 22 | 9.7 | 3.5 | 36.0 | 10 | 7 | | | | 5 | | |
| Romania | 33 | 18.2 | 4.8 | 26.6 | 14 | 11 | 5 | | | | | 3 |
| Slovakia | 13 | 4.3 | 0.8 | 19.0 | 6 | 5 | 1 | | | | 1 | |
| Slovenia | 7 | 1.7 | 0.5 | 26.8 | 3 | 2 | 2 | | | | | |
| Spain | 50 | 34.6 | 15.4 | 44.7 | 23 | 21 | 2 | 2 | | 1 | | 1 |
| Sweden | 18 | 7.1 | 3.2 | 44.7 | 5 | 5 | 4 | 3 | | 1 | | |
| UK | 72 | 45.3 | 15.6 | 34.5 | 5 | 13 | 11 | 5 | 24 | | 13 | 3 |
| Total | 736 | 385.6 | 160.3 | 41.6 | 265 | 184 | 84 | 55 | 54 | 35 | 32 | 27 |

*Notes:*

EPP-ED – European People's Party (Christian Democrats)

S&D – Socialists and Democrats

ALDE – Alliance of Liberals and Democrats for Europe

Greens/EFA – Greens–European Free Alliance

ECR – European Conservatives and Reformists (Euro-unenthusiastic grouping)

EUL-NGL – European United Left–Nordic Green Left

EFD – Europe of Freedom and Democracy (Euro-sceptic grouping)

NA – non-attached

Votes, and turnout, refer to valid votes only.

*Source:* For votes, Mellows-Facer *et al.* (2009), which contains information not available on the EP's own site. For seats, http://www.europarl.europa.eu/parliament/archive/elections2009/en/index_en.html.

in each country by national parties rather than by these transnational groups, and the parties stress national issues when campaigning. Although they may be criticized for this 'parochial' behaviour, the parties are inclined to argue that there is no other way of generating any interest at all among the electorate. The consequence is that the performance of the current national government tends to become the main EP election issue in each individual state. When the EP election falls midway in the domestic electoral cycle, it is seen by voters, the media and the political parties alike as a midterm test of the national government's popularity, so the EP is usually dominated by opposition parties, whereas the Council of Ministers is by definition dominated by government parties (see below). The EP's centre of gravity was generally on the left, or close to the centre, between 1979 and 1999, but since then it has been well on the right (Warntjen et al., 2008: 1249).

Once the elections have been held, the MEPs sit in the Parliament's chambers in Strasbourg and Brussels according to their political group, not according to the country they represent. The EP operates very much along party lines, like national parliaments throughout Europe. In the Parliament elected in 2009 the two main centre-right groups, the EPP and the Liberals, secured nearly half the seats. Even so, the EPP reached an agreement with the Socialists on filling the prestigious position of EP president: for the first half of the parliament's term the office would go to Jerzy Buzek, a Polish EPP member, and in January 2012 he would be succeeded by an MEP from the Socialist group. The MEPs from each national party maintain a separate existence within the EP groups (thus, for example, there is a British Labour group, a French Socialist group, a German SPD group, and so on, within the Socialist group, each with its own internal structure). MEPs vote solidly with their national party group (i.e. German SPD members almost always vote en bloc), and since these national party groups nearly always vote with the parliamentary group (i.e. the German SPD group nearly always votes with the Socialist group) the various groups display high rates of cohesion (Hix et al., 2007: 94). The groups are a little less cohesive than party groups in most domestic parliaments in Europe, but more so than parties in the US Congress, a cohesion that comes partly from high degrees of policy congruence among their members (McElroy and Benoit, 2010). When an MEP is cross-pressured – that is, when their national group does not vote with the political group – they are three times as likely to vote with the national group as with the political group: thus, if the German SPD group decides not to vote with the rest of the Socialist group, the German SPD MEPs are much more likely to vote as the German SPD group does than as the Socialist group does (Hix et al., 2007: 137–138). A group may punish mavericks by not giving them places on delegations or committees (McElroy, 2008), or in extreme cases by fining them, but generally EP groups prefer to let national groups impose discipline on their own members. If a national group chooses to go its own way in a vote, there is nothing the EP group as a whole can do.

The EP does most of its work through committees, of which there are approximately 20 at any one time, corresponding to the main areas of EU activity. Seats on the committees are shared among the political groups in proportion to their size; within each political group, posts are shared among the various countries represented within it. Besides holding committee meetings, the Parliament meets in week-long plenary sessions 12 times a year, at which it considers reports from the committees and votes on declarations or proposed amendments to legislation.

The EP, as we have seen, does not have some of the powers that belong, at least in theory, to domestic parliaments in Europe. It cannot dismiss or appoint the Council of Ministers, which plays an important governmental role, and it cannot initiate or promulgate legislation. One mark of the constraints under which the EP operates is its lack of control over its location. With both the Commission and the Council offices based in Brussels, most MEPs would like the Parliament to be there also. Instead, EP operations are scattered around three countries. It holds its committee meetings in Brussels, which is the seat of most of the real action in the Union, but it must hold nearly all of its plenary sessions in Strasbourg in north-eastern France, and, moreover, most of its administrative staff are based in Luxembourg. Decisions on its location are in the hands of the Council, representing the national governments, and neither the French nor the Luxembourg government has been prepared to give up the prestige and such financial benefits as may arise from having the Parliament meet in its territory. Consequently, truckloads of documents are constantly on the road between Brussels, Luxembourg and Strasbourg, at a considerable cost in terms of time and money; it is estimated that this geographical dispersion consumes around 15 per cent of the EP's budget (Corbett *et al.*, 2007: 32).

The low turnout at EP elections, and the way these are dominated by domestic rather than European political issues, suggests that the Parliament has not managed to make itself very relevant to most Europeans. A survey conducted in 2005 found that only half of Europeans were even aware that the EP *is* an elected body, while in a Eurobarometer survey conducted in the autumn of 2008 only 26 per cent of Europeans, some of whom were no doubt simply guessing, could say that the next EP elections would take place the following year (Farrell and Scully, 2007: 16; Eurobarometer, 2009: 13). This weakens claims by the EP to represent the views of the European public on European issues. The regular proceedings of the EP receive little media coverage in the member states, and when the EP does get into the news, it is because of a sudden political 'crisis' or for all the wrong reasons, such as when allegations surface about MEPs engaging in 'creative accountancy' over their expenses or queueing up to 'sign in' early in the morning and thus qualify for their daily attendance allowance before rushing to the airport to catch a flight home. Members of the EP are often exasperated by the media's approach to coverage of their institution, complaining that the serious work they do in committees and in the legislative process goes virtually unreported while the most minor misdemeanours, real or alleged, are blown up out of all proportion. But although they have a fair point, it remains a fact that the EP has been unable to mobilize European public opinion in its perennial quest to gain greater powers. Although in principle EU citizens want the EP to have more power, both the level of information they possess and their degree of attachment are quite low, and there is little tangible sign of public demand for a more central role for the EP.

Nevertheless, the EP is unquestionably growing in power and significance within the EU's decision-making process. Every reform of the EU's institutions has brought increases in the EP's powers. MEPs are able to use the powers they have, especially those in the areas of the budget or the appointment and dismissal of the Commission, in such a manner as to get their way in other matters. The EP is thus a major actor in the Union's decision-making process, precisely because of the separation of its role from that of the executive. The EP, like the US Congress but unlike parliaments in most European countries, is able to vote against individual items of legislation or to compel changes to the budget without thereby risking bringing down a government. In contrast to some national parliaments, the EP is not, and is unlikely to become, a mere steppingstone on the way to a position in a European government. It is thus likely that MEPs in a more powerful EP will take their parliamentary role more seriously than do many deputies in national parliaments in Europe. Unconstrained by any incentive to be loyal to the executive so as not to jeopardize their promotion prospects – a factor that partly explains the solid party bloc voting among government backbenchers that we witness in national European parliaments, as we saw in Chapter 3 – MEPs may in future become even more significant players within the EU's policy-making process.

### 5.3.3 The Council of Ministers

So far, the Council has been mentioned quite frequently in this chapter, and we have noted that it has considerable power, but its precise nature has not been spelled out. The Council of the European Union (almost always known as the Council of Ministers) represents the governments of the 27 member states of the EU (for the Council, see Hayes-Renshaw and Wallace, 2006; Lewis, 2010). Although there is in principle only one Council, in practice there are several *formations*. This is because each national seat on the Council is filled not by the same person every time but by the national minister with responsibility for the policy area that is to be discussed. Thus, if a forthcoming meeting of the Council is going to discuss EU transport policy, each government sends its transport minister (or at least a very senior civil servant from the transport ministry) to the meeting; if farm prices are to be discussed, it sends its agriculture minister; and so on. The Council meets in one form or another about 80 times a year, with the foreign ministers meeting more than monthly, the finance and agriculture ministers meeting about once a month, and the others less frequently (Hayes-Renshaw and Wallace, 2006: 38–39, 47–48).

At any given time, one of the member states holds what is termed the *Council presidency* (Hayes-Renshaw and Wallace, 2006: 133–161), and meetings of the Council and its many sub-committees are chaired by either the minister or an official from this country. At the moment, the presidency rotates among the member states in a fixed order that runs up to 2020. *Troikas*, each containing one larger country, are assigned 18-month periods, and one member of the country holds the position for six months. In 2011 the schedule called for Hungary to be followed by Poland, in 2012 Denmark would precede Cyprus, in 2013 Lithuania would follow Ireland, and in 2014 Greece would take the first presidency and Italy the second. The period of each country's presidency is too short to make this a very significant role. It is generally reckoned that the 'lead-in' period for a new policy is about 18 months, so the country holding the presidency can rarely bring any new initiative to fruition; the most it can do is speed up or slow-pedal some of those projects already on the books, and perhaps introduce initiatives that it expects might be carried forward. However, there is a 'modest' benefit in policy terms, as the country holding the presidency when a decision is made has some ability to 'pull decision outcomes toward their favoured policy positions' (Thomson, 2008b: 611–613). In recent years there has been more co-ordination between adjacent presidencies in an attempt to avoid the situation where a new presidency might try to reverse the priorities of the preceding one. Multi-Council programmes are now agreed, setting out policy priorities for periods of two to four years.

When the Commission sends a proposal to the Council, the Council forwards a copy to the Parliament and also begins extensive scrutiny of the proposal itself. The Council has a complex network of around 250 working parties and committees, staffed mainly by senior national civil servants. This process is the first stage at which the acceptability or otherwise of the proposal to the 27 national governments is assessed. Not surprisingly, quite a few proposals are killed off at this stage if the relevant committee finds it impossible to reach an agreement, and explicitly rejects or simply shelves the proposal. The best the Commission can hope for is not unanimous approval from the committee, which is unrealistic to expect, but an agreement to pass the proposal on to the next stage of the decision-making process, subject to some or all of the member states entering specific reservations about it.

From the specialist committee, the proposal goes to a body called COREPER, the Committee of Permanent Representatives, which consists of the heads of the permanent delegations maintained in Brussels by each country. These senior diplomats and their staff iron out as many as possible of the problems identified by the specialist committee and, before Council meetings, they brief the ministers about areas where agreement has and has not been reached. All proposals pass from COREPER to a meeting of the Council itself. When a Council meeting is to take place, the relevant ministers arrive from the respective national capitals, and they usually go home again a day or two later.

When the ministers gather in Brussels, they are likely to be faced with a number of proposals that have come through the Union's policymaking process and perhaps with other decisions as well. In areas where COREPER has reached an agreement, the Council needs merely to give formal ratification to the proposal or decision. If COREPER has proved unable to sort out the problems, the ministers themselves will try to break the deadlock, with horse-trading that may cross policy areas (König and Junge, 2009). It seems that the Franco-German connection is still at the centre of Council decision-making, and these two countries possess the most 'network capital' (Naurin and Lindahl, 2008: 74). However, there are no durable coalitions within the Council, and it is not the case that some countries are consistent winners and others consistent losers (Thomson, 2008c: 257).

The manner of Council decision-making can be important in bolstering its power. The treaties provide two main ways for the Council to make decisions: by unanimity, and by qualified majority voting (QMV). Unanimity is needed when the Council wants to amend a Commission proposal against the wishes of the Commission, on major constitutional questions, and in a handful of policy areas (taxation, defence and immigration issues, for example), but successive treaties have greatly reduced the number of other situations in which it is required. QMV is now the standard method of decision-making. When a decision is reached by qualified majority, each minister wields a number of votes corresponding approximately to his or her country's population, although, as with the allocation of EP seats, while Poland, Romania and Netherlands are reasonably accurately represented, larger countries are markedly under-represented and smaller ones over-represented (see Table 5.4). Disproportionality in the allocation of Council seats among countries is more pronounced than in the distribution of EP seats – the least squares index is 8.3, which is comparable to disproportionality at a Hungarian or Lithuanian election, among the most disproportional in Europe (see Table 11.5). The largest five countries, with 63 per cent of the population, have only 41 per cent of the Council votes, while the smallest 19, with 22 per cent of the population, have 43 per cent of the Council votes. The total number of votes among the 27 ministers is 345, and 255 (74 per cent) of these are needed for a majority. Moreover, the votes in favour need also to represent at least 62 per cent of the EU's population. Under the terms of the Lisbon Treaty, this is due to change slightly in 2014 (see Table 5.4).

**TABLE 5.4** Votes per country in the Council of the European Union when decisions are made by qualified majority

| Country | Population Jan 2010 (thousands) | Council votes | Population per Council vote (thousands) | Council votes entitlement if votes were strictly proportional to population |
|---|---|---|---|---|
| Germany | 81 800 | 29 | 2 821 | 56 |
| France | 64 714 | 29 | 2 232 | 45 |
| United Kingdom | 62 008 | 29 | 2 138 | 43 |
| Italy | 60 340 | 29 | 2 081 | 42 |
| Spain | 45 989 | 27 | 1 703 | 32 |
| Poland | 38 167 | 27 | 1 414 | 26 |
| Romania | 21 462 | 14 | 1 533 | 15 |
| Netherlands | 16 578 | 13 | 1 275 | 11 |
| Greece | 11 295 | 12 | 941 | 8 |
| Belgium | 10 827 | 12 | 902 | 7 |
| Portugal | 10 638 | 12 | 887 | 7 |
| Czech Republic | 10 507 | 12 | 876 | 7 |
| Hungary | 10 013 | 12 | 834 | 7 |
| Sweden | 9 341 | 10 | 934 | 6 |
| Austria | 8 375 | 10 | 838 | 6 |
| Bulgaria | 7 564 | 10 | 756 | 5 |
| Denmark | 5 535 | 7 | 791 | 4 |
| Slovakia | 5 425 | 7 | 775 | 4 |
| Finland | 5 351 | 7 | 764 | 4 |
| Ireland | 4 456 | 7 | 637 | 3 |
| Lithuania | 3 329 | 7 | 476 | 2 |
| Latvia | 2 248 | 4 | 562 | 2 |
| Slovenia | 2 047 | 4 | 512 | 1 |
| Estonia | 1 340 | 4 | 335 | 1 |
| Cyprus | 798 | 4 | 200 | 1 |
| Luxembourg | 502 | 4 | 126 | 0 |
| Malta | 413 | 3 | 138 | 0 |
| EU-27 | 501 062 | 345 | 1 452 | 345 |

*Note*: A majority requires 255 votes, and a blocking minority requires 91. As from 1 November 2014, a qualified majority will require the votes of 15 member states (55 per cent), comprising 65 per cent of the EU's population, and a blocking minority will require four member states.

Proportional allocation in last column made by the Sainte-Laguë method.

*Source for population*: Eurostat news release 111/2010, p. 2.

In the past, the Council preferred to operate on the basis of unanimity so as not to overrule any state that had a strong objection to any proposal. The so-called Luxembourg Compromise (an informal understanding) of 1966 was interpreted for the next 20 years as allowing any state to veto any proposal by claiming that its 'vital national interests' were at stake. The result was a very slow-moving decision-making process until, from the mid 1980s onwards, the use of qualified majority voting was expanded by successive treaties. However, it is true that the Council still prefers to operate on the basis of consensus, and that if a country, or a group of countries, has strong objections to a proposal that has majority support, the majority will try to find a way of accommodating the objections rather than railroad the proposal through. As a result, around three-quarters of decisions that could be taken by QMV are in practice taken by consensus (Hayes-Renshaw *et al.*, 2006: 163). This culture of consensus springs largely from a feeling that, in the long run, imposing policies upon countries that intensely dislike them would not be good for the EU's legitimacy or for the successful implementation of its policies. At the same time, however, the fact that decisions *can* be made by a qualified majority vote – and that they have been made in the past, even in the face of vigorous opposition from one or more states – means that those states in a negative minority also have an incentive to work with the majority on an acceptable compromise, since they can no longer simply rely on a veto. In addition, there is a certain amount of 'log-rolling' – states agree to go along with proposals with which they are not entirely happy in the expectation that other countries will do the same when the roles are reversed.

## 5.3.4 The European Council

The European Council consists of the heads of government of the 27 member states (the foreign ministers, the president of the Commission, and another commissioner also attend European Council meetings). It meets at least four times every year, and these summit meetings attract extensive media coverage. All the major steps forward taken by the EU in recent years have been initiated either by the European Council or by the Commission, and at the very least they have needed the backing of the European Council to get going. The Maastricht Treaty of 1992 gave its central role explicit mention, stating that the 'European Council shall provide the Union with the necessary impetus for its development and shall define the general political guidelines thereof', and this position was confirmed and strengthened by the Amsterdam Treaty. Even so, the authority of the European Council is essentially political rather than legal.

The Lisbon Treaty introduced the new position of *president* of the European Council. The president is chosen by the members of the Council for a term of two and a half years, and chairs its meetings, but does not have a vote there. He or she works alongside the *High Representative of the Union for Foreign Affairs and Security Policy*, a member of the Commission who chairs Council of Ministers meetings when these concern foreign policy. The roles of these two figures are not spelled out in the treaty, and it remains to be seen how significant they will be in relation to other actors. The first incumbents were chosen by the heads of government at their meeting in Brussels in November 2009, and the outcome was widely criticized. The president was to be Herman van Rompuy, the prime minister of Belgium, who was unknown outside his own country, and the High Representative was Catherine Ashton of the UK, unknown even within her own country. The low profile of the selections gave the impression that the heads of government were keen to ensure that the appointees would pose no threat to their dominance, and the behind-closed-doors nature of the appointment process added further to the underwhelming nature of the announcement. However, it was soon apparent that both intended to be policy-shapers rather than peripheral figures in search of a role.

Some advocates of closer European integration regret the rise and central position of the European Council when it comes to major decisions. It seems to confirm the position of the member states and their governments, rather than the Union's collective institutions (the Commission and the Parliament), as the central actors in the EU, and gives the impression that the EU is still more of an intergovernmental organization than a supranational one. On the other hand, it could be argued that the EU would be far less relevant to the member states were it not for the direct interest and involvement of the heads of government in shaping its affairs and, moreover, that if EU initiatives and policies are to make fundamental progress, they need behind them the weight that only the heads of government can supply.

The centrality of the European Council, and the important role of the Council of Ministers in general, raises fundamental questions about democratic accountability within the EU. The Commission is accountable to Parliament (which appointed and can dismiss it), and the Parliament is accountable to the European public through the direct elections held every five years. But to whom are the Council of Ministers and the European Council directly accountable? The short answer is: to no one. It is true that all the heads of government attending a European Council meeting, as well as all the ministers attending a Council meeting, are individually accountable to their own parliament for what they have or have not done at the meeting – although how effective parliaments are in enforcing this accountability is another question (see Chapter 3). In addition, the EP has the power to question national ministers when they hold the rotating presidency of the Council. But neither the Council of Ministers nor the European Council as an institution is answerable or accountable to anyone at all, except that of course both must respect the limits of competence imposed by the treaties and by the Court of Justice. The move away from unanimity to QMV as the basis for decision-making has compounded this. Whereas, when decisions required unanimity, each minister could be asked by his or her national parliament why he or she did not veto a proposal, under QMV no single minister has this power. The lack of accountability of important decision-makers has led to much talk of a 'democratic deficit' within the EU, a subject to which we return below.

### 5.3.5 The Court of Justice

The Court of Justice (the ECJ) is based in Luxembourg and consists of 27 judges, one from each member state, appointed for a six-year term (for the ECJ see Arnull, 2006; Alter, 2009). Unlike the situation in most of Europe's constitutional courts (see Chapter 4), judges' terms are renewable. The fact that each judge is appointed by a government, and is dependent on its support for renomination for a further term, causes some concern about how independent the judges can afford to be. The Court interprets and applies EU law and the Union's constitution. Its decisions are binding on all member states, citizens and legal entities within the Union, and this marks one of the main differences between the EU and other international organizations. Under the *doctrine of direct effect*, EU law confers upon individuals rights that public authorities in the member states must respect (Shapiro and Stone Sweet, 2002: 264). Although a state may refuse to accept a judgment made by another international court (such as the International Court of Justice at The Hague or the European Court of Human Rights at Strasbourg), those states belonging to the EU cannot pick and choose among the judgments of the Court of Justice. Its decisions override those of domestic courts, even though this is not explicitly stated in the treaties, and it has pronounced that EU law takes precedence over national law (the *doctrine of supremacy*).

The Court of Justice is in effect the final court of appeal in the EU; there is no higher authority. In giving its judgments, the Court has not confined itself to the treaties (which are concerned mainly with economic matters); it has also looked for inspiration to the constitutions of the member states and to the European Convention on Human Rights. It has taken a creative rather than a positivist approach to its role – that is, it has supplied interpretations to fill gaps in the Union's legislation, and has cited its own case law rather than feeling confined strictly to the letter of the treaties. Based in particular on its activism in the 1960s and 1970s, it has been described as a critical 'motor of integration', and one writer declares that 'no other court ... has ever played so prominent a role in the creation of the basic governmental and political process of which it is a part' (Martin Shapiro, quoted in Kenney, 1999: 145). Judicial activism can be expected to be high when political actors cannot easily constrain a court, and the difficulty of changing the EU's treaties in order to overcome some interpretation put on these by the ECJ, something that needs the approval of every member state and of the EP, thus provides an encouraging environment for members of the ECJ (Dyevre, 2010: 304–310). Examination of the debates in the UK prior to the country's entry shows that MPs there were completely unaware of how much power the ECJ had, and this is one reason for the mistrust shown by many British politicians towards the EU ever since the country became a member (Nicol, 2001). The power of the ECJ is welcomed by those who view it as a neutral referee in the EU system, but others see it as an actor in its own right. It undoubtedly possesses political antennae, and one (contentious) analysis of its judgments suggests that these may be influenced by the preferences of member state governments (Carrubba *et al.*, 2008). The explanation would be that, like domestic constitutional courts (see Chapter 4), it tacitly accepts limits to the scope of the decisions it can make, since a decision that caused resentment among member state governments might lead to disobedience and to a diminution of its authority. Its growing role is also perceived by some as unhealthy because 'legal avenues tend to be exploited disproportionately by corporate bodies', and the ECJ is accused of 'fuelling a more Americanized and adversarial legal culture, which favours those with deep pockets over the resource-poor, compensatory over redistributive justice, and individual over collective benefits' (Bellamy, 2010: 14).

One of the ECJ's functions is to determine the constitutionality of EU laws. It is thus comparable to the constitutional courts that we discussed in the previous chapter. Domestic courts frequently refer cases to the ECJ if a question of the interpretation of Union law is involved. In addition, governments may be taken before the Court for failing to meet their obligations. As a result of such cases, the Court has stated, to give a few examples, that it is not permissible for a member state to fund advertising campaigns designed to promote domestic products; to discriminate against workers – with regard to employment, pay, or other conditions of work or employment – on the basis of nationality; to operate pension schemes with different retirement ages for men and women; or to conduct excessive checking or inspection of imported goods. The growing recourse to the Court has created problems by greatly increasing its workload. In 1989 a *Court of First Instance* (renamed the *General Court* by the Lisbon Treaty) was introduced to share the load and speed up the process of justice, although it still takes around two years on average from the lodgement of a case with the Court for a decision to emerge, partly because of the need to translate every document into each of the 23 languages used in the EU (Nugent, 2010: 218).

As we mentioned, the ECJ is not formally stated in any treaty to be superior to domestic courts, and the relationship between the two is imprecise. After some initial difficulties, the ECJ sought actively to increase its power. It persuaded national courts to defer to it by employing various strategies that took account, for example, of the short-term horizons of political actors, and through a realization on the part of national courts that the growing power of the ECJ would enhance their own power *vis-à-vis* national parliaments and governments (Tallberg, 2003; Stone Sweet, 2004; Alter, 2009). Once national courts started referring cases to it on a large scale, its impact was greatly increased, since, even if governments were prepared to ignore ECJ jurisprudence, 'ignoring their own courts was a different matter entirely' (Alter, 2001: 219). However, the ECJ's position at the top of the European juridical hierarchy is not necessarily secure. Domestic courts, especially constitutional courts, have expressed concern when it seems to them that an EU law or treaty conflicts with the rights guaranteed by the country's constitution, and the judgment of the German Constitutional Court in a challenge to the Maastricht Treaty was anything but deferential towards the ECJ. In its judgment it affirmed that it would treat as invalid any EU action that it regarded as going beyond the EU's authority (Kokott, 1998: 98–107; Stone Sweet, 2000: 174–178).

The key question has often been one of who decides how far the EU's competence runs, a debate known in legal circles by the German term *Kompetenz-Kompetenz*: who has the competence to decide who has the competence? If the EU makes a decision or rule that some argue goes beyond its allotted sphere, who has the right to decide whether it has, or has not, exceeded its authority? In the eyes of the ECJ, the ECJ itself has this right; in the eyes of many constitutional courts, they do, or at least they reserve their position on the question (Stone Sweet, 2004: 91; Arnull 2006: 255–261). Thus it has been argued that the ECJ 'has not established a psychic hegemony over the supreme national courts', which still give the impression that 'they are making a graceful concession when they follow the line laid down by the Court in a particular matter', while Weiler refers to 'a certain credibility issue' given 'troubling' or 'defiant' decisions by courts in Germany, Italy, Denmark, Belgium and Spain in recent years (Allott, 2003: 216–217; Weiler, 2001: 220–221). A number of post-communist constitutions, too, declare explicitly that the constitution is the highest legal source in the land (Albi, 2005: 171–175). National courts may avoid referring cases to the ECJ by declaring, justifiably or otherwise, that the issue is self-evident, or has already been decided by the Court (Raworth, 2001: 137).

Even though, as we have seen, the ECJ is alleged to pay some attention to the views of governments when reaching its judgments, governments are not always compliant with these. They may feel that defiance could lead to a change in the law under which they have been censured, or that the political cost of compliance would be too great, or that by the time the appeal process is exhausted another government will be in office (Alter, 2001: 228). The Court of Justice, unlike domestic courts, has no police force or army to enforce its judgments. Until November 1993, when the Maastricht Treaty came into operation, it did not possess any formal sanctions for use against non-compliers. Since that date it has been able to impose fines on member states for such disobedience, or for failing to implement Union laws. For example, in July 2009 Greece was fined €2 million plus a daily penalty of €16 000 for failing to abide fully by a previous ECJ order to recover state aid given illegally to the state-owned airline (Nugent, 2010: 220). The Court must rely on the law enforcement agencies of the member states and, hence, ultimately on their governments to enforce compliance. In general, it is true, 'the declaratory judgment is its own sanction', and states usually seek to avoid a judgment against them (Freestone and Davidson,

1988: 152). However, this does not always apply, and the Court sometimes experiences great difficulty in trying to secure implementation of its judgments.

In such cases it is confronted not by explicit refusal to comply with a Court judgment but by delaying tactics: states receiving an adverse judgment from the Court sometimes respond by saying that they will need time to consider the full implications of the verdict, a process that in some cases has apparently required several years. Moreover, certain governments seem to be little put out by receiving judgments against them, something we discuss in greater detail later when we look at implementation.

## 5.4  What does the European Union do?

As time has passed, the range of policy areas in which the EU shows an interest has steadily increased. In recent years the emphasis has been on establishing a single market and a single currency across the Union. In addition, in an attempt to give the EU a human face and to moderate some of the effects of giving market forces fairly free rein, members of the Union have set about creating a 'People's Europe' or a 'Social Europe'. In terms of where the EU's money is spent, the main policy area remains agriculture.

### 5.4.1  Single market and single currency

For many years a prominent concern of the Union was the completion of the single internal market. The aim of creating a common European market features strongly in the EEC Treaty of 1957. A common market would mean that goods and services could be marketed and sold with equal ease all across the Union; there would be no barriers to trade within the Union. Real political will was put behind this goal from the mid 1980s onward, and the task of completing the single market was largely completed by 1992. Beyond the single market lies the possibility of a single economy. Economic and monetary union (EMU) is another long-standing goal of European integrationists, and a decisive step was taken in the late 1990s with the establishment of a common European currency, termed the *euro* (the name was another common denominator choice, since virtually every other possibility had some national overtones). To date 17 countries have joined the single currency (see Table 5.1), which is also the currency of some non-members of the EU, notably Kosovo and Montenegro. Members are obliged to join it once they meet the prescribed conditions, but Denmark and the UK have secured the right to opt out, while Sweden is unlikely to join any time soon, its people having voted against the idea in a referendum in September 2003 (Hodson, 2010: 165).

The currency was established under the terms of a *Stability and Growth Pact* (SGP), under whose terms member states are obliged to keep their budget deficits within certain limits, and interest rates are set by the European Central Bank. Doubts were expressed about the project from the start, as it represented an attempt to establish monetary union without economic union, given that the economies of the participating countries are diverse, with a range of economic cycles (Dyson, 2008: 6–9). In addition, Belgium and Italy were admitted even though they did not meet the criteria (they were deemed to be 'heading in the right direction'), and although Greece appeared to meet the criteria, it later transpired that this was only because it had managed to conceal from the EU the full extent of its heavy foreign borrowing. Moreover, enforcement of the rules depends in the first instance upon the other governments taking the initiative in imposing discipline against the offending government, and questions were asked about how likely it was that governments would punish each other, especially given the likelihood that ministers would want to retain each other's goodwill for possible deals in other policy areas. The fears of the doubters were realized in November 2003, when a meeting of EU finance ministers refrained from acting against France and Germany, whose budget deficits were in excess of the permitted level (3 per cent of GDP), despite the protests of the Commission, some member states and the European Central Bank, which warned that the decision undermined the credibility of the currency (Hodson, 2010: 172–173). When the economic crisis became apparent at the end of the 2000s, a number of countries – most notably the so-called PIIGS countries, namely Portugal, Ireland, Italy, Greece and Spain – ran budget deficits way in excess of those permitted under the terms of the SGP, but they were not penalized for doing so because, in the view of the Commission, they really had no alternative in the short term.

### 5.4.2 A people's Europe

There are nowadays very few policy spheres in which the EU is not concerned, at least to some degree. The EU has the aim, even if this is not precisely expressed in any of the treaties, of bringing about an equality of civil and social rights, of living and working conditions, of opportunities, and of income across the Union; this goal is sometimes characterized as building a 'Social Europe' or a 'People's Europe'. To this end it has tended to get involved in virtually all policy areas, including some not enumerated in the founding treaties. It has issued legal instruments covering such diverse subjects as the purity of tap water to which citizens are entitled, the length of time truck drivers can drive without a break, the safety and cleanliness of the sea at bathing beaches, the extent to which countries can reserve their coastal waters for the exclusive use of their own fishing fleets, equal pay for men and women, the rights of consumers, and aid for the Third World.

In addition, the Union has the aim of reducing the significant disparities in wealth that exist within its boundaries, both between and within countries; this is known as *cohesion policy*. Ever since the 1973 expansion there have been large wealth differences among regions, with concern that the moves towards a single market might be of most benefit to a 'golden triangle' covering the south-eastern part of England, parts of France and northern Italy, together with most of western Germany and the Benelux countries, with the rest of the Union becoming ever more peripheral.

Table 5.5 shows the degree of variation between the member states, with GDP per capita in Luxembourg over 15 times the corresponding figure for Bulgaria. The table shows that the budget has some redistributive effect, in that each of the poorest 11 countries receives more from the EU budget than they give to it. The main beneficiary per capita by a long way is Greece. In contrast, the three largest contributors – Germany, France and Italy – contributed half of the revenue in 2008 but received only 34 per cent of the expenditure. To try to even out the fruits of economic growth, the EU has set up a number of 'structural' funds, the most important of which are known as the *Regional Development Fund* and the *Social Fund*, to attempt to promote development in the less wealthy parts of the Union. Under these headings the Union funds schemes to give job training to the unemployed throughout the EU, and to combat unemployment in the peripheral regions. The size of these funds increased greatly in the 1990s, and, at least partly in consequence, wealth per capita in what were then the poorer countries made notable strides towards the EU average.

**TABLE 5.5** Gross domestic product of EU member states, and contributions to and receipts from the 2008 budget

| | Gross domestic product in 2008 per capita ($) | Share of 2008 EU budget revenues contributed (%) | Share of 2008 EU budget expenditure received (%) | Net gain/ loss as % of EU budget | Net gain/ loss per capita (€) |
|---|---|---|---|---|---|
| Luxembourg | 95 700 | 0.2 | 1.3 | 1.1 | 2291.6 |
| Denmark | 56 700 | 2.1 | 1.5 | −0.6 | −134.4 |
| Ireland | 54 600 | 1.4 | 2.0 | 0.5 | 106.6 |
| Netherlands | 47 800 | 6.0 | 2.2 | −3.8 | −265.5 |
| Austria | 46 100 | 2.0 | 1.7 | −0.3 | −49.8 |
| Finland | 45 400 | 1.5 | 1.3 | −0.3 | −72.6 |
| Belgium | 44 800 | 4.2 | 5.8 | 1.7 | 136.4 |
| Sweden | 44 400 | 2.9 | 1.4 | −1.5 | −188.3 |
| France | 41 600 | 16.2 | 13.1 | −3.1 | −66.6 |
| Germany | 39 800 | 20.0 | 10.7 | −9.3 | −134.7 |
| Italy | 36 400 | 13.6 | 9.8 | −3.8 | −80.2 |
| United Kingdom | 36 400 | 9.1 | 7.0 | −2.1 | −45.2 |
| Spain | 36 200 | 9.0 | 11.5 | 2.6 | 46.3 |
| Greece | 31 900 | 2.1 | 8.1 | 6.0 | 547.7 |
| Slovenia | 25 000 | 0.4 | 0.4 | 0.1 | 23.4 |
| Cyprus | 21 700 | 0.2 | 0.1 | 0.0 | −62.4 |
| Portugal | 20 800 | 1.3 | 3.9 | 2.6 | 249.2 |
| Malta | 19 300 | 0.1 | 0.1 | 0.0 | 66.1 |
| Czech Republic | 18 800 | 1.3 | 2.3 | 1.1 | 99.5 |
| Slovakia | 16 400 | 0.5 | 1.2 | 0.6 | 119.2 |
| Estonia | 14 100 | 0.1 | 0.4 | 0.2 | 154.6 |
| Hungary | 12 700 | 0.9 | 1.9 | 1.1 | 105.4 |
| Poland | 11 100 | 3.1 | 7.3 | 4.2 | 109.2 |
| Latvia | 11 000 | 0.2 | 0.6 | 0.4 | 175.6 |
| Lithuania | 10 200 | 0.3 | 1.1 | 0.8 | 241.9 |
| Romania | 7 300 | 1.1 | 2.5 | 1.4 | 67.5 |
| Bulgaria | 6 300 | 0.3 | 0.9 | 0.6 | 80.4 |
| Total/average EU | 31 574 | 100.0 | 100.0 | 0.0 | −12.6 |

*Note*: Countries are ranked in order of per capita gross domestic product. Receipts for Luxembourg and, to a lesser extent, Belgium are distorted by the amount these countries are deemed to receive as a result of hosting EU institutions; 'administration' accounts for 83 per cent of Luxembourg's receipts and 64 per cent of Belgium's, compared with 6 per cent for the EU as a whole, and these two countries receive 78 per cent of total 'administration' expenditure. Excluding this expenditure, Luxembourg's share of expenditure drops to 0.2 per cent (net loss of €50.6 per capita) and Belgium's drops to 2.3 per cent (net loss of €222 per capita), with other countries' figures little affected.

*Sources*: GDP per capita – as Table 1.2; share of EU budget expenditure and revenue 2008: European Commission, *EU Budget 2008: Financial Report* (Publications Office of the EU, Luxembourg, 2009), p. 105; available at http://ec.europa.eu/budget/documents/2010_en.htm.

As to the substance of EU policies, some could be seen as basically left-wing and others as basically right-wing; indeed, the EU comes under attack from both the left and the right. Its strong drive towards the single market and deregulation since the late 1980s, with its insistence on privatization of industries such as telecommunications, have all promoted private enterprise and free trade, and have therefore been pleasing to right-wing parties around Europe, leading to the suggestion that 'the social face of Europe is slowly being replaced with a neo-liberal smile' (Chari and Kritzinger, 2006: 223). On the other hand, it also adopts a very interventionist approach to agriculture, and is active in defending the social rights of sections of society who suffer discrimination of one sort or another, such as women, migrant workers, and workers in general. Its policies to promote gender equality have had particular impact in countries where women have traditionally encountered discrimination. The growing steps towards a single EU economy will make it difficult for any country to pursue policies that drift very far to the right or the left of the consensus, a consensus sometimes termed the 'European social market' or 'neo-liberalism meets the social market' (Hix, 2005: 269–270).

This may be a concern for some governments, although, on the other hand, the claim that 'the EU made us do it' (or 'the EU stopped us from doing it') can be a useful excuse for a government secretly relieved at the chance to wriggle out of election promises they regret having made (Smith, 2000). As this phrase implies, the EU is frequently seen as constraining government policies so tightly that the state is being 'hollowed out', with governments having few real choices to make any more, so political parties cannot credibly promise policies that differ much from the status quo, and political competition becomes 'depoliticized' (Mair, 2007: 163). The result, says Schmidt, is 'politics without policies' at national level, at least in those areas where the EU now makes the decisions, while the EU, because it is not controlled by political parties elected with a mandate, consists of 'policies without politics' (Schmidt, 2006: 223).

In addition, it might be mentioned, the EU's method of making decisions is seen as having centralizing effects within member states (for 'Europeanization' generally see Börzel and Panke, 2010; Ladrech, 2010). It leads to the strengthening of party leaderships *vis-à-vis* party members, and of governments *vis-à-vis* parliaments (Holzhacker, 2007; Carter and Poguntke, 2010). Within governments, it is perceived to lead to power being ever more concentrated in the hands of the prime minister, given the centrality of the European Council in the EU's policy-making process, and in federal systems it strengthens central government at the expense of regional actors (Börzel and Sprungk, 2007). We discuss these matters in more depth in Chapters 2, 3, 10 and 13.

In order to make the EU clearly and directly relevant to its citizens, and to justify the claim that a 'People's Europe' is being constructed, the Union has attempted to create symbols with which Europeans can identify. The EU has its own flag, consisting of 12 gold stars arranged in a circle on a blue background, which can be seen flying from many public buildings across the Union alongside the appropriate national flag, as well as its own anthem (the prelude to Beethoven's 'Ode to Joy'). The passports of all EU countries are now issued in a uniform size and colour, and travellers from one EU country do not have to pass through customs when they visit another. Those living in the 22 countries covered by the Schengen agreements (Bulgaria, Cyprus, Ireland, Romania and the UK are the five countries outside the scheme) do not even pass through a border control when crossing an internal EU frontier. Even if today's Europeans, especially the young ones, are not impressed by the mantra that the EU helps prevent another Franco-German war, since they take peace for granted, they may be enthused by the freedom to take holidays around Europe without having to change currency at the bank or undergo passport checks at every border.

### 5.4.3 Agriculture

In the past, agriculture has not only accounted for the bulk of the EU's budget but has also been one of the areas in which it has been hardest to find agreement. In recent years, though, it has slipped down the political agenda, yet, through the Common Agricultural Policy (CAP), it still consumes a massive amount of the Union's expenditure. Although the proportion of the Union's labour force working in agriculture has fallen from over 25 per cent in the late 1950s to around 9 per cent, the share of Union spending going to agriculture has consistently been far in excess of this: having exceeded 60 per cent in nearly all budgets of the 1970s and 1980s, it fell to around 50 per cent in the 1990s and is now around 40 per cent.

The CAP was designed to guarantee both farm incomes and an adequate supply of food in a Europe haunted by memories of food shortages, but by the 1970s it had become notorious for resulting in massive surpluses, termed *mountains* or *lakes* as appropriate, of food products – especially beef, butter and wine – that could not be sold on the world market because they were so expensive. Farmers had no complaints about this, but elsewhere it was regarded as 'a monument to economic irrationality' (Roederer-Rynning, 2010: 182). EU consumers had to pay well above the market price for their food, while producers in the developing world found themselves unable to gain access to the highly protected EU market and, moreover, faced in their own countries with EU surpluses dumped at artificially low prices. Over time, the costs and contradictions of the CAP became increasingly unsustainable. Domestically, the Union could not afford to support this one sector at such cost, while pressure internationally from the Union's trading partners and from the World Trade Organization made reform a priority.

This took the form of decoupling farmers' income support from their production. In other words, instead of receiving inflated prices for their production, farmers now receive a direct income supplement (based on an average of their previous years' income) and are then free to produce whatever they wish for the open market without price supports. Even so, the CAP remains a very expensive feature of the EU's operations, defended by an 'iron triangle' of farmers' interest groups, national ministries of agriculture, and agricultural officials in the Commission. From 2004 onwards the member states have been obliged to publish details of who receives the money, and it emerged that the biggest recipients were agri-businesses and the wealthiest farmers, the details raising eyebrows in several countries (Fouilleux, 2010: 353). In national terms the CAP is embraced especially by France (Knapp and Wright, 2006: 453–459), Ireland and southern European countries, with Britain, the Netherlands and Scandinavian countries most opposed to continuing it at present levels. Further reform of the CAP, in order to reduce the payments given to farmers so as to free up funds to benefit EU citizens more generally, is widely agreed to be desirable, but in every country, and at EU level, farmers' interest groups are powerful, and governments of all political complexions are reluctant to alienate such a well-organized lobby, as we discuss further in Chapter 13. Of course, farmers are able to obtain such special treatment in other polities too, such as the USA. The result is that money that many feel should be used to train the youth of the EU to take advantage of growth areas such as information technology is instead being channelled into a declining if vital business, creating 'a mismatch between the expenditure priorities of the EU budget and key policy priorities facing Europe' (Laffan and Lindner, 2010: 227).

## BOX 5.1: THE EUROPEAN UNION

### Denmark

Denmark joined the EU in 1973, as part of the first enlargement, along with Ireland and the UK. It held a referendum on the matter in 1972, and 63 per cent voted Yes. Danes are strongly attached to the country's democratic system and wary of any threat to it, so Denmark is one of the countries most resistant to deeper European integration. Its people voted No to the Maastricht Treaty in 1992, as a result of which its government negotiated some special opt-outs at an EU summit in Scotland, and the revised 'Edinburgh Agreement' was approved by Danish voters in a referendum the following year. One aspect of this is that Denmark is not obliged to join the single currency, the euro. As in many countries, the elite is much more integrationist than the population as a whole, and most politicians felt that the Danish opt-outs were and are not in Denmark's interests. There was near all-party agreement at elite level that it would be desirable for Denmark to join the euro, and so a referendum on this was held in September 2000, only for the people to reject the idea by a 53–47 margin. Nevertheless, the Danish krone in practice tracks the value of the euro very closely.

### France

France was one of the six original members of the EEC in 1958. Under General de Gaulle (president from 1958 to 1969), France opposed the admission of Britain, but de Gaulle's attitude towards the EU was not too different from that displayed by certain British governments after 1973. De Gaulle was in favour of the economic benefits that the Union brought, but was very suspicious of any steps that might dilute the traditional sovereignty of the state. Since his departure from office, France has been more willing to contemplate closer integration among the member states, but despite the rhetoric of some of its leading politicians, it is not generally seen as being at the forefront of the integrationists. France has consistently been a strong defender of the Common Agricultural Policy (CAP), from which its agriculture sector benefits greatly. France was accustomed to playing a leading role in the EU, often in combination with Germany, but a number of developments have turned it into more of a reluctant 'downloader' of EU policies than a driving force in the Union: the incorporation of 10 new members in 2004, none of them a traditional ally of France, posed a threat to French centrality in the EU, and indeed English overtook French as the most widely used language in the EU in 1998; hostility to the amount of EU expenditure that goes to the CAP continues to mount around the EU; and the trend of EU economic policy since the early 1990s, favouring competition and deregulation, is perceived domestically as a threat to the French social model. On the plus side, the EU provides an opportunity for France to exert foreign policy influence on a worldwide stage.

### Germany

For Germany, one of the six founders, membership of the EU offered the prospect both of economic gains and of political rehabilitation after the Second World War. As the member state with the largest economy in the Union, Germany has picked up the biggest share of the bill for funding the EU. In the past, most Germans were willing to see this as a price worth paying, even in pure economic terms, for securing access to the huge EU market for their efficient industries, but in recent years there have been signs of a feeling that their country is asked to shoulder an unfairly large proportion of the contributions to the EU's budget. When the single currency was established in 1999, concern was expressed in Germany that too many countries, including some that had not shown convincingly that they were capable of adhering to disciplined economic policies, were being admitted to the scheme. Ironically, Germany soon became one of the first countries to flout the financial discipline that membership of the Eurozone was supposed to impose. Its misdemeanours turned out to be minor, though, compared with the profligacy of Greece in particular, and by the start of the 2010s many Germans lamented the disappearance of the Deutschmark.

## Italy

Italy was one of the founders of the EU, which has brought significant economic benefits to the country, although its wealth is concentrated heavily in the northern half of the country. Italy has a less than glorious record when it comes to implementing Union law and complying with judgments of the Court of Justice. Despite its size, Italy has generally been content to allow other countries, particularly France and Germany, to take the lead in shaping the future direction of the Union. When the single currency scheme was launched in the late 1990s, it was widely assumed that Italy would be unable to meet the conditions for entry; several years of atypically austere budgets enabled the country to (just) meet the entry terms, but the country soon reverted to its traditionally relaxed attitude to budgetary discipline. Among both politicians and the public, enthusiasm for moves towards a federal Europe is high, perhaps because of despair at the quality of domestic governance.

## Netherlands

The Netherlands was one of the founding members of the EU, but as a small country it has accepted that its impact on decisions will be relatively marginal. Attitudes towards the EU in general, as well as specific attitudes towards closer integration, have generally been broadly favourable. Unlike the governments of some other small countries, which fear that a supranational EU government would lead to their interests being overlooked in favour of the larger countries, Dutch governments believe that such supranational bodies, by making decisions in the broader European interest, are more likely to benefit them than a purely intergovernmental arrangement would. The Netherlands was one of the few countries to favour censuring France and Germany for breaching the rules on the size of budget deficits in 2003. Notwithstanding the strongly pro-European sentiment of the Dutch people, voters delivered a 'Nee' in June 2005 in a referendum on the proposed EU constitution, mainly because of a perceived threat posed to Dutch culture by greater integration. The Netherlands' position as a significant net contributor to the EU budget has also contributed to the cooling of enthusiasm for greater integration.

## Poland

Poland is by far the largest of the 10 countries that became members of the EU on 1 May 2004. After 40 years of Soviet-imposed communism the Poles see EU membership as a way to reclaim their historic place at the heart of Europe. With a population of nearly 40 million, Poland accounted for over half of the newcomers' population and 41 per cent of their total GDP. The Europe Agreement was signed in 1991, and Poland applied for EU membership in April 1994. The accession negotiations began in 1998 and were concluded in 2002. During this period important institutional adjustments took place in Poland, driven by EU accession criteria. Poland did a remarkable job getting ready for entry to the EU, with strong economic growth driven by the weak złoty and steep rises in productivity. Poland is the second largest net beneficiary from the EU budget, although, like the Baltic states in particular, it has suffered in that labour market freedom has meant that many of its best-educated and highly skilled young people have moved to western Europe, where wages are

▶ BOX 5.1: CONTINUED

much higher. The accession referendum was passed by a margin greater than 3–1, and since 2004 public support for EU membership has remained high, with overwhelmingly positive assessments of the benefits for the country.

## Spain

Soon after the first democratic election in 40 years was held in 1977, Spain applied for membership of the EU and, after protracted negotiations, it joined on 1 January 1986. The potential economic benefits of membership were a powerful incentive, but just as important were the political implications. Under the long rule of the dictator Franco, Spain had been isolated from west European political thought and developments, even though its economy had grown rapidly, and joining the EU was an ideal opportunity to join the mainstream rather than remain on the fringe. In addition, it was felt that the risk of a military coup by far-rightists attempting to restore a quasi-Francoist dictatorship would be greatly reduced if the country was part of (and was benefiting economically from its membership of) a community committed to the preservation of liberal-democratic values. Spain is one of the more integrationist of the member states, and favours an expansion of the role of the European Parliament. Until the 2004 expansion it was the largest net beneficiary from the EU budget. In a February 2005 referendum Spanish voters endorsed the proposed European constitution by a large margin (over 4 to 1), but on a turnout of little more than 40 per cent. The status of some of Spain's regions, especially Catalunya, has been enhanced by the EU's regional policy, which gives subnational units direct access to EU policymakers.

## United Kingdom

Britain did not hold a referendum on joining the EU in 1973, but in 1975, after some 'renegotiation' of the entry terms, it held one on whether to withdraw, and the people voted 2–1 to remain in the EU. However, Britain was sometimes perceived as having, psychologically at least, one foot inside the EU and one still outside. Under Margaret Thatcher and John Major, its minimalist attitude towards such aspects of European integration as a common currency and guaranteed protection for the rights of workers across the Union irritated many other members in the 1980s and 1990s. Mrs Thatcher succeeded in 1984 in securing a special British 'rebate', amounting to over €6 billion in 2008, to rectify the perceived injustice whereby as one of the less wealthy countries it was a huge net contributor to the budget. Although other countries would like to see this brought to an end, Britain is unlikely to concede the point without significant reform to the highly expensive Common Agricultural Policy, from which it benefits little. After 1997, when Tony Blair entered power, Britain's rhetoric changed greatly, but Blair too had to pay due heed to the strength of Euro-scepticism among the British public and in the popular media, which portray EU membership as 'rule by Brussels' and run frequent stories, often exaggerated or downright false, about the bizarre ideas that 'Brussels bureaucrats' are trying to impose on the British people. The question of relationships with Europe is a major and contentious issue in British politics; it divides each of the two main parties, and has led to the rise of an anti-EU party, UKIP (the UK Independence Party), which won 13 seats at the 2009 EP elections. The return of the Conservatives to power in 2010 has moved the British government back towards a more Euro-sceptic position, and there is no prospect that the UK will join the Eurozone. If the proposed EU constitution had not been scrapped after its referendum defeats in France and the Netherlands in 2005, Britain would have held a referendum on the subject itself, and the constitution's chances of being approved would have been comparable to those of a snowball's life expectancy in hell.

## 5.5 The European Union: intergovernmental or supranational organization?

The EU contains elements of two kinds of polity. One is the intergovernmental organization, in which the governments of sovereign member states co-operate without giving up the ultimate right to make their own decisions. The second is the supranational body, in which the ultimate power rests with the common institutions, and the national governments have room to manoeuvre only within the framework of policy decided at the collective level. Developments such as the increasing power of the European Parliament and the introduction of a common currency suggest that the EU may be moving in the direction of a supranational organization, but, at the same time, the EU still seems to bear many of the characteristics of an intergovernmental organization. We can see the continuing relevance of the intergovernmental model when we examine three aspects of the EU: the relative powers of the main institutions, the implementation of policy, and the financing of the EU.

As we have seen, of the three main political bodies in the EU, one (the Council) is essentially intergovernmental whereas the other two (the Commission and the Parliament) are essentially supranational. Over time the supranational institutions have grown stronger, but not to the extent that many observers would describe the EU itself as basically supranational. Over 20 years ago, the then Commission president Jacques Delors predicted that before long 80 per cent of economic, and perhaps social and fiscal, policymaking in the EU would flow from Brussels. This has not happened, with best estimates putting the figure anywhere between 10 and 40 per cent (Raunio, 2009: 326). The answer to the question attributed (no doubt apocryphally) to Henry Kissinger in the 1970s, 'If I want to talk to the EU, what telephone number do I ring?', remains unclear. His successor now has several options. She could ring the Commission president, the Council president, or the High Representative – but she would probably have serious doubts about how far any of these actors is really in a position to commit the German, French, British or other governments, and might well decide simply to call Berlin, Paris, London, Warsaw and other capitals (Shapiro and Witney, 2009: 27). One attempt to quantify the relative weights of the EU's actors prior to the Lisbon Treaty concluded that these vary according to the precise rules applying in different policy areas, but that, on the whole, both the Commission and the EP had less than a third of the power of the Council, with the Commission and the EP each having a 'power score' roughly equal to that of two or three large member states (Thomson and Hosli, 2006: 412–414). While numerical precision is difficult to reach, the centrality of the European Council, i.e. the 27 heads of government, is not in dispute. If the European Council wants something to happen, it will almost certainly happen; if the European Council does not want something to happen, it will certainly not happen. In this sense, the EU is still predominantly an intergovernmental organization.

Turning to implementation, how fully EU legislation is implemented across the EU is unknown, in the absence of detailed study. It is generally believed that implementation is far from uniform or perfect, and *implementation deficit* is a widely used phrase. We can distinguish two aspects of this: the transposition of directives, and the enforcement of laws. Regarding the first, most of the laws passed by the EU are called *directives*. These stipulate the end to be achieved and a time-frame for achieving it, but permit each member state to decide exactly how that is to be done. Thus researchers have examined patterns in prompt transposition, tardy transposition or non-transposition of directives into domestic law to build a picture of compliance or non-compliance. Second, once EU laws are in place, states might or might not enforce these, and again we can look for variations in national records.

One influential study of the transposition of directives identified three – later, four – ideal-type *worlds of compliance*, at least in certain fields (Falkner and Treib, 2008). In the *world of law observance*, directives are routinely transposed into law on time, and the resulting laws are enforced; Denmark, Finland and Sweden are in this category. In the *world of domestic politics*, compliance is only one goal among many; if there are no domestic concerns, transposition is timely and unproblematic, but if there are political or interest group objections, non-compliance is likely, although once the law is finally promulgated it is enforced. Austria, Belgium, Germany, the Netherlands, Spain and the UK belong to this 'world'. In the *world of transposition neglect*, administrative inefficiency or political lack of interest means that there is usually no activity until the EU exerts heavy pressure, and once the law is in place it may or not be enforced; France, Greece, Luxembourg and Portugal belong here. Finally, in the *world of dead letters*, directives may well be transposed swiftly, but the resulting laws are not enforced; what is on the statute books does not become effective in practice. Italy and Ireland are given as examples, along with the Czech Republic, Hungary, Slovakia and Slovenia, and probably other post-communist countries as well. The same comment has been made about Cyprus (Sepos, 2008: 55).

While other researchers find this 'an interesting idea', it has been criticized for a lack of clarity as to the causal mechanism distinguishing between the types, and the absence of variation among the 'world of domestic politics' countries, where support or opposition would be expected to vary according to the line-up of forces on each issue, also casts doubt on it (Toshkov, 2007: 951, 948). Thomson re-examines the data of Falkner *et al.* and questions the analytic value of the 'worlds of compliance' framework, finding that differences among member states explain little about the transposition of directives. The key factor, he concludes, is simply the extent of policy 'misfit': when the directive conflicts with existing national policy, there will be delay, and where it does not conflict, there won't be (Thomson, 2009; also Thomson *et al.*, 2007).

As well as policy misfit, administrative incompatibility can cause problems. Even if a state is willing to transpose a directive, doing so might prove time-consuming or complicated. Civil servants attempting to do this, or to implement EU legislation, sometimes find themselves unable, because of its vagueness or ambiguity, to understand what obligation it imposes or what action it requires, and the Commission is seen as prone to supply unsatisfactory or tardy answers to questions seeking clarification (Bekkers *et al.*, 1998: 467–468). The structure of national administration may not be conducive to the implementation of EU policy. In the Netherlands, for example, some items of legislation require action from more than one government department, and different departments are accustomed to using different methods of issuing regulations, leading to deadlock or confusion. Matters might be improved if one department was in charge of overall co-ordination, but in fact three different departments are competing for this role, and none possesses the authority to impose itself (Bekkers *et al.*, 1998: 474–475).

When it comes to the implementation of laws, there is widespread suspicion that at least some member states make only token efforts to secure the enforcement of EU decisions about which they happen not to feel strongly, or which they never really supported in the first place. A government that 'loses' in the policymaking stage of the process might not be too concerned, because it knows that when it comes to the second stage, implementation, it will determine what really happens in the country (Hans Samsem, quoted in Demmke and Unfried, 2001: 123). Should such states wish to behave like this, they have many strategies short of outright disobedience, such as lack of implementation, lack of enforcement, lack of application, evasion, non-compliance by the legislature, executive or judiciary, and benign non-compliance (Snyder, 1995: 56). The Common Fisheries Policy, for example, has been something of a disaster, resulting in serious depletion of fish stocks, because a number of governments – such as those of Belgium, France, Portugal and Spain – lack the resources or the will (or both) to implement its restrictions fully and effectively (Lequesne, 2000: 361). Similarly, in the field of environmental law, 'ineffective application and enforcement remains a problem' (Demmke and Unfried, 2001: 81). The introduction of fines, as we mentioned earlier, has given states a strong incentive to be more compliant these days, but these really apply only in cases of outright refusal to obey the rules, as opposed to more subtle methods of evasion.

Table 5.6, which shows the position at the end of 2009, reveals that there is significant national variation in compliance, especially when we take account of the length of time a country has belonged to the EU. The Scandinavian countries – ironically, some of the most Euro-sceptic countries – have good records (Sverdrup, 2004), as do the Netherlands and the UK, while southern European countries, especially Greece and Italy, are least obedient. Generally speaking, the national governments concerned do not take such an indulgent attitude to the enforcement of judgments given by their own domestic courts, although it is probably true to say that the degrees of rigour with which domestic laws and EU laws are enforced in each country are strongly correlated.

One aspect of implementation concerns the question of whether money is spent in the way intended. Undoubtedly, some of it is not. With around 400 000 individual authorizations of payments each year, the convoluted nature of many schemes, especially those involved in the CAP and the cohesion programmes, provide plenty of opportunity for fraud. Best guesses are that anything from 7 per cent to 10 per cent of the EU's budget is used fraudulently, and agricultural products feature prominently in accounts of fraud (Laffan and Lindner, 2010: 224–226). The accession of economically poor post-communist countries in the 2000s is predicted to increase the levels of fraud, given the prior existence of networks that commandeered state assets after the fall of communism, and that may now turn their attention to the distribution of EU funds (Dimitrova, 2010: 144). In an unprecedented move, the EU froze some funds for Bulgaria in 2008 following blatant corruption in the use of past funds, perhaps a sign of things to come (Vachudova, 2009: 44).

Turning to the financial resources of the EU, the relatively low level of finances controlled by the Union institutions as opposed to the national governments also suggests intergovernmentalism. There is a ceiling on the size of the EU's budget relative to the total GNI (gross national income) of the member states for each year: this ceiling stands at 1.24 per cent, and in practice the budget is just over 1 per cent, illustrating the way in which the resources available to the EU institutions are dwarfed by those controlled by national governments. This is partly because some responsibilities usually shouldered by the central government in a federal state, such as defence, are handled at the national level within the EU. In 2011 the EU had a larger population than the USA, but the USA federal budget was nearly 30 times as large as the EU's budget. EU expenditure in the 2011 budget was scheduled to be just over €130 billion, about €264 per person (at prevailing exchange rates in autumn 2010, around US$340, or GB£220).

**TABLE 5.6** Actions of the European Court of Justice with respect to the member states

| | Years of membership | Actions for failure to fulfil obligations | | |
| --- | --- | --- | --- | --- |
| | | Total 1952–2009 | Average per year of membership | 2009 |
| Austria | 15 | 121 | 8.1 | 7 |
| Belgium | 58 | 353 | 6.1 | 13 |
| Bulgaria | 3 | 0 | 0 | 0 |
| Cyprus | 6 | 6 | 1.0 | 3 |
| Czech Republic | 6 | 20 | 3.3 | 4 |
| Denmark | 37 | 34 | 0.9 | 0 |
| Estonia | 6 | 10 | 1.7 | 5 |
| Finland | 15 | 48 | 3.2 | 1 |
| France | 58 | 389 | 6.7 | 8 |
| Germany | 58 | 258 | 4.4 | 5 |
| Greece | 29 | 365 | 12.6 | 12 |
| Hungary | 6 | 6 | 1.0 | 1 |
| Ireland | 37 | 192 | 5.2 | 6 |
| Italy | 58 | 615 | 10.6 | 16 |
| Latvia | 6 | 0 | 0 | 0 |
| Lithuania | 6 | 2 | 0.3 | 0 |
| Luxembourg | 58 | 250 | 4.3 | 5 |
| Malta | 6 | 13 | 2.2 | 3 |
| Netherlands | 58 | 134 | 2.3 | 5 |
| Poland | 6 | 31 | 5.2 | 11 |
| Portugal | 24 | 172 | 7.2 | 17 |
| Romania | 3 | 1 | 0.3 | 1 |
| Slovakia | 6 | 6 | 1.0 | 2 |
| Slovenia | 6 | 2 | 0.3 | 0 |
| Spain | 24 | 219 | 9.1 | 11 |
| Sweden | 15 | 46 | 3.1 | 1 |
| United Kingdom | 37 | 127 | 3.4 | 5 |
| Total | 647 | 3 420 | 5.3 | 142 |

*Note*: The 2004 and 2007 entrants were given interim derogations from a number of directives, which partly accounts for their low figures.

*Sources*: Second and fourth columns from 'Statistics of judicial activity', downloaded from http://curia.europa.eu/jcms/jcms/ Jo2_7032/. Third column, authors' calculations.

The Union is financed on the basis of what are termed *own resources*. This means that it does not receive a block grant from the 27 governments, which would give it an overtly subordinate and dependent position; instead, it has a statutory right to the revenue derived from the flow of money into and around the Union. The main source, accounting for about three-quarters of the revenue, is in effect a direct levy imposed on member states in proportion to their gross national income (GNI). In addition, the EU receives a small share of what national governments collect from the main indirect tax in the Union – the value added tax (VAT) – and it also keeps the duties collected from trade with countries outside the EU.

The discussion above makes it clear that the EU has both intergovernmental and supranational aspects. Focusing on the dominant role of the 27 heads of government, difficulties of uniform implementation of legislation, and the small proportion of resources controlled at EU level emphasize how far the EU still is from being a truly supranational body. Nevertheless, even if it remains more intergovernmental than supranational, it is clearly more than a merely intergovernmental body, and has moved closer to being a genuinely supranational polity than any entity before it. We shall now consider whether it will move further in this direction in the future.

## 5.6 The future of the European Union

The EU is not a static organization. Perhaps it never can be. According to some, it must remain for ever in motion, like a bicycle or certain types of shark, because the status quo is not a stable situation (Wind, 2003: 103). EU treaties embody this aspiration by speaking of 'ever closer union', which to critics savours of 'mission creep' or 'competence creep'. Two separate aspects of its future are uncertain: first, the extent of its membership; and second, the extent to which further integration takes place.

### 5.6.1 EU enlargement

Despite the addition of 12 members in the 2000s, and a degree of 'enlargement fatigue' to add to the 'reform fatigue' currently characterizing the EU, the enlargement process is probably not over. The EU has expressed its willingness to admit those states that have shown their commitment to democracy and the rule of law. Iceland applied for membership in 2009 and, as a wealthy (despite its current economic problems) and stable democracy, is expected to be admitted with little demur if its voters decide they want this. The other candidates are more problematic. Albania, Croatia, Macedonia, Montenegro and Serbia have all applied for membership in recent years, and Turkey's application has been on the table since 1987. The EU has given mildly encouraging signs to the first five, although, alarmed at the problems it took on by admitting Bulgaria and Romania prematurely (as it now sees it) in 2007, it may insist on a long waiting period or even on associate membership. It should be noted that the EU already plays a significant role in those countries, funding major infrastructural projects; any visitor to Albania, for example, will see many signs reminding travellers of the contribution of the EU to the upgrading of the country's road network, and indeed the EU flag is more visible in Albania than in most member states. Switzerland (where in a December 1992 referendum the people narrowly voted against joining the European Economic Area, a free trade area including all the EU member states and a number of non-EU members) and Norway are the only countries that at this stage seem unlikely to want to join the European Union, although Switzerland is a major financial donor to the EU, having agreed in 2006 to give SFr 1 billion (around €760 million) to projects in the post-communist member states as part of its bilateral negotiations with the EU. The most contentious case is that of Turkey. It has a number of long-standing advocates within the Union (and the USA is also very supportive), but other members are decidedly unenthusiastic. It is not only very poor in comparison with the EU, but it is also large (over 70 million people), and overwhelmingly Muslim – although opponents of its admission stress their concerns about its level of internal democracy rather than, at least in public, about its religious composition. Surveys conducted around 2000 showed that Turkey's admission was opposed by more people than opposed the admission of any other country (McLaren, 2007: 253). If Turkey is admitted without the people of the member states having a direct voice in this, the legitimacy and cohesion of the Union will be weakened in the eyes of many citizens, while if its admission is made subject to a referendum in some member states its chances are not bright.

## 5.6.2 EU integration

In principle we would expect enlargement and integration to be inversely related. The wider the range of countries and cultural traditions that are brought within the Union, the harder it will be to create a shared identity. At present, any of the 23 official languages in the EU can be used in any Union forum (the United Nations uses six), thus creating the need for a sizeable army of translators to be present whenever Union business takes place – in 2006 no fewer than 1.1 million pages of documentation were translated within the EP alone (Corbett *et al.*, 2007: 38). In informal discussions, either English or (to an ever-decreasing extent) French tends to be used, as there are few politicians or officials who are not reasonably fluent in at least one of those languages. Language is often a badge of identity, and so the profusion of languages imposes a limit to the closeness of identity that can be expected to develop. One writer does indeed argue that each wave of accessions has led to a decline in the coherence of the system and speaks of the 'Austro-Hungarianization' of the EU, 'a story of steady progress backwards' (Allott, 2003: 222). Nevertheless, proposals for ever-closer integration run hand in hand with the extension of the EU's membership.

Ever since the first of the three Communities, the ECSC, was founded in the early 1950s, there have been some who have hoped, and others who have feared, that the existing Union framework would become the vehicle for a process generally termed *European integration*, ending in the creation of a federal European state, similar in its political structure to the United States of America. The feasibility of this idea has ebbed and flowed over the years, but given the establishment of the Eurozone it could be argued that it would be illogical, inconsistent and undemocratic not to have EU-wide political institutions to monitor economic decisions made at the EU level.

There is some variation among the member states on the question of giving more power to the Union institutions (in other words, the Commission and the Parliament) and taking power away from the national governments (in other words, the Council). Of course, there are also nuances of opinion within each country, and there may be differences between verbal positions and the action a government takes when it comes to the crunch. Even so, a certain degree of generalization is possible. Some countries are traditionally *communautaire*; in the forefront of the integrationists can usually be found Belgium, Italy, Germany and Spain. Others are notoriously recalcitrant when it comes to European integration. The countries that have generally led the resistance to moves towards greater unity are Britain, Denmark and Sweden, but several other states – Austria, Czech Republic, Finland, and probably France, which has been disturbed by some recent developments (Balme, 2009) – would not be far behind them, even though they are usually content to let others take the lead.

What does the European public want? The moves towards European integration that have taken place over the past 50 years have been instigated almost entirely by political elites rather than by the public, and indeed elites are far more enthusiastic about European integration than the general public. A 1996 survey found that 94 per cent of elite members surveyed across Europe expressed support for EU membership, compared with just 48 per cent of the public (Hix, 2008: 59–60). Those who have the educational, linguistic and financial resources to move around the EU and do business across it are, not surprisingly, more enthusiastic than those who do not. The most important decisions have been taken by governments and ratified by parliaments. Most member states held a referendum to decide whether to join in the first place, but only in Denmark and Ireland, because of the contents of their constitutions, have referendums become common on subsequent integrationist measures. In the first decade of the twenty-first century the people of seven countries voted to join the EU, but the outcomes of referendums in existing member states were predominantly negative. Two countries voted against joining the euro: Denmark in 2000 and Sweden in 2003. Ireland voted twice on the Nice Treaty (2001 and 2002) and twice on the Lisbon Treaty (2008 and 2009), in each case delivering a Yes verdict in the second vote after an initial No. In 2005 two countries (Luxembourg and Spain) voted Yes to the proposed EU constitution, and two voted No (France and the Netherlands).

Table 5.7 shows the range of attitudes towards the EU in both affective and evaluative terms. Most people have a favourable attitude, but there are large variations, with the populations of Hungary, Latvia and the United Kingdom particularly unenthusiastic – the first two countries were in economic turmoil when the surveys were conducted. Britain has been an 'awkward partner' ever since it joined, perhaps partly because 'the "winner take all" tradition of British politics [up to 2010, at least] contrasts with coalition and consensus-building in much of continental Europe, which often leads to a confrontational British style' (Bache and Jordan, 2008: 277). At the other end of the scale, several countries exhibit overwhelming support for membership – although we should exercise caution in interpreting the results. For one thing, in three of the 'top six' countries – the Netherlands, Ireland and Denmark – integrationist projects have suffered referendum defeats in recent years. Therefore those countries' enthusiasm for membership indicates satisfaction with the status quo – 'thus far and no further' – rather than a desire for deeper integration.

In addition, the high levels of verbal Euro-enthusiasm in some post-communist states contrast with other evidence of near-indifference. High levels of support are recorded in Table 5.7 for Romania and Slovakia, and yet, as Table 5.3 showed, turnout in the 2009 EP elections was derisory in each country. It has been said that 'after longing for decades to be admitted into the larger European family, both the Romanian elite and the general public seemingly lost interest in the issue the moment the country was formally accepted' (Stan and Zaharia, 2008: 1115), and this may be applicable to some other post-communist countries too. Many civil society actors in such countries are simply too weak to take advantage of the participation opportunities offered by the EU, and may grow weaker instead of stronger, getting 'lost' in the new system

(Gąsior-Niemiec, 2010; Kutter and Trappmann, 2010). For some, the eastern expansion of the 2000s risks calling the whole integrationist project into question, as it limits what the EU can actually do. State capacity in many of the post-communist entrants is weak, leading to concern that while the pre-2004 EU might have coped with only two governance underperformers (Greece and Italy), it is unclear how 'an ever more highly regulated Union can operate when nearly half its members struggle with the tasks of government' (Sissenich, 2010: 22–23).

**TABLE 5.7** Evaluations of membership of the European Union, 2009–2010

|  | Membership a good thing | Membership a bad thing | Our country has benefited | Our country has not benefited |
|---|---|---|---|---|
| Luxembourg | 74 | 8 | 71 | 20 |
| Netherlands | 72 | 8 | 72 | 22 |
| Ireland | 69 | 9 | 79 | 11 |
| Spain | 65 | 10 | 65 | 23 |
| Denmark | 65 | 13 | 76 | 17 |
| Belgium | 65 | 11 | 66 | 28 |
| Slovakia | 64 | 5 | 79 | 14 |
| Romania | 62 | 8 | 62 | 21 |
| Poland | 61 | 8 | 75 | 15 |
| Estonia | 58 | 7 | 77 | 17 |
| Germany | 57 | 14 | 54 | 36 |
| Sweden | 55 | 19 | 51 | 35 |
| Lithuania | 52 | 12 | 68 | 18 |
| Bulgaria | 51 | 7 | 48 | 27 |
| Malta | 50 | 18 | 62 | 25 |
| Greece | 50 | 16 | 65 | 31 |
| Finland | 49 | 21 | 58 | 35 |
| Portugal | 48 | 17 | 60 | 25 |
| Italy | 48 | 15 | 48 | 33 |
| France | 48 | 20 | 53 | 35 |
| Slovenia | 46 | 14 | 62 | 33 |
| Cyprus | 42 | 23 | 49 | 45 |
| Austria | 40 | 20 | 45 | 45 |
| Czech Republic | 38 | 14 | 61 | 32 |
| Hungary | 35 | 20 | 39 | 50 |
| United Kingdom | 29 | 32 | 35 | 50 |
| Latvia | 25 | 22 | 39 | 53 |
| EU-27 | 52 | 16 | 55 | 32 |

*Note*: Figures are averages of the findings of Eurobarometers 71 (June–July 2009), 72 (Oct–Nov 2009) and 73 (May 2010) downloaded from http://ec.europa.eu/public_opinion/index_en.htm.

## 5.7 Representative government and the democratic deficit

A recurring criticism of the EU is that it suffers from a *democratic deficit* – that its decision-makers are not accountable to the European public in the way that we would expect in a democracy, and that the EU as an institution suffers from a legitimacy crisis. Others, however, disagree, saying that there is neither a deficit nor a crisis. We review the arguments, starting with the latter first (drawing especially on Moravcsik, 2002) and then assessing the criticisms (drawing especially on Follesdal and Hix, 2006).

Those who dispute the claim that there is a democratic deficit problem make six points in particular.

First, power does not lie with out-of-control officials as in the stereotype of 'Brussels bureaucrats'; on the contrary, every actor with political power was either directly elected, which MEPs are, or was appointed by national actors with an undisputed democratic mandate (each country's commissioner is nominated by its government, and each Council member is a member of a national government).

Second, the body that the people elect themselves, namely the EP, has ever-increasing power, so through EP elections citizens have a meaningful say in determining the direction in which EU should go.

Third, the EU has a style of government that is very different from the Westminster model – in which the government has almost unchallenged power, and faces an opposition – but that does not make it undemocratic, and indeed it resembles that of the USA (Crombez, 2003). As we mentioned earlier, the EU has been cited as an archetypal example of what Lijphart terms *consensus government*, with many checks and balances to ensure that no one actor has too much power.

Fourth, mechanisms of scrutiny are well developed, and in fact the EU operates more transparently than government in most member states, as shown by the fate of some politicians who 'got away with it' in their own country but were 'found out' at EU level, indicating that the EU 'is, without a doubt, more transparent than all, or nearly all, of its Member States' (Moravcsik, 2001: 174–175).

Fifth, despite Europhobes' allegations that 'Brussels' wants control over everything, the EU is not a state, and impinges only marginally on most people's lives. It does not have the full range of powers and responsibilities that a state has, so it does not need the full mechanisms of democratic accountability that a state does. In terms of its impact on domestic policy, the EU does the kind of thing that at national level is usually deliberately taken out of direct control of governments and given to non-majoritarian institutions, such as setting interest rates, or judging the constitutionality of legislation. As for the EU's role in foreign policy, the United Nations also has power, yet no one suggests that a country's representative there should be directly answerable to the people.

Sixth, critics tend to compare the EU with an idealized vision of perfect democracy, and by that standard they pronounce it wanting. It should instead be compared with the reality of functioning democracy in the member states, by which standard it comes out well.

Those who identify a democratic deficit problem put forward six points to the contrary.

First, for democracy to work there needs to be a *demos,* a people, that thinks of itself as a nation or a unit that should govern itself. That is the case within France, Germany, Poland, and so on, but is not true within Europe as a whole. Others, though, suggest that the sequence is capable of being reversed – in other words, that a regime, in this case the EU, can 'create' a *demos* (Schmitter, 2000: 118).

Second, in a democracy the people can choose their rulers and, if they want, vote them out of office. Within the EU, that does not apply. Citizens are never presented with alternative government teams and allowed to choose between them. There is no competition for votes between competing sets of elites as there is in virtually all definitions of democracy (Schmitter, 2000: 6). Similarly, in a democracy voters can determine the policy direction their country will follow, in that at elections they are presented with alternative sets of policy platforms and can choose between them. That is not the case within the EU. Therefore the EU does suffer a democratic deficit; allowing contestation for political leadership and over policy is an essential element of even the 'thinnest' definition of democracy, but it is conspicuously absent from the EU.

Third, the remoteness of the EU institutions means that it is difficult for citizens even to identify the decision-makers. Most reasonably well-informed citizens across the EU might know who their own country's commissioner is, and could name the Commission president, but probably could not name any other commissioner. In national political systems, if voters are unhappy about education policy, for example, they and the media know whom to ask questions of, but they do not have same knowledge within the EU's political system. In Ireland, 'notwithstanding tangible benefits in terms of economic development, financial transfers and geopolitical positioning, the EU remains a distant and little understood entity for the majority of people' (Laffan and O'Mahony, 2008: 263), and the same would be true for many countries.

Fourth, the EU's decision-making process may be praised for its system of checks and balances, but the other side of this coin is that as a result it is very complex, which is why this chapter is the longest in the book. Voters simply do not know whom to reward or blame for particular actions or inactions; they cannot even identify the 'rascals', never mind throw them out. This lack of knowledge is exploited and reinforced by national governments, who are keen to try to claim credit for anything that works out well, even if some actor within EU really deserves the credit, and to blame the EU for things that do not work out well, even if it was really mainly the government's fault. It also means that citizens who are unhappy about something the EU has done tend to become 'anti-EU', blaming the EU as a whole since there is no identifiable actor to blame; with no identifiable opposition within the system, opposition must become opposition against the system (Hix, 2008: 65–66).

Fifth, even if the EU does not do everything that a state does, it still has significant power, for example over states' economic policy. It certainly has enough power that the power-holders should be as accountable as national-level power-holders are, including the possibility of being voted out of office.

Sixth, despite its transparency in some areas, the Council works behind closed doors (which, arguably, it has to, just as national governments do), so there is an element of secrecy in the way policies are made. Moreover, given the complexity of the decision-making process, most citizens will never know how decisions are made, because it would need too much time and expertise to make meaningful use of the information that is available, so it may as well be secret as far as most people are concerned. Citizens should not have to plough through weighty textbooks or chapters in order to get even a basic idea of how they are governed.

While the first batch of arguments has merit, the fact remains that the EU does make decisions that affect citizens across Europe, and yet ordinary Europeans feel that they have little or no ability to affect those decisions, or to hold the decision-makers accountable. Scharpf, accepting that the decision-making process of the EU lacks legitimacy (the 'government by the people' dimension), maintains that the EU can and does nonetheless enjoy legitimacy in terms of 'government for the people', in other words by producing policy choices 'that can be justified in terms of consensual notions of the public interest' (Scharpf, 1999: 188). The EU's legitimacy, in this perspective, depends on its delivering good government and thus earning *output legitimacy* to make up for the shortage of *input legitimacy*. However, the permissive consensus that scholars used to identify, and which allowed EU elites considerable freedom of action, is increasingly, it is argued, being replaced by a 'constraining dissensus' (Hooghe and Marks 2008). In any event, the EU cannot be said to amount to particularly representative government.

How could the EU's policymaking process be made more responsive and accountable to ordinary citizens? One idea entails introducing direct elections for the president of the Commission, to allow Europeans to choose their chief executive just as Americans do. However, this would be a radical step; the national governments would lose a significant element of the control that they possess at present, and the impact of a directly elected president on the functioning of the EU's political system would be unpredictable, so this idea is unlikely to be adopted in the near future. A more modest proposal would not require any constitutional change, but would involve greater party control of the direction of the EU. At present, even though most of the political actors in the EU system are selected by political parties, parties do not control the way in which members of the Commission or the Council behave (Lindberg *et al.*, 2008). Hix argues that greater party control of the key institutions would improve accountability. A right-wing (or left-wing) majority of governments could select not just a Commission president but a whole Commission of the same ideological hue, and if they had a majority in the EP as well (unlikely, given the anti-government voting behaviour at EP elections) they could determine the course of the EU's policy outputs (Hix, 2008: 110–136). Alternatively, before EP elections the various party groups could declare their choice for the next Commission president, thus putting the heads of government under pressure to nominate the individual backed by the strongest-performing party group when they meet to nominate the president (Hix, 2008: 160–162). However, this would require a degree of co-ordination across the EU that parties have so far shown no sign of being interested in.

## 5.8 Conclusions

Perhaps the biggest problem faced by the EU is the absence of a real European *demos* (people), with a sense of identity as such. The 2010 football World Cup in South Africa featured a number of matches between EU member states, and there was a marked absence of sentiment to the effect that 'it doesn't really matter who wins, as long as it's a team from the EU'. National loyalties were to the fore. When England met Germany the English tabloid media harked back to the two world wars of the twentieth century to remind their readers of past conflicts between the countries from which England had emerged triumphant, while before the final between Netherlands and Spain a Dutch newspaper assured its readers (erroneously, as it turned out) that 'we did it in 1648 so we can do it in 2010' (1648 is the year when the Netherlands won independence from Spain). There are few if any unifying moments in the EU comparable to, say, Thanksgiving Day, Memorial Day, or the 4th of July in the USA, or similar national bonding occasions in every member state. There is little sign that a European identity is growing stronger over time (Thomassen and Bäck, 2009). Across the EU there is no common language and there are no common mass media, elements that would greatly facilitate the emergence of a common identity. Survey evidence shows that the further east one goes in Europe, the less peoples are trusted by their fellow Europeans, and the people of Turkey are trusted least of all, so the admission of 10 eastern European countries in the 2000s reduced the chances of an EU identity emerging, while the admission of Turkey would have an even larger negative effect (Thomassen and Bäck, 2009: 197–198, 204). The absence of a European *demos* creates legitimacy problems for the idea of 'rule by Europe' (see the essays in Auer and Flauss, 1997, especially that by Bryde). Whereas people in one part of France, say, accept the legitimacy of decisions made by the government elected by the French people, even if they do not personally support those decisions, because of a feeling that 'we, the French people' expressed the will behind the decision, the people of France (or any other country) collectively might well not accept as legitimate a policy foisted on them in the name of 'the European people'.

To defend itself against charges that it is keen to accrue as much power to itself as possible, the Commission stresses that the EU should operate according to the principle of *subsidiarity* – that is, that it should perform only those tasks that cannot be performed effectively at a more immediate or local level. Thus the EU should not take decisions or try to take care of business that domestic governments are perfectly capable of looking after. The principle of subsidiarity does not mean, of course, that power should necessarily rest with national governments; if applied fully, it also means that within each country as much power as possible is devolved downwards, to provincial, regional or local governments. In practice, the extent to which subsidiarity is genuinely applied as the basis of decision-making, as manifested in the distribution of power between national and subnational governments, varies widely from country to country around Europe, as we shall see in the next chapter.

## Internet resources

europa.eu
   The main EU portal.

ec.europa.eu/index_en.htm
   The Commission's site.

www.europarl.europa.eu
   European Parliament site.

www.consilium.europa.eu/
   Site of Council of Ministers.

curia.europa.eu
   European Court of Justice site.

ec.europa.eu/public_opinion/index_en.htm
   Reports of the Eurobarometer surveys carried out across the EU twice a year.

ec.europa.eu/dgs/communication/take_part/myths_en.htm
   Site lists 'myths and rumours' that it says have been promulgated about the EU and its so-called 'meddling Brussels bureaucrats' but are not true (although often the explanation is quite convoluted, and the reader is left with the feeling that the stories are not entirely untrue either).

# References

**Albi, Anneli** (2005) *EU Enlargement and the Constitutions of Central and Eastern Europe*, Cambridge University Press, Cambridge.

**Allott, Philip** (2003) 'Epilogue: Europe and the dream of reason', pp. 202–225 in J.H.H. Weiler and Marlene Wind (eds), *European Constitutionalism Beyond the Nation State*, Cambridge University Press, Cambridge.

**Alter, Karen J.** (2001) *Establishing the Supremacy of European Law: The Making of an International Rule of Law in Europe*, Oxford University Press, Oxford.

**Alter, Karen** (2009) *The European Court's Political Power: Selected Essays*, Oxford University Press, Oxford.

**Arnull, Anthony** (2006) *The European Union and its Court of Justice*, 2nd edn, Oxford University Press, Oxford.

**Auer, Andreas and Jean-François Flauss (eds)** (1997) *Le Référendum Européen*, Bruylant, Brussels.

**Bache, Ian and Andrew Jordan** (2008) 'The Europeanization of British politics', pp. 265–279 in Ian Bache and Andrew Jordan (eds), *The Europeanization of British Politics*, Palgrave Macmillan, Basingstoke.

**Balme, Richard** (2009) 'France, Europe and the world: foreign policy and the political regime of the fifth republic', pp. 136–150 in Sylvain Brouard, Andrew M. Appleton and Amy G Mazur (eds), *The French Fifth Republic at Fifty: Beyond Stereotypes*, Palgrave Macmillan, Basingstoke.

**Bekkers, V.J.J.M., A.J.C. de Moor-Van Vught and W. Voermans** (1998) 'Going Dutch: problems and policies concerning the implementation of EU legislation in the Netherlands', pp. 454–478 in Paul Craig and Carol Harlow (eds), *Lawmaking in the European Union*, Kluwer Law International, London.

**Bellamy, Richard** (2010) 'Democracy without democracy? Can the EU's democratic "outputs" be separated from the democratic "inputs" provided by competitive parties and majority rule?', *Journal of European Public Policy*, 17 (1), 2–19.

**Bomberg, Elizabeth and Alexander Stubb** (2008) 'The EU's institutions', pp. 45–70 in Elizabeth Bomberg, John Peterson and Alexander Stubb (eds), *The European Union: How Does it Work?*, 2nd edn, Oxford University Press, Oxford.

**Börzel, Tanja and Diana Panke** (2010) 'Europeanization', pp. 405–417 in Michelle Cini and Nieves Pérez-Solórzano Borragán (eds), *European Union Politics*, 3rd edn, Oxford University Press, Oxford.

**Börzel, Tanja A. and Carina Sprungk** (2007) 'Undermining democratic governance in the member states? The Europeanisation of national decision-making', pp. 113–136 in Ronald Holzhacker and Erik Albaek (eds), *Democratic Governance and European Integration: Linking Societal and State Processes of Democracy*, Edward Elgar, Cheltenham.

**Bouwen, Pieter** (2009) 'The European Commission', pp. 19–38 in David Coen and Jeremy Richardson (eds), *Lobbying the European Union: Institutions, Actors, and Issues*, Oxford University Press, Oxford.

**Bryde, Brun-Otto** (1997) 'Le peuple Européen and the European people', pp. 251–274 in Andreas Auer and Jean-François Flauss (eds), *Le Référendum Européen*, Bruylant, Brussels.

**Burgess, Michael** (2000) *Federalism and the European Union: The Building of Europe, 1950–2000*, Routledge, London.

**Carrubba, Clifford J., Matthew Gabel and Charles Hankla** (2008) 'Judicial behavior under political constraints: evidence from the European Court of Justice', *American Political Science Review*, 102 (4), 435–452.

**Carter, Elisabeth and Thomas Poguntke** (2010) 'How European integration changes national parties: evidence from a 15-country study', *West European Politics*, 33 (2), 297–324.

**Castiglione, Dario, Justin Schönlau, Chris Longman, Emanuela Lombardo, Nieves Pérez-Solórzano Borragán and Miriam Aziz** (2007) *Constitutional Politics in the European Union: The Convention Moment and Its Aftermath*, Palgrave Macmillan, Basingstoke.

**Chari, Raj S. and Sylvia Kritzinger** (2006) *Understanding EU Policy Making*, Pluto Press, London.

Cini, Michelle and Nieves Pérez-Solórzano Borragán (eds) (2010) *European Union Politics*, 3rd edn, Oxford University Press, Oxford.

Corbett, Richard, Francis Jacobs and Michael Shackleton (2007) *The European Parliament*, 7th edn, John Harper Publishing, London.

Crombez, Christophe (2003) 'The democratic deficit in the European Union: much ado about nothing?', *European Union Politics*, 4 (1), 101–120.

Demmke, Christoph and Martin Unfried (2001) *European Environmental Policy: The Administrative Challenge for the Member States*, European Institute of Public Administration, Maastricht.

Dimitrova, Antoaneta L. (2010) 'The new member states of the EU in the aftermath of enlargement: do new European rules remain empty shells?', *Journal of European Public Policy*, 17 (1), 137–148.

Dinan, Desmond (2005) *Ever Closer Union: An Introduction to European Integration*, 3rd edn, Palgrave Macmillan, London.

Dinan, Desmond (ed.) (2006) *Origins and Evolution of the European Union*, Oxford University Press, Oxford.

Dinan, Desmond (2008) 'Governance and institutional developments: ending the constitutional impasse', *Journal of Common Market Studies*, 46 (s1), 71–90.

Döring, Holger (2007) 'The composition of the College of Commissioners: patterns of delegation', *European Union Politics*, 8 (2), 207–228.

Dyevre, Arthur (2010) 'Unifying the field of comparative judicial politics: towards a general theory of judicial behaviour', *European Political Science Review*, 2 (2), 297–327.

Dyson, Kenneth (2008) 'The first decade: credibility, identity and institutional fuzziness', pp. 1–34 in Kenneth Dyson (ed.), *The Euro at 10: Europeanization, Power, and Convergence*, Oxford University Press, Oxford.

Egan, Michelle (2010) 'The single market', pp. 258–274 in Michelle Cini and Nieves Pérez-Solórzano Borragán (eds), *European Union Politics*, 3rd edn, Oxford University Press, Oxford.

Egeberg, Morten (2010) 'The European Commission', pp. 125–140 in Michelle Cini and Nieves Pérez-Solórzano Borragán (eds), *European Union Politics*, 3rd edn, Oxford University Press, Oxford.

Eurobarometer (2009) *The 2009 European Elections: Report*. Special Eurobarometer 303, wave 70.1.

Falkner, Gerda and Oliver Treib (2008) 'Three worlds of compliance or four? The EU-15 compared to new member states', *Journal of Common Market Studies*, 46 (2), 293–313.

Farrell, David M. and Roger Scully (2007) *Representing Europe's Citizens? Electoral Institutions and the Failure of Parliamentary Representation*, Oxford University Press, Oxford.

Follesdal, Andreas and Simon Hix (2006) 'Why there is a democratic deficit in the EU: a response to Majone and Moravcsik', *Journal of Common Market Studies*, 44 (3), 533–562.

Fouilleux, Eve (2010) 'The Common Agricultural Policy', pp. 340–357 in Michelle Cini and Nieves Pérez-Solórzano Borragán (eds), *European Union Politics*, 3rd edn, Oxford University Press, Oxford.

Freestone, D.A.C. and J.S. Davidson (1988) *The Institutional Framework of the European Communities*, Croom Helm, London and New York.

Gąsior-Niemiec, Anna (2010) 'Lost in the system? Civil society and regional development policy in Poland', *Acta Politica*, 45 (1/2), 90–111.

Hayes-Renshaw, Fiona and Helen Wallace (2006) *The Council of Ministers*, 2nd edn, Macmillan, Basingstoke.

Hayes-Renshaw, Fiona, Wim van Aken and Helen Wallace (2006) 'When and why the EU Council of Ministers votes explicitly', *Journal of Common Market Studies*, 44 (1), 161–194.

Hix, Simon (2005) *The Political System of the European Union*, 2nd edn, Palgrave Macmillan, Basingstoke.

Hix, Simon (2008) *What's Wrong with the European Union and How to Fix It*, Polity, Cambridge.

Hix, Simon, Abdul G. Noury and Gérard Roland (2007) *Democratic Politics in the European Parliament*, Cambridge University Press, Cambridge.

Hodson, Dermot (2010) 'Economic and monetary union: an experiment in new modes of EU policy-making', pp. 157–180 in Helen Wallace, Mark A. Pollack and Alasdair R. Young (eds), *Policy-Making in the European Union*, 6th edn, Oxford University Press, Oxford.

**Holzhacker, Ronald** (2007) 'Parliamentary scrutiny', pp. 141–153 in Paolo Graziano and Maarten P. Vink (eds), *Europeanization: New Research Agendas*, Palgrave Macmillan, Basingstoke.

**Hooghe, Liesbet** (2001) *The European Commission and the Integration of Europe: Images of Governance*, Cambridge University Press, Cambridge.

**Hooghe, Liesbet and Gary Marks** (2008) 'A postfunctionalist theory of European integration: from permissive consensus to constraining dissensus', *British Journal of Political Science*, 39 (1), 1–23.

**Irwin, Galen** (1995) 'Second-order or third-rate? Issues in the campaign for the elections for the European Parliament 1994', *Electoral Studies*, 14 (2), 183–199.

**Jones, Robert A.** (2001) *The Politics and Economics of the European Union*, 2nd edn, Edward Elgar, Cheltenham.

**Judge, David and David Earnshaw** (2008) *The European Parliament*, 2nd edn, Palgrave Macmillan, Basingstoke.

**Kenney, Sally J.** (1999) 'The judges of the Court of Justice of the European Communities', pp. 143–171 in Sally J. Kenney, William M. Reisinger and John C. Reitz (eds), *Constitutional Dialogues in Comparative Perspective*, Macmillan, Basingstoke.

**Knapp, Andrew and Vincent Wright** (2006) *The Government and Politics of France*, 5th edn, Routledge, Abingdon.

**Kokott, Juliane** (1998) 'Report on Germany', pp. 77–131 in Anne-Marie Slaughter, Alec Stone Sweet and J.H. Weiler (eds), *The European Court and National Courts – Doctrine and Jurisprudence: Legal Change in its Social Context*, Hart Publishing, Oxford.

**König, Thomas and Dirk Junge** (2009) 'Why don't veto players use their power?', *European Union Politics*, 10 (4), 507–534.

**Kutter, Amelie and Vera Trappmann** (2010) 'Civil society in central and eastern Europe: the ambivalent legacy of accession', *Acta Politica*, 45 (1/2), 41–69.

**Ladrech, Robert** (2010) *Europeanization and National Politics*, Palgrave Macmillan, Basingstoke.

**Laffan, Brigid** (2006) 'Financial control: the Court of Auditors and OLAF', pp. 210–28 in John Peterson and Michael Shackleton (eds), *The Institutions of the European Union*, 2nd edn, Oxford University Press, Oxford.

**Laffan, Brigid and Johannes Lindner** (2010) 'The budget: who gets what, when and how?', pp. 207–228 in Helen Wallace, Mark A. Pollack and Alasdair R. Young (eds), *Policy-Making in the European Union*, 6th edn, Oxford University Press, Oxford.

**Laffan, Brigid and Jane O'Mahony** (2008) *Ireland and the European Union*, Palgrave Macmillan, Basingstoke.

**Lequesne, Christian** (2000) 'The Common Fisheries Policy', pp. 345–372 in Helen Wallace and William Wallace (eds), *Policy-Making in the European Union*, 4th edn, Oxford University Press, Oxford and New York.

**Lewis, Jeffrey** (2010) 'The Council of the European Union', pp. 141–161 in Michelle Cini and Nieves Pérez-Solórzano Borragán (eds), *European Union Politics*, 3rd edn, Oxford University Press, Oxford.

**Lijphart, Arend** (1999) *Patterns of Democracy: Government Forms and Performance in Thirty-Six Countries*, Yale University Press, New Haven, CT, and London.

**Lindberg, Björn, Anne Rasmussen and Andreas Warntjen** (2008) 'Party politics as usual? The role of political parties in EU legislative decision-making', *Journal of European Public Policy*, 15 (8), 1107–1126.

**Mair, Peter** (2007) 'Political parties and party systems', pp. 154–166 in Paolo Graziano and Maarten P. Vink (eds), *Europeanization: New Research Agendas*, Palgrave Macmillan, Basingstoke.

**McElroy, Gail** (2008) 'Committees and party cohesion in the European Parliament', *Osterreichische Zeitschrift fuer Politikwissenschaft*, 37 (3), 357–373.

**McElroy, Gail and Kenneth Benoit** (2010) 'Party policy and group affiliation in the European Parliament', *British Journal of Political Science*, 40 (2), 377–398.

**McLaren, Lauren** (2007) 'Explaining opposition to Turkish membership of the EU', *European Union Politics*, 8 (2), 251–278.

**McNamara, Kathleen R.** (2006) 'Managing the euro: the European Central Bank', pp. 169–189 in John Peterson and Michael Shackleton (eds), *The Institutions of the European Union*, 2nd edn, Oxford University Press, Oxford.

**Mellows-Facer, Adam, Richard Cracknell and Sean Lightbown** (2009) *European Parliament Elections 2009*, Research paper 09/53, House of Commons Library, London.

**Moravcsik, Andrew** (2001) 'Federalism in the European Union: rhetoric and reality', pp. 161–187 in Kalypso Nicolaidis and Robert Howse (eds), *The Federal Vision: Legitimacy and Levels of Governance in the United States and the European Union*, Oxford University Press, Oxford and New York.

**Moravcsik, Andrew** (2002) 'In defence of the democratic deficit: reassessing legitimacy in the European Union', *Journal of Common Market Studies*, 40 (4), 603–624.

**Naurin, Daniel and Rutger Lindahl** (2008) 'East–north–south: coalition-building in the Council before and after enlargement', pp. 64–78 in Daniel Naurin and Helen Wallace (eds), *Unveiling the Council of the European Union: Games Governments Play in Brussels*, Palgrave Macmillan, Basingstoke.

**Nicol, Danny** (2001) *EC Membership and the Judicialization of British Politics*, Oxford University Press, Oxford.

**Nugent, Neill** (2010) *The Government and Politics of the European Union*, 7th edn, Palgrave Macmillan, Basingstoke.

**Pollack, Mark A.** (2003) *The Engines of European Integration: Delegation, Agency, and Agenda Setting in the EU*, Oxford University Press, Oxford and New York.

**Raunio, Tapio** (2009) 'National parliaments and European integration: what we know and agenda for future research', *Journal of Legislative Studies*, 15 (4), 317–334.

**Raworth, Philip** (2001) *Introduction to the Legal System of the European Union*, Oceana, Dobbs Ferry, NY.

**Rihoux, Benoit, Lieven De Winter, Patrick Dumont and Serge Deruette** (2007) 'Belgium', *European Journal of Political Research*, 46 (7/8), 891–900.

**Roederer-Rynning, Christilla** (2010) 'The Common Agricultural Policy: the fortress challenged', pp. 181–205 in Helen Wallace, Mark A. Pollack and Alasdair R. Young (eds), *Policy-Making in the European Union*, 6th edn, Oxford University Press, Oxford.

**Scharpf, Fritz W.** (1999) *Governing in Europe: Effective and Democratic?*, Oxford University Press, Oxford.

**Schmidt, Vivien A.** (2006) *Democracy in Europe: the EU and National Polities*, Oxford University Press, Oxford.

**Schmitter, Philippe C.** (2000) *How to Democratize the EU ... and Why Bother?*, Rowman and Littlefield, Lanham, MD.

**Sepos, Angelos** (2008) *The Europeanization of Cyprus: Polity, Policies and Politics*, Palgrave Macmillan, Basingstoke.

**Shapiro, Jeremy and Nick Witney** (2009) *Towards a Post-American Europe: A Power Audit of EU–US Relations*, European Council on Foreign Relations, London.

**Shapiro, Martin and Alec Stone Sweet** (2002) *On Law, Politics, and Judicialization*, Oxford University Press, Oxford and New York.

**Sieberson, Stephen C.** (2008) *Dividing Lines between the European Union and its Member States: The Impact of the Treaty of Lisbon*, T.M.C. Asser Press, The Hague.

**Sissenich, Beate** (2010) 'Weak states, weak societies: Europe's east–west gap', *Acta Politica*, 45 (1/2), 11–40.

**Smith, Mitchell P.** (2000) 'The Commission made me do it: The European Commission as a strategic asset in domestic politics', pp. 170–189 in Neill Nugent (ed.), *At the Heart of the Union: Studies of the European Commission*, Macmillan, Basingstoke.

**Snyder, Francis** (1995) 'The effectiveness of European Community law: institutions, processes, tools and techniques', pp. 49–87 in Terence Daintith (ed.), *Implementing EC Law in the United Kingdom: Structures for Indirect Rule*, John Wiley, Chichester.

**Stan, Lavinia and Razvan Zaharia** (2008) 'Romania', *European Journal of Political Research*, 47 (7/8), 1115–1126.

**Stone Sweet, Alec** (2000) *Governing with Judges: Constitutional Politics in Europe*, Oxford University Press, Oxford and New York.

**Stone Sweet, Alec** (2004) *The Judicial Construction of Europe*, Oxford University Press, Oxford.

**Sverdrup, Ulf** (2004) 'Compliance and conflict management in the European Union: Nordic exceptionalism', *Scandinavian Political Studies*, 27 (1), 23–43.

**Szczerbiak, Aleks and Paul Taggart** (2004) 'The politics of European referendum outcomes and turnout: two models', *West European Politics*, 27 (4), 557–583.

**Tallberg, Jonas** (2003) *European Governance and Supranational Institutions: Making States Comply*, Routledge, London and New York.

**Thomassen, Jacques and Hanna Bäck** (2009) 'European citizenship and identity after enlargement', pp. 184–207 in Jacques Thomassen (ed.), *The Legitimacy of the European Union after Enlargement*, Oxford University Press, Oxford.

**Thomson, Robert** (2008a) 'National actors in international organizations: the case of the European Commission', *Comparative Political Studies*, 41 (2), 169–192.

**Thomson, Robert** (2008b) 'The Council presidency in the European Union: responsibility with power', *Journal of Common Market Studies*, 46 (3), 593–617.

**Thomson, Robert** (2008c) 'The relative power of member states in the Council: large and small, old and new', pp. 238–258 in Daniel Naurin and Helen Wallace (eds), *Unveiling the Council of the European Union: Games Governments Play in Brussels*, Palgrave Macmillan, Basingstoke.

**Thomson, Robert** (2009) 'Same effects in different worlds: the transposition of EU directives', *Journal of European Public Policy*, 16 (1), 1–18.

**Thomson, Robert and Madeleine Hosli** (2006) 'Who has power in the EU? The Commission, Council and Parliament in legislative decision-making', *Journal of Common Market Studies*, 44 (2), 391–417.

**Thomson, Robert, René Torenvlied and Javier Arregui** (2007) 'The paradox of compliance: infringements and delays in transposing European Union directives', *British Journal of Political Science*, 37 (4), 685–709.

**Toshkov, Dimiter** (2007) 'In search of the worlds of compliance: culture and transposition performance in the European Union', *Journal of European Public Policy*, 14 (6), 933–959.

**Vachudova, Milada Anna** (2009) 'Corruption and compliance in the EU's post-communist members and candidates', *Journal of Common Market Studies*, 47 (s1), 43–62.

**Wallace, Helen, Mark A. Pollack and Alasdair R. Young (eds)** (2010) *Policy-Making in the European Union*, 6th edn, Oxford University Press, Oxford.

**Warntjen, Andreas, Simon Hix and Christophe Crombez** (2008) 'The party political make-up of EU legislative bodies', *Journal of European Public Policy*, 15 (8), 1243–1253.

**Weiler, J.H.H.** (2001) 'Epilogue: the judicial après Nice', pp. 215–226 in Gráinne de Búrca and J.H.H. Weiler (eds), *The European Court of Justice*, Oxford University Press, Oxford and New York.

**Wind, Marlene** (2003) 'The European Union as a polycentric polity: returning to a neo-medieval Europe'?', pp. 103–131 in J.H.H. Weiler and Marlene Wind (eds), *European Constitutionalism Beyond the Nation State*, Cambridge University Press, Cambridge.

**Wyller, Thomas** (1996) 'Norway: six exceptions to the rule', pp. 139–152 in Michael Gallagher and Pier Vincenzo Uleri (eds), *The Referendum Experience in Europe*, Macmillan, Basingstoke.

# 6
# Central, Regional and Local Governance

## Chapter contents

## 6.1 Introduction

National elections, political parties, parliaments and governments are the first things on most people's minds when they think about representative government in modern Europe. However, most of the key public decisions that affect people's everyday lives are not determined by national *electoral* politics. At the level of 'high' politics, for example, every government in Europe had to decide in 2008 how it would respond, without any electoral mandate on the matter, to the unexpected but extraordinarily important events unfolding as part of a world financial crisis. At a less dramatic level, key public decisions must be made about many important matters, including levels of service and spending in major parts of the public sector such as health, education or policing. At regional level, decisions are needed on important matters such as investments in roads, public transport, and other aspects of the communications infrastructure. At a more local level, public decisions involve critical issues such as land-use planning and zoning, making trade-offs, for example, between the need to provide new housing in a particular area and the need to protect the environment and amenities of those who already live there. At the level of the individual citizen, important decisions must be made on matters such as whether particular individuals are eligible, for example, for specified health or welfare benefits, or are personally liable to pay particular taxes.

A large part of the business of running a country, of real-life *governance*, is about administering the machinery of state. It is about *implementing* policy decisions in ways that realize general principles that might have been hotly contested, but nonetheless eventually settled, in the arenas of representative politics. A large part of how representative government really works on the ground, therefore, has to do with the relationship between politics and public administration. After all is said and done, it is pointless winning a crucial political debate on some vitally important matter if the eventual decision is not then implemented. As we saw when looking at the role of the executive in Chapter 2, politics and public administration in representative democracies are formally linked by the two key overlapping roles of a cabinet minister. The same person is at the same time part of the political executive and head of a major administrative department. This focuses our attention on the interaction between politics and public administration at the national level, and in particular on the interaction between senior politicians and senior civil servants.

Another aspect of real-life governance that is of key importance concerns *where* key public decisions are made and implemented. In particular, it concerns whether decisions are made at local, regional, national or supranational level. The jurisdiction of any government is never all-embracing. Even in the most totalitarian of societies, 'the government' does not tell people how many times to chew their food, when to breathe, or what to dream about. As we move from the level of the individual decision-maker to the level of the national government (and beyond this to supranational institutions), we find a large number of different places in which decisions are made. These range from the family, to the street, to the neighbourhood, to the district, to the town, to the county, to the region, to the province, and on to the nation-state. A decision on whether or not to build a new bridge in some particular place, for example, has vastly different consequences for different people, depending on where they live. The lives of those who live beside the bridge may be ruined by its noise and disruption. Those who live in the region but not in the immediate vicinity may save hours of travel time every week. Those who live elsewhere in the country but too far away ever to use the bridge may be forced to pay for part of it with their taxes while getting, as they see it, no benefits from it. The extent to which the interests of these different constituencies of individuals are represented in the eventual decision is affected crucially by whether this is made at local, regional or national level.

The themes we touch on here raise big questions. We look first at the relationship between politicians and the civil service at national level, before moving on to consider the different geographic levels at which decisions might be made.

## 6.2 Politicians and the civil service

A typical modern European government, as we have seen, comprises a cabinet, chaired by a prime minister, and a set of ministers who are usually senior party politicians. After the cabinet has made a decision, responsibility for implementation of this passes to a designated government department, headed by a particular cabinet minister. While ministers are *collectively* responsible for all government decisions by virtue of their membership of the cabinet, each minister is *individually* responsible for the implementation of designated government decisions by virtue of his or her position as the head of a government department. This generates what political scientists call a *principal–agent problem* at several levels. Principal–agent relationships arise whenever one person (an *agent*) is acting on behalf of another (the *principal*). This typically happens because the agent has better information, or is better placed to act, than the principal. For example, if you hire a lawyer to act for you in a complicated legal matter, you do this because the lawyer knows more about relevant aspects of the law and legal procedure than you do, and because he or she may have privileged access to the courts. The potential problem arises because the interests of your agent (the lawyer) are never perfectly aligned with your own. She or he may 'shirk' by not putting in as much work on the case as you would like, or may sacrifice your interests as part of a much larger process of doing deals with other lawyers. Kathleen Eisenhardt provides an accessible review of the principal–agent problem (Eisenhardt, 1989).

At the highest level, being head of a department that implements government policy makes the minister an agent of the government, which is the principal, in the process of policy implementation. Members of the government cannot possibly police the implementation of every policy decision they make. They therefore designate the relevant minister as their agent in this regard. The minister may shirk in this role. She or he may be lazy, inattentive or stupid and for these reasons fail to implement a given policy as the government intended when it made its decision. Or he or she may privately prefer some alternative policy and actually implement this rather than the policy decided by the government.

Moving down the chain of policy implementation, an agency problem also arises within each government department, because the cabinet minister at the department's head cannot possibly know everything about the workings of the department, and will almost certainly not be expert in many of the intricacies involved in serious policy implementation. Thus the minister, now as principal, will need to designate senior bureaucrats as his or her agents in the department, with practical responsibility for actually getting anything done, as well as for the elaboration of detailed policy responses to problems that the minister has been asked to address and bring to cabinet.

Moving even further down the chain, senior civil servants are high-level policymakers who are not responsible for detailed practical decisions about policy implementation – about whether or not to deny some particular person unemployment benefit, for example, or to issue building permits for some local development. Seen in this light, senior civil servants are now in effect principals, to a large extent at the mercy of their more junior colleagues, who are the people who have the detailed information about what is 'really' happening on the ground.

Crudely speaking, therefore, when it comes to any particular policy problem, the cabinet will be in the minister's hands to a large extent, the minister will in turn be in the hands of senior bureaucrats in his or her department, and these senior bureaucrats will also depend upon more junior colleagues. It cannot realistically be any other way, which makes the origins, the 'culture' and the accountability of civil servants a very important political matter.

We return in Chapter 12 to consider the agency relationship between individual ministers in their departments and the cabinet with which they share collective responsibility for the making of key public policy decisions. This relationship is particularly important in coalition cabinets, but is a major factor everywhere in the making and breaking of governments. Here, we focus on the agency relationship between a cabinet minister and bureaucrats for whom he or she is responsible, which has long been a topic of heated debate. There are very different civil service traditions in this regard, both in western Europe and in the former communist states of central and eastern Europe, while radical reform of the civil service has been an important project for all countries experiencing a transition to democracy. In the former communist states, the entire civil service was systematically politicized. In order to ensure that the civil service implemented the wishes and decisions of the communist party, almost all civil service appointments were under the patronage of the party. Only those vetted and approved by the party – the *nomenklatura* – could hold civil service positions, and promotion and advancement depended at least as much on political as on administrative criteria. Under the *nomenklatura* system, therefore, the problem of ensuring civil service responsiveness to political decisions was addressed by politicizing the civil service (Hough and Fainsod, 1979; Kornai, 1992; Baker, 2002).

The evolving western European bureaucratic tradition has seen the civil service as an independent corps of professional administrators rather than a cadre of partisan functionaries. This raises the issue of how independent administrators can be made responsive to political decisions arising from the process of representative government. The formal situation, typically promoted by the civil service itself, is that the civil service is a neutral policy-implementation machine that merely puts into practice the political decisions made by democratically elected public representatives. According to this ideal, policing the bureaucracy is a technical administrative problem of designing the appropriate monitoring systems, because the interests of politicians and bureaucrats will never conflict. A complicated world needs a complicated bureaucracy to administer it, so such monitoring is not a trivial problem. Essentially, however, it is the *technical* problem of designing an administrative system that works well, rather than a *political* problem of controlling a complex system of administrators, each with a private political agenda.

In practice few people, even civil servants, see the civil service as an automatic implementation machine. This raises the matter of political, as opposed to purely technical, control of the state bureaucracy. Here we focus on two important factors that affect the political relationship between ministers and senior bureaucrats. The first concerns the political culture of the civil service itself – in particular, the way in which this derives from patterns of recruitment and training. The second concerns the extent to which ministers can select their senior civil service advisors and thereby feel more confident in political terms that they are being advised by people who are not pursuing conflicting policy objectives.

## 6.2.1 Civil service cultures

Looking first at the culture of the national civil service, we find that western European bureaucracies can be divided into two broad types, to which we can add the highly politicized *nomenklatura* system that was the initial bureaucratic inheritance of central and eastern European countries. Although these differences are helpful in giving us a way to think about things, they are often much smaller in practice than they might seem at first sight.

On the one hand, there is a civil service culture in the British mould. Supporters describe this as 'generalist'; opponents, as 'dilettante'. This type of bureaucracy is characterized by a heavy reliance on senior civil servants with general administrative and managerial skills, as opposed to specific technical expertise. Such administrative systems tend to operate on the basis of peer group pressure and socialization into a particular decision-making culture, as opposed to technical training in particular skills (Hennessy, 1989). The archetypal case of a generalist civil service is found in Britain, and a generalist civil service was inherited on independence by Ireland.

Strong tendencies in this direction can also be seen in Italy, Spain and Portugal (Bekke and van der Meer, 2001; Raadschelders *et al.*, 2007; Ongaro, 2009). The image, and to some extent the reality in Britain, is of a civil service staffed at senior levels by classics scholars from prestigious private secondary schools and universities. Although various commissions of inquiry into the British civil service have commented on this situation and recommended a variety of reforms, it is extraordinarily difficult to reorient an entire civil service culture.

The main European alternative to the generalist civil service culture has a far more technocratic ethos, characterized by much greater reliance on specialists and technical training, either in administrative skills or in specialized roles such as economist, engineer or lawyer. The French civil service, for example, is divided into a series of administrative *corps*, known as the *Grand Corps de l'Etat,* membership of which is absolutely essential for a successful career in the civil service. These *corps* recruit, train and socialize members on the basis of what is effectively an alternative higher education system outside the university sector. They have a series of dedicated schools, in particular the *Ecole Polytechnique,* which specialize in technical education and recruit students on the basis of intensely competitive examinations. A specialized administrative education is given by the *Ecole Nationale d'Administration* (ENA), which recruits students who have an undergraduate degree, once more on the basis of a very competitive examination. Despite periodic attempts to liberalize this process and open up other methods of entry, almost all entrants to the senior civil service in France follow one of these routes (Bekke and van der Meer, 2001; Peters and Pierre, 2004; Ongaro, 2009). Although it might seem as if this pattern of civil service education in France would produce an administrative elite with a high degree of technical expertise, French civil servants may find themselves doing jobs that bear little concrete relationship to their technical training. As with most forms of education almost everywhere, however, what is of primary importance is the process by which students are socialized into a particular culture. The most relevant aspect of this in the present context is the technocratic approach to problem solving by administrative elites, rather than any specific area of substantive expertise, which in all civil services (in common with most other careers) is most effectively learned on the job.

The German civil service is also seen as having a technocratic ethos, although the emphasis in this case is on legal training – a high proportion of German civil servants have a legal background. Civil service recruitment takes place after undergraduate university education, is intensely competitive, and based on a general state examination consisting largely of law and political science – making these subjects preferred choices for undergraduates hoping to enter the civil service. In common with France, however, and unlike Britain, Germany has a civil service whose recruitment and socialization process is education oriented and subject focused: this generates in German civil servants a self-image of the technocratic public administrator. The civil service in central and south-east Europe (Czech Republic, Slovakia, Hungary, Slovenia, Croatia, Serbia and Romania) is in essence fashioned after the German civil service. In these counties too, therefore, there is typically a state exam after undergraduate university education, and the civil service tends to be staffed by people who graduated in law or closely related disciplines.

Although much is made of differences in civil service cultures by those who focus on the internal workings of the bureaucracy, these differences may be less important than the strong general patterns we find at the interface between the political system of representative government and the administrative civil service. It is largely agreed by institutional theorists in the tradition of Wildavsky and economic modellers in the tradition of Niskanen, for example, that bureaucracies should be seen as groups of people concerned to advance their own interests, typically by increasing the size of their agencies and maximizing their budgets (Wildavsky, 1984; Niskanen, 2007). A variation on this view has been put forward by Dunleavy, who argues that civil servants are interested not so much in maximizing budgets as in making their jobs more congenial. This results in what he calls 'bureau shaping' by public administrators (Dunleavy, 1991). Thus civil servants in the department of finance may advise against wholesale tax reform, not because of any impact this might have on the size of their empire, but because such reform might threaten established intradepartmental power structures. The result is a tendency, other things being equal, for bureaucracies to resist political change that runs counter to bureaucratic interests. Such tendencies are likely to affect all civil services, regardless of administrative culture. Arguments about different civil service cultures may thus exaggerate the practical differences we find on the ground, while control of the bureaucracy is a political as well as an administrative problem, the matter to which we now turn.

## 6.2.2 Politicization of senior bureaucrats

The need for political as well as administrative control of the bureaucracy explains why the political orientation of the senior civil service is such an important matter. Even if the civil service were to be nothing more than a well-oiled machine to which politicians issued orders that were carried out to the letter, ministers would still need to rely upon people who shared their own political viewpoints for help with developing new policy proposals. If the members of the civil service do indeed have an agenda of their own, however implicit, then ministers will want people in key positions whom they can trust politically, to reduce the possibility of principal–agent problems and increase the probability that what politicians decide is in fact carried out when policy implementation passes down the line. The more complex and technical the policy area, the less transparent the implementation process, and the harder it is for ministers to monitor civil servants. This increases the incentives for ministers to recruit as advisors policy specialists who share their own political views, either in the senior echelons of their departments or at least with an overview of these.

At the same time the civil service does need to provide a comprehensive source of independent expertise, from which political decision-makers can draw. In an increasingly technical world, this expertise is likely to extend far beyond the knowledge and competence of senior elected politicians, who will inevitably need to rely upon the independent advice of their civil servants if they are to make wise decisions in the public interest. Such independent advice is unlikely to be provided by bureaucrats who are no more than the political lackeys of the parties in power. There is thus a delicate balancing act to be performed in designing a system that guarantees ministers genuinely independent technical advice, yet at the same time reassures ministers that their political preferences, preferences that have furthermore recently been endorsed by the voters, are respected by the senior administrators who have the job of implementing them. Intriguingly, following the collapse of the former Soviet Union, we can observe European countries following two quite distinct trajectories in this regard.

For the former communist states of eastern Europe, the key bureaucratic issue has been *depoliticization* of inherited *nomenklatura* systems (Kotchegura, 2008). This is much more easily said than done. Following periods of 40–50 years during which nearly all of those appointed to civil service positions were politically vetted and approved, the entire civil services in these countries – the entire group of people with practical experience of running the machinery of state – had been appointed by the communist party. It was obviously quite impossible in practical terms to replace this entire administrative cohort overnight. Thus newly democratizing eastern

European states had to rely, for their initial public administration, on civil services whose personnel and bureaucratic cultures were rooted in the Soviet era. While pressure for economic and political reform tended to push these matters ahead of bureaucratic reform as priorities for urgent action, the selection of a civil service 'model' for the transition states was clearly an important issue. On the one hand there was an understandable desire on the part of elected politicians in the post-communist era to ensure that 'their' people were running the civil service, rather than being functionaries of the old one-party state. This led to high levels of turnover in the senior civil service, the personnel of which has changed as governments have changed, a process that tends to undermine the development of an 'independent' professional civil service capable of serving governments of many different political stripes. On the other hand there has been a desire to move away from the highly politicized state bureaucracy of the Soviet era, which will require the evolution over time of mutual trust between politicians and public servants. Since such trust derives from deeply rooted civil service traditions of professionalism and meritocracy, this will require a period of stability in the corps of senior civil servants in each country. This can happen only if incoming ministers forbear from parachuting all of their own people into the top civil service positions as soon as they take office. Given the time it takes for any civil service culture to develop – for the most senior bureaucrats to be drawn from the ranks of those who were socialized into the culture as young administrators – it will be a while before the final shape of the relationship between politicians and civil servants in eastern Europe stabilizes.

For overviews of the post-communist evolution of central and eastern European civil services, see Verheijen (1999), Meyer-Sahling (2004), Dimitrova (2005), Dimitrov *et al.* (2006) and Kotchegura (2008).

In western Europe the trend has if anything been towards *politicization* of the civil service, although nowhere in western Europe do we find the highly politicized system of appointments to the senior civil service that exists in the United States. When a US president changes, so does a high proportion of the most senior bureaucrats in the main departments of state. A large group of lawyers, academics and other professionals known to be sympathetic to the president's views are brought in, typically from outside the government system as a whole, to take over the levers of power. A vestige of a 'spoils' system designed to reward those who helped the president get elected, this system is now used far more to ensure that the president can take effective political control of the senior bureaucracy.

Starting from a position at the opposite extreme to this are Britain and Ireland, where official civil service culture has traditionally been strenuously non-partisan. When a new minister takes office and walks into his or her department for the first time, this is very much a voyage into the unknown. The minister will be greeted by the civil service head of the department, most likely a total stranger who may well have been in the same department for 30 years or more and knows every nook and cranny of it. All the papers of the former minister typically will have been removed, and the new minister will have to become familiar with the new job on the basis of briefings by senior civil servants. If the political 'master' and his or her civil 'servants' really do not get along, it may be possible to get the department head moved, but there will be a very limited choice of candidates from which to pick a successor.

Even in Britain, however, recent trends are towards the creation of a new political cadre of senior advisors to the minister. When Labour returned to power between 1997 and 2010 after a long period of Conservative rule, a politicized cadre of ministerial advisors became players in the policy process, and often came to be seen as gatekeepers to the cabinet's decision-making system. These people were not in any sense career civil servants, but nor were they elected politicians. They acted as senior ministerial advisors, duplicating from an explicitly partisan perspective the type of advisory role also fulfilled by a senior civil servant. Following the 2010 elections and the formation of a Conservative–Liberal Democrat coalition, the incoming prime minister, David Cameron, promised to cap the number of special advisors his government would appoint. It is too early to know, at the time of writing, whether this will in fact happen, but there is little doubt of the long-term trend for ministers to supplement the advice they get from senior civil servants with advice from hand-picked policy advisors who are also on the public payroll.

There is a higher level of politicization of the senior civil service in countries such as Belgium, France and Germany. In France this has been quite explicitly institutionalized into a system of ministerial *cabinets*, teams of trusted ministerial advisors. The head of the team, the *directeur de cabinet*, may indeed be endowed with the authority of the minister. (The term *cabinet* when used in this context is always pronounced as a French word, as if spelled 'cabinay', to distinguish it from the cabinet of ministers, with a 't', that forms the government.) These *cabinets* are teams of about 20 to 30 policy professionals on whom the ministers can rely for two important forms of support that might well otherwise be missing. The first is to ensure that ministerial policies are actually carried out on the ground; members of the *cabinet* in effect are the minister's eyes and ears within the department. The second is to advise the minister on developments outside the department that are likely to have a bearing on the minister's departmental responsibilities. As we have noted, in the complex environment in which any modern cabinet minister must work, ministers are for the most part forced to concentrate on their own departmental briefs. A department's career civil servants may also be preoccupied with specific departmental responsibilities. As a result, there is a danger that developments outside the department may take the minister by surprise, because a real-world policy problem is likely to have an impact on a range of government departments, even if one department has ultimate responsibility for dealing with it. The *cabinet* will keep track of events outside the minister's department, reporting on external developments that the minister needs to be aware of, and acting as a point of contact with other government departments. Although in theory the *cabinet* system gives French ministers the opportunity of appointing outside policy advisors to guard against being railroaded by the civil service, in practice the vast majority of members of a typical ministerial *cabinet* are career civil servants (Kam and Indridason, 2009). Many French ministers are themselves former civil servants, however, and the political affiliations of French civil servants are often more explicit than elsewhere in Europe. This makes it easier for an incoming minister to select a team of civil servants for the *cabinet* who can be relied on to share his or her general political approach.

Ministerial *cabinets* are found in Belgium, where there is also a substantial turnover in the minister's senior civil service team when political power changes hands. This system cannot be found in such an explicit and institutionalized form in any other European country, although there is a trend almost everywhere towards having teams of political advisors tied to particular ministers. In the Netherlands, for example, ministers seek advice from a wide range of policy professionals, commissioning studies and policy reviews that are conducted outside the career civil service, by people whose political affiliations are often quite explicit. This trend is to some extent an explicit recognition in an increasingly technocratic world of something that has always been there. This is the need for ministers to have access to expert advice that they feel comes from an ideologically sympathetic perspective, and which is based outside the civil service department of which they are the political head.

### 6.2.3 Conclusion: increasing accountability of public servants?

Regardless of its culture and style, public administration is ultimately political, and senior civil servants are in many senses politicians in their own right. They make important decisions about policy implementation, albeit under the auspices of their political bosses. These decisions have important implications for the allocation of resources in society, something that is of the very essence of politics. Senior civil servants are also responsible for much of the preliminary work that goes into the development of new policy initiatives, and thus leave their fingerprints all over the making of public policy in many subtle ways. Indeed, for a young person leaving university in almost any European country with the ambition to have a real impact on public life, joining the civil service is an option at least as likely to be effective as becoming a rank-and-file elected politician. The interaction between the senior civil service and the political executive is thus vital for all who are concerned with the shaping and making, as well as with the 'mere' implementation, of important public policy decisions.

At the purely administrative level, furthermore, increasing scepticism about the management style associated with the traditional 'big government' public sector has led to a growing influence of the ideas of 'new public management'. These stress the need for a clear sense of mission in each public sector department, the need for a strategic plan for how to realize this vision, the need for a 'client-centred' approach to service delivery, and the need for the public sector to be held clearly accountable for any failure to deliver. These managerial developments, combined with a situation in which cabinet ministers seem less and less inclined to 'take the rap' for everything in their jurisdiction, are likely to make the public accountability of senior civil servants a matter of increasing public concern (Romzek, 2000).

## 6.3 Levels of governance

Despite many similarities, modern European states vary hugely in terms of the territorial organization of decision-making. Britain and France, not least because of their imperial pasts, have traditionally been very centralized states in which most key decisions are made at the national level. In other countries, especially Switzerland, but also Germany and Austria, for example, decision-making has traditionally been much more decentralized. Taking European countries as a whole, however, the trend for important decisions to be taken at EU rather than national level, discussed in the previous chapter, is counterbalanced by a strong trend within individual countries towards greater decentralization. This involves shifting important policy *decisions*, not just policy *implementation*, to more local or regional arenas. In countries that already have well-established institutions for local decision-making – Sweden and Denmark, for example – even more powers are being handed over to local authorities. For eastern European countries that have undergone a transition to democratic governance, furthermore, it is easy to see that decisions on the decentralization of decision-making have been very significant. Under their former communist administrations, municipalities and regions were to a large extent part of a *top-down* system of local administration, with decisions taken nationally being implemented at local level. A fundamental part of the democratization process in central and eastern Europe, therefore, has been to determine the extent of decision-making autonomy for local government units (Scott, 2009). This was the subject of extended debate in Poland, for example, resulting in provisions in the 1997 constitution that entrenched the principle of *subsidiarity* discussed in the previous chapter, which in this context essentially means that policy decisions should be taken at the lowest level of government that is practically feasible.

There are two different, though related, features of the decentralization of decision-making in modern Europe. The first has to do with the distinction between *federal* and *unitary* states (although, as we shall see, this distinction is becoming blurred by the increasing powers of the regional tier of government in a number of European countries). The second has to do with the system of local government. It is possible for unitary states, as we shall see, to have strong systems of local government, while federal states may have weak local government systems.

## 6.4 Federal government in modern Europe

It is surprisingly difficult to produce an abstract definition of a federal state, although it is also true that most people do know a federal state when they see one. The main European examples of federal states – Switzerland, Germany, Austria and, since 1993, Belgium – differ a lot from each other, and also differ in striking respects from non-European federal states such as the United States, Canada and Australia. The situation is further complicated by the fact that countries such as Spain and Britain, once bastions of centralized governance, now look much more 'federal' after setting up strong regional administrations and assemblies that have substantial powers. In what follows, therefore, we focus our discussion on the territorial distribution of decision-making in Switzerland and Germany, which almost all observers take to be federal states. We also discuss the decisions *not* to adopt federalist arrangements by eastern European states making the transition from communist rule.

### 6.4.1 Federal government in Switzerland

There is a gap between the romantic image and the practical reality of federal government in Switzerland. The romantic image dates the Swiss confederation back to 1291, and portrays this as a loose union of ancient provinces, called *cantons*, which arouse intense loyalties among their citizens and only grudgingly cede very limited powers to the Swiss central government. The practical reality of the modern Swiss state is that it has been governed according to a federal constitution, framed on the basis of European observations of the experience of federalism in the United States, that dated from 1874 and was replaced in 1999. Nonetheless, 25 of the 26 cantons that form the constituent parts of the union are indeed very old, although Jura was formed from a part of Berne in 1980. Earlier Swiss federations had united three of these cantons (from 1315 to 1515), 13 of them (from 1515 to 1798), and all 25 (from 1815 to 1875). None of these cantons was ever really a fully autonomous state as we would now understand the term – another parallel with the constituent states of what is now the United States. Furthermore, when we actually look at what the cantons have the power to do, this turns out to be quite limited, on a par with the power of typical local authorities in many European countries. For a comprehensive discussion of Swiss federalism, see Linder (2010).

What underpins Swiss federalism has as much to do with the social structure as with the constitution. In the first place, a canton does evoke strong feelings of traditional loyalty among at least some of its citizens. Probably more important than historical loyalties to cantons *per se* are two significant sources of social division in Switzerland. These are language – the population is divided between French, German and Italian speakers – and religion – the population is divided between Protestants and Roman Catholics. Looking at the country as a whole, these two cleavages cut across one another; not all members of the same language group have the same religion, and vice versa. Nonetheless, language and religious frontiers do follow the borders of cantons rather closely. Almost all cantons comprise an overwhelming majority of one or the other language group, for example, and are strictly unilingual. The different language groups keep very much to themselves at the local level, and only at the federal level does social and political life become bilingual or even trilingual. Because language defines the communication structure of any society, the distribution of language groups in Switzerland is almost bound to impede any process of centralization. Religious groups are also sorted between cantons in a very structured manner. Individual cantons are either mostly Protestant or mostly Roman Catholic, a relic of the historical role of the cantons in assimilating or resisting the Reformation. Because organized religion provides almost as powerful a cultural network as language, this geographical pattern of religious affiliation also serves to establish the canton as a focus of social and political life.

Despite these diverse traditional sources of loyalty to the canton, there is general agreement that the trend in Switzerland has been towards greater centralization. The list of functions formally allocated to the federal government is long and growing longer; local councils in unitary systems such as Sweden and Denmark typically have more functions than Swiss cantons. Nonetheless, Swiss cantons do have substantial powers, and are responsible for the administration of much of the welfare state, overall policy for which is set at the federal level. They have power to set local taxes, including income taxes, and above all their autonomy is deeply entrenched in the constitution. One very important manifestation of this autonomy is Article 3 of the federal constitution, which vests all future powers in the cantons. New powers can be given to the federal authority only if this is agreed to by the cantons and by the people in a referendum. This clearly limits the growth of federal government. The result is that the share of both taxes and spending under the control of the federal government in Switzerland is much lower, for example, than that controlled by the federal government in the United States, and very much lower than in unitary government systems such as the Netherlands or Spain (Armingeon, 2000). The power of central government in Switzerland is further weakened by the long-standing custom that the presidency of the Swiss Federation rotates between senior politicians on an annual basis, with the result that the majority of Swiss citizens do not know the name of their president. More generally, the particular character of Swiss federalism means that the visibility of Swiss national politicians is lower than that of national politicians in most other modern European states.

A second important manifestation of the constitutional entrenchment of the autonomy of the canton can be seen in the relationship between the two chambers of the Swiss legislature. As in most federal systems, the lower house (the National Council) is elected on a one-person-one-vote basis to represent the population as a whole, and the upper house (the Council of States) is designed to represent the interests of the constituent states of the federation, the cantons. The Council of States thus has two representatives from every full canton. The cantons themselves determine how these representatives are selected, although they are now for the most part directly elected, often by majority rule. If both upper and lower houses do not pass legislation, then it cannot be passed; there is no provision for one house to overturn the vote of the other by special majority.

As we shall see in Chapter 11, cantons also play a part in the very important referendum process in Switzerland. Many proposals put to referendum require the support not just of a majority of voters but also of a majority of cantons. All of this combines to mean that the autonomy of the cantons relative to the central government is entrenched somewhat more deeply than that of the constituent parts of the German federal state, to which we now turn.

## 6.4.2 Federal government in Germany

The historical and cultural context of the German federal state is quite different. The current German constitution, or Basic Law, was effectively framed for what was then West Germany by the victorious Western Allies in 1949. It was an explicit piece of constitutional engineering, using a federal structure to prevent the emergence of the type of powerful centralized state seen in Bismarck's Prussia and Hitler's Third Reich. Indeed, so concerned were the Allies to decentralize the German state that the implementation of an extensive system of local government was already well under way by the end of 1945. Although some of the constituent states (*Länder*) of West Germany – Bavaria, for example – had long historical traditions, many were formed from scratch from the areas that the three Western occupying powers – Britain, France and the United States – happened to control. There was a huge variation in the sizes of the states. Some are no more than medium-sized cities; others, especially North-Rhine Westphalia, are bigger than many European countries.

Not surprisingly in this context, German federal arrangements set out in the Basic Law borrowed heavily from US experience. Furthermore, given the fears of the Allies at the time, the federal structure is given an 'eternal guarantee' in Articles 20 and 79 of the Basic Law: abolishing the federal system in Germany would in effect require a revolution that overthrew the constitution as a whole. As we saw in Chapter 4, however, citizens in a number of countries have introduced completely new constitutions on the basis of the consent of a majority of the population. Thus constitutional guarantees such as these, however 'eternal' they might purport to be, are never really absolute. The reunification of Germany in October 1990 resulted in the assimilation of 16 million people living in five *Länder* from the former East Germany. In addition, with the unification of Berlin, this city became a *Land* in its own right, so there are 16 *Länder* in what is now a united Germany. Obviously, some adjustments were necessary, but the essential structure of the West German federal state, as laid down in the Basic Law, has remained the constitutional basis of the new Germany. For discussions of post-unification federalism in Germany, see Bräuninger and König (1999) and Jeffery (1999).

The division of responsibilities between the *Länder* and the German federal government (the Bund) gives a list of designated powers to either the central government or the *Länder*, and the powers of the *Länder* were strengthened somewhat in 1994. In addition, there are quite a large number of 'concurrent' areas in which both the federal government and the *Länder* may pass laws, although federal law takes precedence over *Land* law in these areas. The federal government deals with matters such as defence, foreign trade and major instruments of macroeconomic policy. Powers explicitly reserved to the *Länder* include control over education and the mass media, but Article 30 of the Basic Law permits *Länder* to legislate on any matter that is not explicitly specified as the preserve of the federal government.

Politically, the *Länder* are represented at the federal level in the upper house of the federal parliament, the Bundesrat. As we saw in Chapter 3, *Länd* members of the Bundesrat are not elected directly (in contrast, for example, to members of the US Senate). Rather, they are delegations from the *Länd* governments, the number of delegates being related, by no means proportionally, to the population of the *Länd* in question. Thus the Bundesrat is sometimes referred to as a *conclave of states*. Each delegation, the members of which are typically members of the *Länd* cabinet, votes as a bloc under the instructions of the *Länd* government. The Bundesrat has considerable powers to block the passage of bills passed by the lower house, the Bundestag, all of which must be submitted to it. If a bill is defeated in the Bundesrat by an ordinary majority, then this veto can be overturned by the lower house with an ordinary majority. If a bill is defeated with a two-thirds majority, then a two-thirds majority in the Bundestag is needed to overturn the veto. And if a bill affects the constitutional position of the *Länder* or the balance of taxes between the federal government and the *Länder* (this includes a lot of bills), then the Bundesrat has an absolute veto. When the two houses are controlled by different party groupings, this division of powers leads to potential confrontation and the clear possibility of legislative gridlock, so that the presence of the *Länder* is definitely felt in federal politics. The two houses, furthermore, can quite easily have different patterns of political control, because *Land* elections do not take place at the same time as federal elections, and voting patterns at the *Land* level may differ from those at the federal level. Research by Bräuninger and König has, however, shown that in many actual policy areas the ability of the federal government to set the policy agenda may well give it more power in practice than formal rules might otherwise indicate.

The legal balance of power between the federal and the *Land* governments is adjudicated by a Federal Constitutional Court (FCC), discussed in Chapter 4. The economic balance of power – so vital in practical politics, whatever the legal position – is guaranteed by the fact that the *Länder* have significant sources of tax revenue from both indirect taxes and a guaranteed proportion of federal income tax revenues. This means that the federal government has not traditionally been able to use the power of the purse strings to bring *Länder* governments to heel, although this situation changed somewhat with the addition of the far poorer eastern *Länder* to the German federation. The extent to which the *Länder* come into open conflict with the federal government, and the extent to which each *Land* pursues policies without regard to what goes on elsewhere, are mediated by a very extensive system of ad hoc committees. These are designed both to resolve potential conflicts before these become explicit and to co-ordinate the activities of different *Länder*, creating a coherent development of public policy across the *Länder* as a whole.

Overall, therefore, despite the fact that many *Länder* are not entities to which citizens have any traditional affiliation, German federalism is underwritten by an explicit and powerful constitutional structure. Furthermore, with the exception of staunchly Roman Catholic Bavaria, *Länder* boundaries do not closely follow those of ethnic, religious or language groups. Essentially, therefore, German federalism is a political and constitutional, rather than a cultural, phenomenon. One implication of this is that German federalism is likely to change as the political environment changes, while both reunification and membership in the European Union (EU) have fundamental implications for German federalism. Reunification, as we have seen, added five *Länder* from the former East Germany, all much poorer than those of the former West Germany. The policy of bringing public and personal services in these new *Länder* towards the standard enjoyed by those in the west generated a need for huge cash transfers, from western *Länder* through the federal government to the eastern *Länder*. This clearly increased the role of the federal government. The impact of the EU is more complex, since the concentration of powers in Brussels has been accompanied by strong support for regions within EU member states. This has the potential to enhance the role of German *Länder* if they become actors in their own right on the European political stage.

Both reunification and European integration have generated lively debates between the *Länder* and the federal authorities in Germany. The fact that they have indicates that the federal ideal is now deeply rooted in the German political system. And the fact that this can be achieved in the relatively short period of time since the introduction of the new Basic Law in 1949 suggests that, notwithstanding some spectacular failures around the world, constitutional engineering can sometimes fulfil its basic objectives.

### 6.4.3 Decisions against federalism in central and eastern Europe

Confronted with the need for a root and branch review of their fundamental constitutional arrangements, the democratizing states of central and eastern Europe had a clear opportunity to choose federal structures, following in the footsteps of post-Nazi Germany. A strikingly different pattern emerged, however. None of the post-communist states of central and eastern Europe opted for a federal system. They all are unitary states, notwithstanding considerable ethnic and cultural internal diversity, and a significant history of federalism in the region. The establishment of a federal Czechoslovakia in 1918 was the modern founding act of statehood for the nations of Slovakia and Bohemia/Moravia. The Yugoslav federation was based largely on the nineteenth-century vision for a south-Slav federation; and the formation of the Soviet Union following the Bolshevik revolution can also be linked to pan-Slavic movements of nineteenth-century nationalists.

To a large extent, however, the historical experience of federalism in eastern Europe was one that its modern citizens were not anxious to repeat, for several reasons. First, previous federations in eastern Europe tended to be dominated by one of the constituent states. The Soviet Union was dominated by Russia; Czechs were dominant over Slovaks in Czechoslovakia; Serbs dominated the Yugoslav federation. This led to what was widely felt to be second-class citizenship for the non-dominant members of the federations concerned. Second, the republics of the socialist federations were also ethnic territories with distinctive cultures, histories and languages. Each constituent part of the federation could typically lay claim to independent sovereignty and a right to secede. Opposition to federalism may come not just from the memory that it was used to oppress minorities, however, but also for fear it could now be used to empower minorities within the transition states of central and eastern Europe. There would be a strong logic for federalism in Romania, for example, giving a degree of autonomy to Hungarian-speaking regions, but that would not be popular with the majority. Finally, one-party communist rule, with its governing principle of democratic centralism, mandated strict discipline and loyalty to the centre among the ostensible leaders of the republics, and required validation of any regional policy or reform by central party leaders. As a result, opposition to communist rule in federal systems was centred largely in the constituent republics. Putting all of this together, we can see why there were so few defenders of the federal idea after the collapse of the communist regimes. Federalism in central and eastern Europe came to be associated with the communist past.

For overviews of federalism in post-communist central and eastern Europe, see Schlesinger (1998) and Roberts (2006).

The transition from communism in eastern Europe was therefore marked by the rapid *dismantling* of federations on a remarkable scale, a process that affected six of the eight eastern European states joining the European Union in 2004. The independence of Estonia, Latvia and Lithuania arose as part of the collapse of the 'federal' Soviet Union. The Czech Republic and Slovakia emerged out of the dissolution of federal Czechoslovakia. Slovenia quickly and successfully declared itself independent from the former Yugoslav federation. In a handful of years, the map of eastern Europe was completely redrawn as a result of the collapse of the communist federations. In these circumstances it is easy to see why citizens of the eastern European transition states saw federalism as something to leave behind them, rather than as a way forward for the future (Rose and Traut, 2001).

## 6.5 The growing importance of regional government

### 6.5.1 Regional government in Spain

Despite the very centralist system of governance in Spain imposed under the dictatorship of General Franco that ended with Franco's death in 1975, many Spanish regions have powerful local traditions and had long demanded autonomy. The province of Catalonia has been at the forefront of these, even receiving limited autonomy between 1913 and 1923 before the imposition of military governments, first under General Primo de Rivera and then under General Franco, that were deeply committed to turning Spain into a strong unitary state. When the Spanish constitution was rewritten at the end of the Franco era, the relative power of regional and central governments became a major bone of contention between left and right. The left wanted Spain to be a federal state; the right was utterly opposed to this. The result was a compromise. The new constitution recognized a series of *autonomous communities*, while some communities with strong historical traditions were granted more autonomy than others.

There are 17 autonomous communities, in effect regional governments, in Spain. Each of these has many of the political and administrative trappings of a mini-state, with a legislature, an executive and a president, as well as a civil service and a high court. Certain important powers are reserved by the constitution to the national government, for example defence, foreign policy, macroeconomic policy and certain major aspects of the social welfare system. Regional powers, which must be exercised in a way that does not conflict with the national constitution, include important areas such as education and health care. The ability of the regions to raise taxes independently, obviously crucial to the possibility of taking truly autonomous decisions on many aspects of public policy, depends upon the national government ceding specific powers of taxation to specific autonomous communities. Throughout the 1980s and 1990s regional governments were financed mainly by grants from the central government. A few regions, including the Basque Country and Navarra, had the power to collect taxes locally, but then pass on a large share of these to the central government. In practice, however, they had to set taxes at the same rate as those for the rest of the country. Recent transfers of taxation powers and service provision to the regional authorities have been associated with increased financial autonomy for the regions, however. The budget for the regions has increased from 3 per cent of national spending in 1981 to more than 35 per cent in recent years; by 2006, only 39 per cent of the total income of the Spanish autonomous communities came from the central government, less than half the equivalent figure for the 1980s (Toboso and Scorsone, 2010).

Some of the autonomous communities in Spain have also maintained a strongly independent local line on many non-financial aspects of public policy. Perhaps the most striking of these is

Catalonia, with a distinctive language, a long history, and Barcelona, one of Europe's major cities, as its capital. The 'government' of Catalonia presents itself in many ways as being on a par with the national government, and in 1992, the year of the Barcelona Olympics, the Catalan president created the position of foreign minister. Furthermore, the Catalan rather than the Spanish national anthem has been played on state visits abroad by the Catalan president. While Catalonia is ahead of the others in presenting itself as having potent features of an independent state, several of Spain's other autonomous communities have 'foreign relations' departments, mostly used to promote regional interests within the EU.

Overall, there can be no doubt that the evolution of regional government in post-Franco Spain challenges the traditional neat separation of countries into those that have a federal system of governance and those that are unitary states. Formally, Spain remains a unitary state, with any power at the disposal of the regions being ceded by the central government. The constraints on central government in taking back these powers – as has indeed previously happened in Spain – depend more upon practical politics than upon the letter of the constitution. Despite its formal unitary status, however, the practical political autonomy of a regional state such as Catalonia is probably far greater than that of a typical *Land* or canton in formally 'federal' Germany or Switzerland. For a discussion of the system of government in post-Franco Spain, see Gunther *et al.* (2004).

## 6.5.2  Devolution of power in the United Kingdom

The very name 'United Kingdom of Great Britain and Northern Ireland' hints strongly at the regional diversity underlying a union of what can be seen as four separate units. Great Britain comprises the countries of England, Wales and Scotland, while how, precisely, to describe Northern Ireland is in itself an intensely political matter. Each of these units has very strong regional traditions. Although the English conquest of Wales dates from 1282, there remains a strong Welsh nationalist movement, and the Welsh language – utterly different from English – remains in widespread everyday use in parts of Wales. English unity with Scotland came much later, with the succession of a Scottish king to the English throne in 1603, consolidated by an Act of Union in 1707. Many Scottish institutions – the legal and educational systems, for example – have remained quite distinct from those in England and Wales. Although Scots Gaelic is very much less current than Welsh as an everyday language, Scottish national identity has remained very strong. This has formed the basis for a very successful and effective Scottish nationalist movement, which was given a huge boost by the discovery of major offshore oil reserves in Scottish waters. These allowed a plausible case to be made that Scotland could be financially self-sufficient. After a long and troubled history of relations between Britain and Ireland, the current province of Northern Ireland came into being with British withdrawal in 1922 from the 26 counties of what was later to become the Republic of Ireland. The remaining six counties of Northern Ireland remained under the control of the British state, and the United Kingdom of Great Britain and Northern Ireland (the UK) came into being.

The post-war emergence of strong nationalist movements in Wales and Scotland – together with continuing sectarian strife between unionist and nationalist communities in Northern Ireland – kept the issue of regional governance very firmly on the UK political agenda from the late 1960s on. Although there were a number of unsuccessful attempts to find a constitutional settlement for Northern Ireland, little was done about the constitutional position of Wales and Scotland during the long period of Conservative government that ran from 1979 to 1997.

Immediately on taking office in 1997, however, Labour prime minister Tony Blair announced referendums on the creation of regional parliaments for Scotland and Wales – in the case of Scotland, with an executive that would have certain tax-varying powers. These were held in September 1997, and resulted in the subsequent creation and election (using a proportional mixed-member electoral system that was in itself a great innovation for Britain) of Scottish and Welsh regional assemblies. The first elections to the new Scottish Parliament and Welsh *Senedd* took place in May 1999, and powers were devolved to these with effect from 1 July 1999.

There is a separate Scottish cabinet – the Scottish Executive – with its own first minister filling a role that could almost be described as that of 'the prime minister of Scotland'. The powers devolved to Scotland are considerably more extensive than those devolved to Wales. There was a striking example of the implications of these powers in 2009, when the Scottish minister for justice exercised his authority by approving the release of a prisoner convicted of involvement in the bombing of a passenger plane over the Scottish village of Lockerbie in 1988. This decision was controversial in Scotland and widely condemned elsewhere, and was made possible by the delegation of justice functions to the Scottish government since devolution.

The Scottish parliament based in Edinburgh has the right, yet to be exercised, to vary the rate of income tax levied in Scotland by up to three pence in the pound. It also has powers over education, health, environment, economic development, local government, transport, sports and agriculture, among other things. Powers reserved to the British parliament in Westminster include defence, foreign policy, large-scale economic management and the social security system. Fewer powers are devolved to Wales; there is no right to vary income tax, and fewer functions can be performed locally, leading some to decry the Welsh Assembly as no more than a talking shop.

For a discussion of regional government in Britain, see Deacon and Sandry (2007) and Bradbury (2008).

As part of the Northern Ireland peace process, the Good Friday Agreement of April 1998 and consequent legislation created a new provincial assembly for Northern Ireland. This is based in Belfast, with substantial powers devolved to a Northern Ireland Executive, with a cabinet and a first and deputy first minister. The rights of both nationalist and unionist communities are protected by a complicated system of qualified majorities needed to pass resolutions in the Assembly, and a requirement that parties be represented in the 'power-sharing' executive in strict proportion to their representation in the Assembly. Elections to the Assembly were held in 1998. After a long delay resulting from protracted negotiations over the decommissioning of IRA weapons, power was devolved to the Northern Ireland Assembly and Executive in December 1999. However, following unionist pressure over the lack of progress on the decommissioning issue, the British government suspended the Northern Ireland Executive in January 2000, even though this had been in operation for no more than a few weeks. *De facto* 'direct rule' over Northern Ireland was thereby restored to Westminster, before being returned to Belfast again in June 2000. The continued stalling of negotiations between all sides led to a further suspension of the Assembly and Executive in October 2002, followed, in an unusual development, by new elections to the suspended Assembly in November 2003. In 2006 the British government and Northern Ireland parties agreed on a roadmap to restore devolution to Northern Ireland. As part of this plan, a significant move towards full devolution was made in 2010, when policing and justice functions were devolved from Westminster to the Northern Ireland Executive.

For a discussion of Northern Ireland politics leading up to the peace process, see McGarry and O'Leary (1997); more generally on recent Northern Ireland politics, see Tonge (2006) and McEvoy (2008).

In a short space of time, therefore, very significant steps were taken to shift power in the United Kingdom away from London and towards regional capitals. The term used to describe this is *devolution*: the granting of power from the centre to some local region. The constitutional implication of *devolved* as opposed to *federal* government is that what has been given away could in theory be taken back by another new government with popular support and a huge parliamentary majority. This did indeed happen when the British government reimposed direct rule on Northern Ireland in 1972 in response to the intense communal violence in the province, setting aside a regional assembly at Stormont that had wielded considerable local power without intervention from Westminster over a 50-year period. Furthermore, the difference between devolved and federal government is highlighted in the clearest possible way by events in Northern Ireland in January 2000 and October 2002. That which the British government had 'given' to Northern Ireland, it could also take away by rushing legislation through the Westminster parliament in a matter of hours, motivated by the political exigencies of the time. However pressing those political exigencies might have been, such action would have been utterly unthinkable in a federal system.

Notwithstanding the Northern Ireland experience, the practical politics of abolishing the Scottish and Welsh assemblies and executives, now that these have been created, makes this a very unattractive prospect in the short to medium term. Indeed, there is nothing in theory to prevent the Scottish Executive from organizing a referendum on the total independence of Scotland from the United Kingdom, thereby provoking a serious constitutional crisis. The Northern Ireland experience, however, shows us that it will take some time before devolution arrangements become deeply enough entrenched to be regarded as an irrevocable move towards a British variant of strong regional government that comes quite close to federalism.

## 6.6 Local government

Many of the services that governments provide, such as health care and education, are delivered to the end user at a local level, in schools, hospitals, and the like. Much of the regulatory activity of government, such as building control or pollution regulation, operates on the ground at the local level. It is thus inevitable in practice that at least some of the machinery for *delivering* public policy outputs must be decentralized and based at a local level near the end user. Whatever the political system, local government, in the sense of local public administration, is inevitable in the real world.

There are also sound theoretical and philosophical reasons for a decentralization of decision-making. Aside from the argument about practical efficiency we just noted, there is the argument that a division of powers helps to avoid a single, monolithic state machine. There is also the argument that increasing the possibilities for ordinary citizens to get involved in the state's everyday workings enhances the legitimacy of the political system. It is no accident that strongly authoritarian regimes such as Franco's Spain or Salazar's Portugal had highly centralized structures of governance. It is, quite simply, very difficult to run an authoritarian regime if real political power is highly decentralized. Having an entrenched decentralized system of governance, therefore, provides a check on the excessive accumulation of power in the hands of some tiny elite. From the perspective of the ordinary citizen, furthermore, the probability of having any real impact on decision-making declines as the decision-making unit gets larger and more remote. A highly centralized state offers little possibility for ordinary citizens to make an impact, either real or imaginary, and may leave citizens feeling powerless and alienated. This in turn may undermine the popular legitimacy of the state. A more decentralized regime may well offer more opportunities for citizen participation, and hence encourage a more widespread feeling that the regime is legitimate and worthy of loyalty.

Despite these general arguments, which apply to all countries, and although all modern European countries have some form of elected local government, the precise form that local government takes, together with the extent to which it is locally politically accountable, varies hugely from country to country. Key variables are: the structure of the local government system, the size and number of local government units; the policy areas where local government has real power; the financial basis of the local government system; and the relative powers of local and national governments in the event of a conflict. Notwithstanding the diversity of European local government systems, we do however see some important general patterns.

### 6.6.1 Structures of local government

Almost every European country has more than one level of local government; most have two levels, some have three. The most basic unit of local government in nearly every European country, often called a *commune* or *municipality*, is typically small and ancient in its origins. As recently as the mid 1990s, for example, one Slovakian mountain municipality comprised no more than 16 citizens. Communes or municipalities in nearly all European countries did, however, undergo major reorganization at some stage during the nineteenth century, when the foundations for most modern systems of local government were laid. As Spence (1993: 74) notes for Italy, 'it is not uncommon for historians to trace the development of the commune as an almost unbroken process beginning in the twelfth century and continuing into the present day.' He goes on to argue, however, that the current structure of Italian local government can be dated to Italian unification in 1861. Similarly, although the English system of parishes and boroughs is very old indeed, the current system of local government can be traced more directly back to a series of major local government reforms beginning in 1835, and the parish no longer has any political significance. In Ireland, the division of the country into the counties that remain today as the basic local administrative units began with the Norman conquest, and was more or less complete by the end of the seventeenth century (Coakley, 2010). France's communes, not surprisingly, can be traced to the Napoleonic era. The Swedish system of local government established in 1863 created municipalities based upon administrative units that were already several hundred years old. In Denmark, the communes were created in 1841 to take over many of the functions formerly fulfilled by parishes. German local government also has a long tradition, as shown by the extensive set of rights enjoyed by its medieval cities. This tradition was broken under Hitler's strongly centralist Third Reich, however, and the current system of municipalities (*Gemeinden*) derives from the arrangements put in place by the Allies in the immediate aftermath of the Second World War. Most central and eastern European states have a long tradition of local government, with systems of municipalities often dating back to the Middle Ages. World wars and the period of communist rule disrupted these, however, and the democratic centralist traditions of twentieth-century communism resulted in local government systems designed to ensure that local authorities did not defy national policymakers.

In almost every European country there is at least one additional tier of local government between the basic unit of the commune or municipality and the national government. These are typically described as *provinces* or *counties*, and there are obviously far fewer of them. There are 19 in Norway, for example, and 12 in the Netherlands. In some countries, especially those with very large numbers of communes or municipalities, the number of provincial areas is larger. There are over 90 departments in France, over 90 provinces in Italy, and over 300 *powiats* drawing together over 2500 municipalities in Poland. In these cases, there is then an additional, regional level at the top of the local government pyramid and below the national government. There are 17 regions in Spain, 15 in Italy and 16 in Poland. The 2006 local government reform in Denmark replaced 14 counties with five large regions that comprise 98 municipalities. In countries such as Spain and Britain, as we have seen, enhancements to the powers of provincial governments have created a system that lies somewhere between traditional federal and unitary models. In other countries, such as the Netherlands, the powers of the regions are weaker.

Thus most modern European states, one way or another, have a system of local government that starts with the commune or municipality and ends with a set of regional or provincial administrations that number somewhere between 12 and 25. For overviews of European local government structures see Norton (1994) and John (2001), and for those in central and eastern Europe see Horvath (2000). Typically, although there are obviously fewer units at each 'higher' level of local government, the relationship between levels is not strictly hierarchical in the sense of one level reporting to, and needing sanction from, the next. Rather, there tends to be a division of labour between levels of local government that is defined either in the constitution or in the national legislation that underpins the local government system. (An exception to this rule is Germany, where the system of municipal government is effectively under the jurisdiction of the regional *Länder* governments.) Indeed, it is sometimes the case that lower levels of local government are considerably more important than higher ones, if we define importance in terms of the range and significance of the public functions for which they have responsibility. Middle-level agencies are often responsible for strategic planning and co-ordination, whereas lower-level agencies actually produce and deliver services on the ground.

This relationship between levels of local government has been extensively debated and thought through, for example, in post-communist Poland. Rather than muddling along with traditional political structures – a luxury always open to long-established western democracies – citizens of eastern European countries had to confront a series of crucial governance issues over a short period of time. While reforming the system of local government might have seemed less exciting than reforming the national political system or setting up massive privatizations of state assets, it was a crucial part of the constitution-building process. Furthermore, having moved rapidly away from a highly centralized state system under communism, decentralization of political power was clearly an important issue in such countries. Thus the new Polish constitution of 1997 begins with a preamble stating the principle of *subsidiarity*. Interpreted literally, subsidiarity implies quite radical decentralization. In the Polish context the constitutional theory is that the local municipality (*gmina*) deals with matters beyond the scope of the individual; the region (*powiat*) deals with matters beyond the scope of the municipality; and the province (*voivodship*) deals with matters beyond the scope of the region. The result is 'a kind of reverse hierarchy. "Superstructures" are added to institutions in those places where smaller organizations, situated closer to citizens, are not able to perform more complex tasks' (Regulski, 2003: 205). The theoretical implication of this is that the state itself will only do things that cannot be done at subnational level, but this is not something that we in practice observe anywhere. As Regulski (2003: 205) observes in a wide-ranging discussion of local government reform in Poland, 'This principle is of fundamental importance. But it was, and still is, very difficult to introduce into practice.' Recent years, moreover, have seen an increased presence of the central state at local levels of administration. For reviews of the recent evolution of local government in central and eastern Europe, see Lankina *et al.* (2008) and Regulska (2009).

This Polish debate shows us clearly that there are two distinct philosophies of local government. On the one hand the subsidiarity principle implies that decisions should be taken at the lowest possible level, with higher tiers of government handling only problems that lower tiers cannot deal with. On the other hand the devolution principle, seen most clearly in Britain and Ireland, gives to local government units, but can also take away, only such powers as are explicitly granted by the national government. For a review of local government systems in many parts of modern Europe, see Loughlin (2001). In practice, the subsidiarity principle for local government is never observed in its purest form. This leads us to the crux of the issue when evaluating any real-world system of local government, which has to do with the real-world significance of the roles it fulfils, and the autonomy it has in fulfilling these.

## 6.6.2 Functions, finances and autonomy of local government

Although discussions of the functions, finances and autonomy of local government might seem to raise quite different issues, they are in practice so intimately interrelated as to be inseparable. This is because, as we have noted, a wide range of government policy outputs must be delivered at a local level. The central government may of course set up local agencies to administer these policies, responsible directly to the central bureaucracy. This was traditionally the preferred solution in Italy, where, before a series of reforms in the mid 1970s, it was estimated that there were about 60 000 such agencies (Spence, 1993). More commonly, however, the central government mandates local government to administer particular policy areas on its behalf. In these cases it is vital to know the extent to which the local government bureaucracy is forced to implement a national policy slavishly, and the extent to which local government agencies may modify national policies on their own initiative.

Although the range of public services *administered* locally is actually rather similar in many European countries, the level of local *autonomy* varies considerably. Because it is usually safe to assume that real political power follows the purse strings, the level of *de facto* autonomy of particular local governments depends to a crucial extent on their ability to raise and spend money independently of the national government. Intimately related to this is the extent to which local people have a real input into local government decision-making. Traditionally, such input was seen in terms of conventional voting in local elections. Recently, however, and in the wake of worries about popular alienation from public decision-making at all levels, local government agencies in a number of countries have set up experiments in innovative ways to involve local people in local decision-making.

It would be an immense task, quite beyond the scope of this book, to run through all the powers of the different levels of local government in each European country. Much of this information can be found in Norton (1994) and John (2001). There are, however, some general patterns. Almost all local councils, even those with relatively fewer powers, play an important role in land-use planning and environmental control: the zoning of development, the processing of individual applications for new development, the issuing of certain licenses and permits, and the monitoring of noxious land uses. Most have a duty to provide a range of services to local residents: fire protection, garbage collection, public utilities and possibly also police – although there is considerable variation in the organization of European police forces, which may also be organized nationally. Other important aspects of the local infrastructure that are often the responsibility of local councils are local public transport and the local road system, as well as one or more of three important aspects of the welfare state: the school system, personal health care and social services, and public housing.

Even though almost no European local council is responsible for every one of these functions, many oversee a number of them. Even in 'centralist' France, it typically falls to local communes to build and maintain local roads, schools, libraries and tourist offices; to dispose of refuse; and to take care of other aspects of minor local infrastructure. In Italy this list is expanded to include local government provision of health care, personal social services, housing, land-use planning, pollution control and local public transport. In Poland almost the entire primary education system was taken over in the late 1990s by the municipalities. In Scandinavia, at the other end of the scale, most aspects of a comprehensive welfare state are supplied on the ground by the local government system. In Sweden in 2005, for example, 28 per cent of the entire workforce was employed by the public sector, 4 per cent by the central government and 24 per cent at the regional and local level (OECD, 2009). The vast bulk of the day-to-day activity of the Swedish welfare state, therefore, is conducted within the local government system. The pattern is similar in other Scandinavian countries.

To what extent is the activity of local councils 'mere' policy implementation at the behest of the national government, a role that could in many ways be performed just as well by a local branch of the central bureaucracy? Here we need to look at both the formal legal position and the power of the purse. In doing so, we must always remember that, in almost all European countries, the powers of local government can be constrained in important ways at the national level. From a constitutional point of view, an interesting illustration of this can be found in the *free commune* or *deregulated local government* experiments that started in Sweden, but quickly extended to Denmark, Norway and Finland. These allowed certain municipalities to be designated as free communes, allowed to make proposals to opt out of national laws in certain specified policy areas in order to develop more effective local arrangements. Areas specifically indicated included land-use planning, the organization of local administration, fees and service charges (in Norway), and education (in Denmark). The first thing that is striking about this, of course, is that such a policy was needed in the first place. This in itself indicates that, despite the size of Scandinavian local government systems, local councils were implementing national policies on most matters rather than deviating from these on the basis of local initiative. The most important thing to note, however, is that the entire experiment was orchestrated by the central government in each country. Only certain municipalities were approved by the central governments for these experiments. And all proposals for local initiatives had to be approved by the national government before they could come into effect; by no means were all of them approved.

The key feature of the Scandinavian free commune experiments, shared by every other European system of local government, is that change could take place only with the approval of the national authorities. In this sense, the constitutions of European unitary states put the boot very firmly on the national, rather than the local, government foot. Unlike federal arrangements, which are typically deeply entrenched in the constitution, making it impossible for them to be changed by the government of the day, the precise system of local government is more typically determined by legislation. This makes it easier to reform the local government system, and also acts as an important constraint on the ability of local councils to defy the national government in any systematic manner.

Clear examples of the cavalier treatment of the local government system by national governments can be seen in both Britain and Ireland, neither of which has traditionally provided any constitutional protection whatsoever for local government. One round of British local government reorganization in 1974, for example, casually swept away counties that had been in existence for many centuries, creating new areas with invented names. In 1985 the powerful, Labour-controlled Greater London Council, which had become a thorn in the side of Margaret Thatcher's Conservative government, was simply abolished. Its powers were redistributed between unelected authorities and smaller local councils, and its main building was sold off to become a hotel and apartment complex. The change of government from Conservative to Labour in 1997 heralded equally dramatic changes in the opposite direction. In addition to the creation, discussed above, of new regional assemblies and administrations for Scotland, Wales and Northern Ireland, the Labour government under Tony Blair engaged in some radical new thinking in relation to local government. This involved a clear preference for creating stronger local executives. A first step towards this was the creation of the very high-profile position of elected mayor of London, the first election for which was held in 2000. Taken together with other local government reforms, this development gave considerable extra power to the London region. A striking example of this power being used in practice was the introduction in February 2003 by Ken Livingstone, then the elected mayor of London, of a *congestion charge* to address the city's chronic traffic problems. In an experiment closely watched throughout the rest of the world, London motorists were forced to pay a fee to drive their cars inside a central congestion zone between 7 am and 6.30 pm, Monday to Friday. Notwithstanding such developments, the lack of an entrenched constitutional position for local government in Britain, together with a long tradition of strong central government, implies that these reforms must be seen as devolutions of power from central or local government. Powers that are devolved by central government can be taken back again in a minute. If any British government chooses to do so, legislation can be pushed through the British national parliament that bans the London congestion charge, even abolishes the position of London mayor altogether, and sells off its newly built headquarters to become yet another hotel and apartment complex.

In Ireland the system of domestic rates (local property taxes), which was a vital part of the revenue base of local councils, was abolished by the central government, without even the need for legislation, in 1978. Irish governments have traditionally had little compunction in postponing scheduled local council elections when these were forecast to prove politically embarrassing. Only in 1999 was a constitutional amendment passed that specifically referred to the local government system, and mandated the holding of local elections every five years. The desire to attract European Union regional funding prompted attempts in 1999 to establish a new tier of government in Ireland – resulting in a new system of 'regions' that bore virtually no relationship to existing geographical or cultural boundaries. Many Irish people have not the slightest idea that such regions exist, and many others do not know which of these regions they live in. Thus local government in Ireland remains weak and ineffective, and attempts to restructure its finances have so far proved unsuccessful. There is an inherently top-down approach to local governance, and debate tends to be conducted in terms of which particular powers can safely be devolved to local authorities without threat to the unitary system, rather than in terms of which functions can be fulfilled only by national governments.

It is inconceivable that a national government in a federal system could behave like this towards its constituent states, since intergovernmental relations are embedded in the constitution. In a very real sense, therefore, local governments in almost every European country ultimately can do only what they are allowed to do by their central government. Powers that are given can be, and sometimes have been, taken away. Despite this ultimate constitutional reality, there is a very wide variation between countries in the level of autonomy that local councils are allowed by central government, and nowhere is this more evident than in the system of local government funding. Everywhere in Europe there are three basic sources of local government financing. These are local taxes on property, business, or income; local service charges; and transfers from higher levels of government. One of the best measures of differences between countries in the degree of local autonomy has to do with how much freedom local councils have to raise money from these various sources as they please, and then to spend this money as they see fit.

At one extreme we find Denmark and Sweden, where the municipalities and county councils are the main tax-gathering agencies for the state as a whole. The 98 Danish municipalities finance their very extensive activities on the basis of local income taxes, the rates of which can be set locally by the municipality, and varied in 2009 from about 22 per cent to about 28 per cent. An additional flat rate health tax of 8 per cent and a small voluntary church tax are also levied at the local level. In Sweden the central government income tax rate has two tiers: one at 20 per cent and the other at 25 per cent. At the same time, the average taxes raised by the counties and municipalities were about 31 per cent of income in 2009. In both of these countries local authorities may also raise a local land value tax, the level of which they are free to determine. There are also transfers of funds from the central government in the form of block grants, which can be used to compensate for the unequal revenue-gathering abilities of different counties and municipalities in a country in which the same welfare system applies to all. The paradox in Sweden is that while the constitution guarantees the political and financial autonomy of the municipalities, it also stipulates that welfare provision is based on equity and equal access, which implies a high degree of centralization. Overall, although much of the expenditure by Swedish and Danish local authorities is on a welfare state determined at national level, the high level of local discretion in raising revenue also provides considerable scope for local policymaking.

At the opposite extreme we find countries such as Ireland, where local councils have very little scope for independent revenue-raising and where, as we have seen, one of the main sources of local revenue was abolished at a stroke in 1978. These revenues were replaced by a block grant that puts the central government overwhelmingly in control of the local government system. Britain, too, has seen major central government attacks on the financial independence of local government. As a result of a series of reforms during the 1980s, local councils were first prohibited from setting rates for local property taxes at will, and both spending and revenue-raising had to comply with strict central government guidelines. Councillors who defied the central government were threatened with the suspension of the council and its replacement with a government-appointed commissioner, or even with imprisonment. Subsequently, domestic rates were abolished and replaced with a local *poll tax*, so called because every adult on the electoral register was liable to pay a fixed charge. This innovation proved massively unpopular, provoking widespread violent demonstrations and contributing in no small way to Margaret Thatcher's downfall. After her departure, the poll tax was replaced with a *council tax*, a modified system of the old property tax, which finances only around one-sixth of total local spending.

## BOX 6.1: REGIONAL AND LOCAL GOVERNMENT

### Denmark

The local level of government in Denmark consists of five regions and 98 municipalities. There is no system of subordination between these two types of administrative unit, as they handle different tasks and have different responsibilities. Among the highly decentralized tasks that are performed at the local level are primary education, a large part of the social welfare provision, health, environment and spatial planning, road management and utilities. Local government elections for the municipal and regional councils take place every four years, under a highly proportional electoral system, and the mayors are elected indirectly by the members of the respective councils. Local governments can arrange advisory referendums, and have been experimenting with different models of advisory committees, sub-councils and consultation forums.

### France

The basic units of local government in France are communes (of which there are thousands), departments (of which there are 96), and regions (of which there are 22). Communes are very old units of local government that may be cities the size of Marseilles or tiny villages. In practice they fulfil a range of different functions, depending on their size; large communes may have an extensive set of functions. Departments are local administrative units of the central state. At the head of each department is a prefect, a civil servant appointed by the Ministry of the Interior. Before local government reforms of 1982, prefects were very powerful, and their power remains considerable. The French regions date from 1964. Each region is headed by a regional prefect, typically one of the departmental prefects in the region. Regions do not have significant powers; the most important units of local government remain communes and departments.

### Germany

Germany is a federal state in which 16 local state governments (*Länder*) have extensive powers entrenched in the constitution. The interests of the *Länder* are further protected by their control of the upper house of the legislature, the Bundesrat. Local government, the basic units of which are about 9000 municipalities (*Gemeinden*), derives its authority from the *Länder*. The municipalities have a very wide range of powers, and can act in all policy areas not specifically allocated to the *Länder* or the federal government. Between the municipalities and the *Länder* are counties (*Kries*), which have a general co-ordinating role. Overall, however, the *Länder* and the municipalities are the key to the German local government system.

### Italy

Italy has a three-tier local government system: regions, provinces and communes. Of these, the provinces have the smallest contemporary role, and the regions and communes have considerable power, most of it granted through recent reforms. The principles of constitutional subsidiarity and legal parity between the central and regional governments were introduced in 2001, and were accompanied by an increase in the taxation powers of the local levels of government. As result of particular ethnic or geographical considerations, five of the 20 regions have an autonomous or semi-autonomous statute. Regional and local elections are held every five years, and mayors, as well as provincial and regional governors, are popularly elected.

### Netherlands

Local government in the Netherlands is based on a system of provinces and municipalities, with lower tiers being subject to the control of higher tiers and the national government. The local administrative head is a burgomaster, appointed by the central government, although there are proposals to replace this position with that of an elected mayor. Almost all of the funding for local government in the Netherlands comes in the form of grants from the central government, most of them earmarked for specific purposes. In consequence, the local government system in the Netherlands does not have a high degree of formal autonomy, although recent experiments in local democracy suggest a desire to increase practical public participation in local decision-making.

### Poland

The 1997 constitution states that Poland is a unitary state, and that local government ensures decentralization of public authority. A three-tiered system took effect on 1 January 1999, according to which Poland is divided into municipalities, counties and regions. Local councils operate at all three levels, making local by-laws, passing budgets, setting local taxes and charges, and adopting resolutions on matters of property rights. Some critics point out that although the distribution of power among different levels of government is set out in the constitution, municipalities, counties and regions have many overlapping tasks. Nonetheless, each level of local government is able to raise its own revenues via local taxes and other charges and, more significantly, has access to a fixed share of the national budget.

### Spain

One of the most striking responses to the ending of a long period of centralized authoritarian rule in Spain was the setting up of a comprehensive system of local and regional authorities, with considerable local autonomy. The major innovation was the introduction of the 17 autonomous regions, each with its own legislature and executive headed by a regional president elected by the legislature. Below the level of region are 50 provinces and about 8000 municipalities, each with its own elected councils. There is some overlap between the powers of different tiers of local government, which causes certain procedures to be rather cumbersome. Although much of the financing of local and regional government comes from the central government, certain regional governments have used their constitutional powers to establish a very independent line. This makes Spain one of the European countries characterized by a high degree of regional autonomy, yet falling short of a constitutionally federal system.

### United Kingdom

The local government system in Britain has long been a political bone of contention, with local authorities challenging national governments' attempts to impose central policies, and national governments responding by taking functions away from local authorities and reducing their power to set local taxes. Local government in Britain is entirely under the control of the national government, can be reformed with ordinary legislation, and has no constitutional protection. The main local authorities are county councils, which retain considerable powers in matters such as policing, housing, transportation and education. Nonetheless, the ability of these councils to adopt independent policies is reduced by the relatively high degree of central government control over local government finances. The recent introduction of Scottish, Welsh and Northern Ireland regional assemblies, the Scottish with tax-varying power, and of an elected mayor for London, does represent a significant move towards decentralization in Britain, however.

Although councils have some other non-tax revenue sources, such as user charges, only 5 per cent of all tax revenues are raised locally. At the same time, selective capping of local spending further restricts the financial autonomy of local authorities.

Most other European countries fall somewhere between these extremes. In the Netherlands, for example, less than 10 per cent of local expenditure is raised locally. The remainder comes from central government grants, many earmarked for particular projects and programmes. Similarly, as we have seen, most of the high-profile regional governments in Spain, including the Catalan government, derive up to 80 per cent of their income from central government grants. In Poland, despite the considerable range of functions fulfilled by the local municipalities, they raise relatively little local revenue. The fundamental source of tax revenue is the national government, which allocates a fixed share of national revenues directly to local authorities. In France and Belgium, in contrast, a far higher proportion of local spending is funded from local taxes, especially on land, property and businesses. Germany cleaves more closely to the Scandinavian pattern, with local government funding coming from income taxes, business and property taxes. In the German case, however, local councils receive a fixed proportion, currently 15 per cent, of all national income tax raised in their area. Local taxes on business are also shared on a rigid basis with higher levels of government, with municipal councils retaining 60 per cent and passing the remainder on to regional and federal government.

### 6.6.3 Popular participation in local decisions

The level of central government control over the local purse strings is obviously one measure of the autonomy of local decision-making in modern Europe. Another is the nature and extent of popular participation in local decisions. One distinctive approach to local participation can be found in Switzerland. Here, local participation can take the form of direct rather than representative democracy, with many local referendums and even a tradition of *Landsgemeinde* (popular assemblies held in the open) for making decisions in several small cantons. Rates of participation in local referendums are often very low, however, and as of 1998 only two of the five cantons that were using the system of *Landsgemeinde*, Appenzell Innerrhoden and Glarus, were still holding open assemblies. The largest open assembly in Switzerland (to which women had been admitted only since 1991) was abolished in Appenzell Ausserrhoden in September 1997. Mandatory fiscal and statutory referendums have also been abolished by some of the cantons in recent years, thus shifting the political power from the electorate to the cantonal parliament, but optional referendums can still be held.

In most of modern Europe the traditional method of involving citizens in local decision-making has been through a system of elections to local councils – in effect, viewing local politics as a microcosm of politics at the national level. There are very wide variations in levels of participation in local government elections across Europe, with the highest levels (of about 75 per cent of registered voters) generally found in Luxembourg, Belgium, Sweden and Austria, and the lowest in Britain (about 35 per cent) and in central and eastern Europe (Council of Europe, 2009). The general trend across Europe, however, has been for turnout in local elections to decline. Combined with steady declines in turnout at national elections and low levels of turnout at European Parliament elections, this has led to a concern that European voters may be getting increasingly alienated from politics. This concern has been accompanied by increased interest at the grassroots level in alternative forms of political expression. As we shall see in Chapter 14, a wide range of formal and informal social groups in what we can generally think of as civil society can all play a part in the process of making decisions.

Popular participation in such groups, which may deal with either single 'pet' issues or matters of more general concern, is an important way to bring people into the decision-making process.

Elite concern at declining turnout in local elections, combined with increasing popular awareness of alternative forms of participation, has generated increasing interest in new ways to involve ordinary people in public decision-making, especially at local level. A common theme is a desire to make decision-making more interactive and *deliberative*. These new approaches set out to go beyond the mere aggregation of individual preferences that is typical of institutions such as elections and referendums. Reasoned discussion, dialogue and debate at the local level are intended to allow a range of options to be developed, examined, challenged and evaluated. Proponents claim the following benefits of this approach: an improvement in citizen awareness and information; an increased sense of local involvement; a general willingness of citizens to take account of the views of others; and an increase in the level of popular acceptance of the decisions that are eventually taken. For a theoretical discussion of the ideas of deliberative democracy, see Elster (1998) and Fishkin (2009).

At a practical level, recent experiments in places such as Denmark and the Netherlands have attempted to put these ideas into practice. In the county of Funen in Denmark, for example, decisions about the future of county hospitals were made on the basis of local deliberative techniques. A traditional survey of 1000 individuals was supplemented with a day-long *deliberative hearing* by 75 representative local citizens. Experts were interrogated, policymakers made presentations, and the eventual policy emerged as a result of intense interactive discussion among what is sometimes called a *citizens' jury*. In the Netherlands, the city of Enschede delegated responsibility for the redesign of a public square to a working group that comprised delegates of interest groups and a sample of directly involved citizens. They organized debates, public excursions to other cities, and a survey to involve citizens in the eventual decision that emerged. This model has been lately adopted in other cities and at the regional level, mainly with respect to environmental policies (Bekkers *et al.*, 2007). Many of these experiments are at an early stage, and they typically have only an informative and consultative role. Nonetheless, they are obviously very significant for the entire concept of representative democracy, especially at local level. In the face of declining levels of turnout in elections to traditional representative institutions, deliberative hearings and citizens' juries suggest that one way forward may not necessarily be found in attempts to force up turnout in conventional elections. Rather, they suggest that the answer may be to find new ways for ordinary people to participate in the key public decisions that affect them.

## 6.7 Conclusions

European variations that we find in patterns of local governance tell us as much about national political cultures as about anything else. In Germany and Scandinavia we see a strong decentralizing ethos. This is reflected both in the large scale of the operations of local or state governments and in their substantial sources of revenue. Elsewhere in western Europe, especially in countries with a long-standing imperial tradition that favours a strong centralized state, local government tends to be significantly weaker, in terms of both what it can do and how it chooses to do it. Governments in such countries seem much less willing to allow local governments to develop alternative power bases that might ultimately challenge their authority. In central and eastern Europe, countries that might have had a long tradition of local government found this significantly disrupted during the period of centralized communist rule. Part of the transition process in these countries has been to redesign systems of local government. This process of local government reform is still evolving, having been given a lower priority than major constitutional reforms of national decision-making structures. The Polish case shows us that, while radical thinking about the subsidiarity principle can inform debate about local government reform, such thoughts are much easier to think than they are to implement on the ground in a political system that already has a national government.

The explicit redesigning of political institutions in central and eastern Europe is also marked by an unwillingness, given recent history, of the new generation of constitutional engineers to take the federalist path. We can see a clear desire for decentralization, following the demise of highly centralized systems of government, but the manifestation of this has been the fragmenting of existing federations into a larger number of smaller independent states, rather than the creation of federal arrangements within existing states. The extent to which decentralization can be achieved in practice will thus depend upon the bedding-in of the new local government systems in eastern Europe.

Overall, however, there can be little doubt that the trend towards shifting the powers of national governments 'up' to the EU level, discussed in the previous chapter, has been combined with a trend towards decentralizing decision-making 'down' from national governments to subnational arenas – at least in terms of political structures and rhetoric, even if not of the practices of real political power. Almost no European politician these days fights elections on the platform of gathering ever more power to the centre, and decentralization is almost universally held to be a 'good thing'. It is also clear, however, that it is hard to decentralize real power in an already centralized state. Not least this is because of the role of the national civil service. An established civil service with a strong sense of self-worth may well develop an identity that links it inextricably with the capital city. Senior civil servants may see postings to provincial locations as demotions or punishments. The doctrine of ministerial responsibility also tends to 'metropolitanize' administration, as top bureaucrats work directly to cabinet ministers who tend to be based in the seat of national power. The ultimate reality is that European states have not grown from the bottom up into the shape they now have. Their boundaries have been set by politics and war at the international level, and their administrative systems thus tend to extend from the top down. In this context, the decentralization of decision-making may be seen as politically expedient, and this is increasingly so, but it tends actually to happen only if it is seen as being expedient when viewed from the perspective of powerful national politicians.

## References

**Armingeon, Klaus** (2000) 'Swiss federalism in comparative perspective', pp. 112–129 in U. Wachendorfer-Schmidt (ed.), *Federalism and Political Performance*, Routledge, London.

**Baker, Randall** (2002) *Transitions from Authoritarianism: The Role of the Bureaucracy*, Praeger, Westport, CT.

**Bekke, Hans and Frits van der Meer (eds)** (2001) *Civil Service Systems in Western Europe*, Edward Elgar, Cheltenham.

**Bekkers, Victor, Geske Dijkstra, Arthur Edwards and Menno Fenger (eds)** (2007) *Governance and the Democratic Deficit: Assessing the Democratic Legitimacy of Governance Practices*, Ashgate, Aldershot.

**Bradbury, Jonathan (ed.)** (2008) *Devolution, Regionalism and Regional Development: The UK Experience*, Routledge, London.

**Bräuninger, Thomas and Thomas König** (1999) 'The checks and balances of party federalism: German federal government in a divided legislature', *European Journal of Political Research*, 36 (6), 207–234.

**Coakley, John** (2010) 'The foundations of statehood', pp. 3–36 in J. Coakley and

M. Gallagher (eds), *Politics in the Republic of Ireland*, 5th edn, Routledge, London.

**Council of Europe** (2009) Report on Developments on Citizens' Participation in Member States, Council of Europe, Utrecht.

**Deacon, Russell and Alan Sandry** (2007) *Devolution in the United Kingdom*, Edinburgh University Press, Edinburgh.

**Dimitrov, Vesselin, Klaus H. Goetz and Hellmut Wollmann** (2006) *Governing After Communism: Institutions and Policymaking*, Rowman and Littlefield, Lanham, MD.

**Dimitrova, Antoaneta L.** (2005) 'Europeanization and civil service reform in central and eastern Europe', pp. 71–90 in F. Schimmelfennig and U. Sedelmeier (eds), *The Europeanization of Central and Eastern Europe*, Cornell University Press, Ithaca, NY.

**Dunleavy, Patrick** (1991) *Democracy, Bureaucracy and Public Choice: Economic Explanations in Political Science*, Harvester Wheatsheaf, Hemel Hempstead.

**Eisenhardt, Kathleen M.** (1989) 'Agency theory: an assessment and review', *The Academy of Management Review*, 14 (1), 57–74.

**Elster, Jon (ed.)** (1998) *Deliberative Democracy*, Cambridge University Press, Cambridge.

**Fishkin, James S.** (2009) *When the People Speak: Deliberative Democracy and Public Consultation*, Oxford University Press, Oxford.

**Gunther, Richard, José R. Montero and Juan Botella** (2004) *Democracy in Modern Spain*, Yale University Press, New Haven, CT.

**Hennessy, Peter** (1989) *Whitehall*, Secker & Warburg, London.

**Horvath, Tamas M.** (2000) *Decentralization: Experiments and Reforms – Local Governments in Central and Eastern Europe*, Open Society Institute, Budapest.

**Hough, Jerry F. and Merle Fainsod** (1979) *How the Soviet Union is Governed*, Harvard University Press, Cambridge, MA.

**Jeffery, Charlie (ed.)** (1999) *Recasting German Federalism: The Legacies of Unification*, Pinter, London.

**John, Peter** (2001) *Local Governance in Western Europe*, Sage, London.

**Kam, Christopher and Indridi Indridason** (2009) 'Cabinet dynamics and ministerial careers in the French Fifth Republic', in K. Dowding and P. Dumont (eds), *The Selection of Ministers in Europe: Hiring and Firing*, Routledge, New York.

**Kornai, János** (1992) *The Socialist System; The Political Economy of Communism*, Oxford University Press, Oxford.

**Kotchegura, Alexander** (2008) *Civil Service Reform in Post-Communist Countries*, Leiden University Press, Leiden.

**Lankina, Tomila V., Anneke Hudalla and Hellmut Wollmann** (2008) *Local Governance in Central and Eastern Europe: Comparing Performance in the Czech Republic, Hungary, Poland and Russia*, Palgrave Macmillan, New York.

**Linder, Wolf** (2010) *Swiss Democracy: Possible Solutions to Conflict in Multicultural Societies*, 3rd edn, Macmillan, London.

**Loughlin, John (ed.)** (2001) *Subnational Democracy in the European Union: Challenges and Opportunities*, Oxford University Press, Oxford.

**McEvoy, Joanne** (2008) *The Politics of Northern Ireland*, Edinburgh University Press, Edinburgh.

**McGarry, John and Brendan O'Leary** (1997) *Explaining Northern Ireland: Broken Images*, Blackwell, Oxford.

**Meyer-Sahling, Jan-Hinrik** (2004) 'Civil service reform in post-communist Europe: the bumpy road to depoliticisation', *West European Politics*, 27 (1): 71–103.

**Niskanen, William A.** (2007) *Bureaucracy and Representative Government*, Aldine-Atherton, Chicago.

**Norton, Alan** (1994) *International Handbook of Local and Regional Government: A Comparative Analysis of Advanced Democracies*, Edward Elgar, Cheltenham.

**OECD** (2009) *Government at a Glance 2009*, OECD Publishing, Paris.

**Ongaro, Edoardo** (2009) *Public Management Reform and Modernization: Trajectories of Administrative Change in Italy, France, Greece, Portugal and Spain*, Edward Elgar, Cheltenham.

**Peters, B. Guy and Jon Pierre (eds)** (2004) *The Politicization of the Civil Service in Comparative Perspective: The Quest for Control*, Routledge, New York.

Raadschelders, Jos, Theo Toonen and Frits van der Meer (eds) (2007) *The Civil Service in the 21st Century: Comparative Perspectives*, Palgrave Macmillan, New York.

Regulska, Joanna (2009) 'Governance or self-governance in Poland? Benefits and threats 20 years later', *International Journal of Politics, Culture and Society*, 22 (4): 537–556.

Regulski, Jerzy (2003) *Local Government Reform in Poland*, Open Society Institute, Budapest.

Roberts, Andrew (2006) 'What kind of democracy is emerging in eastern Europe?', *Post-Soviet Affairs*, 22 (1): 37–64.

Romzek, Barbara S. (2000) 'Dynamics of public sector accountability in an era of reform', *International Review of Administrative Sciences*, 66 (1): 21–44.

Rose, Jürgen and Johannes Ch. Traut (eds) (2001) *Federalism and Decentralization: Perspectives for the Transformation Process in Eastern and Central Europe*, Palgrave, New York.

Schlesinger, Rudolf (1998) *Federalism in Central and Eastern Europe*, Routledge, London.

Scott, James Wesley (ed.) (2009) *De-coding New Regionalism: Shifting Socio-political Contexts in Central Europe and Latin America*, Ashgate, Farnham.

Spence, R.E. (1993) 'Italy', in *Local Government in Liberal Democracies: An Introductory Survey*, J.A. Chandler (ed.), Routledge, London.

Toboso, Fernando and Eric Scorsone (2010) 'How much power to tax do regional governments enjoy in Spain since the 1996 and 2001 reforms?', *Regional and Federal Studies*, 20 (2): 157–174.

Tonge, Jonathan (2006) *Northern Ireland*, Polity Press, Cambridge.

Verheijen, Tony (ed.) (1999) *Civil Service Systems in Central and Eastern Europe*, Edward Elgar, Cheltenham.

Wildavsky, Aron (1984) *The Politics of the Budgetary Process*, Little Brown, Boston, MA.

## CHAPTER 7

# Patterns in Party Politics and Party Systems

## 7.1  Introduction

This book is about the politics of representation in modern Europe. Much of it, in some way or another, is about party politics. We therefore begin by looking at the political parties that lay claim to representing the interests of European voters. Many of these parties, particularly in the long-standing democracies of western Europe, can be classified as belonging to one or another of a small number of party *families* – the Christian democratic family, for example, or the social democratic family, or liberal family, and so on. We consider these party families in detail in the following chapter. In this chapter we explore the way in which the character of political competition in any given country is conditioned by a particular constellation of competing parties that together make up a national party system. We also report the results of recent elections in these countries. As we shall see, although every country has a distinctive blend of party families, and hence a distinctive party system, there are also striking similarities between party systems in different countries. As a general introduction to the key themes that we shall be discussing, therefore, we look in this chapter at the party systems of eight European countries.

The countries that we have chosen, and to which we return systematically at points throughout the text, have not been selected at random; together they capture key variations in the core themes that we discuss. They include all the 'big' countries (Britain, France, Germany, Italy, Poland and Spain), as well as two of the most interesting smaller democracies (Denmark and the Netherlands). They include very old democracies (Britain and France), as well as a younger democracy (Spain) and a relatively new democracy (Poland); party systems dominated by two large parties (Britain and, to a lesser extent, Germany); and systems with many parties (Denmark, Italy, the Netherlands and Poland). They include systems with socialist parties that have long dominated party competition (Denmark and Spain), and with major Christian democratic parties (Germany and, formerly, Italy), with major conservative parties (Britain, and now Italy), as well as ones in which the shape of party politics remains uncertain (Poland) and those in which far-right populist parties have recently emerged to command a large proportion of the vote (Denmark and the Netherlands). Finally, they include systems in which elections are conducted under a plurality voting system (Britain and France), as well as those that employ different forms of proportional representation (PR) (Denmark, Germany, the Netherlands and Spain); and they include systems that almost invariably produce a single-party government (such as Britain), those that almost invariably produce a coalition government (Germany and the Netherlands), and those that sometimes alternate between a single-party and a coalition government (Denmark).

In the older literature on party systems, much was made of the distinction between systems that usually provided single-party government and those that usually led to multiparty coalitions. The former, often typified by the British case, were seen as more moderate as well as more stable, whereas the latter, traditionally associated with the French and Italian cases, were believed to be unstable and potentially more polarizing. This contrast did not seem so plausible when applied to the smaller democracies, however, with countries such as Denmark and Sweden, on the one hand, or the Netherlands and Switzerland, on the other, being characterized by both multiparty coalitions and more moderate, centre-seeking policies. In other words, by taking the smaller European democracies into account, it became evident that multiparty politics and coalition government were not always associated with ideological polarization and instability. Some systems were polarized and volatile, but others were not.

In an effort to account for these differences, Sartori's (1976) typology of party systems took account of the ideological distance of competition as a second independent variable (in addition to the number of parties), and distinguished between systems of moderate pluralism and systems of polarized pluralism. The former tended to have up to five or six parties, with shifting but often stable coalitions, and with parties that tended to reflect more or less moderate ideologies of the left and right. The latter usually had six or more parties, and included two anti-system parties at either extreme of the political spectrum. Competition in these latter systems was therefore highly polarized, and governments, often unstable, struggled to form at the centre. It was these systems, including Italy for much of the post-war period, as well as Fourth Republic France, that were the most unstable.

Most recently, the continued relevance of Sartori's categories has begun to be doubted (Mair, 1997). Despite the emergence of far-right parties in many European polities, the end of the Cold War witnessed the decline of ideological polarization, with the result that there are now few, if any, relevant anti-system parties – that is, parties with an anti-democratic ideology that seek to change not only the government but also the entire political system. Most parties, including the far right, are now coalitionable, and most do gain the opportunity to share government. For this reason it now makes less sense to distinguish between moderate pluralism and polarized pluralism, and these categories no longer sort out the European cases in the ways they once did. Moreover, as we note at the end of the chapter, many European systems are now bipolar in character, with single parties or electoral coalitions competing against one another on election day, and with elections acquiring a much more decisive role in the process of government formation. In the past, elections in multiparty systems were usually followed by weeks or months of lengthy negotiations as the parties bargained with one another as to which coalition might actually form. Indeed, this still happens in the Netherlands and Belgium. In most other countries, however, the parties are now much more likely to specify their alliances in advance, and to form pre-electoral coalitions. In this way, multiparty systems begin to behave like two-party systems, but instead of two individual parties vying with one another, we see two multiparty alliances competing for majority support.

As we argued in the Preface, we in no sense claim that the countries we have selected are 'typical'; it should already be clear that there is no such thing as a typical European country. We have chosen the eight party systems described below because, between them, they include most of the types of variation that we must use if we are to be able to describe the complex mosaic of European party systems.

## 7.2 Eight European party systems

### 7.2.1 Party politics in the United Kingdom

The British party system is often seen as one of the simplest and most clear-cut in Europe. Two large and more or less evenly matched parties have long confronted each other. On one side is the Labour Party, a social democratic party that initially mobilized in order to promote and defend the interests of the working class. The party traditionally enjoyed a close relationship with the trade union movement, and has viewed itself as the political wing of a wider labour movement. Despite this, Labour governments have sometimes found themselves in bitter confrontation with the trade unions over attempts to impose national income policies, notably during the long 1978–1979 'winter of discontent' that led to Labour's defeat in the 1979 general election and ushered in the era of Conservative governments, led by Margaret Thatcher until 1990 and then by John Major until 1997. When the Conservatives eventually lost office, they were replaced by Tony Blair's 'New' Labour, a substantially reformed party that had spent much of its time in opposition trying to distance itself from the unions and from traditional social democratic discourse.

The Conservative Party is Labour's main opponent. Like all traditional Conservative parties in western Europe, the major aims of the Conservatives in the United Kingdom are to defend the rights of private property, to encourage market forces, and to resist the encroachment of the state into spheres of activity (especially economic activity) seen as being properly the realm of unregulated private individuals. For most of its history the party has also defended the traditional moral order, even if this has meant state involvement in regulating personal morality. The Conservatives have also been advocates of tough law-and-order policies and nationalist foreign policy stances based on a strong military profile. This has often led the party to advocate high levels of public spending on policing and national defence, and more recently it has helped push the party into a more Euro-sceptic stance. In contrast to the support for Labour, the Conservatives' strongest support comes mainly from middle-class voters and the more privileged sectors of British society.

**TABLE 7.1** Elections in the United Kingdom since 1997

| Party | 1997 | | 2001 | | 2005 | | 2010 | |
|---|---|---|---|---|---|---|---|---|
| | % of votes | Seats | % of votes | Seats | % of votes | Seats | % of votes | Seats |
| Conservatives | 30.7 | 165 | 31.7 | 166 | 32.3 | 198 | 36.1 | 306 |
| Labour | 43.3 | 419 | 40.7 | 413 | 35.2 | 356 | 29.0 | 258 |
| Liberals | 16.8 | 46 | 18.3 | 52 | 22.0 | 62 | 23.0 | 57 |
| Scottish Nationalists | 2.0 | 6 | 1.8 | 5 | 1.5 | 6 | 1.7 | 6 |
| Welsh Nationalists | 0.5 | 4 | 0.7 | 4 | 0.6 | 3 | 0.6 | 3 |
| Irish Nationalists | 1.1 | 5 | 1.3 | 7 | 1.1 | 8 | 1.0 | 8 |
| Irish Unionists | 1.4 | 13 | 1.5 | 11 | 1.4 | 10 | 0.9 | 8 |
| Referendum Party | – | – | 2.6 | – | – | – | – | – |
| Green Party | – | – | – | – | 1.0 | – | 1.0 | 1 |
| UK Independence Party | – | – | – | – | 2.2 | – | 3.1 | – |
| British National Party | – | – | – | – | 0.7 | – | 1.9 | – |
| Others | 1.6 | 1 | 1.4 | 1 | 2.0 | 3 | 1.7 | 2 |
| All | 100.0 | 659 | 100.0 | 659 | 100.0 | 646 | 100.0 | 649 |

Party composition of government:
1992–1997, Conservative single-party government
1997–2010, Labour single-party government
2010–, coalition of Conservatives and Liberals

Between 1979 and 1997, when the Conservatives won election after election, there was an unprecedented stretch of single-party dominance in British politics, and, following Sartori's classification, this actually transformed the United Kingdom from being a two-party system to a *predominant party system* – that is, a system in which a single party manages to win a majority across four consecutive legislative periods (Sartori, 1976: 192–201). During this period the Conservatives sought to weaken the power of the trade unions, to reduce the size of the state sector, and to sell off many public enterprises to the private sector. In the United Kingdom, which has long had the most majoritarian system in Europe (Lijphart, 1977), the party that wins an election has every opportunity to implement its policy programme. In 1979, for example, when Margaret Thatcher first came to office, the Conservatives held an overall majority of 43 seats in the 635-seat House of Commons; in 1983, when re-elected, they enjoyed a majority of 144 seats in the newly enlarged 650-seat House; and in 1987 they enjoyed a majority of 102 seats. Given such clear majorities, the Conservative governments of the 1980s had little fear of defeat, and hence experienced few real difficulties in pushing through their strongly partisan programme. In 1992, however, they were reduced to have a majority of just 21 seats over all the other parties taken together, and thereafter they were obliged to move a little more cautiously. By the time the 1997 election was held, defections from the Conservative Party in Westminster and a series of bruising by-election defeats had destroyed the party's overall majority, and it ended the parliamentary term as a minority government. It was then replaced by Labour, or by 'New Labour' as it became known under the dynamic new leadership of Tony Blair, which emerged from that election with a lead of some 250 seats over the Conservatives, and with an overall majority of almost 90 seats over all the other parties taken together.

Before the 1997 election, Labour had languished in opposition for 18 years, and had chosen initially to challenge the increasingly right-wing government of Margaret Thatcher by adopting quite a marked left-wing programme. This strategy, to say the least of it, had proved unsuccessful. Indeed, by moving to the left, Labour had alienated many of its more moderate leaders and voters, some of whom then shifted across to the Social Democratic Party (SDP), a more moderate offshoot of Labour that gained many votes in the mid 1980s, and which later merged with the Liberal Party to form the present Liberal Democrats. Following its 1987 defeat, however, Labour slowly began to reorganize and adapt, initially under Neil Kinnock, and later under John Smith and then Tony Blair. By the time Blair had cemented his control over the party, the move towards the moderate centre of the political spectrum had become unstoppable.

Blair discarded many of the older left-wing policies and campaigning styles, and, modelling himself partly on the US Democratic Party under Bill Clinton, made a determined effort to appeal to middle-class voters and to promote centrist policies. 'New' Labour, as he insisted on referring to his party, was different from 'old' Labour. A number of the existing social democratic commitments were maintained, but these were to be recast as 'traditional values in a modern setting.' Part of the change involved the removal of the famous *Clause IV* from the party constitution, a clause that had committed the party – in principle, if not in practice – to wholesale public ownership. New Labour was not going to advocate old-style socialism. Nor was it going to convert completely to the neo-liberalism of the Conservative Party, although it did insist it was pro-business, and it accepted a large number of the Thatcherite reforms enacted by previous Conservative governments. Instead, New Labour was to advocate the so-called Third Way, an approach to policymaking and to governance that owed much to the ideas then being advanced by Blair's intellectual guru, the sociologist Anthony Giddens, then director of the London School of Economics (Marquand, 1999).

Although Labour's additional electoral gains in 1997 amounted to less than 10 per cent, the translation of its higher vote total through the simple-plurality electoral system provided the party with a record majority in Westminster. Moreover, it also left the Conservatives with their smallest ever share of seats. In parliamentary terms this was a landslide, and the Conservatives were left without a single parliamentary seat in either Scotland or Wales. Once they had achieved office, Labour pushed forward a massive programme of reform, not only in the social and economic sphere but also in constitutional terms. In the first three years of office, for example, devolved government was introduced in Scotland, Wales and Northern Ireland; the Bank of England was given its independence; the House of Lords was reformed through the abolition of voting rights for hereditary peers; a system for the direct election of the city mayor was introduced for London; proportional representation was introduced for elections to the new regional assemblies in Scotland and Wales, as well as for the election of British representatives to the European

Parliament; and a form of judicial review was introduced by means of the domestication into British law of the European Convention on Human Rights. This did much to erode Britain's majoritarian style of democracy (for an overview of these changes see Bogdanor, 2004; Flinders, 2005). Labour won again in 2005. In this way, Blair's party came close to matching the succession of Conservative victories, and suggested that rather than having an alternating two-party system, Britain was becoming instead a system of *alternating predominance* – one in which each of the major parties enjoys extended periods in government, but then also suffers extended periods in opposition.

This image of clear-cut confrontation between two sharply distinguished parties, each hoping to form a majority government on its own, is, of course, something of a simplification. There are, for example, several small regionally based nationalist – and anti-nationalist – parties. There is the Scottish National Party, as well as a Welsh nationalist party (Plaid Cymru). In Northern Ireland, which remains an integral part of the United Kingdom, there are two parties that advocate breaking away from the United Kingdom and favour eventual unity with the Irish Republic: the Social Democratic and Labour Party (SDLP) and Sinn Fein, the latter also being formerly the political wing of the armed terrorist organization, the Irish Republican Army (IRA). There are also two unionist parties that fight to preserve Northern Ireland as part of the United Kingdom: the Democratic Unionist Party and the now declining Ulster Unionist Party. But although these parties often win substantial support in their own local areas, and take some seats in the House of Commons, they impinge hardly at all on the British party system taken as a whole. In 2010, for example, the total number of seats won by the regional parties in the House of Commons was only 26, just 4 per cent of the total.

The most important deviation from pure two-party politics in Britain is, of course, the Liberal Democrats, who formally joined government as a junior coalition partner of the Conservatives in May 2010. The Liberal Democrats have traditionally promoted policies that fell between the more radical alternatives of Labour and the Conservatives, and have won support from both major social classes. They received a major electoral boost in the early 1980s when the SDP split from Labour as a result of what it saw as the unwelcome growth of the Labour left. Together, the Liberals and Social Democrats formed an alliance of the centre and posed a serious challenge to the dominance of two-party politics, which itself was particularly polarized during the 1980s. In 1987 the centre alliance won almost 23 per cent of the vote, just 8 per cent less than Labour. Indeed, in the southern part of England, this alliance actually displaced Labour as the major challenger to the Conservatives.

However, even this development had little real impact. Despite the electoral popularity of the Liberal–Social Democratic alliance, the bias against third parties in the British simple-plurality voting system (see Chapter 11) left the two allied parties with only 17 seats for their 23 per cent of the vote. When the chips were down, the alliance did little to disturb the traditional British two-party system – at least at the parliamentary level. Thereafter, the majority of members of the SDP joined the Liberals in the new Liberal Democrat Party, which won almost 17 per cent in 1997 and just over 18 per cent in 2001. On these last two occasions, however, the support for the Conservatives was so low that the Liberals were able to enjoy a tactical advantage, and although their overall share of the vote did not change very much, they managed to win 46 seats in 1997 and 51 seats in 2001.

As the traditional opponent of the newly active, ambitious and yet socially moderate Labour government, the Conservative Party in opposition found itself more and more isolated, and struggled to find a new role in the system. 'The government has stolen our language,' complained the then Conservative leader in an interview with the *Guardian* (17 November 2004), going on to state that 'it becomes very difficult for people to distinguish them from us … I am frustrated.' One way in which the Conservatives tried to carve out a more distinctive profile was by increasingly emphasizing their stance in defence of British independence in Europe. Being significantly more sceptical towards European integration than Labour, and also more sceptical than most mainstream centre-right parties across Europe, the Conservatives increasingly took on the image of a nationalist party. And since they remain so weak in both Scotland and Wales, this image also became one of a specifically English nationalist party. Meanwhile, the Liberal Democrats, buoyed up by their unprecedented success in winning seats, sought to position themselves to the left of Labour, accusing the governing party of having taken over too many of the traditional Conservative economic policies. They also became very critical of Labour's foreign policy, urging closer engagement with Europe, and expressing quite vocal opposition to Blair's support for America in the Iraq war.

This strategy appeared to pay off for the Liberals, and having won a record 62 seats in 2005, they proved able to build on the disillusion with both major parties in the following years. The financial crisis, on the one hand, which damaged Labour's previously strong standing on the economy, and the revelations of sleaze and expense-fiddling in Parliament on the other, which also damaged the Conservative opposition, gave the third party a major boost. In the end, their experience again proved electorally frustrating, and although they managed to increase their share of the vote to 23 per cent in 2010, they actually lost a handful of seats. In this case, however, they also emerged as the king-makers. Labour under Gordon Brown, who had succeeded to the leadership following the resignation of Tony Blair in 2007, proved increasingly unpopular with voters, while the Conservatives, under their new young leader, David Cameron, were slowly winning support. Neither won an overall majority, however (Table 7.1), and for the first time in post-war history a coalition government was formed in Britain. Though closer to Labour in ideological terms, the Liberal Democrats proved more capable of striking a convincing deal with the Conservatives, among the terms of which was the promise of extensive constitutional reform and a referendum on a new and more proportional electoral system. Both the unprecedented fact of a coalition agreement in itself, on the one hand, and the commitment to quite far-reaching institutional reform, on the other, presage a potentially major shake-up of the traditional British party system. This was also the first British government in decades to enjoy a majority of the popular vote, for although previous governments in the 1980s and 1990s had won large parliamentary majorities, they had always done so on the basis of a minority of votes. How long, and how coherently, the government will survive is an open question, of course, especially because, in common with all other European governments at this time, it has had to confront major budgetary problems. The new government must deal with a massive budget deficit and a growing national debt, and has responded to these problems with a harsh austerity programme based on reduced public spending and welfare retrenchment. This, in turn, is likely to provoke a strong opposition from Labour, and thereby a possible return to the traditional rhetoric of left and right, and of class against class.

On the traditional system, see Finer (1980); for more recent assessments see Webb (2000), Dunleavy (2005) and Mair (2009).

## 7.2.2 Party politics in Denmark

In Denmark, as in Britain, there is a major socialist party that initially mobilized in order to promote and defend the interests of the working class, and forged strong links with the trade union movement. There is also a Danish conservative party, which sets out to defend the interests of the middle class and the more privileged sectors of the population. In this sense, Denmark echoes core elements of the British case, with the representation of class interests taking the form of a partisan conflict between left and right. But it is here that the parallels end, for as Table 7.2 shows, the actual balance of forces on left and right in Denmark differs sharply from that in the United Kingdom.

The first point of contrast is that the Danish Social Democrats have been much more successful in gaining office than the British Labour Party, and have held governmental power for long stretches of time. In the period between 1924, when the party first occupied the prime minister's office, and 1983, when a Conservative government first took power, the Social Democrats controlled three in every four governments. At no point did the party ever win an absolute majority of seats, however, and hence they have always relied on forming coalitions with other parties, or have formed minority governments.

**TABLE 7.2**  Election results in Denmark, 1998–2007

| Party | 1998 | | 2001 | | 2005 | | 2007 | |
|---|---|---|---|---|---|---|---|---|
| | % of votes | Seats | % of votes | Seats | % of votes | Seats | % of votes | Seats |
| Social Democrats | 35.9 | 63 | 29.1 | 52 | 25.8 | 47 | 25.5 | 45 |
| Radicals (Social Liberals) | 3.9 | 7 | 5.2 | 9 | 9.2 | 17 | 5.1 | 9 |
| Conservatives | 8.9 | 16 | 9.1 | 16 | 10.3 | 18 | 10.4 | 18 |
| Centre Democrats | 4.3 | 8 | 1.8 | 0 | 1 | 0 | – | – |
| Socialist Party | 7.6 | 13 | 6.4 | 12 | 6 | 11 | 13 | 23 |
| Christian Democrats | 2.5 | 4 | 2.3 | 4 | 1.7 | 0 | 0.9 | 0 |
| Danish People's Party | 7.4 | 13 | 12 | 22 | 13.3 | 24 | 13.9 | 25 |
| Left (Liberals) | 24 | 42 | 31.2 | 56 | 29 | 52 | 26.2 | 46 |
| Progress Party | 2.4 | 4 | 0.5 | 0 | – | – | – | – |
| New Alliance | – | – | – | – | – | – | 2.8 | 5 |
| Unity List | 2.7 | 5 | 2.4 | 4 | 3.4 | 6 | 2.2 | 4 |
| Others | 0.3 | 0 | | | 0.3 | | | |
| All | 99.9 | 175 | 100 | 175 | 100 | 175 | 100 | 175 |

*Note*: Greenland and the Faroe Islands both elect two members to the Danish Parliament (Folketing), but are not part of the Danish party system as such. Generally speaking, they do not vote on issues that do not affect their own constituencies.

Party composition of government:

1993–1994, coalition of Social Democrats, Radicals, Christian Democrats and Centre Democrats

1994–1996, coalition of Social Democrats, Radicals and Centre Democrats

1996–2001, coalition of Social Democrats and Radicals

2001–, coalition of Liberals and Conservatives

The second point of contrast between Denmark and the United Kingdom is that, despite their success, the Danish Social Democrats have never monopolized the representation of the left. From the 1930s to the 1950s the party was challenged by a small Communist Party, which peaked at 12.5 per cent of the vote in elections immediately after the Second World War. In 1960 the Communists faded, and their challenge passed to the newly founded Socialist Party, which then became the most left-wing party in Denmark. In 1967 the Socialist Party split over the question of whether to support the Social Democrat government, and a more radical party, the Left Socialists, emerged, which continued to exist, with low but steady levels of electoral support, until the late 1980s, when it merged with other far-left parties to form the Unity List, which has been in parliament since 1994.

A third point of contrast with Britain is that, unlike the British Conservatives, the Danish Conservatives fall very considerably short of dominating the non-socialist opposition in parliament. While the Conservative Party did hold power for over 10 years from 1982 until 1993, this was the only time that the party had held the office of prime minister since the parliamentary system was established in 1901. Instead, the main opposition to the dominance of the Social Democrats has been the Liberals, who have held power on four separate occasions since 1945. The Conservatives have now fallen to around 10 per cent of the vote, while the Liberals, who were the junior partner in the Conservative-led coalitions of the 1980s, have grown to become the biggest party in Denmark, finally eclipsing the Social Democrats, who had long held that position, in 2001. Further to the right of both Liberals and Conservatives lies the Danish People's Party, which has been the third biggest party in Denmark since 2001. This party originated as a splinter group of the right-wing Progress Party, which had been represented in Parliament since Denmark's 'earthquake' election of 1973, and which had never taken part in any government. In 1999, in a move that is without precedent in European politics, all four Progress Party MPs quit their party.

A final point of contrast with the British party system is shown in the role played by 'centre' parties in Danish politics. While these parties have declined in recent years, they held the balance of power in the political system for most of the twentieth century. The only centre party now left in parliament is the Radical Party, which despite its small size has often played a key role in Danish politics. Its centrist profile can be seen from the fact that it formed part of the Conservative–Liberal coalition governments in the 1980s and early 1990s, and then switched its support to the Social Democratic Party, with which it remained in the government until 2001. Two former centrist parties of note were the Christian Democrats and the Centre Democrats, both of which were first elected to parliament in the 1973 'earthquake' election. While both parties were part of the Conservative–Liberal coalition government in the 1980s and the Social Democrat–Radical government of the 1990s, neither is still represented in parliament, and a successful return seems highly unlikely. The New Alliance Party, which entered parliament in 2007, signalled an attempt to resurrect the centre as a political force in Danish politics. While initially highly successful in polls, an ill-fought election campaign limited it to five MPs, and subsequent infighting and defections have left it with little chance of re-election when Danes next go to the polls.

Thus, while the Social Democratic Party has been the dominant force in Danish politics in the twentieth century, it has been less successful than both its Norwegian and Swedish counterparts, and has never been able to dominate the political process in the same way as its Nordic neighbours. Moreover, since the early 1980s the centre right has proved much more successful than in the preceding half-century, limiting the Social Democrats to eight years in office since 1982.

The key change in recent Danish politics has been the rapid rise of the Danish People's Party (DPP). Created in 1995 by four MPs defecting from the Progress Party, it has proved highly successful since then, growing from 7 per cent of the vote in 1998 to 12 per cent in 2001, and then to a record 14 per cent in 2007 (Table 7.2). Since 2001 the DPP has served as the parliamentary support of the minority Liberal–Conservative government, which is the first time a centre-right parliamentary majority has existed in Danish politics. This has also resulted in the most stable period in government formation and duration in Denmark for many decades. Classified by most observers as a far-right party, and bearing many similarities to the Dutch Freedom Party (see below), the DPP mobilizes on a strongly anti-immigrant and anti-islamization programme, and favours increasing Danish autonomy within the EU. Unlike some other far-right parties in Europe, it has been able to take an active part in governing without losing its electoral appeal, primarily by deftly exploiting the freedom that comes with not being bound by the collective responsibility that taking part in the coalition government would entail. In the 2001 election the strong rightward shift in the electorate (Table 7.2) was attributed to the success of the DPP in claiming that immigration posed severe problems for Danish society and the welfare state, and to the acceptance by the Liberal and Conservative parties that, should the three parties achieve a majority, the DPP would be allowed to promote a very strict immigration policy. Despite starting its political life as somewhat of a pariah, the DPP has thus been able to gain the acceptance of the mainstream parties on the right, and is likely to keep playing a central role in Danish party politics in the years to come.

On traditional Danish party politics, see Pedersen (1987); for analyses of the changes after 2000 see Rydgren (2004) and Green-Pedersen (2006).

### 7.2.3 Party politics in Germany

On the face of it, at least for most of the post-war period, the German party system has appeared very similar to that of Britain. Here, too, there are two main protagonists: the Social Democrats (SPD), the traditional party of the working class, and the Christian Democrats (CDU/CSU), the main representative of conservative interests. Lying strategically – if not always ideologically – between these two parties, with a small but enduring presence, is a liberal party, the Free Democrats (FDP). Although the Free Democrats poll fewer votes than their British counterpart, they have always won quite a substantial representation in the Bundestag, the lower house of the German parliament, as the electoral system ensures that all parties polling 5 per cent or more of the vote (or winning three seats in the single-member districts) are represented in proportion to their electoral support (see Chapter 11).

Despite superficial similarities between the British and German systems, however, there are also striking contrasts. In the first place, the relatively strong parliamentary presence of the Free Democrats ensured that neither of the two major parties was able single-handedly to command a majority of seats in the Bundestag. In Germany, therefore, in contrast to Britain, coalition government was always the norm. Indeed, the last occasion on which a single party secured an overall majority in the Bundestag was in 1957, when the Christian Democrats, under their powerful and popular leader Konrad Adenauer, won just over 50 per cent of the votes and 54 per cent of the seats. Even then, however, a coalition government was formed, with the CDU being joined in government by the now defunct German party, which then held 17 seats in the Bundestag.

**TABLE 7.3** Elections in Germany since 1998

| Party | 1998 | | 2002 | | 2005 | | 2009 | |
|---|---|---|---|---|---|---|---|---|
| | % of votes | Seats | % of votes | Seats | % of votes | Seats | % of votes | Seats |
| Christian Democrats (CDU/CSU) | 35.1 | 245 | 38.5 | 256 | 35.2 | 226 | 33.8 | 239 |
| Social Democrats (SPD) | 40.9 | 298 | 38.5 | 251 | 34.2 | 222 | 23.0 | 146 |
| Free Democrats (FDP) | 6.2 | 44 | 7.4 | 47 | 9.8 | 61 | 14.6 | 93 |
| Greens | 6.7 | 47 | 8.6 | 55 | 8.1 | 51 | 10.7 | 68 |
| The Left | – | – | – | – | 8.7 | 54 | 11.9 | 76 |
| Democratic Socialists[a] (PDS) | 5.1 | 35 | 4.0 | 2 | – | – | – | – |
| Republicans | 1.8 | – | 0.6 | – | 0.6 | – | 0.4 | – |
| German People's Union (DVU) | 1.2 | – | – | – | – | – | 0.1 | – |
| Others | 3.0 | – | 2.0 | – | 3.4 | – | 5.5 | – |
| All | 100.0 | 669 | 100.0 | 611 | 100.0 | 614 | 100.0 | 622 |

Party composition of government:

1998–2005, coalition of Social Democrats and Greens

2005–2009, coalition of Christian Democrats and Social Democrats

2009–, coalition of Christian Democrats and Free Democrats

[a] The Democratic Socialists merged with the Electoral Alternative for Labour and Social Justice (WASG) to form The Left (Die Linke) on 16 June 2007.

In addition to its powerful governmental role, the FDP can be distinguished from the British Liberals in two other respects. First, it promotes an emphatically conservative liberalism. It emphasizes individual as opposed to collective rights, and lays a greater emphasis than even the CDU on the need to roll back the state and maximize private freedoms. Second, the FDP's roots can be found in secular opposition to Catholic politics rather than in liberal opposition to secular conservatism. Despite its brokerage role in government formation, the FDP can therefore be seen as being substantially to the right of the British centre parties, and more akin in many ways to the British Conservatives.

The second major point of contrast with Britain (and with Denmark) concerns the CDU. First, as its name implies, the CDU is not simply a conservative party; it is also a Christian party, a party that has traditionally placed substantial weight on the defence of religious values against the secularism of both the SPD and the FDP. Heir to the primarily Catholic Centre Party of Weimar Germany, which was the major representative of the moderate right in the period prior to the mobilization of Nazism, the post-war Christian Democrats have since broadened their support base through an explicit appeal to Protestant voters. Second, the 'Christian Democrats' are effectively two parties, the CDU proper and its political ally, the Bavarian Christian Social Union (CSU). Unlike the CDU, the CSU is almost exclusively Catholic, and is generally regarded as the most conservative party in Germany. That said, its alliance with the CDU has now endured through generations, and despite the public rows between the two parties regarding economic policy in 2010, it is difficult to imagine them ever going their separate ways.

The third, albeit less marked, contrast with Britain is to be found in the character of the socialist party, the SPD. From its origins in the late nineteenth century as the most radical and powerful socialist party in Europe, when the SPD leadership included some of the foremost Marxist intellectuals in the international socialist movement, the party has developed into one of the most moderate and centrist social democratic organizations in western Europe. The SPD was effectively excluded from office in the early years of post-war West Germany, and it suffered from the reaction against political extremism that flowed in the wake of both Nazism and the communist takeover of East Germany. In 1959, in an effort to acquire a legitimate role in the new state, the party adopted what became known as the Bad Godesberg programme, accepting the principle of the free market economy and a commitment to the North Atlantic Treaty Organization (NATO), and effectively endorsing the policies then being pursued by the incumbent Christian Democratic government. This transformation was finally completed in 1966, when the party joined in a 'grand coalition' with the Christian Democrats. Since then, the degree of ideological conflict between the two major parties has been very muted, and the German party system was often regarded as among the most consensual in western Europe.

The traditional combination of alignments based on class (SPD versus CDU and FDP) and religion (CDU versus SPD and FDP) once led Pappi (1984: 12–14) to speak of the German party system as being characterized by a 'triangular' rather than a unidimensional pattern of competition. Thus the moderate socialism of the SPD and the residual Catholic emphases of the CDU could find common ground in a defence of the welfare state, and of consensual rather than confrontational policymaking. The SPD and FDP, in turn, could find common ground in rejecting the incorporation of Catholic values into public policy (on issues such as abortion and divorce, for example). And the CDU and FDP could – and most often did – find common ground in their defence of the interests of private property and capital.

In the 1980s two factors emerged that helped to undermine this often quite cosy balance. In the first place, a new, radical Green Party emerged, and managed to win sufficient electoral support to push it past the 5 per cent threshold imposed by the German electoral system and to gain strong representation in the Bundestag. This expansion of the number of parties in parliament offered the possibility that party competition could well develop into a confrontation between two rival blocs, with the SPD and the Greens confronting the CDU and the FDP. To be sure, it was always known that there would be much difficult negotiation and internal party conflict before the SPD and the Greens could agree on a common programme for government. Nevertheless, the presence of the Greens did have the potential to destroy the pivotal role of the FDP in German politics and create a two-bloc pattern quite similar to that which, for example, now characterizes party competition in Denmark, France or Italy. This potential was finally to be realized in 1998.

The second, and incomparably the more important, development was the collapse of the East German state and the reunification of the two Germanies in 1990. Greater Germany then accommodated more than 12 million new voters, who had yet to be socialized into stable partisan identities, and whose political behaviour could therefore prove quite volatile for some time to come. In the first democratic elections in East Germany in March 1990, these new electors voted overwhelmingly for the Christian Democrats (who won 47 per cent of the poll), with the Social Democrats winning just 22 per cent and the reformed Communist Party winning 16 per cent. The Christian Democratic successes were later confirmed in the first Bundestag elections of the newly unified state, which were held on 2 December 1990. These were the first all-German elections since Hitler seized power in 1933, and once again they left the coalition of the Christian

Democrats and the liberal FDP with a clear overall majority. Indeed, the FDP success was even more marked than that of the CDU, and the party then polled a substantially larger share of the vote in the eastern part of the country than it did in the west.

For the purposes of that first all-German election, the rule whereby parties require a national minimum of 5 per cent of the vote in order to win representation in the Bundestag (see Chapter 11) was changed so that a party could also win representation if it won 5 per cent either in the area that was formerly West Germany or in the area that was formerly East Germany. This also led to further fragmentation. The former East German Communist Party, now reorganized as the Party of Democratic Socialism (PDS), won only 2.4 per cent in terms of the nation as a whole in 1990, but it won some 10 per cent of the vote in the former East Germany, which was double the threshold and sufficient to win the party 17 seats in 1990. The Greens, on the other hand, were weakened by this rule. They failed to reach the threshold in the west (they polled only 4.7 per cent), and they were able to stay in the Bundestag only because they formed an electoral coalition with Bundnis '90, the alliance of East German citizens' movements that included New Forum, the popular movement that had spearheaded the 1989 protests and revolution. The two groups formally merged in November 1992.

By then, the German party system was more fragmented than at any point in the previous 30 years. Five parties were represented in the Bundestag, ranging from the Greens to the PDS. Political problems had also begun to accumulate in the new Germany. The government was having to cope with the arrival of unprecedented numbers of immigrants, refugees and asylum seekers, and these numbers accelerated in the wake of the collapse of the Soviet Union. Unemployment was particularly high in the former East German area, and voters there were increasingly disillusioned with the lack of economic and social progress, while in the western areas voters were also increasingly discontented about having to bear the burden of the economic costs of reconstruction and resettlement. Symptomatic of this discontent was a small growth in support for extreme-right parties such as the Republicans and the German People's Union (DVU), which together polled some 3 per cent of the vote in 1998. Although these parties later fell back at federal level, the neo-Nazi National Democratic Party and the DVU polled 9 and 6 per cent at *Land* (regional) elections in Saxony and Brandenburg respectively in 2004, and won representation in both *Land* parliaments.

In 1998 bipolar competition became a reality with the arrival in government of a new Red–Green coalition of the SPD and the Green Party under the leadership of Gerhard Schröder. In fact, this was not only the first time that the Greens had become part of a coalition in Germany, it was also the first time that an incumbent German government (the CDU–FDP coalition) had been thrown out of office in its entirety, and a wholly new government installed in its place. As in the United Kingdom, the change of government had been made easier by the increasingly moderate stance adopted by the SPD – although Schröder himself preferred to speak of the 'new middle' rather than the 'third way'. Ironically, one of Schröder's first crises, which was prompted by the sudden resignation of the more left-wing SPD deputy leader Oskar Lafontaine, occurred precisely on the day when Schröder was intending to make a speech heralding the publication of a German translation of Giddens's book *The Third Way*.

Relations between the two new governing parties were not always easy in the beginning, and they experienced a series of defeats in local and regional elections during their term of office. Economic problems also persisted throughout their period of government. But despite the widespread sense of economic doom and gloom (Kitschelt and Streeck, 2003a), and despite a series of small corruption scandals, the two parties narrowly managed to hold on to office in the 2002 election – the losses of the SDP being partially compensated by the narrow gains of the Greens, leaving the coalition with a very small majority in the Bundestag. The gains proved short-lived, however, and voter dissatisfaction grew as the Red–Green coalition seemed unable to lift Germany off the bottom of the European growth league. Dissident elements within the SPD, led by Oscar Lafontaine, joined forces with the PDS in a new party called Die Linke (The Left), and quickly made inroads into SPD support. In the new elections in 2005, Die Linke polled almost 9 per cent, and won more than 50 seats. The Greens held their own, but both the CDU and SPD lost support. Despite this, both latter parties ended up by forming a grand coalition government, the first since 1966, led by Angela Merkel of the CDU, Germany's first female chancellor. Quickly dubbed the losers' coalition, the government survived until 2009, and accumulated a relatively good economic record: unemployment was reduced, the budget deficit began to be tackled, and the government appeared competent in dealing with the first dramatic fallouts from the financial crisis (Faas, 2010). Yet when the new election was called in 2009, neither party was in a strong position. The campaign itself was very consensual and bland, with the SPD proving unable to offer a programme or profile that was really distinct from the CDU. And while the CDU lost marginally in the election, dropping by less than 2 per cent, the SPD was devastated, recording the biggest single loss experienced by any party in post-war German history. The small parties did well. The two left opposition parties grew substantially, and the liberal FDP increased its support by 50 per cent. In the end, despite greater fragmentation, it was therefore the old allies, the CDU and the FDP, who were returned to power. Their relationship did not prove very congenial, however. Chancellor Merkel was accused of indecisive leadership in the face of the severe economic crisis facing both Germany and the Eurozone in 2010, and disputes quickly emerged as to the shape of the new austerity programme, with the FDP fighting for reduced taxes, and with the CDU resisting pressure for even more severe cuts in public spending. Conflicts also began to emerge between the CDU and its more right-wing sister party, the CSU, with the latter opposing Merkel's attempts to adopt a more centrist position. By mid 2010 commentators were predicting an early demise for the new coalition, and a possible return of a CDU–SPD coalition.

On the German party system, see Kitschelt and Streeck (2003b), Lees (2005) and Roberts (2009).

### 7.2.4 Party politics in the Netherlands

Like politics in Denmark, and unlike politics in Britain and the former West Germany, Dutch politics is highly fragmented. It is also increasingly fragmented: new parties emerge with apparent ease, and many flourish and win places in government. The Netherlands is also different in the sense that it is difficult to translate these many parties into coherent blocs or coalitions. Rather, three large parties, none in a position to win a working majority on its own, provide the major alternatives before voters, and in recent years these have been increasingly challenged by new parties that sometimes win enough support to push them into second or third place. The various and often confused manoeuvrings of these parties create a shifting system of coalitions and alliances.

The first of the three traditional large parties is a socialist party, the Labour Party (PvdA), which usually wins between a quarter and a third of the vote. This is also more or less the story of its share of parliamentary seats, since the Dutch electoral system is exceptionally proportional (see

Table 7.4). Both programmatically and in terms of its electoral support, the party stands as the equivalent of the German, Danish and British social democratic parties. Indeed, it sometimes claims to be the true inventor of the 'third way' or 'new middle'. The party based itself traditionally in the working class, and it promotes both the role of the welfare state and a more egalitarian distribution of social and economic resources. Given its relatively small size, however, it has little hope of forming a government of its own, and is obliged to forge alliances with parties to its right.

The second of the three parties is the Christian Democratic Appeal (CDA), which usually vied with the Labour Party as to which would be the biggest single party in the Netherlands. As its name implies, and like the major non-socialist party in Germany, the Dutch CDA is not simply a conservative party. It also seeks to represent the views of Christian voters, both Protestant and Roman

**TABLE 7.4** Elections in the Netherlands since 2002

| Party | 2002 | | 2003 | | 2006 | | 2010 | |
|---|---|---|---|---|---|---|---|---|
| | % of votes | Seats | % of votes | Seats | % of votes | Seats | % of votes | Seats |
| Socialist Party | 5.9 | 9 | 6.3 | 9 | 16.6 | 25 | 9.9 | 15 |
| Green Left | 7.0 | 10 | 5.1 | 8 | 4.6 | 7 | 6.6 | 10 |
| Labour Party (PvdA) | 15.1 | 23 | 27.3 | 42 | 21.2 | 33 | 19.6 | 30 |
| Democrats 66 | 5.1 | 7 | 4.1 | 6 | 2.0 | 3 | 6.9 | 10 |
| Liberals (VVD) | 15.4 | 24 | 17.9 | 28 | 14.7 | 22 | 20.4 | 31 |
| Christian Democrats (CDA) | 27.9 | 43 | 28.6 | 44 | 26.5 | 41 | 13.7 | 21 |
| Freedom Party (PVV) | – | – | – | – | 5.9 | 9 | 15.5 | 24 |
| Christian Union (CU) | 2.5 | 4 | 2.1 | 3 | 4.0 | 6 | 3.3 | 5 |
| Political Reformed Party (SGP) | 1.7 | 2 | 1.6 | 2 | 1.6 | 3 | 1.7 | 2 |
| Pim Fortuyn List (LPF) | 17.0 | 26 | 5.7 | 8 | 0.2 | – | – | – |
| Party of the Animals | – | – | – | – | 1.8 | 2 | 1.3 | 1 |
| Others | 2.4 | 2 | 1.3 | – | 0.9 | – | 1.1 | – |
| All | 100.0 | 150 | 100.0 | 150 | 100.0 | 150 | 100.0 | 150 |

Party composition of government:

2002–2003, coalition of Christian Democrats, Liberals and Pim Fortuyn List

2003–2006, coalition of Christian Democrats, Liberals and Democrats 66

2006–2007, coalition of Christian Democrats and Liberals

2007–2010, coalition of Christian Democrats, Christian Union and Labour

2010–, coalition of Christian Democrats and Liberals, supported by Freedom Party

Catholic. Religious divisions, reflecting conflicts both between the different Christian denominations and between those who are generally pro-clerical and those who are anticlerical, have always been important in Dutch politics. For much of the post-war period, indeed, Protestant and Catholic voters were represented by two separate Protestant parties and one Catholic party. Since 1977, however, and partly as a result of the general weakening of religious ties and the decreasing political salience of interdenominational divisions, these three parties have united behind one pan-Christian party, the CDA. Over and above its defence of religious values, the CDA maintains a moderate conservative position in relation to social and economic policies, drawing electoral support from all major social classes. In the late 1980s and 1990s, however, it entered into quite a serious electoral decline. Indeed, between 1986 and 1998 its vote fell by almost half, and whereas it (or one of its denominational predecessors) played a pivotal and often dominant role in all post-war coalitions, it was forced into opposition between 1994 and 2002. After that it staged an impressive recovery, increasing its support to almost 27 per cent in 2006, when it became once again the biggest single party in the Netherlands and the leader of the governing coalition. By 2010, however, its support had again faded, and it recorded one of its heaviest losses in history.

The third major traditional party in the Netherlands is the Liberal Party (VVD). This party has a much more distinctively middle-class electoral profile than the CDA, and usually won less than 20 per cent of the vote. For long, the Liberals represented the main secular opposition to the Labour Party, and proved far less willing than the CDA to compromise in the direction of Labour's social and economic concerns. At the same time, however, the VVD was also hostile to the representation of religious values in politics. In this respect it sometimes found common ground with the Labour Party in opposition to the CDA. Indeed, the Liberal Party first mobilized in Dutch politics primarily as middle-class opposition to the growing appeal of religious parties. (This links the Dutch Liberals to the German FDP, and sets them apart from the British and Danish Liberals, both of which originated as moderate middle-class alternatives to secular conservative opponents, and both of which are still oriented towards more centrist policies.)

Thus, when it comes to class issues and an economic programme emphasizing the need for a minimum of state intervention and a maximum reliance on market forces, the Dutch Liberals could always identify more strongly with the CDA than with Labour. In terms of the religious–secular divide, however, the Liberals found themselves on the same side as Labour. At the same time, because the CDA's conservative appeal is more moderate than that of the Liberals, the CDA sometimes sought alliances with Labour rather than with the other right-wing party. In this sense, the traditional pattern was similar to that in the former West Germany, and resembled Pappi's triangular party system.

The result, as might be expected, was – and still is – a shifting pattern of coalition government. In 1989 a CDA–Liberal coalition was replaced by a CDA–Labour coalition. This government, in turn, was then replaced by a coalition of Labour, Liberals and the small left-leaning liberal party, Democrats 66, in 1994 – the so-called *purple coalition*, the first Dutch government to exclude the Christian mainstream. That coalition lasted until 2002, and was replaced by a short-lived coalition consisting of the CDA, VVD and the new Pim Fortuyn List, and that in turn was replaced in 2003 by a new coalition of CDA, VVD and Democrats 66. In 2007 the government was formed by the CDA, Labour and the Christian Union, a small Protestant party, but this coalition collapsed in 2010, following disagreements over Dutch involvement in the UN military intervention in Afghanistan.

At centre stage in Dutch party politics, therefore, are three key actors that go in and out of government in a shifting series of alliances. This pattern is complicated by the presence of a number of other parties, on the left and on the right, and both secular and religious. These include the increasingly important Green Left and the Socialist Party, both of which have managed to attract some of Labour's more radical supporters, as well as the Christian Union (CU) and the more fundamentalist Christian Political Reformed Party (SGP). In 2002, however, the traditional patterns of Dutch party politics were suddenly torn apart by the arrival of the right-wing populist Pim Fortuyn List (LPF), a new formation led by the articulate and very flamboyant Pim Fortuyn, who castigated the closed consensual culture that had been formed by the Dutch political class, and who also broke with many of the familiar taboos of Dutch politics by criticizing Islamic culture and by questioning many of the accepted policies regarding immigration, integration and multiculturalism. This was the biggest shake-up ever experienced by Dutch politics, and Fortuyn clearly struck a chord with disillusioned voters on both the left and the right, with opinion polls indicating that his list could win up to 20 per cent of the vote. In the event, it was not to be. In a very dramatic turn of events, Fortuyn was assassinated by an animal rights activist on the eve of polling, and his now leaderless and subsequently fractured party polled 17 per cent of the vote and won 26 seats (the best account and analysis is that by van Holsteyn and Irwin, 2003). Although not as great a success as had been anticipated, this was still a record for any new party in the Netherlands, while the losses experienced by both Labour (from 29 to 15 per cent) and the Liberals (from 25 to 15 per cent) were also at record levels. The opposition CDA, which had refrained from criticizing Fortuyn, proved the most successful of the traditional parties, and it later formed a government with the VVD and the LPF. Conflicts between the parties within the cabinet, however, as well as very sharp disputes between the two leading LPF ministers, forced the government to resign after only a few months in office. In the subsequent election in 2003 the CDA maintained its leading position, the PvdA recovered, and the LPF fell back to just 6 per cent of the vote.

Following, the collapse of the LPF, the established political elites breathed a sigh of relief, convinced that normality seemed to have been restored. However, the short-lived success of the new party, as well as the record levels of electoral volatility, had shown that there existed a serious potential for change in Dutch politics, and this was also evidenced in 2006, when major gains were recorded by the Socialist Party and the new Freedom Party, and again in 2010 when the Freedom Party further increased its support. The Socialist Party, which almost tripled its share of votes and seats in 2006 before falling back again in 2010, is a populist left-wing party, quite similar to the German Linke and also tapping into the same vein of support as the Danish Socialists. These are parties that advance a more radical programme than their social democratic neighbours, and that are often more Euro-sceptic than the governing mainstream. They also represent an important and, as yet, relatively unresearched phenomenon in comparative European politics. The Freedom Party, led by the carefully controlled and highly articulate Geert Wilders, is a right-wing populist party that espouses a strong anti-Islamic programme, and which bears many similarities to the right-wing Danish People's Party. As in Denmark, the mobilization of left- and right-wing challenger parties has tended to polarize the party system, and to raise the temperature of political competition. In 2010 Wilders scored his greatest success, polling almost 16 per cent of the vote, with the Freedom Party in the process the third biggest party in the Netherlands. This, however, says more about how fragmented the party system has become than about Wilders as such. In 2010 the biggest party polled just 20 per cent of the vote, and the prospects for stable long-term coalition formation seemed to have become more clouded. In November 2010 a minority VVD–CDA coalition took office, supported externally by the Freedom Party. This was the first minority government to hold office in the Netherlands, and was not deemed likely to survive its full term.

For an analysis of the traditional Dutch party system, see Daalder (1987); for more contemporary assessments see Mair (2008) and Andeweg and Irwin (2009).

## 7.2.5  Party politics in Italy

Reflecting on the nationalist revolution in early twentieth-century Ireland, the poet W.B. Yeats once wrote that 'things falls apart; the centre cannot hold'. In contemporary Italy, where party politics has been reshaped to a degree unprecedented in any post-war European party system, the centre has also been unable to hold, and the traditional system has fallen completely apart. As things now stand, it has been replaced by a relatively simple bipolar system, in which two broad electoral coalitions confront one another, and in which most other parties have been completely marginalized. However, the glue that holds these coalitions together is very weak, and it is not at all clear whether we can speak of a lasting realignment.

At first sight, the traditional patterns of post-war party politics in Italy did not appear to differ very markedly from those in the other countries surveyed here. In Italy, as in each of the other countries, a left–right opposition lay at the heart of party competition, reflecting the confrontation between parties promoting working-class interests and those promoting the interests of better-off social groups. As in the UK and Denmark, the traditional left, represented in Italy by both a communist and a socialist party, usually won about 40 per cent of the vote. And as in Germany and the Netherlands, there was also a religious–secular divide, although in Italy pro-clerical forces are exclusively Catholic.

The distinguishing feature of the Italian party system was not so much the particular interests that were represented, as the depth of the ideological divisions between the competing parties. The major party on the traditional left was the Italian Communist Party (PCI), which in early 1991, after much agonizing, and in reaction to the collapse of the communist regimes in eastern and central Europe, changed its name to the Democratic Party of the Left (PDS), and more recently to simply Democrats of the Left (DS). It later formed a centre-left alliance with the remnants of the old Christian Democrats, and now both groups compete simply as the Democrats. Before this change, the PCI had been the strongest communist party in western Europe, and averaged 29 per cent of the votes during the 1980s. For most of the post-war era the PCI retained the aura of a far-left opposition, and the strength of PCI support thus marked the Italian party system off from those of many other European democracies. At the opposite end of the left–right ideological spectrum in Italy was the neo-fascist Italian Social Movement (MSI), which usually polled about 6 per cent of the vote.

Ranged between these extremes lay five more central parties. The biggest of these was the Christian Democratic Party (DC), which usually polled about 30 per cent of the popular vote. Like the Dutch CDA, this party combined a moderately conservative economic appeal with the promotion of religious values. Two other parties mobilized on the centre right in Italy: the Liberals and the Republicans between them averaged about 7 per cent of the vote. Although the tiny Liberal Party was the more right-wing of the two, and had an ideological position similar to that of its Dutch and German counterparts, the Republicans reflected the more centrist politics characteristic of the Liberal Party in the UK. Both were largely middle-class parties that endorsed many of the conservative economic appeals of the DC while rejecting its emphasis on religious values.

On the centre left of the system sat the small Social Democratic Party (PSDI), which usually polled about 4 per cent of the vote. More influential on the left was the Socialist Party (PSI), which usually polled about 12 per cent of the vote and shared many of the concerns of the major social democratic parties in the United Kingdom, Denmark, the Netherlands and West Germany.

The traditional Italian party system therefore comprised both a more fragmented and a more polarized set of alternatives than could be found in the other countries we have considered. As a consequence, it was impossible for a clear-cut left- or right-wing bloc to present itself to voters as a realistic governing option. On the left, the combined support of the PCI, PSI and PSDI, together with that of the smaller radical parties, might have appeared sufficient to form a government coalition. Yet, because of the perceived extremism of the PCI, this option seemed impossible to realize. There might also have seemed to be a potential parliamentary majority on the right, but this option also proved impossible to realize, given the far-right position of the MSI – suggestions by the Christian Democrats that they might deal with the MSI proved very unpopular with voters. The consequent exclusion of both ends of the political spectrum from government therefore left the remaining parties searching for a parliamentary majority through the creation of persistent – if unstable – governments of the centre, much like the pattern that prevailed in the French Fourth Republic (see later), and which might yet emerge in the Netherlands and Denmark. The participants typically ranged from the socialists to the Christian democrats to the liberals, who combined into a five-party (*pentapartito*) or four-party coalition straddling the centre left and the centre right (Mershon, 1996).

As is clear from our phrasing, however, all this is now in the past tense, and the Italian party system has been reshaped to an extraordinary degree. Three factors are important here. In the first place, the end of the Cold War led to a decisive shift in which the major party of the left abandoned the traditional communist character of the PCI and moved towards a more conventional social democratic position. This then obliged the other parties, and the voters, to accept that the DS now had the potential to form part of a coalition government, and that, unlike the old PCI, it could no longer be excluded as a matter of principle. This changed the terms of reference of traditional politics.

Secondly, an increasing discontent with the endemic corruption and clientelism that characterized Italian governments fuelled support for the Northern League (Lega Nord), which won almost 9 per cent of the vote in 1992, and which also ended up as the biggest single party in parliament in 1994. The Northern League is a right-wing populist movement based mainly in the richer northern regions of Italy: it demands an end to the system whereby the taxes paid by its relatively prosperous supporters are used to fund welfare programmes and public works in the poorer south and therefore help the government win support in the south. The party also advocates the creation of a federal structure in Italy, with three autonomous regions or 'republics', including its own proposed Padania in the north. Amid all the turmoil of recent Italian politics, the Northern League has steadily gained support and organizational strength, and in organizational terms is now reckoned to be one of the strongest political parties in Italy. Moreover, in the northern part of Italy, where it competes for support, it now often emerges as the biggest single vote winner.

Third, and most important, support for the traditional governing parties – the Christian Democrats (DC) and the Socialists (PSI) – was more or less completely undermined by the revelations of corruption and bribery uncovered by the so-called *mani pulite* (clean hands) investigation. This was an investigation by Italian magistrates that began in Milan in February 1992 and then spread to many other parts of the country. After little more than a year, at the end of March 1993,

**TABLE 7.5** Elections in Italy since 1996

| Party | 1996 | | 2001 | | 2006 | | 2008 | |
|---|---|---|---|---|---|---|---|---|
| | % of votes | Seats | % of votes | Seats | % of votes | Seats | % of votes | Seats |
| Greens | 2.5 | 16 | 2.2 | 17 | 2.1 | 15 | – | – |
| Party of Italian Communists (PdCI) | – | – | 1.7 | 10 | 2.3 | 16 | – | – |
| Communist Refoundation | 8.6 | 35 | 5.0 | 11 | 5.8 | 41 | – | – |
| The Left/The Rainbow[a] | – | – | – | – | – | – | 3.1 | 0 |
| Democratic Party of the Left (PDS) | 21.1 | 171 | 16.6 | 137 | – | – | – | – |
| The Olive Tree/Democratic Party (PD)[b] | – | – | – | – | 31.3 | 220 | 33.2 | 211 |
| Italy of Values | – | – | 3.9 | – | 2.3 | 16 | 4.3 | 28 |
| Socialist Party (PSI)/Dini List[c] | 4.3 | 26 | 2.2 | 2 | – | – | – | – |
| Christian Democratic Centre/ Christian Democratic Union/ Democratic Centre Union (UDC) | 5.8 | 30 | 3.2 | 40 | 6.8 | 39 | 5.6 | 36 |
| People's Party (PPI)/Prodi List | 6.8 | 75 | 14.5 | 80 | – | – | – | – |
| Forza Italia/The People of Freedom (PDL)[d] | 20.6 | 123 | 29.5 | 189 | 23.7 | 137 | 37.4 | 272 |
| Northern League | 10.1 | 59 | 3.9 | 30 | 4.6 | 26 | 8.3 | 60 |
| Social Movement (MSI)/ National Alliance | 15.7 | 93 | 12.0 | 96 | 12.3 | 71 | – | – |
| Radicals/Pannella List[e] | 1.9 | – | 2.3 | – | 2.6 | 18 | – | – |
| Others | 2.6 | 2 | 7.0 | 18 | | | | |
| All | 100.0 | 630 | 100.0 | 630 | 100.0 | 630 | 100.0 | 630 |

Party composition of government:

1996–2001, Olive Tree Alliance with Greens, Communist Refoundation, and Italy of Values

2001–2006, coalition of Forza Italia, National Alliance, Northern League and Christian Democrats (CCD–CDU)

2006–2008, coalition of Democrats of the Left, Democracy and Freedom-the Daisy, Communist Refoundation Party, the Greens, the Italy of Values, and the UDEUR Populars

2008–, coalition of the People of Freedom, and the Northern League

[a] The Left/The Rainbow comprises the Communist Refoundation (RC), the Party of the Italian Communists (PdCI) and the Greens.

[b] The Olive Tree list comprised the Democrats of the Left (DS) and the Daisy (DI). These two parties merged together with the Radical Party, which competed in 2006 under the list 'Rose in the Fist', to form the Democratic Party (PD).

[c] Although the Socialist Party did not contest the 1996 election as an independent party, an official Socialist Party list was included in the list headed by Lamberto Dini.

[d] In 2008 Forza Italia (FI) and the National Alliance (AN) merged to form the People of Freedom (PDL).

[e] In 2006 the Radical Party (PR) competed in the elections with the Italian Social Democrats (SDI), under the banner of 'the Rose in the Fist'.

the investigation had led to accusations of bribe-taking (*tangenti*) against more than 150 members of the Italian parliament, and against almost 900 local politicians. Those accused included many prominent figures in the DC and the PSI. Indeed, almost one-third of PSI MPs were by then under investigation, as were more than one-quarter of its party executives. The PSI leader, Bettino Craxi, fled to Tunisia. The result was that the centre of the old party system, in the form of the DC and PSI in particular, was effectively swept away.

In the 1994 general election, which was the first to be held under the new electoral system (see Chapter 11) – inaugurating the so-called Second Republic – and which witnessed the biggest shift in the political balance ever recorded in post-war Italy, the Northern League won just over 8 per cent of the PR vote and 111 of the 475 single-member districts, and emerged as the biggest single party in the new parliament, with the DS coming a close second with 20 per cent of the PR vote and 77 seats in the single-member districts. The neo-fascist MSI, now reconstituted as the National Alliance, came in third place, with 14 per cent of the PR votes and 86 single-member districts. Perhaps the greatest surprise, however, was the strong showing of Forza Italia (literally, Go, Italy!), which was formed just three months before the election by the media tycoon and owner of AC Milan soccer team, Silvio Berlusconi, and which won 21 per cent of the PR vote and 67 single-member districts.

Together with the Northern League and the National Alliance, Forza Italia had formed a joint right-wing electoral alliance (the Pole of Liberty) in opposition to the DS, and this new alliance emerged from the election with a clear overall majority in the Chamber of Deputies, the lower house of parliament. The three parties later went on to form a government under the premiership of Berlusconi, which included in the cabinet five ministers drawn from the far-right National Alliance/MSI. Berlusconi's government proved fragile, however, not least as a result of tensions between the Northern League and the National Alliance, and it was quickly replaced by a 'technical' non-party government. Then, in 1996, came the second major change of the Second Republic, when the so-called Olive Tree alliance, dominated by the former Communist Party, but led by Romano Prodi, leader of the People's Party, won a narrow overall majority. The new alliance also included the Greens, as well as new groupings that had emerged from the remnants of the old socialist and liberal centre, and won grudging support from the Communist Refoundation. For the first time since 1947 former communists had managed to win government. For the first time, also, there was a complete alternation in government.

Although Prodi later went on to become president of the European Commission in 1999, the new centre-left alliance remained in office until 2001. It proved internally divided, however, and had to be reconstituted on a number of occasions. A major parliamentary defeat in late 1998 led to Prodi's resignation, and his replacement by DS leader Massimo D'Alema, and in April 2000 D'Alema himself was replaced by Giuliano Amato, a former PSI premier. By then, however, the alliance seemed very fragmented, and although still formally united under the Olive Tree (*Ulivo*) label, it went into the 2001 contest as a very varied collection of different and unlikely sounding groups, including the DS, the Daisy (*Margherita* – itself an alliance of several centre parties) and the Sunflower (*Girasole* – an alliance of Greens and former Socialists). On the right, meanwhile, efforts to build a new alliance had succeeded, and in 2001 Berlusconi returned to power at the head of the so-called House of Liberty coalition – including, once again, Forza Italia, the National Alliance and the Northern League. This time the alliance proved quite robust, and it went on to become the longest-serving post-war Italian government. At the same time, it also met with quite severe criticism both at home, in the form of protests and strikes, and abroad, with in both cases an increasing concern being expressed about government policy being used to help promote and protect Berlusconi's personal and business interests.

The election in 2006 was again a bipolar contest, with a broad centre-left coalition led by Prodi winning a narrow majority over a more coherent coalition of Forza Italia, the Northern League and the National Alliance, again led by Berlusconi. This time the left alliance proved particularly unstable, being a coalition made up of smaller coalitions, and of parties inside parties inside parties. In the end there were 12 parties in Prodi's government, and when one eventually abandoned the alliance, aggrieved at the accusations of corruption levelled against its leadership, the government fell. In the ensuing elections of 2008 Berlusconi was returned to power with a large majority, not least as a result of the Northern League doubling its support (Wilson, 2009). This election also marked a formal simplification of the Italian party system and a strengthening of the bipolar tendencies. Forza Italia and the National Alliance had merged into a single party, the People of Liberty (PdL), and worked in close co-operation with the Northern League. The former Communist Party and the loose alliance of centre-left Christian and radical groupings from the old Margherita were combined in the new Democrats Party. The far left, which had played an important role in all post-war Italian parliaments, and which had contested the elections as the Rainbow coalition had failed to pass the threshold, and for the first time went unrepresented in parliament. Other parties that did win representation included Italy of Values, led by the former prosecutor who spearheaded the campaign against political corruption in the early 1990s, and a small centrist Christian Democratic Party, the UDC.

In the new Italy, however, it is less the parties that matter and more the political leaders, and in particular the figure of Silvio Berlusconi, long one of the richest men in Italy and by now the most powerful and successful political leader. Berlusconi has come to dominate Italian politics, and through his wealth and his control of the print and broadcast media he has also come to dominate Italian democracy. That he has survived for so long in the face of a constant flow of scandals and corruption, and against the background of a steadily declining and malfunctioning economy, remains one of the great puzzles of modern European politics. How long his reign will eventually last is impossible to predict, particularly as his alliance with the National Alliance came under great strain in 2010, with Fini, the leader of the latter, breaking with Berlusconi and emerging as a surprisingly strong critic of his attempts to extend his domination of the traditional institutions.

On Italian politics and the party system, see Bull and Rhodes (1997), Bull and Newell (2005) and Newell (2009). On the Berlusconi phenomenon, see Ginsborg (2005).

### 7.2.6 Party politics in France

The current French constitution dates from 1958, which marked the beginning of the French Fifth Republic. Before this, France was governed under the constitution of the Fourth Republic, dating from 1945. During the Fourth Republic the French party system bore many similarities to that of pre-1990s Italy. Politics on the left was dominated by a large pro-Moscow Communist Party (PCF), which polled an average of about 27 per cent of the vote. There was also a steadily weakening Socialist Party, which averaged less than 19 per cent of the vote. The centre was occupied by a Radical Party, which won an average of 12 per cent, and by the Catholic Popular

Republican Movement (MRP), which polled over 25 per cent in the 1940s but which then fell back to just 12 per cent in the 1950s. On the right, a conservative party persisted throughout the period, with around 13 per cent of the vote. In the 1950s, however, the conservatives were marginalized by two rivals on the right, the Gaullists (winning 22 per cent of the vote in 1951) and the far-right Poujadists (winning 12 per cent in 1956), both reflecting opposition to the constitutional arrangements of the Fourth Republic. Faced with anti-constitutional opposition from both left and right, which proved both more extremist and more powerful than in Italy, the centre was unable to hold, and the result was chronic political instability.

Two key changes have occurred in the party system during the early decades of the Fifth Republic (Bartolini, 1984: 104–115). First was the emergence of a much more clearly defined bipolar pattern of competition, much like the two-bloc model that can now be seen in the Italian case, in which the left, represented by the Socialist Party (PS) and the Communist Party, competed against the right, represented by the new Gaullist Party (RPR) and the coalition of forces that organized under the label Union for French Democracy (UDF). The emergence of this bipolar pattern was facilitated by the abandonment of the proportional electoral formula that had been used in the Fourth Republic and its replacement by a double-ballot majority system, which encourages competition between just two candidates in each constituency in the second round of voting (see Chapter 11). It was also encouraged by the introduction of a directly elected president in 1962, which also involves just two candidates competing in the second round of voting (see Table 7.6).

The second change that occurred during the Fifth Republic was a shift in the balance of forces within both the left and the right. For a variety of reasons, both ideological and institutional, the PCF became increasingly marginalized, and the left grew to be dominated by the Socialist Party. Already by the 1980s the PS, together with its electoral allies among the left radicals (MRG), commanded the largest share of the vote in France. The PCF had then fallen to just 10 per cent of the poll and was reduced to playing a supporting role for the PS, and by the first election of the new century the party was reduced to less than 5 per cent of the vote – a far cry from the 20 per cent or more it had enjoyed in the 1960s. In 1981, for the first time ever, the PS emerged with an overall majority of seats in the lower house of the French parliament, although it initially chose to govern in coalition with the PCF. Earlier that same year, with PS candidate François Mitterrand, the left had won the presidency for the first time ever.

There was also a substantial shift in the balance of forces on the right, with the disappearance of the MRP and with the development of a more or less stable and evenly balanced alliance between the Gaullist RPR and the UDF. (The latter, like the early centre-right electoral alliances in Spain (see later), combined liberal, Christian, and conservative forces.) Eventually, in 2002, the two parties merged into the Union for a Popular Majority (UPM), although some elements of the old UDF remained outside the new alliance. Party competition in the Fifth Republic therefore not only took the form of a much better defined confrontation between left and right, but also tended to be dominated by the more moderate of the forces within each bloc. The polarization of the Fourth Republic appeared a thing of the past.

This pattern came to be challenged, however, at least on the right, by the emergence of the far-right National Front. The National Front mobilizes a strongly racist and xenophobic political appeal, and has clocked up some significant electoral successes in the southern parts of France in particular. The problem for the mainstream right is that electoral support for the National Front makes it more difficult for the more moderate elements to achieve a majority in either the presidential or the parliamentary elections. Should they try to come to terms with the National Front, however, and should they attempt to forge a new and more broadly defined alliance on the right, they risk losing their more moderate voters – and some of their leaders – in the centre. The problem is a major one for the mainstream right: in the 1997 parliamentary elections, for example, the National Front polled almost 15 per cent of the vote, although it was denied almost any seats by the double-ballot majority voting systems (Table 7.7). In the presidential elections of 2002 the leader and candidate of the Front, Jean-Marie Le Pen, polled 17 per cent of the first-ballot vote, coming a close second to the Gaullist Jacques Chirac, and knocking the PS candidate Lionel Jospin into third place. In the second ballot, however, Le Pen barely improved his position, and Chirac went on to win by a landslide. Further problems have also been precipitated on the right by conflicts over Europe, with various short-lived Euro-sceptic groups emerging from among the ranks of both the UDF and Gaullists.

It was in an effort to contain this fragmentation, and to finally develop a more coherent anti-socialist alternative, that both major parties eventually merged their forces. This is the most advanced attempt to date to build a genuine catch-all conservative party in France, and it may

**TABLE 7.6** Presidential elections in France since 1995

| Party | 1995[a] | | 2002[b] | | 2007[c] | |
|---|---|---|---|---|---|---|
| | 1st Round % of votes | 2nd Round % of votes | 1st Round % of votes | 2nd Round % of votes | 1st Round % of votes | 2nd Round % of votes |
| Greens | 3.3 | – | 5.2 | – | 1.6 | – |
| Communist Party (PCF) | 8.6 | – | 3.4 | – | 1.9 | – |
| Socialist Party (PS) | 23.3 | 47.4 | 16.2 | – | 25.9 | 46.9 |
| Rally for the Republic (RPR)/Union for a Popular Movement (UMP) | 39.5 | 52.6 | 19.9 | 82.2 | 31.2 | 53.1 |
| Union for French Democracy (UDF) | – | – | 6.8 | – | 18.6 | – |
| National Front (NF) | 15.0 | – | 16.9 | 17.8 | 10.4 | – |
| Other left (various) | 5.6 | – | 22.6 | – | 7 | – |
| Other right (various) | 4.7 | – | 10.4 | – | 3.4 | – |
| Total | 100.0 | 100.0 | 100.0 | 100.0 | 100.0 | 100.0 |

[a] Two candidates from the RPR (Gaullists) ran in the first ballot, Jacques Chirac and Edouard Balladur, and the figure of 39.5 per cent refers to their combined vote. There was no UDF candidate in that first ballot. Chirac, who was the higher-polling Gaullist candidate, and who came in second to the eventual first-ballot leader, Lionel Jospin (PS), then went on to win the presidency in the second ballot.

[b] Jean-Marie Le Pen of the National Front narrowly beat Lionel Jospin (PS) into third place on the first round of voting, and went on to contest the second round against the incumbent, Jacques Chirac. The National Front vote did not increase very much in 2002, but the PS was badly damaged by the participation of many other left candidates in the first round.

[c] Nicolas Sarkozy of the newly founded Union for a Popular Movement (UMP) defeated the Socialist Party's candidate, Ségolène Royal, in the second ballot.

**TABLE 7.7** Legislative elections in France since 1993[a]

| Party | 1993 | | 1997 | | 2002 | | 2007 | |
|---|---|---|---|---|---|---|---|---|
| | % of votes | Seats | % of votes | Seats | % of votes | Seats | % of votes | Seats |
| Greens | 7.6 | – | 6.3 | 8 | 4.4 | 3 | 3.2 | 4 |
| Communist Party (PCF) | 9.2 | 23 | 9.9 | 37 | 4.9 | 21 | 4.3 | 18 |
| Socialist Party (PS)[b] | 18.5 | 60 | 25.5 | 246 | 25.3 | 141 | 26.1 | 205 |
| Other Left | 3.6 | 10 | 5.3 | 29 | 5.4 | 1 | 5.4 | 3 |
| Union for French Democracy (UDF)/ Democratic Movement (MoDem) | 19.1 | 213 | 14.7 | 109 | 4.8 | 29 | 7.6 | 4 |
| Rally for the Republic (RPR)/Union for a Popular Movement (UMP)[c] | 20.4 | 247 | 16.8 | 139 | 33.4 | 365 | 40.3 | 312 |
| New Centre (NC) | – | – | – | – | – | – | 1.6 | 22 |
| Other right | 5.0 | 24 | 4.7 | 8 | 5.5 | 17 | 3.7 | 9 |
| National Front | 12.4 | – | 14.9 | 1 | 11.1 | – | 4.7 | – |
| Others | 4.3 | – | 1.9 | – | 5.2 | – | 3.1 | – |
| All | 100.0 | 577 | 100.0 | 577 | 100.0 | 577 | 100.0 | 577 |

Party composition of government:

1993–1997, coalition of Rally of the Republic and Union for French Democracy

1997–2002, coalition of Socialist Party, Left Radicals, Communist Party, Greens, and other left

2002–2007, coalition of Union for a Popular Movement and Union for French Democracy

2007–, coalition of Union for a Popular Movement and New Centre

[a] Voting percentages are first-ballot results only.

[b] Includes Left Radicals.

[c] In 2002 the RPR joined with the most of the UDF in a new electoral organization, the Union for a Popular Majority, previously known as the Union for a Presidential Majority.

yet serve to bring French politics closer to the British model. The new strategy of the right has also proved successful, at least in the short term. The alliance won power in parliament in 2002, and cemented these gains with a second victory in 2007. The UMP also scored a success in the presidential contest of 2007, when its candidate Nicolas Sarkozy won a decisive victory. The Socialists, who had played a dominant role in French government for most of the 1980s and early 1990s, were now eclipsed, and the party itself was badly divided between different leadership factions, on the one hand, and over economic policies and their position on Europe, on the other. Whether the party can recover a sense of unity in opposition to Sarkozy's handling of the 2008–2010 financial crisis remains open to question.

The best and most comprehensive English-language account of the French party system is Knapp (2004), and in French is Haegel (2007). See also Bornschier and Lachat (2009) and Sauger (2009).

## 7.2.7 Party politics in Spain

Before the collapse of communist rule in eastern Europe in 1989 and 1990, Spain was one of Europe's youngest democracies. The elections held in Spain in 1977, two years after the death of the right-wing dictator General Franco, were the first since Franco had seized power after the defeat of the democratic Republican forces in the 1936–1939 Civil War. As in the early years of many other new democracies, the first period of Spanish democracy was characterized by the creation of many new parties, and by great electoral volatility.

The early stages of the transition to democracy in Spain were dominated by the Union of the Democratic Centre (UCD), a broad coalition of various centre-right and centre-left groups under the leadership of Adolfo Suarez, a former minister in Franco's cabinet and the first prime minister of democratic Spain. This coalition of forces, although electorally successful in 1977 and 1979, was also inherently very fragile and collapsed dramatically in 1982, when its share of the vote fell from 35 per cent to less than 7 per cent. Suarez himself had resigned as prime minister and had abandoned the party in 1981, setting up a new party, the Social and Democratic Centre, that eventually disappeared in the mid 1990s.

With the collapse of the UCD, the key role in the Spanish party system passed to the Socialist Party (PSOE), which polled almost half the votes in 1982 and almost 40 per cent in 1989. With the help of the bias shown towards larger parties in the Spanish electoral system, this level of support guaranteed Socialist Party government in Spain for an extended period from 1982 to 1996, although it lost its overall majority in 1993.

Socialist dominance in Spain was then also facilitated by the fragmentation of the centre-right opposition; indeed, even into its second decade of democracy, Spain remained among the most fragmented of the European party systems. The largest single party on the right is currently the People's Party (PP), formerly known as the People's Alliance, which initially formed the dominant group within the sporadically cohesive People's Coalition, a federation of diverse parties that embraced liberal, Christian democratic and conservative factions, and which grew to almost 35 per cent of the vote in 1993. In the following election the PP overtook the PSOE, emerging as the single biggest party in 1996, and forming a single-party minority government. The party went on to win an overall majority in 2000, but then lost again when the PSOE gained an unexpected victory in the dramatic 2004 election (Table 7.8).

Prior to the 2004 election itself the PP had been expected to win, notwithstanding the anticipated resignation of its long-term leader, José María Aznar. Nevertheless, the slow and inadequate reaction to the ecological disaster that followed from the sinking of the *Prestige* oil tanker off the north-west coast of Spain had damaged the standing of the government, and the Spanish decision to fully back the US and British invasion of Iraq and to commit troops to the war was also proving widely unpopular. In the end, the crucial issue that turned the tide so dramatically was the horrific rail bombing in Madrid on 11 March, which occurred precisely two-and-a-half years after 9/11, and just three days before polling, and which left almost 200 people dead in the city. The damage this caused to the pro-American PP government was then compounded when the government tried to insist that the bombing was the work of the Basque terrorist organization ETA rather than of the Islamic terrorist al-Qaeda, a story that was quickly shown to be implausible. The result, three days later, was a massive swing against the government and a decisive victory for the PSOE and for its new young leader, José Luis Rodríguez Zapatero, who quickly confirmed his long-standing promise to bring Spanish troops home from Iraq.

**TABLE 7.8** Elections in Spain since 1996

| Party | 1996 | | 2000 | | 2004 | | 2008 | |
|---|---|---|---|---|---|---|---|---|
| | % of votes | Seats | % of votes | Seats | % of votes | Seats | % of votes | Seats |
| United Left (IU) | 10.5 | 21 | 5.5 | 8 | 5.0 | 5 | 3.8 | 2 |
| Socialist Party (PSOE) | 37.9 | 141 | 34.1 | 125 | 42.6 | 164 | 43.9 | 169 |
| People's Party (PP) | 38.8 | 156 | 44.5 | 183 | 37.6 | 148 | 39.9 | 154 |
| Convergence and Union (CiU) | 4.6 | 16 | 4.2 | 15 | 3.2 | 10 | 3.0 | 10 |
| Basque Nationalists (PNV) | 1.3 | 5 | 1.5 | 7 | 1.6 | 7 | 1.2 | 6 |
| Union, Progress and Democracy (UPyD) | – | – | – | – | – | – | 1.2 | 1 |
| Republican Left of Catalonia (ERC) | 0.7 | 1 | 0.8 | 1 | 2.5 | 8 | 1.2 | 3 |
| Galician Nationalist Bloc (BNG) | 0.9 | 2 | 1.3 | 3 | 0.8 | 2 | 0.8 | 2 |
| Herri Batasuna (HB) | 0.7 | 2 | – | – | – | – | – | – |
| Others | 4.9 | 6 | 8.1 | 8 | 6.6 | 6 | 5.0 | 3 |
| All | 100.0 | 350 | 100.0 | 350 | 100.0 | 350 | 100.0 | 350 |

Party composition of government:
1996–2004, People's Party single-party government
2004–, Socialist Party single-party government

Zapatero went on to form a minority government – a traditional solution in Spanish politics when the winner of the elections does not get an absolute majority – with the support of the United Left (IU) and pro-Catalan independence Republican Left of Catalonia (ERC). Against a favourable economic background, Zapatero's government focused on moral and ideological issues, criticizing the role of the Catholic church in education, and formally recognizing gay marriage. These issues, together with the approval of the new *Estatuto de Cataluña* (Catalonia's Fundamental Law), the negotiation with ETA (the Basque terrorist pro-independence group), and the Historical Memory Law (which condemns the Francoist regime and rehabilitates all victims of the dictatorship), served to polarize Spanish public opinion to an unprecedented degree (Bernecker and Maihold, 2007). Politics in Spain during this period was seen as involving a new 'war' on values, and various right-wing groups, sometimes with the support of the Church, mobilized against the government. Despite various policy problems and the pending economic crisis, Zapatero won the 2008 parliamentary elections with a 4 per cent margin over the PP. It seemed clear that his turn to the left had won voters over from the smaller left-wing parties, and this, together with the occasional support of different nationalist/regional parties, seemed sufficient to guarantee the PSOE government for four more years.

Although the PSOE and PP now dominate Spanish politics, and although this is effectively a two-party system, they are not the only relevant actors. Other forces on the centre right include the Catalan Convergence and Union (CiU), a loose alliance of conservative, Christian and liberal elements united in their support for greater regional autonomy for Catalonia. Although the CiU is a relatively small party in Spanish terms – it now polls only around 3 to 4 per cent of the vote in Spain as a whole – it has proved remarkably adept at bargaining with its larger opponents in Catalan interests. In return for important economic and political concessions it supported the minority PSOE government from 1993 to 1996, and pursued the same strategy with the minority PP government that came to power following the defeat of the socialists in 1996.

Opposition on the left of the political spectrum was originally focused primarily in the Spanish Communist Party (PCE), which was one of the major parties in the ill-fated Second Spanish Republic (1931–1936), and which had also constituted one of the most powerful clandestine oppositions to Francoism during the period of the dictatorship. The PCE and its leader, Santiago Carrillo, were also at the forefront of the shift towards Eurocommunism in western Europe in the late 1970s, when a number of leading communist parties sought to distance themselves from Moscow and attempted to forge a new, more consciously democratic strategy for reform (e.g., Lange and Vanicelli, 1981). But despite some early speculation that the PCE might emerge as the leading party of the left, and thus occupy a position similar to that of the former PCI in Italy, the party has in fact remained quite marginal. It was only through the later formation of an electoral cartel – the United Left – with a number of other small parties of the left that it could be seen as a serious political force, polling almost 11 per cent of the vote in 1996, but falling to just over 3.5 per cent by the time of the latest election in 2008.

The fragmentation of the Spanish party system has also been compounded by the emergence of a plethora of regional political forces, far too many to be listed separately in Table 7.8. In addition to the Catalan coalition and the pro-independence ERC, parties representing the local interests of Andalusia, Galicia, Aragon, Valencia and the Canary Islands have also won representation in the Cortes, the Spanish parliament. Regionalism is strongest in the Basque country in northern Spain, and has supported two important parties, the Basque Nationalist Party (PNV), a pro-independence conservative party; and Herri Batasuna (Popular Unity), a radical left-wing nationalist party that endorses ETA, the Basque paramilitary organization that is engaged in an armed struggle against the Spanish state. In March 2003 Herri Batasuna was banned by the Spanish Supreme Court on the grounds that it was part of the ETA terrorist network. The Basque region is one of the most distinctive and prosperous in Spain, with a population of over 2 million and with its own language and culture. Two-thirds of Basque voters have supported one or other of the Basque national parties, and the region has been plagued by a level of political dissension and violence almost comparable to that which used to prevail in Northern Ireland.

The most recent political force to appear in Spain has been Union, Progress and Democracy (UPyD), a party founded in September 2007 by Rosa Díez, a former leader of the Basque Socialist Party and head of the PSOE delegation in the European Parliament in 1999. Officially a 'progressive' party, the UPyD did surprisingly well in its first electoral forays, polling more than 300 000 votes in the first months of activity. Nonetheless, and like the IU, it fell victim to the Spanish electoral system, which tends to favour parties with a greater concentration of votes. Despite having the same number of votes as the Basque Nationalist Party (the PNV), which won six seats, it won only one seat in the 2008 election.

The overall picture is thus of a fragmented but increasingly structured party system in which conflicts between the left and the right overlie and intersect conflicts between the centre and the periphery, and between church and state. The recent pattern of alternation in government appears to signal the consolidation of a more sharply defined bipolar pattern of competition, however, and in this sense the Spanish party system is developing along much the same lines as that in Britain, with a major party of the centre left (PSOE) competing against a major party of the centre right (PP), and with a number of smaller and especially regional parties jostling around the edge of this battle. The bipolar confrontation dominates, however, particularly in the wake of the severe cuts announced by the Zapatero government in 2010. Spain has, together with Portugal, Ireland and Greece – the so-called PIGS – been among the countries most severely affected by the growing financial crisis in 2008–2010, and the budgetary adjustment has been among the harshest of all the countries. Whether an ostensibly left-wing government can survive while pushing through such an austerity programme is open to question.

The most comprehensive recent analysis of Spanish politics is Magone (2009), but see also Hopkin (1999), Linz and Montero (2001), Chari (2004) and Bernecker and Maihold (2007).

## 7.2.8 Party politics in Poland

Following a series of reforms introduced in the wake of protests against communist rule in 1956, Poland had been initially allowed to pursue quite a distinctive path within the then all-powerful Soviet bloc. Private agricultural production was accepted, and freedom of religious practice was given to the overwhelmingly Catholic population. This distinctiveness was confirmed in 1980, when following a series of strikes centring on the Lenin shipyards in Gdańsk, the communist government agreed to recognize the existence of the independent trade union Solidarity, led by Lech Wałęsa, who was later to be elected as Poland's first post-communist president. Little more than a year later, however, the tide tuned: the reform policy was reversed in 1981, martial law was imposed and maintained until 1983, Solidarity was banned, and its leadership was arrested. Then, in the late 1980s, fuelled by a severe economic crisis on the one hand, and by the stimulus of the reforms in the Soviet Union on the other hand, the protest movement began to mobilize once more. This time, the pressure for reform proved unstoppable, and eventually a series of round-table negotiations began between the ruling Communist Party and Solidarity. In April 1989 these talks led to a commitment to hold relatively free parliamentary elections, in which the opposition would be allowed to compete for 35 per cent of the seats in the Sejm, the lower house of parliament, and for all of the seats in the Senate, the upper house. The remaining 65 per cent of the seats in the Sejm were to be retained by the Communist Party and their allied satellite party groups, such as the United Peasant Party, Christian Democracy, and the Democratic Party. Communist rule in eastern Europe had first been undermined in 1980 through the official recognition of Solidarity. This new agreement of 1989 was now to echo throughout the Soviet bloc, and was to signal its final demise. Poland was leading the way towards democracy.

Solidarity and its allies, representing a broad anti-communist front and encompassing a wide variety of diverse strands of opinion, went on to win every single one of the contested seats in this new 'managed' election to the Sejm, as well as all but one of the 100 seats in the Senate (Olson, 1993). Moreover, despite being kept to 35 per cent of the seats, they also won effective control of government, in that the communists' ostensibly allied satellite parties suddenly switched their support to the anti-communist alliance. The result was that Poland's first non-communist government took office on 12 September 1989, under the prime ministership of Tadeusz Mazowiecki of Solidarity. Solidarity also gained control of 10 additional ministries, while other parties initially involved in the broad coalition included the United Peasant Party, which was later to reorganize itself as the Polish Peasant Party (PSL), and the Democratic Party, both former communist satellite parties. The communists themselves held four ministries in this interim administration.

As part of the commitments made in the round-table agreement, the new parliament also elected as president the communist party leader and a former prime minister, General Jaruzelski, who had been responsible for the introduction of martial law in 1981. In September 1990, however, Jaruzelski stepped down in order to be replaced by a directly elected president. This new democratic presidential election was then organized in much the same way as those in France, with a second round of voting between the two leading candidates being required if no single candidate won an absolute majority in the first round. The divisions that were later to pull Solidarity apart had by now become apparent, however, and the principal candidates in the first presidential election included the sitting prime minister, Mazowiecki, as well as Lech Wałęsa, who had refused to present himself as a candidate in the partial parliamentary elections of 1989. Wałęsa's supporters had already formed their own political group, the Centre Alliance, which was openly critical of what they regarded as the slow pace of reform under Mazowiecki's government. There was also a third strong outside candidate, Stanisław Tymiński, a Polish-born Canadian businessman, who attempted to hold out the prospect of a miraculous transformation of the Polish economy, and who was later involved in the creation of the so-called Party X. The results proved somewhat of a surprise, with Wałęsa emerging as the strongest candidate in the first round, but without an overall majority (he polled 40 per cent of the votes), and with Tymiński in second place (23 per cent). The sitting prime minister, Mazowiecki, with 18 per cent of the vote, was therefore eliminated. In the second round of voting Wałęsa went on to poll 74 per cent of the vote and was duly elected. Following pressure from Wałęsa, it was agreed that new parliamentary elections would take place in October 1991.

The results of the 1991 election revealed the exceptionally fragmented nature of the emerging party politics. A total of 111 lists were registered for the election, and 29 of these eventually won representation in the Sejm, with the single most successful party, UD, winning just over 12 per cent of the vote and 62 (13 per cent) seats. Nine additional ex-Solidarity parties also won representation; taken together, the combined vote for all of the ex-Solidarity parties totalled almost 52 per cent. The former Communist Party and its one-time allies were represented mainly in the form of the Alliance of Democratic Left (SLD), which emerged as the second biggest party with exactly 12 per cent of the vote and 60 seats, and the Polish Peasant Party (PSL), which won just over 9 per cent of the vote. Among the other parties in the new Sejm was the Beer-Lovers' Party (3 per cent), which had begun as a joke party but which was later backed by a number of leading Polish businessmen.

As in Spain, Poland's first fully democratic election was then followed by a period of quite pronounced political instability. Despite this, however, there were signs that two broad alignments were beginning to take shape. On the one hand there was the Socialist (or former Communist) Party, the SLD, and its main ally, the PSL. This was the old left – the successor parties of the old regime. On the other hand there was the loose grouping around the former Solidarity and its allies, which itself fell into two crudely defined camps – one that was liberal and secular, such as the Freedom Union (UW), and one that was liberal in the pro-market sense, but which was also strongly Catholic. This crude divide between the two alignments was further complicated by the tensions that existed between the two arenas in which competition took place – the presidential arena, on the one hand, and the parliamentary arena, on the other.

By 1995 some of this latter tension evaporated, with Wałęsa being defeated by the SLD's Aleksander Kwaśniewski in the new contest for the presidency. In 2000 Kwaśniewski was re-elected president, and in 2001 the SLD also returned to power in parliament, this time winning a clear majority in alliance with the Labour Union (UP). The main opposition was now represented by yet more newly formed parties – Civic Platform (PO), Law and Justice (PiS) and the League of Polish Families (LPR) – all of which traced their roots back to Solidarity. The 2001 election also saw the emergence of the agrarian populist party Self-Defence (SO), which emerged as the third largest party in the Sejm (Table 7.9). The new post-communist government also proved unstable, however, and ideological differences regarding the economy and the role of the church, as well as over EU accession negotiations, led to the collapse of the coalition in March 2003. Roughly one year later Prime Minister Leszek Miller resigned, pressured mainly by the terrible economic situation, the continuing corruption scandals, and the disintegration of the SLD itself.

The 2005 parliamentary elections were characterized by a clear victory of the post-Solidarity parties (both PiS and PO), partly as a result of the impact of the presidential elections, held almost simultaneously (Tables 7.9 and 7.10). The resignation of the SLD presidential candidate, Wlodzimierz Cimoszewicz, less than a month before the contest, converted the battle for both the premiership and the presidency into a battle between the liberal-conservative PO and the national-conservative PiS, with the latter eventually winning by a narrow margin. Both parties had publicly agreed to join forces in a coalition government, but the imminence of the presidential contest between their two leaders, Lech Kaczyński (PiS) and Donald Tusk (PO), postponed its formation. Although Tusk led after the first round, Kaczyński managed to win the second round with the support of the controversial populist Andrzej Lepper. The result was the formation of a PiS minority government supported by the populist SO, the radical right-wing LPR and the agrarian PSL. A formal coalition was agreed in May 2006, and two months later the leadership of the coalition passed to Jarosław Kaczyński – the identical twin brother of the newly elected president. This new government not only led to the 'legitimization' of parties that had been previously seen as pariahs, but also to the seeming consolidation of a new pattern of competition based on economic differences, the so-called Social versus Liberal Poland. In other words, the ideological conflict between the post-communist and post-Solidarity parties, based on religion and the perception of the communist past, gave way to a more classical confrontation between the economically populist and the more liberal parties.

Fuelled by a critical public opinion and a reinvigorated opposition, the power struggles inside the coalition eventually led to early elections in September 2007 (Table 7.9). Tired of the increasing ideological polarization of the political debate around such issues as lustration (the dismissal of former communists from public offices), and concerned about the increasing role of extreme religious groups (mainly Radio Maria) in political life, voters went to the polls in large numbers (at least by Polish standards) and delivered a clear victory to Civic Platform. Both SO and LPR appeared to exit Polish politics for good. The united left (SLD, UP and SDPL), together with the liberal PD (formerly UW), came in third place, although it was again the agrarian PSL that had the key to the formation of the government. After not much hesitation, Donald Tusk formed a majority government with Pawlak's PSL, delivering a fatal blow to the so-called post-communist cleavage (Grabowska, 2004). Despite some low-level quarrels between the governing forces, and the continuous power struggles between the prime minister and the president, Tusk's cabinet managed to hold firm and become the most popular government in the history of democratic Poland.

**TABLE 7.9** Legislative elections in Poland since 1997

| Party | 1997 | | 2001 | | 2005 | | 2007 | |
|---|---|---|---|---|---|---|---|---|
| | % of votes | Seats | % of votes | Seats | % of votes | Seats | % of votes | Seats |
| Democratic Left Alliance (SLD)[a] | 27.1 | 164 | 41.0 | 216 | 11.3 | 55 | 13.2 | 53 (40) |
| Civic Platform (PO) | – | – | 12.7 | 65 | 24.1 | 133 | 41.5 | 209 |
| Self-Defence (SO) | 0.1 | – | 10.2 | 53 | 11.4 | 56 | 1.5 | – |
| Law and Justice (PiS) | – | – | 9.5 | 44 | 27 | 155 | 32.1 | 166 |
| Polish Peasant Party (PSL) | 7.3 | 27 | 9.0 | 42 | 7 | 25 | 8.9 | 31 |
| League of Polish Families (LPR) | – | – | 7.9 | 38 | 8 | 34 | 1.3 | – |
| Social Democracy of Poland (SdPL) | – | – | – | – | 3.9 | – | – | (10) |
| Democratic Party (PD)[b] | 13.4 | 60 | 3.1 | – | 2.5 | – | – | (3) |
| Movement for the Reconstruction of Poland (ROP) | 5.6 | 6 | – | – | – | – | – | – |
| Solidarity Electoral Action (AWS) | 33.8 | 201 | 5.6 | – | | | | |
| Confederation for an Independent Poland (KPN) | – | – | – | – | – | – | – | – |
| German Minority | 0.6 | 2 | 0.4 | 2 | 0.3 | 2 | 0.2 | 1 |
| Others | 7.3 | – | 0.6 | – | 4.5 | – | 1.3 | – |
| All | 100.0 | 460 | 100.0 | 460 | 100.0 | 460 | 100.0 | 460 |

Party composition of government:

1997–2000, coalition of Solidarity Electoral Action and Freedom Union

2000–2001, Solidarity Electoral Action single-party minority government

2001–2003, coalition of Democratic Left Alliance, Labour Union, and Polish Peasant Party

2003–2005, coalition of Democratic Left Alliance and Labour Union

2005, coalition of Democratic Left Alliance, Labour Union, and Polish Social Democracy

2005–2006, Law and Justice single-party minority government

2006–2007, coalition of Law and Justice, Self-Defence, and the League of Polish Families

2007, Law and Justice single-party minority government

2007–, coalition of Civic Platform and Polish Peasant Party

[a] In the 2001 elections the Democratic Left Alliance (SLD) and Labour Union (UP) formed an alliance. In 2007 the SLD formed an electoral alliance (Left and Democrats, LiD) with the Labour Union, Social Democracy of Poland (SdPL) and the Democratic Party (PD).

[b] The Democratic Party is the legal successor to the Freedom Union (UW), a party founded after the Liberal Democratic Congress (KLD) and the Democratic Union (UD) merged in 1994.

On 10 April 2010, while travelling to Katyn in Russia to commemorate the 70th anniversary of the massacre of thousands of elite Polish officers by Soviet forces during the Second World War, the Polish president was tragically killed in a plane crash. The crash also cost the lives of the Polish army chief, the head of the central bank, and a number of senior MPs and political advisors. In the presidential elections that followed, Bronisław Komorowski of Civic Platform (PO), Speaker of the Sejm and acting president since Lech Kaczyński's death, managed to defeat the latter's twin brother, Jarosław, in the second round of the elections by a margin of 6 per cent.

**TABLE 7.10** Presidential elections in Poland since 2000

| Percentage of votes in 2000 | | Percentage of votes in 2005 | | | Percentage of votes in 2010 | | |
|---|---|---|---|---|---|---|---|
| Candidate (Party) | First ballot | Candidate (Party) | First ballot | Second ballot | Candidate (Party) | First ballot | Second ballot |
| Aleksander Kwaśniewski (Ind./SLD) | 53.9 | Lech Kaczyński (PiS) | 33.1 | 54 | Bronisław Komoroswki (PO) | 41.5 | 53 |
| Andrzej Olechowski (Ind.) | 17.3 | Donald Tusk (PO) | 36.3 | 46 | Jarosław Kaczyński (PiS) | 36.5 | 47 |
| Marian Krzaklewski (AWS) | 15.6 | Andrzej Lepper (SO) | 15.1 | – | Grzegorz Napieralski (SLD) | 13.7 | – |
| Jarosław Kalinowski (PSL) | 6.0 | Marek Borowski (SdPL) | 10.3 | – | Janusz Korwin-Mikke (WiP) | 2.5 | – |
| Andrzej Lepper (SO) | 3.1 | Jarosław Kalinowski (PSL) | 1.8 | – | Waldemar Pawlak (PSL) | 1.8 | – |
| Janusz Korwin-Mikke (UPR) | 1.4 | Janusz Korwin-Mikke (UPR) | 1.4 | – | Andrzej Olechowski (Ind.) | 1.4 | – |
| Lech Wałęsa (Chr. Dem.) | 1.0 | Henryka Bochniarz (PD) | 1.3 | – | Andrzej Lepper (SO) | 1.3 | – |
| Other (N = 5) | 1.8 | Other (N = 5) | 0.7 | – | Marek Jurek (PR) | 1.1 | – |
| | | | | | Other (N = 2) | 0.2 | – |
| | 100.0 | | 100.0 | 100.0 | | 100.0 | 100.0 |

As it could not be any other way in a country where 'the past is never dead' (Jasiewicz, 2009), the Smolensk tragedy and the different ways of looking at Poland's history were central to the presidential campaign, and the results reflected once more the political division between the 'traditional' (i.e. religious and conservative) east and the 'liberal' (i.e. cosmopolitan and secular) west. Although Komorowski could count neither on the formal support of his party's coalition partner (PSL), whose electorate was divided between the two leading contenders, nor on the post-communist SLD, even if some of its popular representatives decided to support the PO candidate at a personal level, it seemed that it was the 'post-communist' voters who finally helped Komorowski to become head of state (see Table 7.10), thus bringing to an end the difficult cohabitation that had begun with the PO parliamentary success three years earlier.

The most remarkable feature about the Polish party system is that it still remains remarkably ill defined and inchoate. Indeed, some 20 years after democratization, and despite the continuing traditional–liberal divide, the party system is still less institutionalized than was the Spanish party system at the beginning of the 1980s. To be sure, some points of stability and political anchoring are evident – most notably in the organizational persistence of the post-communist agrarian PSL, and the role of religion in determining voters' electoral choices. Beyond these points, however, there is little sign of any institutionalization or consolidation. The legacy of Solidarity persists, and the ideological appeal of the Polish version of Christian democracy also persists, but neither tradition seems capable of finding expression in a consolidated or coherent set of party alternatives. For voters, in short – as well as for students of politics – the Polish case sometimes seems impenetrable. Indeed, amidst all the confusions that characterize party competition at the parliamentary level, it is worth noting that voter turnout is the lowest in Europe, while in terms of the comparisons in this volume it is clearly the least consolidated party system in the European Union.

The most comprehensive analysis in English is Millard (2010), but see also Markowski (2001), Szczerbiak (2001) and Jasiewicz (2005).

## 7.3 The diversity of modern European party politics

Each of the party systems that we have considered is characterized by a basic confrontation between the left and the right; each also contains one or more parties that we might think of as being at the centre. Beyond this, however, differences between systems appear to be more striking than similarities. Moreover, when comparing west and east, the differences become even more pronounced.

Let us look at the complexities of the older systems first. In Denmark and the United Kingdom, liberal parties are to be found between the left and the right, and they reflect a more moderate class alternative than that promoted by conservative parties. In the Netherlands and Germany, on the other hand, traditional liberalism has its roots in conservatism – and the liberal parties are mainly to be found on the right. In Denmark and the United Kingdom, class confrontations define the only major dimension in politics, although in Denmark the pattern is more complex, given the secondary role of agrarian and religious interests. In Italy, the Netherlands and Germany, on the other hand, religion traditionally provided a major dimension of party competition.

Differences also extend to the pattern of government formation. In France, Spain, Germany and the United Kingdom the left can hope to govern alone. In the Netherlands and Italy the left has for long been too weak, or too divided, to do so; in each case the left has been obliged to forge coalitions with parties on the centre and right. Finally, although Germany, Denmark and Britain have strongly structured party systems, France and, to a lesser extent, Spain have systems that include loose and often fragmented alliances that lack the cohesion and discipline normally associated with European political parties. The shape of the new Italian party system is still too uncertain to define, while in the Netherlands there have now been a series of successful challengers to the traditional mainstream parties.

Given such diversity, to speak of a 'typical' European party system is clearly unrealistic. Nonetheless, the countries in certain groups do seem quite similar to one another. The Danish party system, for example, has been compared to the party systems in Sweden and Norway by observers who speak of a typical 'Scandinavian' party system (Berglund and Lindstrom, 1978). The Netherlands has been compared to Belgium and Switzerland in an extensive literature that treats them as 'consociational democracies' responding to very deep-seated social and ethnic cleavages (Lijphart, 1977; Luther and Deschouwer, 1999). The deep ideological divisions in the Italian party system before the 1990s have been compared to those in France between 1946 and 1958, and to those in Finland, as examples of 'polarized pluralism' (Sartori, 1976). The southern European democracies of Greece, Spain and Portugal have also been extensively compared in a literature that highlights the common problems experienced by parties in the consolidation of new democracies (Morlino, 1998), and it is now interesting to see in each of these three systems the possible development of a British-style two-party system. In short, although it may be far too simplistic to speak of even west European party politics as being a set of variations on a single theme, it is reasonable to think of them as reflecting variations on a relatively limited set of themes.

### 7.3.1 Left and right

One theme that recurs in almost all the long-established European democracies concerns the role of the left–right dimension in structuring politics. The terms 'left' and 'right' have always been widely accepted as part of the common political currency of Europe. To be on the left has traditionally meant supporting a communist or socialist party claiming to represent the interests of the organized working class. Every European country, without exception, has such a party. This, more than anything else, is the common theme in the politics of representation in Europe, and it also, incidentally, marks off the European experience from that in the United States.

To be on the centre and right has meant supporting those who stand against the communist or socialist parties. On the centre right, however, there are few features common to all the European countries. In some countries, parties of the right have a distinctly religious basis; in others, they are secular. In some countries, parties of the right traditionally have included those reflecting rural or farming interests; in others, they include those representing a particular cultural or linguistic subculture. One of the most striking features of European party politics is thus that although the left has been reasonably homogeneous, and has traditionally been represented by at most two parties, the right has been more fragmented, including religious, secular, agrarian, nationalist and other parties under the same broad umbrella.

Describing the right and the left in terms of the class interests that were traditionally represented by particular parties is only part of the story. There is also clearly a separate ideological sense in which we can speak of such parties as having programmes that are on the left or right of the political spectrum. The problem here is that although it is easy to identify parties that mobilized in defence of particular social interests, it is less easy to specify who is on the left or the right in purely ideological terms.

One example of this is the mobilization of environmentalist, or 'Green', parties in western Europe. This is a relatively new but increasingly relevant and pervasive political family that has emerged from the organizational traditions of neither the left nor the right. Indeed, these parties are sometimes claimed to reflect a wholly 'new' politics that, in terms of both social support and organizational form, represents a genuine challenge to traditional alignments. Increasingly, however, these new parties are seen as moving towards the ideological left of the political spectrum, particularly when they demand both radical economic change and new forms of social justice. In practice, these parties now often find themselves in alliances with social democratic parties. Here too, therefore, organizational and social definitions of the left and the right fit uneasily with more strictly ideological criteria.

When a country had two or more parties on the traditional left – a socialist and a communist party, for example – we might expect them to have acted in concert in an attempt to realize shared goals. In practice, however, this was often not the case. In Italy, during the First Republic, the Socialist Party traditionally cast its lot with the Christian Democratic Party and smaller parties of the right, and refused to consider an alliance with its communist ideological neighbour. Even though the combined vote of the Italian left sometimes exceeded 40 per cent, prior to the 1990s Italian voters were never offered the prospect of a left-wing coalition government. Relations between communists and socialists have also often been very strained in France. Here, however, an eventual alliance of the two parties did lead to an unprecedented left-wing victory in the presidential elections of 1981. Prior to this historic breakthrough, the French socialists had often despaired of finding common ground with their communist neighbours, and had opted instead to chase alliances on the centre and right of the party system.

More recently – in Italy in 1996, in France in 1997, in Germany in 1998 and again in 2002, and in Belgium in 1999 – socialist parties have gained government office through alliances with the newer Green parties, and one of the more important consequences of the rise of Green parties in Europe has been to add sufficient strength to the broad bloc of the left to allow it to regain control of government after long periods of centre-right dominance. Indeed, at the end of 1999, socialist parties – whether alone, or in alliance with Greens or parties of the centre – were in government in all but three (Spain, Luxembourg and Ireland) of the then 15 member states of the European Union. For the first time in post-war history, the major party of the left was in government in all four of the major west European polities at the same time (France, Germany, Italy and the UK). Little more than a decade later, however, following the victory of the Conservative–Liberal coalition in Britain, all four were governed by the right. Indeed, at the end of 2010, six of the seven western countries covered in this chapter were governed from the right. The exception is Spain, where the PSOE still held on to power by the narrowest possible margin.

Maintaining alliances on the right also proves problematic, particularly since the recent rise of the far right (see Chapter 8). Many of the new far-right parties – such as the National Alliance and the Northern League in Italy, the National Front in France, the Flemish Block in Belgium, the Danish People's Party in Denmark, and the Freedom Party in the Netherlands – share many concerns with their more moderate neighbours of the right. However, their sheer radicalism or sometimes even the extremism of their ideological position often makes it difficult for them to form or sustain co-operative arrangements with these neighbours. In party systems that are ideologically polarized, indeed, it is usually easier for parties of the centre right to find common ground with parties of the centre left than it is to find common ground with some of their fellow right-wing parties. This was certainly the case for a long time in Austria, for example, where the increasingly extremist positions adopted by the right-wing Freedom Party under the leadership of Jörg Haider served to isolate his party from coalition-building in the 1990s, while at the same time strengthening his capacity to appeal to voters as an outsider seeking to challenge the control of the established parties. Haider eventually managed to break through to government, marginally outpolling the People's Party in the election of October 1999, and then joining that party in the new government that took office in February 2000. Two years later the Pim Fortuyn List also joined a right-wing coalition in the Netherlands. In both cases it seemed that taboos had been broken, although the experience in government proved unhappy for both parties, each of which lost quite heavily in the subsequent election (see Heinisch, 2003; also Deschouwer, 2009).

Both of these parties also reflected a growing sense of disillusion with politics, which is something that is found in almost all of the countries that have been surveyed here. One consequence of this disillusion is the greater room that is now afforded for the mobilization of protest movements and 'anti-party' – or anti-establishment – parties. The sources of this protest are potentially legion. The persistence of economic problems certainly fuels dissatisfaction, as does the perceived growth in social inequalities. A rising tide of racism creates new tensions that are difficult to resolve. The integration of nation-states within the European Union (see Chapter 5) and the internationalization of economies appear to leave many voters wondering about what responsibilities, if any, still remain with their own national governments (Kriesi *et al.*, 2008). As in the United States, there is also an increasing concern with political corruption and patronage, and a growing sense that politicians are concerned only with looking after themselves. All of these factors help explain the increasing support for parties of the populist right, on the one hand, and for 'new politics' parties of the left, on the other. They also help explain the increasing appeal of flash parties, which suddenly emerge on the campaign trail and equally suddenly disappear. As yet, of course, the anti-party parties to which we refer account for only a very small share of the popular vote in European democracies, and in this sense the traditional patterns still continue to dominate political life. At the same time, however, there is little denying the sense of vulnerability now being felt by some of the most powerful European parties on both the left and the right.

Although the terms 'left' and 'right' might seem to provide a convenient shorthand for describing party politics in different countries using broadly similar terms, superficial similarities nevertheless can be deceptive. Moreover, as the centrist policies of the 'Third Way' or 'new middle' gained wide support in the 1990s, the use of terms such as 'left' and 'right' seemed to become less meaningful. Thus the story is told of how President Chirac of France once listened to a speech by Tony Blair of Britain about the need for more market-friendly policies, and then asked him: 'Let me be clear about this. I am the leader of the Right in France. You are the leader of the Left in Britain. Or is it the other way around?' (Hoggart, 1997). This may change in the coming years, however. The severity of the financial crisis at the end of the first decade of the new century has led most governments to announce major austerity packages, and, as they bite, these may well provoke a return to more traditional left–right conflicts. When it is the socialist parties who are the incumbents, the response of the centre-right opposition tends to be supportive of cutbacks, and hence it is perhaps easier to achieve a consensus. When the centre right is in power, however, and when the social democrats are in opposition, as was the case in most European polities at the onset of the crisis, then opposition to austerity can take the form of calls for higher taxes on the rich and a stronger defence of welfare programmes for the poor, and it is this that might well revitalize the traditional left–right divide.

### 7.3.2 The new bipolar competition

In the 1960s, when the study of comparative European politics was taking off, and when forms of coalition government and government alternation were first beginning to be studied, it was suggested that three different types of party system or even political system were to be found (e.g., Almond, 1960). There was, first, the *adversarial* Anglo-American model with a two-party alternating format, and which in Europe could be found in Britain and nowhere else. Second, there were the so-called *working* multiparty systems, in which one large party tended to confront and sometimes alternate with a coalition of smaller parties, and which tended to be characterized by a reasonably widespread consensus about policymaking and a reasonably centripetal style of competition. Norway and Sweden were the most obvious examples of such a system, with Denmark approximating quite closely. In each of these systems the dominant party was on the centre left. Ireland was similarly structured, although in the Irish case, and exceptionally so, the dominant party was on the centre right. The third conventional model was the so-called *continental* party system, containing more fragmented and more ideologically driven parties, and having a more or less unstable and unpredictable set of coalition alternatives – what Almond (1960) then called 'immobilist', focusing in particular on the cases of France and Italy. What was also particularly distinctive in this latter category, however, was the absence of full-scale government alternation. There was rarely competition between 'Ins' and 'Outs', but instead a frequent reshuffling of coalition partners. Following an election, one or more of these coalescing parties usually stayed in office, while one or more left to make room for new partners. This obviously reduced the clarity of responsibility, turning back-room negotiations rather than the electoral process itself into the decisive forum for determining government formation. Among the democracies in which this model tended to prevail were Belgium and the Netherlands, as well as Germany, Italy, Finland and Luxembourg, with Austria (which tended to opt for a grand coalition) and Switzerland (with its famous and unchanging magic formula) being, in their different ways, also systems in which elite strategies served to confound the capacity of elections to be decisive in establishing the executive. In Europe in the 1960s, in other words, with relatively few democracies to speak of, the continental style of coalition building and partial alternation was the single most dominant form.

Looking at the political landscape of twenty-first-century Europe, by contrast, it is striking to see the sheer number of systems that now fail to match this pattern. In part, this is because systems have changed. The French and Italian systems are the most striking examples of this transformation. As we have seen, France shifted from the quite extreme fragmentation and very unpredictable reshuffling of coalitions that characterized the Fourth Republic to a more stable two-bloc system in the Fifth Republic, not least as a result of contagion from the electoral competition for the presidency. In the wake of a series of key electoral reforms, on the one hand, and following the destruction and remaking of the party system, on the other, Italy also went bipolar, and has so far retained this pattern through the 1990s and beyond. Other cases also shifted, albeit less dramatically and less consistently. Elections in Austria in the late 1990s and early 2000s were temporarily bipolar in character, pitting a new coalition of Christian Democrats and Freedomites against a putative alliance of Social Democrats and Greens. In Germany also, as we have seen, a Red–Green coalition confronted an alliance of the centre right, before the polity switched back to a grand centrist coalition in 2005. Denmark has also become more clearly bipolar, with the decline of the traditional centre parties and the growth in the far right permitting a much sharper competition between left and right.

The change has also been wrought by newcomers, however, with the new democracies of southern and later east central Europe proving predominantly bipolar in character. Greece, Portugal and Spain are both bipolar and essentially two-party, and, together with Malta, now approximate more closely to the traditional British pattern than any of the other systems in Europe. In post-communist Europe, bipolarity also prevails, although in these polities it has usually taken the form of changing electoral coalitions formed within multiparty contexts. In this sense the pattern of competition in the latter region is much less stable than in southern Europe, but nevertheless usually permits voters to make a choice between 'Ins' and 'Outs'.

What had been the modal pattern of party competition in the 1960s – characterized by multiparty contests without a dominant party, and with governments being formed through the reshuffling of coalitions – has therefore now been driven to the margins. Today, this pattern continues to prevail only in Belgium, the Netherlands and Luxembourg, as well as in the fragmented and highly unstructured Finnish system. In Switzerland the traditional pattern also prevails, but here the coalitions are not even reshuffled.

### 7.3.3 Post-communist party systems

One of the major difficulties in determining the character of the new parties and the new party systems that are emerging in post-communist Europe is that they are still very much in a process of formation. It takes time to settle the structure of mass politics (see Chapter 9). Nevertheless, even knowing this, it is still perhaps surprising to see how little stabilization has been evident, particularly in Poland, even after some 20 years of democratic politics. Why might this be the case? One obvious reason is that the voters in these countries have yet to develop the sort of stable set of partisan loyalties that have helped to underpin the stabilization of politics in established party systems, and hence they are likely to prove significantly more volatile than their west European counterparts. The levels of electoral instability recorded in recent Polish elections, for example, are still substantially higher than that recorded in most post-war west European elections (see also Table 9.11 below). Moreover, because many voters initially opted for parties that failed to win representation in parliament, or which subsequently collapsed, and because other potential voters have yet to begin to participate in the electoral process (voter turnout in the Polish parliamentary elections is the lowest in the EU), we can expect to see future elections recording quite substantial shifts in levels of party support. A second reason is that, despite the efforts to clarify the rules of the game as quickly as possible, the precise shape of the institutional environment in these new democracies still remains somewhat uncertain, and demands for further changes in the electoral laws and the structures of government could well prove unsettling for both the voters and the parties. Third, there is the sheer openness of the electoral market, which implies that new parties can be formed and can make an impact with relative ease, and that existing parties can just as suddenly leave the stage. Poland offers numerous examples of such entries and exits, as well as numerous examples of party fission and fusion. Moreover, given that so many of the parties are relatively new creations, and given that they lack any well-established organizational roots or identities, then we cannot expect their supporters or leaders to have developed any strong sense of discipline or loyalty, which implies that these parties will also be quite susceptible to internal splits and fractures (van Biezen, 2003).

But even though the picture that emerges from the post-communist experience is certainly complex, it is still tempting to try to indicate some of the likely sources of future division, and to relate these to the traditional oppositions that have helped to structure the established party systems in western Europe, and which we have already looked at briefly. Issues revolving around the core problem of church–state relations, for example, are clearly apparent in Poland, and there we have seen parties that more or less identify themselves with the sort of policies pursued by traditional Christian democratic parties in the west. Centre–periphery problems are also apparent, with the position of ethnic and national minorities in particular providing the basis for tensions that may yet emerge to threaten the long-term stability of many of these new democracies. Urban–rural divisions are also pronounced, much more so than in the west, and agrarian parties have proved to be significant political forces. Evidence of more conventional left–right oppositions, on the other hand, which have proved so important in the development of west European party systems, are more difficult to characterize. This is partly because the class structure that has emerged from communism is itself so unsettled, with yet little scope, or time, for the development of more typically capitalist class relationships. Nevertheless, even at this early stage, it is possible to identify the existence of a substantial conflict of interest generated by the process of transition itself, with the more liberal reformers pitted against those whose jobs and living standards are inevitably threatened by marketization. This conflict was clearly present in Poland, where it has provided a base of support for the former Communist Party and its allies. It is even to be found in the former East Germany, where resistance to rapid reform has helped to win votes for the former East German Communist Party, the PDS, and later for The Left.

## 7.4 Conclusions

In the end, however, a lot of this sort of analysis must remain somewhat speculative. The patterns in practice are both confusing and diverse, and defy easy generalization. According to an early assessment by Kitschelt (1992), for example, future cleavage structures in the post-communist democracies were going to revolve around at least three overlapping sets of issues: first, the opposition between an inclusive definition of citizenship, which seeks to integrate individual citizens regardless of their ethnicity, class or culture, and a more exclusive definition of citizenship, which emphasizes the importance of homogeneity; second, the opposition between more liberal procedures of decision-making and more authoritarian procedures, an opposition that also includes the question of the role of religious authorities; and third, the opposition between those who favour a political redistribution of resources and those who prefer to rely on market forces (Kitschelt, 1992: 11–14). Some of these oppositions are now clearly to be seen in Poland, in some cases with more sharply defined contours than in others. But precisely because the parties themselves, both as teams of leaders and as organizations, are so fragile and volatile, it is difficult to see any dimension of competition being frozen into place for some time to come. This also means that the parties have an additional source of flux, and this means, in turn, that it is even more difficult to locate them within the traditional family groups that are to be found among the west European democracies. East and west may be coming closer together, but, as we shall see in the following chapters, the differences between the two sets of cases are still more striking than the similarities.

One of the most convenient ways of providing an overview of the combination of uniformity and diversity that characterizes the European party mosaic is to speak of *party families*. Thus, even though there are differences between Christian democratic parties in different countries, there are also striking similarities that go far beyond mere name and religious affiliation. Such parties tend to be located on the centre right of the system, to be flanked by both social democratic and other right-wing parties, to be commonly found at the heart of government coalitions, and so on. Accordingly, we move our discussion forward by looking in the next chapter at the main party families in modern Europe, as well as at how they have developed through the years. Our intention in doing this is to highlight the point that, although no two parties are exactly alike, the parties in particular groups do bear striking resemblances to one another.

## Internet resources

For updates on elections in these and other European countries, see http://electionresources.org/.

Datasets with extensive details of governments, parliaments and parties are hosted on the website of the European University Institute in Florence (at the EUDO pages), and are available through ParlGov Dataverse: http://dvn.eudo.eu/dvn/dv/parlgov.

## References

**Almond, Gabriel A.** (1960) 'Introduction: a functional approach to comparative politics', pp. 3–64 in Gabriel A. Almond and James S. Coleman (eds), *The Politics of Developing Areas*, Princeton University Press, Princeton, NJ.

**Andeweg, Rudy B. and Galen A. Irwin** (2009) *Governance and Politics of the Netherlands*, 3rd edn, Palgrave, Basingstoke.

**Bartolini, Stefano** (1984) 'Institutional constraints and party competition in the French party system', *West European Politics*, 7 (4), 103–127.

**Berglund, Sten and Ulf Lindstrom** (1978) *The Scandinavian Party System(s)*, Studentlitteratur, Lund.

**Bernecker, Walther L. and G. Maihold (eds)** (2007) *España, del consenso a la polarización: cambios en la democracia española*, Vervuert, Madrid.

**Bogdanor, Vernon** (2004) 'Our new constitution', *Law Quarterly Review*, 120, 242–262.

**Bornschier, Simon and Romain Lachat** (2009) 'The evolution of the French political space and party system', *West European Politics*, 32 (2), 360–383.

**Bull, Martin J. and James L. Newell** (2005) *Italian Politics: Adjustment Under Duress*, Polity, Cambridge.

**Bull, Martin and Martin Rhodes (eds)** (1997) *Crisis and Transition in Italian Politics*, special issue of *West European Politics*, 20 (1).

**Chari, Raj S.** (2004) 'The 2004 Spanish election: terrorism as a catalyst for change?', *West European Politics*, 27 (5), 954–963.

**Daalder, Hans** (1987) 'The Dutch Party system: from segmentation to polarization – and then?', pp. 193–284 in Hans Daalder (ed.), *Party Systems in Denmark, Austria, Switzerland, the Netherlands, and Belgium*, Frances Pinter, London.

**Deschouwer, Kris (ed.)** (2009) *New Parties in Government*, Routledge, London.

**Dunleavy, Patrick** (2005) 'Facing up to multi-party politics: how partisan dealignment and PR voting have fundamentally changed Britain's party systems', *Parliamentary Affairs*, 58 (3), 503–532.

**Faas, Thorsten** (2010) 'The German federal election of 2009: sprouting coalitions, drooping social democrats', *West European Politics*, 33 (4), 894–903.

**Finer, S.E.** (1980) *The Changing British Party System, 1945–79*, American Enterprise Institute, Washington, DC.

**Flinders, Matthew** (2005) 'Majoritarian democracy in Britain: Labour and the new constitution', *West European Politics*, 28 (1), 61–93.

**Ginsborg, Paul** (2005) *Silvio Berlusconi: Television, Power and Patrimony*, Verso, London.

**Grabowska, Mirosława** (2004) *Podział postkomunistyczny: Społeczne podstawy w Polsce po 1989 roku*, Scholar, Warsaw.

**Green-Pedersen, Christoffer** (2006) 'Long-term changes in Danish party politics: the rise and importance of issue competition', *Scandinavian Political Studies*, 29 (3), 219–235.

**Haegel, Florence (ed.)** (2007) *Partis politiques et système partisan en France*, Presses de Science Po, Paris.

**Heinisch, Reinhard** (2003) 'Success in opposition – failure in government: explaining the performance of right-wing populist parties in public office', *West European Politics*, 26 (3), 91–130.

**Hoggart, Simon** (1997) 'A perfect reflection of left and right', *Guardian*, 29 March.

**Hopkin, Jonathan** (1999) 'Spain: political parties in a young democracy', pp. 207–231 in D. Broughton and M.S. Donovan (eds), *Changing Party Systems in Western Europe*, Frances Pinter, London.

**Jasiewicz, Krzysztof** (2005) 'Poland: party system by default', pp. 85–118 in David Stansfield, Paul Webb and Stephen White (eds), *Political Parties in Transitional Democracies*, Oxford University Press, Oxford.

**Jasiewicz, Krzysztof** (2009) '"The past is never dead": identity, class, and voting behavior in contemporary Poland', *East European Politics and Societies*, 23 (4), 491–508.

**Kitschelt, Herbert** (1992) 'The formation of party systems in east central Europe', *Politics and Society*, 20 (1), 7–50.

**Kitschelt, Herbert and Wolfgang Streeck** (2003a) 'From stability to stagnation: Germany at the beginning of the twenty-first century', *West European Politics*, 26 (4), 1–36.

**Kitschelt, Herbert and Wolfgang Streeck (eds)** (2003b) *Germany: Beyond the Stable State*, special issue of *West European Politics*, 26 (4).

**Knapp, Andrew** (2004) *Parties and the Party System in France: A Disconnected Democracy?*, Palgrave, London.

**Kriesi, Hanspeter, Edgar Grande, Romain Lachat, Martin Dolezal, Simon Bornschier and Timotheus Frey** (2008) *Western European Politics in the Age of Globalization*, Cambridge University Press, Cambridge.

**Lange, Peter and M. Vanicelli (eds)** (1981) *The Communist Parties of Italy, France and Spain*, Allen & Unwin, London.

**Lees, Charles** (2005) *Party Politics in Germany: A Comparative Politics Approach*, Palgrave Macmillan, Basingstoke.

**Lijphart, Arend** (1977) *Democracy in Plural Societies*, Yale University Press, New Haven, CT.

**Linz, Juan J. and José Ramón Montero** (2001) 'The party systems of Spain: old cleavages and new challenges', pp. 150–196 in *Party Systems and Voter Alignments Revisited*, Lauri Karvonen and Stein Kuhnle (eds), Routledge, London.

**Luther, Richard and Kris Deschouwer (eds)** (1999) *Party Elites in Divided Societies: Political Parties in Consociational Democracy*, Routledge, London.

**Mackie, Thomas T. and Richard Rose** (1991) *The International Almanac of Electoral History*, 3rd edn, Macmillan, Basingstoke.

**Magone, José M.** (2009) *Contemporary Spanish Politics*, 2nd edn, Routledge, London.

**Mair, Peter** (1997) *Party System Change*, Oxford University Press, Oxford.

**Mair, Peter** (2008) 'Electoral volatility and the Dutch party system: a comparative perspective', *Acta Politica*, 43 (2/3), 235–253.

**Mair, Peter** (2009) 'The British party system: a comparative perspective', pp. 283–301 in Matthew Flinders, Andrew Gamble, Colin Hay and Michael Kenny (eds), *The Oxford Handbook of British Politics*, Oxford University Press, Oxford.

**Markowski, Radoslaw** (2001) 'Party system institutionalization in new democracies: Poland – a trendsetter with no followers', pp. 55–77 in Paul Lewis (ed.), *Party Development and Democratic Change in Post-Communist Europe*, Frank Cass, London.

**Marquand, David** (1999) 'Progressive or populist: the Blair paradox', pp. 225–246 in David Marquand, *The Progressive Dilemma*, 2nd edn, Phoenix Giant, London.

**Mershon, Carol A.** (1996) 'The costs of coalition: coalition theories and Italian governments', *American Political Science Review*, 90 (3), 534–554.

**Millard, Frances** (2010) *Democratic Elections in Poland, 1991–2007*, Routledge, London.

**Morlino, Leonardo** (1998) *Democracy Between Consolidation and Crisis: Parties, Groups, and Citizens in Southern Europe*, Oxford University Press, Oxford.

**Newell, James L. (ed.)** (2009) *The Italian General Election of 2008: Berlusconi Strikes Back*, Palgrave Macmillan, Basingstoke.

**Newell, James L. and Martin J. Bull** (2002) 'Italian politics after the 2001 general election', *Parliamentary Affairs*, 55 (4), 626–642.

**Olson, David M.** (1993) 'Compartmentalized competition: the managed transitional election system of Poland', *Journal of Politics*, 55 (2), 415–441.

**Pappi, Franz Urban** (1984) 'The West German party system', *West European Politics*, 7 (4), 7–26.

**Pedersen, Mogens N.** (1987) 'The Danish "working multiparty system": breakdown or adaptation?' pp. 1–60 in Hans Daalder (ed.), *Party Systems in Denmark, Austria, Switzerland, the Netherlands, and Belgium*, Frances Pinter, London.

**Roberts, Geoffrey K.** (2009) *Party Politics in the New Germany*, Frances Pinter, London.

**Rydgren, Jens** (2004) 'Explaining the emergence of radical right-wing populist parties: the case of Denmark', *West European Politics*, 27 (3), 474–502.

**Sartori, Giovanni** (1976) *Parties and Party Systems*, Cambridge University Press, Cambridge.

**Sauger, Nicholas** (2009) 'The French party system: fifty years of change', pp. 79–98 in Sylvain Brouard, Andrew Appleton and Amy G. Mazur (eds), *The French Fifth Republic at Fifty*, Palgrave, London.

**Szczerbiak, Aleks** (2001) *Poles Together: Emergence and Development of Political Parties in Post-Communist Poland*, CEU Press, Budapest.

**van Biezen, Ingrid** (2003) *Political Parties in New Democracies: Party Organization in Southern and East-Central Europe*, Palgrave, London.

**van Holsteyn, Joop J.M. and Galen A. Irwin** (2003) 'Pim Fortuyn and the Dutch election of 2002', *West European Politics*, 26 (2), 41–66.

**Webb, Paul** (2000) *The Modern British Party System*, Sage, London.

**Wilson, Alex** (2009) 'The Italian election of April 2008', *West European Politics*, 32 (1), 215–225.

# Party Families

## Chapter contents

## 8.1 Introduction

As we argued in the preceding chapter, although no two political parties are quite the same, the parties in particular groups may share a considerable family resemblance. Three conventional characteristics can be used to define different party families in Europe (Mair and Mudde, 1998). First, parties can be grouped according to some shared origin: parties that mobilized in similar historical circumstances, or with the intention of representing similar interests, can be treated as having a distinct family resemblance. On these grounds, all traditional socialist or social democratic parties, for example, can be considered as belonging to the same family, as can all agrarian parties. This might be termed the *genetic approach*.

The second sort of family resemblance is defined by the parties themselves, in terms of the way in which they forge links across national frontiers. Such links may take the form of transnational federations, such as that established by various liberal parties. They may also take the form of membership of institutionalized multinational political groups, such as those to be found in the European Parliament (see Chapter 5), and since this now involves the full 27 member states of the European Union, it can offer a reasonably clear guide to the extent of cross-national partisan collegiality in western Europe (for an early application, see Hix and Lord, 1997). In this case we are concerned with *behaviour*.

The final way in which party families can be identified has to do with the extent to which the policies advocated by one party in a country are *similar* to those professed by another party in another country. There are some problems with this, because the 'same' policy may mean quite different things in the practical politics of two different countries, but to ignore professed policies altogether when looking for similarities between parties would clearly be to stick our heads in the sand. It matters what parties say.

Even though no single one of these criteria – genetics, behaviour, or discourse – provides a clear-cut classification, a judicious balance of the three suggests that, as far as modern Europe is concerned, we can think in terms of about nine main party families, and in this chapter we present a brief description of each of these families. We also chart changes in their long-term electoral following over the past half-century of democratic development in western Europe, and we contrast the changing patterns of support they enjoy in different countries. The classification into families in post-communist Europe is more blurred than that in western Europe, however. In the first place, as we have seen, the parties and the still less consolidated or less structured party systems are often very fragmented, and it is sometimes difficult to find a situation that is stable enough to speak of coherent families. Second, the problems facing political actors in post-communist Europe are often still specific to the development from post-communism, and hence have few if any parallels with the west. In terms of the divisions between left and right, for example, we often find the more progressive and radically minded forces being on the centre right, whereas the more conservative forces are sometimes on the left – particularly those in the socialist and post-communist parties with roots in the former regime. Even when we can identify families, therefore, they are sometimes different and particularistic. That said, there are broad pan-European elements constituted by religion, urban–rural divides, and even occasionally by class, and we shall discuss these later in the chapter. As a major first step, however, we shall focus on the long-established democracies of western Europe, since we are here concerned primarily with how the various families have developed across more than a half-century of democratic politics, and hence we need to concentrate on those democracies that have experienced this extended period of party competition. Later in the chapter we shall look at the newer European democracies.

For the purposes of this initial longitudinal analysis, and despite many problems of definition, we have divided these different families of parties into two broad groups: families of the left, which include social democrats, communists, the new left, and the Green parties; and families of the centre and right, which include Christian democrats, conservatives, liberals, agrarian or centre parties, and the far right. For each family, where relevant, we include a table reporting average electoral support in each of the countries in the 1950s, 1960s, 1970s, 1980s and 1990s, as well as in the first decade of the twenty-first century. Though most studies of European politics focus mainly on events in more recent years, we thought it useful to treat these families within the broader post-Second World War historical environment. When presenting these comparative data we concentrate mainly on those countries that have had an uninterrupted history of democratic politics since the 1950s, with separate figures being provided for Cyprus, Greece, Portugal and Spain. Later, we shall also discuss the relevance of these broad family distinctions to the newly emerging post-communist party systems.

We adopt this longitudinal approach to party families for two reasons. First, it helps us to understand the history of European politics, and hence helps us to gain a better sense of the relevant path dependences. Without some sense of the pasts, we can never be in a position to fully grasp the different presents and possible futures of European politics (Goetz et al., 2008). Second, even though each polity is different, a robust comparative politics requires us to identify equivalents and commonalities across national boundaries, and hence to use the same terms of reference to make comparisons across countries, and to identify the questions that need to be answered. To what extent has the left been traditionally divided between socialists and communists in some countries, but not in others? To what extent is the main party of the centre right based on a religious divide, and to what extent is it a secular alternative that dominates? In which countries does the far right mobilize? It is on the basis of the longitudinal data that we present in this chapter that the sense of these questions becomes apparent; later, in Chapter 9, we shall attempt to offer some answers.

## 8.2 Families of the left

There are four relevant party families to be found on the left-wing side of the political spectrum in traditional western European party systems. Social democratic parties are the strongest and most enduring of western Europe's political families, not only on the left but also in European politics taken as a whole. Communist parties are also a very clear-cut group, traditionally comprising those parties that began as pro-Soviet splits from social democratic parties in the wake of the Russian Revolution of 1917. The third and fourth families on the left are the new left and the Greens, which represent more varied collections of more recently formed parties, often grouped together under the general label *left-libertarian parties* (Kitschelt, 1988). All four families can be seen as representing the contemporary left in west European politics; however, they clearly incorporate between them some huge variations both of ideology and of interest representation.

### 8.2.1 The social democrats

Organized social democracy is one of the oldest surviving political forces in western Europe. Even at the beginning of the twenty-first century, the social democrats remain the single most important group in contemporary politics. The majority of the social democratic parties first entered electoral politics in the last quarter of the nineteenth century, and were initially mobilized to represent the political interests of the growing working class, often acting in concert with the trade union movement. In some cases, as in the United Kingdom, a social democratic party was actually created by the trade unions in order to represent their interests in parliament. In other cases, as in the Netherlands, a political party was formed first in its own right and later established links with the trade unions (for a comprehensive account, see Bartolini, 2000). As the franchise was extended to include more and more working-class voters, the social democratic parties grew in support. In the majority of European countries they gained their first experience of government in the years immediately following the First World War. By the late 1940s the position of the social democrats in European politics was well established. It was largely as a result of their intervention that most western European welfare states were expanded during the 1950s and 1960s, and it was largely their voice that was most vocal in resisting later entrenchments (Flora, 1986).

**TABLE 8.1** Mean electoral support for social democratic parties, 1950–2009

| Country | 1950s | 1960s | 1970s | 1980s | 1990s | 2000–2009 |
|---|---|---|---|---|---|---|
| Austria | 43.3 | 45.0 | 50.0 | 45.4 | 37.2 | 33.7 |
| Belgium | 35.9 | 31.0 | 26.6 | 28.0 | 23.8 | 24.6 |
| Denmark | 40.2 | 39.1 | 33.6 | 31.9 | 36.0 | 26.8 |
| Finland | 25.9 | 26.9 | 25.1 | 25.4 | 24.4 | 23.0 |
| France | 25.9 | 18.6 | 22.1 | 35.0 | 24.4 | 27.4 |
| Germany | 30.3 | 39.4 | 44.2 | 39.4 | 36.9 | 31.9 |
| Iceland | 19.5 | 15.0 | 14.8 | 17.1 | 20.3 | 29.2 |
| Ireland | 10.9 | 14.8 | 12.7 | 8.9 | 14.9 | 10.5 |
| Italy | 18.0 | 19.4 | 14.4 | 16.4 | 25.7 | 27.0 |
| Luxembourg | 37.1 | 35.0 | 35.4 | 32.3 | 24.8 | 22.5 |
| Malta | 54.9 | 38.5 | 51.2 | 49.0 | 48.1 | 48.4 |
| Netherlands | 30.7 | 25.8 | 31.9 | 31.0 | 26.5 | 21.2 |
| Norway | 47.5 | 45.4 | 38.8 | 37.4 | 36.0 | 28.5 |
| Sweden | 45.6 | 48.4 | 43.7 | 44.5 | 39.8 | 37.5 |
| Switzerland | 26.0 | 26.0 | 25.7 | 21.2 | 21.0 | 21.5 |
| United Kingdom | 46.3 | 46.1 | 39.1 | 29.2 | 38.9 | 38.0 |
| **Mean (*N* = 16)** | **33.6** | **32.1** | **31.8** | **30.7** | **29.9** | **28.2** |
| Cyprus | | | | 9.7 | 9.5 | 7.7 |
| Greece | | | | 43.5 | 43.8 | 41.6 |
| Portugal | | | | 28.7 | 39.4 | 39.8 |
| Spain | | | | 43.5 | 39.4 | 40.2 |
| **Overall mean (*N* = 20)** | | | | **30.8** | **30.5** | **29.1** |

*Note*: Since Greece, Portugal and Spain did not become fully democratic until the mid 1970s, decade averages are reported only for the 1980s, 1990s and 2000s. Cyprus is also included for the 1980s only. In the 1960s and 1970s elections were infrequent in Cyprus, and the different Greek Cypriot parties sometimes formed a broad national front.

*Sources*: http://parlgov.org/; Mackie and Rose; *European Journal of Political Research; West European Politics*. Because these tables report results for party families, the average figures for each country sometimes refer to two or more parties within any one family.

As Table 8.1 shows, the strongest social democratic presence among the long-established democracies in twenty-first-century Europe can be found in Austria, Germany, Malta, Norway, Sweden and the UK, where in each case the average social democratic share of the vote was still more than 30 per cent during the 1990s. Social democracy proves to be an even more powerful political force in Greece, Portugal and Spain, where democracy was re-established in the 1970s following periods of authoritarian rule, and where social democratic parties now average around 40 per cent of the vote. Socialist governments were re-elected to office in Spain in 2008 and in Portugal in 2009, and defeated the conservatives to return to power in Greece in 2009.

In a second group of countries – Belgium, Finland, France, Iceland and Italy (the now merged former Communist Party and the centre left) – the social democratic share of the vote has recently averaged around 25 per cent, with a slightly lower share of the vote in Luxembourg, the

Netherlands and Switzerland. In Cyprus and in Ireland the social democrats are weaker. In Cyprus this is understandable, given the strength of the local communist party (see below); Ireland is genuinely exceptional, however, in that Labour – and all the left – have always polled so poorly in Ireland. Irish Labour in this sense is the real Cinderella of European social democracy. At the beginning of the 1990s, however, there was an unprecedented if temporary surge of support for the party, which almost doubled its vote to more than 19 per cent, and Labour is also expected to benefit in future elections from widespread discontent with the way in which the recent financial crisis has been handled.

In general, as can be seen from Table 8.1, the electoral position of social democracy has weakened across the post-war period, falling from an average of almost 34 per cent in the 1950s to just more than 28 per cent in the first decade of the twenty-first century. This decline was most marked in Norway and Denmark, as well as in Germany, when the peak in the 1970s is compared with the poor performance in the most recent elections. In the UK the real low point was reached in the 1980s, when support fell below 30 per cent, and when the party was faced by the SDP–Liberal challenge. But the steady electoral decline of social democracy is not completely pervasive. By comparison with the earlier decades, social democrats now poll a greater share of the vote in Iceland and Italy, and are also holding up in France. Among the more recent democracies, the record is also relatively stable in Greece and Spain, while in Portugal the Socialists have increased their share of the vote. Nonetheless, the overall record is one of decline in electoral as well as, more recently, in governmental terms.

These data therefore offer a useful early lesson that it is difficult to generalize about patterns of party support across the established democracies. Not only do the aggregate electoral strengths of the parties differ considerably from one country to the next, but their patterns of development also vary – showing growth in some countries, decline in others, and more or less trendless fluctuations in yet others.

Now that European welfare states have been established for such a long period, it is easy to forget the radicalism that was once an integral part of social democracy in western Europe. In many cases the social democratic parties adopted an explicitly Marxist philosophy, and ultimately envisaged the replacement of capitalism by a genuinely socialist order. During the period in which the franchise was being expanded to include the working class, social democratic parties sought the full extension of political rights and the introduction of social policies designed to protect the interests of workers and of the unemployed.

With time, however, the initial radical impulse of social democracy began to wane. As Michels (1911) argued, electoral imperatives implied more professional organizational techniques, and this did much to blunt the parties' political purism. An important push towards moderation occurred when the Russian Revolution of 1917 precipitated splits in the socialist movement. The consequent creation of communist parties drew away many of the more radical members from the social democratic parties. The moderation of the views of the social democratic parties was also, in part, a product of their very success. The experience of participating in government, particularly in the wake of the Second World War, increased pressures towards ideological compromise, and firmly ensconced social democratic parties at the heart of the political order they initially sought to overthrow. Finally, much of the early radicalism of the social democrats was dissipated as a result of the successful implementation of their short-term policies: full political rights were won, and welfare states grew quickly in most European countries.

As a consequence of all this, the social democrats came to settle for a political role based on managing a mixed economy. They steadily dropped what Kirchheimer (1966) described as their 'ideological baggage' and extended their electoral appeal to the middle class, particularly the middle class working in the rapidly expanding state sector, thus becoming catch-all parties. This drift towards moderation became even more accentuated in the 1990s, as social democratic parties throughout Europe came to terms with the limits to state intervention set by the demands of the international global economy. Within the increasingly integrated European Union area, of course, these limits are even more pronounced (Scharpf, 1999). But although this might be seen to have frustrated social democratic appeals in the late twentieth century, it was quite remarkable to note the extent to which they proved successful at the end of the 1990s, before often losing out again to conservative and centre-right forces in the immediate following elections. Here again, there is a useful and still valid lesson: even when European voters shift to the left or to the right, they rarely stay put, but instead shift back again soon after.

Despite their increased moderation, the policy emphases of contemporary social democratic parties retain a commitment to welfarism and egalitarianism, even though they now tend to place less emphasis on the need to control and regulate economic life. Social democratic party manifestos no longer present a direct ideological challenge to the capitalist order in western Europe. What remains of their traditional radicalism has passed either to increasingly marginalized communist parties or to new left and Green parties that first came to prominence in the 1970s and 1980s. They tend to have become strong supporters of European integration and, more often than not, now follow the Third Way style of politics that was pioneered so successfully by Tony Blair in the UK. In brief, this new approach moved social democratic parties away from their commitment to public ownership and towards a greater acceptance of the market and of market solutions, seeking to establish a middle path – a third way – between traditional socialism and neo-liberalism. The policy would no longer emphasize the need to equalize income and resources, or 'outcomes' across all of the citizenry, but instead would emphasize the need for equality of opportunity. Instead of governments providing citizens with solutions to their problems, they could create the conditions in which citizens would find their own solutions. For Tony Blair, the Third Way was about placing what he called traditional Labour values within a modern setting, and about creating a new synthesis that would rise above left and right, and while explicit references to Third Way thinking are no longer to be seen, the spirit they reflected still prevails today.

Nor did the social democratic parties offer any distinct alternative when it came to finding solutions for the financial and economic crisis that burst over Europe in the months following the collapse of Lehman Brothers and later in the immediate fallout from the Greek monetary crisis. To be sure, there is always a tendency to sink differences and circle the wagons when external threats are posed; but in this case the consensus across the mainstream parties, whether in government or in opposition, was particularly pronounced and particularly striking. On the face of it, these conditions should prove favourable for social democrats to win both support and legitimacy. Financial markets have run into severe difficulties, popular belief in the capacity for self-regulation has waned, and there has been widespread demand for increased state intervention and for state rescue. In other words, there has been a push away from the neo-liberal emphases and towards the sorts of policies and interventions with which social democracy has traditionally been associated. As yet, however, this has not appeared to benefit the social democrats, and in recent elections in France, Germany, Italy and the UK the parties have even lost substantial ground in the most recent elections.

There are a number of possible explanations for this. In the first place, it may be that the social democrats have been simply too convincing in their recent claims to have abandoned their old left-wing traditions, and hence they are no longer believed when they now speak about the need for intervention. Alternatively, while intervention may be needed, and while governments might have to spend in order to bail out failing banks or to bolster weakened currencies, voters might prefer to see these policies carried out by parties who pursue them reluctantly and as a result of exogenous pressures rather than from principled commitment, and hence they opt for the right. A third explanation might simply have to do with where the blame is seen to lie. A large number of European countries voted social democrats into office in the late 1990s and early 2000s, and the policies of these governments – led by Blair in Britain, by Schröder in Germany and by Prodi in Italy – might be believed to lie at the source of the subsequent crisis. The lack of support for social democracy at the end of the decade may therefore reflect the attribution of blame by voters.

On social democracy in general, see Kitschelt (1994), Cuperus and Kandel (1998) and Moschonas (2002).

## 8.2.2 The communists

Even in the past, significant communist parties could traditionally be found in fewer countries than their social democratic rivals, and, in the main, they also proved substantially less successful at winning votes. Moreover, following the collapse of the Berlin Wall in 1989 and the breakdown of the communist regimes in eastern Europe and in the former Soviet Union, those communist parties that remained in western Europe became engaged in a process of reform that sometimes led them to drop their ideological label (as in Finland, Italy and Sweden), or they effectively disappeared as an independent political force (as in the Netherlands and Norway). Only occasionally, as in Cyprus, have they persisted while attempting to hold on to their traditional identity. Even before this, however, as can be seen from Table 8.2, communist parties commanded a substantial proportion of the vote only in Italy and Cyprus, and to a lesser extent in Finland, France and Iceland. Explicit communist parties were effectively non-existent in Ireland, Malta and the United Kingdom, and have now become even more marginalized in Austria, Belgium, Denmark, Norway and Switzerland. Although they have proved more serious contenders for votes in the new southern European democracies – Greece, Portugal and Spain – there has recently been some slippage in their vote in these countries too, and such success as they have had – as in Spain – has required the formation of electoral alliances with other left groupings. In general, across the whole post-war period, average electoral support for communist parties in the long-established democracies fell from almost 8 per cent in the 1950s to less than 4 per cent in the 1990s, and to just over 2 per cent in the first elections of the twenty-first century – this most recent decline being partly accounted for by the split in the Italian Communist Party (PCI), which leaves a relatively small party still in the communist camp (Communist Refoundation), and places a bigger party (the DS and later the Democrats) in the social democratic family. Taking all 20 democracies together, the communists polled an average of just 4.5 per cent in 2000–2009, as against 7.5 per cent in the 1980s.

**TABLE 8.2** Mean electoral support for communist parties, 1950–2009

| Country | 1950s | 1960s | 1970s | 1980s | 1990s | 2000–2009 |
|---------|-------|-------|-------|-------|-------|-----------|
| Austria | 4.3 | 1.7 | 1.2 | 0.7 | 0.4 | 0.8 |
| Belgium | 3.4 | 3.7 | 2.9 | 1.4 | 0.2 | – |
| Denmark | 4.5 | 1.0 | 3.0 | 0.9 | – | – |
| Finland | 22.1 | 21.6 | 17.6 | 13.9 | 10.7 | 9.4 |
| France | 23.9 | 21.4 | 21.0 | 12.4 | 12.6 | 4.6 |
| Germany | 1.1 | – | – | – | 4.0 | 8.2 |
| Iceland | 16.4 | 16.3 | 23.7 | 15.3 | 9.6 | – |
| Ireland | – | – | – | – | – | – |
| Italy | 22.7 | 26.1 | 30.7 | 28.3 | 6.7 | 6.0 |
| Luxembourg | 11.6 | 14.0 | 8.2 | 5.1 | 2.8 | 1.2 |
| Malta | – | – | – | – | – | – |
| Netherlands | 4.4 | 3.2 | 3.4 | 1.1 | – | – |
| Norway | 4.3 | 1.8 | 1.0 | 0.9 | – | – |
| Sweden | 4.2 | 4.2 | 5.1 | 5.6 | 7.6 | 7.0 |
| Switzerland | 2.7 | 2.6 | 2.4 | 0.9 | 1.1 | 0.7 |
| United Kingdom | – | – | – | – | – | – |
| **Mean (N = 16)** | **7.9** | **7.3** | **7.5** | **5.4** | **3.5** | **2.4** |
| Cyprus | | | | 30.1 | 31.8 | 32.9 |
| Greece | | | | 12.1 | 9.5 | 6.8 |
| Portugal | | | | 16.0 | 9.7 | 7.4 |
| Spain | | | | 6.1 | 9.9 | 4.8 |
| **Overall mean (N = 20)** | | | | **7.5** | **5.8** | **4.5** |

Yet even these relatively modest voting figures tend to exaggerate the importance of communist parties in those countries where they might appear on the face of things to have counted as a relevant political force. In Italy, for example, which traditionally hosted the most important of the western European communist parties, the 1980s had already witnessed a major erosion of the distinctively communist element in both party ideology and party organization. In France, on the other hand, the distinctively communist identity of the French Communist Party (PCF) has been jealously guarded at substantial electoral cost. The 1980s witnessed a major electoral decline of the PCF, to the benefit of its more moderate and increasingly successful socialist rival. In Iceland, the People's Alliance (PA) has largely shied away from promoting a distinctive communist identity. It includes quite a substantial social democratic component, and in the 1999 and 2003 elections it took part in a left-wing electoral alliance with the Women's Party and the social democrats. It has since ceased to compete as an autonomous party. The communist party in Finland, which used to be known as the Finnish People's Democratic Union (FPDL), banned prior to the Second World War, enjoyed a peculiar status owing to the country's

## BOX 8.1: THE LEFT

### Denmark

Denmark is home to what has been one of the most successful social democratic parties in Europe. The Danish Social Democrats first came to power in 1924, and remained the dominant actor in Danish politics through to the early 1980s. However, the party never won a majority on its own, and it always relied on the support of smaller parties to its left or right in order to hold office either as a coalition or as a minority government. The party also led various coalition governments during the 1990s, but has been in opposition since 2001. Denmark is also home to one of the oldest and most successful strains of the new left: the Socialist People's Party was formed in 1959, and although it later split in the mid 1960s, it has been represented in parliament ever since. There is no independent Green party represented in the Danish parliament.

### France

The most notable development within the left in France has been the eclipse of the traditionally powerful and strongly pro-Soviet Communist Party (PCF) and the corresponding rise of the Socialists (PS), initially under François Mitterrand in the 1970s and 1980s. The left as a whole was stronger in France in the 1980s than at any other period since the 1950s, but the PS, the dominant group within the left, fell back again in the 1990s. With more internal electoral flux on the left, the Greens finally began to make some headway, and in 1997 they entered government as part of a broad coalition with the Socialist Party and the communists. Since then they have also fallen back. Mitterrand, the socialist candidate, won the presidential elections in 1981 and 1988, but the party's candidate, Lionel Jospin, was defeated in 1995 and 2002, as was Ségolène Royal in 2007.

### Germany

It is in Germany that the Green movement initially mounted what appeared to be the most severe challenge to the traditional left in western Europe. The Social Democrats (SPD) had long enjoyed an effective monopoly of the left, helped largely by the fears of extreme politics in the wake of Nazism, and by the long-term constitutional ban on the Communist Party. Now that monopoly has been broken by the successful mobilization of a Green vote, on the one hand, and by the unexpected success of the former East German communist party, on the other. The latter has now merged into the more radical left party, which wins support throughout Germany. Thanks to an alliance with the Greens, the SPD was able to return to government in 1998 for the first time in 16 years, and the Red–Green coalition was re-elected in 2002. Thereafter, the SPD formed a Grand Coalition with the Christian Democrats, but then lost heavily in 2009 and went into opposition.

### Italy

Italy used to have the largest communist party in western Europe (the PCI), which, since the collapse of the communist regimes in eastern Europe and in the former Soviet Union, split into a major social democratic party, initially known as the Democratic Left, and a smaller and more traditional communist party, Communist Refoundation. The left was always divided in Italy, with the former PCI persistently excluded from government, and with the socialists (PSI) and centrist social democrats (PSDI) forming an essential part of the five-party coalition that held government in Italy throughout the 1980s under the leadership of the Christian Democrats. In 1996, for the first time ever, a coalition led by the left won office in Italy. The coalition included the Democratic Left, the Greens, and left-leaning elements of the old Christian democrats. Following five years of quite pronounced inter-party rivalries, the coalition was defeated by the centre right in 2001, was re-elected in 2006, and defeated again in 2008. The Democratic Left has now merged with other centre-left parties into the broadly based Democrats Party, but has difficulty in mobilizing an alternative to Silvio Berlusconi. The smaller far-left parties are no longer represented in parliament.

## Netherlands

The Dutch left was for a long [time?] often excluded from government, with the Christian Democrats (CDA) and Liberals (VVD) usually managing to win a majority of seats. In fact, between 1958 and 1989, when it finally managed to dislodge the Liberals and replace them as the partner of the CDA in government, the Labour Party (PvdA) had been in government on only three occasions, totalling less than seven years. Electoral support for the PvdA grew in the early 1990s, and in 1994 the party re-entered government as the major party in a centre-left coalition. It was badly defeated in 2002, however, in the wake of the rise of the populist Pim Fortuyn List, before recovering again in 2003. Two parties to the left of Labour, the Green Left and the Socialist Party, have also now established a secure base within the party system.

## Poland

In common with its east central European neighbours, Poland has seen the former Communist Party, the Democratic Left Alliance (SLD), recording substantial electoral successes. The party first came to power in 1993 when it governed in coalition with the old Polish Peasant Party (PSL). The SLD candidate Aleksander Kwaśniewski also won the presidential election in 1995, narrowly defeating Solidarity's Lech Wałęsa in the run-off ballot, and was re-elected in 2000, this time with an absolute majority in the first round. The right won the 2005 election, however, and also gained control of the cabinet in the same year 2005. Since then the former communists have been excluded from power, although their traditional ally, the PSL, now forms part of the coalition with the liberal Civic Platform.

## Spain

The Socialist Party (PSOE) was for long the most successful of the parties in Spain, forming a single-party majority government following the elections of 1982, 1986, 1989 and 1993. In 1996 it was overtaken by the conservative People's Party. The PSOE has also been one of the most moderate of Europe's socialist parties, a factor that did much to slow down the mobilization of a successful opposition on the centre right. The PSOE was unexpectedly returned to government in 2004, following the railway bombing on 11 March in Madrid, and was re-elected in 2008. Despite its initial hopes following the transition to democracy, the Communist Party (PCE) has failed to make a major impact in politics, and has now joined forces with other left-wing critics of the PSOE in a loose alliance called the United Left. Like Greece and Portugal, Spain has never really witnessed the emergence of a new left or Green party, but other left-wing forces are represented within the various nationalist and regionalist groups.

## United Kingdom

Although the Labour Party spent the entire 1980s in opposition, Britain is unique in the extent to which a single party has monopolized the left. Even though a number of leading communists gained prominence inside the trade union movement, the Communist Party has never been successful in

> ## BOX 8.1: CONTINUED
>
> elections, its high point being in 1945 when it won just over 100 000 votes and returned two MPs. Nor has any new left or Green party made any impact in recent Westminster elections, although a Green MP was elected for the first time in 2010. In 1997, following 18 years in opposition, Labour swept back into power under the leadership of Tony Blair. Advocating what he called the 'Third Way', Blair's 'New Labour' government began a massive programme of social and constitutional reform, and was re-elected in 2001 and 2005. In 2010, however, still suffering from electoral disaffection as a result of its support for the US in the Iraq war, and also battered by the fallout from the financial crisis, the party narrowly lost the election and was replaced by a centre-right coalition.

close geographic and cultural links with the Soviet Union. Even here, however, the FPDL was an alliance that included a social democratic component. The strains in this alliance eventually led to a split between more moderate and extreme elements in 1985, and to the creation of the more orthodox Democratic Alternative. Since the late 1990s both sides have now joined together again in the new and more moderate Left-Wing Alliance. Finally, and in a genuinely anomalous position, there is AKEL, the Cypriot Communist Party, which has deliberately retained its core identity and which, despite being banned in the 1930s and again in the 1950s, has managed to hold on to a substantial electoral following since 1960 (Dunphy and Bale, 2007). Indeed, the AKEL candidate, Demetris Christofias, was elected to the presidency of Cyprus in 2008, fuelling much media speculation about communist takeovers of both Cyprus and – more generally – the European Union!

The European communist parties were almost all formed in the immediate wake of the Russian Revolution of 1917, espousing Leninist principles and advocating the revolutionary road to socialism. They thereby established themselves as a radical alternative to the parliamentarism of social democracy. These parties were formally aligned with and took their lead from the Soviet Communist Party. This leadership was organized initially through Comintern, the Communist (or Third) International, which lasted from 1919 to 1943. It was later organized through the less formal Cominform network, which lasted from 1947 to 1956. This alliance with Moscow, together with their evident radicalism, ensured that they were typically regarded as anti-system oppositions, and as such, they often polarized the party systems in which they operated.

Inevitably, they had little experience with government office, although, in the immediate wake of the Second World War, bolstered by the credibility that they had achieved as a result of their crucial role in the anti-fascist resistance, several communist parties were to enjoy brief periods as partners in the widely based coalition governments that sought to re-establish democratic politics in countries such as Austria, Belgium, Denmark, Finland, France and Italy. Since then, communist parties have been involved in government only in Cyprus, Iceland, Finland and, after the early 1980s, France. Beyond this, however, they have sometimes offered the parliamentary support necessary to sustain other parties in office, while not formally joining the cabinet. In Italy, for example, the PCI helped to sustain the Christian Democrats in office in the late 1970s, and Communist Refoundation also helped to keep the PDS-dominated Olive Tree alliance in government in the late 1990s. In Sweden, the small but remarkably persistent Communist Party, now renamed the Left Party, has regularly provided the parliamentary support necessary to maintain the Social Democrats in office.

In part as a response to electoral decline or stagnation, and in part as a means of ending their political isolation, many western European communist parties began to distance themselves from Moscow during the post-war period. This shift heralded the emergence of Eurocommunism in the 1970s, in which the Italian, French and Spanish parties, in particular, sought to elaborate a distinctively non-Soviet strategy for achieving political power. However, this strategy of legitimation did not reap the hoped-for political rewards, and the 1980s witnessed further electoral decline.

Partly as a result of the Eurocommunist strategy, the policy emphases of communist parties ceased to be markedly different from those of their social democratic rivals, and they also began to emphasize questions of welfare, social justice, and the need for democratic decision-making. Where they do still differ from the social democrats is in their emphasis on state involvement in the economy, and in their greater scepticism about the free market. They stress the need for a controlled economy, as well as for more public ownership, and they are much more critical about the benefits of European integration. They are also much more explicit in their claim to represent the specific interests of the traditional working class and trade unions, in contrast to the more catch-all electoral appeal of social democracy.

On communist parties in western Europe more generally, see March and Mudde (1989) and Botella and Ramiro (2003).

### 8.2.3 The new left

The third party family on the left is usually described as the 'new' left, although by now some of the parties involved have been competing for three decades or more. As can be seen from Table 8.3, patterns of popular support for the new left make it easier to understand the general decline of social democratic and communist voting. Through to the 1980s, the trend in support for the new left ran counter to that for the traditional left, rising from just 1 per cent in the 1960s in western Europe as a whole to almost 3 per cent in the 1980s before falling back again – to the benefit of the Greens – in the 1990s and then picking up again thereafter. This suggests a reshuffling rather than a decline of the left.

The first new left parties emerged in the 1960s. These tended more towards an orthodox Marxist position, having often emerged as a result of divisions within the established communist parties. The later new left parties, on the other hand, tended to be stimulated by the wave of student radicalism of the late 1960s, and they have also been spurred on by the growing ecology movement. Indeed, it is often difficult to distinguish these new left parties from more orthodox Green parties (see below), and since the emergence of the latter, the two groups have frequently worked in concert. The Dutch Green Left, for example, is an alliance between Greens, new left parties, and the old Communist Party. Herbert Kitschelt (1988), in one of the earliest comparative analyses of these groups, grouped both types of parties under the label *left-libertarian*.

As Table 8.3 shows, new left parties have established themselves in only a scattering of the western European polities, and even where they exist, they often remain quite marginal. It is only occasionally, as in Denmark in the 1980s, when two new left parties were competing, or in Norway in 2001, or again in Denmark in 2007, that the new left vote has reached double figures. Outside Denmark and Norway, new left support has proved notable only in Iceland (where it has included the Women's Alliance) and Sweden. In this sense it may be regarded as a largely Scandinavian phenomenon.

Not least as a result of their diverse origins, the policy emphases of new left parties reflect a wide-ranging set of concerns. On one hand the new left parties echo traditional communist

**TABLE 8.3** Mean electoral support for new left parties, 1960–2009

| Country | 1960s | 1970s | 1980s | 1990s | 2000–2009 |
|---|---|---|---|---|---|
| Austria | – | – | – | – | – |
| Belgium | – | – | – | – | – |
| Denmark | 7.7 | 8.3 | 14.4 | 7.7 | 8.5 |
| Finland | – | – | – | – | – |
| France | – | – | – | – | 3.1 |
| Germany | – | – | – | – | – |
| Iceland | – | – | 7.8 | 7.4 | 2.6 |
| Ireland | – | 1.4 | 3.9 | 3.2 | 0.7 |
| Italy | 2.2 | 3.3 | 4.0 | – | – |
| Luxembourg | – | – | – | – | 2.6 |
| Malta | – | – | – | – | – |
| Netherlands | 3.0 | 4.0 | 2.6 | 2.4 | 9.6 |
| Norway | 4.0 | 6.9 | 6.8 | 8.4 | 11.9 |
| Sweden | – | – | – | – | – |
| Switzerland | – | 0.9 | 2.3 | 0.3 | 0.9 |
| United Kingdom | – | – | – | – | – |
| **Mean (N = 16)** | **1.1** | **1.6** | **2.6** | **1.8** | **2.5** |
| Cyprus | | | – | – | – |
| Greece | | | – | – | 5.3 |
| Portugal | | | – | – | – |
| Spain | | | – | – | – |
| **Overall mean (N = 20)** | | | **2.1** | **1.4** | **2.3** |

parties in their opposition to market forces, and their concern for public ownership and a controlled economy. Again like traditional communist parties, and quite unlike their Green allies, they emphasize an explicit appeal to the traditional working class. And although they stress a commitment to the welfare state, social justice and environmental protection, in common with all left parties, they also promote a more libertarian trend of freedom and democracy. Finally, they also tend to be more sceptical about European integration.

### 8.2.4 Green parties

Radical left politics can be seen as having developed in four distinct phases. As we have seen, the first, most important, and most enduring of these phases was the emergence of social democratic parties in the late nineteenth century. The second phase involved the split in social democracy in the wake of the Russian Revolution and the consequent emergence of the communist alternative. Here, too, the new parties proved reasonably enduring and, in certain limited instances, grew to a majority position on the left. The third phase was the mobilization of the

**TABLE 8.4** Mean electoral support for Green parties, 1980–2009

| Country | 1980s | 1990s | 2000–2009 |
|---|---|---|---|
| Austria | 4.1 | 6.6 | 10.3 |
| Belgium | 6.0 | 10.9 | 7.4 |
| Denmark | 0.7 | 2.2 | 2.7 |
| Finland | 2.7 | 7.0 | 8.3 |
| France | 0.9 | 8.4 | 4.8 |
| Germany | 5.1 | 6.4 | 9.1 |
| Iceland | – | 3.1 | 16.0 |
| Ireland | 0.4 | 2.1 | 4.3 |
| Italy | 1.3 | 2.7 | 1.4[a] |
| Luxembourg | 6.4 | 9.3 | 11.7 |
| Malta | – | 1.5 | 1.0 |
| Netherlands | 1.1 | 5.6 | 5.6 |
| Norway | 0.1 | 0.1 | 0.2 |
| Sweden | 2.9 | 4.3 | 4.9 |
| Switzerland | 5.0 | 6.3 | 9.2 |
| United Kingdom | 0.3 | 0.3 | 0.8 |
| **Mean ($N = 16$)** | **2.3** | **4.8** | **6.1** |
| Cyprus | – | 1.0 | 2.0 |
| Greece | 0.2 | 0.6 | 1.1 |
| Portugal | – | 0.3 | 0.2[b] |
| Spain | – | 1.0 | – |
| **Overall mean ($N = 20$)** | **1.9** | **3.9** | **5.1** |

[a] The percentage of vote for the Green Party in 2006 is not computed, as they participated together with the Communist Refoundation (RC), the Party of the Italian Communists (PdCI) and the newborn Democratic Left in the 'Left/Rainbow' electoral alliance.

[b] In 2005 the Portuguese Green Party (MPT) allied with the Social Democratic Party (PSD).

new left in the 1960s and 1970s, a movement that managed to establish itself in mainstream politics in only a handful of countries, and in these largely at the expense of the traditional communist parties. Finally, in the late 1970s and 1980s came the fourth phase – the emergence of 'Green', or ecology, parties. Green parties tend to poll only a small percentage of the total vote. Nevertheless, their recent growth and pervasiveness have generated substantial interest among students of the European party mosaic.

By the beginning of the twenty-first century, as Table 8.4 shows, Green parties had gained a respectable share of electoral support across the large majority of western European countries. To be sure, the Green alternative remains essentially marginal by comparison with that of its larger rivals, and on the average accounted for little more than 2 per cent of the vote in the established democracies in the 1980s, for less than 5 per cent in the 1990s, and for just over

6 per cent – a growing trend – in the first decade of the new century. Although not so new any more, the Greens clearly do represent a growing phenomenon, and average figures mask the sometimes substantial increase in Green support that has occurred in the some recent elections. Indeed, in the 2010 election in the UK, the Green Party even managed to win one seat. The averages also mask substantial variations between countries. In Belgium, for example, average Green support exceeded 10 per cent in the 1990s, although the party then fell back in the elections of 2003, when it polled less than 6 per cent after an unhappy experience as a coalition partner in the national government. Moreover, in Austria, Iceland and Luxembourg – small countries, to be sure – the Greens polled more than 10 per cent of the vote in the 2000–2009 period. The Netherlands also comes close to this level, although the Green alternative there is one that competes as part of an electoral coalition involving also the new left and the former Communist Party.

In the United Kingdom, although usually performing poorly in Westminster elections, the Green Party did poll almost 15 per cent of the vote in the 1989 British direct elections to the European Parliament, but fell back to just less than 9 per cent a decade later. Green parties have not made any significant impact in the new democracies of southern Europe, although Green members of parliament were first elected in 1989 in Greece, in 2001 in Cyprus, and as part of the broad United Democratic Coalition in 1987 in Portugal.

Even though a major electoral breakthrough has so far eluded Green parties in Europe, in other respects they have achieved some notable political successes, entering government coalitions in Belgium, Finland, France, Germany, Ireland and Italy. Indeed, they have also notched up a major success in Latvia, where Europe's first-ever Green prime minister was appointed. In Luxembourg, the Netherlands and Switzerland it is also possible that the Greens might one day enter government. This might also constitute the most important contribution of these relatively small parties – that they provide the additional support necessary to allow the formation of centre-left governments. Without the Greens, for example, it would have been impossible for any left-wing coalition to displace the centre-right governments in France, Germany or Italy during the latter half of the 1990s.

The policy emphases of Green parties, as might be expected, give pride of place to the need to protect the environment. This involves promoting policies that would curb economic growth and require substantial regulation of industrial and commercial activity. Green manifestos also emphasize the need for international peace and disarmament, and urge an increase in the level of development aid provided to developing countries. They emphasize social justice, particularly the need for equal treatment of women, as well as of ethnic and racial minorities. Green parties also stress participatory democracy, and even attempt to structure their own organizations in such a way as to allow maximum grassroots involvement. Finally, and as with the other smaller parties of the left, they tend to question the value of further European integration – or, even when they accept this development, they push strongly for it to be accompanied by more democratic decision-making. Bearing in mind the rapidly rising salience of the issues valued by the Green parties, we might also probably judge their success in terms of the extent to which these issues now rank so highly on the policy agendas of all political parties on the left.

On Green parties in general, see Müller-Rommel and Poguntke (2002), Rihoux and Rüdig (2006) and Frankland *et al.* (2008).

## 8.3  Families of the centre and right

The party families of the right are more heterogeneous than those of the left, and, as we shall see, they also show much more evidence of flux in their aggregate electoral support over time. These families include the Christian democrats, made up of parties that temper mainstream conservatism with a defence of religious values; conservative parties, distinguished from the Christian democrats by a more strident anti-socialist rhetoric, as well as by the absence of traditional links with organized religion; and liberal parties, a heterogeneous group that includes centrist parties such as the British Liberals and quite right-wing parties such as the Dutch Liberals. There is also a group of agrarian or centre parties that originally mobilized in defence of farming interests in a variety of western European countries. Finally, there is a family of far-right parties, characterized by the promotion of populist and xenophobic political appeals, and now competing as a serious challenger in a growing number of European polities.

### 8.3.1  The Christian democrats

For most of the post-war period, the Christian democratic family constituted the largest single group on the centre right of western European politics. This family has a base in most established western European democracies, the main exceptions being Iceland and the United Kingdom. It has also emerged as at least a marginally relevant political force in Portugal.

The Christian democratic family contains a number of distinct strands. The first is primarily Roman Catholic in origin, and includes Christian parties that began to mobilize in the mid to late nineteenth century, and which are now among the strongest parties in Europe. This strand is made up of Christian democratic parties in Austria, Belgium, Italy, Luxembourg, Malta and Switzerland, although the Swiss party now also wins support from Protestant voters.

The second strand in Christian democracy comprises two parties that draw substantial support from both Catholics and Protestants. The German Christian Democratic Union (CDU) and its Bavarian sister party, the Christian Social Union (CSU), were both formed in 1945 in the period of immediate post-war reconstruction. They built on the legacy of the former Catholic Centre Party, one of the dominant parties in Germany before the Nazi regime. In 1945, however, in a deliberate effort to erode the divisions that had been so evident in the pre-war period, the new CDU sought the support of both Catholics and Protestants. This cross-denominational appeal became even more pronounced after German unification, since the eastern parts of Germany contained quite a high proportion of Protestant voters. The CSU, on the other hand, remains almost wholly Catholic. The second biconfessional Christian democratic party is the Dutch Christian Democratic Appeal (CDA), which was originally divided into three separate parties, the Catholic People's Party and two smaller but persistent Protestant parties, the Anti-Revolutionary Party (ARP – the revolution to which it was opposed was the French revolution of 1789) and the Christian Historical Union (CHU). These formed a federation in 1975 and then fused into a single party in 1980. Both the CDU and the CDA, with their substantial Protestant components, can be differentiated from the essentially Catholic parties in the first strand of Christian democracy. In all other respects, however, not least in their inheritance of a long tradition of confessional politics, and in the strong bargaining positions they now enjoy in their respective party systems, these two strands of Christian democracy fill rather similar roles in party politics.

The third strand is largely Protestant, and is of more recent origin – the parties involved often first contested elections only after the Second World War. It is also more marginal in electoral terms. It comprises the Christian democrats of Denmark, Norway and Sweden, together with the minor evangelical and reformed Protestant parties in the Netherlands and Switzerland. The Swedish party enjoyed quite a strong surge of support in the 1990s, and took part in the Swedish centre-right coalition government in the mid 1990s. Although falling back again in the new century, it still polled almost 7 per cent in the most recent election. The Christian People's Party in Norway also did particularly well in the 1990s, polling almost 14 per cent of the vote in 1997, and going on to become the senior partner in the new minority centre-right coalition that displaced the minority social democratic government after that election. Thereafter, though still managing to poll more than 12 per cent in 2001, its vote has steadily declined.

Over and above these cases of quite explicit Christian parties, a Christian democratic element can also be identified in France and Ireland. The French case is the more interesting of the two, because a substantial Catholic party, the Popular Republican Movement, was among the most influential in the French Fourth Republic (1946–1958). With the shifting centre-right alliances that have characterized French politics since 1958, however, the distinct Christian alternative has all but disappeared. Much of its more conservative support was eventually captured by the Gaullists, and the more moderate elements operated under the Centre Social Democrat label within the loose alliance called the Union for French Democracy.

In Ireland, where the population is still almost 90 per cent Catholic and where rates of church attendance were, with Poland, still among the highest in late-twentieth-century Europe, there is no tradition of organized Christian democracy. Since Catholics were in an overwhelming majority in the population, and since the mainstream parties were strongly committed to defending Catholic values in public policymaking, the Church never felt the need to promote a distinct party organization. In recent years, however, one of the leading parties of the centre right, Fine Gael, has affiliated with the Christian democratic group in the European Parliament, the European People's Party. Hence, although historically outside the Christian democratic tradition, Fine Gael has proved willing to adopt this transnational organizational identity.

As Table 8.5 shows, and notwithstanding the more recent successes of the smaller Protestant parties, Christian democracy as a whole has experienced quite a substantial erosion of electoral support towards the end of the twentieth century, falling from an average of almost 23 per cent in the 1950s to less than 18 per cent in the most recent elections. Across all 20 west European democracies its average support now comes to less than 15 per cent, with explicitly Christian parties making little headway in the newer southern European democracies. Without the exceptionally strong support for the Maltese party, which may be regarded as being close to the order of the conservative party family (see below), the decline would be even more pronounced. Excluding Malta, the Christian democrats fall to less than 16 per cent in 2000–2009, and to just 13 per cent when all 19 other systems are taken into account. Trends do fluctuate, however, Among the most dramatic declines were those experienced in Austria and most especially the Netherlands in the 1990s, and while both parties picked up support again in the new century, the Dutch CDA fell back heavily in 2010. There has also been a marked decline in Belgium, where the Catholic parties (one Flemish, one Walloon) have lost more than half their support, and where, as in the Dutch case, they lost their almost permanent hold on government. In Italy the Christian democratic vote has been drastically reduced, with the allegations of corruption

**TABLE 8.5** Mean electoral support for Christian Democratic parties, 1950–2009

| Country | 1950s | 1960s | 1970s | 1980s | 1990s | 2000–2009 |
|---|---|---|---|---|---|---|
| Austria | 43.8 | 46.9 | 43.2 | 42.2 | 28.7 | 34.2 |
| Belgium | 45.4 | 36.3 | 33.7 | 27.8 | 23.1 | 23.3 |
| Denmark | – | – | 3.9 | 2.4 | 2.2 | 1.6 |
| Finland | – | 0.6 | 2.9 | 2.8 | 3.4 | 5.1 |
| France[a] | – | – | – | – | – | – |
| Germany | 47.7 | 46.3 | 46.0 | 45.9 | 40.1 | 35.8 |
| Iceland | – | – | – | – | 0.2 | – |
| Ireland[b] | 28.1 | 33.4 | 32.8 | 33.9 | 26.3 | 24.9 |
| Italy | 41.3 | 38.6 | 38.5 | 33.6 | 17.8 | 5.2 |
| Luxembourg | 37.5 | 34.3 | 31.2 | 33.3 | 30.3 | 37.1 |
| Malta | 35.9 | 52.7 | 48.3 | 50.9 | 50.5 | 50.6 |
| Netherlands | 53.2 | 49.8 | 37.8 | 36.6 | 23.3 | 32.2 |
| Norway | 10.3 | 9.0 | 11.9 | 8.7 | 10.8 | 9.6 |
| Sweden | – | 1.1 | 1.6 | 2.4 | 7.7 | 7.9 |
| Switzerland | 24.2 | 24.4 | 23.2 | 22.2 | 18.8 | 17.2 |
| United Kingdom | – | – | – | – | – | – |
| **Mean (N = 16)** | **22.9** | **23.4** | **22.1** | **21.5** | **17.6** | **17.8** |
| Cyprus | | | | – | – | – |
| Greece | | | | – | – | – |
| Portugal | | | | 6.9 | 7.3 | 8.8 |
| Spain | | | | 2.2 | – | – |
| **Overall mean (N = 20)** | | | | **18.4** | **15.1** | **14.7** |

[a] Since the mid 1970s the Christian democrats in France, together with conservative and liberal forces, have contested elections as part of the UDF Alliance and later, in a link with the Gaullists, as part of the UMP; their electoral support has therefore been grouped together with that of the conservatives.
[b] For the purposes of this analysis, the Irish party Fine Gael is classified as Christian democratic.

destroying the party after 1992, and leaving behind a group of divided smaller parties that split between the alliances of left and right. Indeed, in Italy the Catholic vote was almost completely taken over by Berlusconi's alliances, leaving only a small independent force in the centre.

Elsewhere, particularly in Germany and Switzerland, the Christian vote has also fallen. What is striking, however, is that, with the possible exception of the small Protestant parties in Sweden and Finland, no country has experienced a sustained increase in Christian democratic support over the post-war period. This is despite what many scholars indicate is the growing importance of religion in domestic politics. Since 9/11, for example, differences between the predominantly Christian populations of western Europe and the expanding Muslim minority have been highlighted by many right-wing parties and public commentators, and issues of religious freedom have become more contentious in the wake of various restrictions on the wearing of Islamic dress. In May 2010, for example, the French interior minister proposed a complete ban on burqas: 'We are an old country anchored in a certain idea of how to live together. A full veil which completely hides the face is an attack on those values, which for us are so fundamental,' he argued. 'Citizenship has to be lived with an uncovered face. There can therefore be absolutely no solution other than a ban in all public places' (*Guardian*, 19 May 2010).

The dominant strand in western European Christian democracy was always represented by the Catholic parties in particular. Even in the case of the biconfessional parties, the Catholic heritage has been well to the fore. This particular heritage dates back to the nineteenth century, when Catholic mobilization took place in response to secularizing and anticlerical impulses from both conservatives and liberals (Kalyvas, 1996). Since then, however, those issues that first generated these conflicts between church and state have largely been settled, and the parties themselves have developed into mainstream components of the centre right. Their religious emphases surface only in response to the appearance on the political agenda of moral issues such as abortion, euthanasia and divorce, on which the established Christian churches have strong views, as well as through the emerging tension between Christians and Muslims. The smaller Protestant parties share these positions, but add a concern for reversing what they see as the general trend towards permissiveness and ungodliness. The Norwegian and Swedish parties, for example, have campaigned strongly against both alcohol and pornography, and one of the more fundamentalist of the Dutch parties, the Political Reformed Party (SGP), has long refused to allow women to stand for election on the party lists, or to vote in internal party meetings.

Christian parties can be distinguished from their conservative counterparts (see later) because their popular base, their social concerns, and their reluctance to promote policies that might lead to social conflict have always inclined them (the Catholic parties in particular) towards a more centrist, pro-welfare programme. Indeed, the impetus behind the development of welfare states in post-war Europe derived almost as much from Catholic pressure as it did from social democracy. This was particularly true in countries such as Belgium, the Netherlands and Italy, where social democracy has always remained relatively weak (van Kersbergen, 1995; van Kersbergen and Manow, 2009). In short, Christian democratic parties have traditionally tended to be state-oriented parties, sharing common ground with the social democrats in their opposition to neo-liberal, libertarian, and individualistic policies. Apart from some of the smaller Protestant parties, which are often Euro-sceptic, these Christian parties have also been among the strongest advocates of European integration.

On Christian democracy, see Kalyvas (1996), Gehlen and Kaiser (2004) and van Hecke and Gerard (2004); on church–state issues more generally see Madeley and Enyedi (2003) and de Vreese and Boomgaarden (2009).

### 8.3.2 The conservatives

Across western Europe in general, conservative parties have begun to poll almost as big a share of the votes as the Christian democrats. Indeed, if we exclude the small island state of Malta, where the Christian democrats are closely akin to a conservative party, the conservatives now poll more votes than the Christian democrats. This is not so much due to the conservatives' own success – they have stayed remarkably steady across the decades (see Table 8.6) – but because their overall vote has held firm, while that of the Christian democrats has sometimes failed badly. Whereas the Christian democrats polled half as much again as the conservatives in the 1950s, by the new century the two families were more or less on a par. Conservative parties also poll particularly well in Greece, Spain and Cyprus, where they constitute the principal opposition to the left. Across all 20 democracies the conservatives now poll an average of more than 18 per cent of the vote, substantially more than the Christian democrats. What is most striking about the conservative vote is that even this high level of average support is depressed by the fact that conservative parties do not compete in a number of countries. Where they do exist, conservative parties often do very well, winning around 40 per cent in France, Iceland, Ireland, the UK, Greece, Spain, and now Italy. The conservatives also poll well in Cyprus, but there too, as in Malta, it is sometimes difficult to separate conservatism from Christian democracy.

**TABLE 8.6** Mean electoral support for conservative parties, 1950–2009

| Country | 1950s | 1960s | 1970s | 1980s | 1990s | 2000–2009 |
|---|---|---|---|---|---|---|
| Austria | – | – | – | – | – | – |
| Belgium | – | – | – | – | – | 2.1 |
| Denmark | 18.4 | 21.3 | 10.5 | 19.5 | 13.3 | 9.9 |
| Finland | 14.2 | 14.2 | 19.6 | 22.9 | 19.5 | 20.5 |
| France[a] | 44.2 | 55.6 | 50.3 | 42.7 | 39.7 | 49.1 |
| Germany | – | – | – | – | – | – |
| Iceland | 41.3 | 39.5 | 36.8 | 38.4 | 38.8 | 31.3 |
| Ireland | 46.0 | 45.7 | 49.1 | 45.9 | 39.2 | 41.6 |
| Italy | – | – | – | – | 13.9 | 30.2 |
| Luxembourg | – | – | – | – | – | – |
| Malta | – | – | – | – | – | – |
| Netherlands | – | – | – | – | – | – |
| Norway | 18.7 | 20.2 | 20.9 | 28.1 | 15.7 | 6.1 |
| Sweden | 17.0 | 14.4 | 15.4 | 21.1 | 22.3 | 20.7 |
| Switzerland | – | – | – | – | 1.2 | 1.3 |
| United Kingdom | 47.6 | 42.7 | 41.0 | 42.2 | 36.3 | 32.0 |
| **Mean (N = 16)** | **15.4** | **15.8** | **15.2** | **16.3** | **15.0** | **15.3** |
| Cyprus | | | | 32.8 | 35.2 | 37.7 |
| Greece | | | | 41.8 | 44.0 | 40.9 |
| Portugal | | | | – | – | – |
| Spain | | | | 25.9 | 33.3 | 40.7 |
| **Overall mean (N = 20)** | | | | **17.5** | **16.9** | **18.2** |

[a] Since the mid 1970s the UDF Alliance, which is treated here as a conservative party, has brought together under one umbrella Christian democrats, conservatives and liberals.

## BOX 8.2: THE CENTRE AND RIGHT

### Denmark

The right is traditionally very divided in Denmark, as it is in all of the Scandinavian polities. The Liberals are currently the largest of the older components, and are a centrist party that has recently moved to the right. In addition, there is a Conservative party and a Radical (former agrarian) party, as well as a small Christian party. Needless to say, the problem for the right in Denmark was getting all of these different actors together in a coherent coalition that could challenge the long-dominant Social Democrats for office. Most recently, Danish politics has been polarized as a result of the major electoral success of the far-right Danish People's Party (DPP), the successor to the anti-tax Progress Party, which mobilizes on a strident anti-immigrant platform. The strength of the DPP enabled the centre right to win an overall majority for the first time in 2001, but while the DPP supports the present government coalition of Liberals and Conservatives, it is not formally a member of the government.

### France

The 1980s and 1990s witnessed increasing divisions and fluctuations within the French centre and right. The traditional dominance of the Gaullists (RPR) was challenged by the growth in the more centrist liberal–Christian–conservative alliance of the UDF, led by Giscard d'Estaing. The problem for the Gaullists was compounded by the electoral successes of the National Front, an extreme right-wing party that campaigned mainly on immigration issues. In 1981, for the first time in the history of the Fifth Republic, the centre right lost the presidency to the socialist candidate, François Mitterrand. They lost again in 1988, but Jacques Chirac of the RPR regained the office in 1995, and despite a strong first-round challenge from the National Front, was re-elected in 2002. The centre right was also successful in 2007, when Nicolas Sarkozy was elected. The centre right has also been divided by conflicts over Europe, with an anti-European faction of the RPR winning significant support in the elections to the European Parliament in 1999, but in 2002 a successful effort was made to unite Gaullists, UDF and other centre-right forces within the Union for a Popular Majority (UMP), which won an overall parliamentary majority in the elections of that year and again in 2007.

### Germany

The centre right dominated governments in Germany during the 1980s and for much of the 1990s. In 1982 the small and quite conservative Liberal Party (FDP) withdrew from its 13-year coalition with the Social Democrats and joined forces with the Christian Democrats (CDU/CSU) under Helmut Kohl. This coalition survived in office until 1998, when it was displaced by an alliance of the SPD and Greens. The CDU in particular suffered a loss of support because of popular discontent with the costs and difficulties that followed German unification. The party also suffered from a series of corruption scandals. Under the popular leadership of Angela Merkel, a former East German political activist, the party returned to power as part of a Grand Coalition with the Social Democrats in 2005, and were re-elected in coalition with their old FDP ally in 2009. Although extreme-right parties have managed to win some electoral support in recent elections, particularly at the *Land* or regional level, they have not yet managed to break through the 5 per cent electoral threshold for the federal parliament.

### Italy

The centre right was the dominant political force in Italy throughout most of the post-war period, and the Christian Democrats (DC) played the dominant role in every government, being the party that provided the prime minister in all but a handful of the 50 post-war governments. Today, although the DC has all but disappeared, the centre right is dominant once again, this time under the powerful leadership of media tycoon and billionaire Silvio Berlusconi. Berlusconi has forged a successful merger between his own Forza Italia party and the former fascist National Alliance, and the new party, the People of Liberty (PdL), shares power with the Northern League (Lega Nord), a regional party that comes close to replicating the appeal of the far right in neighbouring Austria and Switzerland. This powerful coalition is scarcely challenged by the weak left opposition, and also controls most of the public and private media.

## Netherlands

The Dutch right has always been divided. The dominant Christian Democratic Appeal (CDA) was formally established in 1980, when the traditional Catholic People's Party (KVP) merged with two smaller Protestant parties (the ARP and the CHU), and was in government continually until 1994. This was usually together with its main rival on the centre right, the conservative Liberal Party (VVD), and these two parties continue to vie with one another as to who will be the biggest party in parliament. Following the sudden rise of the populist right Pim Fortuyn List (LPF) in 2002, the VVD lost heavily, whereas the opposition CDA gained support. A new government was then formed of CDA, VVD and LPF, but this soon collapsed in disarray, and was replaced following the 2003 election by a government of CDA, VVD and the small liberal D66. Later again, the CDA governed with Labour and a small Protestant Christian party, but when that government fell, the CDA lost heavily. Although the LPF has since disappeared, a new far-right party, the Freedom Party, under the leadership of Geert Wilders, has begun to attract a large share of electoral support. In November 2010, echoing its Danish counterpart, it offered parliamentary support to a minority coalition of VVD and CDA.

## Poland

The centre right in Poland has proved extraordinarily unstable and fragmented, and despite Poland's position as the forerunner in the challenge to the old communist regime, the initiative has often slipped from the hands of the reformers movement and into those of the former communists. Part of the problem in the centre right was the division between Catholic and secular forces, and part was also driven by personality conflicts. Solidarity had proved enormously successful in uniting all of these disparate forces within one highly purposive and effective movement. But once power was achieved, the tensions emerged, and the movement broke down into various conservative Catholic groupings and various liberal, secular elements. These groups did manage to come together sufficiently to form a government between 1997 and 2001, but fell apart again in the wake of their main candidate's poor performance in the 2000 presidential election. The right, this time dominated by more populist elements, won power again in 2005, with the more radical alternatives being replaced by a coalition of the liberal Civic Platform and the Peasants Party in 2007.

## Spain

Following the initial but short-lived success of the Union of the Democratic Centre (UCD), the centre right in Spain proved weak and fragmented. With time, however, the conservative People's Party (PP) developed a dominant position, emerging from a difficult history fraught with alliance and schism, and bringing together conservative, liberal and Christian factions. In 1993 the PP recorded its first big success, polling almost 35 per cent of the vote, less than 4 per cent behind the PSOE, and in 1996 it overtook the PSOE to become the single biggest party, taking office as a minority government. It went on to win an overall majority in 2000, but lost unexpectedly to the PSOE in 2004. Although extreme right-wing elements can be found in Spanish politics, such as the National Unity Movement, they have achieved no significant electoral support.

▶ **BOX 8.2: CONTINUED**

**United Kingdom**

The centre and right were traditionally quite hostile to one other in Britain. The Conservative Party held government from 1979 to 1997, for most of that time under the dynamic leadership of Margaret Thatcher. The result was that many supporters of the centre parties found increasingly common ground with Labour in their opposition to Conservative policies. At the beginning of the 1980s it seemed that the centre, in the form of the old Liberal Party and the newly formed Social Democratic Party, was going to become a major force in British politics. However, votes failed to be translated into parliamentary seats, given the electoral system, and the challenge fizzled out. The Social Democrats then disbanded their new party, and the majority of the members merged with the Liberals to form the new Liberal Democratic Party. The Liberals first began to work closely with the new Labour government of Tony Blair, but later moved to a more critical stance. Meanwhile, tiring of their years in opposition, the Conservatives began to adopt a more moderate and compromising rhetoric. When the 2010 election resulted in a parliament in which no single party commanded a majority of seats, the Liberals found themselves as king-makers, and quickly decided to join with the Conservatives in a reformist coalition. Though still very small, and though winning no seats, the far-right British National Party outpolled the Greens in 2010.

As with liberal and Christian families, there are several strands within conservatism in western Europe. One increasingly important strand includes what we might think of as 'national' parties, which marry a conservative socio-economic appeal with an emphasis on the pursuit of the national interest. This strand includes the Independence Party in Iceland, Fianna Fáil in Ireland, the French Gaullists, the British Conservatives, and the Cypriot Democratic Coalition. All five parties, which also tend to be the most successful in the family, stress the importance of national shibboleths, and all decry the 'anti-national' character of sectional or class politics. This strand also includes some strong Euro-sceptic elements, particularly in France and Britain, while in Fianna Fáil the attitude towards Europe is one of pragmatic support. The PdL (and formerly Forza Italia) in Italy can also be considered to belong to this 'national' group, as might many of the major centre-right parties in post-communist Europe, where conservatives have emerged as one of the major political alternatives (see below). A second distinctive strand within European conservatism is made up of traditional conservative parties in Denmark, Finland, Norway and Sweden. These are characterized by a more moderate opposition to state intervention, married to a commitment to a consensual approach to policymaking. The development of these latter parties has also been constrained by their relatively limited support. Unlike their larger counterparts in the UK, France and Ireland, these parties have almost always had to govern in coalition, and have always had to fight to win the leading position on the centre-right.

Although the conservatives are more clearly on the right than the Christian democrats, the two families can in many ways be viewed as functional equivalents. Both represent the major alternative to the appeal of social democracy, and, what is more telling, the two families rarely flourish within the same party system. Where secular conservatism is strong, Christian democracy tends to be weak or non-existent (in the Scandinavian countries, the United Kingdom, Greece and Spain). Where Christian democracy is strong, secular conservatism tends to be weak or non-existent (in Austria, Belgium, Germany, Malta and the Netherlands). In Italy, it is precisely the conservative Forza Italia and later PdL that have been taking the place of the shattered Christian Democrats.

The policy priorities of the conservative family are quite distinctive. Although the conservatives share some degree of commitment to welfarism with all other party families, this ranks lower in conservative party programmes than in the programmes of other parties on the right. Rather, conservative parties emphasize the need to support private enterprise and to encourage fiscal austerity. They also emphasize government efficiency, as well as law and order. Moreover, in many countries they also stress the importance of traditional national values, combining economic liberalism with sometimes heavy-handed social interventionism.

The literature on conservative parties is relatively scarce, but see Girvin (1988).

### 8.3.3 The liberals

Electoral support for liberal parties in western Europe has increased slightly across the post-war period, and now stands at an average of some 10 per cent of the total vote. The liberal presence is also pervasive. Malta is now the only established European democracy that does not have a relevant liberal party, whereas among the newer southern European democracies, liberal parties, broadly defined, are strong in Cyprus and Portugal, weak in Spain, and non-existent in Greece. Ireland has also witnessed the emergence of a liberal party in the 1980s, the Progressive Democrats. This party polled more than 11 per cent of the vote in its first electoral outing in 1987, and although its vote declined thereafter, the party has succeeded in entering government coalitions with Fianna Fáil. The party has recently been wound up. The fact that Ireland did not have a liberal presence before the late 1980s suggests an intriguing but probably spurious relationship between small island polities, on the one hand – Iceland, Ireland, Malta – and a rejection of liberalism, on the other. Cyprus would present a problem here, however, since the liberals poll quite a substantial vote. Finally, although a strong liberal tradition exists in France, the present liberal tendency was largely subsumed within the loose, wide-ranging alliance of the Union for French Democracy (UDF), and is now even more diluted within the new centre-right alliance, the Union for a Popular Majority (UMP).

As Table 8.7 shows, despite the fact that the liberal parties are present in almost all European countries, there is substantial variation in liberal strength. During the 1990s, for example, the liberals were very successful and won an average of more than 20 per cent of the vote in Belgium, Luxembourg, the Netherlands and Switzerland – all of which belong to the well-known group of consociational democracies (Lijphart, 1977; Luther and Deschouwer, 1999). The Dutch figure is truly striking, for although it encompassed two parties, the left-leaning Democrats 66 and the more conservative Liberal Party, there was an almost fourfold growth from just less than 10 per cent in the 1950s to almost 35 per cent in the 1990s. That said, both parties suffered badly in the wake of the rise of the populist Pim Fortuyn List, falling back to an average of less than 20 per cent in the elections in 2000–2009 before picking up again in 2010. Liberals also poll reasonably well in the UK, averaging more than 17 per cent in the 1990s, and winning a record 62 seats in the House of Commons in 2005. In May 2010 they joined the Conservatives as the junior partner in Britain's first coalition government since the Second World War.

Elsewhere, however, liberals are quite marginal in electoral terms, failing to come even close to double figures in all other countries where they compete. The exception is Portugal, where the liberals have become the main opposition to the social democrats, and where they have risen to an average of more than 30 per cent of the vote. Yet, even in countries where liberal support falls below 10 per cent, the parties concerned often exert a political influence far exceeding that

**TABLE 8.7** Mean electoral support for liberal parties, 1950–2009

| Country | 1950s | 1960s | 1970s | 1980s | 1990s | 2000–2009 |
|---|---|---|---|---|---|---|
| Austria | 8.4 | 6.2 | 5.6 | 7.4 | 5.0 | 1.0 |
| Belgium | 11.5 | 18.3 | 15.4 | 21.1 | 22.6 | 25.6 |
| Denmark | 8.1 | 9.3 | 8.3 | 5.6 | 4.0 | 8.4 |
| Finland | 7.1 | 9.7 | 5.4 | 0.9 | 1.7 | 0.2 |
| France | – | – | – | – | – | – |
| Germany | 8.6 | 9.4 | 8.2 | 8.9 | 8.0 | 10.6 |
| Iceland | – | – | – | – | 1.8 | 6.0 |
| Ireland | – | – | – | 3.5 | 4.7 | 3.4 |
| Italy | 4.8 | 8.1 | 5.4 | 6.9 | 5.8 | 14.0[a] |
| Luxembourg | 12.6 | 13.6 | 21.8 | 17.5 | 20.7 | 15.6 |
| Malta | – | – | – | – | – | – |
| Netherlands | 9.9 | 12.8 | 19.7 | 25.5 | 34.6 | 19.7 |
| Norway | 9.8 | 9.5 | 5.8 | 3.4 | 4.1 | 4.9 |
| Sweden | 22.1 | 16.3 | 11.8 | 10.8 | 7.0 | 10.4 |
| Switzerland | 31.4 | 32.9 | 31.1 | 30.1 | 24.8 | 18.6 |
| United Kingdom | 5.1 | 9.9 | 14.7 | 23.9 | 17.3 | 20.2 |
| **Mean (_N_ = 16)** | **8.7** | **9.8** | **9.6** | **10.3** | **10.1** | **9.9** |
| Cyprus | | | | 23.6 | 20.6 | 18.5 |
| Greece | | | | – | – | – |
| Portugal | | | | 27.3 | 39.4 | 32.7 |
| Spain | | | | 4.6 | 3.2 | – |
| **Overall mean (_N_ = 20)** | | | | **11.1** | **11.3** | **10.5** |

[a] Includes the percentage of vote for the Daisy (DS), but only in 2001.

suggested by their low legislative weight. Their position, which is sometimes close to the centre of the party system, allows them to take on a crucial role as junior partners in coalition governments of the centre-right as well as the centre-left (Keman, 1994). Indeed, liberal parties are governing parties *par excellence* – including now in the United Kingdom, where they have also formed coalitions with Labour in the regional parliaments of Scotland and Wales.

The liberal political family is often seen as a centre group in western European politics, but in practice these parties represent a diverse range of ideological concerns. Historically, liberal parties have been associated with the impulse to extend the franchise, to promote individual rights, and to resist religious influences in political life. Prior to the emergence of social democracy, liberal parties thus constituted the first real opposition to conservatism and the right. Some of these concerns have survived and are more or less common to all European liberal parties – an emphasis on individual rights and a residual (though increasingly less relevant) anticlericalism. Over time, however, other liberal concerns have mutated, and two clear strands of European liberalism can now be identified.

Within the first strand, an emphasis on individual rights has led to a concern for fiscal rectitude and opposition to all but minimal state intervention in the economy. This right-wing strand of liberalism has been particularly important in Austria, where the Freedom Party used to be regarded as the most rightist of European liberal parties, but which is now better grouped with the far right (see later). The right-wing strand is also important in Belgium, Germany, Italy, Luxembourg, the Netherlands and Switzerland, and this is the position towards which the Progressive Democrats in Ireland originally gravitated. This brand of liberalism has tended to emerge in countries that are also characterized by strong Christian democratic parties, and hence where the anticlerical component of liberalism was once important. Indeed, anticlericalism in these countries has two distinct forms, being represented on the left by socialist or communist parties and on the right by secular liberal parties.

The second strand of European liberalism reflects a more centrist, if not left-leaning, position in which a concern for individual rights and progressive politics has engendered an emphasis on social justice and egalitarianism. This is the strand that has tended to emerge in countries where the main right-wing group is a conservative party that has taken over the more anti-interventionist liberal tendency, and where the anticlerical component in liberalism has proved less relevant. This strand is evident in Denmark, Norway and Britain, and is also represented by Democrats 66 in the Netherlands. Sweden can also be regarded as belonging to this group, although the party there made a sharp rightward turn in the 2002 election.

Above all, European liberal parties have demonstrated a strong appetite for participation in government, and the policies implied by the different ideological strands of liberalism have not been allowed to get in the way of this. In Belgium and Luxembourg, for example, governments tend to alternate between coalitions of the centre left (Christians and social democrats) and of the centre right (Christians and liberals). In Germany, on the other hand, notwithstanding their philosophy, the liberals have played the role of centre parties in government-formation negotiations, switching support from time to time between social democrats and Christian democrats. In Scandinavia yet another pattern is apparent: the dominance of the social democrats encourages liberals, as well as agrarian or centre parties, to join forces with the other bourgeois parties to construct a 'broad-right' anti-socialist coalition. In each case, however, the liberals are regular participants in the politics of government formation.

The presence of two major strands of liberal ideology and the diversity of liberal party strategies suggest that any overall depiction of liberal party policy concerns may be misleading. Although the more left-leaning British, Danish and Norwegian liberals traditionally placed a major emphasis on the need for a controlled economy, this emphasis was largely absent from the programmes of the Austrian, Dutch and Italian liberals. In common with most other parties, however, all liberal parties share a commitment to welfarism, and, in common with the left and the agrarian parties, they also stress the need for environmental protection.

What can also be taken as reasonably characteristic of all liberal parties is an emphasis on freedom, democracy, decentralization and social justice, reflecting a continuing and pervasive concern for individual rights and freedoms, as well as a reluctance to tolerate more authoritarian styles of governing. In a curious way, therefore, liberal parties now reflect a set of political appeals that echoes elements of both the new left and the traditional right. This may well stem from the shared contemporary orientation of all three groups towards an essentially middle-class electoral constituency.

On liberal parties in general, see Kirchner (1988).

### 8.3.4 The agrarian or centre parties

As can be seen from Table 8.8, although agrarian parties – or the now self-styled 'centre' parties – exist only in a small number at all in many west European countries, where they do exist, they tend to be quite large. Agrarian parties did once contest elections in both Ireland and the Netherlands, but they were essentially a Scandinavian phenomenon, with a strong presence in Denmark, Finland, Iceland, Norway and Sweden. Outside the Nordic area an agrarian party persisted for a long time in Switzerland, but later, under the leadership of Christoph Blocher, promoted a largely anti-immigrant stance and moved to the far right, with which they have been grouped from the 1990s onwards in Table 8.9. Beyond the established democracies, agrarian parties also competed in elections in a number of post-communist democracies, but even there they are now less popular than before (see later).

As their name suggests, agrarian parties were primarily special-interest parties. They were initially mobilized in the late nineteenth and early twentieth centuries to represent the specific concerns of farmers and the agricultural sector. With the economic and demographic decline in

**TABLE 8.8** Mean electoral support for agrarian/centre parties, 1950–2009

| Country | 1950s | 1960s | 1970s | 1980s | 1990s | 2000–2009 |
|---|---|---|---|---|---|---|
| Austria | – | – | – | – | – | – |
| Belgium | – | – | – | – | – | – |
| Denmark | 22.9 | 20.0 | 15.1 | 11.4 | 21.0 | 28.8 |
| Finland | 23.6 | 23.7 | 24.1 | 25.2 | 24.6 | 23.9 |
| France | – | – | – | – | – | – |
| Germany | – | – | – | – | – | – |
| Iceland | 22.6 | 28.2 | 23.0 | 20.0 | 20.2 | 14.7 |
| Ireland | 2.0 | 0.5 | – | – | – | – |
| Italy | – | – | – | – | – | – |
| Luxembourg | | | | | | |
| Malta | – | – | – | – | – | – |
| Netherlands | – | 3.5 | 1.3 | – | – | – |
| Norway | 9.5 | 9.9 | 9.8 | 6.6 | 12.3 | 17.7 |
| Sweden | 11.0 | 14.2 | 21.8 | 12.2 | 7.0 | 7.1 |
| Switzerland[a] | 12.1 | 11.2 | 10.8 | 11.1 | – | – |
| United Kingdom | – | – | – | – | – | – |
| **Mean (N = 16)** | **6.6** | **6.9** | **6.7** | **5.4** | **5.3** | **5.8** |
| Cyprus | | | | – | – | – |
| Greece | | | | – | – | – |
| Portugal | | | | – | – | – |
| Spain | | | | – | – | – |
| **Overall mean (N = 20)** | | | | **4.3** | **4.3** | **4.6** |

[a] From the 1990s onwards, the Swiss People's Party is treated as far right rather than agrarian.

this sector over time, agrarian parties have attempted to extend their appeal to middle-class urban voters. This shift was most clearly signalled by a change of name to Centre Party in Finland, Norway and Sweden (in 1965, 1959 and 1957, respectively). Since then the Swedish party has faded, but in Norway – as also in Denmark – the former agrarians recorded their best results in the first decade of the new century.

One result of this process of adaptation is a curious amalgam of agrarian party policy concerns. Despite their move away from a distinctively rural base, the centre parties continue to stress the interests of agriculture and farmers, and are the only party family to do so. This is also true of the Swiss People's Party, even following its rightward drift (Kriesi and Trechsel, 2008: 93–98). Two other emphases also reflect their particular heritage, one on decentralization, which harks back to their essentially peripheral roots, and the other on a form of environmental protection that, in its anti-industrial bias, is also characteristic of such parties. At the same time, however, the former agrarian parties also emphasize welfare provision, social justice, and the need for a controlled economy, which suggests a leftist orientation; and they favour both private enterprise and the maintenance of traditional moral values, which suggests quite a conservative impulse.

Although this mix of policy concerns allows the parties to appeal to both the right and the left, their earlier positions in Scandinavian party systems suggested a reasonably close alignment with the social democrats. In both Norway and Sweden in the 1930s, for example, some of the most important welfare legislation was passed by social democratic governments supported by the old agrarian parties – a powerful if now old-fashioned version of a 'Red–Green' alliance that helped lay the basis for the present advanced welfare states in these countries.

Nowadays, however, the Scandinavian parties attempt to play the role of genuine centre parties, bridging the gap between the social democrats and a fragmented bourgeois opposition. In this sense they can now be difficult to distinguish from more orthodox liberal parties (see above), especially when, as in Denmark, there is even a confusion in the names used by the parties (the name in English of the Danish Liberal Party is the Social Liberals, whereas the agrarian/centre party is known simply as the Liberals). Indeed, the similarities among these groups are highlighted by the fact that the strongest agrarian parties emerged in systems where liberalism is weak (the Scandinavian countries), whereas the strongest liberal parties tend to be found in countries where there was no agrarian presence (see also Steed and Humphreys, 1988). In general, however, agrarian or centre parties can be regarded as having drifted from the left towards the right over time. This is obviously most marked in Switzerland. On the infrequent occasions when they win government office, they now tend to be the moderate allies of bourgeois coalition partners. As a party family, however, they have now all but disappeared, or have forfeited their distinct identity.

On the emergence and development of agrarian/centre parties, see Urwin (1980) and Arter (2001).

### 8.3.5 The far right

The most striking development in the politics of the right during recent decades has been the growth of parties of the far right. Indeed, whereas such parties were to be found only in Italy, France, and marginally in Germany in the 1950s, they now compete more or less seriously in Austria, Belgium, Denmark, France, Italy, the Netherlands, Norway and Switzerland. In some cases the parties involved are relatively new, and have quickly built up substantial electoral support: the Dutch Freedom Party and Danish People's Party are both among the clearest examples of such mobilization. In other cases the growth in support for the far right has come as a result of the conversion of existing and older parties to a far-right position. The Austrian Freedom Party (FPÖ) and the Swiss People's Party (SVP) are among the clearest examples in this category. The FPÖ competed for decades in Austrian elections, representing a rather right-wing liberal position that was also sympathetic to the integration and rehabilitation of former Nazis in post-war Austrian politics, but only moved to the far right at the end of the 1980s (Art, 2006). In Switzerland the former agrarian SVP moved from mobilizing opposition to Swiss membership of the United Nations and the European Economic Area in the late 1980s to adopting a very strident anti-immigrant stance. In the case of both parties, as can be seen from the figures in Table 8.9, the shift to the right proved very rewarding in electoral terms.

As yet, far-right parties have not begun to compete in a significant way in Cyprus, Iceland, Ireland, Malta or the United Kingdom, and they also are not present in Greece, Portugal or Spain. That said, far-right elements exist as smaller groups or as factions within conservative and liberal parties in many of these countries, and in the United Kingdom the far-right British National Party won two seats in the 2009 European elections, and outpolled the Greens in 2010. These parties have also made their mark in the post-communist systems, and most notably in Hungary, where the fascist-like Joppik Party – a party that includes a uniformed militia called the Hungarian Guard, and which has a record of anti-Semitic and anti-Gypsy rhetoric (Phillips, 2010) – polled 17 per cent of the vote in the 2010 elections. Through still relatively small in European terms, far-right parties have quadrupled their vote in the last decades, rising from an average of just over 2 per cent in the 1980s to almost 8 per cent in the new century (Table 8.9), when they also outpolled the Greens. Though falling back since then in some cases, including Austria in 2000–2009, they have built significant new support in Belgium, Denmark, the Netherlands, Norway and Switzerland. The principal protagonists on the far right now include the National Front in France, the Northern League in Italy, the Freedom Party and Alliance for the Future of Austria (BZÖ) in Austria, the Flemish Block in Belgium, the Progress Party in Norway, the Danish People's Party in Denmark, the Freedom Party in the Netherlands, and the former agrarian Swiss People's Party. Although parties such as the German People's Union are not yet significantly relevant actors at the national level, a historical legacy and sporadic successes at the regional and local levels suggest that these might also not be discounted.

Traditionally, parties of the far right have been small parties, although in some countries they have proved sufficiently popular to have had a major impact on the direction and pattern of party competition at the national level. In the wake of the collapse of the centre in Italian politics, the former Italian Social Movement (MSI), which was reconstituted as the National Alliance, suddenly polled exceptionally well in the 1994 elections, as did the Northern League, which in many ways is similar in outlook to the Austrian Freedom Party. Both parties then entered government with Forza Italia in 1994 and again in 2001 and 2008, and the National Alliance later formally merged with the Forza Italia party in the new People of Liberty (PdL). In the Netherlands the first successful 'far-right' party – the designation is disputed – the Pim Fortuyn List, briefly took part in a government with the Christian Democrats and Liberals. In Denmark the Danish People's Party offers external support to the centre-right government, as does the Freedom Party in the Netherlands, and in Austria the FPÖ governed in coalition with the Christian Democrats.

**TABLE 8.9** Mean electoral support for far-right/populist parties, 1950–2009

| Country | 1950s | 1960s | 1970s | 1980s | 1990s | 2000–2009 |
|---|---|---|---|---|---|---|
| Austria[a] | – | – | – | – | 22.0 | 17.8 |
| Belgium | – | – | – | 1.5 | 9.7 | 13.8 |
| Denmark | – | – | 11.0 | 6.6 | 7.5 | 13.2 |
| Finland | – | – | – | – | 0.3 | – |
| France | 4.3 | – | – | 6.7 | 14.2 | 4.7 |
| Germany | 1.1 | 2.1 | – | 0.3 | 2.5 | 0.5 |
| Iceland | – | – | – | – | – | – |
| Ireland | – | – | – | – | – | – |
| Italy | 11.1 | 6.3 | 6.7 | 6.6 | 20.9 | 14.8[b] |
| Luxembourg | – | – | – | 1.2 | 1.2 | 0.5 |
| Malta | – | – | – | – | – | 0.3 |
| Netherlands | – | – | – | 0.6 | 1.8 | 9.6 |
| Norway | – | – | 3.5 | 7.1 | 10.8 | 18.4 |
| Sweden | – | – | – | – | 2.6 | 2.2 |
| Switzerland[c] | – | – | 4.8 | 4.3 | 25.4 | 29.2 |
| United Kingdom | – | – | – | – | – | – |
| **Mean (N = 16)** | **1.0** | **0.5** | **1.6** | **2.2** | **7.4** | **7.8** |
| Cyprus | | | | | – | – |
| Greece | | | | | – | 2.9 |
| Portugal | | | | | – | – |
| Spain | | | | | – | – |
| **Overall mean (N = 20)** | | | | **1.8** | **5.9** | **6.4** |

[a] The Austrian Freedom Party is classified as far right from the 1990s onwards.
[b] It does not include the vote for the National Alliance (AN) in 2008, as the latter merged with Forza Italia to form the People of Liberty (PdL).
[c] The Swiss People's Party is treated as far right from the 1990s onwards.

Some of these parties, including the French National Front and the Belgian Vlaams Blok, are extremely right wing and highly xenophobic; some also claim to be heirs to the fascist and anti-system right-wing movements that rose to prominence in interwar Europe (Art, 2006). In November 2004, for example, the Vlaams Blok was banned by the Belgian Supreme Court on the grounds that it incited racism. This was the culmination of a three-year lawsuit and, perhaps ironically, came just at the moment when the party itself was adopting a more moderate-sounding programme. The ban has little real impact, however, in that the party has simply reconstituted itself under the new name Vlaams Belang (Flemish Interest). At their core, however, there are at least two appeals that characterize all of the new far-right parties, and which have acquired particular force in recent years. First, almost without exception, they mobilize against immigration and against those policies that are seen to promote multiculturalism. These are nationalist parties in the main, sometimes extremely so, and they have also served as a focus for the more strident opposition to European integration. Second, as 'outsider' parties, they mobilize against the political establishment, and what they see as the self-serving character of the political class. In this they have been bolstered by the increased allegations of political corruption that are now current in many of the west European polities (Heywood, 1997), as well as by the more generalized disillusion, indifference and sometimes even anti-party sentiment that characterizes many European voters (Mudde, 2004). This latter protest is often self-sustaining. Because these parties are so extreme, there is a reluctance on the part of the established parties to consider them as suitable coalition allies. And as long as they remain excluded from processes of government formation, they can continue to assert a populist – and often popular – anti-establishment appeal. This is certainly a large part of the reason why Jörg Haider's Freedom Party proved so successful in the Austrian elections of the 1990s. Once it was admitted to government in 2000, on the other hand, its support began to fall. The same was true of the Pim Fortuyn List in the Netherlands, even though Fortuyn himself rejected the far-right label, and identified more closely with politicians such as Berlusconi rather than with Haider or Le Pen. As Heinisch (2003) has argued, while these new right-wing populist parties may be successful in opposition, they can fail in government. This is not true of the Italian Northern League, however, which has become organizationally stronger and electorally more successful during its recent years in government with Berlusconi (see also Deschouwer, 2009).

More generally, the relative electoral success of these new parties can also be linked to the growth of Green and left-libertarian protest on the left of the political spectrum. Ignazi (2004), for example, has suggested that the rise of the extreme right in recent years may reflect the other side of the 'new politics' divide, in which the growing support for new left and Green parties is now being counterbalanced by a shift towards a new right – the one side representing the interests of those who have found themselves benefiting from post-industrialism, the other representing the interests of those who are being left behind (see also Müller-Rommel, 1998). In France, Austria and Switzerland, for example, it is striking to see the extent to which these new parties of the right have made inroads into some of the traditional working-class constituencies of the social democratic and communist left.

On the far right in general, the best recent analyses are Mudde (2007) and Bornschier (2010).

## 8.4 Other parties

Although most European countries are presented as being 'nation-states', in which the boundaries of nation and state coincide, many incorporate important local minorities of distinct national, linguistic and ethnic groups. These groups are often represented by parties that have their basis in local ethnic or regional identities, with demands that range from greater regional autonomy to full-fledged separatism. These parties, while linked to one another by their strong regional or ethnic concerns, vary immensely in their other policy positions, and in their general positioning on the left–right scale.

Regional or ethnic parties can be found in one form or another in almost all western European states, as well as in a number of post-communist states. But despite what are often quite high levels of electoral support in local power bases, these parties are relevant at the national level in only a handful of countries. Belgium, given its deep ethnic and linguistic divisions, provides the most striking examples, including various Flemish (Dutch-speaking) and Walloon (French-speaking) regional parties. Indeed, given that even all the mainstream Belgian parties have separate Flemish and Walloon organizations, and given that the Walloon organizations do not compete for Flemish votes, and vice versa, it is now almost impossible to speak of a single Belgian party system at the electoral level.

Also of some significance have been the Swedish People's Party, the political voice of the Swedish-speaking minority in Finland, and a regular participant in Finnish coalition governments; the nationalist Sinn Fein Party, which formerly offered political support to the Irish Republican Army, and which mobilizes both in the Irish Republic and, within the United Kingdom, in Northern Ireland; various Basque separatist parties in northern Spain, including Herri Batasuna, which supports the armed struggle of Basque paramilitary organizations, and which was banned by the Spanish Supreme Court in 2003; and, in the United Kingdom, the Scottish and Welsh nationalists, together with constitutional nationalists and unionists in Northern Ireland. The UK has also recently witnessed the emergence of the UK Independence Party (UKIP), which polled particularly well in the elections to the European Parliament in 2004 and 2009, but which has yet to make any real impact on elections to Westminster. In Belgium the Vlaams Belang, which we group under the far right, is a strong advocate of Flemish independence.

In general, the strongest support for these parties within the west European area is to be found in Belgium, Spain and the United Kingdom. Although these parties remain a tiny electoral minority within most of western Europe, it is important to remember that these movements do command substantial support in their local areas. Roughly two Basque voters in three support Basque nationalist parties, for example. In Northern Ireland virtually all of the vote is won by nationalist or regional (including unionist) parties. Indeed, none of the mainland British parties is even willing to nominate its own candidates for elections in the province, and when the British Conservative Party tested the waters in Northern Ireland in a by-election in 1990 it was utterly trounced by local parties. In the 2010 elections the Conservatives established a link with the Ulster Unionist Party, but this experiment also ended in electoral disaster.

On regionalist parties in general, see De Winter *et al.* (2006) and Hepburn (2009).

There are also additional parties that compete in European elections, but which defy simple categorization in terms of party families. These include a number of small Danish parties, including the long-standing Justice Party. Pensioners' parties have occasionally competed in Finland, Italy, Luxembourg and the Netherlands (as well as in post-communist Slovenia, where the pensioners' party DeSUS polled 4 per cent of the vote in 2004). Europe's first 'antiGreen' party, the aptly named Automobile party, was founded in Switzerland in 1985, but was later absorbed by the far right. It is also important to note that independent candidates and loose, ill-defined alliances can from time to time be significant in a variety of countries – most notably in France, Ireland and the United Kingdom, where electoral systems place few obstacles in the way of independent candidatures.

It is in Portugal and Spain, however, where 'other' parties have been most important – at least in the early years of their democracies. As these new party systems emerged in the wake of the transition to democracy in the late 1970s, a number of temporary and shifting alliances appeared, often involving protagonists who shared little other than a desire to ensure the consolidation of democratic practices. These alliances were oriented towards particular domestic problems of democratic transition and consolidation, bearing little relationship to the interests and programmes of parties in the established democracies. In Portugal, for example, a group known as the Democratic Alliance polled more than 48 per cent of the vote in 1980 and then fell apart into various factions and units. Two elections later, in 1985, the Democratic Renewal Party was created; it won more than 18 per cent of the vote before falling back to 5 per cent in 1987. The number and size of these loose electoral alliances in 1980s Portugal and, to a lesser extent, Spain offered an ample indication of the difficulties involved in consolidating a new party system, a problem that has also proved very apparent in the newly emerging post-communist party systems. Indeed, it is because so many of the new democratic parties in post-communist Europe are short-lived and merging and dividing, and because so many defy easy categorization within the familiar western party families, that we treat them separately here.

## 8.5 The post-communist party families

Although we still have to be very cautious about predicting the future shape of the parties and the party systems in the new post-communist democracies, there are nevertheless some common threads that can already be picked out regarding the types of party which have developed, and the sorts of family they have developed. Five of these are particularly important. First, there are those new parties that emerged in opposition to the former regime, and which, at the same time, reflected broad-based alliances containing diverse strands of ideological and partisan opinion. Examples include the former Solidarity opposition in Poland, the Popular Front in Latvia, the Civic Forum in the Czech Republic, and People Against Violence in Slovakia. These alliances often broke up soon after the transition to democracy, and split into various conservative, liberal or even nationalist groupings. Second, there are those new parties that also emerged in opposition to the old regime but which, from the beginning, were already characterized by a more distinctive political ideology, such as the Democratic Forum (HDF) or Alliance of Free Democrats (AFD) in Hungary, or the Confederation for an Independent Poland. With time, however, the distinction between this and the first category has become blurred as a result of the disintegration of the broad anti-communist fronts. Third, there are the successors of the former ruling communists themselves, which have since reformed and reconstituted themselves as parties that claim to support the new democratic systems, but which continue to favour state intervention, and which argue against the wholesale introduction of liberal market policies, such as the Polish Democratic Left Alliance (SLD), or the Hungarian Socialist Party (MSzP). Fourth, there are the old 'satellite' parties that once formed part of the former communist political leadership, such as the Polish Peasant Party (PSL), which seek to restore an independent electoral credibility. Finally, there are also the historic pre-communist parties, such as the Latvian Social Democratic and Farmers' parties, or the Hungarian Smallholders' Party, many of which re-emerged after 1989 in the hope of capitalizing on their earlier legitimacy. To these might also be added some of the small Christian democratic parties that also trace their roots back to the interwar years.

Despite such common threads, however, there is clearly no uniform pattern, and the precise shape of each individual system has been at least partially determined by the specific legacy of the pre-communist regime, on the one hand, as well as by the particular way in which the post-communist transition proceeded, on the other. In Poland, as in the Czech and Slovak republics, for example, the regime was attacked from the ground, and the transition involved the mobilization of a broadly based opposition movement that was later to fragment into a variety of different political parties in the wake of the first democratic elections. In Hungary, on the other hand, where the regime had begun to reform itself in the mid 1980s, different parties began to emerge and to compete with one another well before the first elections, and an embryonic multiparty system was already in place before the communist regime actually collapsed. In Latvia and the other Baltic states the struggle against communism was also a struggle for national independence, and the dominant forces in the new democracies were nationalist in character. In these states there also existed the specific problem of an ethnic Russian minority, and hence issues relating to ethnicity and citizenship rights figured high up on the new political agenda.

All of these national experiences, as well as the more or less enormous burden of reconstruction shouldered by each of the polities, inevitably led to a set of political oppositions that was without real parallel in western Europe. This, at least, is one way of looking at the issue. Dealing with Russian, Roma or irredentist minorities, for example, is not something that has figured very strongly in the recent experiences of western political leaders. Converting an outdated, bureaucratic and state-controlled economy into a late-twentieth-century market economy is also not a problem that has been faced in the west – except in the eastern part of Germany, of course, where unification of west and east has not yet had the effect of pulling the east up to the living standards of the west. Nor have the present batch of western leaders ever been obliged to engineer a democratic constitution more or less from scratch, or to build a competitive party system. In contemporary western Europe, democracy has been inherited. In post-communist Europe it has had to be constructed. It is then hardly surprising that political alignments should look different once we go beyond the west, or that they should sometimes prove more challenging.

But there is also another side to the story (Lewis, 2006, 2007). Even when political institutions and party systems are constructed from scratch, it is often with one eye on the experiences of more seasoned models. Lessons have been learned from the west, and existing party models, and even current issue positions, have sometimes been absorbed by the new polities. In addition, regardless of the location of the polity or its level of institutional development, some key problems are of pan-European concern, and hence prompt the emergence of similar political coalitions and alignments – issues relating to the reorganization of welfare states, for example, or those relating to the positions to be adopted in the new international order. The development of comparable political profiles has also been fostered by the enlargement of the European Union, forcing adaptation to the common *aquis*, on the one hand, and bringing many of the new post-communist parties into transnational and specifically European party federations, on the other (Bressanelli, 2010; McElroy and Benoit, 2010). In other words, even when the post-communist path to party politics has been forged by national and systemic peculiarities, it is often standardized by the need for the new actors to forge links with like-minded forces throughout the enlarged European Union (Zielonka and Pravda, 2001).

In sum, although substantial differences exist between the development of west European party systems and the development of post-communist party systems, and although it is therefore not always easy to detect family resemblances between the two groups of countries, some links can nevertheless be established (Hlousek and Kopecek, 2010). Christian democratic parties can be found in each of the two groupings, for example, even though this family still has a more powerful hold among the west European polities. Conversely, conservative parties prove to be stronger in the post-communist world, even though in this case they are concerned more with reforming than with conserving, as such. In many cases these parties grew out of the popular coalitions and citizens' movements that initially challenged the communist regimes, and hence they reflect the sort of radical and protest-based traditions that, in the west at least, are normally associated with the left. In this sense it is the socialist, or ex-communist, parties that might be seen as the real conservatives of post-communist Europe – parties that once held a monopoly of political power, and which now, as democrats, seek to slow down the speed of liberal reform. These parties have no equivalent in the west, of course; their social democratic counterparts in the west come from a wholly different political tradition, while their fading ex-communist counterparts were never regime parties. In some cases, however, such as in the Czech Republic, there is now a major social democratic party that shares common roots with the social democratic parties in the west, and which traces its identity back to the pre-communist interwar years. In this sense we can speak of two distinct socialist party families in post-communist Europe: the ex-communists, who are strongest in Bulgaria, Hungary, Poland and Romania, and who also appear to have a growing appeal in the Czech Republic; and the more conventional social democrats, who are strongest in Latvia, the Czech Republic and Slovakia.

The differential levels of support for the various families in the different post-communist countries are summarized in Table 8.10, and are obviously based on only two decades of competition. Given the lack of continuity of many party organizations in post-communist Europe, as well as the formation and collapse of so many short-term electoral alliances, it is as yet almost impossible to trace meaningful long-term patterns. As can be seen from the table, many of the parties in post-communist Europe can be associated with one or other of the cross-national families that have been discussed earlier. There is a small set of Green parties, for example, although these are even weaker in the new Europe than in the old. The Czech Greens, one of the largest of this small polling group, did join the centre-right government in 2007, and held three cabinet seats. Moreover, one party not incorporated in the table is the Hungarian 'Politics Can Be Different' (LMP), a Green liberal party that won an impressive 7.5 per cent of the vote on its first outing in the election of April 2010. There are also agrarian parties, representing a strong rural interest in countries such as Estonia, Latvia and Poland, and which are much more closely tied to the farming vote than is now the case with the older agrarian parties in Scandinavia. Nevertheless, one of the surprises of post-communist party development is how weakly these parties have performed, in that it had been widely anticipated that they would poll particularly well following the transition to democracy. However, as Mudde (2002: 229) notes, 'today, farmers in the region are "rural workers" rather than "peasants", and they give their support to (former) Communist parties rather than populist peasant parties'. Another group that is common to the west is that of the far-right and/or populist parties, with levels of electoral support averaging around the same level as in the west. That said, it is possibly even more difficult in these settings to draw a line between the far right, as such, and a more contingent populist appeal. In the Slovak case, for example, the high figure for the 1990s refers to both Meciar's Movement for a Democratic Slovakia-People's Party (HZDS) as well as the Slovak National Party (SNS), a party that recently served in the government coalition. But whereas the far-right and/or populist parties have gained support in recent elections in the west, there is some evidence of decline – in the Czech Republic, Latvia, Romania and Slovakia – in the new Europe. This is as yet an uneven and uncertain picture, however, and the far right has clearly gained in Bulgaria, Lithuania and – especially in 2010 – Hungary.

Christian democrats also poll less than in the west, which is perhaps also surprising, given that, especially in Poland, they formed a core part of the old opposition to the former communist regimes. On the other hand, it is sometimes very difficult to distinguish Christian and conservative

TABLE 8.10 Electoral support for party families in the new Europe

| Country | Period | (Ex)Communist / Socialist[a] | Social democrat | Green | Liberal | Conservative/ Christian democrat | Agrarian | Populist / far right | Ethnic / regional | Others / not aligned |
|---|---|---|---|---|---|---|---|---|---|---|
| Bulgaria | 1990s | 33.0 | 1.9 | – | 3.8 | 35.9 | 4.6 | – | 7.5 | – |
|  | 2000s | 22.0 | 0.3 | – | 21.9 | 29.4 | 0.1 | 8.8 | 11.6 | – |
| Czech Republic | 1990s | 11.8 | 21.7 | 0.4 | 8.4 | 36.8 | 2.2 | 6.0 | 2.5 | – |
|  | 2000s | 15.7 | 31.3 | 4.4 | 0.4 | 40.7 | – | 0.5 | 0.2 | – |
| Estonia | 1990s | – | 10.3 | 0.9 | 45.9 | 18.3 | 2.4 | – | 4.0 | 5.2 |
|  | 2000s | – | 8.8 | 3.6 | 48.5 | 24.9 | 10.1 | – | 1.6 | – |
| Hungary | 1990s | 38.5 | – | – | 16.2 | 33.5 | 11.2 | 2.4 | – | – |
|  | 2000s | 30.7 | – | – | 2.8 | 48.3 | 0.4 | 10.6 | – | – |
| Latvia | 1990s | – | 19.9 | – | 21.7 | 13.5 | 7.3 | 22.5 | 3.8 | 2.4 |
|  | 2000s | – | 20.5 | – | 7.5 | 47.3 | 13.1 | 6.2 | 3.0 | – |
| Lithuania | 1990s | 28.4 | 6.5 | – | 18.1 | 25.1 | 2.0 | 4.8 | 2.1 | 8.9 |
|  | 2000s | 16.3 | – | – | 30.7 | 17.2 | 5.2 | 12.1 | 4.3 | 7.6 |
| Poland | 1990s | 19.8 | 8.0 | – | 18.8 | 23.6 | 14.0 | 7.4 | 1.0 | – |
|  | 2000s | 21.8 | 3.9 | – | 28.0 | 24.7 | 16.0 | 5.7 | 0.3 | – |
| Romania | 1990s | 28.6 | 2.0 | – | 2.3 | 28.4 | – | 13.8 | 8.9 | – |
|  | 2000s | 35.0 | – | – | 9.3 | 32.0 | – | 8.1 | 9.5 | – |
| Slovakia | 1990s | 18.3 | – | – | – | 21.6 | – | 40.6 | 9.7 | 2.7 |
|  | 2000s | 6.1 | 21.3 | – | 4.7 | 25.1 | – | 23.5 | 11.5 | – |
| Slovenia | 1990s | 11.6 | – | 3.6 | 31.8 | 31.2 | – | 5.9 | – | 3.2 |
|  | 2000s | 20.4 | – | 1.1 | 18.7 | 41.5 | – | 5.9 | – | 5.8 |

[a] In post-communist Europe this refers to the former regime parties.

parties in the new Europe, and it is often the case that both types of party are affiliated to the same European people's party group in the European Parliament. For this reason, and in contrast to the treatment in the long-established democracies, we combine the two groups together into a single category in Table 8.10. This may also tell us something important about these two families. As noted earlier, Christian democratic parties trace their origins to the defence of primarily Catholic values in late nineteenth- and early twentieth-century Europe (see also Chapter 9), and hence emerged within a particular historical conjuncture. Where these parties failed to emerge, the centre right was usually dominated by secular conservative parties, and the two families have since tended to be the functional equivalent of one another in their role as the mainstream alternative to social democracy. In the later democratizing polities, however, there was little opportunity for Christian democracy as such, and hence the centre right was more or less monopolized by conservatives in countries such as Greece, Portugal and Spain. And while religious divisions have proved more important in the post-communist polities – especially in Poland – here too the bias towards the conservative alternative is quite marked. It is in this very general sense that we can speak of a waning of the Christian democratic alternative over time (see Bale and Szczerbiak, 2008).

What is also striking about the post-communist voters is the extent to which they still support the old regime parties, with both decades recording an average of close to 20 per cent of the vote for the former communist parties. This average figure is somewhat misleading, however, in that the former communists are strongest in south-eastern and east central Europe – Bulgaria, Romania, Hungary, Poland, the Czech Republic and Slovakia – and win no support at all in Estonia or Latvia. Indeed, among the Baltic states, the post-communists are successful only in Lithuania, where they were led by the charismatic Algirdas Brazauskas, and proved one of the only post-communist parties to succeed in the founding elections. In other cases the success of the post-communist parties came in later elections, with the founding elections being dominated by opponents of the old regime (on these different patterns, see Grzymała-Bussel, 2002). The second striking feature, and on a scale that is massively greater than in the west, is the size of the vote that goes to liberal parties – centrist and reformist parties that are sometimes difficult to distinguish from the conservatives, but which have always been in the forefront of the struggle for democracy, and which are present in all of the polities except Slovakia in the 1990s. These parties are particularly strong in the Baltic states, and more recently in Bulgaria and Poland. The third important feature here is the vote that goes to parties representing ethnic or regional minorities, such as the Russians in the Baltic states or the Hungarians in Slovakia. Problems of this sort are much more pronounced than in the west, and often reflect an incomplete or forced nation- and state-building process.

## 8.6 Conclusions

But even if this mode of classification allows most of the main parties to be grouped within one or other of the more or less conventional political families, any comparison of the post-communist alignments with those of the west must be extremely careful. Despite recent electoral flux, the main parties in western Europe are still organizationally stable and ideologically embedded. Social democratic parties are easily recognized as such, and continue to have much in common with regard to their ideological profile and policy preferences. The same is true for most of the Catholic or Catholic-influenced Christian democratic parties, and also even for many of the secular conservative parties. Moreover, these are often old parties, which contest election after election with the same organization and under the same label, and which manage to protect their identities even when entering coalitions or electoral alliances. In such a context it is therefore still very meaningful to speak of party families. In post-communist Europe, by contrast, the parties are fragmented and often short-lived. With each election we tend to see a host of new party labels of new electoral alliances. Between elections we see constant splits and divisions within existing parties. The result is that while a crude profile of the distribution of support between party families can be established – as in Table 8.10 – there is no guarantee that anything like this pattern will still be seen in five or ten years hence, particularly as far as the distribution of support on the centre right is concerned. Indeed, as Sitter (2002: 447) has noted, it is the character of the right that remains one of the most powerful forces driving multiparty competition in the new post-communist systems.

In general, therefore, and despite exceptions on both sides, contemporary post-communist party politics can be distinguished from western European party politics by virtue of its lack of institutionalization (Casal Bertoa and Mair, 2010). As we shall see in the following chapter, however, this distinction may yet fade away – not only because post-communist systems will become more institutionalized, but also because western systems are themselves likely to become less structured.

## References

**Art, David** (2006) *The Politics of the Nazi Past in Germany and Austria*, Cambridge University Press, Cambridge.

**Arter, David** (2001) *From Farmyard to City Square: The Electoral Adaptation of the Nordic Agrarian Parties*, Ashgate, Aldershot.

**Bale, Tim and Aleks Szczerbiak** (2008) 'Why is there no Christian democracy in Poland – and why should we care?' *Party Politics*, 14 (4), 479–500.

**Bartolini, Stefano** (2000) *The Political Mobilization of the European Left, 1860–1980: The Class Cleavage*, Cambridge University Press, Cambridge.

**Bornschier, Simon** (2010) *Cleavage Politics and the Populist Right*, Temple University Press, Philadelphia, PA.

**Botella, Joan and Luis Ramiro** (eds) (2003) *The Crisis of Communism and Party Change: The Evolution of Western European Communist and Post-Communist Parties*, Institut de Ciències Polítiques i Socials, Barcelona.

**Bressanelli, Edoardo** (2010) 'The European Parliament after Lisbon: the policy position and coherence of the political Groups', paper presented to the 24th conference of the Italian Society of Political Science, Venice, 16–18 September.

**Casal Bertoa, Fernado and Peter Mair** (2010) *Two Decades On: How Institutionalized are the Post-Communist Party Systems?*, EUI Working Paper SPS 2010/3, European University Institute, Florence.

**Cuperus, René and Johannes Kandel** (1998) *European Social Democracy: Transformation in Progress*, Friedrich Ebert Stiftung/Wiardi Beckman Stichting, Amsterdam.

**Deschouwer, Kris (ed.)** (2009) *New Parties in Government*, Routledge, London.

**De Vreese, Claes H. and Hajo G. Boomgaarden** (eds) 'Symposium: Religion and the European Union', *West European Politics*, 32 (6), 1182–1283.

**De Winter, Lieven, Margarita Gómez-Reino and Peter Lynch (eds)** (2006) *Autonomous Parties in Europe: Identity Politics and the Revival of the Territorial Cleavage*, 2 vols, Institut de Ciències Polítiques i Socials, Barcelona.

**Dunphy, Richard and Tim Bale** (2007) 'Red flag still flying? Explaining AKEL – Cyprus's communist anomaly', *Party Politics*, 3 (3), 287–304.

**Flora, Peter** (1986) 'Introduction', pp. v–xxxvi in Peter Flora (ed.), *Growth to Limits: The West European Welfare States since World War II, vol. 1: Sweden, Norway, Finland, Denmark*, de Gruyter, Berlin.

**Frankland, E. Gene, Paul Lucardi and Benoit Rihoux (eds)** (2008) *Green Parties in Transition*, Ashgate, Farnham.

**Gehlen, Michael and Wolfram Kaiser** (2004) *Christian Democracy in Europe since 1945*, Frank Cass, London, 2004.

**Girvin, Brian (ed.)** (1988) *The Transformation of Contemporary Conservatism*, Sage, Beverly Hills.

**Goetz, Klaus H., Peter Mair and Gordon Smith (eds)** (2008) *European Politics: Pasts, Presents, Futures*, special issue of *West European Politics*, 31 (1/2).

**Grzymała-Busse, Anna Maria** (2002) *Redeeming the Communist Past: The Regeneration of Communist Parties in East Central Europe*, Cambridge University Press, Cambridge.

**Hecke, Steven van and Emmanuel Gerard (eds)** (2004) *Christian Democratic Parties in Europe since the End of the Cold War*, Leuven University Press, Leuven.

**Heinisch, Reinhard** (2003) 'Success in opposition – failure in government: explaining the performance of right-wing populist parties in public office', *West European Politics*, 26 (3), 91–130.

**Hepburn, Eve (ed.)** (2009) *New Challenges for Stateless Nationalist and Regionalist Parties*, special issue of *Regional and Federal Studies*, 19 (4/5).

**Heywood, Paul** (1997) 'Political corruption: problems and perspectives', *Political Studies*, 45 (3), 417–435.

**Hix, Simon and Christopher Lord** (1997) *Political Parties in the European Union*, Macmillan, Basingstoke.

**Hlousek, Vit and Lubomir Kopecek** (2010) Origin, Ideology and Transformation of Political Parties: East-Central and Western Europe Compared. Farnham: Ashgate.

**Ignazi, Piero** (2004) *Extreme Right Parties in Western Europe*, Oxford University Press, Oxford.

**Kalyvas, Stathis N.** (1996) *The Rise of Christian Democracy in Europe*, Cornell University Press, Ithaca, NY.

**Keman, Hans** (1994) 'The search for the centre: pivot parties in west European party systems', *West European Politics*, 17 (4), 124–148.

**Kirchheimer, Otto** (1966) 'The transformation of the west European party systems', pp. 177–200 in Joseph LaPalombara and Myron Weiner (eds), *Political Parties and Political Development*, Princeton University Press, Princeton, NJ.

**Kirchner, Emil J. (ed.)** (1988) *Liberal Parties in Western Europe*, Cambridge University Press, Cambridge.

**Kitschelt, Herbert P.** (1988) 'Left-libertarian parties: explaining innovation in competitive party systems', *World Politics*, 40 (2), 194–234.

**Kitschelt, Herbert P.** (1994) *The Transformation of European Social Democracy*, Cambridge University Press, Cambridge.

**Kriesi, Hanspeter and Alexander H. Trechsel** (2008) *The Politics of Switzerland*, Cambridge University Press, Cambridge.

**Lewis, Paul G.** (2006) 'Party systems in post-communist central Europe: patterns of stability and consolidation', *Democratization*, 13 (4), 562–583.

**Lewis, Paul** (2007) 'Political parties', pp. 174–192 in Stephen White, Judy Batt and Paul G. Lewis (eds), *Developments in Central and East European Politics 4*, Palgrave Macmillan, Basingstoke.

**Lijphart, Arend** (1977) *Democracy in Plural Societies*, Yale University Press, New Haven, CT.

**Luther, Richard and Kris Deschouwer (eds)** (1999) *Party Elites in Divided Societies: Political Parties in Consociational Democracy*, Routledge, London.

**Mackie, Thomas T. and Richard Rose** (1991) *The International Almanac of Electoral History*, 3rd edn, Macmillan, Basingstoke.

**Madeley, John and Zsolt Enyedi (eds)** (2003) *Church and State in Contemporary Europe*, special issue of *West European Politics*, 26 (1).

**Mair, Peter and Cas Mudde** (1998) 'The party family and its study', *Annual Review of Political Science*, 1, 211–229.

**March, Luke and Cas Mudde** (2005) 'What's left of the radical left? The European radical left after 1989: decline and mutation', *Comparative European Politics*, 3 (1), 23–49.

**McElroy, Gail and Kenneth Benoit** (2010) 'Party policy and group affiliation in the European Parliament', *British Journal of Political Science*, 40 (2), 377–398.

**Michels, Robert** (1911/1962) *Political Parties: A Sociological Study of the Oligarchical Tendencies of Modern Democracy*, The Free Press, New York.

**Moschonas, Gerassimos** (2002) *In the Name of Social Democracy: The Great Transformation from 1945 to the Present*, Verso, London.

**Mudde, Cas** (2002) 'In the name of the peasantry, the proletariat, and the people: populisms in Eastern Europe', pp. 214–232 in Yves Mény and Yves Surel (eds), *Democracies and the Populist Challenge*, Palgrave, London.

**Mudde, Cas** (2004) 'The populist zeitgeist', *Government and Opposition*, 39 (4), 541–563.

**Mudde, Cas** (2007) *Populist Radical Right Parties in Europe*, Cambridge University Press, Cambridge.

**Müller-Rommel, Ferdinand** (1998) 'The new challengers: Greens and right-wing populist parties in western Europe', *European Review*, 6 (2), 191–202.

**Müller-Rommel, Ferdinand and Thomas Poguntke (eds)** (2002) *Green Parties in National Governments*, Frank Cass, London.

**Phillips, Leigh** (2010) 'What's behind Hungary's far-right Jobbik', *Bloomberg Businessweek*, 20 April (www.businessweek.com/globalbiz/content/apr2010/gb20100420_420459.htm).

**Rihoux, Benoit and Wolfgang Rüdig** (2006) 'Analyzing Greens in power: setting the agenda', *European Journal of Political Research*, 45 (1), 1–33.

**Scharpf, Fritz** (1999) *Governing in Europe: Effective and Democratic?* Oxford University Press, Oxford.

**Sitter, Nick** (2002) 'Cleavages, party strategy and party system change in Europe, east and west', *Perspectives in European Politics and Society*, 3 (3), 425–451.

**Steed, Michael and Peter Humphreys** (1988) 'Identifying liberal parties', pp. 376–395 in *Liberal Parties in Western Europe*, Emil J. Kirchner (ed.), Cambridge University Press, Cambridge.

**Urwin, Derek W.** (1980) *From Ploughshare to Ballotbox: The Politics of Agrarian Defense in Europe*, Universitetsforlaget, Oslo.

**van Kersbergen, Kees** (1995) *Social Capitalism*, Routledge, London.

**van Kersbergen, Kees and Philip Manow (eds)** *Religion, Class Coalitions, and Welfare States*, Cambridge University Press, Cambridge.

**Zielonka, Jan and Alex Pravda (eds)** (2001) *Democratic Consolidation in Eastern Europe*, vol. 2: *International and Transnational Factors*, Oxford University Press, Oxford.

# CHAPTER

# 9

# Cleavage Structures and Electoral Change

## Chapter contents

## 9.1 Introduction

Enormous historical legacies underpin the appeals that political parties make to the citizens of the various European polities, and similar legacies help determine how citizens respond to those parties. Indeed, Seymour Martin Lipset and Stein Rokkan, in one of the most cogent and influential accounts of the development of modern European politics (Lipset and Rokkan, 1967), begin their analysis with events that took place more than four centuries ago, at a time when the very idea of mass political parties, let alone that of mass democracy, was unthinkable. Those events and subsequent developments over the succeeding centuries continue to provide the parameters of contemporary politics in Europe.

To take a very clear-cut example, we saw in the preceding chapter that one of the most evident distinctions between the established European party systems concerns whether the major party of the centre right is a Christian democratic or a conservative party. We also saw that when there is a major Christian party, that party typically depends on a substantial Catholic vote. And the presence or absence of this Catholic vote derives, in turn, from a history of religious division that dates back to at least 1517, when Martin Luther pinned his 95 theses to the door of a church in Wittenberg, thus initiating the Protestant revolt against the Church of Rome and marking the beginning of what we now know as the Reformation.

The ensuing clash between traditional Catholic Europe and reforming Protestant Europe constituted the first serious division in what had previously been a unifying Christian culture. The western area of Europe was effectively fractured in two, and the boundary between the two parts can be seen on a map of Europe by drawing a line between the Dutch city of Rotterdam in the north-west and the Italian city of Venice in the south-east. To the south and west of this line lie most of the countries that remained loyal to Rome, and which remain predominantly Catholic today: France, Spain, Belgium, Luxembourg, Italy and Austria, as well as the southern part of the Netherlands and southern Germany. To the north and east of this line, but still within the area of western Europe, lies the Protestant domain: the Scandinavian countries in particular, as well as northern and eastern Germany and the northern part of the Netherlands. Britain was also to form part of the Protestant north, whereas Ireland remained mainly Catholic (see also Table 1.1).

In most but not all of the Catholic countries, as we have seen, the major party of the centre right has been or still remains an essentially Catholic Christian democratic party. In all of the Protestant countries the major party of the centre right is a conservative party. In the Netherlands the continental fissure also split the polity, leading, as we have seen, to the early mobilization of both Catholic and Protestant Christian parties.

What is clear beyond any shadow of a doubt is that the religious history of the previous four centuries still overhangs the development of party politics in contemporary Europe – as well as helping to set the long-standing division between west and east (Prodromou, 1996). Given this, it is hardly surprising that the broad outline of the party systems in the long-standing democracies of western Europe has proved so enduring.

In this chapter, therefore, we discuss the traditional cleavage structures that have underpinned European politics, and we explore how they might have changed in recent years. We also explore whether the changes that have occurred might be leading towards the realignment of party systems or towards dealignment. As in the previous chapter, we shall often make a distinction between the traditional west European democracies, on the one hand, and the new post-communist democracies, on the other. Although the two sets of polities often share similar cleavage structures, the questions that we address to long-standing party systems are necessarily different from those we address to newly formed party systems.

## 9.2 The meaning of cleavage

Before we consider the actual substance of the divisions that underpin contemporary European politics, whether in the east or in the west, it is important to be clear about precisely what we mean by the notion of a *cleavage*, which implies much more than a mere division, more even than an outright conflict, between two sets of people. In the 1980s, for example, before the end of the Cold War, there was a sharp division in a number of countries between those who favoured the continued deployment of nuclear missiles and those who favoured nuclear disarmament. This division cut deep, and often led to violent conflict, in the form of protests and street demonstrations. It was also pervasive, being an important item on the political agenda in countries as diverse as the United Kingdom, Italy, West Germany and the Netherlands. But the nuclear missile issue, although acute, pervasive, divisive and conflictual, did not constitute a fundamental cleavage in the sense identified by Lipset and Rokkan, for whom a cleavage has three quite specific connotations (Bartolini and Mair, 1990: 212–249; Bartolini, 2000).

First, a cleavage involves a social division that separates people who can be distinguished from one another in terms of key social-structural characteristics such as occupation, status, religion or ethnicity. Thus a cleavage may separate workers from employers, or Catholics from Protestants, or, as in Belgium, those who speak French from those who speak Dutch, or, as in Latvia, for example, those who are ethnically Latvian from those who are ethnically Russian. A cleavage cannot be defined at the political level alone (as with the division over nuclear disarmament, for example).

Second, the groups involved in the division must be conscious of their collective identity – as workers or employers, or as Latvians or Russians, for example – and be willing to act on this basis. This sense of collective identity is of crucial importance in the emergence and maintenance of cleavages. Without it, no 'objective' social division will be transformed into a salient socio-political cleavage. For example, although the gender division between men and women remains one of the most significant social divisions in all western societies, it has never really generated the sense of collective gender identity that could turn gender into a salient basis for a major political division (Lovenduski, 1986; Kaplan, 1992). Despite widespread feminist mobilization, Iceland is still the only west European country to have ever produced a distinct and important women's party.

Third, a cleavage must be expressed in organizational terms. This is typically achieved as a result of the activities of a trade union, a church, a political party, or some other organization that gives formal institutional expression to the interests of those on one side of the division. In Britain, for example, although an objective social reality of distinctive national groups has always existed in Scotland and Wales, and although there has also been a clear collective sense of national identity within these groups, Welsh and Scottish nationalist politics have only sporadically achieved organizational expression. Hence the nationalist cleavage in Britain has often been dormant, although currently it has acquired a relatively strong articulation. In Ireland, by contrast, and in Irish relations with Britain, it was one of the dominant elements in mass politics prior to Irish independence, and continued to shape electoral alignments well into the twentieth century. In Northern Ireland, of course, it was, and still is, all-consuming.

It is important to maintain an emphasis on each of the three components of a cleavage, because this helps us to understand how cleavages can persist or decay. A change in the cleavage structure of a society can occur as a result of changes in the social divisions that underpin cleavages, as a result of changes in the sense of collective identity that allows cleavages to be perceived by those involved, or as a result of changes in the organizational structure that gives political expression to cleavages. (For two valuable recent assessments, see Bornschier, 2010; Enyedi and Deegan-Krause, 2010.) As we shall see, recent experiences in Europe suggest evidence of change in all three components.

## 9.3  Traditional cleavage structures

In their seminal analysis of European political development, Lipset and Rokkan (1967) argued that the parameters that determined contemporary political alignments resulted from the interaction of four major historic cleavages. The first of these was the cleavage that divided the dominant culture (in the centre of the state and nation) from subject cultures (in the periphery). The second was the cleavage that divided church from state. The third was the cleavage dividing those involved in the primary economy (typically in the countryside) from those in the secondary economy (typically in the town). The fourth was the cleavage that divided employers from workers (Lipset and Rokkan, 1967: 13–26; reprinted in shorter form in Mair, 1990: 99–111; see also Rokkan, 1970: Chapter 3).

### 9.3.1  The centre–periphery cleavage

The first of the cleavages to which Lipset and Rokkan refer is that between the *subject culture* and the *dominant culture*, now more commonly described as the cleavage between a country's socio-political *centre* and its *periphery*. This centre–periphery cleavage derives from the era during which both the boundaries and the political authority of modern European states were being forged. When these modern states were being built, an inevitable clash emerged. On one side were those, typically at the centre of the political system, who sought to standardize the laws, markets and cultures that lay within state boundaries. On the other side were those, normally on the periphery of the new states, who sought to preserve their independence and autonomy.

The desire for autonomy was rooted in a variety of factors (Keating, 2008). In some cases linguistic or minority national groups resisted the encroachment of what they regarded as essentially foreign government. In other cases religious groups resisted the new codes, customs and values imposed from the centre. Either way, pockets of resistance to centralization persisted in many of the developing nation-states. In some cases this resistance led eventually to secession, as when southern Ireland left the United Kingdom. In some cases it led to the granting of substantial local autonomy within the largest state, as with the separate Dutch-speaking (Flemish) and French-speaking (Walloon) communities in Belgium. In some cases it ended with effective absorption, as with the Breton minority in north-west France. The most common outcome, however, of this conflict between state-builders and subject populations was a diffuse but persistent tension between the two. This created a centre–periphery cleavage in many European countries that remains visible to this day. It manifests itself in patterns of political attitude and voting behaviour, as well as in the persistence of small ethnic, linguistic or other cultural minorities. The centre–periphery cleavage is salient even among some of the 'smaller' democracies in which the geographic, as opposed to the socio-political, distance between the centre and the periphery is not very large. It is also marked in a number of the post-communist countries, not least as a result of boundary problems that were never solved, or were sometimes even created, during the communist period. The division between ethnic Latvians and Russians is one obvious case in point, as is that between the Slovak majority and Hungarian minority in Slovakia.

### 9.3.2 The church–state cleavage

The process of state-building also created a second cleavage, at once more sharply defined and more critical. This involved the conflict between state-builders and the church, a conflict epitomized by the secular challenge posed by the French Revolution more than 200 years ago. This was, and remains, a conflict about rights and privileges. It had to do with whether policies on crucial questions of public morality and, above all, education would be determined by the state or by the church.

The church–state cleavage developed in very different ways in Protestant and Catholic societies. The newly formed Protestant churches were essentially national churches that had largely become 'agents of the state' (Lipset and Rokkan, 1967: 15). They thus had little incentive to challenge the policies of the state. Indeed, it was often only as a result of an alliance with the state that these churches had been able to establish themselves as legal entities. (This was not always the case. In the Netherlands, for example, the more fundamentalist Protestant adherents of the Dutch Reformed Church also opposed the secular ideas of the French Revolution in 1789, prompting the creation of the Anti-Revolutionary Party, a party that remained a significant independent electoral force until the end of the 1970s, when it merged with two other Christian parties into the CDA.)

In the case of the Catholic church, the potential for conflict with the state was enormous. First, the Catholic church saw itself as being 'above' the state, owing its allegiance to a supranational religious organization based in the Vatican. Second, the Catholic church persistently sought to insulate its adherents from secularizing tendencies, creating an autonomous cultural environment that proved resistant to state penetration. Thus Catholics sought to maintain their own independent schools, and rejected state provision of secular education. They also sought to ensure that state laws on issues of public morality, such as divorce and censorship, would reflect Catholic values. Conflict between church and state was thus almost inevitable. This was obviously true in those countries where Catholics constituted a substantial religious minority, as in the Netherlands and Germany. It was also true, however, in countries such as France and Italy. In both countries, although the population was nominally all Catholic, the French Revolution has prompted a major secular impetus that found expression in the anticlericalism of the early liberal and radical parties. In the exceptional case of Ireland, where the vast majority of the population remained practising Catholics, secularism failed to take root, and, until relatively recently, state policy actually enshrined the Catholic belief system. Following the fall of communism, issues of religious freedom and control also re-emerged in eastern Europe, and proved especially pronounced in Catholic Poland.

Thus the practical impact of the church–state cleavage was very unevenly distributed, proving a major source of political mobilization only in those countries with a substantial Catholic minority. In those countries, as we have seen, Christian democratic parties now constitute a powerful electoral force. In the Protestant north and east of Europe, on the other hand, an accommodation between church and state was reached without too much difficulty.

No substantial religious cleavage emerged, and so room was left for the mobilization of alternative cleavages (for a recent overview, see Madeley and Enyedi, 2003; see also Kalyvas, 1996; Ertman, 2009).

That said, there is now increasing evidence of a partial revival of the religious cleavage, albeit in a different form than used to be the case in Europe. In this new guise, a religious cleavage emerges between a largely immigrant, or immigrant-descended Muslim minority, on the one hand, and the indigenous Christian and/or secular majority, on the other. This division has always been present, but it has only recently become politicized, not least as a result of reactions to 9/11. The issues involved are in some ways familiar: as in past conflicts between Catholics and the state, the question is whether and to what extent the Muslim minority can be expected to integrate, or whether separate schools and cultural practices can be tolerated. At the beginning of the twenty-first century these issues took on a particularly sharp and often polarized character in Belgium, Denmark, France and the Netherlands in particular, fuelling violence and protest actions, on the one hand, and encouraging support for far-right populist parties, on the other. But while the protagonists who are now involved may be new, the sense of cleavage, and the logic of the division itself, is familiar.

### 9.3.3  The rural–urban cleavage

The third cleavage identified by Lipset and Rokkan concerns the conflict between the traditionally dominant rural interests and the new commercial and industrial classes of the cities. This conflict was already apparent in the medieval period, but became particularly acute with the beginning of the Industrial Revolution. Although acute, however, the rural–urban cleavage was not always persistent. In Britain and Germany in particular, but also in most of the rest of continental western Europe, divisions between the two groups did not form an enduring partisan conflict. In Scandinavia, on the other hand, as well as in parts of eastern Europe, urban interests proved much more dominant, and sustained rural opposition to the urban elites resulted in the creation of powerful agrarian parties that persisted – albeit in a modified form – into the beginning of the twenty-first century.

But although the rural–urban cleavage may now be largely dormant in relation to conflicts between traditional landed and urban interests, there is also a sense in which the cleavage may now be acquiring a new, post-industrial relevance. Three factors are involved here. First, like the United States, many European countries now face severe problems in balancing the interests of city and country, problems that often derive from the concentrations of urban poverty and racial tension in inner cities, the remedies for which are seen to demand increasing government intervention and expenditure. At the same time, many more wealthy citizens flee inner cities in search of suburban and/or rural comforts, eroding the tax base of cities while continuing to take advantage of their services, and thus generating a new clash of interests between city and country. Second, at least within the countries of the European Union (see Chapter 5), a new and sometimes violent conflict has arisen as a result of the drive to free the movement of agricultural produce between countries while reducing subsidies to farmers. City dwellers clearly favour the cheaper food produced by both strategies, but farmers are increasingly discontented with the threatened slump in their standard of living. Third, urban–rural interests may also clash over values, and over the manner in which the countryside is managed. In Britain in 2003 and 2004, for example, a very bitter and sometimes violent row broke out between supporters of the primarily urban Labour Party and members of the newly formed Countryside Alliance over the question of whether fox-hunting should be banned. This was a long-favoured preference of Labour, but was resisted very heavily by those involved in the sport. Relations between Labour and many country-dwellers had already been soured by opposition to the slaughter policy pursued by Labour during the outbreak of a foot and mouth epidemic among cattle and sheep. In this case the traditional cleavage, although marginal, was experienced with great intensity.

Farmers now make up a very small proportion of the workforce in most western European countries, of course, and so it is unlikely that they could generate and sustain major new agrarian political movements. But there are often enough of them (in France, for example) to tip the balance between the existing parties, and they can therefore pose a threat to their traditional representatives on the centre right. They also form an important lobby group (see Chapter 13), and anyone who recalls the very bitter conflict between the United Kingdom and France over beef exports in the late 1990s will need no reminding of the political weight that farmers can wield.

### 9.3.4 The class cleavage

By far the most important cleavage to emerge from the Industrial Revolution was the conflict between the owners of capital together with their allies among the established elites, on the one hand, and the newly emerging working class, on the other. The process of industrialization meant that, throughout nineteenth-century Europe, workers became increasingly concentrated in an essentially urban factory system. This provided a social environment in which they began to develop organizations, both trade unions and political parties, that sought to improve their conditions of work and to enhance their life chances. The increasing concentration of production enabled the organizations of the emerging working class to compensate for their lack of economic resources by mobilizing large groups of workers in collective action.

However, although the class cleavage is present in all western European countries, its organizational expression shows at least two contrasting patterns (Bartolini, 2000). In all countries during the Industrial Revolution, and in the majority of countries thereafter, the political demands of workers were expressed by a socialist party. In the wake of the Russian Revolution of 1917, as we have seen, more radical workers shifted towards a communist alternative, and in a small number of countries support for such parties equalled and even surpassed that of the Socialist Party. According to Lipset and Rokkan (1967: 21–23), much of the explanation for the relative success of communist parties lies in how bourgeois elites first responded to the workers' demands. Where they were more accommodating and pragmatic, as in Scandinavia and Britain, workers eschewed radical alternatives and became integrated into national politics. Where the bourgeois response was more repressive, and the extension of political and social rights to the working class was resisted most adamantly – as in France, Germany, Italy and Spain – workers adopted a more radical agenda, preparing the ground for the later acceptance of communist parties. Thus, even though class cleavage has been characteristic of all European democracies, the political expression of working-class interests has in some countries been divided between a socialist party and a communist party, although this political division between socialists and communists does not itself have the properties of a separate cleavage as we have outlined them.

## 9.3.5 The interaction of different cleavages

History has left a complex mosaic of social and political divisions in Europe. The cleavage between workers and employers has found expression in almost every European country, both east and west, but cleavages relating to centre–periphery, rural–urban divisions, or to church–state relations emerged in ways that were specific to particular countries. Thus, although the major *similarities* between the western European political systems in particular derive from the class cleavage, the major *differences* between them can be explained to a large extent by the idiosyncratic development of other, often pre-industrial, social cleavages.

One way to distinguish these western European countries is in terms of the interaction between the various cleavages that are present in the system. As the class cleavage emerged in Austria, for example, it overlapped the important church–state cleavage. This resulted in a Christian Democratic Party, which represents both 'owners' and the church, and a Socialist Party, which represents both workers and anticlericals. The two key cleavages cut along the same lines.

In the United Kingdom, in contrast, a single social cleavage has come to dominate politics. Church–state tensions were largely resolved through the creation of a national church during the Reformation, and the rural–urban cleavage was resolved when the landed aristocracy and the emerging industrial capitalists made common cause during the nineteenth century. The most important centre–periphery tensions largely evaporated in 1921, with the secession of southern Ireland from the United Kingdom, a radical break that also helped to solve lingering problems of church–state relations reflected in opposition between the overwhelmingly Catholic Ireland and largely Protestant Britain. Until the partial re-emergence of Scottish and Welsh nationalism in the 1970s, therefore, nothing remained to interact with the class cleavage in Britain itself, and the result has been the emergence of two large political blocs that were distinguished from each other almost exclusively on the basis of their traditional class appeals. As Pulzer (1967: 98) once famously noted: 'Class is the basis of British politics; all else is mere embellishment and detail.'

In other cases, important cleavages cut across one another. In the Netherlands, as we have seen, the church–state cleavage first resulted in the creation of the three different forces, representing Catholics, Protestants and anticlericals. When the class cleavage emerged, however, it cut across the church–state cleavage. This implied the formation of a new party, the Labour Party (PvdA), which opposed both the religious parties and the bourgeois anticlerical Liberal Party. In France, too, the church–state cleavage cuts across the class cleavage. The Catholic Popular Republican Movement (MRP) opposed the secular socialists and the communists on the one hand and the secular bourgeois liberals and radicals on the other, finding reasonably common ground with the more religiously inclined conservative Gaullist movement. In terms of social and economic policy, however, the MRP looked left and found itself making common cause with the workers' parties against the liberals, radicals and Gaullists.

Overall, therefore, what we might think of as the *cleavage structure* of a particular society has two distinct features. The first has to do with the particular cleavages that have survived historically as important lines of social and political division. The second has to do with the extent to which these important lines of division cut across one another. Thus a religious cleavage and a class cleavage may both run along the same lines (if all workers are Catholic, for example, and all owners are Protestant), or they may cut across one another (if whether or not someone is a Protestant or Catholic has no bearing on whether he or she is a worker). It is this pattern of

## BOX 9.1: TRADITIONAL CLEAVAGE STRUCTURES

### Denmark

The rural–urban cleavage has been particularly important in Danish politics, as in Scandinavian politics more generally, and Danish farmers have traditionally supported the Liberal Party. In recent decades, as the Liberals have extended their appeal into the towns and cities, the relevance of this cleavage has clearly waned. The main cleavage within traditional politics has been the class cleavage, promoting both the Social Democrats and the Socialist People's Party on the left, and the Conservatives on the right. There is also a small religious cleavage, involving mainly campaigns against permissiveness and alcohol consumption. In recent years, in common with the Netherlands, a new anti-immigration divide has begun to fuel support for the far right.

### France

Three cross-cutting cleavages have been of major importance in post-war France: a class cleavage, separating the right from the left; a religious cleavage, separating the Gaullists, the National Front and the Catholic groups within the UDF from the socialists, the communists, and the liberal and conservative elements within the UDF; and a centre–periphery tension that pervades all parties and reflects the inevitable and persistent response to the domination of Paris. Whether new divisions concerning Europe, concerning immigrants, or even concerning religion have the capacity to become translated into real cleavages is still an open question. Although the broad left–right division has remained remarkably stable in France, the individual parties and other organizations that mobilize on left and right have never been particularly strong.

### Germany

For much of the post-war period, the class cleavage has been the dominant cleavage in Germany, cross-cut by a formerly much stronger church–state cleavage. Rural–urban tensions, which proved important in the nineteenth century, have now effectively disappeared. Since the reunification of east and west in 1990, Germany has experienced the re-emergence of a version of the centre–periphery cleavage, with the interests of the relatively poorer east conflicting with those of the richer west. Germany was also seen as one of the first countries to reflect an important divide between the old and the new politics on the left, although it now seems that the new politics challenge is being increasingly absorbed within conventional left–right competition.

### Italy

Much like France, post-war Italy also experienced the three separate but cross-cutting cleavages of class, religion, and centre–periphery. Growing secularization undermined the salience of the religious divide, and led Italy to adopt legislation permitting both divorce and abortion. In the 1990s the dominant Christian Democrat Party broke apart, and was replaced in part by the secular Forza Italia, led by Silvio Berlusconi. The class cleavage has also waned, particularly since the split in the Communist Party and the formation of the more moderate Democratic Party. Centre–periphery tensions, on the other hand, are acquiring a new and more powerful resonance. This is not only reflected in the growth of the Northern League, but is also exacerbated by the persistent inequalities between the richer north and the poorer south.

### Netherlands

Cleavages of class and religion are also the dominant cleavages in Dutch politics, although increased secularization and a blurring of class boundaries have tended to erode the strongly 'pillarized' subcultures on which the traditional cleavage structure in the Netherlands rested. Although there are few if any remaining centre–periphery tensions in the Netherlands – the country is simply too small for these – local identities prove remarkably strong, and continue to be sustained by the very uneven geographic distribution of the different religious groups. In recent years the rise of the far right has pushed established social divisions between the indigenous and immigrant populations to the top of the political agenda.

### Poland

One of the key divisions within contemporary Polish politics concerns the scale and pace of the transition to a full market economy, and the relative success of the SLD in the first post-communist elections offered a good indicator of the desire among many voters to maintain a reasonable level of welfarism and social protection. A second major division in Poland is reflected in the survival of the church–state cleavage. Poland is a predominantly Catholic country, with some of the highest levels of religiosity and church attendance in modern Europe, and the post-communist period has seen frequent clashes between advocates of Catholic values, on the one hand, and more liberal or secular forces, on the other. Inevitably, these disputes became particularly acute during the period in which the new institutions were being designed. A third divide opposes the urban, industrial and service economy to the traditional rural economy, which remains very important in Poland. Finally, overlapping with many of these conflicts, as well as building upon them, there is a new divide between westernization and nationalism, a divide that also finds expression in the opposition between various pro- and anti-EU forces. On this last issue there is now probably more consensus among the political elites than among the general public.

### Spain

Two cleavages clearly dominate Spanish politics: the class cleavage and the centre–periphery cleavage. Although the strength of the Socialist Party might suggest that class is substantially more important, no other western European country contains such a range or variety of regionalist and nationalist parties. At the same time, however, the class cleavage also operates within the regional party systems, with left–right divisions cutting across local solidarities. Despite a long tradition of church–state conflict, religion has had a surprisingly marginal impact on politics since the transition to democracy.

### United Kingdom

Britain has perhaps the simplest cleavage structure in Europe. Class was by far the dominant traditional cleavage, with the less significant religious and rural–urban divisions having waned in the nineteenth century. A robust centre–periphery cleavage does persist, however, reflecting the multinational character of the United Kingdom state, and pitting Scottish, Welsh and Irish nationalists against the English centre. Most recently, it seems that the bitter conflict resulting from the cleavage between nationalists and unionists in Northern Ireland is finally coming to an end. This has always been the most bitterly contested division in the politics of the United Kingdom, but since it is largely confined to Northern Ireland, it has had little effect on mass politics in mainland Britain.

interaction between cleavages that has underpinned the traditional structure of party competition in most western European states, and which also played a major role in shaping the interwar patterns of those states that were later to come under Soviet control.

## 9.4 The persistence of cleavages and the freezing of party systems

Following the path-breaking work of Lipset and Rokkan, it became common to speak of the *freezing* of western European party systems at about the time of the 1920s as a result of the remarkable persistence of the cleavages that underpin party politics. Cleavages could persist for four main reasons. First, they could persist when the interests with which the cleavage was concerned remained relevant, and the groups that were polarized retained a sense of collective identity. Second, major alternative political identities were likely to be mobilized only when substantial bodies of new votes were incorporated into mass politics, and no such large-scale incorporation has occurred since the granting of universal suffrage. Third, the rules of the game are such that they tended to favour the persistence of those parties that devised the rules in the first place. Fourth, parties could attempt to isolate their supporters from competitors and thereby 'narrow' the electoral market. Let us look at these elements more closely.

Cleavages persist first because they concern people who are divided from one another on the basis of real and enduring issues. As long as workers continue to feel that they have a common interest that is distinct from the interest of employers, or farmers, for example, and as long as this remains relevant at the level of politics and government, the cleavage around which workers are aligned is likely to persist. Conversely, if the social distinctiveness of being a worker becomes blurred, or if it is no longer seen to be relevant politically, the class cleavage might become dormant. (This is precisely the argument that is now cited to emphasize the changing character of contemporary European politics.)

Second, cleavages persist because European electorates are now fully mobilized (Lipset and Rokkan, 1967; Rokkan, 1970). This is an important argument, and it helps explain why the freezing of many European party systems is typically said to have occurred around the 1920s. According to Lipset and Rokkan, the political alignments that are forged when a group of voters is newly enfranchised tend to prove both strong and enduring. Hence the importance of the 1920s, the period when universal suffrage was generally introduced. This is not, of course, to suggest that the cleavages that were relevant in the 1920s will always remain salient. Rather, it implies that subsequent political realignments involve winning the support of voters who are already aligned in terms of a particular cleavage structure, a more difficult task than attracting new voters with no established alignments. Another way of thinking of this is to consider the period leading up to universal suffrage as having set the parties in motion. Thereafter, these self-same parties will tend to hold on to their monopoly of representation.

The third explanation for the persistence of cleavages has to do with the laws that govern the conduct of elections. As we shall see in Chapter 11, the first-past-the-post electoral system that operates in Britain (and the United States) is often said to favour the development of a two-party system. The proportional representation (PR) systems that operate in the majority of western European states are more conducive to multiparty politics. It might be argued that by not penalizing minority parties, PR electoral systems help maintain minor cleavages. Conversely, first-past-the-post systems, by squeezing out small parties, may eliminate minor cleavages and allow the most salient cleavage to dominate the system as a whole. As Lipset and Rokkan (1967: 30; see also Sartori, 1987) forcefully remind us, however, the rules of the game do not emerge out of thin air; rather, they are legislated by political parties. They will therefore tend to protect established interests. Similarly, in a separate analysis of electoral systems, Rokkan (1970: 147–168) argued that the adoption of PR *resulted from*, rather than *led to*, multiparty politics. Proportional representation electoral systems were adopted in countries where there were distinct cultural or linguistic minorities. When the mass working class was enfranchised in countries where other cleavages were already present, the rules of the game were often modified to ensure the continued representation of the existing smaller parties. This, of course, facilitated the persistence of the cleavages along which they aligned.

A fourth factor that encourages the persistence of cleavages has to do with party organization (see Chapter 10). In a desire to insulate party supporters from the competing appeals of their opponents, many European parties initially involved themselves in a host of social activities. They attempted to establish a presence in many different areas of their individual supporters' lives, organizing social clubs, welfare services, recreational facilities, and the like, thus offering adherents a range of services to sustain them 'from the cradle to the grave'. Although such behaviour was mainly a characteristic of working-class socialist parties (the best account is in Roth, 1963), this process of *encapsulation* was also attempted by some of the Christian parties, notably the old Catholic People's Party in the Netherlands (Bakvis, 1981) and the People's Party in Austria (Diamant, 1958; see also Houska, 1985). This process of integrating and encapsulating supporters thus characterized many of the new mass parties that challenged the most elitist traditional cadre parties in the era of popular enfranchisement (Duverger, 1954; Neumann, 1956; Katz and Mair, 1995). These mass parties helped to create and sustain specific political subcultures in which they hoped that party voters would express a more permanent sense of 'belonging' rather than make a more instrumental, and changeable, policy-oriented voting decision. These mass parties attempted to corner the electoral market by building long-term voter attachments. To the extent that they succeeded, they stabilized cleavage structures, and the party systems on which these were based.

The persistence of cleavages and party systems is underlined most clearly in Lipset and Rokkan's work, which has since become the benchmark for many subsequent analyses of western European party systems. Writing from the perspective of the late 1960s, and noting that the last new cleavage that had emerged had been the class cleavage, solidified some 40 years before, Lipset and Rokkan (1967: 50) rounded off their analysis with the much cited conclusion that 'the party systems of the late 1960s reflect, with few but significant exceptions, the cleavage structures of the 1920s. ... The party alternatives, and in remarkably many cases the party organizations, are older than the majorities of the national electorates.' This was to become known as the *freezing hypothesis* – the hypothesis that party systems in western Europe had 'frozen' into place in the 1920s, and hence that any subsequent changes will have proved either marginal or temporary (Mair, 2001).

The freezing hypothesis offered an influential theoretical and historical explanation for the stability of European electoral behaviour in the 1950s and 1960s. This was the period in which the potentially vulnerable new West German party system had begun to be stabilized by the success of Konrad Adenauer's Christian Democrats, and by the abandonment of radical policies by the Social Democrats in 1959. It was the period in which the policies of the Labour Party in Britain had become almost indistinguishable from those of the centrist Conservative government in a process of convergence that became popularly known as 'Butskellism', a neologism derived from the names of R.A. Butler, then Conservative treasury minister, and Hugh Gaitskell, then leader of the Labour Party. It was the period in which the polarized party system of Italy seemed set to stabilize under the centre-right control of the Christian Democrats, and in which the unstable French Fourth Republic had been replaced by the potentially more stable presidential system of the Fifth Republic. It was the period of unchanging social democratic hegemony in Scandinavia. In more general terms, it was a period described by some observers as one in which there was a 'waning of opposition' (Kirchheimer, 1957, 1966) and an 'end of ideology' (Bell, 1960).

This seemingly pervasive political consensus, together with the marked increase in mass prosperity that characterized western Europe in the first post-war decades, clearly enhanced the prospects for democratic stability in the continent. It also seemed to be accounted for rather neatly by the processes of inertia suggested by Lipset and Rokkan. When Rose and Urwin set out in the late 1960s to conduct the first real empirical test of the freezing hypothesis, they found that

> **"** whatever index of change is used ... the picture is the same: the electoral strength of most parties in Western nations since the war has changed very little from election to election, from decade to decade, or within the lifespan of a generation ... the first priority of social scientists concerned with the development of parties and party systems since 1945 is to explain the absence of change in a far from static period in political history.
>
> *(Rose and Urwin, 1970: 295)* **"**

## 9.5 From persistence to change

Thus political scientists became convinced during the late 1960s that western European party politics had settled down into a very stable pattern. However, while Lipset, Rokkan and others were putting the finishing touches to their various analyses of persistence, the image of tranquillity began to be rudely shattered. Signs of change had actually been apparent already in 1968, when student protests and violent street demonstrations raged throughout western Europe and the United States. There were also signs of a challenge to the consensus within more mainstream politics, however.

In Norway, for example, the country on which Rokkan based much of his initial theories, the stability of politics was fractured in the early 1970s when a referendum on Norway's entry into the then European Community reawakened the dormant centre–periphery conflict, and provoked major splits in the traditional parties. In the United Kingdom in 1974, nationalist parties from Scotland and Wales won a record share of the vote, while in Northern Ireland the political violence that had erupted in 1968 continued unabated, claiming almost 500 lives in 1972 alone. In Belgium, the rise of Flemish and Walloon nationalist movements provoked major splits in all three traditional parties, and effectively led to the emergence of two separate party systems – one Dutch-speaking and one French-speaking. In the Netherlands, the major Catholic party and its two traditional Protestant opponents were forced into an electoral alliance in order to stave off their severe electoral losses. Meanwhile, in Italy in 1976, the Communist Party won its highest share ever of the vote, and came within 5 per cent of overtaking the ruling Christian Democrats – a gain that prompted a stern warning from the US State Department about the dangers of bringing communists into government. In France in 1974, a candidate supported by both the socialists and the communists came within 1 per cent of finally snatching the presidency from the centre right. In short, it now seemed to be the case that 'a week is a long time in politics', as former British Labour leader Harold Wilson once observed. *Stability* was the catchword of the 1950s and the 1960s. *Change* was to become the catchword of the 1970s.

Nowhere were these watershed changes of the 1970s better illustrated than in Denmark in 1973. For many scholars this was also seen at the time as a major turning point, especially since Denmark had long been regarded as 'one of the most dull countries to deal with for a student of voting behaviour' (Pedersen, 1987). This dull image was to be utterly transformed by the election of December 1973, however, when the number of parties winning representation in the Danish parliament suddenly doubled from five to ten, and when the combined vote share of the four parties that had traditionally dominated Danish politics – Social Democrats, Social Liberals, Liberals and Conservatives – fell more or less overnight from 84 per cent to just 58 per cent. Indeed, it was precisely in that election of some 30 years ago that the first signs of the re-emergence of the far right were seen, in that a very right-wing anti-tax party, the Progress Party, suddenly emerged as the second largest party. These dramatic changes occurred during a period of only 27 months following the previous Danish election, and are summarized in Table 9.1.

Table 9.1 shows big changes in the vote shares of the parties, and on this basis we can calculate what is now known as *the index of aggregate electoral volatility*, one of the standard measures of electoral change (Pedersen, 1979, 1983). The Progress Party gained almost 16 per cent of the vote. Other gains were made by the Centre Democrats (7.8), Communists (2.2), Christians (2.0) and Justice Party (1.2). The Social Democrats lost 11.7 per cent of the vote. Other losses were suffered by the Conservatives (–7.5), Liberals (–3.3), Social Liberals (–3.2) and Socialist People's

**TABLE 9.1** Denmark's 'earthquake' election of 1973

|  | 1971 | | 1973 | |
|---|---|---|---|---|
|  | **% of votes** | **Seats** | **% of votes** | **Seats** |
| Social Democrats | 37.3 | 70 | 25.6 | 46 |
| Conservatives | 16.7 | 31 | 9.2 | 16 |
| Liberals | 15.6 | 30 | 12.3 | 22 |
| Social Liberals | 14.4 | 27 | 11.2 | 20 |
| Socialist People's Party | 9.1 | 17 | 6.0 | 11 |
| Christian People's Party | 2.0 | – | 4.0 | 7 |
| Justice Party | 1.7 | – | 2.9 | 5 |
| Left Socialists | 1.6 | – | 1.5 | – |
| Communists | 1.4 | – | 3.6 | 6 |
| Progress Party | – | – | 15.9 | 28 |
| Centre Democrats | – | – | 7.8 | 14 |
| Others | 0.2 | – | – | – |
| Total | 100.0 | 175 | 100.0 | 175 |

*Source*: Unless otherwise stated, the sources for all tables in Chapter 9 are as those for Table 8.1 above.

Party (–3.1). If we summarize these changes by reference to Pedersen's index, then we see that the aggregate (or total) electoral volatility in Denmark between 1971 and 1973 was 29.1 per cent, a very high figure indeed.[1] During the 1960s, for example, volatility in Denmark averaged 8.7 per cent. In the 1950s it averaged just 5.5 per cent (see Table 9.9 later). This election, although old, is therefore a valuable illustration of how extensive electoral change can be.

The first comprehensive analysis of changing levels of electoral volatility in western Europe came, appropriately enough, from a Danish researcher, Mogens Pedersen (1979, 1983), whose work had been stimulated partly by the extraordinary level of change in his own country. Pedersen documented the changes that were also evident in Norway and the Netherlands and, to a lesser extent, in Switzerland, the United Kingdom, Finland and Sweden. His work challenged the conclusions of both Lipset and Rokkan and Rose and Urwin, and suggested that there had been a significant 'unfreezing' of European party systems. A similar conclusion was reached by Maguire, who replicated and updated Rose and Urwin's analysis at the end of the 1970s. Just one decade later, using identical statistical measures to Rose and Urwin, Maguire found evidence of much greater instability and argued that western European party systems 'cannot now be regarded as inherently stable structures' (Maguire, 1983: 92). Although the priority stated by Rose and Urwin at the end of the 1960s had been to explain stability, by the end of the 1970s, for Maguire, the priority had become to explain why many party systems seemed to be subject to sudden change (see also Dalton *et al.*, 1984; Crewe and Denver, 1985).

## 9.6  Change in European cleavage structures and electoral behaviour

The argument that post-1970s party systems in western Europe had entered a period of quite sudden and pervasive change is by now a received wisdom, with much of this change being attributed to fallout from the decline of traditional cleavages (e.g., Inglehart, 1984; Franklin *et al.*, 1992; Dalton and Wattenberg, 2000). Indeed, contrary to the conclusions reached by Lipset and Rokkan, most observers now prefer to speak of the *de*freezing of traditional political alignments and party systems. Needless to say, these arguments apply only to the long-standing party systems of Europe. In the post-communist systems in particular, there was no structure of mass democratic politics that could have become frozen through the century, and hence the notion of defreezing is hardly relevant. That said, students of contemporary post-communist alignments do point to continuities with the alignments that once characterized the interwar democracies in eastern Europe, suggesting that even if the traditional cleavage structure was dormant under communism, it has now been at least partially revived (Kitschelt *et al.*, 1999).

Among the long-standing democracies, and following our earlier definition, cleavages can be subject to erosion or change in three distinct ways. First, the strength of cleavages may be affected

---

[1] Calculations of levels of aggregate volatility must be treated very carefully, however, as the figures may be artificially raised as a result of one-off party splits and mergers. In this Danish example, for instance, the Centre Democrats were not a wholly new party, but rather a split from the Social Democrats. A more realistic index of volatility would therefore measure change in 1973 by comparing the combined vote share of the divided parties (25.6 + 7.8 = 33.4 per cent) with the previous vote share of the Social Democrats (37.3 per cent) in order to produce a figure of 3.9 per cent for the net party change and a figure of 21.2 per cent for the election as a whole (see Bartolini and Mair, 1990: 311–312). Subsequent calculations of levels of electoral volatility reported in this chapter follow this latter rule.

by changes in the social structure, such as through shifting or blurring class and occupational boundaries, or through changes in religious affiliation. Second, the strength of cleavages may be affected by changes in collective identities and behaviour, such as when workers might no longer feel a sense of collective identity as workers, or when Catholics might no longer act in concert in support of particular political preferences. Third, the strength of cleavages may be affected by the organizational and ideological behaviour of parties, such as when parties begin to downplay their appeals to specific social or cultural constituencies.

For the purposes of this chapter, we now want to look briefly at the evidence of change in cleavage strength in the first two of these three factors, focusing mainly on the period from the 1950s to the 1980s, when a lot of the social change in particular is believed to have taken place. From the 1990s onwards the pace of change slackened, and most of the trends bottomed out. Later, in Chapters 10 and 14, we shall be paying much closer attention to party organizational and programmatic change (see also Kirchheimer, 1966; Katz and Mair, 1995).

## 9.6.1 Changing social structure

The last half-century in western Europe has witnessed a profound change in social structure and life chances, a change that has clearly fed into and fuelled the changing patterns of politics and political representation. It is not only important here to recognize that the last half-century has seen a major sea change in the way people earn their livings. This will already be all too familiar to even the most cursory observer. What is at least as important is to recognize that, within the different sectors, technological changes and economic modernization have led to the erosion of many traditional social boundaries. As the population has become more educated and more prosperous, lifestyles have begun to converge, and previous lines of division between different sectors of the population have tended to become blurred. In 1960, for example, women constituted an average of just 31 per cent of the west European labour force, whereas in 2005 the figure in most countries in Europe, including the post-communist democracies, was around 45 per cent. Yet another indicator of change can be seen in the decline in the numbers of people belonging to the traditional blue-collar working class. The proportion of manual workers in the labour force fell from an average of close to 50 per cent in western Europe in 1960 to substantially less than 40 per cent at the turn of the century, with the service sector emerging as by far the largest employment sector (Crouch, 2008). In other words, as Ambrosius and Hubbard (1989: 76, 78) put it, dating the change to the 1960s in particular, post-war western Europe has witnessed the crossing of a major 'socio-historical watershed', while modernization in the eastern Europe after 1990 has led to a rapid convergence in occupational structures and lifestyles across the entire European Union.

Nor was it just the economic and occupational categories that were changing in the 1960s and after. Religious identities and practice were also subject to erosion as western Europe in general drifted towards a more secular society. One of the first comprehensive studies to tap into this change, the World Values Survey of 1981–1982, revealed some striking contrasts (Inglehart, 1990: 191). Thus while some 83 per cent of those surveyed in the oldest cohorts (aged 65 or more) in western Europe proved willing to describe themselves as 'a religious person', this was true of only 53 per cent of those who were then in the youngest cohorts (aged 15 to 24). Already by then, of course, religious practice had also fallen off considerably. In West Germany in the late 1980s, for example, only 25 per cent of the electorate regularly attended church – as against 40 per cent in the 1950s. Among Catholics alone, regular church attendance had fallen from over 50 per cent to just 30 per cent in the same period. In Ireland, where Catholicism had long held a particularly powerful sway, figures indicated that weekly church attendance had fallen from 81 per cent in 1990 to just 67 per cent four years later (Hardiman and Whelan, 1998: 72). This figure is likely to have fallen even further following the more recent revelations of child abuse in Catholic schools and other institutions. More generally, a survey of values in Europe 2000 found that the proportion of Europeans who regularly attended church was only 30 per cent, with a further 30 per cent never attending, and with the remaining 40 per cent attending only on special occasions (Halman *et al.*, 2005: 63).

It is perhaps in the Netherlands that this widespread process of secularization has proved the most striking – and it also in the Netherlands that it has been most tellingly documented, and can best be illustrated (see Andeweg and Irwin, 2009). Religious identity and practice have always constituted a key component in Dutch culture, where the long-standing tolerance of religious differences had been fostered by the existence of quite a sharp – or *pillarized* – division between three main Christian denominations: Catholic, Protestant and Calvinist. In 1956 members of these three main denominations accounted for more than 75 per cent of the Dutch electorate, and among those members the numbers regularly attending church services accounted for more than half the electorate (Table 9.2). In other words, these religious affiliations were more than simply nominal, and the Netherlands was clearly a deeply religious country. By 1977 the proportion of church attenders had fallen to 42 per cent, and by 2006 to just 17 per cent. By the new century, in other words, the Netherlands had been effectively secularized.

## 9.6.2 Changing voting behaviour

In addition to these dramatic changes in the social structure of many European countries, most of which have accelerated during the 1990s, there is also evidence of a waning of the sense of identification between particular groups and political parties that formerly represented their interests. In other words, even among the diminished pool of workers or religious practitioners there is evidence to suggest that there was a major falling off in collective partisan preferences through the 1970s and 1980s. This is also most clearly evidenced in Andeweg and Irwin's (2009) Dutch data (pp. 112–113), which are summarized in Table 9.2. As can be seen from the table, the picture in 1956 was one of a very structured electorate. Some 52 per cent of voters were practising Christian churchgoers, and might have been expected to vote for one or other of the Christian parties. A further 33 per cent of the electorate was secular working class, and hence might be expected to vote for the Labour Party. And this is clearly how voters did behave in 1956: 95 per cent of the practising Catholics voted for the Catholic Party, while 63 per cent of the Dutch Reformed Protestants voted for one of the Protestant parties, as did 93 per cent of the other, and often stricter, Protestant communities. Moreover, some two-thirds of the secular working class voted for the PvdA. If we sum these figures in a crude aggregation, then we can see that a total of 85 in every 100 Dutch voters belonged to either a Christian or working-class 'pillar', and that 68 of these 85 voted according to their pillar political identity – that is, they voted along the expected cleavage lines. By 1977, on the other hand, the number belonging to these pillars had fallen to 70 in every 100, and of these only 45 voted along the expected lines. By 2006 the number had been reduced to 47 – fewer than half the voters – and of these only 19 voted along cleavage lines. In 1956, in other words, more than two-thirds of Dutch voters followed traditional cleavage voting patterns. By 2006 this proportion had been reduced to less than 20 per cent. Not only had the groups themselves declined in numbers – barely 7 per cent of the electorate were practising Catholics in 2006 – but the levels of voting cohesion within each group had

**TABLE 9.2** The decline of cleavage voting in the Netherlands

| | 1956 | | | 1977 | | | 2006 | | |
|---|---|---|---|---|---|---|---|---|---|
| | % in electorate | % of group voting along cleavage lines | % cleavage vote | % in electorate | % of group voting along cleavage lines | % cleavage vote | % in electorate | % of group voting along cleavage lines | % cleavage vote |
| Practising Catholics | 30 | 95 | 28.5 | 24 | 66 | 16.0 | 7 | 61 | 4.3 |
| Practising Dutch Reformed | 12 | 63 | 7.6 | 9 | 52 | 4.7 | 2 | 58 | 1.2 |
| Practising other Protestants | 10 | 93 | 9.3 | 9 | 75 | 5.3 | 8 | 43 | 3.4 |
| Secular working class | 33 | 68 | 22.4 | 28 | 67 | 18.8 | 30 | 32 | 9.6 |
| Total | 85 | 80 (mean) | 67.8 | 70 | 65 (mean) | 44.8 | 47 | 49 (mean) | 18.5 |

*Source:* Calculated from Tables 4.2 and 4.3 in Andeweg and Irwin (2009: 112).

also dramatically declined. As Andeweg and Irwin (2009: 113) conclude, the structured (or cleavage) model in the Netherlands 'is almost literally dying. It no longer provides a useful model to understand Dutch voting behaviour.'

The contraction of both the traditional working class and the churchgoing public in contemporary western Europe, together with a declining political cohesion even among those who retain traditional social-structural identities, has inevitably undermined the potential role of traditional social cleavages. This has resulted in the erosion of two of the most important subcultures in modern Europe, creating conditions in which individual preferences may replace collective identification as a basis for party choice.

Other forces also appear to be pushing European electorates in this direction. Already in the late 1980s, for example, Dalton (1988: 18–24) suggested that Europe was experiencing the emergence of a more politically sophisticated electorate. This new electorate was characterized by high levels of education, and had access, particularly through television, to a huge amount of information about politics. Dalton argued that this led voters to relate to politics on an individual rather than a subcultural basis. This trend was also compounded by a shift towards the privatization of consumption – of housing, health care, education, car ownership, and so on – promoting individualistic and fragmented political responses that some suggested were likely to push patterns of partisan preference in western Europe much closer to those in the United States.

More generally, following one of the most comprehensive attempts to address this problem from a comparative perspective, Mark Franklin and his colleagues concluded that the end of the 1980s had witnessed a fundamental weakening of the relationship between social structure, including both class and religion, and voting behaviour. The main findings of these authors are summarized in Table 9.3, and show that whereas social-structural variables (including class,

**TABLE 9.3** The declining impact of social structure on left voting, 1960s to 2004[a]

|  | % Variance explained around 1960s | % Variance explained in 1989 | % Variance explained in 2004 |
| --- | --- | --- | --- |
| Belgium | 29.9 (1973) | 9.5 | 2.8 |
| Britain | 20.6 (1964) | 7.4 | 4.1 |
| Denmark | 23.0 (1971) | 9.6 | 6.9 |
| France | 8.3 (1968) | 5.6 | 4.9 |
| Germany (West) | 8.2 (1968) | 6.7 | 4.8 |
| Ireland | 11.2 (1969) | 4.9 | 4.2 |
| Italy | 24.4 (1968) | 10.0 | 11.4 |
| Netherlands | 35.0 (1967) | 10.7 | 6.7 |
| Norway | 42.0 (1969) | 14.6 | 6.9 |
| Sweden | 29.0 (1964) | 18.0 (1985) | 9.6 |
| **Mean** | **23.2** | **9.7** | **6.2** |

[a] This table summarizes the amount of variance in electoral support for parties of the left that can be explained (at the individual level) by a combination of social-structural variables including class, religion, trade union membership, church attendance, and so on.

*Source:* Adapted from Franklin *et al.* (1992/2009: 100, 116, 162, 194, 232, 247, 267, 313, 430).

religion, gender, region, trade union membership, church attendance, and so on) were able to explain an average of some 23 per cent of the variance in left voting when the first mass surveys were undertaken in these countries, this figure had fallen to just less than 10 per cent by the end of the 1980s. The decline was most pronounced in Belgium, the Netherlands and Norway, and only in Italy did social-structural factors explain a greater share of the variance in the more recent period. The argument advanced by this study did not suggest, however, that these changes had been brought about by the emergence of new cleavages, or even by a change in the traditional cleavage structures themselves. Rather, in much the same way as Dalton had argued, they suggested that the traditional cleavages had simply become less relevant to partisanship as a result of what they defined as the growing *particularization*, or individualization, of voting choice (van der Eijk *et al.*, 1992). In later data, collected with reference to the elections to the European Parliament in 2004, the decline appeared to have continued. By then the overall figure had fallen to just 6 per cent, with all countries other than Italy falling to levels that could scarcely be imagined in the 1960s.

Let us try to knit these various strands together. A cleavage, it will be recalled, is sustained by three separate elements: a distinct social base, a sense of collective identity, and a clearly defined organizational expression. In its most extreme form, a cleavage is therefore sustained through the creation of distinctive subcultures within which voting is an expression of social identity rather than a reflection of instrumental choice. In short, voters *belong*. As Richard Rose once put it, at a time when this sense of belonging was particularly pronounced, 'to speak of the majority of voters at a given election as choosing a party is nearly as misleading as speaking of a worshipper on a Sunday "choosing" to go to an Anglican rather than a Baptist or a Catholic church' (Rose, 1974: 100).

Already by the end of the 1980s, however, there was ample evidence to suggest that these traditional demarcation lines were becoming blurred, with the strength of cleavage voting becoming even more eviscerated by the time of the first elections in the new century. Class divisions were becoming less pronounced, and widespread secularization had reduced the impact of religious divisions. Even within what remained of the traditional social groups, behaviour was tending to become less collective, and the traditional variations in political preference between groups were tending to wane. Finally, as we shall see in later chapters, and in what seems to be a response to these changes, political parties had begun to loosen their bonds with specific groups of voters, and had begun to appeal much more emphatically to the electorate at large. In short, the evidence suggested – and still does suggest – a consistent trend towards a much less structured electorate, and towards the fragmentation and particularization of political preferences.

However, before going on to look at where these changes might be heading, we do need to introduce a couple of important caveats. First, although class and religion may now have less impact on voting behaviour than was the case in the 1950s and 1960s, their impact has not disappeared entirely (e.g., Elff, 2007). In Britain, for example, the higher service class still continues to register a preference for the Conservatives, and both the skilled and unskilled working class still tend to opt for Labour. In the increasingly secular Netherlands a majority of the now diminished set of religious practitioners still votes for the CDA. Indeed, according to a recent analysis of Dutch voting behaviour by Pellikaan (2010), religious differences also continue to matter, albeit indirectly, in that they have helped lead to the emergence of two divergent left–right scales among citizens, one reflecting the preferences of the voters for the secular parties and the other reflecting those of the voters for the religious parties.

Second, while class and religion may now offer fewer direct voting cues, other identities retain a powerful impact. The large majority of Basque voters in Spain still vote for Basque parties. An even larger majority of Catholics in Northern Ireland still vote for Irish nationalist parties. Almost all Swedish-speaking Finns – they are not very numerous – still support the Swedish People's Party. In Belgium virtually every Flemish voter supports a Flemish party, and virtually every French-speaking voter supports a Walloon party. Indeed, these sorts of identity might even be becoming more pronounced. In 1972 – and again in 1994 – the old centre–periphery cleavage in Norway was suddenly reawakened by the prospect of Norwegian entry into the European Union. A similarly dormant north–south conflict was reawakened in Italy thanks to the mobilization efforts of the Northern League. And while class politics may be waning in Britain, there is ample evidence to suggest that Scottish, Welsh, and – through the Conservatives' new appeals – even English nationalism is growing in importance.

## 9.7 Change towards what?

In a wide-ranging early discussion of electoral change in advanced industrial democracies, Russell Dalton and his colleagues (Dalton *et al.*, 1984) put forward two general models that seek both to explain the nature of the changes occurring in western European politics and to predict their potential consequences. Their first explanation is based on the role of cleavages. It suggests that as traditional cleavages wane in importance and new cleavages emerge, voters go through a process of *realignment*. Their second explanation concentrates on the declining role of political parties. It suggests that, almost regardless of the new issues and concerns arising in post-industrial societies, political parties as such will become less and less relevant to the representation of interests. Citizens will turn increasingly towards interest groups and other social movements in order to press their demands, producing a widespread process of *dealignment*. Although both explanations emphasize the declining political relevance of factors such as class and religion, the realignment thesis stresses the growth of other concerns, whereas the dealignment thesis suggests that electorates will become ever more unstructured. We shall now turn briefly to assessing each of these arguments.

### 9.7.1 Towards realignment?

Despite Lipset and Rokkan's earlier emphasis on the freezing of party systems, it has been argued that the new issues that arise in post-industrial societies may reflect the emergence of a wholly new cleavage, one that, like more traditional cleavages, is characterized by a social base, a collective identity, and an organizational expression. One version of this argument builds on Inglehart's (1990, 1997) influential theories of *postmaterialism* and *postmodernization*, and suggests that a new politics has emerged that may be associated with a distinct social base within the new middle class, particularly among younger voters and those with a university education, and the values of which are also distinctive, laying particular stress on environmental protection, feminism, and the extension of democratic and social rights. This new politics was also reflected in the emergence of a distinct organizational expression, most clearly represented in the rise of Green parties in most parts of western Europe, as well as in the earlier 'new left' parties, which are increasingly seen as part of the wider new politics constituency. It is in this sense that what has become known as postmaterialism can be seen to constitute the basis for a new cleavage, the mobilization of which implies a potential realignment of party politics (see also Inglehart, 1984).

There are two reasons to suggest that this particular scenario may be exaggerated, however. First, and most obviously, despite the evident resonance of some of the issues associated with the new politics, the parties associated with the new politics remain an essentially marginal electoral force. As we saw in Chapter 8, Green parties polled an average of some 5 per cent of the vote in western Europe in the 1990s, and around 6 per cent in the first elections of the new century, with a further 2 to 3 per cent going to the new left. These figures are not to be dismissed, and they also conceal quite a bit of variation across the different polities. Nonetheless, they fail to signify a dramatic sea change in aggregate voting alignments.

The second reason why it may be precipitate to speak of realignment in this particular case is that, despite their own initial claims, the appeals of parties associated with the new politics are not really so very different from those of more traditional parties. There is a sense in which they need not be seen to represent a new dimension in mass politics, cutting across the left and the right; rather, they can be regarded as a new variation within the left. During their initial formation, Green parties often deliberately avoided applying terms such as 'left' or 'right' to their own politics. As Jonathon Porritt, a leading member of the British Green Party, then put it:

> 66 We profoundly disagree with the politics of the right and its underlying ideology of capitalism; we profoundly disagree with the politics of the left and its adherence, in varying degrees, to the ideology of communism. That leaves us little choice but to disagree, perhaps less profoundly, with the politics of the centre and its ideological potpourri of socialized capitalism.
>
> *(Porritt, 1984: 43)* 99

With time, however, the capacity to maintain this distinctive approach was undermined. As Green parties began to win seats in local assemblies and national parliaments, they found themselves obliged to come to terms with mainstream politics, and like their long-established competitors, they found it difficult – and undesirable – to stand aloof from day-to-day political bargaining. Even more important, in such situations the Green parties have become increasingly associated with other parties of the left. Thus, in both Belgium and Germany, Green parties have forged local alliances with established left-wing parties, and both later joined governments together with the social democrats. A similar process happened in France and Italy. In the Netherlands, the tiny Green Party actually joined with the Communist Party and two small new left parties to form an electoral cartel, the Green Left. Indeed, already by the end of the 1980s, Porritt's own emphasis had changed: no longer rejecting notions of left and right, he argued that a crucial issue was the extent to which 'today's Green parties [should] identify themselves specifically as parties of the left' (Porritt, 1989: 8). This positioning is not unambiguous, however. The new Green party in Hungary, which won more than 7 per cent of the vote in the 2010 elections, is a 'Green–Liberal' party – Politics Can be Different (LMP) – and the Greens have also joined centre-right governments in the Czech Republic, Finland and Ireland, trying to make the most of their sometimes pivotal position in coalition bargaining. Moreover, as ideological competition across the mainstream tends to moderate more generally, coalition-making between parties, of whatever hue, tends to become more promiscuous.

Nevertheless, if postmaterialist concerns do signify a potential for change within western European party systems, this seems likely to be a limited realignment that changes some of the terms of reference of the left-wing divide while leaving its essential basis intact. Thus one of the few studies to address these questions to the politics of gender, which has long been a major concern of postmaterialism, found that attitudes towards gender inequalities did not actually constitute part of any new cleavage but, rather, were strongly associated with and absorbed within the older left–right divide (Evans, 1993). This sort of change and adaptation is by no means novel. As we saw in Chapters 7 and 8, the terms of reference of the left–right divide have often been in flux, and it can even be argued that it is primarily because of this flux that the distinction itself has remained so relevant for so long, in that the terms 'left' and 'right' are capable of taking on new meanings for successive generations of voters and parties in European politics. As Smith once put it, 'it is precisely the "plasticity" of left and right which enables [parties] to combine coherence and flexibility, to absorb new issues and ward off challenges' (Smith, 1989: 159). Hence adaptation could be seen on the left, when the initial monopoly of the social democratic parties was challenged fundamentally by the mobilization of communist parties in the wake of the Russian Revolution of 1917, and again by the new left parties of the late 1960s and 1970s. The Green challenge of the late 1980s and the 1990s, to the extent that this challenge is contained within the broad left, may simply be another step in a long and continuing process of adaptation.

On the right, despite overall long-term continuity, the political terms of reference have also changed continually. New politics at this end of the spectrum has also enjoyed greater success, with the rise of far-right parties in such countries as Austria, Belgium, Denmark, France, Italy, the Netherlands and Norway, and with their overall mean levels of support rising from less than 1 per cent in the 1960s to some 8 per cent in older democracies in the new century. Moreover, albeit often with difficulty, they have also sometimes joined government – in Austria, Italy and the Netherlands, for example – or supported minority governments as external partners (in Denmark). Although this might offer stronger evidence of realignment than the Green case on the left, here too we may simply be seeing another step in the extended process of adaptation. As far-right parties gain votes, their desire for influence becomes more apparent, and hence their programme becomes somewhat more pragmatic. We shall come back to this issue later in the chapter.

Taking left and right as a whole, however, the most remarkable feature of all is the extraordinary persistence across the post-war decades. To be sure, the individual countries have varied in terms of their own national records (see Chapter 8). In addition, as we have seen, there has also been some limited reshuffling at the European level both *within* the left and *within* the right. But for compelling evidence of overall persistence, we need look no further than the summaries in Tables 9.4 and 9.5, as derived from the various family tables in Chapter 8.

**TABLE 9.4** The persistence of the left, 1950–2009 (in 16 countries)

| Party family | 1950s | 1960s | 1970s | 1980s | 1990s | 2000–2009 |
|---|---|---|---|---|---|---|
| Social democrats | 33.6 | 32.1 | 31.8 | 30.7 | 29.9 | 28.2 |
| Communists | 7.9 | 7.3 | 7.5 | 5.4 | 3.5 | 2.4 |
| New left | – | 1.1 | 1.6 | 2.6 | 1.8 | 2.5 |
| Greens | – | – | – | 2.3 | 4.8 | 6.1 |
| All left | 41.5 | 40.5 | 40.9 | 41.0 | 40.0 | 39.2 |

*Note*: Figures refer to mean aggregate electoral support per decade: see the tables in Chapter 8.

**TABLE 9.5** The persistence of the centre and right, 1950–2009 (in 16 countries)

| Party family | 1950s | 1960s | 1970s | 1980s | 1990s | 2000–2009 |
|---|---|---|---|---|---|---|
| Christian democrats | 22.9 | 23.4 | 22.2 | 21.5 | 17.6 | 17.8 |
| Conservatives | 15.4 | 15.8 | 15.2 | 16.3 | 15.0 | 15.3 |
| Liberals | 8.7 | 9.8 | 9.6 | 10.3 | 10.1 | 9.9 |
| Agrarian/centre | 6.6 | 6.9 | 6.7 | 5.4 | 5.3 | 5.8 |
| Far right | 1.0 | 0.5 | 1.6 | 2.2 | 7.4 | 7.8 |
| All centre and right | 54.6 | 56.4 | 55.3 | 55.7 | 55.4 | 56.6 |

*Note*: Figures refer to mean aggregate electoral support per decade: see the tables in Chapter 8.

Table 9.4 summarizes changes in the mean levels of electoral support across the past six decades for the different families of the left in the long-established democracies. For the left as a whole this has been remarkably invariant, declining ever so slightly from 41.5 per cent in the 1950s and 40.5 per cent in the 1960s to 39.2 per cent in the first decade of the new century. To put it another way, the difference between the average left vote in the 1960s, when Lipset and Rokkan were first discussing the freezing of party systems, and the left vote in 2000–2009 is just 1.3 per cent. And this continuity has ensued despite what has been a wholesale transformation in society, economy and culture. Within the left, and among the individual families, there is of course substantial variation. Both the social democrats and the communists have fallen by more than 5 per cent across the last five decades, with the slack being taken up by the new left and especially by the Greens. In this sense the left as a whole appears to have become more modern – or postmodern – than was the case in the earlier post-war years. Moreover, as we have seen in the previous chapter, there have also been major ups and downs in the different countries, and these averages clearly conceal substantial national fluctuation. But despite greater fragmentation and fluctuation within the left, alliances between the different left parties are just as feasible now as during the 1950s and 1960s – perhaps even more so since the more hard-line communists have been partially edged out by the more accommodating Greens and new left. The left may now be more varied than before. It is certainly not weaker.

Table 9.5 summarizes the parallel changes in the mean levels of support for the different families of the centre and right. Here, too, the sheer persistence over time is striking. These families of the centre and right together accounted for 54.6 per cent of the European vote in the 1950s, and stayed steady through to the 56.6 per cent recorded in the new century. (Because of the presence of 'other' parties – see Chapter 8 – the two sets of families do not sum up to exactly 100 per cent.) Indeed, the difference between the figure for the 1960s and that for 2000–2009 is just 0.2 per cent. In this group of families, however, reshuffling has been more pronounced. While the conservatives have remained more or less unchanged at the European level, Christian democratic parties have fallen by almost a quarter. Particularly in the bigger countries, an increasingly secular society is clearly less hospitable to these latter parties. The small agrarian-centre group has also shed votes, and while part of these losses has been made up by liberal gains, it is the far right that has compensated for the bulk. In the short run, at least, this may also work to undermine the overall position of the right, in that some of these new extreme parties are difficult and unreliable coalition allies. One result of their success might therefore be to weaken the strategic position of the right by pushing the parties of the centre into closer alignment with the left; should the far-right parties moderate, however, the right will be strengthened strategically (see Bale, 2003).

In short, if realignment is taken to mean the replacement by an alternative divide of the fundamental division between the right and the left, then the evidence in favour of realignment is far from convincing. If it is taken to mean a significant shift in party fortunes *within* either the left and/or the right, on the other hand, then a limited realignment may well be taking place. Then again, this is not a particularly new phenomenon – we have seen reshuffling before.

## 9.7.2 A new cleavage?

If, on the other hand, as Ignazi (2004) initially suggested, there is something qualitatively different about the 'new politics' of the left and of the Green parties, and if this is now being challenged by the mobilization of 'new right' parties, then we could be witnessing the emergence of a new cleavage in European politics. Two important arguments have recently been developed along these lines, and both are worthy of review. Both also associate the emergence of the new divide with the increasing impact of Europeanization and globalization, as well as with the declining significance of national boundaries in contemporary Europe. The first of these is the thesis advanced by Liesbet Hooghe and Gary Marks (e.g., 2009), who argue that the conventional economic left–right divide in European party competition has now been supplemented by a new non-economic divide that pits Green/alternative/libertarian positions against those of traditionalism/authority/nationalism. The one set of positions, which they refer to as the *gal* pole, promotes multiculturalism and social egalitarianism, whereas the second set, the *tan* pole, emphasizes the importance of traditional boundaries, identities and political practices. The one is progressive, the other conservative, and unlike the positions located along the conventional economic left–right divide, these two poles also map strongly onto the divisions between those who favour (the gal group) and those who oppose (the tan group) European integration. With modernization, they argue, and with more pronounced Europeanization, politics has therefore moved beyond the left–right conflict over policy outputs ('who gets what') and has come to embrace additionally the issues of identity and community ('who is one of us') (Hooghe and Marks, 2009: 16). In this reading, European political competition has become more clearly two-dimensional, with a progressive–conservative divide concerning identities cutting across a traditional left–right divide concerning resources. The greater fragmentation of the old left–right blocs as a result of the emergence of postmaterialist parties on the left and populist parties on the right is not therefore simply the result of growing polarization or reshuffling; rather it represents a fundamental new divide.

The second argument that builds on a similar logic is advanced by Kriesi *et al.* (e.g., 2008), who argue that European integration and globalization have opened up and 'unbundled' the boundaries of the European nation-states (see also Bartolini, 2005). Kriesi and his colleagues (pp. 3–22) also refer to this process as one of *denationalization*, and argue that electorates are then challenged by the impact of supranational institutions, by new waves of immigration, and by the liberalization and integration of markets. This leads to the emergence of a new structural conflict between the *winners* and *losers* of globalization. The latter are those whose life chances were reasonably protected under the old regime of embedded liberalism and strong national boundaries, whether through the restriction of labour markets or through the development and maintenance of strong welfare states. The winners, by contrast, are those who are well positioned to take advantage of the new opportunities that globalization or Europeanization offers, and whose skills and resources become more highly prized. This new conflict cuts across the traditional left–right alignments, not least because it includes a cultural as well as an economic dimension, with cultural divides crystallizing around issues relating to immigration and European integration. The losers in this new conflict tend to oppose further European integration, and call for restrictions on immigration, thus bringing them close to the camps of the new populist right. The winners, by contrast, who also tend to be more highly educated, are more supportive of European integration and have more liberal attitudes towards immigration and multiculturalism. Here too, then, the increasing fragmentation of the old left–right blocs is not simply a reshuffling of forces, but rather a sign that a new cleavage may be emerging.

Both of these arguments are very strongly grounded with empirical evidence regarding party positions and programmes, on the one hand, and voter attitudes and behaviour, on the other. Both also clearly point to an important new dimension of conflict in European politics that plays out in similar ways in a multiplicity of different political systems. In this sense, both point to a divide that has all the potential for effecting a substantial realignment of voting preferences. At the same time, however, it may be simply too soon to speak of such a radical departure. For all their recent successes, for example, the parties of the far right, like those of the new left and Greens, all of which symbolize the new forces of change, still account for only a relatively small share of the popular votes. Taken together, average electoral support for the far right, the Greens and the new left totalled a little more than 16 per cent of the vote among the long-established democracies in the first decade of the twenty-first century; even when taken together, in other words, they were all still being outpolled by the ailing Christian democrats.

There are also other problems with these arguments. The Hooghe–Marks gal–tan divide, for example, which was first highlighted by expert studies of party positions, centres on the divide over European integration. In practice, however, despite many predictions to the contrary; despite the claim by van der Eijk and Franklin (2004: 47) that the European issue was equivalent to a 'sleeping giant', which had become 'ripe for politicization'; and despite the strident political debates that resulted in the defeat of the European referendums in France, the Netherlands and Ireland, the European dimension has still failed to emerge as a major source of conflict in national electoral campaigns. In other words, experts may deem the parties to be divided over Europe in interesting ways, but the issue itself seems relatively marginal as far as voters and electoral competition are concerned (see also Mair, 2007: 154–156).

Kriesi *et al.*'s (2008) distinction between the winners and losers of globalization, and the interesting way in which this is seen to tie into a cultural as well as an economic divide, is in this sense more interesting and more robust. It is also a distinction that can be related to the emergence of the divide within the contemporary labour force between insiders and outsiders, the former having relatively secure employment and stable life chances, while the latter work with short-term or part-time labour contracts, and are predominantly women, immigrants and young persons. According to David Rueda's (2007) analysis of this issue, for example, it is to the former group that traditional social democratic policies are oriented. The question here, however, is whether these sorts of divide are likely to prove enduring, in an economic and cultural sense, and whether, as Kriesi *et al.* assert, they have the basis to form a genuinely new cleavage. As argued earlier, not all divides are sufficiently strongly structured or persistent to merit being defined as cleavages, and these recent and as yet relatively uncertain conflicts may not reach that particular threshold. These are new conflicts, to be sure, but ones that are perhaps less suited to be treated within the terms of reference of Lipset and Rokkan, and which might be better understood when placed in the framework proposed by Schattschneider (1960), who spoke in more general terms of the *conflict of conflicts*, and of how new dimensions of competition competed for attention with older ones.

Moreover, it is also not at all certain how sharp these distinctions will remain within a context of more generalized retrenchment and crisis. The winners of globalization may have enjoyed many benefits during the boom years of the 1990s and early 2000s, but they may no longer see themselves as winners in times of fiscal and monetary crisis, and in periods in which the assets offered by house prices and generous pension rights appear less assured.

### 9.7.3 Towards dealignment?

The argument that there has been a *dealignment* of western European party systems rests on three types of evidence: first, a decline in the extent to which voters identify with political parties, and prove willing to turn out to vote for them; second, the emergence of new political parties, and the growth in electoral support for such parties; and third, the general increase in levels of electoral volatility. As we shall see, evidence regarding all three factors suggests that the hold of traditional parties in Europe is indeed being undermined, but, as we shall also see, even this conclusion should not be overstated.

#### *Party identification and voter turnout*

One of the clearest symptoms of the process of dealignment in western Europe can be seen in the declining levels of party identification, the psychological attachment that is seen to tie individual voters to particular party alternatives. At first sight, the evidence of such decline seems quite convincing. In one assessment, for example, Dalton *et al.* (2002: 24–29) collated various Eurobarometer surveys and national election studies covering some 14 European polities over the period from the 1960s through to the end of the 1990s, and found that the evidence of declining partisanship was unequivocal. In all but two of the polities (the exceptions were Belgium and Denmark), the trend in levels of popular identification with parties was clearly downwards – sometimes very markedly so. Moreover, in *all* 14 polities, this time without exception, the trend in levels of strong party identification was also clearly down. In other words, substantially fewer voters now feel a strong sense of attachment to their party of choice than used to be the case in Europe. A similar pattern is evident in the comparable data that are summarized for a group of key European polities in Table 9.6, and which in some cases go up to 2001 and 2002. Here, a decline in the general level of party identification is evident in each of the countries, albeit more pronounced in some cases (e.g., Ireland) than in others (e.g., Denmark). Moreover, here also it is the decline in the numbers

**TABLE 9.6** The decline of party identification

| Country: dates | % Party identifiers | | % Strong party identifiers | |
|---|---|---|---|---|
| | Past | Present | Past | Present |
| Austria: 1954, 2001 | 73 | 55 | 71 | 25 |
| Denmark: 1971, 1988 | 56 | 50 | 30 | 23 |
| Germany: 1972, 2002 | 75 | 65 | 17 | 12 |
| Ireland: 1978, 1994 | 29 | 18 | 14 | 6 |
| Italy: 1978, 1996 | 77 | 56 | 46 | 30 |
| United Kingdom: 1964, 2001 | 93 | 84 | 44 | 15 |

*Note*: Data refer to the proportion of survey respondents reporting an attachment or a close attachment to a party.

*Source*: Eurobarometer, as derived from data reported in Mair *et al.* (2004).

of voters with a strong sense of identification that is most evidently marked, and which is also sometimes very sharp (Austria, the UK). Although the sense of attachment to party has not been completely obliterated in western Europe, these figures suggest that it is clearly waning.

In practice, however, we must be careful not to read too much into such figures. In the first place, information on party identification is based on survey data, and the cross-national use of survey data is notoriously fraught with problems. Questions must be translated into different languages, and anyway the same questions tend to mean rather different things in different countries, often leading to contradictory results (Sinnott, 1998). In addition to these methodological problems, there have been conceptual problems in applying what is essentially a US notion of party identification in the European context (Thomassen, 1976). For a range of institutional reasons (the voter registration process, the holding of primaries, the holding of separate presidential and parliamentary elections), US voters may be able to distinguish between identifying with a party, on the one hand, and voting for that party, on the other. European voters, in contrast, often change their party identification at the same time as they change their vote. Thus, even though party identification can remain quite stable in the United States, notwithstanding some electoral volatility, it does not tend to have the same degree of independent stability in Europe.

A second reason to be cautious when interpreting data on the dealignment of party identification in Europe is that many European voters have traditionally tended to identify primarily with social groups and only indirectly with political parties. Sections of the Italian electorate, for example, may have identified with the Christian Democrats only to the extent that they also identified with the Catholic church, which was associated with the DC. In the same way, sections of the British electorate may have identified with the Labour Party only to the extent that they had a working-class identification, which then translated into a sense of belonging to the Labour Party as the party of the working class. In other words, precisely because many European parties were traditionally cleavage-based, the primary loyalty of a voter may be to the class or social group that defines a cleavage rather than to the party that represents it, although this pattern is likely to have changed in line with the general decline of cleavage voting in recent years.

Perhaps the most serious problem with applying the notion of party identification in the European context is that there is evidence that voters in more fragmented party systems can identify with more than one party at the same time (van der Eijk and Niemoeller, 1983). Voters on the left, for example, may identify with both a socialist party and a communist party, maintaining a stable sense of belonging to the left bloc as a whole, while shifting their preferences from one party to another according to the particular circumstances of a given election. Given the evidence that we have seen of the aggregate persistence of left and right over time, as well as that of the reshuffling that has taken place within each of these blocs, this interpretation seems at least intuitively plausible (see also Bartolini and Mair, 1990).

Thus, despite the fact that the evidence of declining party identification in Europe seems quite powerful and consistent, interpreting this evidence is quite difficult. Rather than showing that European party systems are becoming dealigned, patterns in these data may be a product of applying an inappropriate concept to European multiparty parliamentary democracies.

The evidence is somewhat clearer with regard to trends in voting turnout. Participation levels in national elections in western Europe have usually far exceeded the levels recorded in the United States, but ever since observers began debating the extent to which traditional parties and party systems were being transformed there has been a general expectation that these high levels of electoral participation would begin to decline. As we shall see in Chapter 11, voting has actually been obligatory in a small number of European polities. Even beyond these polities, however, turnout has been very high. In Malta, for example, where turnout is not obligatory, virtually every able voter now turns out on election day. In Denmark, Germany, Iceland, Italy, Luxembourg, the Netherlands, Norway and Sweden turnout levels well in excess of 80 per cent have not been uncommon. It is really only in Switzerland, and then only since the 1970s (when Swiss women were first given the vote) that the exceptionally low level of turnout in national elections approximates to that in the United States, although it should also be pointed out that, even in other countries, levels of turnout in elections to the European Parliament (Table 5.3 above) now often fall below those recorded in the US. Moreover, as we shall see later, levels of participation are also markedly low in many of the post-communist democracies.

Nor, perhaps surprisingly, was there much change in this pattern of high turnout at national elections – at least through to the 1980s, and at least at the cross-national European level. In the 1950s, for example, turnout levels averaged 84 per cent (Table 9.7). In the 1960s the average

**TABLE 9.7** Mean levels of electoral participation, 1950–2009

| Country | 1950s | 1960s | 1970s | 1980s | 1990s | 2000–2009 |
|---|---|---|---|---|---|---|
| Austria | 95.3 | 93.8 | 92.3 | 91.6 | 83.8 | 80.5 |
| Belgium | 93.1 | 91.3 | 92.9 | 93.9 | 92.5 | 92.9 |
| Denmark | 81.8 | 87.3 | 87.5 | 85.6 | 84.4 | 86.0 |
| Finland[a] | 76.5 | 85.0 | 81.1 | 78.7 | 70.8 | 68.8 |
| France | 80.0 | 76.6 | 82.3 | 71.9 | 68.9 | 62.4 |
| Germany | 86.8 | 87.1 | 90.9 | 87.1 | 79.7 | 75.9 |
| Iceland | 90.8 | 91.3 | 90.4 | 89.4 | 86.4 | 85.4 |
| Ireland | 74.3 | 74.2 | 76.5 | 72.9 | 67.2 | 64.8 |
| Italy | 93.6 | 92.9 | 92.6 | 89.0 | 85.5 | 81.8 |
| Luxembourg | 91.9 | 89.6 | 89.5 | 88.1 | 87.1 | 90.3 |
| Malta | 78.7 | 90.3 | 94.0 | 95.2 | 94.7 | 94.8 |
| Netherlands[b] | 95.4 | 95.0 | 83.5 | 83.5 | 76.0 | 79.8 |
| Norway | 78.8 | 82.8 | 81.6 | 83.1 | 77.1 | 76.2 |
| Sweden | 78.7 | 86.4 | 90.4 | 89.1 | 85.0 | 81.1 |
| Switzerland[c] | 69.0 | 64.2 | 52.3 | 48.2 | 43.8 | 46.7 |
| United Kingdom | 79.1 | 76.6 | 75.1 | 74.1 | 75.4 | 63.2 |
| **Mean (*N* = 16)** | **84.0** | **85.3** | **84.6** | **82.6** | **78.6** | **76.9** |
| Cyprus | | | | 95.2 | 92.2 | 90.4 |
| Greece | | | | 83.5 | 81.6 | 74.1 |
| Portugal | | | | 78.0 | 64.3 | 61.8 |
| Spain | | | | 73.5 | 77.6 | 72.7 |
| **Overall mean (*N* = 20)** | | | | **82.6** | **78.7** | **76.5** |

*Note*: As in Chapter 8, for Cyprus, Greece, Portugal and Spain, decade averages are reported only since the 1980s.

[a] From 1975 onwards, Finnish citizens residing abroad were given the right to vote, but the figures reported here refer only to the turnout among Finnish residents.

[b] From 1971 onwards (that is, including all 1970s elections), it was no longer obligatory for Dutch voters to attend at the ballot box.

[c] Women in Switzerland were given the vote in federal elections for the first time in 1971.

was 85 per cent, falling to just below 85 per cent in the 1970s and to just under 83 per cent in the 1980s. There was not much variation here.

In the 1990s, on the other hand, the picture began to look quite different. Among the 16 long-established democracies, turnout averaged less than 79 per cent in the 1990s, falling below the 80 per cent mark for the first time in post-war history, and dropping by a full 4 per cent with respect to the 1980s. More strikingly, all but five of these countries (Belgium, Denmark, Malta, Sweden and the UK) recorded their own lowest decade average in the 1990s, while, with the exception of the UK, all recorded a lower turnout in the 1990s than in the 1980s. This was a marked change, and it suggested that European voters might be becoming more disengaged from the conventional political process. Such evidence would clearly serve the dealignment thesis. The evidence of the first elections of the new century also confirms this pattern. In 2000–2009 turnout fell even further, to below 77 per cent among the 16 long-established democracies, and to a similar level when all 20 democracies are measured. To be sure, the differences are small – but they are still moving in a consistent direction, and have resulted in a turnout level that is now lower than in any of the decades since the Second World War.

### Support for new political parties

The second obvious symptom of partisan dealignment is a trend towards increasing electoral support for new political parties. As political responses to the parties have become more individualized, and as the links between parties and voters have become more attenuated, the space for the creation of new parties has increased. In some cases, as with the Green parties of the far right, new parties reflect the emergence of new issues. In other cases, however, new parties are simply the results of splits in old parties. In Britain, Denmark and the Netherlands in the 1970s and 1980s, for example, key figures abandoned mainstream socialist parties and formed new parties of the centre left. In Belgium the politicization of the linguistic divide in the 1970s led not only to the creation of new parties but also to splits in each of the main traditional parties, a dynamic that continues to disrupt the Belgian party system even into the present century.

In fact, and as can be seen from Table 9.8, aggregate electoral support for new parties has risen steadily over the past half-century. The operational definition of new parties that we are using here is a very simple – and generous – one: recalling that Lipset and Rokkan spoke in the late 1960s of the fact that many of the parties then contesting elections 'were older than the national electorates', we can make a very simple distinction between the so-called 'old' parties, being those that first began contesting elections prior to the 1960s, and 'new', or 'post-freezing' parties, being those that first began to contest elections from 1960 onwards. Indeed, these latter have proved thick on the ground: of the almost 300 separate parties that contested at least one election in the long-established democracies between 1960 and 2000, some 60 per cent have been formed after 1960. To put it another way, only some 40 per cent of parties contesting elections during these past four decades were around when Lipset and Rokkan proposed the freezing hypothesis (Mair, 1999).

Given these large numbers, and given that the later the period the more likely it is that the numbers will have accumulated, it is not then very surprising to see their aggregate support building up. During the 1960s, when only some 30 of these new parties had already been formed, their total vote averaged just over 4 per cent (Table 9.8). In the 1970s this grew to just over 9 per cent, and then to more than 14 per cent in the 1980s. In the 1990s the new party share totalled more than 22 per cent, and in 2000–2009 was almost 30 per cent: by the new century, therefore, almost one in every three votes being cast in national elections in the established democracies was going to a party that had been formed after 1960.

**TABLE 9.8** Mean aggregate electoral support for new political parties, 1960–2009

| Country | 1960s | 1970s | 1980s | 1990s | 2000–2009 |
|---|---|---|---|---|---|
| Austria | 1.7 | 0.1 | 4.1 | 11.5 | 17.8 |
| Belgium | 2.8 | 11.4 | 12.9 | 23.7 | 23.8 |
| Denmark | 8.7 | 26.9 | 30.7 | 24.9 | 27.4 |
| Finland | 1.6 | 8.2 | 13.7 | 22.3 | 20.5 |
| France | 16.3 | 29.1 | 27.1 | 41.7 | 58.2 |
| Germany | 4.3 | 0.5 | 7.5 | 13.9 | 15.2 |
| Iceland | 2.4 | 4.7 | 19.3 | 21.6 | 53.6 |
| Ireland | 0.3 | 1.4 | 7.9 | 10.0 | 7.6 |
| Italy[a] | 9.5 | 3.3 | 7.1 | 66.8 | 100.0 |
| Luxembourg | 3.1 | 12.0 | 11.5 | 22.4 | 23.3 |
| Malta | 13.1 | 0.0 | 0.1 | 1.5 | 1.0 |
| Netherlands | 2.3 | 26.6 | 44.5 | 45.9 | 60.1 |
| Norway | 3.9 | 13.6 | 15.1 | 19.7 | 30.8 |
| Sweden | 1.1 | 1.6 | 4.5 | 14.5 | 15.0 |
| Switzerland | 0.4 | 5.3 | 12.2 | 14.9 | 11.0 |
| United Kingdom | 0.0 | 0.8 | 11.6 | 2.3 | 2.7 |
| **Mean (*N* = 16)** | **4.4** | **9.1** | **14.4** | **22.4** | **29.3** |

*Note:* 'New parties' are here defined as those that first began to contest elections no earlier than 1960 and that poll at least 1 per cent in one election.

[a] Calculated on basis of PR votes only since elections of 1994.

In some of the countries involved, this growth has clearly been substantially above this average. In the newly made Italian party system, where new parties accounted for the vast majority of votes cast in the 1990s, they now enjoy a monopoly of the vote. None of the older protagonists continues to compete. In the Netherlands, where the CDA also counts as a new party, their share averaged almost 46 per cent in the 1990s, and then rose to more than 60 per cent in the first decade of the new century, helped along in part by the success of the Pim Fortuyn List and later by the Socialists and the Freedom Party. In France, where party longevity is the exception, new parties averaged more than 40 per cent in the 1990s, and almost 60 per cent thereafter. Indeed, it is really only Malta and the United Kingdom that have proved completely inhospitable to new parties, notwithstanding the flurry of success enjoyed by the SPD in Westminster elections in the 1980s.

Taking these figures at face value, we might be inclined to read them as signifying a fundamental transformation in party alignments in the established democracies. The fact that the old parties formed before the 1960s have accounted for fewer than half those contesting elections over the past 50 years, and the fact that the new parties formed since 1960 pulled in almost a third of the votes in the new century elections, must surely signal a major change.

But what sort of change is this? As we have already seen (Tables 9.4 and 9.5), most of the traditional party families are managing to hold their own in aggregate electoral terms. We have also seen that the really new families – the new left and Greens, on the one hand, and the new far right, on the other – have not proved great vote winners to date, at least not across western Europe as a whole. Moreover, some of the most successful 'new' politics parties of the far right – including the Freedom Party in Austria and the National Alliance (ex-MSI) in Italy – are themselves quite old parties, albeit now dressed in new ideological costumes.

What this therefore seems to suggest is that many of the votes going to new parties are actually going to new organizational alternatives that operate within recognizable – if not wholly traditional – parameters. This is not exactly the old politics; after all, newly formed organizations are unlikely to present themselves as wholly belonging to the past. But nor is it necessarily the new politics. At best, it may be old politics in a new form. Hence it is not too surprising to find that the most successful of these new formations over the past 40 years include parties such as the Dutch CDA, Forza Italia and the Democrats in Italy, the UDF and later the UMP in France, and the Left Wing Alliance in Finland. To be sure, these are all new parties. But their politics will be familiar to even the most old-fashioned observer of west European politics.

Here again, then, we seem to see evidence that speaks more of dealignment than realignment. Loyalties to traditional parties are certainly ebbing. Otherwise, even these familiar-sounding new parties would never have enjoyed any real success. Moreover, there are certain groups of new parties that emerge in a number of countries, albeit without achieving a great success in any of them – the recent experience of pensioners' parties offers a useful example here (Hanley, 2010). But while voters may well be willing to consider new alternatives, especially since the 1990s, and in this sense may be regarded as increasingly dealigned, it seems that, as yet, they are unwilling to transfer across to a wholly new politics.

### Electoral volatility

The third collection of evidence in favour of the dealignment thesis involves increased aggregate electoral volatility (Pedersen, 1979, 1983), which, precisely because it measure levels of flux from one election to the next, offers a very useful summary indicator of short-term changes in party support.

When the trend towards increased electoral volatility was first noted in certain countries in the 1970s, it was not in fact then seen to apply to western Europe as a whole. Pedersen's own evidence from the 1970s, for example, pointed to an actual decline in volatility in France and West Germany and, albeit less marked, in Italy. In each of these countries, the party system was restructured in the early post-war years, following the re-establishment of the democratic process, and each party system was soon to be stabilized by a strong centre-right party. In many other European countries, however, the 1970s did witness an erosion of the 'steady-state' politics of the 1950s and 1960s, and since then the expectation has been that this sense of flux would eventually pass on to even the more stable polities.

Even by the 1980s, however, these expectations had not been borne out. Indeed, in western Europe as a whole (Table 9.9) the 1980s witnessed a marginal decline in volatility, a decline that was particularly marked in Denmark, the Netherlands, Norway and the United Kingdom. Moreover, what could also be seen by the 1980s was that the level of aggregate vote shifts between the main class blocs on the left and right was much less than the volatility

**TABLE 9.9** Mean aggregate electoral volatility, 1950–2009

| Country | 1950s | 1960s | 1970s | 1980s | 1990s | 2000–2009 |
|---|---|---|---|---|---|---|
| Austria | 4.1 | 3.3 | 2.7 | 5.5 | 9.4 | 15.5 |
| Belgium | 7.6 | 10.2 | 5.3 | 10.0 | 10.8 | 14.5 |
| Denmark | 5.5 | 8.7 | 15.5 | 9.7 | 12.4 | 10.4 |
| Finland | 4.4 | 7.0 | 7.9 | 8.7 | 11.0 | 6.8 |
| France | 22.3 | 11.5 | 8.8 | 13.4 | 15.4 | 13.5 |
| Germany | 15.2 | 8.4 | 5.0 | 6.3 | 9.0 | 9.0 |
| Iceland | 9.2 | 4.3 | 12.2 | 11.6 | 13.7 | 12.4 |
| Ireland | 10.3 | 7.0 | 5.7 | 8.1 | 11.7 | 7.5 |
| Italy[a] | 9.7 | 8.2 | 9.9 | 8.6 | 22.9 | 14.0 |
| Luxembourg | 10.8 | 8.8 | 12.5 | 14.8 | 6.2 | 6.8 |
| Malta | 9.2 | 14.4 | 4.6 | 1.4 | 3.6 | 1.3 |
| Netherlands | 5.1 | 7.9 | 12.3 | 8.3 | 19.1 | 22.3 |
| Norway | 3.4 | 5.3 | 15.3 | 10.7 | 15.9 | 13.7 |
| Sweden | 4.8 | 4.0 | 6.3 | 7.6 | 13.8 | 14.9 |
| Switzerland | 2.5 | 3.5 | 6.0 | 6.4 | 8.0 | 7.9 |
| United Kingdom | 4.3 | 5.2 | 8.3 | 3.3 | 9.3 | 6.0 |
| **Mean (N = 16)** | **8.0** | **7.4** | **8.6** | **8.4** | **12.0** | **11.0** |
| Cyprus | | | | 12.8 | 8.4 | 7.9 |
| Greece | | | | 11.3 | 5.5 | 7.1 |
| Portugal | | | | 15.0 | 11.9 | 10.2 |
| Spain | | | | 14.2 | 8.8 | 8.5 |
| **Overall mean (N = 20)** | | | | **9.4** | **11.3** | **10.5** |

*Note*: The values refer to levels of aggregate electoral volatility, measured as the sum of the percentage vote gains of all the winning parties (or the sum of the percentage vote losses of all the losing parties) from one election to the next. See Pedersen (1979, 1983). As in Chapter 8, for Cyprus, Greece, Portugal and Spain, decade averages are reported only since the 1980s.
[a] Calculated on basis of PR votes only since elections of 1994.

within these class blocs (Bartolini and Mair, 1990; Mair, 1997: 76–90). In other words, at least as far as the class cleavage is concerned, a much greater proportion of electoral instability proved to be the result of switching votes between friends rather than between enemies, a trend that is also compatible with the notion that European voters may identify with more than one party at the same time.

But although this bloc volatility continues to remain relatively low, it is striking to note that elections since the 1990s now reveal that aggregate volatility as a whole has increased quite suddenly and quite markedly (Table 9.9), averaging some 11 per cent among the long-established democracies. The 1990s marked the first post-war decade in which the mean level of volatility across western Europe as a whole pushed above 10 per cent, marking an increase of almost half as much again relative to the 1980s. The growth in volatility in the 1990s has also proved remarkably consistent, with almost three-quarters of the individual countries registering their own peak post-war levels. The exceptions to this pattern include Denmark, where the really big electoral earthquakes hit in the 1970s, and France and Germany, which experienced considerable volatility in the wake of immediate post-war reconstruction. Luxembourg and Malta also peaked during earlier decades. Remarkably, however, it was only in Luxembourg that volatility in the 1990s proved lower than in the 1980s. Moreover, despite a slight average decline, the elections that have so far taken place in the new century confirm this new trend. Austria, Belgium, the Netherlands and Sweden have gone on to new record highs, with the sudden growth in support for the far right (in the Netherlands in 2002), or its sudden decline (Austria in 2002), producing election outcomes that rank among the most volatile in western European history (Table 9.10 below). But although these elections were exceptional, they can be related to a trend towards greater electoral instability. Among the nine post-war elections included in Table 9.10, for example, five have occurred since 1990. Here again, then, as we have seen with regard to levels of turnout and support for new parties, we see evidence to suggest that the period around the turn of the new century is different from what has gone before. Here again, we may be witnessing the first real signs of dealignment.

**TABLE 9.10** The most volatile elections since 1900 in Europe's long-established democracies

| Country | Year | Level of volatility (%) |
| --- | --- | --- |
| Italy | 1994 | 36.7 |
| Germany | 1920 | 32.1 |
| France | 1906 | 31.1 |
| Netherlands | 2002 | 30.7 |
| France | 1910 | 30.5 |
| Germany | 1924 | 27.1 |
| France | 1958 | 26.7 |
| Switzerland | 1919 | 23.4 |
| Italy | 1948 | 23.0 |
| Switzerland | 1917 | 22.8 |
| Italy | 2001 | 22.0 |
| Netherlands | 1994 | 21.5 |
| Denmark | 1973 | 21.2 |
| Germany | 1953 | 21.2 |
| Austria | 2002 | 21.1 |
| Ireland | 1927 (Sept) | 20.8 |

*Note*: All elections with a level of volatility greater than 20.0 per cent.

## BOX 9.2: TRENDS IN ELECTORAL VOLATILITY

### Denmark

Having gone through a prolonged period of electoral stability, Denmark, like its Scandinavian neighbours, experienced a major upsurge in electoral volatility in the early 1970s. Indeed, it was the 'earthquake' election in 1973 that first drew scholarly attention to the supposed unfreezing of the established party systems in Europe more generally. Since then volatility has been reduced, and has come close to the European average in the last two decades. Despite the shake-up to the party system following the rise of the far-right Danish People's Party, Denmark now records a lower level of volatility than either Norway or Sweden.

### France

Largely as a result of its relatively unstructured party system, and shifting patterns of alliance and schism between the different political leaders, France has always had one of the most volatile electorates in western Europe. As the party system began to consolidate under the Fifth Republic, however, volatility tended to decline, falling below 10 per cent for the first time in the 1970s. In the 1980s volatility began to increase once again, and the elections of the 1990s proved more volatile than any since the 1950s.

### Germany

Germany was traditionally characterized by an extremely volatile electorate, particularly during the interwar and early post-war years. During the 1960s, however, as the West German party system became consolidated, volatility tended to decline. Although the emergence of the Greens led to a more unsettled situation in the 1980s, the level of volatility has nevertheless not grown substantially. The highest level recorded in recent elections was a net shift of just over 12 per cent in 2009, with the next highest being just over 11 per cent in the very exceptional unification elections of 1990. Since the 1950s, mean volatility per decade has always remained below 10 per cent, being one of the lowest among all established democracies.

### Italy

Despite immensely unstable governments, Italy was for long characterized by a surprisingly stable pattern of electoral alignments, with volatility levels remaining below 10 per cent in each of the decades from the 1950s to the 1980s. In the 1990s, on the other hand, with the complete remaking of the party system, volatility rose to record levels. In 1994, for example, the first election of the so-called Second Republic, volatility exceeded 36 per cent, a level that had never previously been seen among the long-established European democracies in the twentieth century. Even in 2001, when things had begun to settle down, and the two-bloc system appeared reasonably consolidated, volatility still reached 22 per cent, almost double the west European average. It has since fallen back again.

### Netherlands

The Netherlands, along with Denmark and Norway, was one of the classic examples of increasing electoral volatility during the late 1960s and the 1970s. Thereafter volatility tended to decline, and the party system stabilized around the new patterns that began to emerge in the 1960s. In the election of 1989, for example, the net shift in votes was a little over 5 per cent, less than half the levels recorded in the early 1970s. This all changed again in the 1990s, however, and volatility reached a record high of almost 22 per cent in the election of 1994. This big jump in volatility reflected the sharp decline in support for both the Christian Democrats and Labour. Four years later, in 1998, things had still not settled down, with volatility reaching almost 17 per cent, well above the levels recorded in the 1950s, 1960s, 1970s and 1980s. By 2002 and 2003 the level of electoral change had reached dramatic proportions, and the volatility recorded in 2002 was the fourth highest ever recorded among the long-established European democracies since 1900. Even in 2010, when no new party emerged, volatility was among the highest ever recorded in post-war western Europe.

## Poland

Like many post-communist democracies, Poland has recorded levels of volatility that are far in excess of those recorded in the long-established democracies. This is partly due to the sheer volume of splits and mergers among parties, particularly within the group that came out of the former Solidarity. What had once been a united anti-communist movement rapidly disintegrated into various parties and factions, divided by religion, economic philosophy and personality disputes. Volatility has also been the result of adaptation to electoral engineering, including the imposition of thresholds and the consequences this has for representation, on the one hand, and coalition building, on the other. Although flux still characterizes the former anti-communist opposition, elements of stability have emerged through the persisting electoral success of the former communist party. Having averaged some 25 per cent in the elections of the 1990s, volatility fell slightly in the first decade of the new century.

## Spain

While Spain, like many other new party systems, appeared to have a relatively unstable electorate during its first elections, the high mean levels of volatility nevertheless disguise a pattern that is actually quite difficult to characterize. Although mean volatility in the 1980s was over 14 per cent, almost double that in the same period in the 'older' party systems of Europe, this high figure derives entirely from the very exceptional election of 1982, when support for the Union of the Democratic Centre fell from 35 per cent to less than 7 per cent, and when the vote for the Socialist Party rose from 31 per cent to 47 per cent. Overall volatility in that election reached a remarkably high level of over 36 per cent, the same as that recorded in Italy in 1994. In the previous and subsequent elections, however, average volatility was much lower, and in the 1990s Spain's position relative to the older west European systems had been reversed – it recorded a level of volatility that was only some two-thirds of that in the long-established democracies. Levels have remained low in the first elections of the new century.

## United Kingdom

Notwithstanding the temporary and radical electoral flux created by the growth of the third-party vote in the 1970s, as well as the threat posed by the alliance parties in the 1980s, electoral volatility has always proved relatively muted in post-war British elections. The most volatile post-war election was that in February 1974, when both the Scottish and Welsh Nationalists, as well as the Liberals, experienced a major surge in their fortunes, and when the overall electoral support won by the Conservatives and Labour fell to a post-war low. The level of volatility in that election was almost 15 per cent. In 1997, with the Labour landslide, volatility rose sharply again to more than 13 per cent, falling back to averaging just 6 per cent in the 2000s. Even the election that led to the path-breaking coalition of Conservatives and Liberals in 2010 was not marked by a high level of volatility.

## 9.8 Evaluating change and stability

The older studies of the established democracies that set out to chart and explain change often concluded with the observation that change is neither so extensive nor so pervasive as was first imagined. 'Even if change is widespread,' concluded one early account, 'it is important not to overstate its extent. Although few party systems have been as constant as they once appeared to be, all exhibit substantial elements of continuity' (Wolinetz, 1988: 296). Taking all the evidence presented in this chapter together, we can see that this conclusion probably still holds, and that the long-established democracies are characterized at least as much by continuity as they are by change. To be sure, the image of transformation is seductive; but the shock of the new can blind us to the persistence of the old (see Enyedi and Deegan-Krause, 2010, for a recent evaluation).

The continuities can be easily summarized. The overall balance between the broad left bloc and the broad centre-right bloc is remarkably constant. There is also a very low level of aggregate vote redistribution across the key left–right boundary. The principal political protagonists, most notably the social democrats and the conservatives, have proved very resilient. New parties, despite their pervasiveness and their electoral success, do not seem to have challenged the core of traditional alignments.

The changes are also evident, however, particularly since the 1990s. There is a growing individualization of political preferences and a weakening of collective identities. There is a decline in the distinctiveness of the social bases of party support. There have been changes in the terms of reference of the division between the left and the right. The balance of support for parties within each bloc has sometimes changed. And a 'new politics' dimension has emerged in many of the more established European democracies. Above all, one of the most important party families, the Christian democrats, has experienced a major decline in its aggregate electoral support. Perhaps most important of all, it seems that voters have become less willing to participate, while those who still do turn out to vote are now more willing to play around with their individual party preferences.

The overall picture, then, may still be one of *peripheral* change, with the *core* of most of the party systems remaining intact (Smith, 1989), and with the voters who continue to opt for these parties proving increasingly disengaged. European voters are less tied to parties than before, and have shown themselves more willing to shift their preferences from one party to another. But they do so cautiously. On the left, voters may shift from a socialist party to a Green party, but they tend to remain on the left. Votes on the right may shift from a Christian party to a secular party, or from a conservative party to a far-right party, but they tend also to stay on the right. Only occasionally do we see changes such as those that have been documented in the shift of traditional working-class voters from social democratic or communist parties to the parties of the far right. Ties to individual parties may have weakened, but ties to the broader identities of the left and the right are still relatively intact. In this important sense, the notion that European party systems are frozen should not be dismissed too easily.

It must be emphasized, moreover, that the long-term stabilization of western European party systems is not simply a function of the ties that bind distinct social groups (Catholics, workers, farmers, and so on) to parties or to blocs of parties. To be sure, social structure has certainly proved to be an important stabilizing element, especially in systems with strong social cleavages or subcultures, such as Italy, the Netherlands and Sweden. But if social structure were the only freezing agent, then we should already have witnessed much greater change in electoral align-ments in the 1970s and 1980s than was actually the case. The fact is that many of the old tradi-tional party families in Europe remain alive and kicking despite what we have seen to be the widespread weakening of religious and class identities, and the long-term process of individuali-zation. To suggest that social structure alone is the freezing agent is to suggest that a frozen party system can exist only in a country in which there is also a frozen society, and this is patently implausible.

Party systems are in fact frozen by a variety of factors, of which social structure is just one of the more important (Bartolini and Mair, 1990: 251–308; Sartori, 1990; Mair, 1997: 199–223). They are also frozen by the constraints imposed by institutional structures such as the electoral system (see Chapter 11), and by the organizational efforts of the parties themselves (see Chapter 10). Most important, party systems are also frozen by the constraints imposed by the structure of party competition. In Italy, for example, the basis for a wholesale change in electoral preferences in the 1990s was laid partly by the 'legitimation' of the left, which undermined the terms of reference by which Italian party competition had been structured since the late 1940s. Italian voters, as well as the Italian parties themselves, had long been constrained by the belief that there was no alternative to Christian Democratic government. And once such an alternative finally did emerge through the transformation of the unacceptable PCI into the highly acceptable PDS, this particular anchor was cut loose and voters began to shift in relatively great numbers.

Up to now, however, the sorts of dramatic changes that have recently had an impact on the Italian party system remain exceptional, and whether similar ruptures will yet come to affect other long-standing European party systems is still to be seen. For example, it remains to be seen whether the new experiment in coalition politics in the UK in 2010 will undermine what has been up to now one of the most resilient party systems in Europe. In a similar vein, it remains to be seen whether the striking success of the far-right Swiss People's Party will finally spell a definite end to the Swiss 'magic formula' for government formation, whereby the same four parties have coalesced together in government for the past 50 years. It also remains to be seen whether the huge flux that characterized Dutch politics throughout the first decade of the new century will signal a new and lasting change in patterns of government formation and party competition.

Finally, and most importantly, it also still remains to be seen whether contemporary new divides will be strong enough and persistent enough to develop into new cleavages, or even into a recrudescence of old cleavages. The growing tension between indigenous and immigrant pop-ulations, for example, particularly relating to the position of Islamic communities and practices, might well lead to a revitalization of old-style church–state issues. From another perspective, as suggested by Kriesi and his colleagues, the winners of globalization might well end up in a struc-tured conflict with the losers, forcing a new alignment in many of the European polities in both east and west. Alternatively, the growth of Euro-scepticism in both western and post-communist Europe, and growing opposition to the deepening and widening of European integration, might also begin to force a new alignment, thus waking van der Eijk and Franklin's 'sleeping giant'. One direction in which such politicization might lead is towards a wholly new divide, with pro- and anti-EU parties lined up in a new set of alliances; or, as in the Norwegian case, it might simply play out within a revitalization of older alignments defined by centre and periphery. Older alignments might also be reawakened by the continuing fallout from the 2008–2010 finan-cial crisis. Facing the pressure of new austerity programmes, European politics might revert once again to the traditional struggle of rich against poor, and of working class against middle class (see, for example, Vail and Bowyer, 2011). All of this may also have a depoliticizing effect, however, and hence one of the most important questions for the future is whether voters might become even more disengaged, and whether aggregate voting outcomes will begin to reflect an ever more random distribution of preferences, leading to the possible erosion of long-familiar structures. In the wake of the very severe financial crisis in Iceland, for example, some 33 per cent of voters in the local elections in Reykjavik in 2010 opted for the 'Best' Party, a new formation whose programme was devoted to promising free towels at all swimming pools and a new polar bear for the city zoo. In such scenarios, new and potentially revitalized divides might not actually develop, or at least they might not translate so directly into the national electoral arena, and hence the result could be continuing dealignment, disaffection, and cynicism. Alternatively, as in Greece in 2010, when faced with the proposals for new austerity programmes, the result might be the mobilization of mass protests and strikes.

## 9.9 Parties and voters in post-communist Europe

One of the most important lessons that we have learned from looking at the development of parties and party systems in western Europe is that the structure of mass politics takes time to stabilize. When mass politics begins, in other words, it is often unsettled. As was the case in Portugal and Spain in the late 1970s and 1980s, as well as in the rest of Europe in the wake of full democratization in the early part of the twentieth century, the formative years of mass politics are often characterized by significant volatility and change. New parties emerge and then disappear. Parties fuse with one another and then split away again. And the process by which voters learn about the limits and possibilities afforded by new electoral systems, on the one hand, and about the constraints and opportunities imposed by the new structures of party competition, on the other, can often take years to develop. In post-communist Europe, then, as was noted in Chapter 7, as well as in most other new democracies, we cannot expect to witness the immediate settling down or institutionalization of stable party systems (Enyedi, 2006).

There are three principal factors involved here, each of which sets the post-communist experience off from that in western Europe, and each of which was also likely to have promoted quite high levels of electoral instability (see Mair, 1997: 175–198; see also Tóka, 1998; Kitschelt *et al.*, 1999). First, and most obviously, the path towards democracy in post-communist Europe has been radically different from that taken in most of western Europe. Not only are we talking here about a massive and quite overloaded process of transition – from communism to multiparty democracy, and from command economies to the free market – but we are also talking about a different mode of democratization. When most of the west European polities democratized at the beginning of the twentieth century, the process involved opening up to the mass of new voters a regime in which political competition was already an accepted principle. In other words, the regimes were competitive, but exclusive – they denied the mass of ordinary citizens the right to participate. Democratization involved enfranchisement, the advent of mass suffrage. In post-communist countries, by contrast, the process occurred the other way around. The principle of mass participation had been accepted under communism – indeed, if the mock elections that took place under communism recorded turnouts of less than 90 per cent, the regime took umbrage – but not the right of competition. Elections were held, but they were not free elections. Given these different paths to democracy, then, we should not necessarily expect that the resultant parties and party systems will prove easily comparable (van Biezen, 2003).

Second, the electorates in post-communist Europe are different. One obvious difference in this regard is the absence of a long-standing cleavage structure (see Tóka, 1998), at least in the sense that has been discussed earlier – a structure that is characterized by distinct social divisions, a strong sense of collective identity within different groups in society, and strong organizations to which citizens might feel a sense of belonging. Social divisions in post-communism are still essentially fluid, with the transition from a command to a market economy initially breaking down those few lines of social stratification that previously existed. And although this market economy is beginning to lead to new lines of stratification, these are emerging in the wake of societies that experienced through transition what Batt (1991: 50) once tellingly described as 'an unprecedented degree of social destructuring, volatility and fluidity'. To be sure, identities other than those eroded by the communist economic system have survived – national or ethnic identities in a number of the post-communist states, such as in Latvia, for example; a religious, Catholic, identity in Poland in particular; the Hungarian minority in Slovakia; and so on. But these are the exceptions. The emergence of cleavages is also hampered by the fact that the parties in these new democracies have not yet invested a great effort to build a popular sense of identification and belonging among voters. There are exceptions, of course. The Czech and Slovak parties, for example, have grown to dominate their respective systems, and they have also been intent on building powerful organizational networks within their polities (Kopecký, 2005). Indeed, prior to the 2010 election, when two new parties suddenly emerged and captured more than a quarter of the vote, the Czech Republic was believed to have one of the most stable party systems in the post-communist region. In the main, however, post-communist parties scarcely exist beyond parliament, with little continuity over time in terms of identity or organization, and with little evidence of any substantial organizational presence on the ground. As such, they do little to promote the structuring of electoral choice (see Chapter 10 below; see also Lewis, 2001; van Biezen, 2003). In short, the electorates in post-communist countries tend to be different in the sense that, as Rose (1995) put it in an early analysis, they are demobilized – lacking in any strong affective ties to the parties that compete for their votes, and often sceptical about the idea of party itself. It is not so much that these voters are *dealigned*, as is perhaps increasingly the case in contemporary western Europe; rather, they are not *yet* aligned.

Third, the parties themselves are different. This is not so much a matter of differences in ideology or programmatic identity – although these are also important – as of organizational behaviour and practice. In brief, parties in new democracies in general, and those in the post-communist democracies in particular, are less frequently characterized by a sense of organizational loyalty and commitment. Where conflicts arise inside a party, then, the solution is often to split the party apart, with the dissenting factions establishing their own separate alternative organizations. At the same time, when common interests are perceived among different parties, even in the short term, the decision is often made to merge the parties into a broad electoral or even organizational coalition. The result is a constantly shifting array of actors, with parties entering elections in one guise, and then adopting yet another in parliament itself, and with relatively little continuity in alternatives from one election to the next.

To be sure, there is quite substantial variation among across the post-communist systems in this regard. At one extreme lie the Polish and Latvian cases, where the huge variety of party alternatives move in and out of diverse alliances from one election to the next, and where, within parliament itself, there is a constant shifting between parliamentary factions and clubs, such that it becomes almost impossible even to identify some of the individual parties or to pin them down to particular positions. In the Czech Republic and Hungary, by contrast, at least until 2010 when both were severely disrupted, the alignments at both the electoral and parliamentary level seemed much more predictable, although in the Hungarian case electoral support did always shift quite considerably from one election to the next (Table 9.11). Such complex processes of party fission and fusion are very uncommon in long-established party systems – almost by definition. Among the west European cases discussed above, for example, it is really only in France and Belgium, and, since 1994, in Italy, that this sort of reshuffling is so pervasive. Indeed, were such organizational behaviour to be a feature of these western systems, then it would be almost impossible to speak of them in terms of party 'systems' as such. For a system of parties to emerge in the first place, and for it to persist, it must necessarily be characterized by regularity and predictability. This is what any system entails. And this is also why it still remains quite difficult to speak of real 'party systems' in a number of the new post-communist democracies. Neither the parties themselves, nor their modes of interaction, have always been fully regularized (Casal Bertoa and Mair, 2010).

This sense of flux is also clearly compounded by unpredictability at the level of the voters themselves. Over and above the uncertainties that follow from the relative absence of affective loyalties to parties, as well as those that can be associated with the continuing institutional fluidity (see above), there are also uncertainties regarding how even short-term voter preferences will be reflected. Two factors are important here. First, turnout levels are still often relatively low by European standards (Table 9.11), and hence a lot of voters may not yet have become socialized into the electoral process. In this sense, they remain demobilized and unpredictable. Second, because of the high thresholds imposed by the new electoral systems (Chapter 11), and because both the voters and some of the parties have needed time to learn how to operate within the constraints imposed by these systems, a lot of votes in the formative elections were initially

**TABLE 9.11** Aggregate change in parliamentary elections post-communist Europe

| Country | 1990s | | 2000–2009 | |
| --- | --- | --- | --- | --- |
| | Turnout | Electoral volatility[a] | Turnout | Electoral volatility[a] |
| Bulgaria | 72.7 | 30.2 | 60.9 | 43.7 |
| Czech Republic | 77.8 | 21.8 | 61.3 | 16.7 |
| Estonia | 63.8 | 24.0 | 61.5 | 28.4 |
| Hungary | 63.8 | 29.0 | 69.2 | 13.3 |
| Latvia | 80.1 | 43.3 | 66.9 | 29.8 |
| Lithuania | 64.1 | 42.6 | 51.0 | 36.9 |
| Poland | 46.4 | 25.2 | 46.9 | 23.6 |
| Romania | 74.2 | 17.8 | 54.3 | 23.0 |
| Slovakia | 80.1 | 19.9 | 62.4 | 20.1 |
| Slovenia | 74.5 | 25.3 | 64.7 | 21.9 |
| **Mean (N = 10)** | **69.8** | **27.9** | **59.9** | **25.7** |

[a] Because precise information is often missing on the relationship between some of the parties that contest sequential elections, these provisional estimates of electoral volatility have a substantial margin of error. In general, they are likely to overestimate the real levels of aggregate volatility.

wasted by the failure of the parties concerned to win through to parliamentary representation. In the Czech Republic in 1992, for example, parties failing to reach the threshold accounted for almost 19 per cent of the total vote. In Slovakia in 1992 the equivalent figure was almost 24 per cent, and in Poland in 1993, following the imposition of the new thresholds, more than 34 per cent of votes were cast for unsuccessful parties. These balances have come down in recent years as the parties and the electorates have learned to play the electoral game more efficiently, and as fewer votes are wasted. Nonetheless, the phenomenon does persist to some extent in certain countries: in the most recent elections in the Czech Republic and Lithuania, for example, some 20 per cent of votes went to parties or candidates who failed to win representation, as did 16 per cent of the votes in the recent elections in Slovakia.

Putting all of these factors together, the picture that emerges is one of instability and flux among voters and their parties (see also Pop-Eleches, 2010). This picture is summarized in Table 9.11, which reports levels of turnout and electoral volatility in elections in parliamentary elections in the 10 post-communist countries that concern us in this volume, and which offers a useful contrast with the patterns evident in the long-established western European democracies during the same period (Tables 9.7, 9.9). Through the 1990s, when these new party systems were first emerging, turnout averaged some 70 per cent, almost 10 per cent less than the 'trough' recorded among the established European democracies during the same period. Of course, there are also sharply contrasting patterns recorded here, with average turnout levels in Latvia, Slovenia, the Czech Republic and Slovakia approximating to the west European levels, while that in Poland just managed to exceed that in Switzerland. This alone might suggest that it is also difficult to generalize even among this limited set of countries. On the other hand, by the beginning of the new century turnout had actually fallen, to just less than 60 per cent, and this decline was marked in all of the countries with the exceptions of Hungary, where turnout rose, and Poland, where it remained effectively unchanged at a remarkably low level of 46 per cent. This also serves to widen the gap with the long-established democracies. In this sense it is worth underlining that the *average* turnout among the post-communist countries in 2000–2009 is lower than in *each* of the west European countries, with the single exception of Switzerland.

It is even more striking to observe the contrast in volatility levels (see also Tavits, 2008). Across all 10 post-communist countries in the 1990s volatility averaged 27.9 per cent, falling slightly to 25.7 per cent in the first decade of the new century. This average is more than double the equivalent figures in western Europe (Table 9.9); indeed, the *average* figure of 25.7 per cent is higher than all but seven of the most volatile *single* elections ever recorded among the long-established democracies (Table 9.10). What is also evident from the figures in Table 9.11 is that there is a reasonably marked difference between the small Baltic states, on the one hand, which remain extraordinarily volatile, and the slightly more stable east-central European states, on the other hand. In Latvia and Lithuania, in particular, volatility in the 1990s averaged more than 40 per cent, as against little over 20 per cent in the other states. That said, volatility later declined in both countries, but grew in Bulgaria, Estonia and Romania. The figure for the Czech Republic in the latter decade is actually quite exceptional for the region, being lower than that recorded in many of the long-established polities during the same period, but this also rose in 2010 when two new parties made substantial inroads into what seemed to be becoming an established political landscape. These figures need to be treated with caution, however. As noted above, these are nascent party systems, and they are often constituted by non-institutionalized parties. Groups of leaders adopt particular labels in elections, but are then quite prepared to reshuffle their alliances within parliament. Moreover, when labels change, or when parties split or merge, it is often difficult for the outside observer to trace the precise details of who has gone where, or with whom. The result is that new parties are deemed to have emerged and old parties are deemed to have failed, even though core elements of continuity might well be present. This also means that the real levels of aggregate volatility are probably lower than those that we indicate, and hence that the contrast with the stable and highly transparent party politics is probably exaggerated. To be sure, the electorates in post-communist Europe are less stable than those in the west, but it is sometimes difficult to be precise when pinning this difference down.

When turnout levels began to dip in the established democracies in the 1990s, and when levels of volatility began to climb, it suggested the onset of a new period of dealignment. Party systems and electoral support patterns had been frozen in the past, but they now appeared to be thawing out. With even lower turnout levels and even higher peaks in volatility becoming apparent in post-communist Europe, the interpretation must necessarily be different. These systems are not emerging out of a frozen landscape – at least as far as democratic party systems are concerned. Rather, they are being formed for the first time. In other words, while the western systems may be becoming dealigned, these post-communist systems might well be on the way to an initial alignment. In this sense, we may conceive of each set of systems as beginning from opposite ends of some notional continuum, in which the western systems come from a point of stability and head towards a more uncertain and unpredictable future, while the post-communist systems emerge from a point of total uncertainty and unpredictability – an inevitable characteristic of newly created party systems – and perhaps head towards a more stable future (see also Ágh, 1998; Sitter, 2002). It is therefore interesting to note the small decline in average volatility levels across the decades in Table 9.11. This would suggest that we might eventually see them meeting in the middle, converging on a point that is neither frozen not wholly fluid, and in which broad continuities combine with sometimes rapid and short-term change. What also follows from this, of course, and what may well be the most interesting aspect of this contrast between the two sets of systems, is not that the post-communist countries are catching up with the already developed party politics of the west, but rather that the patterns evident in the post-communist countries may well represent one version of the possible future facing their western neighbours (see also Bohle and Greskovits, 2009).

## 9.10 East versus west, or east *and* west?

Although parties and party systems in post-communist democracies may not be stabilized by new cleavage structures – the consolidation of new cleavages is unlikely to prove possible in the increasingly individualized Europe of the twenty-first century – they may well be stabilized by persisting dimensions of competition. In other words, key issues and alternatives are likely to remain relevant for quite some years to come, even if the manner in which individual voters line up on these issues may reflect quite particularistic concerns. Tóka (1998: 607), for example, has convincingly argued that post-communist alignments will be likely to hinge quite firmly on value preferences and on what he calls 'value voting', with the important dimensions being those constituted by religion versus secularism, left versus right, and nationalism versus anti-nationalism. In contemporary politics, he noted, such values are likely to remain relatively independent of circumstances related to status and demography, and, when it comes to generating partisan commitment, they 'are at least as effective as is the political mobilization of organizational networks ... Rather than stick with parties whose followers or leaders "look like them", voters are most likely to stick with the parties with whom they agree on major issue dimensions.' Here too, then, we can see a possible convergence between the directions in which the eastern and western systems are heading, with the freeing of political preferences from long-term social determinants. What we also see, particularly in recent elections, is an interesting convergence of trends – with both east and west opting for the (old) left in the late 1990s, and now with both moving to the right.

## 9.11 Conclusions

In this chapter we have offered a very brief overview that sets the experience of post-communist Europe against the more lengthy analysis that we devoted to the development of cleavages and mass politics in western Europe. As we noted earlier, these two separate worlds are not easily integrated with one another. The western polities have, in the main, more than a half-century of peaceful democratic development already behind them. The post-communist polities, on the other hand, have experienced a long history of authoritarianism, and only managed to effect a transition to democracy at the end of the twentieth century. What this brief overview indicates, however, is that the evident contrasts between these two parts of Europe may not last for long. It is not that the post-communist polities are necessarily 'catching up' with their more long-established western counterparts. That would leave a misleading impression. Instead, the politics of post-industrial society at the beginning of the new century, whether practised in east or west, is sufficiently different from what went before that both sets of countries may well be converging on a new equilibrium. In the end, it may not be the former contrasts between the traditional capitalist democracies and the new post-communist democracies that matter, but rather the difference between both sets of polities now, on the one hand, and the patterns that formerly prevailed through most of the twentieth century, on the other. Whether this also applies to the way in which contemporary political parties are organized is a question that will be addressed in Chapter 10.

## References

**Ágh, Attila** (1998) *The Politics of Central Europe,* Sage, London.

**Ambrosius, Gerold and William H. Hubbard** (1989) *A Social and Economic History of Twentieth-Century Europe,* Harvard University Press, Cambridge, MA.

**Andeweg, Rudy B. and Galen A. Irwin** (2009) *Governance and Politics of the Netherlands,* 3rd edn, Palgrave, Basingstoke.

**Bakvis, Herman** (1981) *Catholic Power in the Netherlands,* McGill-Queens University Press, Kingston and Montreal.

**Bale, Tim** (2003) 'Cinderella and her ugly sisters: the mainstream and the extreme right in Europe's bipolarising party systems', *West European Politics,* 26 (3), 67–90.

**Bartolini, Stefano** (2000) *The Political Mobilization of the European Left, 1860–1980: The Class Cleavage,* Cambridge University Press, Cambridge.

**Bartolini, Stefano** (2005) *Restructuring Europe: Centre Formation, System Building, and Political Structuring Between the Nation State and the European Union,* Oxford University Press, Oxford.

**Bartolini, Stefano and Peter Mair** (1990) *Identity, Competition, and Electoral Availability: The Stabilization of European Electorates, 1885–1985*, Cambridge University Press, Cambridge.

**Batt, Judy** (1991) *East Central Europe from Reform to Transformation*, The Royal Institute of International Affairs/Pinter Publishers, London.

**Bell, Daniel** (1960) *The End of Ideology*, The Free Press, New York.

**Biezen, Ingrid van** (2003) *Political Parties in New Democracies: Party Organization in Southern and East-Central Europe*, Palgrave, London.

**Bohle, Dorothee and Béla Greskovits** (2009) 'Varieties of capitalism and capitalism "tout court"', *European Journal of Sociology*, 50 (3), 355–386.

**Bornschier, Simon** (2010) *Cleavage Politics and the Populist Right*, Temple University Press, Philadelphia, PA.

**Casal Bertoa, Fernando and Peter Mair** (2010) *Two Decades On: How Institutionalized are the Post-Communist Party Systems?*, EUI Working Paper SPS 2010/3, European University Institute, Florence.

**Crewe, Ivor and David Denver (eds)** (1985) *Electoral Change in Western Democracies: Patterns and Sources of Electoral Volatility*, Croom Helm, London.

**Crouch, Colin** (2008) 'Change in European societies since the 1970s', *West European Politics*, 31 (1/2), 14–39.

**Dalton, Russell J.** (1988) *Citizen Politics in Western Democracies: Public Opinion and Political Parties in the United States, Great Britain, West Germany, and France*, Chatham House, Chatham, NJ.

**Dalton, Russell J. and Martin P. Wattenberg (eds)** (2000) *Parties without Partisans: Political Change in Advanced Industrial Democracies*, Oxford University Press, Oxford.

**Dalton, Russell J., Scott C. Flanagan and Paul Allen Beck (eds)** (1984) *Electoral Change in Advanced Industrial Democracies: Realignment or Dealignment?*, Princeton University Press, Princeton, NJ.

**Dalton, Russell J., Ian McAllister and Martin P. Wattenberg** (2002) 'Parties and their publics', pp. 19–42 in Kurt Richard Luther and Ferdinand Müller-Rommel (eds), *Political Parties in the New Europe*, Oxford University Press, Oxford.

**Diamant, Alfred** (1958) 'The group basis of Austrian politics', *Journal of Central European Affairs*, 18 (2), 134–155.

**Duverger, Maurice** (1954) *Political Parties*, Methuen, London.

**Elff, Martin** (2007) 'Social structure and electoral behavior in comparative perspective: the decline of social cleavages in western Europe revisited', *Perspectives on Politics*, 5 (2), 277–294.

**Enyedi, Zsolt** (2006) 'Party politics in post-communist transition', pp. 228–238 in William J. Crotty and Richard S. Katz (eds), *Handbook of Political Parties*, Sage, London.

**Enyedi, Zsolt and Kevin Deegan-Krause (eds)** (2010) *The Structure of Political Competition in Western Europe*, special issue of *West European Politics*, 33 (3).

**Ertman, Thomas** (2009) 'Western European party systems and the religious cleavage', pp. 39–55 in Kees van Kersbergen and Philip Manow (eds), *Religion, Class Coalitions, and Welfare States*, Cambridge University Press, Cambridge.

**Evans, Geoffrey** (1993) 'Is gender on the "new agenda"?', *European Journal of Political Research*, 24 (2), 135–58.

**Franklin, Mark N., Tom Mackie and Henry Valen (eds)** (1992) *Electoral Change: Responses to Evolving Social and Attitudinal Structures in Western Countries*, ECPR Press, Colchester, 2009 (reprint of original 1992 edition with additional material).

**Halman, Loek, Ruud Luijx and Marga van Zundert (eds)** (2005) *Atlas of European Values*, Brill, Leiden.

**Hanley, Sean** (2010) 'The emergence of pensioners' parties in contemporary Europe', pp. 225–244 in Jörg Tremmel (ed.), *A Young Generation Under Pressure?*, Springer Verlag, Berlin.

**Hardiman, Niamh and Christopher Whelan** (1998) 'Changing values', pp. 66–85 in William Crotty and David E. Schmitt (eds), *Ireland and the Politics of Change*, Longman, New York.

**Hooghe, Liesbet and Gary Marks** (2009) 'A postfunctionalist theory of European integration: from permissive consensus to constraining dissensus', *British Journal of Political Science*, 39 (1), 1–23.

**Houska, Joseph J.** (1985) *Influencing Mass Political Behavior: Elites and Political Subcultures in the Netherlands and Austria*, University of California at Berkeley, Institute of International Affairs.

**Ignazi, Piero** (2004) *Extreme Right Parties in Western Europe*, Oxford University Press, Oxford.

**Inglehart, Ronald** (1984) 'The changing structure of political cleavages in western society', pp. 25–69 in Russell J. Dalton, Scott C. Flanagan and Paul Allen Beck (eds), *Electoral Change in Advanced Industrial Democracies: Realignment or Dealignment?*, Princeton University Press, Princeton, NJ.

**Inglehart, Ronald** (1990) *Culture Shift in Advanced Industrial Society*, Princeton University Press, Princeton, NJ.

**Inglehart, Ronald** (1997) *Modernization and Postmodernization: Cultural, Economic, and Political Change in 43 Societies*, Princeton University Press, Princeton, NJ.

**Kalyvas, Stathis N.** (1996) *The Rise of Christian Democracy in Europe*, Cornell University Press, Ithaca, NY.

**Kaplan, Gisela** (1992) *Contemporary West European Feminism*, Allen & Unwin/UCL Press, London.

**Katz, Richard S. and Peter Mair** (1995) 'Changing models of party organization and party democracy: the emergence of the cartel party', *Party Politics*, 1 (1), 5–28.

**Keating, Michael** (2008) 'Thirty years of territorial politics', *West European Politics*, 31 (1/2), 60–81.

**Kirchheimer, Otto** (1957) 'The waning of opposition in parliamentary regimes', *Social Research*, 24 (2), 127–156.

**Kirchheimer, Otto** (1966) 'The transformation of western European party systems', pp. 177–200 in Joseph LaPalombara and Myron Weiner (eds), *Political Parties and Political Development*, Princeton University Press, Princeton, NJ.

**Kitschelt, Herbert, Zdenka Mansfeldova, Radoslaw Markowski and Gabor Toka** (1999) *Post-Communist Party Systems: Competition, Representation and Intra-Party Cooperation*, Cambridge University Press, Cambridge.

**Kopecký, Petr** (2005) 'Building party government: political parties in the Czech and Slovak Republics', pp. 119–146 in David Stansfield, Paul Webb and Stephen White (eds), *Political Parties in Transitional Democracies*, Oxford University Press, Oxford.

**Kriesi, Hanspeter, Edgar Grande, Romain Lachat, Martin Dolezai, Simon Bornschier and Timotheos Frey** (2008) *West European Politics in the Age of Globalization*, Cambridge University Press, Cambridge.

**Lewis, Paul (ed.)** (2001) *Party Development and Democratic Change in Post-Communist Europe*, Frank Cass, London.

**Lipset, Seymour M. and Stein Rokkan** (1967) 'Cleavage structures, party systems and voter alignments: an introduction', pp. 1–64 in S.M. Lipset and Stein Rokkan (eds), *Party Systems and Voter Alignments*, The Free Press, New York.

**Lovenduski, Joni** (1986) *Women and European Politics: Contemporary Feminism and Public Policy*, Wheatsheaf, Brighton.

**Madeley, John T.S. and Zsolt Enyedi (eds)** (2003) *Church and State in Contemporary Europe*, special issue of *West European Politics*, 26 (1).

**Maguire, Maria** (1983) 'Is there still persistence? Electoral change in Western Europe, 1948–1979', pp. 67–94 in Hans Daalder and Peter Mair (eds), *Western European Party Systems: Continuity and Change*, Sage, London.

**Mair, Peter (ed.)** (1990) *The West European Party System*, Oxford University Press, Oxford.

**Mair, Peter** (1997) *Party System Change: Approaches and Interpretations*, Clarendon Press, Oxford.

**Mair, Peter** (1999) 'New political parties in long-established party systems: how successful are they?', pp. 207–224 in Erik Beukel, Kurt Klaidi Klausen and Poul Erik Mouritzen (eds), *Elites, Parties and Democracy: Festschrift for Mogens N. Pedersen*, Odense University Press, Odense.

**Mair, Peter** (2001) 'The freezing hypothesis: an evaluation', pp. 27–44 in Lauri Karvonen and Stein Kuhnle (eds), *Party Systems and Voter Alignments: Looking Back, Looking Forward*, Routledge, London.

**Mair, Peter** (2007) 'Political parties and party systems', pp. 154–166 in Paolo Graziano and Maarten P. Vink (eds), *Europeanization: New Research Agendas*, Palgrave Macmillan, Basingstoke.

**Mair, Peter, Wolfgang C. Müller and Fritz Plasser (eds)** (2004) *Political Parties and Electoral Change*, Sage, London.

**Neumann, Sigmund** (1956) 'Toward a comparative study of political parties', pp. 395–421 in Sigmund Neumann (ed.), *Modern Political Parties*, University of Chicago Press, Chicago.

**Pedersen, Mogens N.** (1979) 'The dynamics of European party systems: changing patterns of electoral volatility', *European Journal of Political Research*, 7 (1), 1–26.

**Pedersen, Mogens N.** (1983) 'Changing patterns of electoral volatility: explorations in explanations', pp. 29–66 in Hans Daalder and Peter Mair (eds), *Western European Party Systems: Continuity and Change*, Sage, London.

**Pedersen, Mogens N.** (1987) 'The Danish "working multiparty system": breakdown or adaptation?', pp. 1–60 in Hans Daalder (ed.), *Party Systems in Denmark, Austria, Switzerland, the Netherlands and Belgium*, Frances Pinter, London.

**Pellikaan, Huib** (2010) 'The impact of religion on the space of competition: the Dutch case', *Politics and Religion*, doi:10.1017/S1755048310000143.

**Pop-Eleches, Grigore** (2010) 'Throwing out the bums: protest voting and unorthodox parties after communism', *World Politics*, 62 (2), 221–260.

**Porritt, Jonathon** (1984) *Seeing Green: The Politics of Ecology Explained*, Blackwell, Oxford.

**Porritt, Jonathon** (1989) 'Foreword,' pp. 7–9 in Sara Parkin, *Green Parties: An International Guide*, Heretic Books, London.

**Prodromou, Elizabeth H.** (1996) 'Paradigms, power, and identity: rediscovering orthodoxy and regionalizing Europe', *European Journal of Political Research*, 30 (2), 125–154.

**Pulzer, Peter** (1967) *Political Representation and Elections in Britain*, Allen & Unwin, London.

**Rokkan, Stein** (1970) *Citizens, Elections, Parties*, Universitetsforlaget, Oslo.

**Rose, Richard** (1974) *The Problem of Party Government*, Macmillan, London.

**Rose, Richard** (1995) 'Mobilizing demobilized voters in post-communist societies', *Party Politics*, 1 (4), 549–563.

**Rose, Richard and Derek Urwin** (1970) 'Persistence and change in western party systems since 1945', *Political Studies*, 18 (3), 287–319.

**Roth, Günther** (1963) *The Social Democrats in Imperial Germany: A Study in Working-Class Isolation and National Integration*, Bedminster Press, Totowa, NJ.

**Rueda, David** (2007) *Social Democracy Inside Out: Partisanship and Labor Market Policy in Advanced Industrialized Democracies*, Oxford University Press, Oxford.

**Sartori, Giovanni** (1987) 'The influence of electoral laws: faulty laws or faulty method?', pp. 43–68 in Bernard Grofman and Arend Lijphart (eds), *Electoral Laws and Their Political Consequences*, Agathon Press, New York.

**Sartori, Giovanni** (1990) 'The sociology of parties: a critical review', pp. 150–182 in Peter Mair (ed.), *The West European Party System*, Oxford University Press, Oxford.

**Schattschneider, E.E.** (1960) *The Semisovereign People*, Holt, Rinehart & Winston, New York.

**Sinnott, Richard** (1998) 'Party attachment in Europe: methodological critique and substantive implications', *British Journal of Political Science*, 28 (4), 627–650.

**Sitter, Nick** (2002) 'Cleavages, party strategy and party system change in Europe, east and west', *Perspectives on European Politics and Society*, 3 (3), 425–451.

**Smith, Gordon** (1989) 'Core persistence: system change and the "people's party"', *West European Politics*, 12 (4), 157–168.

**Tavits, Margit** (2008) 'On the linkage between electoral volatility and party system instability in central and eastern Europe', *European Journal of Political Research*, 47 (5), 537–555.

**Thomassen, J.J.A.** (1976) 'Party identification as a cross-cultural concept: its meaning in the Netherlands', pp. 63–80 in Ian Budge, Ivor Crewe and Dennis Farlie (eds), *Party Identification and Beyond*, Wiley, London.

**Tóka, Gábor** (1998) 'Party appeals and voter loyalties in new democracies', *Political Studies*, 46 (3), 589–610.

**Vail, Mark I. and Benjamin T. Bowyer** (2011) 'Economic insecurity, the social market economy, and support for the German left', *West European Politics*, 34 (4).

**van der Eijk, Cees and Mark Franklin** (2004) 'Potential for contestation on European matters at national elections in Europe', pp. 32–50 in Gary Marks and Marco R. Steenbergen (eds), *European Integration and Political Conflict*, Cambridge University Press, Cambridge.

**van der Eijk, Cees and B. Niemoeller** (1983) *Electoral Change in the Netherlands*, CT Press, Amsterdam.

**van der Eijk, Cees, Mark N. Franklin, Tom Mackie and Henry Valen** (1992) 'Cleavages, conflict resolution, and democracy', pp. 403–426 in Mark N. Franklin, Tom Mackie and Henry Valen (eds), *Electoral Change: Responses to Evolving Social and Attitudinal Structures in Western Countries*, ECPR Press, Colchester, 2009 (reprint of original 1992 edition).

**Wolinetz, Steven B. (ed.)** (1988) *Parties and Party Systems in Liberal Democracies*, Routledge, London.

# CHAPTER 10

# Inside European Political Parties

## Chapter contents

## 10.1 Introduction

As earlier chapters in this book have made clear, political parties play a vital role in European politics. They control governments, dominate parliaments, and have a strong role in the appointment of members of constitutional courts. In many parts of the world, parties are inclined to be peripheral or transient bodies: they may be built around a single leader and cease to exist when this leader disappears from the scene, as has occurred in some developing countries. They may play a secondary role in what are primarily candidate-centred politics, as in the United States. In Europe, however, parties really matter, and many authors have quoted with approval Schattschneider's statement that 'modern democracy is unthinkable save in terms of the parties' (Schattschneider, 1977: 1). During most of the nineteenth century, much political thinking frowned upon parties as divisive, and a negative force in politics, but by the end of the century there was a sometimes grudging acceptance of the necessity in a mass democracy of competition between more or less cohesive parties (Scarrow, 2006a).

We have seen in earlier chapters that some European parties have a long history, surviving world wars and fundamental changes of regime. We saw in Chapter 3 that the institutions of European parliamentary democracy mean that on the whole it is party, rather than candidate, that Europeans vote for at election time. National government in Europe (though not government in the EU) is party government, although other organizations, such as interest groups, sometimes appear to challenge this, as we shall see in Chapter 13. Consequently, the internal affairs of parties, although they are regarded by many Europeans as mundane and uninteresting, may make a significant difference to the politics of a country, by determining the nature of both the politicians and the policy packages among which voters choose at elections. In this chapter, therefore, we move inside parties and ask what sort of bodies they are. We consider how well they are organized; how they make decisions; where they get their resources; how they are adjusting to important social changes, such as the increasing role of the mass media in politics; and how political parties make their distinctive contribution to the politics of representation in Europe.

## 10.2  What do parties do?

Political parties are present in, and indeed are at the core of, politics in all European countries. Even though many Europeans are cynical about parties and their motives, European politics would scarcely operate without them. They perform a number of functions that are crucial to the operation of modern political systems. Among these functions, we shall pick out four that are particularly important.

First, political parties structure the political world. As we have seen in earlier chapters, and will also see in Chapter 12, parties are the key actors in the operation of governments and parliaments. If there were no parties – in other words, if every member of parliament was an independent, with no institutionalized links with other members – the result would be something close to chaos. The only west European country that has come anywhere close to this situation in living memory was Fourth Republic France prior to 1958, when the parliamentary groups were numerous and internally incohesive, rendering stable government and cohesive policymaking impossible, except to the extent that the civil service filled the breach. Parties also structure the political world for many voters, who see politics in terms of the fortunes of parties as much as the fate of issues, especially at election times. Most individual voters don't have time to work out their view on every political issue, and many tend to follow their party's judgement on matters about which they have not thought deeply.

Second, parties recruit and socialize the political elite. To become a member of parliament in Europe it is virtually essential first to be selected by a political party as an election candidate. Likewise, to become a government minister in most countries it is usually necessary to be a senior member of a political party. Thus gaining access to political power requires being accepted by a party, and usually being a leading figure in it. Parties also socialize the political elite; most government ministers have spent a number of years as party members, working with other party members and learning to see the political world from the party's perspective. In doing this, they become accustomed to working with others, learning about teamwork, about the need to coordinate their activities with other figures in the party and, most importantly, about the constraints that party discipline imposes on them. The control that European parties possess over elite recruitment and socialization marks one major difference between most of Europe, on the one hand, and the USA and certain other presidential systems on the other. In the latter, the country's political leader often does not emerge from within the party organization, and in some cases complete political outsiders, such as Hugo Chávez in Venezuela or Alberto Fujimori in Peru, can come through and win political power. This means that the political direction of such systems is inclined to be inherently less stable, whereas in Europe, where political parties control the channels of elite recruitment and socialization, the behaviour of political leaders is usually more predictable, for better or worse.

Third, parties provide linkage between rulers and ruled, between civil society and the state. They constitute one of the mechanisms by which voters are linked to the political world, providing a flow of information in both directions. As we shall see later, there are many doubts as to whether parties are still performing their linkage role effectively.

Fourth, parties aggregate interests. Unlike interest groups, which we look at in Chapter 13, they put forward and try to implement packages of proposals, not just policies in one area of government. Most parties at elections put forward manifestos containing policies on many different issues, and thereby stand ready to give direction to government. By doing this they offer meaningful choices to voters between alternative policy packages, and thus play a crucial part in the process of converting voters' preferences into government policy. Party control of government, whether by one party or by a coalition of parties, should mean some more or less coherent programme that the government aims to follow, rather than a situation where disparate individual ministers each pursue their own ideas.

## 10.3 Basic party organization

Party organizations differ in detail around Europe, but the basic organizational elements are very similar. Members of parties belong to a local unit based on a geographic area, usually known as the *branch*. Ideally, the party will aim to establish branches all over the country in order to maintain a presence on the ground and to mobilize potential voters. The branches usually have a role in selecting election candidates, and they are entitled to send delegates to the party's *annual conference*, which in many parties is nominally the supreme decision-making body. Delegates at the annual conference usually elect most members of the party's *national executive*, which runs the party organization between conferences, adjudicating on internal disputes. This works in conjunction with the party's *head office*, staffed by the party's own employees, who constitute a permanent party bureaucracy. The other main element in the party is the *parliamentary party* or *caucus*, comprising the party's elected deputies.

In the case of some parties, this basic picture is complicated by the presence of other bodies. A few parties, such as the French Socialists, are highly factionalized. Such parties contain a number of clearly defined groups, often quite institutionalized, with a continuous existence over time; the various factions jostle for power and position within the party, sometimes quite co-operatively and in other cases more competitively (Boucek, 2009). Factionalization is generally something that parties aim to avoid: factions were an important element in the death of the Italian Christian Democrats (DC) in the early 1990s. Other parties have in the past had interest groups affiliated to them; examples include the Labour parties in Britain, Denmark, Norway and Sweden, although in each case, especially the first two, the links have become much weaker in recent years (Allern *et al.*, 2007). In federal countries the party organizations in the various states may have considerable freedom of action. This is especially true of the German Christian

Democrats and the Austrian People's Party (the latter also has interest groups, in the form of farmers', workers' and business leagues, attached to it).

Party constitutions usually give the impression that the party is a smoothly functioning organization in which important decisions are reached through a fully participatory process. The reality, as might be expected, is often rather different. Although some parties do operate reasonably peacefully (though not necessarily very democratically), others are wracked by constant internal tension. One very common source of conflict concerns the ideological 'purity' of party policy. The battle lines are often drawn between party activists, for whom it may be of prime importance that the party adhere to the ideals that led them to join it in the first place, and party legislators, who may well wish to trim ideological sails in order to get into office. Internal conflict along these lines was very prominent, for example, in the British Labour Party during most of the 1980s. In any case, what is important to remember is that every European political party is a political system in its own right. In order to understand what parties do, therefore, it is important to understand what is happening inside them.

## 10.4 Party membership

### 10.4.1 Who becomes a party member?

Belonging to a party in Europe is slightly more formal than in some other parts of the world, involving more than just expressing an inclination towards the party in question (Heidar, 2006). Typically, to become a party member one has to pay an annual membership fee and indicate (by signing some kind of pledge) that one accepts the basic principles of the party. This is a token requirement in most cases, although Europe's only remaining strong communist party, AKEL in Cyprus, takes it seriously and is selective about whom it admits (Christophorou, 2007: 184). Members are also expected, at least in theory, to attend regular local branch meetings.

Not surprisingly, most people who vote for a party do not go to the trouble and expense of actually joining it. Party members make up only a minority of party supporters as a whole. Just how large or small this minority is varies a lot, both from country to country and from party to party within countries. Indeed, it can be difficult to pin down exactly how many people really do belong to parties. Some parties are simply not sufficiently centralized to know how many members they have. In Switzerland, the most decentralized country in Europe, for example, party headquarters may have little knowledge of the position in the various cantons around the country. Similarly, most of the Green parties that began to emerge as a significant political force in the 1980s shunned the formal organizational structure of the established parties on principle, although in many cases they have had to think again about this in order to compete effectively with other parties (Burchell, 2001). Other parties may have a good idea of their membership but be reluctant to disclose the information publicly. In Poland, for example, one writer comments that all parties maintain high levels of secrecy regarding data on membership because of the embarrassingly low figures (Jasiewicz, 2007: 102). In France, party secrecy and outright misrepresentation mean that various researchers have come up with different figures (Billordo, 2003). Sometimes, a party event lifts the lid on the true picture. For example, in Portugal the main opposition party, the PSD, held a leadership election in 2007, and although at the time it claimed to have 146 000 members, it turned out that only 63 000 were eligible to vote as actual dues-paying members (Magone, 2008: 1113).

Consequently, even when we do manage to get membership figures for a particular party, we need to treat these sceptically. Parties have an incentive to claim more members than they really have, in the hope of increasing their legitimacy. Whether higher (claimed) numbers really mean more legitimacy is doubtful, though, given that scarcely any citizens either know or care how many members any particular party claims to have. One of the few parties with no desire to inflate its figures is the recently founded Freedom Party in the Netherlands, which has just two members: its founder Geert Wilders, and his foundation (Andeweg and Irwin, 2009: 66). As we shall see, questions have been raised as to whether any party really needs members these days. There are internal balance of power reasons, too, why membership figures may be exaggerated. The figures passed on to head office by the local organizational units around the country may not be reliable; the number of delegates each branch can send to the annual conference may depend on how many members it has, for example, so the larger it claims to be, the more delegates it can send. Local members may even pay membership dues for 'ghost' members, creating 'paper' branches, in order either to boost local representation in national bodies or to boost their own position in local intra-party competition, over candidate selection for example. Another problem is the relatively subjective definition of membership in some cases. There may be people in some parties who invariably help the party campaign during elections but who never actually join, and thus are not formally considered members. Other parties might still count as members people who, in fact, drifted away years ago but never explicitly resigned; a number of parties in southern Europe record such people as 'sympathisers', retaining their contact details as possible election-time workers (Bosco and Morlino, 2007: 7–8; van Biezen, 2008: 310). There is also a degree of 'noise' in the annual membership figures, which may fluctuate randomly or in a manner linked to the electoral cycle.

A good, through probably extreme, example of the difficulty of counting members comes from one of the countries that on paper appears to have an exceptionally high proportion of party members, namely Iceland. Perhaps appropriately, given the island's geographical location in mid-Atlantic, the concept of party membership bears as much resemblance to the American model as to the standard European one. At the time of the 2007 election, the parties' records claimed that around 38 per cent of the electorate belonged to a party. Evidence from surveys found that around 30 per cent of respondents reported that they were party members – a lower figure, but still very impressive (Hardarson and Kristinsson, 2008: 374). However, Kristjánsson suggests that most of those describing themselves as party members really meant only that they had a feeling of identity with a party, not an organizational connection. None of the parties collects annual dues from members, nor do they purge their membership lists, so anyone who ever joined is counted as a member until death. In reality, he suggests, all party work is carried out by about 0.5 to 1 per cent of the electorate (Kristjánsson, 2003).

Still, when all the qualifications are made, we can come up with at least some reasonably hard facts on party membership in individual countries. The pattern for each country is summed up in Table 10.1. It can be seen that, in most countries, only a small fraction of those who vote for a party are sufficiently committed to join it and, as we shall see, only a minority of this minority can be considered active in the party. There are only three countries, besides the dubious case of Iceland, where a tenth or more of electors join a party: Austria, Cyprus and Malta. These are all fairly small countries, and indeed there is an inverse relationship between country size and membership levels (Weldon, 2006: 471–473). The way in which the parties in Austria saturate society is well documented; over one in six of all Austrians belong to a political party, and the parties

**TABLE 10.1** Party membership as a percentage of the electorate

|  | Percentage of electorate that belongs to a political party | Trend in membership in recent decades |
| --- | --- | --- |
| Austria | 17.3 | Decline from 1980 to 1999, stability since then |
| Belgium | 5.5 | Decline from 9% in 1980 |
| Bulgaria | 5.6 | Little change since 2002 |
| Cyprus | 16.2 | No information |
| Czech Republic | 2.0 | Decline from 7% in 1993 |
| Denmark | 4.1 | Decline from over 20% in 1960s |
| Estonia | 4.9 | Modest increase since 2002 |
| Finland | 8.1 | Decline from 16% in 1980 |
| France | 1.8 | Decline from 5% in 1978 |
| Germany | 2.3 | Figure has halved since 1980 |
| Greece | 6.6 | Figure doubled 1980–1999, stability since then |
| Hungary | 1.5 | Decline from 2.1% 1999 |
| Iceland | 38.0[a] | Dramatic growth – but see note below |
| Ireland | 2.0 | Decline from 5% 1980 |
| Italy | 5.6 | Decline from 10% in 1980; but has risen from 1998 level of 4% |
| Latvia | 0.7 | Stability at very low level since mid 1990s |
| Lithuania | 2.7 | Slight increase since mid 1990s |
| Luxembourg | – | Figure stood at 10% in late 1980s |
| Malta | 30.0 | Dramatic increase in early 1980s, stability since then |
| Netherlands | 2.5 | Decline from 1980 to 1999, stability since then |
| Norway | 5.0 | Now around one-third of the 1980 figure |
| Poland | 1.0 | No significant or sustained changes |
| Portugal | 3.8 | Down from 5% 1991 |
| Romania | 3.7 | No information |
| Slovakia | 2.0 | Down from 4% in 2000 |
| Slovenia | 6.3 | Down from 10% 1998 |
| Spain | 4.4 | Steady increase from 1.2% in 1980 |
| Sweden | 3.9 | Decline from 8% 1980 |
| Switzerland | 4.8 | Down from 11% 1977 |
| United Kingdom | 1.2 | Now less than a third of 1980 figures |
| Average | 6.7 | |
| Average excluding Iceland and Malta | 4.6 | |
| Average post-communist countries | 3.0 | |

[a] For Iceland, see caveat in text, p. 330.

*Sources*: For Iceland, Hardarson and Kristinsson (2008: 374); for Malta, data are from 2004 and come from party websites. For all other countries, data are from van Biezen *et al.* (2009).

permeate many aspects of ordinary life by providing social outlets together with a patronage system so extensive that even the most menial public sector job can be hard to obtain unless one belongs to the party in whose gift it lies. An even higher proportion of Maltese electors are members of a party: the two main parties, the Maltese Labour Party (MLP) and the Partit Nazzjonalista or Nationalist Party (PN) have a social club in virtually every town of any size (for example, see the website of the PN's branch in Mellieha at http://www.mellieha.com/pn/), which is the centre of social life for many members, and they have a range of ancillary organizations plus their own radio stations. The PN has separate associations for workers, the self-employed, pensioners, women, and young people; it runs its own travel agency; and it has a section called 'Team Sports PN' that organizes tournaments for members and supporters in various sports, such as football, athletics and snooker (information from the party's website at www.pn.org.mt). Some of the Cypriot parties, too, are deeply embedded in a subculture (Dunphy and Bale, 2007: 300).

It is generally accepted that membership figures are declining right across western Europe, even if the biggest drops took place between 1980 and 2000, with near-stability since then in most countries. From a survey of membership data in 27 European countries between 1980 and the late 2000s, van Biezen et al. (2009) found that the trend was downwards everywhere except Greece and Spain; for the period since the late 1990s, there was also growth in Estonia and Italy. Moreover, even the 1980 figures represent a decline from earlier decades. We can illustrate the decline by considering a few specific examples. In Denmark, over a fifth of all registered voters were party members in the early 1960s, but by 2008 only one in 25 belonged to a party. In Britain, individual membership of the Labour Party fell from a peak of just over a million in 1952 to fewer than 200000 in 2008, and the drop in Conservative membership has been just as precipitous. Even allowing for the likelihood that computerization and more efficient database management means that parties now have a more realistic (and lower) idea of how many members they really have, the overall picture of decline is clear.

We can explain the decline in membership by considering the reasons why people might join a party in the first place. It was suggested in the 1960s by Clark and Wilson that there are three main motives that might lead someone to join a party (see Clark and Wilson, 1961; Ware, 1996: 68–78). One is *material*, the desire to gain some tangible reward, such as a public office or a public resource controlled by the party, or to build a political career. This has been important in such countries as Austria, Belgium, Greece, Italy and Spain (Hopkin, 2006). Even so, it is generally a minor factor, and is under attack in those countries where the 'party card' is still an asset when it comes to being given a public sector job. The second motive is *solidary*, referring to the desire for social contact and a sense of comradeship in a common enterprise; with the rise of a wide range of leisure opportunities and the decline in cohesiveness among subcultures and communities, this is of diminishing importance. The third is *purposive*, in other words directed towards a specific end, referring to a desire to advance certain policy goals. This, too, is under challenge, although perhaps not as much as the first two: the attraction of joining a party in order to promote a particular issue is weakened by the rise of social movements, single-issue pressure groups, and community action groups, which provide other, perhaps more satisfying, ways of participating. For such groups a particular issue is its members' top priority, whereas for a party any issue is just one among many, and may get lost from view if the party enters government.

Across western Europe, then, membership levels are declining. In the post-communist countries these levels were low to start with (for parties in post-communist countries generally, see Bugajski, 2002). Under the communist regimes, many people felt that it was unwise or pointless to become politically active, and this pattern has generally continued since the collapse of communism. In some, such as Poland, the very concept of party partisanship had negative connotations going back before the communist era. Polish parties score very low in terms of trust, and are regarded as 'selfish, quarrelsome, divisive and possibly corrupt' (Kostelecky, 2002: 153; Sanford, 2002: 195). Thus membership is low as a result of both supply-side and demand-side factors: the great majority of Poles see no point in joining a party, while existing party leaders, for their part, feel no burning desire to try to recruit members (Szczerbiak, 2001b). This applies in virtually all post-communist countries. Membership is particularly low in Latvia, something that has been attributed partly to the 'open list' electoral system (see Chapter 11 for discussion of such systems). This means that, for candidates, building support among voters is more important than having a strong base within the party organization (Smith-Sivertsen, 2004). Even when membership is apparently quite high, we need to treat the figures with some suspicion. When Estonian membership lists were made public in 2002, it turned out that some 'members' were unaware of their supposed membership, while one party's membership claims surpassed the number of votes it won at the following year's election (Sikk, 2006: 344, 360).

Parties in post-communist countries are characterized by low and often declining membership, and weak links with civil society (Jungerstam-Mulders, 2006; Kopecký, 2008: 2). Many are short-lived, which, as we saw in Chapter 7, makes it difficult to speak of a party 'system' in most countries. Parties come and go rapidly; an average of 5.6 new parties have emerged at each election since the end of communism, and in several elections new parties have won more than half of the votes (Tavits, 2008: 114). Even if there is a degree of continuity between previous and apparently new parties (Lewis, 2007: 179–180), it is easy to understand why parties do not manage to build up a loyal body of members. For example, in Bulgaria the former king, Simeon II, founded a party, the NDSV, before the 2001 election, and it won 43 per cent of the votes despite having scarcely any members or organization. By 2009 it had disappeared as an electoral force – but Simeon's former bodyguard formed another new party, GERB ('Citizens for European Development of Bulgaria'), which won almost half of the seats at the 2009 election. Meanwhile, in 2008 a Lithuanian television personality founded a 'National Resurrection Party', which he promised would deliver 'plenty of mirth and merriment' and used the slogan 'the ship is sinking, at least with us it will be more fun'. Such parties might exist as light relief in many countries – but in Lithuania the NRP became the third strongest party after the election, and joined the next government. Such fluidity has general problems for society; mandate responsiveness is weak, given the vague promises that parties make and the uncertainty as to whether parties will be around long enough to accept responsibility for decisions they made while in office (Roberts, 2010: 88). The transience of parties means they cannot establish a membership base, and the lack of such a base helps explain their transience and policy vagueness. They have been branded with labels such as 'voicemail parties', 'virtual parties', 'couch parties' (all their members could fit on one couch), or 'head without a body parties' (they have leaders and MPs but scarcely any members).

One reason why membership was low from the start in post-communist countries is that nearly all the parties were founded after 1989 from the top down by elites looking to build support organizations, rather than emerging, as many of their western counterparts did in the early twentieth century, from significant social forces in society (Mair, 1997: 183–187). A related reason is that by the time these parties were formed, parties no longer needed a lot of members.

Therefore, rather like countries that missed out on the Industrial Revolution being able to skip straight from an agricultural economy to a high-tech one, post-communist countries simply arrived at once at the low membership levels to which western parties seem to be gradually dwindling. Post-communist parties emerging in recent times could be deliberately designed by elites as low-membership organizations, whereas most western parties retain an organizational structure that evolved many decades ago to meet the needs of ordinary members. We return to this later in the chapter.

As a general rule, party members are not entirely socially representative of party voters. Anders Widfeldt analysed surveys of the public across Europe in the late 1980s; since these surveys enquired about party membership, Widfeldt was able to compare members of a party with other supporters of the party. He found that women were consistently under-represented: in 34 of the 37 parties for which there were data, the proportion of men was higher among party members than among other party supporters. Likewise, young people were under-represented among party members while the middle-aged were over-represented, and working-class people were under-represented in virtually every party compared with their strength among other party supporters. He concludes: 'the members of political parties in western Europe are, on the whole, not socially representative of party supporters. Party members tend to be disproportionately male, middle-aged and middle-class' (Widfeldt, 1995: 165). There was no consistent pattern as to which parties had memberships that were closest to being a social cross-section of party supporters; in some countries, this might be true of right-wing parties, while in other countries left-wing parties had this position.

These broad findings tally with information on some specific parties that have been studied in greater detail. An Internet survey in Britain in 2008, for example, found that, compared with the electorate as a whole, members were more likely to be retired, and they were five years older than the average adult. They were more likely than the electorate at large to be highly educated, high earners and in professional jobs, and, most strikingly, two-thirds were male (Whiteley, 2009).

The decline in membership numbers means that parties have become less firmly implanted in civil society than they were in earlier decades, and calls into question their ability to perform their linkage role. One analysis suggests that memberships are now so small and socio-demographically unrepresentative that 'it might be reasonable to regard them not as constituting part of civil society – with which party membership has traditionally been associated – but rather as constituting the outer ring of an extended political class' (van Biezen et al., 2009: 10). The shrinkage in membership is one reason why well-resourced parties nowadays spend their money on setting up focus groups; in an ideal world, parties would have their ears close enough to the ground not to need focus groups to tell them what the public is thinking. At the same time, while it is easy to be cynical about parties that pre-test their policies in the same way as a soft-drinks manufacturer would seek consumer feedback on a new product, we should not adopt too rosy a view of the past. Party members are not necessarily a reliable touchstone of what the voters are thinking, since their views may be out of line with those of voters, as we discuss later in this chapter. Moreover, while parties risk appearing unprincipled if they adapt their policies according to what focus groups or opinion polls tell them, they will be accused of arrogance if they stick to a fixed set of 'principled' policies regardless of what the voters think about these. Even so, falling membership numbers do pose problems for parties, as we explain later in the chapter.

## 10.4.2 The activities of party members

What do party members do? In virtually all parties nowadays, members tend to be most active at election time, playing an important role in campaigning at the grassroots level. In particular, they have a part to play in mobilizing the faithful, by putting up posters, looking after party stalls and handing out leaflets in public places, and even, in a few countries such as Britain and Ireland, going from house to house and knocking on doors to rekindle dormant loyalties and to show that the party has a local presence. Between elections, undoubtedly, many party branches are not especially active. The more committed members attend branch meetings regularly, to discuss ways of expanding the organization at the local level, or to decide their stance on issues due to arise at the next annual conference.

In most parties, only a small proportion of members can really be considered activists, that is, regular attenders at local branch meetings and participants in the party's internal affairs (Heidar, 2006). Surveys in Britain, Denmark and Ireland have found a majority of members reporting that they do not spend any time at all on party activities in the average month (Gallagher and Marsh 2004: 413; Pedersen *et al.*, 2004: 375; Seyd and Whiteley, 2004: 359). It is also true that branch meetings may not be needed to bring members together these days; communication is possible by means of telephone, email or – especially in rural areas – by face-to-face contact in the course of daily life (Gallagher and Marsh, 2002: 103; Heidar and Saglie, 2003a: 771–776; Heidar and Saglie, 2003b: 231–232). Even so, the general impression is that most party organizations are merely 'ticking over' for most of the time, springing to life during election campaigns.

One concern for parties is that the humdrum nature of internal party life may mean that party organizations now come to attract only people who are interested in precisely that: party organization. Ware (1992: 79) quotes from a study of British Conservative members that concluded that 'what all activists were interested in was not politics but organization.' A few years earlier, a Conservative minister had put the point more pungently in his private diary, noting that his local party organization members were 'boring, petty, malign, clumsily conspiratorial and parochial' (quoted in Kingdom, 2003: 313). The question of who will become the next constituency organization chairperson animates some members much more than the party's policy on economic growth. Other parties, too, have concluded that the frequency of meetings meant that the organization was becoming 'introverted' or 'inward-looking', and was 'literally talking to itself' rather than engaging with the public (Gallagher and Marsh, 2002: 81). Members, or potential members, with ideas and enthusiasm find little to attract them in such an environment. However, a study of young members (in the 18–25 age bracket) did not discover such a negative picture, although it is possible that the more 'moral-minded' (idealistic) and 'social-minded' members will drift away from the parties they joined, and that the 'professional-minded' young members, who look forward to a career in politics, gradually become as organization-oriented as the existing long-term members (Bruter and Harrison, 2009).

It was not always like this. As mentioned in the preceding chapter, belonging to a party in the early years of the twentieth century could mean living within what was virtually a separate subculture in society. This was especially true of left-wing parties with a mass membership, such as the German SPD. Belonging to the SPD was almost a way of life. The party had its own newspaper, which members bought, read, and discussed with one another, and its branch offices all over Germany were centres of social activity for members, running stamp-collecting clubs and sports teams, organizing outings, and so on. It ran its own health service, paid for by members

## BOX 10.1: MEMBERSHIP OF POLITICAL PARTIES

### Denmark

Membership in Denmark, as in most countries, has declined steadily since the 1960s, when over a fifth of Danes belonged to a party. By 1980 the figure was down to 7 per cent, and in 2008 it was just over 4 per cent. Nonetheless, political parties, like just about every other political institution or body in the country, are highly regarded by Danes: when citizens across the EU were asked in 2009 whether they trusted or distrusted political parties, Denmark was the only country in which trust outweighed distrust.

### France

Reliable figures on party membership in France are hard to come by, but estimates concur on figures that represent a low and declining proportion of voters. The UMP has most members, followed by the PS, which has never been a mass membership party. The Communist Party claims to have over half as many members as the PS, although, given its record of electoral decline over the last two decades, some analysts are sceptical. Members in all parties, with the occasional exception of the Socialists, have a reputation for being deferential towards their leaders.

### Germany

Party membership in post-war Germany has fluctuated somewhat, but has been consistently low by general west European standards. The Social Democrats (SPD) had the largest number of members prior to the 1990s, but by the end of that decade they had been overtaken by the combined strength of the two parties in the main right-wing bloc, the CDU and CSU. The CDU, in particular, traditionally attached low priority to the recruitment of members, but after losing office in 1969 it set about strengthening its organization so as to challenge the dominance of the SPD on the ground. Its membership more than doubled during its 13-year period in opposition; in government from 1982 to 1998 membership fell slightly, but not to the same extent as SPD membership. The FDP has far fewer members, and the Greens are smaller still. Following the reunification of Germany in 1990, all the parties sought to extend their membership in the former East Germany, but only the Free Democrats had much success in this, and the low levels of membership in all post-communist countries mean that unification was one factor in reducing overall German party membership. Die Linke (The Left) has significant numbers of members from both east and west, and overall has a few thousand more than the FDP. The Greens, like their counterparts elsewhere, and despite (or because of) their ethos of membership participation in internal party decision-making, have relatively few members.

### Italy

The party with the most members in post-war Italy was the Communist Party (PCI), which in the early 1990s was reborn as the PDS and then the DS (Democratic Left), with far fewer members than the PCI, before merging with another party in 2007 to form the DP. In the late 1980s two of the government parties, the Christian Democrats (DC) and the Socialists (PSI), had over two million members between them, but these parties both disintegrated as a result of the scandals that convulsed Italian politics in the early 1990s, and the evidence suggests that most of their members drifted away from politics. Forza Italia was founded by the media tycoon Silvio Berlusconi in 1993, and was initially described as a 'virtual party' with no real organizational structure and a small membership base, but by 2008 it had reached 400 000 members compared with 615 000 for the DP. Forza Italia's increase in enrolment is one reason why Italy is among the few countries to show membership growth since the turn of the century. The Lega Nord remains strongly organized, and its membership levels grew in the second half of the 2000s.

## Netherlands

Over the last 40 years, the membership of the Dutch parties has declined from a level that was never particularly high by general European standards. The drop has been most pronounced among the religious parties (now combined in the CDA); membership fell from about half a million in 1950 to around 68 000 in 2009. The membership of the Socialist PvdA halved from the early 1980s to the mid 2000s. In most parties, the activity of sections such as youth movements and women's groups seems to have declined. The Freedom Party was founded in 2005, becoming the third largest party in parliament at the 2010 election, and has deliberately eschewed the conventional membership model; from the start it has had just one member, its leader Geert Wilders.

## Poland

In reaction to the pervasive control of the Communist Party from the late 1940s onward, the Law on Political Parties adopted in 1990 required only 15 signatures (raised to 1000 in 1997) for a political party to be registered. There are many officially registered active parties, but most have few members. Party membership in Poland remains low, hovering around 1 per cent of the electorate. According to claimed figures, the two parties with most members in 2009 were two of the parties that had existed under communism, the Peasant Party (PSL) and the post-communist SLD, which accounted between them for almost two-thirds of the country's party members, even though at the 2007 election they won only 22 per cent of the votes. Parties were mostly founded by political entrepreneurs rather than emerging from significant social forces, and thus, by design, they do not give a strong role to members in internal decision-making. When Europeans were surveyed in autumn 2009 about their trust in parties, Poles were near the bottom of the list, with only 7 per cent expressing trust and 88 per cent distrust.

## Spain

The Spanish parties had exceptionally small memberships in the years after the return to democracy in the late 1970s, but, unlike most European parties, they have been gaining rather than losing members since then. The right-wing PP more than doubled its membership during the 1990s, and the Socialists (PSOE) also showed a steady increase. Overall levels have risen from 1 per cent in 1980 to 2 per cent in 1990, 3 per cent in 2000 and 4 per cent in 2008, yet are still below the European average. The legacy of dictatorship is sometimes suggested as an explanation for the phenomenon, as it led to a political culture that did not encourage active participation in politics, just as in communist regimes.

## United Kingdom

Party membership in Britain has declined markedly since the 1950s, even allowing for the patchy data available on membership. Research in the early 1990s discovered that the average Conservative member was aged 62; these members have a reputation for being more right-wing than Conservative MPs, and are noted for their strong Euro-scepticism. The party had an estimated two to three million members in the 1950s and 1960s, but this had declined to only a quarter of a million by the end of the 2000s. Labour's figures followed a bell curve during the twentieth century. Up to the mid 1940s the party had on average around a third of a million members each year, but then membership rose to a peak of over a million in the early 1950s. The pattern since then has been one of steady decline, back to fewer than 200 000 in 2008. The membership of all the other British parties is small.

through a health insurance scheme, and sought to look after members and their families from the cradle to the grave. In 1906 it founded a training school in Berlin for the political education of members, grooming the most committed to take up places in the ranks of its full-time employees. Given that many members worked in factories alongside fellow party members and belonged to trade unions associated with the party, they were virtually cocooned from contact with the rest of German society.

But even in the heyday of mass parties, in the first half of the twentieth century, few European parties managed to 'encapsulate' their members to this extent. Not only has the number of party members generally diminished, as we have seen, but the commitment of those members may well have waned – although we should not imagine that a few decades ago party members behaved very differently, since the available evidence suggests that levels of activism among members were low throughout the twentieth century (Scarrow, 1996: 181–194; Allern and Pedersen, 2007: 79). The 'golden age' of mass and active party membership is yet another golden age that perhaps never really existed. Certainly, some of the reasons why people might once have joined parties now have much less force. The modern welfare state has taken over many of the functions that party insurance schemes once performed. A rise in living standards, a huge increase in leisure outlets, and the advent of television and the Internet have all combined to reduce the appeal of spending evenings playing table tennis in the local party hall. Fewer people are living in a party-dominated subculture, and the parties in Malta and, perhaps, Cyprus are now virtually unique in Europe in their capacity to structure their members' leisure activities to a significant extent. Television has undermined much of the rationale for party newspapers, so few European parties nowadays run their own papers, and when they do, these often make a loss. The dedicated party activist, spending much of his or her free time debating and propagating the party's policy and ideology, is becoming a creature of the past, maybe indeed of a mythical and non-existent past.

All of this does not mean that ordinary members no longer play a role within European parties. On the contrary, they are important in giving these parties a character quite distinct from that of their American counterparts. The role of European party members in certain key areas gives parties a reasonable degree of coherence, as we see when we look at power within parties.

## 10.5 Power within parties

Who controls European parties? Who wields power within them? Who determines the packages they offer to the voters at elections, and the policies they implement if they get into office? In reality, there is no one answer to this question. It is just not the case that all power lies in one place and every other part of the party is powerless. Usually, the internal affairs of parties are characterized by a continuous process of accommodation and mutual adjustment. When it comes to the crunch, most party members at every level would rather keep the party together as an effective body than precipitate a destructive split – although, of course, sometimes internal differences are so great that a split does take place and a new party is formed, a development that is more common in new party systems than in established ones. More commonly, there is a constant process of give and take, and the party remains together precisely because a balance of power is respected and no one element tries to achieve complete control. The various elements in the party organization – the leader, MPs, rank-and-file members, and so on – may jostle for position, but there is rarely open warfare of the sort that in the United States is prone to break out at primaries. After all, they all belong to the same party and can be assumed to have a broadly similar political outlook. They are bound to disagree on details, but the leader and parliamentarians usually have some freedom of manoeuvre, provided that they stay within the broad parameters of what is acceptable to the membership.

There are several important areas of activity where conflict can arise within a party, and where we might look in order to try to identify the most powerful actors within the party. Three, in particular, have the potential to be key battle sites. The first is the writing of the party's manifesto, the set of policies upon which it fights elections. The second is the election of the party leader, and the third is the selection of the party's parliamentary candidates. We shall examine each of these in turn.

### 10.5.1 The party manifesto and programme

Two of the party's policy documents are especially significant: the party manifesto, the formal declaration in which a party tells the voters what it will aim to do if it gets into government; and the party programme, the statement of the party's aims and aspirations, which is generally updated every few years. Party members often differ among themselves as to what should be put in these documents, partly because not all members have exactly the same policy preferences, and partly because some members are more concerned than others with winning votes as opposed to maintaining ideological purity. Arguments about the party's policies often surface at annual conferences, where tension is sometimes apparent between parliamentarians and rank-and-file members. The rank and file, especially in radical parties, is inclined to suspect the deputies of being seduced by the club-like atmosphere of parliament, of forgetting their roots, and of being willing to betray the party's principles in order to get into the comfortable seats of power. The deputies, in turn, may view some members as being unworldly zealots who are unaware that compromises and bargaining are necessary in order to achieve at least part of what the party stands for, and are obsessed with policies that have no hope of ever being acceptable to the wider electorate.

Although some party activists may feel like fighting over every semicolon in the party's manifesto and programme, in the belief that they are taking part in a battle for the party's soul, others conclude, as indeed do most political scientists, that this is probably not the most important arena of intra-party conflict. Parties feel that they have to have a manifesto, to show that they are to be taken seriously – and they would certainly be criticized if they didn't have one. However, there is no real expectation that many people will read it; realistically, everyone, including the party, knows perfectly well that most voters don't bother to read manifestos. At most, the party hopes that some of the main, or at least most vote-catching, ideas will be highlighted by the media. And although a manifesto is in theory a commitment by the party to do certain things if it gets into government, in practice few voters are so naive as to believe that a party, once in government, feels bound to do everything mentioned in its manifesto and to do nothing that is not mentioned there. Parties always have good excuses for not fulfilling their manifesto pledges; they will be able to point to some unexpected development that threw their plans off course, such as a worldwide economic downturn, for example. As we shall see in Chapter 14, even academics who have spent a lot of time on the question find it a challenge to establish the extent to which parties actually do what they promised to do, so the average voter is unlikely to keep a running tally of pledge fulfilment.

Many election manifestos are drawn up by groups close to the party leadership, with little real membership involvement. If manifestos and policy programmes come to be drawn up in such a way that the leadership is not keen on the result, then these documents are likely simply to gather dust from the moment they are published. If a particular party is in government, furthermore, its ministers, while always trying to keep the party onside, are unlikely to feel bound by the details of a manifesto that they can dismiss as the brainchild of some starry-eyed young enthusiasts hired by head office. Examples abound of parties, especially left-wing parties, where membership participation in drawing up supposedly key documents has meant very little. For example, the Spanish Socialists engaged in a massive exercise from 1987 to 1990 to draw up a new programme, involving 950 000 people and 14 900 debates, but once it was adopted little more was heard of it (Gillespie, 1993: 93–94). In other words, the content of manifestos and programmes can hardly be said to determine the behaviour of the party's ministers should it get into office. Most members are well aware of this, and do not believe that, even if they have a major input into the manifesto, they will really be determining the behaviour of their party ministers in a future government, and this naturally makes them less likely to care deeply about the contents of the manifesto.

While members do not have a real input into the manifesto as a whole, increasingly parties are holding internal referendums among their members on specific policy issues (for a list see Sussman, 2007: 2). For example, the French Socialist Party, the PS, held a referendum in 2004 to decide its attitude towards the planned EU Constitutional Treaty, an issue that divided the party at every level. Both sides were equally resourced by the party in terms of subsidies, local meetings, and space in the party media, and the outcome was fairly close, 59–41 in favour of supporting the treaty (Crespy, 2008; Wagner, 2008). Likewise, in both Denmark and Sweden parties have held a referendum to decide their attitude towards the EU. We discuss the implications of this growing use of internal party referendums later in the chapter.

## 10.5.2 Election of the party leader

A second important area of potential conflict is the election of the party leader. The leader of any organization can be expected to be more powerful than other members, and leaders of political parties are especially important because, during election campaigns, much of the focus of the media is upon the party leaders. In the case of some parties it may be hard to say who exactly the leader is: there may be a party chairperson, a party president and a parliamentary leader, with different people holding these positions and no clear designation of one as 'the' leader. For some of these parties, such as the Norwegian centre-right Høyre, it is conventional to see the real leader as the person who would become prime minister if the party came to hold that position in a future government (Heidar, 1997: 133). The same is true in many other countries, even if it is not quite an acid test. In Denmark there is considerable variation among the parties as to the official position that the 'real' leader holds (Bille, 2000: 140). The fact that most prime ministers are party leaders makes the election of a leader an important process within parties. Of the last 11 British prime ministers, going back to Anthony Eden, only five have entered 10 Downing Street following an election victory. The other six – Eden, Harold Macmillan, Alec Douglas-Home, James Callaghan, John Major and Gordon Brown – took over in mid-term following the resignation of the incumbent, and they became prime minister solely because they were picked as the new *party* leader (Kenig, 2009: 241). Not all party leaders become prime ministers, but pretty much every prime minister needs to become a party leader first.

Among those parties for which we can clearly identify the leader, there are several distinct methods of selection. In some parties – examples can be found in Denmark, Ireland and the Netherlands – the parliamentary group, comprising the party's elected deputies, plays a major or indeed exclusive role in choosing the leader. In many other parties – including a number in Austria, Finland, Germany, Norway and Sweden – a party congress or convention picks the leader. A model that is becoming more common allows a direct vote among the entire membership, a method used in some or all parties in Belgium, Britain, Denmark, France, Germany, Iceland and Ireland (LeDuc, 2001; Quinn, 2004; Bosco and Morlino, 2007: 9; Wauters, 2010). Thus, in Britain, David Cameron was chosen as Conservative leader by a postal ballot of all party members in 2005. In 2010 all Labour members had a vote in the election to pick the successor to Gordon Brown, but as part of an 'electoral college' in which the votes of members, MPs and members of affiliated trade unions each counted for a third of the total vote. David Miliband won most support among party members and MPs, but was beaten by his brother Ed due to the latter's strong lead among trade union members. The motive for giving all members a vote may be to attract new members by giving them a meaningful role within the party or, to take a more cynical view, to bypass the influence of supposedly more 'extreme' party activists, something that we discuss more fully later.

Some parties are throwing caution to the winds and opening up leadership elections to all comers. This creates the risk that the supporters of other parties might deliberately saddle a rival with the least appealing option on offer, although this does not seem to have happened yet. In Italy in October 2005 the centre-left parties held a primary at which anyone, having paid a small amount to help defray the cost of the exercise, could cast a vote to decide who should be their prime ministerial candidate. Over four million people turned out to vote, and Romano Prodi was the comfortable winner. Two years later, when the two main parties of the centre left merged, they repeated the exercise to decide who should lead the new party; this time 3.5 million voted, and the mayor of Rome, Walter Veltroni, won 75 per cent of the votes. The two main Greek parties have used a similar, albeit more controlled, method to select their leaders, although PASOK's 'election' was more of a coronation, as there was only one candidate.

In any case, and whatever the leadership selection method, the leader's job will be very difficult if he or she does not have the confidence of the party's parliamentarians. This was shown in October 2003 when Britain's Conservative MPs voted out Iain Duncan-Smith, who had been chosen as leader by the members just two years earlier in a decision that rapidly came to seem a mistake (Denham and O'Hara, 2008: 85–96). Duncan-Smith was widely regarded as 'not up to the job', and became a figure of fun in the media. After his removal from office, MPs prevented members from having any say in choosing his successor by rallying behind a single candidate, Michael Howard. Under the party's rules, while members choose the leader, it is MPs who nominate the candidates, so the members' power of choice can be rendered worthless if the MPs collectively agree on just one name.

### 10.5.3 Selection of the parliamentary candidates

A third area of prime importance for politics within parties is candidate selection (Gallagher and Marsh, 1988; Narud *et al.*, 2002; Rahat, 2007; Field and Siavelis, 2008; Hazan and Rahat 2010). The selection of the individuals who are entitled to use the party's label when they stand for election plays a crucial role in the political recruitment process. Only the people selected as candidates can become members of parliament, and in virtually every country most or all government ministers are present or former members of parliament. After the 2010 election in the United Kingdom, for example, 564 of the 649 MPs elected represented either the Conservative Party or the Labour Party. Each of these parties nominated 630 candidates, one in each mainland British constituency (apart from the constituency of the Speaker of the Commons). The people who selected these 1260 Conservative and Labour candidates therefore exercised an enormous power over who could and who could not get into the House of Commons and, beyond that, into government. Moreover, many seats in Britain (approximately 500 of them) are known to be 'safe seats' for one or other party, at least under the SMP electoral system used up to now, and in these cases selecting the candidate is tantamount to picking the MP. In some other countries, too, the candidate selectors can reasonably be seen as choosing members of parliament. For example, in a number of European countries such as Italy and Spain, as we shall see in the next chapter, the electoral system presents voters with a number of 'closed' party lists, each list containing the names of candidates in a fixed order that the voters cannot alter. If a party wins, say, five seats in a particular district, these seats go to the top five names on the list, and it is the candidate selectors who determine which individuals are chosen to occupy these positions. When the voters have no power to choose among the candidates of their favoured party, and when ordinary MPs have significant influence over policy outcomes – so that, in effect, the candidate selectors are directly picking the people who will wield real power – candidate selection is particularly important (Cross, 2008).

In 1997 Tony Blair became prime minister of Britain, swept into office with a huge majority on a powerful wave of personal popularity. However, in order to attain this position, Blair had had to become Labour leader, for which he needed to be a Labour MP, and in order to achieve that, he had to be selected as a Labour candidate in a constituency that his party had a chance of winning. By far the most difficult hurdle that he had to overcome was the last of these. In the early 1980s he made unsuccessful attempts to be picked as the Labour candidate in a number of constituencies where Labour might win the seat. Finally, shortly before the 1983 election, he sought to be selected as the party's candidate in the safe Labour seat of Sedgefield in the northeast of England, a constituency with which he had no previous connection. He had first of all to persuade the sceptical members of a Labour branch in the constituency to nominate him for inclusion on the panel from which the shortlist would be picked. The branch did this, but all seemed lost when he was omitted from the shortlist of six that was drawn up by the handful of people who constituted the constituency executive committee. However, one of the members of the branch that had nominated him had become so impressed by Blair that he persuaded the committee at a late stage to add Blair to the shortlist. The 119 members entitled to make the decision then met all seven people seeking the nomination, after which they picked Blair as the Labour candidate; he duly won the seat at the election and, given that it was a safe Labour seat, became in effect an MP for as long as he wanted to remain in the Commons (Rentoul, 1995: 91–137). If he had not managed to secure selection as a Labour candidate by a small number of people in one of the proverbial smoke-filled rooms, either in Sedgefield or in another constituency that was winnable for Labour, he could never have become prime minister.

Aspiring politicians who do not meet with the approval of these powerful gatekeepers, the major parties' candidate selectors, can either start their own party, with very limited chances of success, or find that their political careers are dead in the water. Candidate selection is thus a crucial step in the political recruitment process. For this reason, it is also a key area of internal party activity. If one section of a party, such as the party leader or the national executive, has control over the selection process, then this section can almost be said to control the party. Candidate selection is thus a vital matter in every individual European political party; it is also important – indeed, it is one of the key factors – in making European political parties very different from American parties.

This is because European parties control their own candidate selection – albeit, as we shall see, with considerable variation as to who exactly within the party can be said to occupy this controlling position. The only European country with parties that use American-style open primaries, in which anyone who wishes to participate can do so, is Iceland, where primaries have been used since 1914 and have become common since the early 1970s. At the 2007 election it was found that 30 per cent of voters had taken part in a primary at that election: 69 per cent of self-described party members, and 16 per cent of non-members (Hardarson and Kristinsson, 2008: 375). It has at most been dabbled with by parties elsewhere. In 2009 the British Conservatives held an open primary in the Totnes constituency, sending ballot papers and pre-paid reply envelopes to all 69 000 people on the electoral register. Over 16 000 votes were cast, and the selected candidate went on to win the seat at the 2010 election. However, the exercise cost the party £38 000, implying a cost of around £24 million to do this in every constituency, so on financial grounds alone this approach is likely to be used infrequently. Besides, when every voter in the constituency is able to play a part in this process, local party members and activists have no more power than anyone else, and might well wonder why they bother paying a membership fee and working for the party.

In every other country in Europe the power to choose candidates is kept within the party. Perhaps surprisingly, given the importance of candidate selection in affecting the composition of parliament, the process is regulated by law in only a few countries. In Finland parties are legally obliged to open up the process of candidate selection to a direct vote of all their members, while in Germany the law ensures that candidates are selected by local party organizations, with the parties' national executives having no power to overturn the decisions reached locally. Parties in every other country are in effect treated as private bodies, and can make whatever arrangements they wish when they pick parliamentary candidates, reflecting a strong constitutional norm of freedom of political association.

The furthest that any party outside Iceland goes down the road towards opening up its selection process to all and sundry is to adopt 'party primaries' (sometimes known as OMOV, standing for one member one vote), which allow each paid-up party member a direct say in the choice of parliamentary candidates. This method of choosing candidates, although still employed by only a minority of parties, is becoming more common (Scarrow et al., 2000; Bille, 2001; Hazan and Rahat, 2010: 91–103). It is a method employed in Austria, Britain, Finland (where, as we have seen, it is obligatory under law), Ireland (by two of the largest three parties, Fine Gael and Labour) and the Netherlands (by D66). In addition, in some other countries, such as Belgium, Denmark and Germany, there is provision for party primaries, although in practice other methods of candidate selection are sometimes employed. In Denmark the process, always fairly open and democratic, has become even more so, with the role of individual members increasing even as the number of members has declined (Bille, 2001: 373–378). This method increases the quantity of participation in the process, but not necessarily the quality, in the sense that many members are recruited by aspiring candidates solely to support them in the vote, have no commitment to the party, and leave once they have cast their vote in the party primary (Hazan and Rahat, 2010: 98–103). In addition, while party primaries provide an incentive to membership, they provide a disincentive to activism, since the most passive member has just as much power as the most active.

More commonly, candidate selection involves interplay between the local and central party organizations, with the balance varying from case to case. Often, the key decisions are taken locally, with national actors sometimes attempting to influence the process. In other parties the balance is different, in that the ultimate decisions are taken nationally, with local organizations trying to influence the outcome.

The nature of the candidate selection process is affected by the electoral system. This does not determine either the nature or the outputs of candidate selection, but it 'constrains and conditions the parties' menu of choices concerning candidate selection' (Hazan and Voerman, 2006: 159). If a country is divided into single-member constituencies, then, quite obviously, each party will select only one candidate in each constituency, whereas in proportional representation (PR) systems based on multi-member constituencies it is common for several candidates from the same party to be picked. The evidence from many countries, as we discuss in greater detail in the next chapter, is that under PR the selectors then aim to 'balance the ticket', ensuring that both men and women are represented, along with individuals who will appeal to different sectoral or geographical interests within the constituency (Gallagher, 1988). However, the degree of centralization of the process is difficult to explain simply in terms of the political institutional features of a country, and one of the few identifiable patterns is that large parties tend to have a more centralized procedure than small ones (Lundell, 2004). In addition, there is often considerable variation between different parties in the same country – as, for example, in Poland – which shows that neither institutional nor cultural features of a country can entirely determine the nature of candidate selection (Szczerbiak, 1999, 2001a: 58–62).

Does it matter who selects the candidates? It could indeed matter if different actors within the party had different values and priorities, in which case whoever gains control of candidate selection could ensure that only those people holding certain political views are picked as candidates, and hence have a chance of becoming parliamentarians. In addition, variations in this essentially private process might have a discernible impact upon the socio-demographic composition of parliament, if these variations lead to differences in the proportions of women, young people and ethnic minorities in parliament.

When we try to identify the values that selectors impart to the candidate selection process, we find that selectors everywhere tend to appreciate certain characteristics in aspiring candidates: having local roots is always welcomed (even in Britain, although it is by no means essential there), as is possessing a solid record as a party member. Sometimes, though, parties are willing to offer a candidacy to non-members who have proven appeal, in the hope of thereby boosting the party's votes. Another universal pattern is that incumbent MPs are only rarely deselected, that is, they are nearly always picked to run again.

Most candidates in most parties are of higher socio-economic status than the voters for the same parties, but this is not necessarily due to bias on the selectors' part. British candidate selectors are sometimes accused of favouring wealthy, upper-class men when making their choices, although an investigation of the selection process at the 1992 election concluded that the backgrounds of successful seekers after a nomination were not very different from those of unsuccessful ones, and so, apart from some possible discrimination against women by Labour selectors, there was little evidence of bias on the part of selectors (Norris and Lovenduski, 1997). Given the under-representation of women in every European parliament (we discuss this further in the next chapter), several countries or parties have chosen to adopt gender quotas, under which, typically, at least a third (or 40 per cent) of candidates must be male and the same proportion must be female (Krook, 2009). These have made a difference, quotas being strongly correlated with the proportion of MPs who are female (Tripp and Kang, 2008: 350).

France took a slightly different route, with the introduction in 2000 of the so-called *parity law*, under which, at National Assembly elections, parties are expected to ensure that precisely half of their candidates are male and half female. If they fall short of this target their state-supplied finance is reduced somewhat, but not by enough to encourage any party to pass over a strongly placed male candidate in favour of a less electorally appealing female. As a result, the smaller parties all scrupulously respect the 50–50 balance, but the larger ones, especially the right-wing UMP, prefer to suffer some financial penalty rather than risk losing an election (Murray, 2007).

Generally, how far the selectors' own views impinge upon the nature of the candidates they select is a rather under-researched question. In some cases there are suspicions that the members deliberately reject aspiring candidates whose views are not the same as their own. In Britain's Conservative Party in recent years, it has become difficult for anyone without Euro-sceptic views to gain selection as a candidate, with the result that the parliamentary party has become overwhelmingly Euro-sceptic (Webb, 2000: 185). In the 1980s there was a widespread perception that members of the Labour Party were left-wing 'extremists', and that they were picking candidates of a similar persuasion and thereby potentially making the party unelectable. However, a study of British Labour Party activists found that although they saw themselves as further to the left than Labour voters, they deliberately selected Labour candidates whose views were more moderate than their own, especially in marginal constituencies, so as not to damage the party's electoral chances (Bochel and Denver, 1983: 60).

In principle, as the selectorate becomes wider and more inclusive, we might expect party cohesion in parliament to decline, but an effect might appear only once the level of inclusiveness passes a certain threshold, such as opening up the process to all party voters as in the USA (Hazan and Rahat, 2006: 379–382). Before that threshold is reached, it may not matter greatly exactly *who* within the party chooses the candidates, but it does matter a lot that it is *someone* within the party, and not the voters at large, who chooses them. Even if different actors within the party have different priorities and views on some issues, they all belong to the same party and are thus likely to have a broadly similar political outlook. Epstein (1980: 219, 225) points out that it is not necessary for the leadership to pick all the candidates directly, because the results of locally controlled selection are usually perfectly acceptable to it. Local party activists, just like the national leadership, want deputies who are loyal to the party line as defined nationally. For political parties, keeping candidate selection firmly under their own control has two great advantages. First, it helps retain the loyalty of ordinary party members. Deciding who will be allowed to use the party's name and resources in the election campaign is often the only real power members have, so allowing them to do this increases the party leaders' ability to retain a substantial body of co-operative members. Second, it enables the parties to behave as cohesive and disciplined bodies in parliament, and in political negotiations with other parties (see Chapter 3), and this in turn means that the party label conveys valuable information to voters at election time. European party organizations control access to their label at elections, and can withhold it from parliamentarians who are not sufficiently loyal to it in parliament. Their American counterparts, lacking this power, cannot do this. The threats and blandishments of interest groups, political action committees (PACs) and constituents at large may all have to be taken seriously by American Congress members, but in Europe individual MPs must put the party first, last, and always. Defying the party line in parliament may lead to deselection at the next election, and MPs will have little chance of re-election without the party label. Outside the party there is no salvation, or at least no long-term prospect of a political career.

## BOX 10.2: SELECTION OF PARLIAMENTARY CANDIDATES

### Denmark

As in other Scandinavian countries, local party organization has considerable freedom of action, and local rather than national-level actors are generally more influential in candidate selection. Most parties select their candidates through party primaries, with every member having a vote. Because Denmark is smaller than its Nordic neighbours, it lacks a strong centre–periphery cleavage, and as a result local roots are not as important as in, say, Norway, where generally only local people have a chance of being selected. In Denmark it is common for Copenhagen residents to be selected as candidates in constituencies outside the capital.

### France

Parties in France tend to be dominated by a small number of prominent individuals (notables), a fact that manifests itself in the candidate selection process. Before the formation of the UMP in 2002 the two main right-wing parties, the RPR and UDF, usually fought elections in tandem, so they came to arrangements as to which of them should contest each constituency. The central authorities of the parties, especially the national executives, played a decisive role in this, and were also important in picking the candidates, although they were always sensitive to the views of local notables. Communist Party candidates are chosen by the national executive. Local members have rather more say in the Socialist Party, although here, too, some central involvement is necessitated by the factionalized nature of the party; the factions are required to come to some overall arrangement on sharing the candidacies in order to preserve party unity. As in most countries, local roots are very important; most parliamentary deputies are simultaneously councillors (usually mayors) of their town or village, and resentment is created when candidates are 'parachuted' by the central party authorities into a constituency with which they have no links. The parity law passed in 2000 makes it compulsory for parties to pick equal numbers of men and women at all levels of election except for elections to the National Assembly, where, instead, they are asked to do so but suffer only financial penalties if they do not. These penalties would hit small parties hard, so in consequence they are highly obedient to the law's provisions, whereas the larger parties can better afford to take the financial penalty, which in any case they may recoup if they win more seats with a gender-unbalanced set of candidates than they would have done had they run as many women as men. The PS used a party primary to select Ségolène Royal as its presidential candidate in 2007, and the UMP also decided to employ this method to select its candidate, although in the event there was no election, as Nicolas Sarkozy was the only nominee.

### Germany

Candidate selection is regulated by law, which ensures that the central authorities of the parties have very little power. Selection is carried out by local conventions consisting of delegates from party branches within the constituency. Once these local bodies have made their choice, the central bodies cannot enforce changes. There is very little variation between the parties. Although the German electoral system provides two routes to parliament (see Chapter 11), the parties do not look for different qualities in the candidates they nominate for the list seats and for the constituency seats; indeed, there is considerable overlap between the two sets of candidates, with about 80 per cent of MPs being both list and constituency candidates.

### Italy

The electoral system adopted in the mid 1990s, which was based primarily on single-member constituencies, led to negotiations and deals among parties of the left and of the right as to which among a number of allied parties should present a candidate in each specific constituency. These deals were especially complicated on the left, because the centre left is more fragmented than the centre right. Once the allied parties decided which one would contest which seat, candidate selection itself was a relatively oligarchical process. The electoral system adopted in 2006 gave the large parties an incentive to go it alone and leave their smaller former allies to fall by the wayside, thus obviating the need for negotiations and deals with them. Candidate selection in the left-wing DP is similar to that in the old PCI, with national leaders having the choice of the safest seats, and the provincial and regional organizations making selections that require approval at national level. In the main right-wing party, the 'People of Liberty' (in which Forza Italia is the largest component), the dominance of the leader Silvio Berlusconi is reflected in the way candidates are picked, and, similarly, within the Lega Nord the leader, Umberto Bossi, retains considerable power over candidate selection, as over other matters of internal party life. In the Alleanza Nazionale, which merged with Forza Italia into the 'People of Liberty', candidate selection was mainly under the control of the leadership group around the party leader, Gianfranco Fini.

## Netherlands

There is some variation among the Dutch parties. The largest two, the CDA and the PvdA, took some power away from party members in the 1990s, the central party organization exercising greater influence with the aim of selecting more women and young candidates than had been picked by the members, who had tended to place a high value on service to the party organization. These parties now allow members to vote on who should be the top name on the list, but members cannot affect the placings of other candidates. In the liberal VVD the national executive was already the most important actor; this party has been affected less than the CDA and PvdA by demands for democratization since the 1970s. A fourth party, Democrats 66, in contrast, places heavy stress on internal democracy and gives a postal vote in the candidate selection process to every paid-up member, and it is the only party where members can really have an impact on the order in which the candidates are ranked, something that is very important in the Netherlands, as the electoral system means that it is the candidate selectors who pretty much determine which candidates will be elected to the seats that the party wins.

## Poland

In most of the Polish parties the first stage of the candidate selection procedure is almost completely decentralized, with central involvement consisting at most of issuing general guidelines regarding the types of quality that local parties should look for. In most cases the initial local candidate lists are composed without any interference from the party leaders. However, under electoral law, candidate lists can be submitted only by a nationally approved plenipotentiary, and in addition most parties' statutes give the leadership the right to make changes to the local selections. The extent to which the centre actually does intervene varies from party to party. In the PSL (Peasant Party), local selections are left more or less untouched. In some other parties, such as Law and Justice (PiS), the centre is more interventionist – it might 'parachute in' a candidate without local connections or veto someone whom it feels will damage the party's image, and sometimes it alters the order of names on the list. Even though Poland has an open-list electoral system, the top two positions on the list are regarded as most likely to attract preference votes. For the first time, the Civic Platform (PO) selected its candidate for the 2010 presidential election, Bronisław Komorowski, by a party primary, in which fewer than half of its 40 000 members voted, and Komorowski went on to be elected president.

▶ **BOX 10.2: CONTINUED**

### Spain

Because Spanish parties are leader dominated and have relatively few members, it is not surprising to find that candidate selection is controlled largely by the leadership group. Although the leadership usually feels it wise to pay some regard to the feelings of the local party organization, and especially regional 'barons', when settling on its lists around the country, it nonetheless retains a fairly free hand in deciding who should carry the party flag. Local activists occasionally show their displeasure with the centrally made selections by running dissident lists in the election, but these rarely achieve any success.

### United Kingdom

Candidate selection in Britain used to be dominated by local party activists, but in recent years there has been a movement towards giving ordinary members a direct voice. In the 1990s Labour adopted a 'one member one vote' system, known by the acronym OMOV, allowing each member a direct vote in the selection process. This method is also employed by Britain's third party, the Liberal Democrats. The Conservative Party combines centralization and membership involvement. It maintains a list of about 800 centrally approved aspirant candidates, who have to go through a rigorous screening procedure, and constituency organizations are expected to draw up a shortlist from these names, with ordinary members making the final choice from this shortlist. Aspiring Conservative candidates who do not share the Euro-sceptic attitudes of party members face an uphill struggle to win selection. Candidate selection in Britain is unusual in that, whereas parliamentarians in virtually every other country have roots in the constituency they hope to represent, selectors in Britain often pick someone with no previous connection with the constituency – although even in Britain local roots are becoming more important.

For parliamentarians, this has the advantage of protecting them from the risk of being picked off one at a time by outside interests who might put pressure on them to defect from the party line, and from the threat of being targeted at the next election by powerful and well-funded single-issue groups. Whatever an interest group might threaten to do to a deputy who doesn't vote as it wants, it is nothing compared with what the party will do if the deputy doesn't vote as *it* wants. At the same time, the prospect of being deselected by the candidate selectors is a remote one for deputies who are loyal to the party. Most European parties have adopted a style of organization that keeps deputies on a fairly long leash held by the ordinary members, but does not go so far as to make them mere poodles of unelected activists. Clearly, one could argue either in favour of the European model of strong and disciplined parliamentary parties, or in favour of the American pattern of greater independence of the individual Congress member. Hazan and Rahat (2010: 165–178) argue that a three-stage process that would allow all party members to choose from a shortlist drawn up by smaller groups within the party would better serve the wider democratic process than either open US-style primaries or a closed process from which most party members are excluded. Regardless of which method has most merits, it is beyond dispute that disciplined and cohesive political parties are central to European parliamentary democracy, and that party control of candidate selection is essential to this. American-style direct primaries are incompatible with strong political parties (Ranney, 1975), and, in the last analysis, all of the differences that are to be found within Europe are probably less significant than the differences between European and American candidate selection practices as a whole.

### 10.5.4  Sources of party finance

Because European parties do so much more as party organizations than US parties, they need more resources. This is not to suggest that there is more money floating around in European politics than there is in the United States – almost certainly, the reverse is true. But in the United States a significant proportion of political funds are raised and spent by and on candidates rather than parties, whereas in Europe parties are much more central in raising and spending money, as in everything else.

European parties need money for two main reasons. First, they need it to run their organizations: to pay their head office staff and their equipment, telephone and other bills; to hold annual conferences and other meetings; and in some cases to support research institutions linked to the party. Second, they need cash to fight election campaigns, and this has become the main item of expenditure for nearly all parties. In the past, parties in most European countries were not allowed to buy television advertising space, although this is now possible in a growing number of countries (including Austria, Germany, Italy, the Netherlands and Sweden). Even where this is still illegal, parties find plenty of other ways to spend money at election time: on newspaper and poster advertising; on the public relations firms that increasingly design election campaigns; on private focus group and survey research; perhaps on a helicopter to whisk the party leader around the country on the campaign trail; on mobile phones to keep candidates in touch with party headquarters; and on balloons, buttons, and general razzmatazz.

Parties get their money from a variety of sources (general overviews are given in Katz, 1996: 124–132; Williams, 2000; Pinto-Duschinsky, 2002; Fisher and Eisenstadt, 2004; Scarrow, 2007; Nassmacher, 2009). Dues paid by members play a role, but nowadays these rarely produce more than a quarter of a party's income; the Netherlands, where membership dues constitute about half of party revenues and the state only a quarter, is a notable exception here (Andeweg and Irwin, 2009: 78). A second source of income is that a party may request, or insist, that its parliamentary deputies and government ministers pay a proportion, perhaps as much as 10 per cent, of their official salary into party coffers, which is particularly common among left-wing parties. Third, parties may engage in fund-raising activities, such as the garden fetes and church hall bazaars for which the British Conservatives are famous. Some parties publish their own newspapers, but these days, as mentioned, they are more often a drain on a party's coffers than a contributor to them.

Besides these three sources arising *internally*, that is, from the party's own activities, there are also three important *external* sources of money. First, major interest groups back political parties whose policies they think will help them. In particular, business gives money to right-wing parties, and trade unions give money to left-wing parties. Second, donors, whether private or corporate, are important to some parties, especially in post-communist countries, where the middle class is weak and there is a 'general lack of a culture of supporting charities and public associations' (Smilov, 2007: 15). Third, in the great majority of European countries the state gives public money to political parties. Moreover, in almost every country there are benefits in kind, including free party broadcasts and mailings during election campaigns, as well as grants to the parliamentary groups to enable them to pay for secretarial and research assistance.

These external sources of funding – contributions from interest groups or donors and from the state – are related, because concern about the consequences of parties becoming financially dependent on vested interests is one of the factors that has brought about the rise of state financing. Obviously, neither business corporations, wealthy donors nor trade unions give money to parties simply as a charitable exercise. At the very least, they hope to help their chosen party get into government and implement policies broadly sympathetic to their own preferences. Some sponsors may have more tangible benefits in mind. A business or a wealthy individual may give money to a party in the hope (or even on condition) that, once in government, it will give the donor special access to decision-makers, or even that the party's ministers will make a specific decision, perhaps on a tax liability or a request for land-use planning permission, that will repay the investment several times over. This is particularly likely to happen when, as is the case in many countries, there are no laws, or at most ineffective laws, compelling parties to disclose their financial sources.

The first European country to introduce state funding of its parties was West Germany in 1959. The German scheme has subsequently been expanded and altered several times, and now involves huge sums of money (Detterbeck, 2008). Parties winning more than 0.5 per cent of the vote in an election receive €0.85 for each of the first four million votes and €0.70 for each vote over and above this that they received at the most recent Bundestag, European Parliament and *Länder* elections, plus matching funds (at a rate of €0.38 per euro) for the membership fees and donations (up to €3300) that they receive. Since the constitution says that parties cannot be 'predominantly' funded by the state, public funding cannot exceed the amount that any party raises itself. In 2007 the CDU/CSU received €44 million, the SPD €32 million, the Greens €10 million and Die Linke €8 million. Fifteen other parties also qualified, and the total disbursed was €107 million (details at Bundestag website – see list of Internet resources at the end of this chapter). The result is that the German parties are awash with funds, and even after covering the costs of exceptionally large party bureaucracies and research institutes, they have enough left over to help like-minded parties in the poorer post-communist countries. In Germany's case, the past history of dictatorship may create a heightened willingness to spend a lot of money on preserving the institutions of liberal democracy.

Other countries have rather more modest schemes, although the principle is the same: parties receive money in approximate proportion to their electoral strength. In most countries all the money is paid by the national government to the parties' national headquarters, while in others, especially in Scandinavia, a significant part of the cash flows from local government to the parties' local organizations (Gidlund and Koole, 2001: 123). With expenditure rising constantly, and most other sources of revenue proving erratic or unreliable, state-supplied income now looms large in the finances of parties in countries that have public funding schemes. In many countries that have state funding this source of party income exceeds all other sources combined (Mair, 1997: 141–142; Heidar and Svåsand, 2004: 308). This applies to most parties in post-communist countries as well, although these have two other potential sources of income. Some parties benefited from the less than transparent distribution of state assets at the end of the communist era, and some secured admission to one of the main European party groups (such as the socialist or the Christian democratic group), which had the potential to bring significant material benefit. Although the financial resources of post-communist parties are not great in absolute terms, the parties' low number of members means that their ratio of head office employees to members is much higher than in the west (van Biezen, 2003: 207). In addition, local organizations are reliant on deputies' salaries, strengthening the deputies' powerful position within the organization (Jasiewicz, 2007: 105).

The pros and cons of public funding of political parties have been debated in many European countries. One argument, as we have seen, is that it frees parties from having to dance to the tune of wealthy financial backers, and thus reduces corruption in politics generally. In practice it certainly does not eliminate the 'sleaze factor' entirely, as periodic scandals demonstrate.

In Italy, for example, an extensive scheme of state funding of parties did not prevent a number of parties from engaging in corruption on a massive scale, in the Tangentopoli (Bribesville) affair of the 1990s that we outlined in Chapters 4 and 7 above. In France, traditional 'occult practices' still exist despite state finance, which is also criticized for being structured in such a way that it has led to an explosion in the number of parties, many launched by entrepreneurs primarily in order to get their hands on the available money (Clift and Fisher, 2005: 250). In Portugal, a degree of corruption coexists with state funding, aided by the indifference of citizens (de Sousa, 2004). In post-communist countries, too, the laws on transparency read well on paper but are laxly enforced, leading to a general impression among many voters of ongoing corruption. At Bulgaria's 2009 election the electoral commission decreed that a fifth of the parties' campaigning materials had to be devoted to messages such as 'Buying and selling votes is illegal', despite which it was estimated that over 3 per cent of votes could be considered 'bought' (Kanev, 2007; Spirova, 2010: 277).

Defenders of state financing maintain that there would be even more of this kind of thing if parties were entirely dependent on private sources. They also dispute the suggestions of critics that it will lead to a decline in party membership and will make leaders less accountable to members as the leaders realize they no longer need members' dues; the evidence is that the introduction of state finance makes no difference to membership trends (Pierre *et al.*, 2000). In some countries, such as Germany and Netherlands, the schemes are designed to encourage parties to recruit more members rather than try to do without members. Right-wing critics argue that party funding should be left to the market and is none of the state's business, whereas left-wing critics claim that state funding turns parties into mere agents of the state or 'public utilities' instead of the autonomous forces they should be (Lipow, 1996: 49–65). Undoubtedly, public funding, by requiring state involvement in monitoring the parties' use of this money, does bring the state into parties' internal affairs, thus arguably transforming them into 'public service agencies' (Mair, 2006: 25). The experience of many countries suggests that laws on party finance are unlikely to change established patterns, and that the most that can be hoped for is greater transparency. Even this has difficulties: if there are no rules the public tends to be suspicious about what is going on away from its gaze, and if there are rules that are feebly enforced the suspicions are even greater, whereas if the rules are strongly enforced and lead to high transparency there is a good chance that the media will be able to feed on a seemingly endless diet of 'scandals', thus reinforcing the public cynicism that it was hoped state finance and transparency would dispel.

Supporters of state financing emphasize that not all parties can find wealthy interest groups willing to give them money. Parties whose policies appeal to no wealthy interest group – Green parties, for example, or centre parties – may receive only small sums from members and sympathetic individuals. Private money may wield undue influence in intra-party battles. For example, in the days leading up to the ousting of Iain Duncan-Smith as British Conservative leader in 2003, several large donors had stated that they would stop giving money to the party unless he were replaced (Denham and O'Hara, 2008: 92). Moreover, state financing is awarded according to a predetermined formula, and thus seems to make competition 'fairer'. It also seems to come without strings attached, although sometimes it is conditional upon parties making what are seen as acceptable policy choices: the Belgian Vlaams Blok lost state funding in 2004 on the ground that its policies amounted to advocating racism (Bale, 2007: 152), while in France, as we have seen, parties lose financially if they do not select equal numbers of male and female candidates. Concern has been expressed that the parties already in parliament can form a tacit 'cartel', using their control of the state to vote themselves public money in a manner that reinforces their position by placing parties outside the cartel at a disadvantage (Katz and Mair, 1995: 15–16). The evidence is, though, that challenger parties fare no worse in countries that provide state funding than elsewhere, and there is no sign of any over-time effect either (Pierre *et al.*, 2000; Scarrow, 2006b).

Although some people claim that political parties are private bodies, and as such have no right to expect money from the public purse, others point out that they fulfil a public function: they are essential to the workings of a democracy and therefore need to be sustained. Furthermore, the role of government has expanded greatly since the nineteenth century, and government is controlled by a ruling party or parties. Unless parties have the money to explore and expand policy options, and to conduct research into the feasibility of their ideas, the country as a whole could suffer from the inadequately thought-out policies they promote.

The flow of money into a party is likely both to reflect and to reinforce the balance of power within the party. For donors other than the state there is little point in giving money to people or groups within a party who have no power – it makes sense, obviously, for them to give money to those who wield the power, and who can make the policy decisions that the donors wish to see. By doing this, of course, they further strengthen those to whom they give money. The pattern in Europe generally since the 1960s has been one of a dramatic increase in the amount of money going to central party bodies, both to the parliamentary party and to head office (Katz and Mair, 1992; Farrell and Webb, 2000).

Although every European party would no doubt like more money to finance its activities, most parties with reasonable levels of electoral support have sufficient resources to get their message across at elections. Individual party candidates fight elections on a national party platform and thus do not need much money to mount a personal campaign. The need for a personal campaign arises only when a preferential electoral system pits two or more candidates of the same party against each other (see Chapter 11). Even in those cases, the amounts of money involved are not huge: the elected candidates in a Finnish constituency in 1999 spent an average of just over €11 000 each, for example, a sum that would not get anyone far in a US campaign (Ruostetsaari and Mattila, 2002: 100). Moreover, a European candidate who flaunts his or her wealth on a personal campaign rather than fighting as part of the party's team might well incur disapproval, perhaps from voters as well as from party members. Consequently, candidates do not need huge sources of private funding to bankroll their election campaigns, and are less dependent on non-party groups than their US counterparts. Once again, we see in Europe the dominance of party over candidate, in marked contrast to the situation in the United States.

## 10.6  The changing shape of European parties

Political parties, like other organizations, change and adapt in response to changes in their environment. There have been many attempts to assess evolving patterns of European party organizations. In the 1950s the French writer Maurice Duverger argued that during the nineteenth century most parties had been what he termed *cadre parties*, which were dominated by local notables, who in most cases were the parties' MPs. At local level these notables had their own support groups, but the people in these groups were not really party members, as they did not pay a membership fee and had no formal rights within the party. These parties, said Duverger, were swept aside, or at least compelled to change their organizational structure, later in the nineteenth century and in the first half of the twentieth century by the *mass party*. He maintained that the mass party, with a large number of fee-paying members, a sizeable permanent bureaucracy in the head office, and a clear policy programme, was the 'new' or 'modern' form of party, and he foresaw a convergence towards this model (Duverger, 1964: 427).

In contrast, Leon D. Epstein, writing in the 1960s, believed that mass parties belonged only to particular places and periods. He identified a number of *counter-organizational tendencies* – such as the increasing use of the mass media, especially television, during election campaigns, which reduced the need for thousands of ordinary party members to go out spreading the word in order to get the message across – which, he argued, would increasingly undermine the rationale for the existence of large-scale mass political parties (Epstein, 1980: 233–260). In a similar vein, Otto Kirchheimer (1966) argued that changes in European society were bringing about changes in the type of party likely to flourish (on Kirchheimer, see Krouwel, 2003; Hale Williams, 2009). Class lines were becoming less sharp, and the growth of the welfare state and the mixed economy had cut the ground from under the feet of old-style anti-system socialist parties, which had been dedicated to a radical transformation of society, with members living within a virtual subculture. The type of party best suited to current conditions was what Kirchheimer called the *post-war catch-all party* that tried to win votes from nearly all sections of society, and would concentrate on general, bland 'valence' issues such as better health and education services. Panebianco (1988: 262–274) elaborated this idea with the *electoral–professional* model, emphasizing in particular the central role of professionals with the expertise to perform certain tasks, such as designing election campaigns. Some of the arguments put forward as to why power seemed to be drifting remorselessly from parliaments to governments applied to intra-party relations too, such as the need for quick decisions and the inability of ordinary members, 'amateurs', easily to familiarize themselves with the details of complex issues. Although it was a later development, the growing role of the European Union has been seen to have the same effect, making it more difficult for party members to hold leaders accountable (Aylott *et al.*, 2007; Carter and Poguntke, 2010).

From this point of view, a party does not really need a large number of committed members. In the 1980s Gunnar Sjöblom took this line of thought one step further and argued that members might actually be a handicap to a party, or at least to its parliamentarians. He suggested that various changes in society, such as increased mobility and the growing role of the mass media in conveying political messages, were leading to greater volatility among voters. People were suffering from *information overload*; they were confused by a never-ending stream of reports about proposals, decisions and speculation, and were increasingly likely to vote on the basis of *political paraphernalia* – trivial factors such as the style or appearance of the party leader (Sjöblom, 1983: 385). In this situation, members with a strong commitment to certain principles were a definite liability to the vote-hungry parliamentarians, who wanted the party to be able to change tack rapidly to take advantage of the shifting winds of public opinion. Party members trying to drum up support by faithfully plugging a traditional message were likely to have a counterproductive effect. Consequently, argued Sjöblom (1983: 395), 'it may be to the advantage of a party to have few and/or passive members.' Indeed, the deputy leader of the Spanish Socialist Party said over 20 years ago that he would sooner have 10 minutes of television broadcasting time than 10000 members (Gillespie, 1989: 366).

This argument seems to become even more persuasive when we think about the types of people who might make up the bulk of party members. We pointed out earlier (p. 332) that the factors that motivate people to join a party might be categorized as material, solidary or purposive, and although each of these motives seems to be losing power, it may be that the first two have lost more of their force than the last. If this is the case, those joining for the third reason will form an increasing proportion of members, their ideological commitment no longer diluted by the more pragmatic members who joined for less explicitly political purposes. There is a plausible argument, backed up with evidence, to the effect that party members tend to be more extreme – that is, further from the centre of the political spectrum – in their views than party voters (May, 1973). (The evidence is less clear-cut on the question of whether members are also more extreme than MPs, as May also claimed.) For example, in Sweden, members of the main left-wing party hold views further to the left than that party's voters, and members of the main right-wing party hold views that are further to the right than that party's voters (Widfeldt, 1999: 263). This line of argument was expressed colourfully in the 1930s by an observer of the British Labour Party, who claimed that its local constituency organizations were 'frequently unrepresentative groups of nonentities dominated by fanatics and cranks and extremists' (quoted in McKenzie, 1982: 194). In addition, even if researchers feel that the jury is still out on whether every aspect of May's law is true, party leaders may feel it to be true and thus want to reduce the power of activists. Besides, quite apart from the policies that activists want, leaders might well believe that it is best not to give members too much of an opportunity to make their views known, because the public prefers united parties to parties characterized by internal debate, argument and apparent disunity (Maravall, 2008). Certainly, it is quite plausible that members impose programmatic 'costs' upon the party leadership by demanding that the party adopt certain policy stances as the price of their continued loyalty, and it may be that the policies they demand are sometimes ones that the voters as a whole do not find attractive (Strøm, 1990). Members, then, might saddle the party with vote-losing policies, in which case parliamentarians might prefer to dispense with members and instead communicate with the public entirely through the mass media.

This possibility suggests that parties will be less keen than in the past to recruit members and, as we have seen in this chapter, party membership levels have indeed been falling across Europe in recent decades. This does not necessarily mean that parties are becoming weaker, any more than, say, a car factory is weaker because it employs far fewer workers now than four decades ago, yet still produces the same number of cars. Rather, it is partly a reflection of the fact that the kinds of task for which parties once needed a mass membership, such as providing cheap labour and a source of finance, are now taken care of by other means, principally the mass media, computerized databases and state funding. The automobile factory is now less rooted in the community than it was when it had a mass workforce on the production line, but if it is still delivering a product that consumers want, it could be judged as being as successful as ever. The same, clearly, could be said about parties. This is one reason why many post-communist parties have very few members; they were founded in a technological era and a funding environment where a mass membership would simply be seen as a 'deadweight' (Kitschelt et al., 1999: 395–397).

The organizational structure of parties, too, seems to be changing, in response to the same set of factors. The main trend is one that we have already mentioned in connection with candidate selection and the election of leaders: the use of direct rather than representative democracy within parties. Increasingly, members are being given a vote on subjects that were previously decided by members' delegates within the organization, such as branch officials or conference delegates. This move tends to give party leaders greater freedom of action, since members, deciding as individuals how to vote by postal ballot on some leadership proposal, are less likely to block initiatives from the top than were branch activists, who were better able to mobilize and to act collectively. The potentially troublesome activist layer, comprising people who according to May's law are the most likely to hold extreme views, thereby become marginalized (Hopkin, 2001; Katz and Mair, 2002: 128–129).

Some analysts feel that this reduces intra-party democracy, since they regard atomized members as more docile, more passive, or more easily manipulable by the leadership than a membership acting collectively through the previously dominant branch structure. They speak of the arrival of the *plebiscitary party*, in which all proposals come from the top, with members' role being simply to ratify these ideas; this kind of party 'is characterised by a veneer of democracy overlaid by centralisation and control' (Lipow, 1996: 1–2; Whiteley and Seyd, 2002: 213–217). The role of members now is to 'pay up and shut up'. Others, though, note that the old structures were often far from a paradigm of democracy, and that today's party members, being better educated and having access to far more independent sources of political information than previous generations, are perfectly capable of making 'informed and rational' judgements, and are not just putty in the hands of party leaders (Scarrow *et al.*, 2000: 150). Just as with national-level referendums, which we discuss in the next chapter, the process might be abused by an authoritarian leader who is really offering only the opportunity to endorse his proposals, but they might also be occasions of genuine choice, which certainly applied to the French PS membership vote on the EU Constitutional Treaty, which we discussed earlier (p. 340).

As parties move away from the structure of the mass party, which was dominant in Europe from around 1900 to 1960, their organizational form defies easy labelling. The concept of the *cartel party* (Katz and Mair, 1995), which we have already mentioned, has been very influential. It emphasizes the reliance of parties on state funding rather than members' dues, and sees parties as having moved from their original role of linking civil society with the state to a position where they are virtually agents of the state. It suggests, further, that parties collude with each other rather than compete full-bloodedly as in the past. Internally, it envisages parties as *stratarchies*, with each level being virtually autonomous rather than being answerable to actors at other levels within the party. Carty (2004) also accepts the notion of parties as stratarchies and suggests that parties can be seen as *franchise systems*, which, like a hamburger chain, have a centrally designed product plus a local network to distribute it. There is an implicit contract between the head office and the local outlets, under which each has its rights and its responsibilities, and as long as everyone is keeping to their part of the bargain, each level leaves the other alone.

Koole (1996), in contrast, disputes the existence of stratarchy, arguing that every level of the party has a strong stake in what actors at other levels are doing. He emphasizes the reliance of party leaders and national executives upon endorsement or election by ordinary members, the potential damage to a party's national image by the behaviour of a rogue candidate at local level, and the impact upon local elections of what a party is doing at national level, as reasons why actors at one level have good reason to take a great deal of interest in trying to influence what is going on at other levels. He also disputes the idea that parties systematically collude with each other, arguing that electoral competition is fiercer than ever (Koole, 1996; see also Kitschelt, 2000; for response, see Katz and Mair, 2009). Koole has put forward the model of the *modern cadre party*, one in which the parliamentary group is dominant, yet to some degree accountable to the members, so that there remains a degree of internal democracy (Koole, 1994). However, given that the original cadre parties had no members in the conventional sense of the word, and that there was no pretence that MPs were accountable to an extra-parliamentary organization, the name chosen for this model is perhaps misleading. Consequently, Heidar and Saglie (2003b), identifying pretty much the same features as Koole, prefer the name *network party*, emphasizing the way in which policies are devised in informal networks rather than through the formal processes implied by the party constitution. They characterize Norwegian parties as 'mass parties without a mass membership', and suggest plausibly that the picture they find in Norway would apply to most of modern Europe. Whatever name is chosen, there is agreement on the most important aspects of the substance: parties are financed primarily by the state, dominated by the upper echelons (the leader and MPs), have a membership base that almost always amounts to less than 10 per cent of their voters, and yet preserve the formal mechanisms of internal party democracy, which, however attenuated, act as a continuing constraint on the leaders' freedom of manoeuvre.

## 10.7 The future of European parties

Despite the plethora of writings that discuss the 'crisis' of parties or the 'decline in party', political parties in modern Europe seem very likely to survive the falling membership levels and other trends that we have discussed. Gloomy analysts have been talking in terms of party decline for pretty much as long as parties have existed (Scarrow, 2000: 80). To see why parties are likely to survive, we can usefully distinguish three levels of party, an approach devised in the 1960s by the American political scientist V.O. Key. First, there is the *party in the electorate* or *party on the ground* – the parties' implantation in civil society. As we have seen, there is a lot of evidence that parties are indeed becoming weaker at this level. Second, there is the *party in public office* – its elected representatives and their direct organizational support. Third, there is the *party in central office* – the headquarters and central organs of the party. There are no signs of decline at the second and third levels (Webb, 2002). Most observers believe that power increasingly lies with the parliamentary group, whose members are becoming ever more autonomous (Katz and Mair, 2002; Pedersen, 2010). It has been argued that power in post-communist parties and in southern Europe, at least according to their rulebooks, lies with the party in central office and the national executive, and perhaps with regional 'barons', rather than with the parliamentary group, although in some cases MPs control many of the positions on national executives (van Biezen, 2003; Bosco and Morlino, 2007: 19–22). In terms of their resources – grassroots membership being the obvious exception – parties are becoming steadily stronger, and they continue to dominate parliaments and governments (Mair, 1997: 120–154; Strøm, 2000).

Moreover, it is not just academics but most Europeans themselves who accept that parties are essential – necessary evils, in many people's eyes – for the functioning of representative government in modern Europe. Parties are certainly not popular. When EU citizens were asked in autumn 2009 whether they 'tend to trust' political parties, just 16 per cent said they did, while 79 per cent said they did not (Eurobarometer 72, question A10.7). In only one country, Denmark, did trust outscore distrust. In post-communist countries the image of parties was especially poor, just 10 per cent on average expressing trust and 85 per cent distrust. Even so, voters, when asked, acknowledge that parties are necessary to make politics 'work', even if they do not particularly love the parties they have (Torcal *et al.*, 2002: 266; Holmberg, 2003: 291; Dalton and Weldon, 2005: 934–935). Even in Poland, where the view of parties is very negative, there is a grudging appreciation that parties perform useful functions, and that things would probably be (even) worse without them (Jasiewicz, 2007: 96–97). The apparent indispensability of parties is demonstrated by their dominance of politics in post-communist countries since 1989: despite the widespread public antipathy to them, parties in these countries play pretty much the same role as their west European counterparts. In some ways, they are even more central to politics. Although in resource terms they may seem weaker than their western counterparts, civil society and interest groups are weaker still, leaving parties virtually unchallenged as key political actors (Evanson and Magstadt, 2001).

It seems likely not only that parties will continue to exist but that they will continue to have members, albeit not as many as in the period from the 1950s to the 1980s. Even on the most self-interested calculus, parliamentarians are aware that members have their uses. When Silvio Berlusconi founded Forza Italia in 1993 it was often seen as a virtual party that would not bother to recruit members, but by 2007 it had over 400 000 of them (van Biezen et al., 2009: 32). No matter how high-tech election campaigns become, members demonstrating an active local party presence are still of benefit to the candidates. The presence of active local members tends to result in more votes for the party at election time (Gallagher and Marsh, 2002: 135–139; Seyd and Whiteley, 2002: 111–137). Even though television is the main political arena during election campaigns, this is an addition to rather than a replacement for the work done by the local party organization. And although this local organization may not do a great deal between elections, there is a need to keep some kind of network in place at all times so that there is something that can be activated at elections; if the local organization is allowed to atrophy, it will become very difficult to revive the party's unpaid workforce (Ware, 1992: 89). In addition, as we have already mentioned, specific actors within the party may have incentives to recruit members, seeing them as a resource in intra-party battles such as candidate or leadership selection.

Susan Scarrow (1996: 42–45) points out that, in theory at least, there are a number of other benefits that having members brings to a party. They bring legitimacy benefits, by fostering the impression, accurate or otherwise, that party leaders are at the apex of a principled movement rather than being merely a self-interested clique answerable to no one. Voters still expect their parties to be visible locally as well as in the mass media; media strategies designed to market party elites need 'validation' on the local level (Boll and Poguntke, 1992: 140). Members may also act as ambassadors to the community, perhaps influencing the views of their friends and neighbours; studies in Britain and in Denmark have found that members are a visible and articulate local manifestation of the party, frequently discussing politics with non-members (Martin and Cowley, 1999; Pedersen, 2003: 297). In addition, members provide a source both of linkage with the wider electorate and of new ideas, as well as providing a recruitment pool from which party candidates and leaders can be drawn.

Thus to talk about the decline of party in Europe is contentious. European parties could be seen to be failing (Mair, 2006: 29), or a more benign interpretation is that they are adapting rather than declining or disappearing. In terms of the functions of parties, which we outlined earlier in this chapter, parties may not play the linkage role that they once did, but in other respects they face no serious challengers – which is why, though unloved, they dominate post-communist political life. Parties are still indispensable after all these years. As Webb (2002: 458) puts it:

 Parties continue to perform vital tasks with a relatively high degree of effectiveness and are central mechanisms of popular choice and control. If they did not exist in the advanced industrial democratic world, somebody would undoubtedly have to invent them.

Parties thus continue to be vital organs of representation in European politics. Despite suggestions that their members' views and backgrounds are likely to be unrepresentative of voters, we have seen that in many ways the political values and social profile of party members are not such as to distort the process of representative government, or the packages of policies on offer to voters, in any major way. European parties will continue to be fundamentally different from American ones for as long as they retain control over the selection of their candidates, and there is no prospect of their relinquishing that prerogative. Elections in Europe will continue to centre on parties, and on the programmes that they offer, rather than on candidates. Electors will continue to vote for parties; seats in parliaments will continue to be divided among parties. The link between votes and seats is forged by electoral systems, and it is to this subject that we now turn.

## Internet resources

The Richard Kimber site is the most useful general site. In addition, we include links to a range of members of different party families and countries around Europe.

www.politicsresources.net/parties.htm
   Richard Kimber's politics resources site, with links to sites of parties in numerous countries plus a number of party constitutions.

www.politicalresources.net/
   Links to party sites around the world.

www.cdu.de/en/3440.htm
   Site of Germany's CDU, Europe's largest Christian democratic party; substantial number of English-language pages.

nu.pvda.nl/
   Dutch Labour Party site; some pages in English.

www.conservatives.com/
   Britain's Conservative Party site, including the opportunity to join as a 'member' or a 'friend'.

www.ilpopolodellaliberta.it/
   Site of the People of Liberty, the main right-wing party in Italy, dominated by Silvio Berlusconi.

www.platforma.org/
   Poland's Civic Platform (Platforma Obywatelska); some pages in English.

www.venstre.dk/
   Denmark's Liberal Party (Venstre); English-language version available.

www.frontnational.com/
   Site of France's FN – surprisingly, available in French only.

www.ciu.cat/
Site of Convergence and Union (CiU), perhaps Europe's largest regional party – although it would see itself as a national party in Catalunya rather than as a regional party in Spain. Site available in Catalan only.

www.Greenparty.ie/en
Site of Ireland's Green Party, with prominent appeals for visitors to donate money to the party.

www.akel.org.cy/nqcontent.cfm?a_id=1&lang=l3
Site of AKEL, the main left-wing party in Cyprus and Europe's strongest remaining communist party.

www.bundestag.de/htdocs_e/bundestag/function/party_funding/index.html
Detailed documents (all in English) giving details of the public funding of German parties.

## References

**Allern, Elin H. and Karina Pedersen** (2007) 'The impact of party organisational changes on democracy', *West European Politics*, 30 (1), 68–92.

**Allern, Elin Haugsgjerd, Nicholas Aylott and Flemming Juul Christiansen** (2007) 'Social Democrats and trade unions in Scandinavia: the decline and persistence of institutional relationships', *European Journal of Political Research*, 46 (5), 607–635.

**Andeweg, Rudy B. and Galen A. Irwin** (2009) *Governance and Politics of the Netherlands*, 3rd edn, Palgrave Macmillan, Basingstoke.

**Aylott, Nicholas, Laura Morales and Luis Ramiro** (2007) 'Some things change, a lot stays the same: comparing the country studies', pp. 190–210 in Thomas Poguntke, Nicholas Aylott, Elisabeth Carter, Robert Ladrech and Kurt Richard Luther (eds), *The Europeanization of National Political Parties: Power and Organizational Adaptation*, Routledge, London.

**Bale, Tim** (2007) 'Are bans on political parties bound to turn out badly? A comparative investigation of three "intolerant" democracies: Turkey, Spain, and Belgium', *Comparative European Politics*, 5 (2), 141–157.

**Bille, Lars** (2000) 'A power centre in Danish politics', pp. 130–144 in Knut Heidar and Ruud Koole (eds), *Parliamentary Party Groups in European Democracies: Political Parties behind Closed Doors*, Routledge, London.

**Bille, Lars** (2001) 'Democratizing a democratic procedure: myth or reality? Candidate selection in western European parties, 1960–1990', *Party Politics*, 7 (3), 363–380.

**Billordo, Libia** (2003) 'Party membership in France: measures and data-collection', *French Politics*, 1 (1), 137–151.

**Bochel, John and David Denver** (1983) 'Candidate selection in the Labour Party: what the selectors seek', *British Journal of Political Science*, 13 (1), 45–69.

**Boll, Bernhard and Thomas Poguntke** (1992) 'Germany: the 1990 all-German election campaign', pp. 121–143 in Shaun Bowler and David M. Farrell (eds), *Electoral Strategies and Political Marketing*, Macmillan, Basingstoke.

**Bosco, Anna and Leonardo Morlino** (2007) 'What changes in south European parties? A comparative introduction', pp. 1–28 in Anna Bosco and Leonardo Morlino (eds), *Party Change in Southern Europe*, Routledge, London.

**Boucek, Françoise** (2009) 'Rethinking factionalism: typologies, intra-party dynamics and three faces of factionalism', *Party Politics*, 15 (5), 455–485.

**Bruter, Michael and Sarah Harrison** (2009) 'Tomorrow's leaders? Understanding the involvement of young party members in six European democracies', *Comparative Political Studies*, 42 (10), 1259–1291.

**Bugajski, Janusz** (2002) *Political Parties of Eastern Europe: A Guide to Politics in the Post-Communist Era*, M.E. Sharpe, Armonk, NY.

**Burchell, Jon** (2001) 'Organisational reform within European Green parties', *West European Politics*, 24 (4), 113–134.

**Carter, Elisabeth and Thomas Poguntke** (2010) 'How European integration changes national parties: evidence from a 15-country study', *West European Politics*, 33 (3), 297–324.

**Carty, R. Kenneth** (2004) 'Parties as franchise systems: the stratarchical organizational imperative', *Party Politics*, 10 (1), 5–24.

**Christophorou, Christophoros** (2007) 'Party change and development in Cyprus (1995–2005)', pp. 176–205 in Anna Bosco and Leonardo Morlino (eds), *Party Change in Southern Europe*, Routledge, London.

**Clark, Peter B. and James Q. Wilson** (1961) 'Incentive systems: a theory of organizations', *Administrative Science Quarterly* 6, pp. 129–66.

**Clift, Ben and Justin Fisher** (2005) 'Party finance reform as constitutional engineering? The effectiveness and unintended consequences of party finance reform in France and Britain', *French Politics*, 3 (3), 234–257.

**Crespy, Amandine** (2008) 'Dissent over the European Constitutional Treaty within the French Socialist Party: between response to anti-globalization protest and intra-party tactics', *French Politics*, 6 (1), 23–44.

**Cross, William** (2008) 'Democratic norms and party candidate selection: taking contextual factors into account', *Party Politics*, 14 (4), 596–619.

**Dalton, Russell J. and Steven A. Weldon** (2005) 'Public images of political parties: a necessary evil', *West European Politics*, 28 (8), 931–951.

**Denham, Andrew and Kieron O'Hara** (2008) *Democratising Conservative Leadership Selection: From Grey Suits to Grass Roots*, Manchester University Press, Manchester.

**de Sousa, Luís** (2004) 'The regulation of political financing in Portugal', *West European Politics*, 27 (7), 124–145.

**Detterbeck, Klaus** (2008) 'Party cartel and cartel parties in Germany', *German Politics*, 17 (7), 27–40.

**Dunphy, Richard and Tim Bale** (2007) 'Red flag still flying? Explaining AKEL – Cyprus's communist anomaly', *Party Politics*, 13 (3), 287–304.

**Duverger, Maurice** (1964) *Political Parties*, 3rd edn, Methuen, London.

**Epstein, Leon D.** (1980) *Political Parties in Western Democracies*, rev. edn, Transaction Books, New Brunswick, NJ.

**Evanson, Robert K. and Thomas M. Magstadt** (2001) 'The Czech Republic: dominance in a transitional system', pp. 193–209 in Clive S. Thomas (ed.), *Political Parties and Interest Groups: Shaping Democratic Governance*, Lynne Rienner, Boulder, CO, and London.

**Farrell, David M. and Paul Webb** (2000) 'Political parties as campaign organizations', pp. 102–128 in Russell J. Dalton and Martin P. Wattenberg (eds), *Parties without Partisans: Political Change in Advanced Industrial Democracies*, Oxford University Press, Oxford.

**Field, Bonnie N. and Peter M. Siavelis** (2008) 'Candidate selection procedures in transitional polities: a research note', *Party Politics*, 14 (4), 620–639.

**Fisher, Justin and Todd A. Eisenstadt (eds)** (2004) *Comparing Party Finance Across Democracies: Broadening the Debate*, special issue of *Party Politics* 10 (6).

**Gallagher, Michael** (1988) 'Conclusion', pp. 236–283 in Michael Gallagher and Michael Marsh (eds), *Candidate Selection in Comparative Perspective: The Secret Garden of Politics*, Sage, London.

**Gallagher, Michael and Michael Marsh (eds)** (1988) *Candidate Selection in Comparative Perspective: The Secret Garden of Politics*, Sage, London and Newbury Park.

**Gallagher, Michael and Michael Marsh** (2002) *Days of Blue Loyalty: The Politics of Membership of the Fine Gael Party*, PSAI Press, Dublin.

**Gallagher, Michael and Michael Marsh** (2004) 'Party membership in Ireland: the members of Fine Gael', *Party Politics*, 10 (4), 407–425.

**Gidlund, Gullan and Ruud A. Koole** (2001) 'Political finance in the north of Europe (the Netherlands and Sweden)', pp. 112–130 in Karl-Heinz Nassmacher (ed.), *Foundations* for Democracy: Approaches to Comparative Political Finance, Nomos Verlagsgesellschaft, Baden-Baden.

**Gillespie, Richard** (1989) The Spanish Socialist Party: A History of Factionalism, Clarendon Press, Oxford.

**Gillespie, Richard** (1993) '"Programa 2000": the appearance and reality of socialist renewal in Spain', West European Politics, 16 (6), 78–96.

**Hale Williams, Michelle** (2009) 'Kirchheimer's French twist: a model of the catch-all thesis applied to the French case', Party Politics, 15 (5), 592–614.

**Hardarson, Ólafur Thordur and Gunnar Helgi Kristinsson** (2008) 'The parliamentary election in Iceland, May 2007', Electoral Studies, 27 (7), 373–377.

**Hazan, Reuven Y. and Gideon Rahat** (2006) 'The influence of candidate selection methods on legislatures and legislators: theoretical propositions, methodological suggestions and empirical evidence', Journal of Legislative Studies, 12 (2), 366–385.

**Hazan, Reuven Y. and Gideon Rahat** (2010) Democracy within Parties: Candidate Selection Methods and Their Political Consequences, Oxford University Press, Oxford.

**Hazan, Reuven Y. and Gerrit Voerman** (2006) 'Electoral systems and candidate selection', Acta Politica, 41 (1), 146–162.

**Heidar, Knut** (1997) 'A "new" party leadership?', pp. 125–147 in Kaare Strøm and Lars Svåsand (eds), Challenges to Political Parties: The Case of Norway, University of Michigan Press, Ann Arbor, MI.

**Heidar, Knut** (2006) 'Party membership and participation', pp. 301–315 in Richard S. Katz and William Crotty (eds), Handbook of Party Politics, Sage, London.

**Heidar, Knut and Jo Saglie** (2003a) 'A decline of linkage? Intra-party participation in Norway, 1991–2000', European Journal of Political Science, 42 (2), 761–786.

**Heidar, Knut and Jo Saglie** (2003b) 'Predestined parties? Organizational change in Norwegian political parties', Party Politics, 9 (9), 219–239.

**Heidar, Knut and Lars Svåsand** (2004) 'Political parties in Norway', pp. 295–317 in Hanne Marthe Narud and Anne Krogstad (eds),

Elections, Parties, and Political Representation, Universitetsforlaget, Oslo.

**Holmberg, Sören** (2003) 'Are political parties necessary?', Electoral Studies, 22 (2), 287–299.

**Hopkin, Jonathan** (2001) 'Bringing the members back in: democratizing candidate selection in Britain and Spain', Party Politics, 7 (7), 343–361.

**Hopkin, Jonathan** (2006) 'Clientelism and party politics', pp. 406–412 in Richard S. Katz and William Crotty (eds), Handbook of Party Politics, Sage, London.

**Jasiewicz, Krzysztof** (2007) 'Poland: party system by default', pp. 85–117 in Paul Webb and Stephen White (eds), Party Politics in New Democracies, Oxford University Press, Oxford.

**Jungerstam-Mulders, Susanne (ed.)** (2006) Post-Communist EU Member States: Parties and Party Systems, Ashgate, Aldershot.

**Kanev, Dobrin** (2007) 'Campaign finance in Bulgaria', pp. 33–51 in Daniel Smilov and Jurij Toplak (eds), Political Finance and Corruption in Eastern Europe: The Transition Period, Ashgate, Aldershot.

**Katz, Richard S.** (1996) 'Party organizations and finance', pp. 107–133 in Lawrence LeDuc, Richard G. Niemi and Pippa Norris (eds), Comparing Democracies: Elections and Voting in Global Perspective, Sage, Thousand Oaks, CA.

**Katz, Richard S. and Peter Mair (eds)** (1992) Party Organizations: A Data Handbook, Sage, London.

**Katz, Richard S. and Peter Mair** (1995) 'Changing models of party organization and party democracy: the emergence of the cartel party', Party Politics, 1 (1), 5–28.

**Katz, Richard S. and Peter Mair** (2002) 'The ascendancy of the party in public office: party organizational change in twentieth-century democracies', pp. 113–135 in Richard Gunther, José Ramón Montero and Juan J. Linz (eds), Political Parties: Old Concepts and New Challenges, Oxford University Press, Oxford and New York.

**Katz, Richard S. and Peter Mair** (2009) 'The cartel party thesis: a restatement', Perspectives on Politics, 7 (7), 753–766.

**Kenig, Ofer** (2009) 'Democratization of party leadership selection: do wider selectorates produce more competitive contests?', *Electoral Studies*, 28 (8), 240–247.

**Kingdom, John** (2003) *Government and Politics in Britain: An Introduction*, 3rd edn, Polity, Cambridge.

**Kirchheimer, Otto** (1966) 'The transformation of the western European party system', pp. 177–200 in Joseph LaPalombara and Myron Weiner (eds), *Political Parties and Political Development*, Princeton University Press, Princeton, NJ.

**Kitschelt, Herbert** (2000) 'Citizens, politicians and party cartellization: political representation and state failure in post-industrial democracies', *European Journal of Political Research*, 37 (7), 149–179.

**Kitschelt, Herbert, Zdenka Mansfeldova, Radoslaw Markowski and Gábor Tóka** (1999) *Post-Communist Party Systems: Competition, Representation and Inter-Party Competition*, Cambridge University Press, Cambridge.

**Koole, Ruud** (1994) 'The vulnerability of the modern cadre party in the Netherlands', pp. 278–303 in Peter Mair and Richard S. Katz (eds), *How Parties Organize: Change and Adaptation in Party Organizations in Western Democracies*, Sage, London.

**Koole, Ruud** (1996) 'Cadre, catch-all or cartel? A comment on the notion of the cartel party', *Party Politics*, 2 (2), 507–523.

**Kopecký, Petr** (2008) 'Political parties and the state in post-communist Europe: the nature of symbiosis', pp. 1–23 in Petr Kopecký (ed.), *Political Parties and the State in Post-Communist Europe*, Routledge, London.

**Kostelecky, Tomás** (2002) *Political Parties after Communism: Developments in East-Central Europe*, Woodrow Wilson Center Press, Washington, DC.

**Kristjánsson, Svanur** (2003) 'Iceland: a parliamentary democracy with a semi-presidential constitution', pp. 399–417 in Kaare Strøm, Wolfgang C. Müller and Torbjörn Bergman (eds), *Delegation and Accountability in Parliamentary Democracies*, Oxford University Press, Oxford.

**Krook, Mona Lena** (2009) *Quotas for Women in Politics: Gender and Candidate Selection Reform Worldwide*, Oxford University Press, Oxford.

**Krouwel, André** (2003) 'Otto Kirchheimer and the catch-all party', *West European Politics*, 26 (6), 23–40.

**LeDuc, Lawrence** (2001) 'Democratizing party leadership selection', *Party Politics* 7 (7), 323–341.

**Lewis, Paul G.** (2007) 'Political parties', pp. 174–192 in Stephen White, Judy Batt and Paul G. Lewis (eds), *Developments in Central and East European Politics 4*, Palgrave Macmillan, Basingstoke.

**Lipow, Arthur** (1996) *Political Parties and Democracy: Explorations in History and Theory*, Pluto Press, London and Chicago.

**Lundell, Krister** (2004) 'Determinants of candidate selection: the degree of centralization in comparative perspective', *Party Politics*, 10 (1), 25–47.

**Magone, José M.** (2008) 'Portugal', *European Journal of Political Research*, 47 (7/8), 1108–1114.

**Mair, Peter** (1997) *Party System Change: Approaches and Interpretations*, Clarendon Press, Oxford.

**Mair, Peter** (2006) *Polity-Scepticism, Party Failings, and the Challenge to European Democracy*, Netherlands Institute for Advanced Study, Wassenaar.

**Maravall, José María** (2008) 'The political consequences of internal party democracy', pp. 157–201 in José María Maravall and Ignacio Sánchez-Cuenca (eds), *Controlling Governments: Voters, Institutions, and Accountability*, Cambridge University Press, Cambridge.

**Martin, Alan and Philip Cowley** (1999) 'Ambassadors in the community? Labour Party members in society', *Politics*, 19 (9), 89–96.

**May, John D.** (1973) 'Opinion structure of political parties: the special law of curvilinear disparity', *Political Studies*, 21 (1), 135–151.

**McKenzie, Robert** (1982) 'Power in the Labour Party: the issue of "intra-party democracy"', pp. 191–201 in Dennis Kavanagh (ed.), *The Politics of the Labour Party*, George Allen & Unwin, London.

**Murray, Rainbow** (2007) 'How parties evaluate compulsory quotas: a study of the implementation of the "parity" law in France', *Parliamentary Affairs*, 60 (4), 568–584.

**Narud, Hanne Marthe, Mogens N. Pedersen and Henry Valen (eds)** (2002) *Party Sovereignty and Citizen Control: Selecting Candidates for Parliamentary Elections in Denmark, Finland, Iceland and Norway*, University Press of Southern Denmark, Odense.

**Nassmacher, Karl-Heinz (ed.)** (2009) *The Funding of Party Competition: Political Finance in 25 Democracies*, Nomos Verlagsgesellschaft, Baden-Baden.

**Norris, Pippa and Joni Lovenduski** (1997) 'United Kingdom', pp. 158–186 in Pippa Norris (ed.), *Passages to Power: Legislative Recruitment in Advanced Democracies*, Cambridge University Press, Cambridge.

**Panebianco, Angelo** (1988) *Political Parties: Organization and Power*, Cambridge University Press, Cambridge.

**Pedersen, Helene Helboe** (2010) 'Differences and changes in Danish party organisations: central party organisation versus parliamentary party group power', *Journal of Legislative Studies*, 16 (6), 233–250.

**Pedersen, Karina** (2003) 'Party membership linkage: the Danish case', PhD thesis, Department of Political Science, University of Copenhagen.

**Pedersen, Karina, Lars Bille, Roger Buch, Jørgen Elklit, Bernhard Hansen and Hans Jørgen Nielsen** (2004) 'Sleeping or active partners? Danish party members at the turn of the millennium', *Party Politics*, 10 (4), 367–383.

**Pierre, Jon, Lars Svåsand and Anders Widfeldt** (2000) 'State subsidies to political parties: confronting rhetoric with reality', *West European Politics*, 23 (3), 1–24.

**Pinto-Duschinsky, Michael** (2002) 'Financing politics: a global view', *Journal of Democracy*, 13 (3), 69–86.

**Quinn, Thomas** (2004) 'Electing the leader: the British Labour Party's electoral college', *British Journal of Politics and International Relations*, 6 (6), 333–352.

**Rahat, Gideon** (2007) 'Candidate selection: the choice before the choice', *Journal of Democracy*, 18 (8), 157–170.

**Ranney, Austin** (1975) *Curing the Mischiefs of Faction: Party Reform in America*, University of California Press, Berkeley and London.

**Rentoul, John** (1995) *Tony Blair*, Little, Brown, London.

**Roberts, Andrew** (2010) *The Quality of Democracy in Eastern Europe: Public Preferences and Policy Reforms*, Cambridge University Press, Cambridge.

**Ruostetsaari, Ilkka and Mikko Mattila** (2002) 'Candidate-centred campaigns and their effects in an open list system', pp. 92–107 in David M. Farrell and Rüdiger Schmitt-Beck (eds), *Do Political Campaigns Matter? Campaign Effects in Elections and Referendums*, Routledge, London.

**Sanford, George** (2002) *Democratic Government in Poland: Constitutional Politics since 1989*, Palgrave Macmillan, Basingstoke.

**Scarrow, Susan** (1996) *Parties and their Members: Organizing for Victory in Britain and Germany*, Oxford University Press, Oxford.

**Scarrow, Susan E.** (2000) 'Parties without members? Party organization in a changing electoral environment', pp. 79–101 in Russell J. Dalton and Martin P. Wattenberg (eds), *Parties without Partisans: Political Change in Advanced Industrial Democracies*, Oxford University Press, Oxford.

**Scarrow, Susan E.** (2006a) 'The nineteenth-century origins of modern political parties: the unwanted emergence of party-based politics', pp. 16–24 in Richard S. Katz and William Crotty (eds), *Handbook of Party Politics*, Sage, London.

**Scarrow, Susan E.** (2006b) 'Party subsidies and the freezing of party competition: do cartel mechanisms work?', *West European Politics*, 29 (4), 619–639.

**Scarrow, Susan E.** (2007) 'Political finance in comparative perspective', *Annual Review of Political Science*, 10, 193–210.

**Scarrow, Susan, Paul Webb and David M. Farrell** (2000) 'From social integration to electoral contestation: the changing distribution of political power within political parties', pp. 129–153 in Russell J. Dalton and Martin P. Wattenberg (eds), *Parties without Partisans: Political Change in Advanced Industrial Democracies*, Oxford University Press, Oxford.

**Schattschneider, E. E.** (1977) *Party Government*, Greenwood Press, Westport, CT (originally published 1942).

**Seyd, Patrick and Paul Whiteley** (2002) *New Labour's Grassroots: The Transformation of the Labour Party Membership*, Palgrave Macmillan, Basingstoke.

**Seyd, Patrick and Paul Whiteley** (2004) 'British party members: an overview', *Party Politics*, 10 (4), 355–366.

**Sikk, Allan** (2006) 'From private organizations to democratic infrastructure: political parties and the state in Estonia', *Journal of Communist Studies and Transition Politics*, 22 (2), 341–361.

**Sjöblom, Gunnar** (1983) 'Political change and political accountability: a propositional inventory of causes and effects', pp. 369–403 in Hans Daalder and Peter Mair (eds), *Western Europe Party Systems*, Sage, London.

**Smilov, Daniel** (2007) 'Introduction: party funding, campaign funding and corruption in eastern Europe', pp. 1–31 in Daniel Smilov and Jurij Toplak (eds), *Political Finance and Corruption in Eastern Europe: The Transition Period*, Ashgate, Aldershot.

**Smith-Sivertsen, Hermann** (2004) 'Why bigger party membership organisations in Lithuania than in Latvia 1995–2000?', *East European Quarterly*, 38 (8), 215–259.

**Spirova, Maria** (2010) 'The 2009 parliamentary elections in Bulgaria', *Electoral Studies*, 29 (9), 276–278.

**Strøm, Kaare** (1990) 'A behavioral theory of competitive political parties', *American Journal of Political Science*, 34 (4), 565–598.

**Strøm, Kaare** (2000) 'Parties at the core of government', pp. 180–207 in Russell J. Dalton and Martin P. Wattenberg (eds), *Parties without Partisans: Political Change in Advanced Industrial Democracies*, Oxford University Press, Oxford.

**Sussman, Gary** (2007) 'Are party ballots approximating national referendums?', *Representation*, 43 (1), 1–18.

**Szczerbiak, Aleks** (1999) 'Testing party models in east-central Europe: local party organization in postcommunist Poland', *Party Politics*, 5 (5), 525–537.

**Szczerbiak, Aleks** (2001a) *Poles Together? The Emergence and Development of Political Parties in Post-Communist Poland*, Central European University Press, Budapest.

**Szczerbiak, Aleks** (2001b) 'The new Polish political parties as membership organizations', *Contemporary Politics*, 7 (7), 57–69.

**Tavits, Margit** (2008) 'Party systems in the making: the emergence and success of new parties in new democracies', *British Journal of Political Science*, 38 (8), 113–133.

**Torcal, Mariano, Richard Gunther and José Ramón Montero** (2002) 'Anti-party sentiments in southern Europe', pp. 257–290 in Richard Gunther, José Ramón Montero and Juan J. Linz (eds), *Political Parties: Old Concepts and New Challenges*, Oxford University Press, Oxford and New York.

**Tripp, Aili Mari and Alice Kang** (2008) 'The global impact of quotas: on the fast track to increased female legislative representation', *Comparative Political Studies*, 41 (1), 338–361.

**van Biezen, Ingrid** (2003) *Political Parties in New Democracies: Party Organization in Southern and East-Central Europe*, Palgrave Macmillan, Basingstoke.

**van Biezen, Ingrid** (2008) 'Party development in democratic Spain: life-cycle, generation, or period effect?', pp. 23–43 in Bonnie N. Field and Kerstin Hamann (eds), *Democracy and Institutional Development: Spain in Comparative Theoretical Perspective*, Palgrave Macmillan, Basingstoke.

**van Biezen, Ingrid, Peter Mair and Thomas Poguntke** (2009) 'Going, going … gone? Party membership in Europe at the beginning of the 21st century', paper presented at the ECPR Joint Sessions in Lisbon.

**Wagner, Markus** (2008) 'Debating Europe in the French Socialist Party: the 2004 internal referendum on the EU Constitution', *French Politics*, 6 (3), 257–279.

**Ware, Alan** (1992) 'Activist–leader relations and the structure of political parties: "exchange models" and vote-seeking behaviour in parties', *British Journal of Political Science*, 22 (2), 71–92.

**Ware, Alan** (1996) *Political Parties and Party Systems*, Oxford University Press, Oxford.

**Wauters, Bram** (2010) 'Explaining participation in intra-party alliances', *Party Politics*, 16 (6), 237–259.

**Webb, Paul** (2000) *The Modern British Party System*, Sage, London.

**Webb, Paul** (2002) 'Conclusion: Political parties and democratic control in advanced industrial societies', pp. 438–460 in Paul Webb, David M. Farrell and Ian Holliday (eds), *Political Parties in Advanced Industrial Democracy*, Oxford University Press, Oxford.

**Weldon, Steven** (2006) 'Downsize my polity? The impact of size on party membership and member activism', *Party Politics*, 12 (2), 467–481.

**Whiteley, Paul** (2009) 'Where have all the members gone? The dynamics of party membership in Britain', *Parliamentary Affairs*, 6 (6), 242–257.

**Whiteley, Paul F. and Patrick Seyd** (2002) *High-Intensity Participation: The Dynamics of Party Activism in Britain*, University of Michigan Press, Ann Arbor, MI.

**Widfeldt, Anders** (1995) 'Party membership and party representativeness', pp. 134–182 in Hans-Dieter Klingemann and Dieter Fuchs (eds), *Citizens and the State*, Oxford University Press, Oxford.

**Widfeldt, Anders** (1999) *Linking Parties with People? Party Membership in Sweden 1960–1997*, Ashgate, Aldershot.

**Williams, Robert (ed.)** (2000) *Party Finance and Political Corruption*, Macmillan, Basingstoke.

# Elections, Electoral Systems and Referendums

## Chapter contents

## 11.1 Introduction

Elections are central to representative government in Europe. Their significance is both practical and symbolic. In practical terms, they play a large role in determining who becomes part of the political elite. In addition, they have a major bearing on the formation of governments, although, given the frequent complexity of government formation in modern Europe, their impact in this respect may be only indirect (see Chapter 12). As we saw in the previous chapter, elections have become the focal point of activity for most European parties.

Elections are also important symbolically in most competitive party systems, legitimizing a country's political system in the eyes of its citizens. They offer a means of participating in politics at relatively low cost to the individual in terms of time, money and mental effort. For most people, indeed, voting in elections is their only active participation in the political process. Elections also give citizens the feeling that they are exercising choices about who should represent them in the national parliament and about who should form the next government, even though the vote of any individual elector is highly unlikely to have much impact on either matter.

Elections themselves consist everywhere of citizens casting votes for candidates and/or political parties, but there is considerable variation across Europe in the precise set of electoral laws that determines how the votes that are cast are transformed into seats in the legislature in each country. In this chapter we consider the variations in electoral systems in some detail, because these variations can have a significant bearing on some of the major differences in party politics across Europe. A country's electoral system can affect the nature of its party system, the socio-demographic composition of its parliament, the accuracy with which voters' preferences are reflected in the composition of the legislature, and the likelihood that governments will be formed by a coalition of parties rather than by just a single party.

Elections decide which parties and which candidates hold seats in parliaments, but they do not necessarily reflect a judgement on issues. At general elections it is usually the case that many different issues are discussed during the course of the campaign, and even if a particular party pays special attention to one issue, the degree of popular support for that party cannot necessarily be interpreted as the voters' verdict on the issue in question. In a number of European countries, therefore, referendums are used precisely in order to obtain the voters' decision on a specific issue. To some this is basically a good thing, because it provides for greater popular participation in the decision-making process; to others it raises the fear that existing political institutions such as parliaments, governments and political parties will be weakened. Therefore we end this chapter by assessing the role of referendums in modern European politics, and asking whether use of the referendum amounts to 'direct democracy' and in this sense constitutes a challenge to representative government.

Before looking in detail at the nature and impact of electoral systems and the effects of referendums, we briefly outline some central aspects of the legal framework regulating elections in Europe, specifically the nature of the electorate and the timing of elections.

## 11.2 Elections in Europe

### 11.2.1 Who votes?

Elections in all European states are now held under a universal adult franchise. In most countries universal male suffrage had been won by the time of the First World War (Przeworski, 2009) and female suffrage by the Second World War, although women did not receive the vote until immediately after the Second World War in Belgium, France, Greece, Italy and Malta, and not until the 1970s in Switzerland. Evolving legal definitions of adulthood have brought down the voting age in many countries, characteristically to 18, although in a few countries it remains at 19 or 20. Austria perhaps started a trend when in 2007 it reduced voting age to 16. Certain categories of citizens are disfranchised in many countries, including people serving prison sentences and those confined to mental institutions. In only a few countries can non-citizens vote in national elections. Generally speaking, the qualifications needed to be an election candidate are the same as those for being a voter (for details, see Katz, 1997: 246–261; Massicotte et al., 2004: 15–65).

In European countries it is the responsibility of the state to ensure that the electoral register – the list of eligible voters – contains the names of all who are entitled to vote. This means that European electoral registers tend to be more accurate than those in the United States, for example, where the onus is on individuals to register themselves as voters. The proportion of the voting-age population that turns out to vote is higher in Europe than in the United States, in most countries reaching between 70 and 85 per cent. It is particularly low in Switzerland and in some post-communist countries (below 40 per cent in Romania's 2008 election), and especially high in Denmark, Iceland and Malta, along with some countries where voting is or has been compulsory (Belgium, Cyprus and Luxembourg), in all of which turnout routinely exceeds 85 per cent. Since the late 1970s, however, turnout has been decreasing at elections all across Europe (see Table 9.7 above).

## 11.2.2 When do people vote?

In most countries, the law or constitution prescribes a maximum period between elections, but not a minimum; this is four years in most European countries and five years in the rest (see Table 12.1). Within the prescribed limits, the timing of parliamentary elections is usually, on paper at least, at the discretion of the government of the day. To be precise, governments, or sometimes specifically the prime minister, typically have the power to recommend the dissolution of parliament to a head of state, who almost invariably takes this advice. In France, it is the president who has the right to call parliamentary elections at any time – even against the wishes of the government, which may be of a different political complexion – though not more than once a year. (We discussed this power of the French president in detail in Chapter 2.) French presidential elections are held at fixed five-year intervals (the term was seven years prior to 2002), and in a few European countries parliamentary elections too take place at set intervals: in Lithuania, Norway, Sweden and Switzerland, for example, parliaments have a fixed lifespan of four years. Most countries hold elections at weekends, but a few vote on a working day (Massicotte et al., 2004: 117).

Most European governments have complete legal freedom of action as to exactly when they call an election, subject to specified maximum terms. This can make the timing of elections a matter of strategic consideration. In a few European countries, such as Norway and Sweden, the timing of elections is fixed by law, as it is in the United States; in others it is more or less determined by practice and convention, so all political actors have a pretty good idea several years in advance as to when the next election is coming round. For example, in Luxembourg it has become accepted that elections take place every five years, on the same day as elections to the European Parliament. In other countries, however, election dates are decided either by the government of the day or by events outside its control, such as a collapse in the government's parliamentary support, matters that we return to in greater detail in the following chapter. (For analysis of strategic election timing in Britain, see Smith, 2004; see also Strøm and Swindle, 2002.)

Parliamentary elections, of course, are not the only opportunity that people have to vote in modern Europe. In all countries there are also elections for local councils (these are quite important in Scandinavia), and in several there are regional or provincial elections (for example, in Austria, France, Germany, Italy, Spain and the United Kingdom), as we saw in Chapter 6. The 27 member states of the European Union (EU) hold elections to choose members of the European

Parliament; these elections, which we discussed in detail in Chapter 5, take place every five years. In 13 countries, as we noted in Chapter 2, the president is directly elected by the people (see Table 2.2). In addition, as we shall see in the last section of this chapter, the referendum is employed in a number of European countries. This profusion of voting opportunities may contribute to declining turnout, by inducing 'voter fatigue' and creating uncertainly as to which if any contest 'really matters'.

## 11.3  Types of electoral system

In this chapter we concentrate mainly on parliamentary elections, the most important political contests in every European country with the possible exception of Cyprus, France and Romania, which are not straightforward parliamentary systems. In particular, we shall concentrate on electoral systems, the mechanisms that turn the votes cast by people on election day into seats to be occupied by deputies in the parliament. The electoral system structures the choices that the voters can make and then converts these choices into a legislature.

A wide variety of electoral systems are in use across Europe, and there is an equally wide selection of literature describing and tracing the history of these systems (see Gallagher and Mitchell, 2008; Farrell, 2010). This variety reflects in part the different weights attached to different criteria in different countries. Most countries use some form of proportional representation (PR). There is considerable debate in the literature as to whether the general move from plurality to PR around the turn of the twentieth century, and the adoption of electoral reform generally, should be seen as motivated by a combination of partisan motives and non-partisan reasons such as improving the operation of the political system (Blais *et al.*, 2005, Gallagher, 2008b: 535–539; Katz, 2008; Shugart, 2009; Kreuzer, 2010; Renwick, 2010;) represents a risk-minimizing response to an increasingly uncertain political environment (Colomer, 2004); is due almost solely to partisan calculations (Benoit, 2004; Boix, 2010; Andrews and Jackman, 2005, who note that such calculations could prove flawed in conditions of high uncertainty); or should be seen primarily as the consequence of the organization of economic interests, with proto-corporatist countries opting for PR and pluralist ones sticking with plurality systems (Cusack *et al.*, 2010). (For discussion of corporatism and pluralism, see Chapter 13 below.) Given that electoral systems are chosen by political actors, rather than being randomly assigned to countries, we obviously cannot assume automatically that electoral systems 'cause' any observed aspects of political behaviour.

It is a striking fact that no two European countries have electoral systems that are identical in every detail. This brings a glint to the eye of connoisseurs of detail, but might seem to be worrying for those trying to get an overview of European practice. Fortunately, we can identify some broad principles behind electoral system design, even if the precise implementation of those principles varies somewhat from country to country.

Electoral systems in western Europe have been fairly stable since 1945; only in Greece could the electoral system be said to have been used as a political football, although Italy has seen instability over the last 20 years (Bull and Newell, 2009: 44–53; Renwick, 2010: 111–128), and France has a long record of opportunistic changes in earlier periods. In Greece the electoral system was changed seven times over the 12 elections of the 1974–2009 period, invariably by the governing party trying to gain partisan advantage. In post-communist Europe the picture

| | Basic category | Members of lower house | Number of constituencies (districts) | Significant changes since 1945/1990[a] |
|---|---|---|---|---|
| Austria | PR list | 183 | † | Introduction in 1992 of a third tier, increase from 9 to 43 districts, and minor expansion of effectiveness of preferential voting |
| Belgium | PR list | 150 | 11 | Abolition of higher tier, and significant expansion of effectiveness of preference voting, prior to 2003 election |
| Bulgaria | Mixed parallel | 240 | 32 | Replaced regional PR list system before 2009 election |
| Cyprus | PR list | 56 | † | This replaced 'reinforced PR' 1995 |
| Czech Republic | PR list | 200 | 14 | Importance of preference votes increased before 2006 election |
| Denmark | PR list | 175 | † | Change of formula from DH to MSL 1953 |
| Estonia | PR list | 101 | † | Abandonment of STV after 1990 election |
| Finland | PR list | 200 | 15 | None |
| France | Non-PR (two-round) | 577 | 577 | Many (see text pp. 375–376) |
| Germany | Mixed compensatory | 598 | † | Minor changes in 1953, 1956, 1984 and 1990 |
| Greece | PR list | 300 | † | Many changes, usually designed to benefit the government of the day |
| Hungary | Mixed partially compensatory | 386 | † | None |
| Iceland | PR list | 63 | † | Changes in 1987 and 2000 |
| Ireland | PR STV | 166 | 43 | None |
| Italy | PR list | 630 | 1 | Major changes in 1993 and 2005 |
| Latvia | PR list | 100 | 5 | Threshold raised from 4% 1995 |
| Lithuania | Mixed parallel | 141 | 72 | Several; most recently, weight of preference votes in awarding list seats to individual candidates increased in 2008 |

**TABLE 11.1** Electoral systems in Europe, 2010

**TABLE 11.1** (*continued*)

| | Basic category | Members of lower house | Number of constituencies (districts) | Significant changes since 1945/1990[a] |
|---|---|---|---|---|
| Luxembourg | PR list | 60 | 4 | None |
| Malta | PR STV | 65 | 13 | Winner in votes guaranteed majority of seats since 1987 |
| Netherlands | PR list | 150 | 1 | Minor increase in effectiveness of preferential voting 1998 |
| Norway | PR list | 169 | † | Change of formula from DH to MSL 1953; addition of 8 national seats before 1989 election (increased to 19 before 2005 election) |
| Poland | PR list | 460 | 41 | Changes prior to four of first five post-communist elections |
| Portugal | PR list | 230 | 20 | None since 1975 |
| Romania | PR list?[b] | 315 | 1 | System adopted 2008 |
| Slovakia | PR list | 150 | 1 | Weight of preference votes increased prior to 2006 election |
| Slovenia | PR list | 90 | † | Introduction of 4% threshold prior to 2000 election |
| Spain | PR list | 350 | 52 | None since 1977 |
| Sweden | PR list | 349 | † | Change of formula from DH to MSL 1952; introduction of higher-tier seats in 1970; introduction of meaningful preference voting 1998 |
| Switzerland | PR list | 200 | 26 | None |
| United Kingdom | Non-PR (plurality) | 650 | 650 | None (yet) at national level |

*Note*: In the case of post-communist countries, only changes since 1990 are noted.

[a] Abbreviations for electoral formulae: DH, D'Hondt; MSL, modified Sainte-Laguë; STV, single transferable vote.

[b] The Romanian system is unique (see text, pp. 386–387) and is difficult to fit into any of the conventional categories.

† Indicates country has 'complex districting', i.e. higher-tier constituencies to iron out discrepancies arising from lower-level constituencies. In these circumstances it is difficult to give a meaningful figure for the number of constituencies, as the units in which people vote may have no significance when it comes to the allocation of seats.

*Sources*: Mackie and Rose (1991); Rose and Munro (2003); annual updates in the *Political Data Yearbook* of the *European Journal of Political Research*; election reports in *Electoral Studies*; Birch (2003).

varies: in some countries there has been stability and continuity (Slovenia, Hungary and the Baltic states) whereas in others (such as Poland and Romania) the electoral system has been the object of a number of political battles, with many attempts to make changes, some of them successful (Birch *et al.*, 2002).

For all this diversity, there are several systematic patterns in the profusion of electoral systems to be found across the continent. One vital distinction is between plurality or majority systems (we shall refer to these as *majoritarian systems*) on the one hand and *proportional representation systems* on the other. The latter put more stress on the concept of proportionality, the numerical accuracy with which the votes cast for parties are translated into seats won in parliament. Under a PR system, if a party receives, say, 25 per cent of the votes, it can expect to win close to 25 per cent of the seats. If every party participating in an election was guaranteed exactly the same share of seats as it won of the votes, we would describe that system as perfectly proportional, although this would not necessarily mean that the system was 'perfect' in a normative sense. In practice, no electoral system can guarantee perfect proportionality, but PR systems attach greater priority to getting somewhere close to this goal. Plurality systems do not, of course, set out deliberately *not* to achieve high proportionality, but by prioritizing other criteria they accept a certain level of disproportionality as inevitable. An overview of European electoral systems in these terms is shown in Table 11.1.

## 11.4 Plurality and majority systems

Throughout the nineteenth century, elections in most countries were held under plurality systems, but a combination of factors led almost all countries to adopt some form of PR in the twentieth century (Colomer, 2004). At the moment, only two European countries do not use an electoral system that has at least an element of PR: these are the United Kingdom and France.

The electoral system used in the United Kingdom for House of Commons elections is the least complicated of all systems. It is the same as that employed for most elections in the United States, Canada and India, for example. The country is divided into 650 areas, known as *constituencies* or (in the USA) *districts*, each of which returns one member of parliament (MP) to the House of Commons. (Constituencies everywhere in Europe are geographically delineated; for an innovative argument in favour of the random assignment of citizens to non-geographic constituencies, see Rehfeld, 2005.) Within each constituency, the candidate with the most votes, whether or not this is a majority over all others combined, wins the seat. The system is best named the *single-member plurality (SMP) system*, though it is often called 'first past the post', in a rather dubious analogy with horse racing, or simply 'the British system'. Voters, on entering the polling station, are given a ballot paper listing all the candidates, and they write an X next to the name of the candidate they wish to vote for. An example of the operation of the system in a constituency in Cornwall, on the Celtic fringe of England, in the 2010 general election is shown in Table 11.2.

This system has the merit of simplicity for voters. It is also defended on the ground that as the MP, in this case George Eustice, is the only representative for the constituency, responsibility for its interests lies unequivocally with him. This, it is claimed, helps forge a bond between an MP

**TABLE 11.2** The British electoral system in operation, Camborne and Redruth constituency, 2010 election

|  | Votes | % of votes |
| --- | --- | --- |
| George Eustice (Conservative) | 15 969 | 37.6 |
| Julia Goldsworthy (Liberal Democrat) | 15 903 | 37.4 |
| Jude Robinson (Labour) | 6 945 | 16.3 |
| Derek Elliott (UK Independence Party) | 2 152 | 5.1 |
| Loveday Jenkin (Mebyon Kernow) | 775 | 1.8 |
| Euan McPhee (Green Party) | 581 | 1.4 |
| Robert Hawkins (Socialist Labour Party) | 168 | 0.4 |
| Total | 42 493 | 100.0 |

and his or her constituents that would be lost if several MPs were responsible for the same constituency, as each might then 'shirk'. In terms of the national impact, as we discuss later, the system is praised for its tendency to produce single-party majority governments, although it did not do this in 2010.

But the plurality system has many critics. Three of the main points made against it are illustrated by the Camborne and Redruth result. First, Eustice was elected despite winning less than 40 per cent of the total votes; in fact, 62 per cent of the voters were not represented by a candidate of their favoured party. It is almost certain that most Labour voters would have preferred the election of the Liberal Democrat candidate to the actual outcome, and so in a straight fight between the Conservative and the Liberal Democrat, the latter would have won. Therefore the British system is criticized for not necessarily producing the MP who would be most representative of the voters' wishes and, worse, for producing results that are in some sense arbitrarily determined by the nomination of 'vote-splitting' losing candidates.

Second, the Camborne and Redruth contest presented Labour supporters in particular with a tactical choice: should they vote for the Labour candidate, or should they vote for the Liberal Democrat in order to keep the Conservative out? If they vote sincerely, in accordance with their true preferences, then this might have the effect of helping to bring about the election of the candidate they like least. Although no electoral system is completely 'strategy-proof', the plurality system is almost guaranteed to force at least some voters to think strategically if there are more than two serious candidates.

Third, if the pattern of the Camborne and Redruth result, with over 60 per cent of the votes wasted on losing candidates, were repeated over the entire country, the House of Commons could be very unrepresentative of public opinion. In practice, the lack of 'fairness' in individual constituencies evens itself out to some extent across the country; an overall election is never as 'unfair' as a sample constituency outcome repeated 650 times over (Gallagher and Mitchell, 2008: Appendix C). Consequently, between 1945 and the 1970s, when nearly all the votes were won by the two main parties, Labour and the Conservatives, the national outcome in terms of seats was not grossly unrepresentative. But when a third party (the Liberals in 1974 and 1979, the alliance between the Liberal and the Social Democratic Party in 1983 and 1987, and the Liberal Democrats from 1992 onwards) began winning significant support, the national outcome fell much further short of perfect proportionality, with the third party the main victim. This is illustrated by the result of the 2010 election (see Table 11.3), when the largest two parties received 87 per cent of the seats for 65 per cent of the votes. At the previous three elections Labour had won a comfortable, sometimes an overwhelming, majority of seats despite receiving a minority of the votes (only 35 per cent in 2005).

The plurality electoral system in the United Kingdom has come under increasing challenge in recent years. Indeed, the country now employs a variety of different electoral systems in different settings (Mitchell, 2008; see Box 11.1). After its 1997 election victory the incoming Labour government soon lost enthusiasm for the idea of electoral reform, with which it had dallied while in opposition; the idea somehow looked less attractive once Labour became the main beneficiary of the existing system (Blau, 2009). The Conservatives have always been against any change to the status quo. The third party, the Liberal Democrats, have consistently favoured the introduction of proportional representation, but before 2010 were never in a position to do anything about it. As Paul Mitchell puts it, when a party has the will to change an electoral system it does not have the power, and when it has the power it does not have the will (Mitchell, 2008: 174).

The failure of any party to win an overall majority at the 2010 election opened the door to at least modest electoral reform. In the negotiations that led to the formation of the Conservative–Liberal Democrat coalition government, the Conservatives would not countenance putting PR on the agenda but were compelled to agree to the holding of a referendum on changing to the *alternative vote* (AV) – the single transferable vote in single-member constituencies (in the USA this is known as 'instant runoff'). Under AV, voters would rank the candidates in order of preference by placing a number ('1', '2', etc.) next to each name. The counting process would no longer finish with the counting of the first preferences; instead, if no candidate had a majority, the lowest-placed candidate would be eliminated and his or her votes transferred to the other candidates, in accordance with the second preferences marked on the ballots. So, in Camborne and Redruth, the three minor party candidates, and then the Labour candidate, would have been successively eliminated. Assuming that a majority of Labour voters gave their second preference to the Liberal Democrat candidate rather than to the Conservative, the Liberal Democrat would almost certainly be carried above the Conservative and would therefore win the seat.

---

**TABLE 11.3** Votes and seats in the United Kingdom general election of 2010

|  | % of votes | % of seats |
|---|---|---|
| Conservatives | 36.1 | 47.2 |
| Labour | 29.0 | 39.7 |
| Liberal Democrats | 23.0 | 8.8 |
| Others | 11.9 | 4.3 |
| Total | 100.0 | 100.0 |

*Source*: Table 7.1.

The alternative vote is a majority system, as opposed to the British plurality system, because the counting process continues until one candidate has a majority (50 per cent plus 1) over all other remaining candidates.

No European country uses the alternative vote to elect its parliament (although it is employed in Australia), but a system that has some of the same properties is used in France. There, as in Britain, deputies are returned from single-member constituencies, but there is provision for two rounds of voting, on successive Sundays. If a candidate wins a majority of votes in the first round, he or she is elected, but that occurs in only a minority of constituencies (in 109 out of 577 constituencies in 2007). Otherwise, the first round of voting is followed by a second, which only the top candidates are allowed to enter (see Box 11.1). The candidate with the most votes (a simple plurality) in the second round wins the seat, even if he or she fails to achieve an overall majority. (French presidential elections are held under the same system, except that only the top two candidates from the first round are allowed to proceed to the second, thus guaranteeing that the eventual winner will emerge with an absolute majority.) This system is also used in Hungary and in Lithuania to elect some of the MPs, as we discuss later (Benoit, 2008).

This *two-round double ballot system* (2RS) has at least one advantage over the British one: it gives supporters of losing first-round candidates a chance to switch their second-round vote to one of the serious contenders. But, even if it does have the potential to give a slightly greater choice to the voters, the French system, like the British, does not overcome the problem of disproportional overall results. In 2007, for example, the UMP won only 40 per cent of the votes but 54 per cent of the seats, and the bonus of the largest party is usually much greater than this. Like the British system, the French 2RS assists the largest parties and penalizes smaller ones. It brings particular benefits to parties close to the centre, such as the UMP and the Socialists, and works against more extreme parties, such as the Communists (PCF) or the far-right Front National (FN). Such parties, even if their candidates make it into the second round, are very unlikely to win the run-off against a more centrist candidate, and so they win a smaller share of the seats than of the votes. The PCF has some scope for deal-making with the Socialists, albeit on the Socialists' terms, and thus wins some seats, but the FN is generally treated as a pariah by the other parties, and usually ends up with few or no seats; it won none at either the 2002 or 2007 elections despite receiving 4 million votes at the two elections combined. For supporters of the double-ballot system this pronounced penalization of 'anti-system' parties is a definite merit (Sartori, 1997: 67).

One disadvantage of 2RS when compared with the alternative vote is that the candidates whom it allows through to the second round are decided entirely by first-round support without any consideration of broad support. This was dramatically illustrated at the French presidential election of 2002, when almost everyone expected that the second round would be fought between the main right-wing candidate, the incumbent Jacques Chirac, and the Socialist leader Lionel Jospin. Instead, because of fragmentation of the left-wing vote, Jospin was pushed narrowly into third position by the far-right candidate Jean-Marie Le Pen, whom Chirac defeated by 82 per cent to 18 per cent in the second round. Under the alternative vote, vote transfers from the lower-placed candidates of the broad left would have taken Jospin into second or perhaps even first place by the end of the count; under the two-round system this counted for nothing, because his first-round votes were slightly fewer than Le Pen's.

In France, as we have mentioned, the electoral system has over the years been manipulated by ruling parties for their own benefit (for details, see Elgie, 2008; Blais and Loewen, 2009).

The two-round system was used for most of the period between 1831 and 1939, although other systems were often tried for short periods. After the Second World War a PR system was briefly used, but in the early 1950s a new system was introduced, with the clear aim of discriminating against the Communist Party. The two-round system was brought back under de Gaulle in the late 1950s, and this ushered in a period of electoral system stability apart from a short-lived deviation in the late 1980s. The Socialists replaced 2RS with PR for the 1986 election, partly to minimize their electoral losses, but the incoming right-wing administration promptly reintroduced 2RS, under which subsequent parliamentary elections have been held.

## 11.5 Proportional representation

Discontent with the anomalies produced by plurality or majority systems, combined inevitably with self-interested calculations by those parties that were faring, or seemed likely to fare, badly under such systems, led to discussion of electoral reform throughout Europe in the second half of the nineteenth century. As the franchise expanded to include the working class, the prospect of seeing left-wing parties sweep the board under the existing system brought about a sudden appreciation of the principle of PR on the part of the existing conservative and liberal parties in most countries. By the end of the Second World War nearly all countries had electoral systems based on PR. The key element in any PR electoral system is the multi-member constituency. Seats are allocated to parties within each constituency in broad proportion to the votes each party receives. Proportional representation systems cannot be based solely on single-member constituencies with no higher level of seat allocation, because a single seat cannot be divided up proportionately, no matter what method is used to allocate it. As a general rule, indeed, the larger the district magnitude (i.e., the number of members returned from each constituency), the more proportional the national election result is likely to be. This, it should be stressed, applies only when a PR formula is used. If a plurality or majority formula is employed in multi-member constituencies, as when American public representatives are elected from 'at-large' districts, the result is highly disproportional, being even more crushing to minorities than a series of single-seat constituencies.

There are important variations between PR systems, but it is as well to remember that while it is easy to be put off by the apparent complexity of some systems (a useful argument for politicians opposed to the introduction of any new system, who can say 'our voters would never be able to understand that'), the underlying principles are usually fairly straightforward. Basically, PR systems can be grouped into three categories: list systems, mixed systems, and STV. We shall examine each in turn.

### 11.5.1 List systems

The basic principle of a list system is that each party presents a list of candidates in each constituency. Each list usually contains as many candidates as there are seats to be filled in the constituency. The seats are then shared out among the parties in proportion to the votes they win, in accordance with a predetermined formula. Although PR is scarcely used at any level of elections in the United States, Americans were the first to think about ways of achieving proportional representation. They were interested not in the proportional allocation of seats to parties in accordance with the votes that each party receives but in the proportional allocation to states of seats in the House of Representatives in accordance with the population of each state. Most of the PR methods used in Europe today were either used or discussed in the United States long before Europeans thought of them.

List systems differ from one another in a number of respects, and we discuss these in sequence. They are:

a the formulae used to award seats to parties within each constituency;

b the matter of whether or not there is a second, higher, tier at which seats are awarded, to override any imbalances that may arise at the constituency level;

c the existence of thresholds; and

d the degree of choice, if any, given to voters to express a preference for one or more specific candidates on the party list.

The picture is summarized in Table 11.4.

### Electoral formulae

A number of different methods are used to decide how seats are shared out among parties, the most common being largest remainders (using the Hare or Droop quota), highest averages using the D'Hondt method, and highest averages using the modified or pure Sainte-Laguë method. In the United States largest remainders with the Hare quota is known as the Hamilton method and D'Hondt as the Jefferson method, used for apportioning seats in the House of Representatives from 1790 to 1830. The 'pure' Sainte-Laguë method is known in the United States as the Webster method; the modified version used in some Scandinavian countries has the effect of making it more difficult than under the pure version for small parties to win seats. We shall not elaborate the differences between these formulae in any detail here (the mechanics are explained in Gallagher and Mitchell, 2008: Appendix A), because these differences are less important than the similarities. However, it should be noted that, of these five methods, both pure Sainte-Laguë and largest remainders with the Hare quota are completely even-handed as between large and small parties; modified Sainte-Laguë and largest remainders with the Droop quota tilt the balance slightly towards larger parties; and the D'Hondt method favours large parties even more. All variants of PR are essentially similar in that they set out to award seats as 'fairly' as possible to each party according to how many votes it won, although they are based on slightly different ideas as to exactly what is meant by the concept of 'fairness' (Gallagher, 1991). They share a common attachment to the idea of proportionality, and in this they differ fundamentally from the plurality method, where other criteria take priority.

### District magnitude and higher tiers

The seat allocation method is just one factor determining how proportional the distribution of seats will be in relation to the way votes were cast. A second and often more important factor is district magnitude. If the average district magnitude is small, an election outcome is unlikely to be highly proportional, no matter what allocation formula is used. Spain employs relatively small constituencies (district magnitude averages seven seats), and in addition its rural areas are significantly over-represented in parliament (Hopkin, 2008). Consequently, the major parties there derive a sizeable bonus, and there is usually significant deviation from perfect proportionality, albeit not on the same scale as in countries using the British plurality system. Ireland employs constituencies whose district magnitude averages only four seats, the lowest for any PR system in Europe, and this largely accounts for the country's above-average levels of disproportionality.

**TABLE 11.4** Features of European electoral systems, 2010

| | Constituency level seat allocation formula[a] | Higher-tier seat allocation? (formula) | Threshold (for participation in higher-tier seat share-out unless otherwise specified) | Choice of candidate within party? |
|---|---|---|---|---|
| *PR list systems* | | | | |
| Austria | Hare | Yes (DH) | 4% of votes nationally or 1 constituency seat | Yes, but largely ineffective |
| Belgium | DH | No | 5% needed within a constituency for any seats there | Yes |
| Cyprus | Hare | LR-Hare | 1.8% national vote or 1 constituency seat | Yes |
| Czech Republic | DH | No | 5% of votes nationally for any seats | Yes |
| Denmark | DH | Yes (LR-Hare) | 2% of votes nationally needed for parliamentary representation | Yes |
| Estonia | Hare | Yes (DH) | 5% of votes | Yes |
| Finland | DH | No | – | Yes |
| Greece | DH | Yes (LR) | 3% of votes nationally needed for parliamentary representation | Yes |
| Iceland | DH | Yes (DH) | 5% of votes nationally | Yes, but largely ineffective |
| Italy | LR-Hare | No[†] | 4% of votes nationally | No |
| Latvia | SL | No | 5% of votes nationally for any seats | Yes |
| Luxembourg | DH | No | – | Yes |
| Netherlands | DH | No[†] | 0.67% of votes nationally needed to qualify for seats | Yes, but largely ineffective |
| Norway | MSL | Yes (MSL) | 4% of votes nationally | Yes, but largely ineffective |
| Poland | DH | No | 5% of votes nationally needed for any seats | Yes |
| Portugal | DH | No | – | No |
| Romania | See pp. 386–87 | DH | 5% or 6 constituency seats | No |
| Slovakia | LR-Droop | No[†] | 5% of votes nationally needed for any seats | Yes |
| Slovenia | Droop | Yes (DH) | 4% of votes nationally | Yes |
| Spain | DH | No | – | No |

**TABLE 11.4** (*continued*)

| | Constituency level seat allocation formula[a] | Higher-tier seat allocation? (formula) | Threshold (for participation in higher-tier seat share-out unless otherwise specified) | Choice of candidate within party? |
|---|---|---|---|---|
| Sweden | MSL | Yes (MSL) | 4% of votes nationally or 12% in one constituency needed for parliamentary representation | Yes |
| Switzerland | DH | No | – | Yes |
| *Mixed systems* | | | | |
| Bulgaria | Plurality | Yes (LR-Hare) | 4% of votes nationally | No |
| Germany | Plurality | Yes (LR-Hare) | 5% of votes or 3 constituency seats | No |
| Hungary | 2-round | Yes (DH) | 5% of votes nationally | No |
| Lithuania | 2-round | Yes (LR-Hare) | 5% of list votes | Yes |
| *Other PR systems* | | | | |
| Ireland | STV | No | – | Yes |
| Malta | STV | Yes[‡] | See[‡] | Yes |
| *Non-PR systems* | | | | |
| France | 2-round | No | – | No |
| United Kingdom | Plurality | No | – | No |

[a]Formulae: DH, D'Hondt; LR, largest remainders; MSL, modified Sainte-Laguë; STV, single transferable vote.

*Notes*: In some countries, especially post-communist ones, there are higher thresholds for coalitions.

[†] For seat allocation purposes, there is only one (national) constituency.

[‡] In Malta, whichever of the two main parties wins a plurality of first preference votes is awarded extra seats to give it an overall majority of seats, if it has not won a majority from the constituencies. This is the only situation in which there is any higher-tier allocation.

*Sources*: As Table 11.1.

One way of overcoming the problem is to use larger constituencies, averaging around 12 seats or more, as in Finland, Latvia and Luxembourg. This is taken to the extreme in the Netherlands and Slovakia; in each case, the whole country forms one giant constituency. There are other countries, too, such as Italy and Slovenia, in which even though MPs are deemed to be representatives of a particular subnational constituency, the allocation of seats to parties is determined entirely by their national share of the vote, meaning that for seat allocation purposes those countries in effect constitute just one constituency. Employing large constituencies is sometimes criticized on the grounds that voters are likely to feel remote from their deputies. Another method is to have a second level of allocation at which disproportionalities arising at the constituency level can be ironed out (Taagepera and Shugart, 1989: 126–133). In some countries a certain proportion of seats is set aside at the start for this purpose: about 20 per cent in Denmark and Iceland, and 11 per cent in Norway and Sweden. These 'higher-tier' seats are then awarded to the parties in the appropriate numbers to compensate them for any shortfall in the seats they won in the constituencies, and thereby bring the overall distribution of seats as close to perfect proportionality as possible. In other countries, such as Austria, the number of higher-tier seats is not fixed in advance, but the effect is just the same. What happens here is that each party's 'wasted' votes from the constituencies – that is, the votes it has not used to earn seats – are pooled on a national or regional basis, and a distribution of the unallocated seats takes place in accordance with each party's unused vote totals (Müller 2008). This ensures that very few of a party's votes are wasted.

### 11.5.2 Mixed systems

For about a decade from the late 1980s mixed systems were the favoured option of electoral reformers in many countries (for mixed systems see Massicotte and Blais, 1999; Shugart and Wattenberg, 2003; Gallagher and Mitchell, 2008: Chapters 10–15). Much of the growth in usage has been outside the region we are covering (Japan, Mexico and New Zealand are the most prominent examples), but four of the 30 countries covered by this book now employ a mixed system. The essence of these systems is that MPs can be elected by two different routes. There is a wide range of possible (and even actual) variants, but the most widely employed is the one where the voter has two votes: one to choose a local constituency MP, and the other to choose a party list. There is terminological profusion when it comes to naming this kind of system: it is known not only as mixed but also as *mixed member, additional member* (particularly in Britain) or *personalized PR* (particularly in Germany).

The link between the two types of seat – constituency and list – can be made in two different ways. In one, termed *compensatory* mixed systems or MMP (*mixed-member proportional*), the list seats are awarded to parties to ensure that their overall seat total (list seats plus constituency seats) is proportional to their list votes. Thus, if a party has been under-represented at constituency level, which is usually the case for small parties, it is allocated relatively more list seats to 'compensate' it and bring it up to its overall 'fair' share. The other type of mixed system is *parallel*, where the list seats are shared out purely on the basis of list votes, without taking any account of what has happened in the constituency component. Parallel mixed systems produce a less 'fair' overall outcome than compensatory ones, because the list seats are not used to counterbalance the disproportionalities produced in the constituency component.

Germany's is the archetypal mixed system (Saalfeld, 2008). The country is divided into 299 single-member constituencies, in each of which the seat goes to the candidate with the most votes, just as in Britain. The sharing out of the national seats is then carried out in such a way as to ensure that each party's total number of seats (constituency seats plus national seats) is proportional to its share of the list votes – in other words, it is a compensatory system (see Box 11.1). Usually, the two main parties, the SPD and the CDU/CSU, win the great majority of the constituency seats: 282 out of 299 at the 2009 election, for example. Consequently, the other parties are reliant on the list seats to achieve their overall fair share. A peculiarity of the German system is the possibility of *overhang seats*, which can distort the overall proportionality of the system (see Box 11.1 and Behnke, 2007).

In contrast, Lithuania employs the other type of mixed system, the parallel version. There are 71 single-member constituencies, in which the French two-round system is used, and a list component with 70 seats. Once again each voter has two votes, one in the constituency and one for a list. Because it is a parallel system, the list seats are awarded entirely on the basis of the list votes won by each party, without regard to what happened in the single-member constituency component. This is better for the large parties, which, given the 5 per cent threshold for qualification for list seats, get a bonus from the list section to add to the one they already got from the single-member constituency component. In 2000, for example, the social democratic coalition in Lithuania took 40 per cent of the list seats with just 31 per cent of the list votes – having already won 32 per cent of the single-member constituencies with just 20 per cent of the votes. Bulgaria, too, employs a parallel system, and indeed Bulgaria's system only just qualifies for description as a mixed system, since the mix is very unbalanced: 31 MPs are elected from single-member constituencies and the other 209 from lists.

Mixed systems grew in popularity in the 1990s because they could be perceived as offering 'the best of both worlds' (Shugart and Wattenberg, 2003). Citizens have an individual MP to represent them, as they would under a non-PR system, but the provision of a list component means that, overall, the relationship between seats and votes is much closer than it would be under a non-PR system. This combination of proportionality and local representation is what made mixed systems the alternative of choice for electoral system reformers and designers in a number of countries. However, some of the early gloss has worn off them. Empirically, it is not true that they produce two 'types' of MP: constituency MPs who are focused on casework, and list MPs who focus on national political issues. Most list candidates also stand in a constituency. In Germany, Scotland and Wales it is common for list MPs to set up offices in the single-member constituency where they are based and, while constituency MPs are a little more constituency-focused and list MPs have a little more contact with interest groups, differences between the two groups are minor (Lundberg, 2006). In addition, mixed compensatory systems are open to manip-ulation by the parties, which led to problems in Italy while it employed such a system, and con-tributed to the abandonment of mixed systems in 11 countries in the 2000s (D'Alimonte, 2008: 258–260; Lundberg, 2009: 18). One cross-national study has concluded that mixed systems in fact constitute the worst of both worlds: 'mixed electoral systems have statistically significant lower levels of accountability, government effectiveness, control of corruption, representation of women in parliament and voter turnout' (Doorenspleet, 2010: 43).

### 11.5.3 Thresholds

Even PR electoral systems, despite their name, sometimes have features that give an inbuilt advantage to larger parties. This is due either to self-interest on the part of the larger parties (who usually make the rules), or to a disinterested concern that perfect proportionality could lead to a proliferation of small parties in parliament and thus to difficulty in forming a stable government – or to a combination of both factors. It is common, therefore, for electoral systems to employ a threshold that a party must overcome before it qualifies for seats. The best-known example is the German system, which allows only those parties that have either won at least 5 per cent of the list votes, or won at least three constituency seats, to share in the national list allocation. Only once has a party qualified for list seats without winning 5 per cent of the list votes: this occurred in 1994, when the former communists, the PDS, qualified via the three-constituencies route, thanks to their strength in east Berlin. In order to prevent fragmentation, and to encourage the consolidation of a coherent party system, post-communist countries generally impose higher thresholds than their west European counterparts: often parties must reach 4 or even 5 per cent of the vote in order to qualify for *any* seats (Table 11.4). Some countries apply a threshold at the level of individual constituencies: for example, in Belgium no party can receive any seats within one of the multi-member constituencies unless it has won at least 5 per cent of the votes there.

## BOX 11.1: ELECTORAL SYSTEMS

### Denmark

Denmark's system has undergone only minor modifications since 1920. In essence it is a highly proportional open-list system; in other words, parties receive a seat share that corresponds closely to their vote share, and in most cases voters have the power to decide which of their favoured party's candidates they wish to see take the party's seats. About half of all voters cast a preference vote for an individual candidate. The country is divided into 10 multi-member constituencies, which between them have 135 so-called *constituency seats*, and within these constituencies seats are awarded to parties by the D'Hondt method. This on its own would produce a reasonably proportional outcome, but to raise the level of proportionality even higher there are an additional 40 seats that are awarded to the parties in such a way as to iron out disproportionalities arising from the distribution of the constituency seats. These 40 seats are awarded to candidates who missed election in the constituencies; there is no separate national list. There is a threshold for receiving any of these 40 higher-tier seats: parties must receive 2 per cent of the votes nationally (or meet one of two other requirements) in order to qualify for inclusion in the share-out.

### France

France does not use proportional representation to elect deputies to the National Assembly. Instead, it employs a *two-round* or *double ballot* system. Metropolitan France is divided into 555 single-member constituencies (the overseas territories and departments return an additional 22 deputies). Within each constituency there can be two rounds of voting on successive Sundays. If a candidate wins an overall majority in the first round, he or she is elected as the deputy for the constituency, but in the great majority of constituencies no candidate achieves this, and the second round takes place a week later. Only candidates whose first round votes exceeded 12.5 per cent of the electorate (which on the basis of turnout at the 2007 election equates to just over 20 per cent of the votes cast) are permitted to participate in the second round, unless the operation of this rule would leave fewer than two candidates entitled to take part, in which case the top two are both allowed through. In the second round the candidate with the most votes, whether or not this amounts to a majority, wins the seat. Hence the system is sometimes described as *majority–plurality*, in that a majority in the first round, or a plurality in the second, suffices for election.

### Germany

The German electoral system provides two routes to the lower house of parliament, the Bundestag. When voters enter the polling booth, they are faced with a ballot paper with two columns. One gives them a vote in the election of a member of parliament (MdB) for the local single-member constituency; half of the 598 members of parliament are elected from single-member constituencies in exactly the same way as in the United Kingdom. The second column enables them to cast a list vote; the other half of the parliament is elected from party lists. The overall allocation of seats in the Bundestag is decided by these list votes. Each party is awarded as many list seats as it needs to ensure that its total number of seats (constituency seats and list seats combined) is proportional to the share of list votes it received. However, parties do not receive any list seats unless they have either won at least 5 per cent of the list votes or won three constituency seats. If a party wins more constituency seats within any *Land* (province) than it is entitled to on the basis of its list votes, it is allowed to keep these extra seats (which are termed *Überhangmandate*), and the size of the Bundestag is expanded accordingly. At recent elections these *Überhangmandate*, which represent a distortion of proportionality and have caused considerable debate, have significantly increased the size of the government's majority: from 2 to 10 in 1994, from 8 to 21 in 1998, and from 21 to 42 in 2009. The Federal Constitutional Court has expressed serious concern about this, and has asked that a way of abolishing the *Überhangmandate* be found by 2011.

## Italy

From the end of the Second World War until 1993, Italy had a very proportional type of PR system, based on open lists within large constituencies. Politicians found guilty of corruption in the early 1990s were inclined to blame the electoral system for forcing them into clientelistic 'vote-buying' exercises of one sort or another, so the electoral system moved to the top of the hit-list of Italy's political reformers, and was fundamentally altered in 1993. The new system was a compromise between those who wanted to adopt the British single-member plurality system and those who wanted to retain PR. It was a mixed system that was partially compensatory, in that the share-out of list seats took some but not full account of the seats that parties won in the single-member constituencies. It was still difficult for any one party to win an overall majority of seats, so in 2005 Prime Minister Berlusconi introduced a new system, under which seats are awarded to parties in accordance with their share of the national vote. There is a threshold of 4 per cent of the votes to qualify for any seats (2 per cent for parties that are part of a coalition). Although there are 26 regional units for seat allocation purposes, the determination as to how many seats each party receives is made entirely on the basis of national votes, so for seat allocation purposes the whole country in effect constitutes one large constituency. The majoritarian twist given to the system by Berlusconi is that the largest party or coalition automatically receives 347 of the 630 seats (except, of course, in the unlikely event that its share of the votes would entitle it to more than 347 seats anyway, in which case the system operates along regular PR lines), thus guaranteeing it an overall majority in the Chamber of Deputies. Voters have no power to express support for individual candidates on their party's list.

## Netherlands

The Tweede Kamer (Second Chamber) contains 150 deputies and, when it comes to awarding seats to parties, the whole country is treated as one 150-member constituency. Each party presents a list of candidates, and the parties receive seats in proportion to their votes; the seat allocation formula used is the D'Hondt highest averages method. Parties receiving fewer than two-thirds of 1 per cent of the total votes cast do not qualify for any seats; this is the lowest threshold, as a share of the national vote, employed by any country in Europe. It rarely happens that the threshold debars a Dutch party from receiving seats. Voters can cast a preference vote for a candidate on a party list, but in practice the casting of preference votes in the Netherlands has very little impact on the composition of the parliament. Because there are no subnational constituencies, the system is sometimes criticized for being impersonal. The government that took office in 2003 outlined plans for a mixed system that would see half of the deputies elected from small multi-member constituencies and the other half from a national list, but this idea came to nothing, as did more modest plans, advocated in 2006 by a citizens' assembly, to increase the impact of preference votes.

## Poland

The 460 members of the Sejm are elected from 41 constituencies, in which seats are awarded to parties by the D'Hondt method. Parties require 5 per cent of the votes nationally to qualify for any seats (coalitions need 8 per cent). Voters can cast preference votes for individual candidates on a party's list, and these preferences determine which candidates are elected. Poland's electoral system

▶ **BOX 11.1: CONTINUED**

was changed before the elections of 1991, 1993 and 2001, and there was a minor change involving the seat allocation formula before the 2005 election, but it now seems to have acquired stability.

### Spain

The Congress of Deputies is elected from 52 constituencies, each of which is based on a province and returns on average only seven deputies, a relatively small figure for a PR electoral system. There is significant malapportionment, with the smaller rural provinces being over-represented compared with the cities. Within each constituency, the D'Hondt highest averages formula is employed; this tends to favour the large parties rather than the small ones. Parties must reach a threshold of 3 per cent within a constituency to receive any seats there, although this has relevance only within the largest two constituencies, Madrid and Barcelona; in the other constituencies a party whose support was below 3 per cent would have virtually no chance of winning a seat anyway. There is no higher-tier allocation to compensate parties for any under-representation in the constituencies. Voters have no choice of candidate; they simply cast a vote for one of the party lists that are offered.

### United Kingdom

The UK employs the single-member plurality system. The country is divided into 650 constituencies, each returning one Member of Parliament (MP) to the House of Commons. Within each constituency the candidate winning the most votes, whether or not this amounts to a majority, becomes the MP. Other bodies within the UK are most commonly elected by forms of PR: mixed compensatory systems (the Scottish Parliament and Welsh Assembly), proportional representation by the single transferable vote (the Northern Ireland Assembly, Northern Ireland MEPs, and Scottish local government), or a closed PR list system (the 69 members of the European Parliament elected from England, Scotland and Wales).

Thresholds are usually employed to limit the degree of proportionality achieved, and could, if set too high, significantly distort the election outcome. For example, in the 1980s the Greek electoral system imposed a threshold of 17 per cent for qualification for higher-tier seats, which gave a sizeable bonus to the large parties. This was termed *reinforced PR* – which was also used in Cyprus – but in fact it was not proportionality but the parliamentary strength of the largest parties that was reinforced (Dimitras, 1994: 160). A variation on the conventional concept of thresholds is the awarding of a seat bonus to the largest party, with the aim of ensuring that it achieves an overall majority in parliament. In Italy the largest party or coalition is awarded 55 per cent of the seats unless its votes entitle it to that many seats anyway (Renwick *et al.*, 2009), and at the Greek elections of 2007 and 2009 the largest party received a bonus of 40 seats (to be raised to 50 at the next election).

The effect of thresholds can be seen most starkly in Poland. At its first post-communist election, in 1991, there were no thresholds, and an amazing 29 different parties won seats. For the next election, in 1993, thresholds were introduced (5 per cent within constituencies and 7 per cent to qualify for national list seats). This time only seven parties won any seats, and 40 per cent of the votes were cast for parties that won no seats. By the time of the following election in 1997, parties and voters showed that they had learned the lesson of the threshold: the fragmentation of the vote and overall disproportionality both plummeted, and only 12 per cent of votes were wasted on parties that failed to reach the threshold. Like several other post-communist countries, Poland imposes two thresholds: one for single parties, and a slightly higher one (8 per cent in this case) for coalitions.

## 11.5.4  Which candidates get the list seats?

So far, we have been discussing the ways in which the seats are divided up among the parties under list and mixed systems. Once this has been decided, a second question arises: which candidates on the party's list are awarded the seats that the party has won? This is dealt with in different ways. In some countries the order of candidates drawn up by the party organization is a fixed ranking that the voters cannot alter. These systems are termed *non-preferential*, with *closed* or *blocked* lists, and aspiring candidates compete with each other inside the party to be placed as high as possible on the party list. In a second group of countries, in contrast, there is no default order; the voters alone decide which candidates are elected. These systems are termed *preferential*, with *open* or *unblocked* lists. Under such systems there is intra-party electoral competition, because candidates of the same party are competing against each other for personal votes. In between these two are cases where the party's ranking, termed a *flexible* list, may stand as a default ordering but can be overturned if enough voters combine against it. These cases may in practice be either essentially preferential or essentially non-preferential, depending on just what degree of co-ordination is needed among voters to overturn the ordering decided on by the party organization; in some countries it is very easy for voters to do this, and in others it is virtually impossible. The systems in operation are listed in Table 11.4, which shows that in around half of the 30 countries we cover voters have an effective power to choose among candidates of their favoured party (for a more detailed analysis see Shugart, 2008: 36–44). The trend, although it is a gradual one, is in the direction of allowing voters a greater degree of choice among candidates of their favoured party.

There are relatively few examples of PR list systems where the lists are completely closed. Countries in this category include Italy, Portugal and Spain; the lists used on the one recent occasion when France used PR, in 1986, were also closed. In all of these cases the order of candidates' names on the list is decided by the parties, and voters cannot alter it. Moreover, where mixed systems are used, the lists are usually in practice closed (as in Germany and Hungary, though not in Lithuania). In these countries, then, candidate selection plays an especially important role in the political recruitment process, as we saw in the previous chapter, because the selectors are in effect choosing the MPs.

Countries in the second category, employing genuinely open lists where the voters determine which of a party's candidates are elected, include Finland, Luxembourg, Poland and Switzerland. In Finland the voters are all-powerful; they are obliged to express a preference for one specific candidate, and, within each party, those candidates receiving the most preferences win the seats. In Switzerland and Luxembourg voters express as many preferences as there are seats in the constituency. They can cast a *list vote* for a party, which has the effect of giving one preference vote to each of the party's candidates, or they can cumulate two preference votes on one candidate. They can give their preferences to candidates on more than one party's list, an option known as *panachage*, which is confined to these two countries. Everywhere, candidates near the top of the lists tend to receive the most preference votes: this could be either because the candidate selectors place the most attractive candidates in the most prominent positions, or because being near the top of the list attracts votes from party supporters who do not know much about individual candidates (on Switzerland, see Lutz, 2010). Most likely, both factors operate. Thus, in Poland, about a third of all preference votes go to the candidate placed top of the list, and around 40 per cent of these list-heading candidates are elected – although in 2001 one candidate placed as low as 38th on a list also won enough preference votes to be elected (Millard, 2004: 93–94). Where voters can express a choice among candidates of the same party, the relative importance of individual candidates seems to be increasing (Karvonen, 2010: 63).

Turning to the third category, the party candidate selectors draw up a list upon which the candidates appear in a particular order, and the voters have a greater or lesser degree of power to overturn this order. The general trend is one of growing weight given to preference votes. Sometimes, the voters can decide either to cast a list vote, endorsing the order drawn up by the party, or to cast a personal vote for an individual candidate on the list; what varies is how likely these personal votes are to make any difference to the outcome. A number of post-communist countries chose such systems, under which a degree of co-ordination by voters is needed to disturb the order drawn up by the party. As a result, whereas in open-list countries all MPs owe their election to preference votes, and in closed-list countries no MP does, in this third category of countries a proportion of MPs are elected as a result of the impact of preference votes. In Estonia around 15 per cent of MPs are elected thanks to preference votes, while in Slovakia the proportion is smaller – 5 per cent in 2006. A low figure may, of course, simply indicate that the candidate selectors correctly anticipated the preferences of party voters, not that preference voting is ineffective. In both of these countries, along with the Czech Republic and Lithuania, the role of preference votes in deciding which candidates win the seats has been increased by rule changes in recent years. In Sweden preference votes had little impact prior to 1998, but then the rules were changed: candidates who receive preference votes from at least 8 per cent of their party's voters now leapfrog candidates who were placed above them on the list but receive fewer preference votes. Because most preference votes are cast for candidates already near the top of the list, not many MPs are elected out of list order due to preference votes (ten in 2002 and six in 2006). Under the Danish system the parties can choose how to present their lists; some forms give considerable choice to the voters, whereas others restrict it, and the degree of voter choice can vary from party to party as well as between and even within constituencies (Elklit, 2008). In practice, it is the voters who wield the decisive voice, as in the overwhelming majority of cases – 88 per cent in the 2000s – the parties choose the open-list option (Karvonen, 2010: 46).

In certain other countries, though, there are systems that in theory offer the opportunity for preferential voting for candidates but in practice are such that voters' preferences rarely overturn the ordering set by the parties. In Norway personal votes have never made any difference to the personnel elected, because they have been unable to have an effect unless at least half of a party's voters make exactly the same change to the list. In Iceland no candidate was elected out of list order, due to preference votes, between 1946 and a slight increase in the weight of preference votes at the 2007 election. In Austria, similarly, even though a change to the electoral law in 1992 was supposed to make preferential voting more effective, scarcely any candidates have been elected out of list order since then. The system in the Netherlands differs in some of the details, but the essential feature is the same: the party supplies a default order of candidates, and such a high degree of concerted action by voters has been needed to overturn it that the party's rank ordering has almost always stood. Only three candidates were elected due to preference votes between 1945 and 1994. A change in 1998 liberalized the position slightly, but at the following four elections together only five candidates were elected out of list order (Andeweg and Irwin, 2009: 103).

While we do not have space to describe every country's electoral system in detail, it is worth explaining Romania's electoral system in depth, since it is difficult to fit it into the scheme that we are employing here. People vote in what looks to all intents and purposes like a single-member constituency, as in Britain, with one candidate from each party. Seats are awarded to the parties, though, not on the basis of which candidate won in each of the 334 constituencies, but on the basis of the parties' national vote totals. The unique feature of the Romanian system is the way in which seats are allocated to individual candidates: a complicated procedure under which, simplifying somewhat, those of its candidates who won the largest shares of votes in their constituencies receive its seats, subject to the restriction that no more than one candidate who stood in any single-member constituency can be elected. The rationale of this unique system is that while the overall results respect proportionality, each constituency has a single identifiable MP. The downside is that the candidate who supposedly 'represents' the constituency may not be the person who won the most votes there; in 2008, 120 of the 334 constituency winners did not win election, and in some cases the person deemed elected from a constituency had been comprehensively defeated there (Downs, 2009: 512; Maxfield, 2009).

### 11.5.5 The single transferable vote

The PR-STV electoral system was devised in Britain in the middle of the nineteenth century. It is used to elect the parliaments of Ireland and Malta, it was employed to elect Estonia's parliament at the 1990 election, and in November 2010 it was used in Iceland for the nationwide election of 25 members of a constitutional convention (for assessments of STV see Bowler and Grofman, 2000). In Ireland the then largest party, Fianna Fáil, twice (in 1959 and 1968) attempted to have the system replaced by the British plurality system, but on each occasion the electorate rejected the proposed change in a referendum. Like list systems, STV aims to give proportional representation to the shades of opinion within the constituency. Unlike them, it does not presuppose that those opinions are organized in terms of parties.

Voters cast a vote by ranking as many as they wish of the candidates, regardless of party, in order of their preference; they place a '1' next to the name of their favoured candidate, a '2' next to the name of their second favourite, and so on (for detailed explanations of how STV works see Gallagher and Mitchell, 2008: 593–596; Sinnott, 2010: 119–124). The counting of votes revolves around the Droop quota. This is calculated as the smallest integer greater than $[v/(s + 1)]$, where $v$ is the number of valid votes and $s$ the number of seats in the constituency. The Droop quota is therefore one more than a quarter of the votes in a three-seat constituency, one more than a fifth in a four-seater, and so on. Any candidate who achieves the Droop quota is certain of election and does not need votes over and above this number, which are surplus to requirements.

Any candidate whose total of first-preference votes equals or exceeds the Droop quota is declared elected. Unless it should happen that sufficient candidates are elected at this stage, the count then proceeds by distributing the surplus votes of the elected candidate(s) – that is, the votes they possess over and above the quota. These votes are transferred to the other candidates, in proportion to the next preferences marked for them. The purpose of doing this is that, if it were not done, some votes would be 'wasted' by remaining in the possession of a candidate who did not need them. If no candidate has a surplus, the candidate with the fewest votes is eliminated, and his or her votes are transferred to the other candidates, again in accordance with the next preferences marked. This process continues until all the seats have been filled.

What are the pros and cons of STV when compared with other PR systems? (It is worth emphasizing that PR-STV in multi-member constituencies is indeed a form of PR, involving as it does the distribution of seats among candidates based on their support, even though it is possible to find examples in the comparative literature that wonder aloud whether it really is a form of PR or for no clear reason categorize it as 'semi-PR'. If all voters were to cast their votes entirely along party lines, it would produce outcomes very similar to those delivered by the D'Hondt method or largest remainders with the Droop quota.) Its advocates emphasize several points. First, PR-STV gives voters the opportunity to convey a lot of information about their preferences; they may rank all the candidates in order of choice, whereas under almost every other system they are limited to expressing a 'Yes' verdict on one (or a few) and 'No' on the rest. Second, when ranking candidates, voters are not constrained by party lines, since they can vote for candidates without regard to party affiliation. For some voters, party is not all-important. These might be voters whose main concern is with an issue that cuts across party lines (such as abortion, European integration, or nuclear power, for example); or voters who want to affect the social composition of parliament, and thus wish to vote, say, for women or young candidates across party lines; or voters who want to elect a representative whose home base is in their own area of the constituency. Such voters can give their first preference vote to, say, a pro-EU candidate from one party and their second preference to a pro-EU candidate from a different party. List systems do not offer this opportunity, and the apparent exceptions – those of Switzerland and Luxembourg, which offer *panachage* – are not really comparable.

This is because of the third argument in favour of STV, namely, that voters control the way their votes will be used. No vote can help a candidate unless it expresses a preference for him or her. This sets STV apart from all list systems, where a preference given to one candidate of a party might end up helping another candidate of the same party – a candidate whom, perhaps, the voter does not like. Under STV, voters can continue to give preferences after their first, knowing that a preference given to a candidate can never help that person against a candidate to whom the voter gave a higher preference. This is not the case under *panachage*; the voter giving a preference to a candidate of one party does not know which candidate of that party it will ultimately help, as it is added to the party's pool and could benefit any of its candidates.

Fourth, STV gives voters the opportunity to express an opinion as to the direction their party should take. If there is more than one tendency or faction within a party, voters can express higher preferences for candidates from the one they favour, and affect the composition of the parliamentary group accordingly. STV shares this quality with preferential list systems and American primaries. In addition, voters can, by the way they order candidates of other parties, send signals about the coalition partner(s) they would like their own party to take, and indeed help designated partners to benefit from their vote if their own party cannot make use of it.

Fifth, it ensures that voters can vote sincerely, knowing that even if their first-choice candidate is unpopular, the vote will not be wasted, as it can be transferred to another candidate in accordance with the second preference the voter has marked on the ballot paper.

But STV also has its critics, which helps to explains why it has inspired so little enthusiasm on the European mainland. They make three points in particular. First, they are not impressed with the opportunity it gives voters to cross party lines. On the contrary, they feel that this might weaken the internal unity of parties and make them less cohesive. In elections, candidates of one party, rather than being able to concentrate on propagating party policies, must be alive to the possibility of attracting lower preferences from other parties' supporters. This might make the parties 'fuzzy at the edges' as candidates adopt bland positions for fear of alienating any voter who might possibly give them a lower preference. Critics of STV argue that modern democratic politics, certainly in parliamentary systems, needs strong, cohesive parties to work properly, a subject that we discussed in Chapters 3 and 10, and that the idea of voting for candidates rather than parties, although all very well for other kinds of elections, is inappropriate for parliamentary elections. This argument is difficult to evaluate, because STV is used in too few countries for us to be able to tell whether it will tend to weaken parties. It must be said, though, that there is no evidence at all that parties in either Ireland or Malta are any less cohesive and disciplined than parties anywhere else (Gallagher, 2008a: 523–525).

The second criticism is that STV can realistically be used only in relatively small constituencies, thus raising the prospect of disproportionality (lack of complete correspondence between parties' shares of the votes and the seats). For example, STV is difficult to operate in constituencies larger than about 10 seats, because the ballot paper could then contain 30 to 40 names, and most voters' preferences would become meaningless after the first half-dozen or so. In both Ireland and Malta the largest constituency size currently used is five seats. Because votes are assumed to be cast for candidates rather than parties, it is impossible, without contradicting the principles on which STV is based, to have higher-tier seat allocation (without the use of a second vote, as in Germany), although, as Table 11.4 explains, Malta does have such an allocation in reserve. In practice, though, the possibility of disproportionality does not seem to be a major problem, as over the long term election results in Ireland and Malta have been as proportional as those of other PR systems.

Third, it has been argued that STV facilitates the election of independent candidates, who may be able to wield undue power over a government that lacks a secure majority. Independents, like centre-party candidates, stand to benefit from an electoral system in which voters can rank order the options as, precisely because they do not have a party label and thus do not alienate anyone, they may well be the second choice of many voters. Empirically, it is true that the election of independents is quite common in Ireland (13 were elected in 2002 out of 166 MPs), whereas elsewhere in western Europe independent members of parliament are virtually unknown. In times of minority government in Ireland, some independent deputies have been able to extract concessions from the government on local matters. Sinnott argues that STV thus makes possible circumstances in which independents wield disproportionate power and create a potentially serious underlying threat to the stability of government (Sinnott, 2010: 127). However, no independent has been elected to the parliament of Malta since independence in 1964.

## 11.6 Why electoral systems matter

The plethora of electoral systems used across Europe suggests that there is no simple answer to the question 'Which is the best electoral system?' If there was such a system, presumably every country would use it. But although there has been no trend towards a uniform electoral system, we have seen that the great majority of countries have systems based on PR, and in about half of the cases they allow voters to choose between candidates of their favoured party. Only Britain and France use systems that do not embody the principle of PR. All the remaining countries that we are looking at employ some type of PR: in 22 countries a list system is used, four employ a mixed system, and Ireland and Malta have the single transferable vote. We have already reviewed the arguments about the relative merits of list systems and STV; we must now look at the wider question of the advantages and disadvantages of PR systems generally in comparison with plurality systems (for general discussions of the consequences and merits of different electoral systems, see Lijphart, 1994; Gallagher and Mitchell, 2008; Baldini and Pappalardo, 2009).

One obvious criterion for judging electoral systems is proportionality: how closely does the distribution of seats in parliament reflect the preferences of the voters as expressed in an election, and are some electoral systems better than others on this dimension? Another criterion is stable effective government. This is sometimes argued to be in conflict with the first, in that a very proportional electoral system might lead to a highly fragmented parliament from which it is difficult to put together a majority government, while a system that gives the largest parties a sizeable seat bonus is less proportional but more likely to produce stable government. Others, though, are not convinced that government stability is any lower under PR systems. There are other criteria, too, that could be taken into account in an assessment of the merits of electoral systems. Do some systems produce better policy outputs, and do some give a better chance than others to women and minorities to win election to parliament? The overall picture, based on the most recent elections in each of our 30 countries, is summarized in Table 11.5.

## 11.6.1 Proportionality

The proportionality of election results – the degree to which parties' shares of the seats correspond to their shares of the votes – does indeed tend to be significantly greater under PR than under plurality systems. Table 11.5 shows clearly that there was a large difference between the plurality systems of Britain and France, on the one hand, and all PR systems on the other hand, at the most recent elections. Among PR systems, there is some variation. The most proportional outcomes occur in countries that use large district magnitudes (Austria, Cyprus, Denmark, the Netherlands and Sweden), and also in Malta, despite its small district magnitude of just five seats per constituency. Although the Czech Republic, Hungary, Latvia, Poland and Slovakia also award seats in large districts, their employment of a 5 per cent national threshold creates disproportionality, because a significant number of people vote for parties that fail to reach the threshold. Disproportionality is also prone to be high when thresholds and/or small district magnitude assist the large parties and penalize small ones, as in Greece and Ireland (Anckar, 1997). The pattern in Table 11.5 matches that found by Lijphart (1994: 96–97) for the period 1945–1990.

## 11.6.2 The number of parties

The formulation of the best-known causal relationship in the study of the effects of electoral systems is attributed to Maurice Duverger. It holds that the single-member plurality system favours a two-party system, the double-ballot majority system tends to produce multipartism tempered by alliances, and PR tends to lead to the formation of many independent parties (Duverger, 1986: 70). Under the French two-round system many parties may contest the first round of voting, but there are strong incentives for parties to form alliances for the second-round contests. The British-style SMP system is associated with a two-party system because of both mechanical and psychological effects, as Duverger terms them. The mechanical effect is simply that smaller parties with support spread across the country do not reap a proportional reward in seats for their share of the votes. Whereas under a PR system a party winning, say, 10 per cent of the votes in every part of the country would end up with about 10 per cent of the seats, under an SMP system such a party would probably win no seats, because it would not be the strongest party in any constituency. The psychological effect comes about precisely because voters are aware of the mechanical effect: they know that if they cast their vote for a small party,

**TABLE 11.5** Aspects of electoral outcomes in Europe

| | Elections | Disproportionality | Effective number of parties (elective level) | Effective number of parties (legislative level) | % of seats in parliament held by women |
|---|---|---|---|---|---|
| Austria | 2002–2008 | 2.4 | 3.8 | 3.5 | 28 |
| Belgium | 2003–2010 | 4.1 | 9.3 | 7.8 | 39 |
| Bulgaria | 2001–2009 | 6.3 | 4.7 | 3.7 | 21 |
| Cyprus | 2001–2006 | 2.0 | 4.0 | 3.8 | 12 |
| Czech Republic | 2002–2010 | 6.7 | 5.2 | 3.8 | 22 |
| Denmark | 2001–2007 | 1.4 | 5.1 | 4.9 | 38 |
| Estonia | 1999–2007 | 3.8 | 5.8 | 4.8 | 23 |
| Finland | 1999–2007 | 3.2 | 5.8 | 5.1 | 40 |
| France | 1997–2007 | 17.7 | 5.4 | 2.8 | 19 |
| Germany | 2002–2009 | 3.4 | 4.7 | 3.4 | 33 |
| Greece | 2004–2009 | 7.2 | 2.9 | 2.5 | 17 |
| Hungary | 2002–2010 | 8.3 | 2.9 | 2.2 | 9 |
| Iceland | 2003–2009 | 2.6 | 4.2 | 3.8 | 43 |
| Ireland | 1997–2007 | 6.3 | 4.0 | 3.1 | 14 |
| Italy | 2006–2008 | 4.7 | 4.8 | 4.1 | 21 |
| Latvia | 2002–2010 | 4.9 | 6.2 | 5.0 | 20 |
| Lithuania | 2004–2008 | 8.1[a] | 7.3[a] | 5.6 | 19 |
| Luxembourg | 1999–2009 | 3.6 | 4.4 | 3.9 | 20 |
| Malta | 1998–2008 | 1.7 | 2.0 | 2.0 | 9 |
| Netherlands | 2003–2010 | 1.0 | 5.9 | 5.7 | 41 |
| Norway | 2001–2009 | 3.0 | 5.3 | 4.7 | 40 |
| Poland | 2001–2007 | 6.0 | 4.6 | 3.6 | 20 |
| Portugal | 2002–2009 | 5.3 | 3.3 | 2.7 | 27 |
| Romania | 2000–2008 | 5.2 | 4.4 | 3.5 | 11 |
| Slovakia | 2002–2010 | 6.7 | 6.8 | 5.0 | 15 |
| Slovenia | 2000–2008 | 3.4 | 5.4 | 4.7 | 14 |
| Spain | 2000–2008 | 4.9 | 3.0 | 2.5 | 37 |
| Sweden | 2002–2010 | 1.9 | 4.7 | 4.3 | 45 |
| Switzerland | 1999–2007 | 2.7 | 5.6 | 5.0 | 29 |
| United Kingdom | 2001–2010 | 16.5 | 3.5 | 2.4 | 22 |
| **Mean** | | **5.8** | **4.9** | **4.0** | **25** |

[a] These figures for Lithuania refer to list votes only.

*Notes*: Figures for disproportionality and effective number of parties are averages over the most recent three elections. For Cyprus, Italy and Lithuania, figures are averages for last two elections. Disproportionality refers to vote–seat disproportionality as measured by the least squares index (Gallagher and Mitchell, 2008: Appendix B). The scale runs from 0 to 100, 0 representing full proportionality and 100 representing total disproportionality. Effective number of parties at elective and at legislative level refers to the level of fragmentation in terms of votes and seats respectively (Laakso and Taagepera, 1979).

*Sources*: Election indices calculated from data at http://www.tcd.ie/Political_Science/Staff/michael_gallagher/ElSystems/index.php. For women in parliaments, figures as of 31 December 2010 from the website of the Inter-Parliamentary Union (www.ipu.org).

this vote is likely to be wasted, and therefore the votes for such parties do not reflect their true level of underlying support. We saw in the earlier discussion of the Camborne and Redruth result in Britain in 2010 (Table 11.2) that the electoral system compelled supporters there of Labour and some other parties to decide whether to waste their vote on a candidate who was virtually certain to lose or to vote instead for one of the two candidates who had a real chance. In this example Labour was the main party affected, but in most constituencies the Liberal Democrats are the third party and hence the main losers. The psychological effect also applies to the best potential candidates, to campaign workers and to financial donors, all of whom see little point in giving their time or money to a certain loser and thus gravitate to the parties that are already strongest.

The precise meaning, status and accuracy of Duverger's predictions have been the subject of an extensive literature (see, for example, Cox, 1997: 13–33; Benoit, 2006; Gallagher, 2008b: 545–548), and this is not the place to explore these issues fully. However, we can examine the evidence to see whether there are indeed fewer parties under non-PR than PR systems. In order to do this, we need some satisfactory measure of the number of parties. Simply counting the number of parties is not sufficient; for example, in the British House of Commons around eight or ten different parties are usually represented (there were 10 in 2010), but Britain has never had anything like a genuine nine-party system, that is, one with nine parties each of similar size. To deal with this, Laakso and Taagepera devised a measure that takes into account not only the number of different parties but also the relative size of each, which they call the *effective number* of parties. It is essentially a measure of fragmentation, registering the extent to which strength is concentrated or dispersed. The intuitive meaning to be put on an effective number of, say, 4.2 parties is that there is the same degree of fragmentation as if there were 4.2 equal-sized parties (Laakso and Taagepera, 1979). This number can be calculated both at the elective level, by measuring the degree to which votes are dispersed among the parties, and at the legislative level, by doing the same for seats.

Table 11.5 shows that the pattern of party competition in Europe in the 2000s corresponded well to Duverger's predictions. In the two plurality countries, Britain and France, the reduction from the elective to the legislative level, brought about by the 'mechanical' effect of the electoral system, is very marked. In Britain, something like a three-party system at the elective level is reduced to something much closer to a two-party system in parliament – though the 2010 election produced the most fragmented parliament since before the Second World War. In France, the votes at elections are spread among many more parties than in Britain but, partly as a result of the alliances and deals that Duverger predicts, parliamentary strength is far less fragmented than this. In PR systems, although the fragmentation in parliament is less than that seen at the electoral level, the reduction is more moderate, as we would expect.

However, it is not invariably the case that PR is associated with multipartism. Certainly this is true in some countries, most notably Belgium, where fragmentation has reached remarkable levels; at the 2010 election the strongest two parties received only 31 per cent of the votes between them. In Finland, Latvia, Lithuania, Netherlands, Slovakia and Switzerland, too, the effective number of parties in parliament exceeds 5. Yet in some other PR countries (Greece, Hungary, Ireland, Malta, Portugal and Spain) parliamentary strength is little if at all more fragmented than in France or the UK.

The case of Malta in particular shows that the relationship between electoral systems and party systems is not a deterministic one. Since independence, Malta has had the purest two-party system in Europe; since the start of the 1970s, the combined vote share of Labour and the Nationalists has averaged over 99 per cent, neither party has fallen below 46 per cent of the votes, and no other party has won a seat. This shows that while PR systems may well give parliamentary expression to a multiparty system if other factors, such as the number of political or social cleavages, cause voters to create one in the first place, PR does not by itself bring a multiparty system into being.

Electoral systems, then, do play a major part, albeit not a deterministic one, in influencing the shape of party systems. If Britain and France had 'pure' PR systems, their parliaments would look very different (see Table 11.6). In France, under PR Nicolas Sarkozy's UMP would have been well short of an overall majority in 2007, and would have had to form a minority government or try to put together a coalition, either a centrist coalition with the Socialist Party or a right-wing coalition with a number of smaller groups. The Front National would have won significant representation. The UK would have had what is clearly a three-party system. Any two of the three main parties could numerically have formed a majority coalition, and the Liberal Democrats would have had a pivotal position given the political impossibility of a Conservative–Labour coalition. Parties to the right of the Conservatives were unrepresented in the actual election, but would have won over 30 seats between them under nationwide PR. Of course, the figures in the table are not in any way a prediction, because if PR were actually in operation we could expect voting patterns to alter, for the reasons we have already discussed, and the smaller parties would be expected to win many more votes than they do at present. The plurality electoral system may be all that has kept Britain (and, indeed, the United States) looking like a two-party system since the 1970s, and it has certainly been the key to two-party domination of the legislature.

A plurality electoral system, with its tendency to produce competition between just two large parties, reflects the view that a majority should prevail over a minority. This in itself is an impeccable democratic principle. But it encounters problems in societies that are divided into a number of segments or interests, and on issues where there are more than two positions. When there is no majority to represent, plurality systems tend to produce outcomes that favour inordinately the larger minorities and discriminate against the smaller ones. PR systems, in contrast, seek to reflect in parliaments the divergences that exist in society.

### 11.6.3 Coalition or single-party government?

One common argument against PR systems is that the very accuracy with which they reflect parties' electoral strengths in parliament creates problems when it comes to forming a government. It is extremely rare, under any type of electoral system, for one party to win a majority of the votes cast, so a single-party majority government is likely only if the largest party receives a bonus of seats that takes it over the magic 50 per cent mark. Obviously, this is most likely to happen under a plurality system, where proportionality is lower and the largest party often wins a substantial bonus. For example, in Britain's 2005 election Labour received only 35 per cent of the votes, but won 55 per cent of the seats, a bonus of 20 per cent. Under a PR system, assuming that disproportionality is not introduced as a result of small district magnitudes, no party's seat bonus is very large. Consequently, a single-party majority government is possible only if one party actually wins a majority of votes or comes very close to it, so that it needs only a small bonus to

**TABLE 11.6** Election results in France and the United Kingdom under existing systems and under nationwide PR

| France 2007 | | | United Kingdom 2010 | | |
|---|---|---|---|---|---|
| Party | Seats in actual election | Seats under nationwide PR | Party | Seats in actual election | Seats under nationwide PR |
| UMP | 313 | 227 | Conservative | 307 | 238 |
| PS | 186 | 142 | Labour | 258 | 191 |
| MoDem | 3 | 44 | Liberal Democrats | 57 | 152 |
| FN | 0 | 25 | UKIP | 0 | 20 |
| PCF | 15 | 25 | BNP | 0 | 12 |
| Far left | 0 | 20 | SNP | 6 | 11 |
| Greens | 4 | 19 | Green Party | 1 | 6 |
| Diverse right-wing | 9 | 14 | Sinn Féin | 5 | 4 |
| New Centre | 22 | 14 | Democratic Unionist Party | 8 | 4 |
| Miscellaneous left-wing | 15 | 11 | Plaid Cymru | 3 | 4 |
| PRG | 7 | 8 | SDLP | 3 | 2 |
| MPF | 1 | 7 | Ulster Unionists | 0 | 2 |
| Hunting, Fishing | 0 | 6 | English Democrats | 0 | 1 |
| Other ecologists | 0 | 5 | Alliance Party | 1 | 1 |
| Regionalists | 1 | 5 | Respect | 0 | 1 |
| Other far-right | 0 | 3 | Traditional Unionist Voice | 0 | 1 |
| Others | 1 | 2 | Others | 1 | 0 |
| Total | 577 | 577 | Total | 650 | 650 |

*Note*: The figures for seats under nationwide PR assume that all votes would have been cast exactly as they actually were, and that seat allocation is determined by the Sainte-Laguë method on the basis of national support without the use of any threshold. If either country introduced nationwide PR the likelihood is that there would be thresholds, in the UK probably applied separately within England, Scotland, Wales and Northern Ireland so as not to deprive parties based there of representation.

achieve a parliamentary majority. Empirically, single-party governments are much more likely under majoritarian electoral systems.

Still, the relationship between electoral systems and government types is not entirely straightforward. It is true that, in most countries, all or virtually all governments are coalitions. It is also true that Britain, owing to its non-PR electoral system, did not have a coalition government between 1945 and 2010. However, the British electoral system has not always produced a stable majority government: as well as 2010, no party won an overall majority in February 1974, and the slim majorities won in 1950, 1964 and October 1974 led to short-lived governments and/or to instability. In France, too, the plurality system did not produce a majority government in either the 1988 or the 1997 elections, and indeed, bearing in mind that the RPR and UDF were separate (albeit allied) parties, the Fifth Republic has had very few single-party governments (see Box 11.2). Likewise, in countries using PR systems, even though coalitions are far more common, there are still many cases of single-party government. The Austrian Socialist Party, Ireland's Fianna Fáil, the Norwegian Labour Party and the Swedish Social Democrats have all had long spells in office alone, although most of these parties have now lost their former dominant status. All Maltese governments are single-party majority governments, and other countries with PR have experienced single-party government for periods. As we noted in Chapter 7 (pp. 231–233 above), there is a trend towards bipolarity in a number of European multiparty systems, and elections are increasingly occasions when voters can choose between identifiable government options.

Some defenders of non-PR systems have argued that even if these systems do not produce proportional representation in any given parliament, they are likely to produce proportional tenure in government over a series of parliaments. The rationale for this is that a large party winning, say, between 40 and 50 per cent of the votes will have all the government power for about half the time, whereas under PR, it is argued, small centrist parties may be almost permanent fixtures in government, thus earning tenure in government way above their electoral support. However, empirical analysis does not support the claim that non-PR systems perform better on this criterion than do PR ones (Vowles, 2004). Under both kinds of electoral system, large parties' share of time in office tends to be greater than their share of electoral support, while extreme parties fare badly. The supposed bias towards centrist parties under PR largely disappears when account is taken of the (usually small) share of cabinet seats they occupy while in office. While single-party government gives some voters pretty much all of what they want and takes no account of the views of the others, coalitions give many voters at least some of what they want.

## 11.6.4  Policy outputs

Which kind of system better represents the policy preferences of voters, and which leads to better policy outputs? There is general agreement that voters' preferences are better represented in parliaments by PR systems, but there is some disagreement as to the implications for congruence between voters and governments. Powell (2006) found that governments negotiated after PR elections had policy positions that were significantly closer to the citizen median than those elected under majoritarian elections, bolstering his conclusion from an earlier study that 'the proportional vision and its designs enjoyed a clear advantage over their majoritarian counterparts in using elections as instruments of democracy' (Powell, 2000: 254). However, neither Blais and Bodet (2006) nor Golder and Stramski (2005) found any significant differences between the two types of electoral system when it came to congruence. Powell later sought to reconcile these contrary findings by concluding that whereas PR elections usually lead to governments that are more congruent with the voters' preferences, this was not the case in the period 1996–2004, when there was no difference (Powell, 2009: 1492). The explanation for the pattern is that under PR governments are always quite close to citizens' preferences, whereas under non-PR systems the level of congruence depends on how close the winning party is to the median voter, something that can vary a lot over time according to the level of polarization in the party system (Kim *et al.*, 2010).

Other researchers have explored the question of whether government outputs are different, even 'better', under one type of system than another. Arend Lijphart, from a study of government performance in 36 countries, concluded that electoral systems can have an impact on many

## BOX 11.2: THE IMPACT OF ELECTORAL SYSTEMS

### Denmark
The use of large constituencies together with higher-tier seats produces outcomes that are among the most proportional in Europe, although parliamentary strength is not highly fragmented. Individual MPs are accountable to voters as a result of the use of open rather than closed party lists. No party ever wins a majority of seats, but this does not mean that all governments are coalitions, because single-party minority governments are common. Electoral reform is not an issue in Denmark, with scarcely any calls for fundamental change to the system.

### France
As in Britain, the electoral system, being based on single-member constituencies, greatly favours the large parties. Single-party majority government, though, is uncommon; only four times in the post-1958 Fifth Republic has one party won a majority of seats (the Gaullists in 1968, the Socialists in 1981, and the UMP in 2002 and 2007). The potential of single-member constituency systems to produce startling results was demonstrated by the March 1993 election, one of the most disproportional ever to have taken place in any country, when the two main right-wing parties won 460 of the 577 seats in parliament despite having attracted only 38 per cent of votes in the first round of voting (which under a 'pure' PR system would have earned them just 221 seats). The main beneficiaries of the high disproportionality that is usually produced by the French system are the mainstream right-wing parties and, to a lesser extent, the Socialists. The main losers are small parties, together with the extreme parties: the communists on the left and the FN on the right.

### Germany
Under the Weimar Republic established after the First World War, Germany had highly proportional election results and very unstable governments. The electoral system adopted after the Second World War is seen by supporters as having produced the best of both worlds: election results are still highly proportional, but there is no problem of government instability. The threshold that parties need to reach before qualifying for list seats has prevented the development of a situation where a multitude of small parties hold the balance of power. During the 1960s and 1970s only three parties (the SPD, the CDU/CSU and the FDP) were represented in the West German Bundestag, before they were joined by the Greens in the 1980s and the PDS (later the Left Party) in the 1990s. There is no great difference in the behaviour of constituency MPs and list MPs; indeed, most list MPs also stand in a constituency, and most constituency MPs also appear on a list.

### Italy
Italy's pre-1993 electoral system guaranteed a high degree of proportionality, and a large number of minor parties usually gained representation. Voters' ability to indicate a preference for individual candidates on their chosen party's list generated considerable intra-party competition in and between elections; this was especially pronounced within the then-dominant Christian Democrats, and reinforced the highly factionalized nature of that party. The system adopted in 1993 was designed to have a very different impact. It eliminated the element of intra-party competition for preference votes and encouraged the formation of pre-election coalitions. A further step was taken in this direction by the 2005 change, which gave Italy an electoral system designed to produce majority government by a single party or pre-declared coalition, because the majority of seats were automatically given to the winner, so that voters would be faced with a clear choice between a

government of the right or of the left. Both elections held so far under this system, in 2006 and 2008, produced majority governments.

## Netherlands

Because the Netherlands returns all its members of parliament in one nationwide constituency, proportionality is high, with the largest parties receiving a negligible bonus of seats over and above their share of the votes. The absence of any subnational constituencies has led to complaints that connections between citizens and MPs are weak. There have been attempts over the years to try to counteract this by introducing provisions under which 'personal votes', that is, preference votes cast for individual candidates, would be more effective in determining which individual candidates are elected, and a change made before the 1998 election made it slightly easier for these personal votes to have an impact. Even this limited opportunity has been resented by the Dutch parties, which sometimes demand pledges from their candidates that if they are elected 'out of order', owing to preference votes, at the expense of a candidate higher on the list, they will resign their seat in favour of the candidate whom the party organization had placed higher on the list. Indeed, a candidate elected 'out of order' on the Socialist Party's list for the upper chamber elections in 2007 was expelled from the party when he refused to give up his seat.

## Poland

The first free election, that of 1991, was remarkable for the numbers of parties that competed (111) and won seats (29), and the success of the Polish Friends of Beer Party (Polska Partia Przyjaciół Piwa), which won 16 seats, gained news coverage around the world (although it was claimed that the party had a serious anti-alcoholism message and was aiming to wean drinkers away from the harder stuff). Thresholds introduced for subsequent elections have drastically reduced the number of parties securing representation in the Sejm, and have consequently increased government stability. Parliamentary strength now shows only moderate fragmentation. Despite the degree of activism and protest under the communist regime (higher than in other communist countries), turnout levels are low, with only two post-communist elections (just) bringing more than 50 per cent of the electorate out to vote.

## Spain

Spain's electoral system is a version of PR, but it does not produce highly proportional outcomes. The main reason is the low number of members returned from the average constituency, together with malapportionment (the deliberate over-representation of rural areas). In consequence, the largest parties receive a significant bonus from the electoral system and are able to govern, sometimes as a minority government, without the need for coalition partners. Small parties with a strong regional base also fare well, but small parties whose support is spread thinly across the country are invariably under-represented.

## United Kingdom

The single-member constituency electoral system gives a large bonus of seats to the two largest parties, Labour and the Conservatives, which regularly win nearly all the seats in parliament even though smaller parties may take up to a third of the votes. An observer sitting in the gallery of the House of Commons would infer from the distribution of seats among the parties that Britain has something close to a two-party system, but this impression is created largely by the electoral

> ### BOX 11.2: CONTINUED
>
> system. If Britain were to adopt a proportional electoral system, smaller parties would win many more seats in the Commons (see Table 11.6), and the possibility of single-party majority government, the norm in the post-war period, would be virtually eliminated. Electoral reform has often been discussed, but neither of the major parties, especially when in power, has been keen on a move to proportional representation. It has long been a priority for the Liberal Democrats, consistently under-represented in parliament and frozen out of office since 1945 despite being electorally one of the strongest liberal parties in Europe. Their entry to government in 2010 as part of a coalition with the Conservatives enabled them to secure a commitment on a referendum to change to the alternative vote. That is not a form of proportional representation, but it would benefit the Liberal Democrats, compared with the status quo, if they are the second choice of both Conservative and Labour voters.

aspects of public policy. In countries that are close to the model of *consensus democracy*, of which a PR electoral system is a key component, the record of government tends to be 'kinder and gentler' when it comes to welfare spending, protection of the environment, use of harsh penal measures, and aid to developing countries, than it is in *majoritarian democracies*, which use plurality or majority electoral systems. When it comes to macroeconomic performance and control of violence, too, consensus democracies have a slightly better record (Lijphart, 1999: 258–300). Similarly, Vernby (2007) argues that strikes are less frequent when PR is used. Other analyses agree with Lijphart – though do not necessarily see it in a positive light – that in countries that use PR there will be higher government spending, a larger welfare state, higher government deficits, and more redistribution of resources. According to Persson and Tabellini (2005: 270), a switch from PR to a majoritarian electoral system will reduce overall government spending by about 5 per cent of GDP. One explanation offered is that centre-right governments dominate under majoritarian systems, whereas centre-left governments dominate under PR (Iversen and Soskice, 2006). Among PR systems, Gerring and Thacker (2008) maintain that, on balance, closed-list systems deliver the best policy outputs. The huge range of variables that contribute to government outputs means that the precise contribution of the electoral system remains open to considerable debate.

### 11.6.5 The backgrounds of parliamentarians

Proportional representation elections produce parliaments that differ from those produced by plurality elections. This is true not just as far as the representation of parties is concerned; it also applies to the profile of the individuals who sit on the parliamentary benches.

This has long been apparent when we look at the proportion of women in legislatures around the world. Other things being equal, the use of PR tends to facilitate the election of women (Norris, 2004: 179–208; Salmond, 2006; Paxton *et al.*, 2010), although it is not the only factor. Given that variation within each type of electoral system is greater than variation between types, it may well be that the actions of parties and the state, in particular whether gender quotas are adopted, have a greater impact on female representation in parliament than the electoral system does (see Chapter 10 for discussion of gender quotas). Britain and France, the two countries that do not use PR, used to be laggards in this table, but while they are still below average, they have significantly closed the gap in recent years. In nine countries a third or more of parliamentarians are women, with the Scandinavian countries and the Netherlands leading the way. Of course, these countries have a progressive attitude towards female participation in politics and in society generally (see the gender empowerment index in Table 1.1), and their choice of an 'inclusive' electoral system could be seen as a manifestation of this attitude as well as simply a cause of the composition of parliament.

The reason why PR facilitates the election of women to parliament is to be found primarily in the multi-member constituencies necessitated by PR. Under a single-member constituency system, the candidate selectors might be reluctant to pick a woman as the party's sole candidate, using the excuse, genuine or otherwise, that they believe some voters will be less likely to vote for a woman than for a man. But when several candidates are to be chosen, it is positively advantageous for a ticket to include both men and women, for an all-male list of three or more candidates is likely to alienate some voters.

The evidence as to whether, within the PR group, either STV, open-list systems or closed-list systems give any special advantage to women is inconclusive. In closed-list systems, where the voters cannot alter the candidate selectors' rankings, the selectors could, if they wished, bring about gender equality in parliament by employing the 'zipper' system of alternating women and men on the list; placing a woman first, a man second, a woman third, and so on. On the other hand, in countries where the selectors might wish to do this, it is quite likely that the voters too will believe in gender equality and will not use their preference votes specifically against women candidates. If this is the case, an open-list system and PR-STV will neither assist nor damage women's electoral chances. The empirical evidence is inconclusive. Table 11.5 shows that of the eight countries with most women, four (Sweden, Finland, Denmark and Belgium) employ open-list systems, while in the other four (Iceland, Netherlands, Norway and Spain) the voters have little or no opportunity to alter the rankings of the candidate selectors. The number of women elected in the two PR-STV countries is even lower than in the plurality countries (the averages are 11 per cent and 20 per cent respectively), but this is generally attributed less to their use of STV and more to the fact that both countries, Ireland and Malta, are strongly Catholic; it is clear that, other things being equal, attitudes towards a political role for women are more favourable in Protestant countries.

There is less research on other under-represented groups, but the same argument applies. Those who pick the party's candidate in a single-member constituency may be reluctant to take the risk of selecting a representative of an ethnic, religious or linguistic minority, but candidate selectors in a multi-member constituency will usually feel it wise to ensure that the ticket includes a cross-section of the groups to which the party is hoping to appeal. Legislatures produced by PR elections thus tend to be more representative of the population that elects them, in terms of both the backgrounds of the parliamentarians and the relationship between votes won and seats received by political parties. When voters can choose among candidates of one party, as under open-list PR or PR-STV, the proportion of MPs with local roots is higher than it is under closed-list systems (Shugart et al., 2005). However, a study of data from 30 countries found little electoral system impact on contact between citizens and MPs, neither when comparing PR with non-PR systems nor when comparing open-list and closed-list varieties of PR (Curtice and Shiveley, 2009).

Over and above the tangible difference that preference votes in open-list systems can make to the backgrounds of MPs and to the closeness of MPs' connection to their voters, the very fact of being able to choose their representatives may have a positive impact on voters' feelings about the entire political system. For one thing, turnout is higher in PR elections (Blais and Aarts, 2006; Selb, 2009). More broadly, analysis of surveys from 29 nations concludes that 'there is firm support for the view that preferential voting can make a difference – in this instance to levels of voter satisfaction with democracy' (Farrell and McAllister, 2006: 742). Such systems, according to the data, promote a greater sense of fairness about election outcomes among citizens.

## 11.7 Referendums

Elections are archetypal institutions of representative democracy, but in a number of countries the people make certain decisions themselves, by means of the referendum. In a referendum the people decide directly on some issue, rather than electing representatives to make decisions on their behalf. In the great majority of European countries a referendum can be triggered only by one of the institutions of representative government, such as the government, a parliamentary majority, a specified minority in parliament, or the president. In a number of countries – Hungary, Italy, Latvia, Lithuania, Luxembourg, Slovakia, Slovenia and Switzerland – the people themselves can bring about a popular vote by means of provisions for the initiative, without needing the endorsement of any other political actor. In post-communist countries the number of signatures needed makes it difficult to get a proposal off the ground (Albi, 2005: 141–145). In Slovakia, for example, it is 350000, equal to about one in seven of those who voted in the 2010 general election – and, moreover, the result has no force unless a certain level of turnout is reached (see below).

The use of the referendum varies hugely across Europe (see Table 11.7). Between 1945 and 2010, over 660 referendums took place in the 30 European countries we are examining – and one country, Switzerland, was responsible for almost two-thirds of these. Referendums are relatively common in Italy and Ireland, with Lithuania, Slovakia and Slovenia catching up fast. In contrast, Germany held no national referendums, and Austria, Belgium, Finland, Iceland, Norway and the UK held very few (on the UK see Bogdanor, 2009: 173–196). Attempts to find parsimonious explanations for this variation have been largely unsuccessful. The use of referendums worldwide increased steadily during the course of the twentieth century (LeDuc, 2003: 21).

Most commonly, referendum issues are ones that cut across party lines, and given that party systems are usually based on the left–right dimension, as we saw in Chapter 8, socio-economic issues are not usually the subject of referendums. Instead, questions that concern national sovereignty or moral issues are often seen as particularly suitable for a direct vote by the people. In relation to sovereignty, 17 countries have held referendums on membership of the European Union. Of the first 15 members, Austria, Denmark, Finland, Ireland and Sweden held a referendum before joining, and nine of the ten 2004 entrants (Cyprus was the exception) did the same, as did Romania (Szczerbiak and Taggart, 2004). Several other countries have held referendums on aspects of European integration, as we saw in Chapter 5. Iceland and Norway held referendums on independence – in each case there was near unanimity in favour – as did the three Baltic states in the early 1990s (the votes were heavily in favour, but there was strong opposition from Russians living in these countries).

**TABLE 11.7** National referendums, 1945–2010

| Country | Number of referendums | Country | Number of referendums |
|---|---|---|---|
| Austria | 2 | Latvia | 8 |
| Belgium | 1 | Lithuania | 19 |
| Bulgaria | 0 | Luxembourg | 1 |
| Cyprus | 2 | Malta | 2 |
| Czech Republic | 1 | Netherlands | 1 |
| Denmark | 18 | Norway | 2 |
| Estonia | 4 | Poland | 7 |
| Finland | 1 | Portugal | 4 |
| France | 14 | Romania | 4 |
| Germany | 0 | Slovakia | 15 |
| Greece | 4 | Slovenia | 16 |
| Hungary | 12 | Spain | 4 |
| Iceland | 1 | Sweden | 5 |
| Ireland | 30 | Switzerland | 416 |
| Italy | 69 | United Kingdom | 1 |
| | | Total | 664 |

*Notes:* In cases of countries that have not been continuous democracies since 1945, the period covered is the time during which they were democracies. All figures refer to national-level referendums only.

*Source:* www.c2d.ch/, the site of the Research Centre on Direct Democracy (C2D); see web links at the end of the chapter.

The people of Cyprus, too, voted on a sovereignty issue in April 2004, when a simultaneous vote was held in both parts of the divided island on an EU plan to reunify the island. If both sections had voted in favour, the island would have been reunited and would have joined the EU a week later as one political entity. However, while Turkish Cyprus supported the proposals (65 per cent were in favour), Greek Cyprus voted three to one against. The outcome was that only the Greek part of Cyprus joined the EU – leading to some unhappiness among other EU member states, who felt that the Greek Cypriots had in effect prevented Turkish Cyprus from gaining EU entry.

Moral issues occasionally feature as referendum topics. In Italy, after parliament had legalized divorce in 1970, opponents of this measure brought about a popular vote in 1974 to strike it down, and the people's decision to retain the divorce laws confirmed the liberalizing trend in Italian society. In Ireland, too, the legalization of divorce required the approval of the people in a referendum; in 1986 the vote was against change, but when a further referendum was held in 1995, there was a slim majority in favour, thus opening the door to the provision of divorce. Italy, Ireland and Portugal have also held referendums on abortion.

Several post-communist regimes made provision for the referendum and also for the initiative, allowing a number of citizens to promote laws or to challenge existing ones. This was taken furthest in Lithuania, whose number of referendums soon reached double figures (Krupavicius and

## BOX 11.3: THE REFERENDUM

### Denmark

Amending the Danish constitution requires the consent of the people, as expressed through a referendum, as does any step that reduces the country's sovereignty (unless parliament approves the measure with a five-sixths majority). In addition, a third of members of parliament can demand a referendum on any bill passed by parliament, although this has not happened since 1963. The most contentious referendums have been on aspects of European integration. The country voted by a comfortable majority to enter the EU in 1973, but in 1992 it became the first country to say No to an integrationist step when the people voted 51–49 against the Maastricht Treaty, although they approved an amended version, with Danish opt-outs, the following year. In September 2000 the people voted 53–47 against joining the single European currency, the euro. The parties in parliament are much more pro-integration than the Danish people, and they prefer not to put European issues to a referendum if this can be avoided.

### France

France has a long history of referendums, going back to 1793. Most of its pre-1945 referendums were widely seen as dubiously democratic, being used by authoritarian rulers to legitimize their positions (some writers use the term *plebiscitarian* for such referendums). More recently, the transition from the Third to the Fourth Republic was achieved by referendums in the mid 1940s, and in 1958 voters approved the inauguration of the Fifth Republic. The character of the Fifth Republic was transformed by the referendum called by Charles de Gaulle in October 1962 on direct election of the president. De Gaulle had been made president in 1958 by the established parties, and by 1962 he had fulfilled the tasks they had hoped he would undertake. They may have planned to dispense with his services once his term ended, but de Gaulle outflanked them by his decision to call a referendum. The people voted in favour of the change, and this considerably enhanced the power and prestige of the president, at least when the president's party holds a parliamentary majority, as we saw in Chapter 2. In 1969, though, a referendum brought about de Gaulle's downfall; he had tied his continuation in office to the success of an administrative reform proposal, and when the people rejected this measure, he resigned from office. From then to the end of the century there were only three further referendums. In May 2005 the French 'Non' to the proposed EU constitution, by a margin of 55 to 45, caused consternation among political elites across Europe. In 2008 constitutional provision was made for popular involvement in bringing about a referendum on certain types of government actions, but this would need a petition signed by 10 per cent of the electorate as well as the agreement of a fifth of MPs.

### Germany

Two referendums were held under the Weimar Republic in the 1920s, and a further four took place under the Nazis in the 1930s. Needless to say, the last four were not in any way democratic exercises, and Hitler's use of the referendum brought the institution into lasting disrepute in Germany. The post-war German constitution makes no mention of national referendums, and none has been held since 1938, although referendums occur at state level. Even though the fears, dating from the Nazi era, about the possible undemocratic overtones of referendums may seem exaggerated, there seems little likelihood that Germany will make use of the referendum in the near future.

## Italy

Italy is second only to Switzerland in the number of popular votes that take place. It is one of the few European countries where the voters themselves can bring about a popular vote by means of the initiative, without needing the agreement of the government, parliament, or political parties. Some Italian referendums have been particularly important: in 1974 Italians voted to retain the laws permitting divorce, which the Catholic church and conservative groups had hoped would be struck down by the referendum, and in the early 1990s the votes to reform the electoral system constituted decisive blows against the corrupt and tottering political establishment. The rule that a referendum result is not valid unless turnout reaches 50 per cent allows opponents of popular proposals to thwart them by not turning out.

## Netherlands

Prior to 2005 the Netherlands was unique in western Europe in never having held a national referendum. Despite this, or possibly because of it, the question of whether referendums support or damage democracy was debated more intensively in the Netherlands than virtually anywhere else. A number of referendums were held at local level on an experimental basis, and the country finally introduced legislation that would allow national referendums. The first of these took place in 2005 on the subject of the proposed EU constitution. The Dutch 'Nee', by a 62–38 margin, just three days after the French had said the same, killed off the constitution, and may also have killed off enthusiasm among the generally pro-European-integration Dutch political elite for the idea of holding more referendums.

## Poland

The political space (unique in the communist world) that was won in Poland during the 1980s by the Solidarity movement saw the holding of two referendums in November 1987 on political and economic reforms proposed by the regime; that they were not mere formalities was shown by the fact that neither set of proposals won the support of as many as 70 per cent of those voting and, moreover, a further 30 per cent heeded Solidarity's call to boycott the referendums. Only seven referendums have been held in post-communist Poland. In 1996 only 32 per cent bothered to vote in a set of five referendums on privatization. Second, in 1997 the people voted narrowly (53–47) to adopt a new constitution, and in 2003 they voted by nearly four to one in favour of joining the EU. Referendum results are not binding unless turnout reaches 50 per cent (if it does not, the votes are deemed merely 'consultative'), and given that Poland's citizens have proved difficult to mobilize politically – the country has consistently low turnout – this gives the same opportunity to opponents of change as is provided by a similar rule in Italy, that is, the chance to block a popular proposal by simply not voting.

## Spain

Spain has used the referendum institution sparingly. Two non-democratic referendums took place under the authoritarian Franco regime, and after Franco's death in 1975 two further referendums authorized the transition to democratic politics, with a vote in favour of the political reform programme in 1976 and approval of a new constitution in 1978. The only national referendums since then came in 1986, when the people voted narrowly in favour of Spain's remaining within NATO, and in 2005, when on a low turnout there was a strong vote in favour of the proposed EU constitution, three months before the referendum defeats in France and the Netherlands put an end to the idea. In addition, a number of referendums have taken place at regional level.

▶ **BOX 11.3: CONTINUED**

**United Kingdom**

Before 2011 only one national referendum had taken place in the United Kingdom; that was in 1975, when by a two-to-one majority the people voted to remain within the European Community, which the UK had joined in 1973. However, the referendum has been used rather more within the component parts of the United Kingdom. In 1979 and 1997 there were referendums in Scotland and Wales on the devolution of powers – in each nation the 1979 proposals did not receive enough support, but the 1997 proposals did, and they led to the creation of the Scottish parliament and the Welsh assembly that we discussed in Chapter 6. In addition, the package of proposals agreed by political leaders in Northern Ireland in April 1998 (the 'Good Friday Agreement') was put to the people of the province a month later, and received endorsement by 71 per cent to 29 per cent. Whether a referendum is held on a given issue is decided by the government of the day, meaning that the process is open to manipulation for political advantage. The Conservative–Liberal Democrat government that took office in May 2010 promised a referendum on electoral reform within a year.

Zvaliauskas, 2001; Møller, 2002). One of the proposals in 1996, very unusual for a referendum topic, was to amend the constitution to specify that at least half of the annual budget should be spent on social welfare, health care, education and science, and similarly in 2008 Latvia held a referendum on whether to increase pensions significantly. However, high thresholds have led to a low acceptance rate (see below). It is clear that some proposals in several post-communist countries have been promoted by parties more in order to impress or mobilize a group of voters than in any serious expectation of seeing their proposals passed.

The impact of the referendum has, not surprisingly, been greatest in Switzerland, where 50 000 people can, by signing a petition, launch an initiative and bring about a popular vote on any bill recently passed by parliament. Over the years only about 7 per cent of bills have been challenged in this way; about half of these bills have been endorsed by the people and the other half have been rejected (Trechsel and Kriesi, 1996: 191). The impact on policymaking is to incline those drawing up legislation to consult widely, in order to bring onside any group that might otherwise launch an initiative against the bill. Proposals for constitutional change need to be approved by both a majority of the voters and a majority of the 26 cantons (see Chapter 6).

In Italy, too, the use of the referendum has been very significant. Here, most popular votes have been *abrogative initiatives* – that is, they are launched by a petition signed by a prescribed number of voters, and they have the aim of repealing an existing law (Uleri, 1996). In the early 1990s two popular votes on aspects of the electoral system dealt hammer blows to the corrupt political establishment dominated by the Christian Democrats (DC) and the Socialists (PSI). The overwhelming support for both reforming measures was interpreted as an expression of popular disgust at the behaviour of the ruling elite, which bowed to public pressure and left power, leading to a change in the lower-house electoral system and to elections held three years ahead of schedule in March 1994. The Constitutional Court, which we discussed in Chapter 4, plays an important 'gatekeeper' role by deciding whether questions may be put to a vote of the people.

The rules in Italy require that for a law to be struck down by a referendum there must be not only a majority of votes in favour of such a proposal but also a turnout of at least 50 per cent. Consequently, if public opinion is known to be strongly supportive of some proposal, opponents are best advised not to vote at all in the hope of thereby invalidating the result by preventing turnout reaching the 50 per cent threshold. In 1991 the Italian prime minister Bettino Craxi (later disgraced and indicted for corruption) advised Italians to 'go to the beach' rather than vote on a change to the electoral system – although most of them defied him and voted. In 2005 large majorities voted to nullify laws prohibiting aspects of medically assisted fertilization, but because only about a quarter of the electorate turned out, with the Catholic church advising abstention, their votes had no effect.

The disadvantages of imposing thresholds in referendums are both manifold and manifest, yet several post-communist countries went down this route (Brunner, 2001: 222–223; Albi, 2005: 139–145). The most common requirement is a turnout of at least 50 per cent, a hangover from the days of communism, when this threshold was nominally in place for all elections. Some countries complicate matters further by having different thresholds for different kinds of referendum (for example, 'ordinary' referendums or constitutional amendment referendums). Only a few countries have no such high hurdles: Estonia and the Czech Republic, where a simple majority suffices, Latvia, where turnout must reach half the number who voted in the previous general election, and Hungary, where the majority supporting a proposal must amount to at least a quarter of the electorate. The result of these often high requirements, coupled with declining turnout in most post-communist countries, is that 'more than half of referendums within recent years have failed to meet the quorums' (Albi, 2005: 139).

The referendum is an institution that might seem to be inherently in conflict with the system of representative government that this book is about. Indeed, some critics of the referendum argue against it precisely on the ground that it will weaken or undermine representative institutions. Perhaps, in countries where the people can launch an initiative against a law passed by parliament, governments and parliaments may avoid taking tough but necessary decisions for fear of a popular vote overturning these. There are also elitist concerns that the mass public, being ill-informed and easily manipulable, will be too easily swayed by a handful of media barons without thinking deeply about the issues. In this rather far-fetched line of thought, the use of referendums could transform a representative democracy into a *plebiscitarian democracy*. A different kind of objection is that the people, far from being too subservient to political or media leaders, will prove contrary, voting against sensible propositions simply in order to punish an unpopular establishment. This argument was heard in the wake of defeats for the proposed EU constitution in referendums in France and the Netherlands in 2005, and for the Lisbon Treaty, which replaced it, in Ireland in 2008. The issues of constitutional redesign within the EU were too complex for ordinary voters, it was said, and many people voted instead on the basis of extraneous factors such as the supposed threat of the 'Polish plumber' in France or, in Ireland, the illusory spectre of European conscription. Finally, the inherently majoritarian nature of the referendum device means that minority rights could be overridden. This claim was frequently heard in the aftermath of a referendum in Switzerland in November 2009, when the people, against the advice of nearly all the political parties and against the wishes of Muslims resident in the country, voted 57–43 to ban the building of any further minarets.

Despite these fears, representative institutions have not been seriously challenged by the referendum (Gallagher, 1996; Setälä and Schiller, 2009). For one thing, in most countries that hold referendums, elected representatives control access to them. Typically it is the government, acting by virtue of its support in parliament, that determines the wording and timing of proposals to be voted on. Consequently, it is, as Butler and Ranney (1994: 21) observe, 'hard to believe that ... the referendum seriously subverts representative democracy.' Qvortrup (2005: 152–161) argues that it is likely to strengthen rather than weaken representative government. In Switzerland representative institutions are by now well accustomed to operating in conjunction with the referendum. Only in Italy can the referendum be said to have had a destabilizing effect; initiatives played a major role in bringing down the corrupt *partitocrazia* in the early 1990s, and could in theory make life difficult for more creditable political actors in future. The argument that many people are incapable of focusing on the matter at hand and tend to vote on the basis of extraneous matters, especially at European integration referendums, is disputed by Binzer Hobolt, who concludes that 'voters are smarter than they are often given credit for', and that issue voting is prevalent at such referendums (Binzer Hobolt, 2009: 248–249). Attitudes towards the EU also dominated at the Dutch referendum on the EU Constitutional Treaty in 2005 (Lubbers, 2008). And, while the people may sometimes vote against projects favoured by most MPs, as with the Swiss vote against the building of minarets, this could be viewed as the people making legitimate if contentious policy choices rather than simply being misguided.

The idea of replacing representative government by some kind of *direct democracy* in which citizens would vote on virtually every issue is clearly completely unrealistic in a modern complex society. The sensible question to ask is thus not whether direct democracy, which in any case is an ill-defined concept, is better than representative democracy. It is, rather, whether representative government and the referendum are inherently in conflict, or whether the latter can usefully complement the former. For the most part, the record in modern Europe suggests that it can.

## 11.8 Conclusions

Studies of electoral systems have come a long way in recent decades (Shugart, 2008). During the first half of the last century some writers used to argue seriously that the adoption of PR in any country was virtually bound to lead to the collapse of democracy and the establishment of a dictatorship. Others claimed that PR was almost a guaranteed recipe for harmony, enlightened government and a contented citizenry. Expectations of the difference that electoral systems can make are now more realistic.

Even so, there is no doubt that electoral systems do matter. Proportional representation systems lead to parliaments that more closely reflect the distribution of votes than do plurality systems, are more likely to be associated with a multiparty system, and facilitate the entry of women and ethnic minorities into parliament. The open-list and STV variants enable voters to make a choice of candidates within a party, and hence give individual MPs an incentive to be responsive to voters' demands. In contrast, majoritarian systems may lead to parliaments whose composition does not closely reflect the way people voted, but they score higher than PR when it comes to giving voters a chance to identify the government options at an election, and to throw a government out of office.

One of the areas in which electoral systems have their most visible consequences is government formation. PR formulae are much less likely than a plurality or majority system to manufacture single-party governments. Because it is very uncommon for a single party to win a majority of the votes cast, PR systems tend to be characterized by coalition government, the subject to which we now turn.

## Internet resources

www.ipu.org
> Site of the Inter-Parliamentary Union, with information on each member country's electoral system and electoral rules, plus data on the number of women in parliament, and links to national parliaments' sites.

www.unc.edu/~asreynol/ballots.html
> Andrew Reynolds's site at the University of North Carolina, with ballot papers from over 100 countries, showing the choices and constraints facing voters in different countries.

www.tcd.ie/Political_Science/staff/michael.gallagher/ElSystems/index.php
> Site with data on indices of disproportionality and party system fragmentation at elections in over 90 countries, plus information on electoral systems, and downloadable files for calculation of indices.

aceproject.org/
> Site of the Electoral Knowledge Network, with information on every country's electoral system.

psephos.adam-carr.net/
> Adam Carr's site, based in Melbourne, describing itself as 'the largest, most comprehensive and most up-to-date archive of electoral information in the world, with election statistics from 175 countries'.

www.nsd.uib.no/european_election_database/
> Detailed results, at regional and/or constituency level, of parliamentary and other elections in 31 European countries for the period since 1990.

fruitsandvotes.com
> Site maintained by Matthew Shugart; discussion of electoral system effects in many countries (and organic growing).

www.c2d.ch/
> Site of the Research Centre on Direct Democracy (C2D), based in Aarau in Switzerland, with data on past referendums worldwide and news about forthcoming ones.

## References

**Albi, Anneli** (2005) *EU Enlargement and the Constitutions of Central and Eastern Europe*, Cambridge University Press, Cambridge.

**Anckar, Carsten** (1997) 'Determinants of disproportionality and wasted votes', *Electoral Studies*, 16 (4), 501–515.

**Andeweg, Rudy B. and Galen A. Irwin** (2009) *Governance and Politics of the Netherlands*, 3rd edn, Palgrave Macmillan, Basingstoke.

**Andrews, Josephine and Robert Jackman** (2005) 'Strategic fools: electoral rule choice under extreme uncertainty', *Electoral Studies*, 24 (1), 65–85.

**Baldini, Gianfranco and Adriano Pappalardo** (2009) *Elections, Electoral Systems and Volatile Voters*, Palgrave Macmillan, Basingstoke.

**Behnke, Joachim** (2007) 'The strange phenomenon of surplus seats in the German electoral system', *German Politics* 16 (4), 496–517.

**Benoit, Kenneth** (2004) 'Models of electoral system change', *Electoral Studies*, 23 (3), 363–389.

**Benoit, Kenneth** (2006) 'Duverger's law and the study of electoral systems', *French Politics*, 4 (1), 69–83.

**Benoit, Kenneth** (2008) 'Hungary: holding back the tiers', pp. 231–252 in Michael Gallagher and Paul Mitchell (eds), *The Politics of Electoral Systems*, paperback edn, Oxford University Press, Oxford.

**Binzer Hobolt, Sara** (2009) *Europe in Question: Referendums on European Integration*, Oxford University Press, Oxford.

**Birch, Sarah** (2003) *Electoral Systems and Political Transformation in Post-Communist Europe*, Palgrave Macmillan, Basingstoke.

**Birch, Sarah, Frances Millard, Marina Popescu and Kieran Williams** (2002) *Embodying Democracy: Electoral System Design in Post-Communist Europe*, Palgrave Macmillan, Basingstoke.

**Blais, André and Kees Aarts** (2006) 'Electoral systems and turnout', *Acta Politica*, 41 (2), 180–196.

**Blais, André and Marc André Bodet** (2006) 'Does proportional representation foster closer congruence between citizens and policy makers?', *Comparative Political Studies*, 39 (1), 1243–1262.

**Blais, André and Peter John Loewen** (2009) 'The French electoral system and its effects', *West European Politics*, 32 (2), 345–359.

**Blais, André, Agnieszka Dobrzynska and Indridi H. Indridason** (2005) 'To adopt or not to adopt proportional representation: the politics of institutional choice', *British Journal of Political Science*, 35 (1), 182–190.

**Blau, Adrian** (2009) 'Electoral reform in the UK: a veto player analysis', pp. 61–89 in André Blais (ed.), *To Keep or to Change First Past the Post? The Politics of Electoral Reform*, Oxford University Press, Oxford.

**Bogdanor, Vernon** (2009) *The New British Constitution*, Hart, Oxford.

**Boix, Carles** (2010) 'Electoral markets, party strategies, and proportional representation', *American Political Science Review*, 104 (2), 404–413.

**Bowler, Shaun and Bernard Grofman (eds)** (2000) *Elections in Australia, Ireland, and Malta under the Single Transferable Vote: Reflections on an Embedded Institution*, University of Michigan Press, Ann Arbor, MI.

**Brunner, Georg** (2001) 'Direct vs. representative democracy', pp. 215–227 in Andreas Auer and Michael Bützer (eds), *Direct Democracy: The Eastern and Central European Experience*, Ashgate, Aldershot.

**Bull, Martin J. and James L. Newell** (2009) 'Still the anomalous democracy? Politics and institutions in Italy', *Government and Opposition*, 44 (1), 42–67.

**Butler, David and Austin Ranney** (1994) 'Theory', pp. 11–23 in David Butler and Austin Ranney (eds), *Referendums around the World: The Growing Use of Direct Democracy*, Macmillan and St Martin's Press, Basingstoke and New York.

**Colomer, Josep M.** (2004) 'The strategy and history of electoral system choice', pp. 3–78 in Josep M. Colomer (ed.), *Handbook of Electoral System Choice*, Palgrave Macmillan, Basingstoke.

**Cox, Gary W.** (1997) *Making Votes Count: Strategic Coordination in the World's Electoral Systems*, Cambridge University Press, Cambridge.

**Curtice, John and W. Phillips Shiveley** (2009) 'Who represents us best? One member or many?', pp. 171–192 in Hans-Dieter Klingemann (ed.), *The Comparative Study of Electoral Systems*, Oxford University Press, Oxford.

**Cusack, Thomas, Torben Iversen and David Soskice** (2010) 'Coevolution of capitalism and political representation: the choice of electoral systems', *American Political Science Review*, 104 (2), 393–403.

**D'Alimonte, Roberto** (2008) 'Italy: a case of fragmented bipolarism', pp. 253–276 in Michael Gallagher and Paul Mitchell (eds), *The Politics of Electoral Systems*, paperback edn, Oxford University Press, Oxford.

**Dimitras, Panayote Elias** (1994) 'Electoral systems in Greece', pp. 143–175 in Stuart Nagel (ed.), *Eastern Europe Development and Public Policy*, Macmillan, Basingstoke.

**Doorenspleet, Renske** (2010) 'Electoral systems and democratic quality: do mixed systems combine the best or the worst of both worlds? An explorative quantitative cross-national study', *Acta Politica*, 40 (1), 28–49.

**Downs, William M.** (2009) 'The 2008 parliamentary election in Romania', *Electoral Studies*, 28 (3), 510–513.

**Duverger, Maurice** (1986) 'Duverger's law: forty years later', pp. 69–84 in Bernard Grofman and Arend Lijphart (eds), *Electoral Laws and Their Political Consequences*, Agathon Press, New York.

**Elgie, Robert** (2008) 'France: stacking the deck', pp. 119–136 in Michael Gallagher and Paul Mitchell (eds), *The Politics of Electoral Systems*, paperback edn, Oxford University Press, Oxford.

**Elklit, Jørgen** (2008) 'Denmark: simplicity embedded in complexity (or is it the other way round?)', pp. 453–472 in Michael Gallagher and Paul Mitchell (eds), *The Politics of Electoral Systems*, paperback edn, Oxford University Press, Oxford.

**Farrell, David M.** (2010) *Electoral Systems: A Comparative Introduction*, 2nd edn, Palgrave Macmillan, Basingstoke.

**Farrell, David and Ian McAllister** (2006) 'Voter satisfaction and electoral systems: does preferential voting in candidate-centred systems make a difference?', *European Journal of Political Research*, 45 (5), 723–749.

**Gallagher, Michael** (1991) 'Proportionality, disproportionality and electoral systems', *Electoral Studies*, 10 (1), 33–51.

**Gallagher, Michael** (1996) 'Conclusion', pp. 226–252 in Michael Gallagher and Pier Vincenzo Uleri (eds), *The Referendum Experience in Europe*, Macmillan and St Martin's Press, Basingstoke and New York.

**Gallagher, Michael** (2008a) 'Ireland: the discreet charm of PR-STV', pp. 511–532 in Michael Gallagher and Paul Mitchell (eds), *The Politics of Electoral Systems*, paperback edn, Oxford University Press, Oxford.

**Gallagher, Michael** (2008b) 'Conclusion', pp. 535–578 in Michael Gallagher and Paul Mitchell (eds), *The Politics of Electoral Systems*, paperback edn, Oxford University Press, Oxford.

**Gallagher, Michael and Paul Mitchell (eds)** (2008) *The Politics of Electoral Systems*, paperback edn, Oxford University Press, Oxford and New York.

**Gerring, John and Strom C. Thacker** (2008) *Good Government: A Centripetal Theory of Democratic Governance*, Cambridge University Press, Cambridge.

**Golder, Matt and Jacek Stramski** (2005) 'Ideological congruence and electoral institutions', *American Journal of Political Science*, 54 (1), 90–106.

**Hopkin, Jonathan** (2008) 'Spain: proportional representation with majoritarian outcomes', pp. 375–394 in Michael Gallagher and Paul Mitchell (eds), *The Politics of Electoral Systems*, paperback edn, Oxford University Press, Oxford.

**Iversen, Torben and David Soskice** (2006) 'Electoral institutions and the politics of coalitions: why some democracies redistribute more than others', *American Political Science Review*, 100 (2), 165–181.

**Karvonen, Lauri** (2010) *The Personalisation of Politics: A Study of Parliamentary Democracies*, ECPR Press, Colchester.

**Katz, Richard S.** (1997) *Democracy and Elections*, Oxford University Press, Oxford.

**Katz, Richard S.** (2008) 'Why are there so many (or so few) electoral reforms?', pp. 57–76 in Michael Gallagher and Paul Mitchell (eds), *The Politics of Electoral Systems*, paperback edn, Oxford University Press, Oxford.

**Kim, HeeMin, G. Bingham Powell and Richard C. Fording** (2010) 'Electoral systems, party systems and ideological representation: an analysis of distortion in western democracies', *Comparative Politics*, 42 (2), 167–185.

**Kreuzer, Marcus** (2010) 'Historical knowledge and quantitative analysis: the case of the origins of proportional representation', *American Political Science Review*, 104 (2), 369–392.

**Krupavicius, Algis and Giedrius Zvaliauskas** (2001) 'Lithuania', pp. 109–128 in Andreas Auer and Michael Bützer (eds), *Direct Democracy: The Eastern and Central European Experience*, Ashgate, Aldershot.

**Laakso, Markku and Rein Taagepera** (1979) '"Effective" number of parties: a measure with application to west Europe', *Comparative Political Studies*, 12 (1), 3–27.

**LeDuc, Lawrence** (2003) *The Politics of Direct Democracy: Referendums in Global Perspective*, Broadview Press, Peterborough, Ontario.

**Lijphart, Arend** (1994) *Electoral Systems and Party Systems: A Study of Twenty-Seven Democracies, 1945–1990*, Oxford University Press, Oxford.

**Lijphart, Arend** (1999) *Patterns of Democracy: Government Forms and Performance in Thirty-Six Countries*, Yale University Press, New Haven, CT, and London.

**Lubbers, Marcel** (2008) 'Regarding the Dutch "Nee" to the European Constitution: a test of the identity, utilitarian and political approaches to voting "No"', *European Union Politics*, 9 (1), 59–86.

**Lundberg, Thomas Carl** (2006) 'Second-class representatives? Mixed-member proportional representation in Britain', *Parliamentary Affairs*, 59 (1), 60–77.

**Lundberg, Thomas Carl** (2009) 'Post-communism and the abandonment of mixed-member electoral systems', *Representation*, 45 (1), 15–27.

**Lutz, Georg** (2010) 'First come, first served: the effect of ballot position on electoral success in open ballot PR elections', *Representation*, 46 (2), 167–181.

**Mackie, Thomas T. and Richard Rose** (1991) *The International Almanac of Electoral History*, 3rd edn, Macmillan, London.

**Massicotte, Louis and André Blais** (1999) 'Mixed electoral systems: a conceptual and empirical survey', *Electoral Studies*, 18 (3), 341–366.

**Massicotte, Louis, André Blais and Antoine Yoshinaka** (2004) *Establishing the Rules of the Game: Election Laws in Democracies*, University of Toronto Press, Toronto.

**Maxfield, Ed** (2009) 'Romania's parliamentary elections, 30 November 2008', *Representation*, 45 (4), 485–493.

**Millard, Frances** (2004) *Elections, Parties, and Representation in Post-Communist Europe*, Palgrave Macmillan, Basingstoke.

**Mitchell, Paul** (2008) 'United Kingdom: plurality rule under siege', pp. 157–184 in Michael Gallagher and Paul Mitchell (eds), *The Politics of Electoral Systems*, paperback edn, Oxford University Press, Oxford.

**Møller, Luise Pape** (2002) 'Moving away from the ideal: the rational use of referendums in the Baltic states', *Scandinavian Political Studies*, 25 (3), 281–293.

**Müller, Wolfgang C.** (2008) 'Austria: a complex electoral system with subtle effects', pp. 397–416 in Michael Gallagher and Paul Mitchell (eds), *The Politics of Electoral Systems*, paperback edn, Oxford University Press, Oxford.

**Norris, Pippa** (2004) *Electoral Engineering: Voting Rules and Political Behaviour*, Cambridge University Press, Cambridge and New York.

**Paxton, Pamela, Melanie M. Hughes and Matthew A. Painter** (2010) 'Growth in women's political representation: a longitudinal exploration of democracy, electoral system and gender quotas', *European Journal of Political Research*, 49 (1), 25–52.

**Persson, Torsten and Guido Tabellini** (2005) *The Economic Effects of Constitutions*, MIT Press, Cambridge, MA.

**Powell, G. Bingham** (2000) *Elections as Instruments of Democracy: Majoritarian and Proportional Visions*, Yale University Press, New Haven, CT, and London.

**Powell, G. Bingham** (2006) 'Election laws and representative governments: beyond votes and seats', *British Journal of Political Science*, 36 (2), 291–315.

**Powell, G. Bingham** (2009) 'The ideological congruence controversy: the impact of alternative measures, data, and time periods on the effects of election rules', *Comparative Political Studies*, 42 (12), 1475–1497.

**Przeworski, Adam** (2009) 'Conquered or granted? A history of suffrage extensions', *British Journal of Political Science*, 39 (2), 291–321.

**Qvortrup, Mads** (2005) *A Comparative Study of Referendums: Government by the People*, 2nd edn, Manchester University Press, Manchester and New York.

**Rehfeld, Andrew** (2005) *The Concept of Constituency: Political Representation, Democratic Legitimacy, and Institutional Design*, Cambridge University Press, Cambridge.

**Renwick, Alan** (2010) *The Politics of Electoral Reform: Changing the Rules of Democracy*, Cambridge University Press, Cambridge.

**Renwick, Alan, Chris Hanretty and David Hine** (2009) 'Partisan self-interest and electoral reform: the new Italian electoral law of 2005', *Electoral Studies*, 28 (3), 437–447.

**Rose, Richard and Neil Munro** (2003) *Elections and Parties in New European Democracies*, CQ Press, Washington, DC.

**Saalfeld, Thomas** (2008) 'Germany: stability and strategy in a mixed-member proportional system', pp. 209–230 in Michael Gallagher and Paul Mitchell (eds), *The Politics of Electoral Systems*, paperback edn, Oxford University Press, Oxford.

**Salmond, Rob** (2006) 'Proportional representation and female parliamentarians', *Legislative Studies Quarterly*, 31 (2), 175–204.

**Sartori, Giovanni** (1997) *Comparative Constitutional Engineering: An Inquiry into Structures, Incentives and Outcomes*, 2nd edn, Macmillan, Basingstoke.

**Selb, Peter** (2009) 'A deeper look at the proportionality–turnout nexus', *Comparative Political Studies*, 42 (4), 527–548.

**Setälä, Maija and Theo Schiller (eds)** (2009) *Referendums and Representative Democracy: Responsiveness, Accountability and Deliberation*, Routledge, Abingdon.

**Shugart, Matthew Søberg** (2008) 'Comparative electoral systems research', pp. 25–56 in Michael Gallagher and Paul Mitchell (eds), *The Politics of Electoral Systems*, paperback edn, Oxford University Press, Oxford.

**Shugart, Matthew Søberg** (2009) 'Inherent and contingent factors in reform initiation in plurality systems', pp. 7–60 in André Blais (ed.), *To Keep or to Change First Past the Post? The Politics of Electoral Reform*, Oxford University Press, Oxford.

**Shugart, Matthew Soberg and Martin P. Wattenberg (eds)** (2003) *Mixed-Member Electoral Systems: The Best of Both Worlds?*, Oxford University Press, Oxford.

**Shugart, Matthew Søberg, Melody Ellis and Kati Suominen** (2005) 'Looking for locals: voter information demands and personal vote-earning attributes of legislators under proportional representation', *American Journal of Political Science*, 49 (2), 437–449.

**Sinnott, Richard** (2010) 'The electoral system', pp. 111–136 in John Coakley and Michael Gallagher (eds), *Politics in the Republic of Ireland*, 5th edn, Routledge and PSAI Press, Abingdon and New York.

**Smith, Alastair** (2004) *Election Timing*, Cambridge University Press, Cambridge.

**Strøm, Kaare and Stephen M. Swindle** (2002) 'Strategic parliamentary dissolution', *American Political Science Review*, 96 (3), 575–591.

**Szczerbiak, Aleks and Paul Taggart (eds)** (2004) *Choosing Union: the 2003 EU Accession Referendums*, special issue of *West European Politics*, 27 (4).

**Taagepera, Rein and Matthew Soberg Shugart** (1989) *Seats and Votes: The Effects and Determinants of Electoral Systems*, Yale University Press, New Haven and London.

**Trechsel, Alexander H. and Hanspeter Kriesi** (1996) 'Switzerland: the referendum and initiative as a centrepiece of the political system', pp. 185–209 in Michael Gallagher and Pier Vincenzo Uleri (eds), *The Referendum Experience in Europe*, Macmillan and St Martin's Press, Basingstoke and New York.

**Uleri, Pier Vincenzo** (1996) 'Italy: referendums and initiatives from the origins to the crisis of a democratic regime', pp. 106–125 in Michael Gallagher and Pier Vincenzo Uleri (eds), *The Referendum Experience in Europe*, Macmillan and St Martin's Press, Basingstoke and New York.

**Vernby, Kåre** (2007) 'Strikes are more common in countries with majoritarian electoral systems', *Public Choice*, 132 (2), 65–84.

**Vowles, Jack** (2004) 'Electoral systems and proportional tenure of government: renewing the debate', *British Journal of Political Science*, 34 (1), 166–179.

# Making and Breaking Governments

**12**

## Chapter contents

## 12.1 Introduction

We are by now very familiar with the fact that most modern European democracies, including recently democratized countries of central and eastern Europe, have *parliamentary government* regimes in which the executive is responsible to the legislature. One important consequence of this is that governments are not chosen directly by the people. Rather, the people first vote to choose a parliament, and this elected parliament then has the constitutionally embedded power both to choose the government and to dismiss it from office. The system of parliamentary government means that, whatever the fine constitutional theory, the raw political reality is that parliamentary elections are much more about choosing governments than they are about choosing a set of people to legislate, to pass laws. Bagehot's memorable description of the British system of government, first published in 1885, applies more generally to parliamentary government: '[t]he legislature chosen, in name, to make laws, in fact finds its principal business in making and in keeping an executive ...' (Bagehot, 2000: 61). The real prize that is won or lost at parliamentary elections, for most politicians at least, is a place in the government.

Very few European political parties ever win an overall majority of parliamentary seats. This is because it is unusual for any political party to win a majority of *votes* in any modern European democracy, while we saw in the previous chapter that the proportional representation (PR) electoral systems used in almost all European countries generate legislatures in which the distribution of *seats* reflects this pattern. This means there is no unambiguous choice of government that has been indicated by citizens voting in the election. When no single party wins a parliamentary majority, it is axiomatically the case that a *legislative coalition* of two or more different parties is needed to provide majority support for any government. Note that government positions may be filled by politicians from just one party in such minority settings, but politicians from more than one party must *support* this government in key parliamentary votes. It is a matter of simple arithmetic that there are several different ways to put together a majority coalition when there is no single majority party. Several different possible governments could therefore command the support of a legislative majority. In this importance sense, citizens in most European countries have not definitively 'chosen' a government by the time that votes have been counted. The precise composition and nature of the government are settled, after the election is over, following intensive and high-stakes negotiations between senior politicians.

Even when one single party wins a legislative majority, any government is nonetheless a coalition of diverse interests. In Britain (and indeed in the United States), such coalitions of interest are found for the most part inside political parties. Even in Britain, however, the electoral system generated a 'hung' parliament in May 2010, followed by a coalition between Conservatives and Liberal Democrats. In most continental European countries election results are translated more or less proportionally into parliamentary seat distributions, and bargaining to form a government takes place both within and between political parties. These election results mean that many governments in modern Europe are executive coalitions in which more than one party is represented at the cabinet table. Most European single-party cabinets, furthermore, are not made up of parties that control parliamentary majorities on their own. They are single-party 'minority' cabinets that must rely for their continued existence on parliamentary support coalitions of two or more parties. A coalition of parties then *supports* the government in parliament, even if only one party fills the seats at the cabinet table.

The constitutional regime of parliamentary government implies by definition that, even after a government has been installed by parliament, this is by no means the end of the story. The ability of any government to hold on to the reins of power depends crucially on continuing support in parliament, even if this support does not come from the same group of legislators who supported the government in the first place. This implies an ongoing process of bargaining and negotiation between senior politicians, dealing with the shocks and unanticipated events that inevitably arise. A distinctive implication of parliamentary government is thus that the government can be brought down at any moment, at least when parliament is in session, by the defection of key elements of its parliamentary support coalition. In reality, as we shall see, political life in a modern European democracy is typically much less chaotic than this might seem to imply.

In the rest of this chapter, as we explore the making and breaking of governments in modern Europe, we first look in more detail at how the constitutional regime of parliamentary government defines the rules of the political game, before examining factors that affect the formation of European cabinets and the allocation of cabinet portfolios among parties. We then move on to explore why some European governments last as long as is constitutionally possible while others form, collapse, and re-form at a much faster pace.

## 12.2 Making and breaking governments: the rules of the game

### 12.2.1 Parliamentary votes of confidence and no confidence

The defining constitutional principle in a parliamentary democracy, that the executive is responsible to the legislature, is implemented in practice using the procedural device of a parliamentary motion of no confidence in the government. The right to propose a motion of no confidence, the precedence that this motion takes over other business, and the inability of the government to use its control over the legislative agenda to avoid this motion being put to a vote, must all be deeply embedded in parliamentary rules of procedure that cannot be changed at the whim of the government. Constitutionally, if such a vote is carried, the government is deemed dismissed if it does not resign voluntarily. Even where, as in Britain and Finland for example, there is not a binding constitutional constraint that governments must retain the confidence of the legislature, there is nonetheless a very strong constitutional convention that a government will in fact resign if defeated in a no-confidence vote. Switzerland is the main exception to this arrangement in modern Europe. The seven-member Swiss cabinet, its Federal Council, is elected by a legislature with a four-year term. Once formed, the government does not have to face legislative confidence votes, so that Switzerland is typically not seen as a parliamentary government system. The incidence of these and other institutional features that structure the making and breaking of governments in modern Europe is documented in Table 12.1.

The vote of no confidence may or may not be supplemented by other rules of parliamentary procedure. These include a rule in many countries that losing the vote on final passage of the government's annual finance bill, or *budget*, is the same as losing a vote of no confidence. If the government cannot get its budget through the legislature, it is deemed to be dismissed. There is also often a provision for a government facing a vote of no confidence to transform this into a vote of *confidence*, or indeed to propose its own motion of confidence at any time. This can be used by the government to force the legislature to 'put up or shut up' and in this way stake the future of the government on passage of the confidence vote, since it falls if the vote is lost.

The fact that government accountability in parliamentary systems is ensured by the legislative vote of confidence/no confidence has important consequences for the degree of control that the people, via their elected public representatives, have over what governments actually do. While the legislature may seem to have sweeping powers to make and break governments, these powers may in practical terms be rather like the power of a sledgehammer to crack a nut. The main form of legislative control over the executive is to throw the entire executive out on its ear. But many matters on which the legislature disagrees with the executive may not be important enough to warrant such extraordinary measures, and the executive may thus get its way on these. This situation can be exploited by a canny government, which can use its power to bring matters to a head by threatening a vote of confidence in order to force a troublesome opposition to back down. In this way an incumbent government in a parliamentary democracy can get far more of its own way, in effect by 'daring' the legislature to throw it out when there may be no viable alternative, than the formal constitutional position might suggest. John Huber provides a fascinating elaboration of this in the case of France (Huber, 1996).

**TABLE 12.1**  Constitutional factors in government life cycles

| | Does head of state play active role in govt formation? | Is formal investiture vote needed? | Must govt resign if it loses confidence vote? | Can govt dissolve legislature? | Can legislature dissolve legislature? | Maximum time between elections |
|---|---|---|---|---|---|---|
| Austria | No | No | Yes | Yes | Yes | 5 years |
| Belgium | No | Yes | Yes[c] | Yes | No | 4 years |
| Bulgaria | No | No | Yes | No | No | 4 years |
| Cyprus | Yes | No | No | No | Yes | 5 years |
| Czech Republic | Yes | Yes | Yes[a] | No | Yes | 4 years |
| Denmark | No | No | Yes | Yes | No | 4 years |
| Estonia | Yes | Yes | Yes | No | No | 4 years |
| Finland | No | Yes | Yes | Yes | No | 4 years |
| France | Yes | No | Yes[a] | Yes[b] | No | 5 years |
| Germany | No | Yes | Yes[c] | Yes | No | 4 years |
| Greece | No | Yes | Yes[a] | Yes | No | 4 years |
| Hungary | No | Yes | Yes[c] | No | Yes | 4 years |
| Iceland | No | No | Yes[a] | Yes | No | 4 years |
| Ireland | No | Yes | Yes | Yes | No | 5 years |
| Italy | Yes | Yes | Yes | Yes | No | 5 years |
| Latvia | Yes | Yes | Yes | No | No | 4 years |
| Lithuania | Yes | Yes | Yes | Yes | Yes | 4 years |
| Luxembourg | No | Yes | Yes | Yes | No | 5 years |
| Malta | No | No | Yes | Yes | No | 5 years |
| Netherlands | Yes | No | Yes | Yes | No | 4 years |
| Norway | No | No | Yes | No | No | 4 years |
| Poland | Yes | Yes | Yes[c] | No | Yes | 4 years |
| Portugal | Yes | Yes | Yes[a] | No | No | 4 years |
| Romania | Yes | Yes | Yes | No | No | 4 years |
| Slovakia | Yes | Yes | Yes[a] | No | No | 4 years |
| Slovenia | Yes | Yes | Yes[c] | No | Yes | 4 years |
| Spain | Yes | Yes | Yes[c] | Yes | No | 4 years |
| Sweden | No | Yes | Yes[a] | Yes | No | 4 years |
| Switzerland | No | Yes | No | No | No | 4 years |
| United Kingdom | No | No | No | Yes | No | 5 years |

[a] Absolute majority of legislature is required to pass a no-confidence vote.
[b] After one year.
[c] Motion of no confidence in prime minister must specify successor.

## 12.2.2 Investiture requirements

In some countries, Belgium and Italy for example, an incoming government must win an explicit formal legislative investiture vote before it can take office. In other countries, Denmark and Finland for example, there is no constitutional requirement for a formal investiture vote. Notwithstanding superficial appearances, the requirement for an explicit investiture vote is not a defining *constitutional* feature of parliamentary government. This is because, from the first moment it presents itself to parliament, any government must be able to survive a possible vote of no confidence, which amounts to the existence of an implicit investiture requirement, and members of any potential government must take this into account during the process of cabinet formation.

Nonetheless, the existence of a formal investiture requirement is *politically* important, as Kaare Strøm has demonstrated. This is because the absence of a strict legislative investiture test makes it easier to form minority governments, in which the government parties themselves do not have a legislative majority but must instead rely on 'outside' support from other legislative parties (Strøm, 1990). Once a government has been installed, particular issues leave a minority government open to challenge; a particular piece of legislation or a particular policy may rouse the anger of sections of the opposition. As we shall see below, however, one strategy for minority governments, if they are not forced to face the test of putting together an overall majority on investiture, is to skip from one legislative majority to another on an issue-by-issue basis, with each majority made up of different parties. In such cases, Denmark is usually cited as the classic example: the government's majority may comprise one set of parties for one issue and a quite different set for a different issue. In countries that do have a formal investiture requirement, however, this is not possible. The incoming government must present the legislature with a general policy programme and a set of nominations for all cabinet positions. It must win majority support in the legislature for the entire package, and cannot rely on different majorities on different issues, because the single investiture vote passes judgement on all of these important matters taken together. It is thus not surprising that this more 'rational' system of forming a government in a parliamentary democracy would be selected, as we can see from Table 12.1, by the democratizing states of central and eastern Europe, forced to consider the matter when drafting new constitutions.

## 12.2.3 *Formateurs:* the role of the head of state

All governments derive both their fundamental legitimacy and their legal recognition under the constitution from somewhere. There is always some constitutionally designated officer, typically the head of state in a modern European democracy, charged with investing each new government with its constitutional authority. We can divide countries into those where the head of state plays an active role in the government formation process and those where he or she has a purely formal swearing-in function, doing little more than handing over the seals of office and shaking the hand of the incoming prime minister. Where the head of state does play an active role, this typically involves choosing a particular senior politician to initiate the process of forming a government, effectively designating this person as a potential prime minister. This designated government builder is typically referred to by political scientists, adopting the usage of a number of European countries, as a *formateur*. Where the head of state does not play an active role in government formation, some other facet of the local institutional context, whether constitutionally mandated or the result of strong local conventions, structures the process of negotiation between senior politicians that results in the emergence of a candidate for the position of prime minister.

In Greece, for example, it is formally laid down in the constitution that in the event that no single party has a legislative majority, the head of state first designates the leader of the largest party as *formateur*. If this person fails to form a government, then the head of state must then ask the leader of the second-largest party to be *formateur*, and so on. Operating strictly on this principle, the role of the head of state in government formation could, less congenially, be carried out by an automaton. This might seem a 'natural' and intuitive rule that also gives parties strong incentives to compete vigorously with each other at election time for the position of largest party. However, Greece and Bulgaria are the only countries in modern Europe to have this formal constitutional provision.

In some countries, Britain and Ireland for example, there is a strong convention that the initiative in government formation lies with the outgoing government. Even if the government has lost support in the election that has just been held, the outgoing prime minister is still given a chance to form another administration, to be the first *formateur*. This may often be a mere formality; a badly beaten prime minister typically concedes defeat on election night. Nonetheless, outgoing British prime minister Gordon Brown stayed in office for several days after losing the May 2010 election, before conceding he could not form a government. In such cases the outgoing prime minister had a clear 'first mover' advantage in the government formation process.

In other European countries, Finland, Poland and Romania for example, the head of state may use his or her discretion and judgement when selecting a *formateur*. The most extreme case of this arises under the French semi-presidential system, according to which the president simply picks the *formateur* he or she most favours, subject to the need for this person to be able to command a legislative majority. More generally, the 'stronger' the presidency in any given country, the more active a role the president may play in the government formation process. Even in countries where the constitution provides that the head of state should behave like a machine, however, a particularly intractable political situation may force a president or monarch to use discretion to break a deadlock. In all of these cases it is possible that the personal political preferences of the head of state may have a significant effect on the outcome of the government formation process.

The choice of *formateur* in the government formation process is of particular interest to political scientists, since the first *formateur* – whether the incumbent PM, leader of the largest party, or the president's favourite – is typically seen as having a big bargaining advantage (Ansolabehere *et al.*, 2005; Kang, 2009; Laver *et al.*, 2010). This is because, with rational foresight and assuming the first *formateur*'s party is a pivotal member of at least some legislative majority, the first *formateur* should be able to figure out a coalition deal that will be accepted by a coalition of legislators who, between them, command a legislative majority, and should thereby be able either to gain or to retain the office of prime minister.

## 12.2.4  The status quo and 'caretaker' governments

As we noted in Chapter 2, democratic constitutions take extravagant care to ensure that there is always a legally installed incumbent government. There is never a moment with no government, leaving the doors of government buildings swinging in the breeze and tumbleweed blowing down the corridors. The binding constitutional constraint that ensures this is that *the incumbent government remains in place until formally replaced by an alternative*. Once the legislature has been dissolved and an election called, or once a government has been defeated or resigned, the incumbent government nonetheless remains in office to run the country as a *caretaker* administration.

There is variation from country to country in the extent to which caretaker governments can embark on new policy initiatives. In some countries, such as Ireland, a caretaker government can and does use the full range of powers available to any normal government. It is not uncommon for crucial decisions to be taken, and political appointments made, by a caretaker. In other countries, such as Denmark and Poland, a caretaker government is strictly constrained by constitutional conventions to do only what is absolutely necessary to keep the ship of state afloat. Laver and Shepsle (1994: 291–292) provide a comparative overview of the powers of caretaker governments in different European states. Whatever the powers of a caretaker government, the constitutional bottom line is that the ministers and policies of the incumbent government remain in place during the making of any new government. The alternative to forming a new government is never a void, but is the continuation of the incumbent caretaker administration (Laver *et al.*, 2010). This situation can last a long time. The Belgian government sworn into office on 20 March 2008, to take an extreme example, emerged from negotiations that started after the general election of 10 June 2007, during which the outgoing Belgian cabinet remained in office, and daily life in Belgium continued as normal.

## 12.2.5 Agreeing a joint programme of government

Over and above picking a prime minister, two other important matters must be settled in government formation negotiations. The first concerns who will hold the various cabinet positions, a matter to which we shortly return. The second is a joint policy programme for the government, a particularly important matter for governments that are coalitions of different parties, each with a different policy programme. Thus the German federal election of September 2009 resulted in significant losses for one of the members of the outgoing government, the centre-left Social Democratic Party (SDP), modest gains for the centre-right Christian Democratic Union (CDU), led by the outgoing chancellor Angela Merkel, and significant gains for the CDU's traditional coalition partner, the right-wing Free Democrats (FPD). Merkel set about trying to negotiate an agreement with the FDP, and more than three weeks of tough policy negotiations ensued. A policy deal between the two parties was announced in the early hours of the morning of Saturday 24 October 2009. The proposed allocation of cabinet portfolios to senior members of each party was announced the same day. The main substance of the policy negotiations between the two prospective coalition partners concerned the level of tax cuts that would be introduced, notwithstanding a growing German budget deficit. This was a very important matter on which the parties differed radically at the start of the negotiations, yet had to agree a joint policy on before they could go into government together.

While party leaders who are thinking about going into government together must always come to some agreement about how to resolve their policy differences, the way in which this agreement is made public differs from case to case. Sometimes it is published as an explicit, comprehensive and formal joint programme of government, although data collected by Strøm *et al.* (2008) for post-war western European coalition cabinets suggest that this happens in only about 40 per cent of all cases. Sometimes it may be a less comprehensive and/or more informal agreement disseminated via press releases and briefings. Sometimes (according to Strøm *et al.* for about 10 per cent of coalition cabinets), there is no explicit agreement at all, although, even in this event, an *implicit* policy agreement between the parties manifests itself in the policy proposals that emerge from the government once the legislature is in session. However this is manifested, some form of agreement between coalition partners is always arrived at. Leaders of different parties cannot go into government together if they expect to fall out immediately over the crucial joint policy decisions they will surely have to make. While there are obviously no hard data on this, most of the time, when party leaders are engaged in extended negotiations over government formation, they are not talking about how to share out the cabinet portfolios; they are talking about how to reconcile their policy differences.

## 12.2.6 Choosing a set of cabinet ministers

Forming a government involves, almost by definition, choosing the senior politicians who will hold cabinet portfolios. This chosen set of cabinet ministers must be acceptable to a majority of legislators, if the government is to gain and retain office. The set of proposed cabinet ministers is therefore one of the major factors that legislators take into account when deciding whether or not to support the government. Making nominations for cabinet appointments is thus one of the most important practical sources of prime ministerial power in Europe, particularly as European cabinet nominees are not subjected to the intense process of individual scrutiny and investigation faced by their US counterparts. In single-party majority cabinets the power of the prime minister to hire and fire cabinet ministers is limited only by the internal politics of the governing party (Kam, 2009). In coalition cabinets, however, each party leader typically nominates ministers to the subset of portfolios that have been allocated to his or her party during government formation negotiations. A prime minister may veto an occasional controversial nomination by another party leader, but in effect the power to choose cabinet ministers for 'their' portfolios rests with the leaders of each government party.

Since being a cabinet minister is such a difficult and important job, we might expect that only a limited set of politicians are up to it. It is here that the twin roles of the cabinet minister, as political head of a department of state and at the same time as a party representative in government, may come into conflict. Politically, cabinet ministers may be chosen for their loyalty to the party, or their ability to represent varying strands of party opinion. The vagaries of internal party politics may mean that a party leader feels compelled to include internal party opponents in the cabinet. Other leaders may choose to banish such opponents to the political wilderness and reward only loyal colleagues. Whatever political considerations are taken into account, there will be a limited set of senior party politicians that the leader wishes to appoint to cabinet positions. Over and above the incentives arising from practical politics, party leaders must also take into account the administrative ability to run a major government department, but this ability need not correspond in any way to the ability to get elected to parliament. No party leader wants to put a complete idiot in charge of a government department, since this is likely to have bad repercussions for the party as a whole, but room for manoeuvre in cabinet nominations will already be seriously limited by practical politics before administrative ability is taken into account. The process of choosing cabinet ministers, therefore, is by no means guaranteed to pick the team of people best able, in administrative terms, to run the major departments of state.

Typically, cabinet ministers are past or present parliamentarians, although this varies a lot between countries, and in some countries a minister must resign from the legislature on being appointed to the cabinet. France, Norway and the Netherlands are examples of this. At one end of the spectrum is a small group of countries, notably Britain and Ireland, in which cabinet ministers are almost always members of parliament. At the other end is a group of countries in which it is by no means necessary or even typical for cabinet ministers to be past or present parliamentarians. Austria, the Netherlands, France, Finland, Norway and Sweden are in this category, as well as a significant number of cabinets in post-transition central and eastern Europe. In the first years after transitions from communist rule, many of the new political faces were western-educated expatriates returning home, and/or opposition leaders who had been dissidents or otherwise outside the political system. Subsequently, voters in central and eastern Europe have tended to be cynical and distrustful of political elites (Mishler and Rose, 1997), providing incentives to form cabinets comprising young, western-educated and non-political technocrats, examples of which can be found in Estonia, Slovakia and Bulgaria. When cabinet ministers are not members of parliament, especially in western Europe, by far the most likely former occupation is civil servant. In the Netherlands, Sweden, Finland, Norway and France, about one-quarter of all cabinet ministers are former civil servants; elsewhere the proportion is much smaller (Blondel, 1991; Almeida et al., 2003; Dowding and Dumont, 2009).

## 12.3 Government formation

As we have seen, the typical European election does not definitively settle the matter of who forms the government, although even in a coalition system elections are often more decisive than many people realize. If members of the incumbent government want to continue in office, and if the election result makes this feasible, then the incumbent government may well be able to remain in office; no serious consideration may be given to a change of government. Table 12.2 presents some striking findings on this for western Europe, using data collected by Strøm et al. (2008). The table deals only with minority legislatures in which no single party controlled a majority of seats. It sorts government formation situations in post-war western Europe into those that immediately followed an election and those for which there was no intervening election, and thus followed a defeat or resignation of the incumbent government. When government formations immediately followed an election, we see that the incumbent cabinet and prime minister went back into office in fully one-third of all cases. In stark contrast, when government formation was taking place without an intervening election, the incumbent prime minister and parties were almost never returned to office. The situation shown in Table 12.2 is, however, quite different in central and eastern Europe, where incumbents have been so rarely returned to power, in part because of a strong pattern of anti-incumbent voting, that some authors have talked in terms of *hyperaccountability* (Roberts, 2008).

**TABLE 12.2** Government turnover with and without intervening elections

|  | Different PM and cabinet | Same PM and cabinet | Total |
|---|---|---|---|
| Post-election cabinet | 129 | 61 | 190 |
| No intervening election | 147 | 3 | 150 |
| Total | 276 | 64 | 340 |

*Source*: Replication dataset for Strøm *et al.* (2008).

This table does not of course tell us *why* the same government was often returned to office following an election, although it is quite consistent with the interpretation that government turnover *between* elections happens when legislators have some specific alternative in mind, while scheduled elections may 'automatically' trigger government formation in situations where there is no alternative to the incumbent that is also preferred by some legislative majority. What we do see unambiguously from Table 12.2 is that, election results permitting, a continuation of the status quo government is a distinct possibility.

The situation after the 2002 election in Ireland was a case in point. When the election was held, the incumbent government – formed in 1997 – was a coalition comprising the large centre-right Fianna Fáil Party and a small party, the Progressive Democrats (PDs), widely seen as having a more right-wing economic programme. This government did not in itself command a majority of the Irish parliament, the Dáil, but was kept in power by a small group of independent deputies in exchange for having the ear of government in relation to the problems of their local constituencies. The Fianna Fáil–PD coalition had presided over the 'Celtic Tiger' boom that resulted in sustained growth of the Irish economy (now a distant memory), and the two government parties fought the 2002 Dáil election on the basis that they would continue in government together if they were able to do so. When the votes were counted, they had increased their combined share of seats, now commanding a parliamentary majority between them. While some members of Fianna Fáil, now close to a parliamentary majority in its own right, might have flirted with the idea of going it alone as a one-party minority government, the outcome of the government formation process, to nobody's surprise, was that the incumbent Fianna Fáil–PD coalition government continued in office. In this particular case, Irish voters can be seen to have 'chosen' their coalition government at the parliamentary election. They had a clear opportunity to punish the incumbent coalition, and they chose not to do so.

Election results can also lead to predictable *changes* of coalition government. The Italian general election of 2008, for example, followed the collapse of the centre-left government led by Romano Prodi, and was fought between two rival electoral coalitions. An electoral coalition on the centre right was led by former prime minister Silvio Berlusconi, and linked a new party, Il Popolo della Libertà, itself a merger of Forza Italia and Alleanza Nazionale, to the strongly regionalist party Lega Nord. An opposing party, the Partito Democratico, had been forged by merging several smaller parties on the centre left, and was led by Walter Veltroni. The centre-left coalition in effect fought the 2008 election as the incumbent with an agreed candidate for prime minister, on the basis that they would continue in government if able to do so. The centre-right cartel of parties fought the 2008 election as an alternative government, also led by an agreed candidate for prime minister in Silvio Berlusconi. In this case, therefore, Italian voters had a clear choice between two possible government coalitions when they went to the polls, and in the event chose Berlusconi's centre-right government. Italian voters had spoken, and had played a big part in changing their government, even in a political system with a large number of parties. On the effect of pre-electoral coalitions on government formation, see Golder (2005, 2006).

Thus we should not get too bewitched by the idea that the battle for political control in most European countries is settled, not by voters, but by party leaders wheeling and dealing in smoke-filled rooms. Even in countries where coalition governments are an established part of the political landscape, election results may be politically decisive, and voters may have a direct say in government formation. They may confirm an incumbent coalition in office, as in Ireland in 2002, or they may make it possible for a prearranged coalition in opposition to take over the reins of power, as in Italy in 2008. Notwithstanding this, and going to the constitutional heart of the matter in European parliamentary democracies, the final say in government formation always lies with elected politicians, not voters. Whatever the election result, no government can form without an agreement between senior politicians. Once formed, any government can fall if this agreement collapses. The constitutional and political bedrock is that the government remains in office as long as, but no longer than, a majority of parliamentarians prefer it to any feasible alternative. This means that the way politicians feel about the precise composition of any putative government is an absolutely vital matter. Before we can tell a sensible story about how European politicians set out to bargain their way into government, and before we can discuss the factors that Europe's parliamentarians take into account when trying to decide which government to support, we must consider what it is that motivates these people.

### 12.3.1 Office-seeking politicians?

As we have seen, each European government comprises a cabinet led by a prime minister. The prime minister is typically, although not invariably, leader of one of the main political parties. Thus, in order to become a prime minister, it is almost always necessary first to become a party leader, a fact that adds much of the fire and brimstone to leadership contests in European political parties, discussed in Chapter 10 above. After the prime ministership, cabinet ministries are the most powerful political offices in the land. A seat at the cabinet table represents the pinnacle of a political career for most successful politicians. Cabinet ministers are typically, although not invariably, senior party legislators, though who is or is not 'senior' in a political party is a far less clear-cut matter than who is the party leader. Indeed, a party leader can turn colleagues into senior politicians at the stroke of a pen, by nominating them to the cabinet.

The fact that the positions of prime minister and cabinet minister are such glittering political prizes provides one distinctive perspective on the making and breaking of governments in modern Europe. This perspective sees politicians as being interested mainly in the *intrinsic* rewards of office. To be a cabinet minister, after all, is to be a famous and powerful person. The desire for such fame and power, for the 'smell of the leather' in the ministerial car, may well be the most important motivation for many politicians, even if few would ever admit this openly or even to themselves. In many ways, achieving high office is in itself the mark of 'success' in any political career.

### 12.3.2 Policy-oriented politicians?

Another important set of reasons for trying to get into government has to do with influencing public policy. If politicians want to make a difference to public policy, the most effective way they can do this is to get into the cabinet. This motivation, of course, is far more acceptable to the wider political world than naked political ambition, and is the objective most politicians promote in public. Few politicians, whatever their real hopes and fears, look for votes on the grounds that what they want to do if elected is make lots of money, get their picture in the newspaper every day, ride around in the back seat of a chauffeur-driven limousine, and have a large staff to boss around. Most European politicians, like their US counterparts, campaign on the basis of promises about all the good that they can do for their country if voters put them in a position of power. They usually claim that they don't want all of this power for its own sake, but rather in order to implement cherished and lofty policy objectives for the benefit of everyone.

The desire to consume the intrinsic rewards of office and the desire to have an impact on public policy are quite different plausible motivations for the politicians involved in the making and breaking of governments (Müller and Strøm, 1999). As we now show, however, different interpretations of government formation in modern Europe flow from these alternative assumptions about what motivates politicians.

### 12.3.3 Office-seeking politicians and 'minimal winning' governments

Perhaps the best-known approach to analysing government formation in modern Europe is based on the assumption that politicians are driven above all else by the desire to enjoy the rewards of office for their own sake. This approach leads to predictions that the governments that form will be just enough to take the prize and no bigger, that 'minimal winning' cabinets are likely to be the European norm. Minimal winning cabinets carry no passengers; they include only parties whose seats are essential to maintain the government's parliamentary majority.

The logic of this argument is straightforward. If being in government is valued in and for itself, then the set of cabinet positions is like a fixed sack of trophies to be shared out by the winners of the government-formation game. Any cabinet party whose votes are not essential to the government's parliamentary majority will be enjoying some of these scarce trophies without contributing any of the political resources needed both to capture them and to hold on to them. Office-seeking politicians are likely to exclude such 'passenger' parties from the cabinet. This logic implies that government coalitions should comprise as few parties as possible, consistent with the need to win confidence votes in the legislature. The result is a minimal winning government. If a government does indeed include parties whose seats are not needed for its legislative majority, then it is called an *oversized* or *surplus majority* government. Both names, of course, suggest the rather curious, and as we shall see unwarranted, implication that some governments can in some sense have too much support. Nonetheless, if a cabinet includes a party whose votes are not essential to keeping the government in office, then we do have to ask what else this party is contributing. The notion of the minimal winning cabinet thus provides a useful basis from which to start thinking about the making and breaking of European governments. For reviews of 'office-driven' models of government formation, see Laver (1998) and Laver and Schofield (1998). In a careful and widely cited empirical review by Martin and Stevenson of the formation of various types of government in parliamentary democracies, furthermore, one of the headline conclusions is that 'it is immediately clear ... that minimal winning theory is a significant improvement on the intuitive idea that majority cabinets are more likely to form than cabinets that control only a minority of legislative seats' (Martin and Stevenson, 2001: 41). In short, there is a systematic tendency for real governments to contain sufficient parties to allow them to control a legislative party, but no more than this. This effect remains even after controlling for policy differences between the partners in government (see below), and does indeed suggest that politicians have office pay-offs on their minds when they bargain over government formation.

The office-seeking assumption about the motivations of politicians also provides the basis for a number of *power indices*, which measure the extent to which parties can exploit their bargaining positions in the legislature. Two well-known power indices are the *Shapley-Shubik* and *Banzhaf* indices, each named after their inventors. Such power indices have been the subject of intense and ongoing intellectual controversy (Albert, 2003). Nonetheless, the intuition behind them all is that they help highlight ways in which the distribution of bargaining power can sometimes differ quite starkly from the distribution of seats in the legislature. One classic example occurs when there are two large parties, each falling somewhat short of a parliamentary majority, with the balance of power held by a much smaller party. Imagine a legislature in which two parties win about 45 per cent of the seats, and a smaller party wins about 10 per cent. In this situation, and if politicians are concerned above all else to get into office, the political facts of life are that neither of the two large parties can take power on its own, but that any two parties can take power as a coalition. All three parties have equal bargaining power despite their unequal size, giving the smaller party a level of power quite disproportionate to its size. This is actually quite similar to a situation that often arose in pre-unification Germany, with the much smaller Free Democrat Party holding the balance of power in this sense. This allowed the Free Democrats to be a maker and breaker of German governments despite their small size, and indeed to be in most post-war German coalition cabinets, often with the more coveted cabinet portfolios.

### 12.3.4 Policy-oriented politicians and ideologically compact governments

If the politicians who make and break governments want to leave their mark on public policy rather than merely consume the fruits of office, this generates a different interpretation of government formation. Public policy applies to everybody – to those who are in government and those who are not, to voters and non-voters alike. Crucially, public policy cannot in any sense be 'used up' at a faster rate if there are more parties in the government. Thus the defence policy of any given country is a policy that applies to all who live there, whether they are in the government or outside it, citizens or politicians. If more people join the government, the policy is in no sense diluted; it is no better and no worse than it was before. Those who want a major change in defence policy will be delighted when this happens, whether they are in or out of office at the time.

If politicians are driven by nothing but the desire to affect public policy when they set out to bargain their way into government, then the logic of minimal winning cabinets is eroded. If some other politician shares your policies, then there is no reason in the world, if all you care about is policy, to keep this person out of office. This approach suggests that the cabinets that take office will contain parties whose policies are as compatible as possible. They will be ideologically compact in the sense that cabinet parties will tend to be closer together, rather than further apart, in their ideological positions. In the extreme, if parties care only about policy, then this should lead to cabinets that are so compact that they comprise only a single party, even a very small one, with a very central policy position. If the other parties do not care at all about getting into office, then they may regard the policies of this very central government as being better than those of any other government that is likely to form. They may thus allow the central party to take power on its own and implement its policy programme. As we shall soon see, this logic underpins the formation of the minority governments that are common in modern Europe.

It is obviously rather extreme to assume either that politicians care only about feathering their own nests or that they care only about the good of the country. The truth is probably somewhere in between, and some accounts of the politics of government formation in modern Europe are based on the assumption that politicians care both about getting into office for its own sake and also about having an impact on public policy. This leads to predictions that minimal winning governments will tend to form, because office motivations are important, but that these will be ideologically compact, because policy is also important. This leads in turn to the prediction that *minimal connected winning* cabinets will form; these are cabinets comprising parties that are adjacent to each other in policy terms, and which cannot lose a party off either 'end' without losing their majority. Figures 12.1 to 12.3 later in this chapter give examples of these.

Many authors have constructed *policy-driven* models of government formation in modern Europe. These differ in a number of important respects, although most assume that there is more to policy-driven government formation than a single left–right dimension of public policy. Other policy dimensions that might have a bearing upon government formation in particular countries include foreign policy, environmental policy, and the liberal–conservative dimension of social and moral policy on matters such as abortion or gay marriage. Some models of government formation focus more or less exclusively on the policy positions of the political parties and their relative strengths in the electorate and/or legislature (Schofield, 2008). Others focus more on institutional features of the government formation process, including: the order in which parties are chosen to be *formateurs* (Baron, 1991); the vote of confidence procedure (Strøm, 1990; Huber, 1996); and the need to allocate control of particular policy areas to particular cabinet ministers (Laver and Shepsle, 1996) and junior ministers (Thies, 2001). Looking at more behavioural matters, Carrubba and Volden focus on the need for coalition partners to put together 'log-rolls', whereby one partner makes concessions in policy areas that are lower on its list of priorities, in exchange for concessions from a coalition partner on policy areas much closer to its heart (Carrubba and Volden, 2001; Volden and Carrubba, 2004). A common feature of most of these models is a predicted tendency for coalition governments to adopt positions relatively close to the centre of whichever policy dimensions are salient, and this is indeed a strong empirical pattern (Martin and Stevenson, 2001). The net result is that government formation in a coalition system is likely to produce government policies that are less extreme than the policies of many parties winning seats in the legislature. In this important sense, the politics of coalition may well have a moderating effect on public policy outputs.

### 12.3.5  Minority governments

At first sight the idea of a minority government, made up of parties whose members do not themselves control a majority of seats in parliament, seems at best a paradox and at worst downright undemocratic. If there is a minority government, after all, there must be a majority opposition in parliament. In the typical European country with a PR electoral system, furthermore, this majority opposition will have been supported in the most recent election by a majority of voters. This opposition controls enough seats in parliament to bring down the government but, for some reason, chooses not to do so. When there is a minority government, furthermore, a cabinet has taken office with no parliamentary guarantee that it can stay there for any length of time, because it can be defeated at any moment at the pleasure of the opposition. Yet Kaare Strøm has argued convincingly that minority governments should be seen as a normal and 'democratic' outcome of the process of representative government in modern Europe, rather than as a sign of its failure (Strøm, 1990).

The main reason why minority governments are so common has to do with the role of party policy. If politicians are driven solely by the desire to get into power, then it is hard to see why they would languish in opposition when they have the muscle to force their way into government and take control of the spoils of office. If politicians care about policy outcomes, however, there may well be circumstances in which their policy objectives are better served from a seat on the opposition benches than one at the cabinet table. This is why Strøm looked at the influence over policy that can be wielded by the opposition, and in particular at influence exercised via the legislative committee system. This influence arises because it is actually quite rare for big decisions on important policy issues to be slugged out on the floor of the legislature. Many more political wars are waged in committees. As we saw in Chapter 3, different European countries differ considerably in terms of the effectiveness of their committee systems and the policy influence that committees give the opposition. The more powerful the committee system and the greater the influence of the opposition, the lower the incentives for opposition parties to get into the government. When there are lower incentives to get into government, there is a greater likelihood of minority governments.

Perhaps the clearest and most universal explanation of the ability of minority cabinets to stay in power, however, is based on policy divisions within the opposition. On this account, a minority government can survive, and can be quite stable, if the opposition parties are sufficiently divided on policy that they cannot agree on a specific replacement. Although control over a parliamentary majority guarantees victory, failure to control a majority does not spell inevitable defeat if the opposition is divided. If some party has a sufficiently central policy position that it can split every possible winning coalition of its political opponents in this way, it can form a viable minority government. Laver and Shepsle (1996) call this a *very strong* party; its strength derives from the fact that any government that excludes it is likely to be defeated on policy grounds in favour of a minority government comprising just the very strong party. In such a situation, a very strong party obviously can credibly demand to be allowed to govern alone, even in a minority position, a conclusion for which Martin and Stevenson (2001:48) found systematic empirical support.

This logic may well underwrite a number of minority governments formed by the Social Democrats in Denmark, for example, in political situations where a party with an ideological position close to the centre of the ideological spectrum won considerably less than a majority of seats but faced a divided opposition. Some of the opposing parties were to the left; some to the right. As a result of this ideological positioning of the parties, it was difficult to envisage a coalition of ideologically diverse opponents that could somehow combine to evict the Social Democrats in favour of an alternative they could all agree on. Because it was very difficult for this reason to evict the strong centre party from office, this party was in a very powerful bargaining position and could well have decided to go it alone. Even without a majority it could not be beaten. Indeed, the ability of a particular party to go it alone as a minority government, in the face of a divided opposition, is one of the acid tests of real bargaining power in the making and breaking of governments.

## 12.3.6 Surplus majority governments

Just as some cabinets may be able to survive with less than a parliamentary majority, others may include parties whose seats are not crucial to the government's majority in the legislature. There may be several reasons for the formation of such *surplus majority* or *oversized* governments.

Immediately after the Second World War, for example, governments of *national unity* were formed in many western European countries, with the idea of involving all sections of society in the huge job of post-war reconstruction. These were typically 'grand' coalitions comprising all, or nearly all, major parties. Examples can be found in Austria, Belgium, Finland, France, Germany, Italy, Luxembourg and the Netherlands. In most cases, and perhaps somewhat surprisingly in the circumstances, these grand coalitions tended to be short-lived. 'Normal' party competition soon re-established itself, and government formation quickly came to involve some parties going into power and consigning others to the opposition. A similar pattern can be seen in the founding governments that were formed at the beginning of the transitions to democracy in central and eastern Europe. There was a strong tendency, not for grand coalitions of all parties, but certainly for oversized coalitions involving more parties than were needed to control a parliamentary majority. Although long-term trends have yet to emerge over the short period since the start of post-communist transitions in the early 1990s, there does seem to be some movement away from surplus-majority governments, as party competition in central and eastern Europe becomes consolidated.

Moving beyond post-war or post-communist transitions, one reason why we find surplus majority governments in long-established party systems has to do with the constitution. Different countries have different requirements for constitutional amendments but, as we saw in Chapter 4, one such requirement involves winning a *qualified* majority vote in the legislature. This is a majority of more than 50 per cent of legislators – two-thirds or three-quarters, for example. If constitutional reform is on the political agenda in such settings, a cabinet may need a legislative majority of more than 50 per cent. Additional parties may then be included in the cabinet in order to achieve this higher threshold. In Belgium, for example, divisions between the two main language communities have resulted in constitutional requirements that any law affecting relations between the communities requires the assent of a majority in each language group, and two-thirds of legislators overall. This means that Belgian cabinets may sometimes need a two-thirds legislative majority in order to govern effectively. Such cabinets may superficially look oversized, but they are in practice no larger than legally necessary in the circumstances.

Other benefits may arise from carrying 'passengers' in cabinet coalitions, especially for a large government party. Once a government has taken office, any party that is crucial to the government's majority can bring down the entire executive by withdrawing its support. If their votes are critical to the government majority, even tiny parties have a potent threat with which to try squeezing concessions from their cabinet colleagues. To forestall this possibility, a large party may choose to surround itself with a protective screen of weaker 'passengers' so that no single other party is critical to the cabinet's parliamentary majority. In this event, none of the weaker passengers can make serious demands once the government has formed, because every one of them is expendable. To put it rather crudely, powerful parties might actually choose to carry passengers so that one or two can be tossed overboard without too much fuss if they start to get greedy.

This argument was recently elaborated by Carruba and Volden, who studied the need for governments to get diverse packages of policy proposals through the legislature (Carrubba and Volden, 2001; Volden and Carrubba, 2004). This means that government parties will have to do 'log-rolling' deals with each other. Party A concedes to Party B on some issue it opposes but does not care too much about. It does this in exchange for a concession from Party B to Party A on a matter that Party B opposes but is close to Party A's heart. Each party benefits from log-rolling like this – getting its way on what it cares most about by giving way on what it cares less about. Any policy agreement between prospective coalition partners can be seen as a log-rolling deal of this type. These deals are not put into practice, however, in a single giant 'omnibus' law that deals with absolutely everything, but in a *sequence of legislative proposals*. This means that any log-roll underpinning a coalition cabinet is vulnerable to defections by parties that achieve their objectives early in the sequence. Once way to minimize the risk of this is to put together an oversized government, which reduces the incentive of any one member to defect, since the government can remain in office and continue to implement its policy programme, even after such a defection.

Surplus majority governments are therefore easier to understand than it might seem at first sight. As we shall shortly see, they are also quite common in practice, particularly in the former communist states of central and eastern Europe. Drawing together the various possible explanations that have been set out above, we can come to a conclusion quite similar to the one that we came to for minority governments – that policy is important in government formation. Almost all of the theoretical ways in which we make sense of surplus majority governments have to do, one way or another, with the desire of potential members of the government to fulfil their policy objectives. This is true whether these objectives reflect what politicians feel deeply in their hearts about policy, or whether they reflect a more pragmatic desire to redeem policy pledges made to voters at the previous election.

### 12.3.7  A minimal winning cabinet in Germany

We shall shortly be looking at the types of representative government that form right across modern Europe, but the best way to get a feel for this is to look at some specific examples. We begin with a straightforward and instructive example of a minimal winning cabinet. The top part of Figure 12.1 provides some information about the situation in Germany following the general election of 27 September 2009. This resulted in the five parties represented being in the parliament that was given the job of choosing a government. The policy positions of these parties are placed on a general left–right dimension capturing most aspects of policy. The number of seats won by each party, out of a total of 622, is also given. The ordering of party positions on

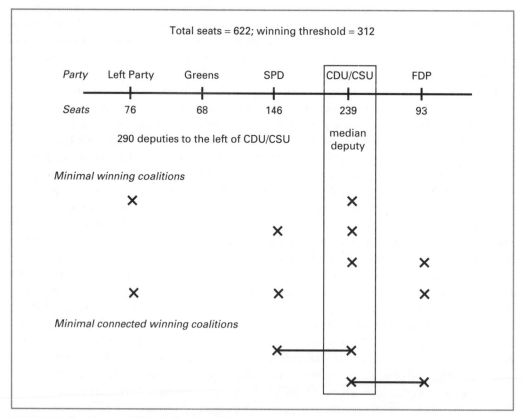

**FIGURE 12.1**  Coalition possibilities in Germany, 2009

economic policy is taken from a collection of expert surveys of party positions in a wide range of countries (Benoit and Laver, 2006). From left to right, the parties involved were the Left Party, Greens, the Social Democrats (SPD), the Christian Democrats (CDU/CSU), and the Free Democrats (FDP). The incumbent government at the time of the election was a coalition between the SPD and the CDU/CSU, led by the CDU leader Angela Merkel.

The essential parliamentary arithmetic of government formation in Germany after the 2009 election, which determined the different ways to put together a parliamentary majority of 312 seats, is shown in the bottom part of Figure 12.1. Leaving party policy positions completely on one side, the four minimal winning coalitions are listed. There are three minimal winning coalitions involving the CDU/CSU, which can join with the Left Party, the SPD or the FDP. There is also a minimal winning coalition excluding the CDU/CSU. Obviously, any other party or parties could be added to each minimal winning coalition to create surplus majority coalitions. Minority governments would comprise less than the minimal winning coalitions, but minority governments still need to win votes of confidence: they thus need the explicit or implicit support of a majority coalition in the legislature, even if the cabinet partners themselves do not constitute a majority.

One thing is very striking about German government formation in 2009: the Greens were members of no minimal winning coalition. The 2009 German parliamentary arithmetic put the Greens, with 68 seats, in a *very* different bargaining position from that of the Left Party, only slightly larger at 76 seats. Quite simply, the Greens were not an *essential* member of *any* parliamentary majority and, in the indelicate language of government formation studies, were a *dummy* party likely to be to watching government formation from the sidelines. A dummy party in a multiparty system is the equivalent of the losing party in a two-party system, with no direct leverage over the making and breaking of governments. We also see quite clearly how bargaining leverage in government formation can be quite disproportional. The three medium-sized parties won quite different seat totals at the election: the Left Party won 76 seats, the SPD won 146 seats, and the FDP won 93 seats. Yet these parties were all substitutes for each other in the brutal arithmetic of forming a government. What is sometimes known as the *decisive structure* of government formation was that the Christian Democrats could choose any one of the three medium-sized parties as a partner in a majority coalition, or all three of them could combine to keep the Christian Democrats out of office.

If party policy is important in government formation, as it usually is, then we also need to consider policy differences between the parties in the various potential governments. Looking at the bottom part of Figure 12.1 again, we see that there were two minimal connected winning coalition cabinets after the 2009 German election. These were coalitions comprising only parties that were adjacent to each other on the left–right scale. Both of these involved the Christian Democrats, who could combine to form a minimal connected winning cabinet with either the SPD to the left of the FDP to the right. The other two minimal winning cabinets did not comprise ideologically adjacent parties – and such cabinets may be considered less likely to form than those comprising parties whose policy positions are closer together.

Notice that the CDU/CSU were in an especially powerful position following the 2009 election, by virtue of the fact that they controlled the 'median' legislator on the key left–right dimension of economic policy. Counting legislators from the left or the right of the scale, the median legislator is the person who turns a losing coalition into a winning one. Since 312 legislators are needed for a winning coalition, the 290 legislators to the left of the CDU/CSU need to be supplemented by some from that party. Likewise, the 93 legislators to the right of the CDU/ CDU require the addition of most of the Christian Democrat deputies before they control a majority. As we shall see in another context, the fact that the Christian Democrats controlled the median legislator means that they could possibly have formed a minority government without co-operating with any other party. This is because there is neither a majority on the left, nor on the right, that can agree on an alternative that they prefer to the policy position of CDU/ CSU. However, as we saw in Table 12.1, there is an important constitutional provision in Germany called the *constructive vote of no confidence*, which requires the motion of no confidence in the government that is passed by a majority of the legislature to specify a successor to the incumbent government. This is designed to make minority governments much less likely, and indeed there has been no minority government in post-war Germany.

Given all of this, and assuming that the diverse party policy positions are important in the formation of German governments, the leader of the CDU/CSU was in pole position, and was essentially able to choose whether she preferred the SPD or the FDP as a coalition partner. Since the outgoing government had been a somewhat fraught coalition between the CDU and SPD, Angela Merkel choose the FDP and succeeded in forming a coalition cabinet with them, albeit after a period of fairly intense negotiations over a joint policy platform for the new government.

### 12.3.8 Minority cabinets in Norway

As we have seen, while any government does need to win confidence votes in parliament if it is to stay in power, the parties in the cabinet do not themselves need to control a legislative majority, and may instead form a minority administration. This is what happened after the September 1997 general election in Norway. Some information on the Norwegian party system after this election is given in the top part of Figure 12.2. Once more, party positions on a left–right dimension are shown, as estimated by the Benoit-Laver expert survey, together with legislative seat totals. Ranging from left to right, the parties are the Socialist Left, Labour, Centre Party, Christian People's Party (KrF), Liberals, Progress Party, and Conservatives. A complicating factor that does not show up in this figure is that the Progress Party had controversial policies on certain issues, notably immigration policy, which meant it was not seen as an acceptable partner in government by parties of either the centre left or the centre right.

The traditional pattern of government formation in Norway over most of the post-war era had been an alternation in power between two blocs of the centre right and the centre left. Centre-right governments were coalitions of medium-sized and small parties, anchored by the Conservatives. Centre-left Norwegian governments were typically single-party Labour administrations, often kept in office on the basis of outside support from other left-wing parties. The outgoing government in 1997 was a single-party minority administration controlled by the Labour Party. While the Norwegian economy was in good shape, it quickly became clear that the incumbent Labour Party was not doing well in the opinion polls. While the right as a whole remained divided over the controversial issue of EU membership, an issue that had dominated Norwegian politics in the 1990s, the three parties of the centre – Liberals, KrF and Centre Party – announced their intention to form a government should Labour be defeated.

When the election results were declared, it became clear that the two left-wing parties had dropped to their lowest combined level of support since 1936 and, with 74 seats, not only fell well short of the 83 seats required to form a government but also faced a majority centre-right

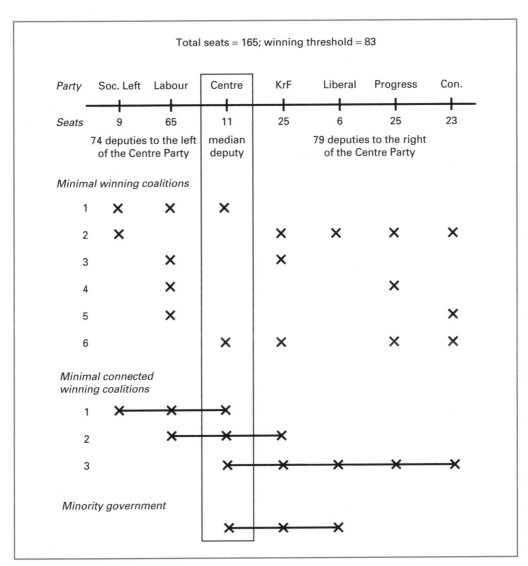

**FIGURE 12.2** Coalition possibilities in Norway, 1997

opposition with enough votes to defeat them at every turn. The Labour government resigned. The bottom part of Figure 12.2 shows that the arithmetic of coalition formation in Norway after this election was quite complicated, with six different possible minimal winning coalitions and three minimal connected winning coalitions. The small Centre Party now controlled the median legislator, albeit with only 11 seats of the 165 in the legislature. This put the Centre Party in pole position during negotiations over government formation, and it is in theory possible that it could have formed a minority administration all on its own, albeit with such a tiny number of deputies that its general legitimacy might well have been called into question. This is because there was neither a legislative majority to the left, nor to the right, of the Centre Party that could agree on some alternative.

In the event, the government that formed was the small centrist coalition proposed during the election campaign, a coalition that fell far short of a parliamentary majority and excluded the traditional anchor of right-wing governments in Norway, the Conservative Party. Indeed, the administration that took over the government in October 1997 controlled only 42 of the 165 seats in the Norwegian legislature. Divisions within the right had thus broken the typical pattern of two-bloc politics in Norway. This minority government conformed very closely to the pattern of a small government at the centre of the party system that could continue in office because it divided the opposition. In order to defeat it, parties from both the right and the left of the minority government had to be able to agree upon some alternative. In effect, both Labour and the Conservatives had to find something that they both liked better than the incumbent minority government, an unlikely prospect. Led by Kjell Magne Bondevik of the Christian People's Party, this government lasted three years, despite controlling far less than a majority of parliamentary seats, before being forced to resign in March 2000 after losing a vote of confidence in the Norwegian parliament. It was replaced in March by another minority government, this time led by Jens Stoltenberg of the Labour Party, which stayed in office until the next scheduled elections in September 2001. These elections resulted in heavy losses for Labour and significant gains for the Conservatives, opening the way for Bondevik to form his second centre-right minority administration, this time including the Conservatives, a minority government that stayed in office for a full four-year term that lasted until the scheduled parliamentary elections of September 2005.

### 12.3.9 Surplus majority cabinets in Italy

Just as cabinets can sometimes be stable while controlling less than a majority of legislative seats, they may sometimes include more members than are strictly needed in order to control the legislature. This may be because the government needs a qualified majority of more than 50 per cent for certain vital votes, as in Belgium, or there may be less tangible political considerations. Italy, for example, has a long tradition of surplus majority coalitions, one of which formed in May 1994. As we saw in Chapter 7, Italian politics had been thrown into convulsions prior to the 1994 election by serious corruption scandals that undermined each of the main traditional parties. Many traditional parties declined dramatically or disappeared altogether, while many new parties had formed. In an attempt to produce a more stable party system, the electoral system had been reformed to one in which 75 per cent of all seats were allocated in single-seat constituencies on a first-past-the-post basis, while the remaining 25 per cent were allocated in regional constituencies using list-PR. The new system created very strong incentives for the formation of pre-electoral coalitions of parties. This was because, in order to avoid electoral disaster, *cartels* of parties needed to get together to decide which of them would fight which single-seat constituency.

The result of all this, for the 1994 election, was that while at least 15 different parties contested the PR element of the election, three party cartels formed to contest the single-seat constituencies. These were the Freedom Pole, the centrist Pact for Italy, and the Progressive Alliance on the left. In the event, the election was won by the set of parties comprising right-wing Freedom Pole, with media mogul Silvio Berlusconi, founder of the new party Forza Italia, as its candidate for prime minister. The list of possible minimal winning coalitions in this complex setting was immense. However, there were only three possible minimal connected winning coalitions. Two of these involved a large number of parties, while the third involved the three larger parties of the right – Forza Italia, Lega Nord and Alleanza Nazionale. A government based on the Freedom Pole, with Berlusconi at its head, did in fact take office after 12 days of hard bargaining. The government was remarkable in a number of ways. None of the main parties had been in government before, and Alleanza Nazionale was a party that could trace its traditions back to Italy's wartime fascists. Forza Italia was a brand new, media-driven party, while Lega Nord was driven mainly by the demand for greater autonomy for northern Italy. These three parties between them controlled a legislative majority but, despite this, two smaller parties that had also been part of the right-wing electoral cartel were given seats in the cabinet. These were the UdC and CCD, both splinters from the former Christian Democrats. Neither of these parties was needed to keep the government in office in terms of legislative seats, but both nonetheless formed part of this surplus majority administration.

As we shall see when discussing Table 12.6, surplus majority governments, despite having additional legislative support, tend on average to last less long than those with bare majorities. This may be the case because those political circumstances that encourage a prospective government to take on surplus partners may well be more troubled, and thus unstable, than the norm. As it happens, this particular surplus majority government did not last long. A number of serious divisions quickly opened up between Lega Nord and Forza Italia. Among other things, these concerned the issues of federalism – a fundamental matter for Lega Nord – as well as the fight against corruption and antitrust legislation, the latter very sensitive, given Berlusconi's dominant position in the Italian media. The government ceased to be viable after the withdrawal of the Lega Nord, a pivotal rather than a surplus member of the coalition whose votes were essential to its survival. Facing a motion of no confidence that he would surely have lost, Silvio Berlusconi resigned in late December 1994.

## 12.4 Types of government in modern Europe

Although the preceding case studies give us a feel for types of government that form in modern Europe, they cannot give us a systematic picture of this. Table 12.3 summarizes the types of government that have formed since the Second World War in a wide range of European countries. Looking first at the bottom line, we see a wide diversity of government types. Only about 13 per cent of governments are single-party majority administrations, with this type of government typical in Britain and Greece, which both have electoral systems highly likely to produce single-party parliamentary majorities even when no single party wins a majority of the popular vote. Single-party majority governments in modern Europe thus tend to be artefacts of particular electoral systems. About one-third of the large number of governments categorized were minimal winning coalitions, and this type of government can be found in virtually every European country, even in Britain following the May 2010 election. Taking these two types of government together, under half of European administrations are conventional majority cabinets, in the sense that the government parties control a parliamentary majority between them, but there are no surplus members whose votes are not needed for this. Conversely, well over half of the governments analysed either had too few parties to control a majority, or had more parties than they needed to do so.

Over one-third of post-war European cabinets were minority administrations. The body of the table also shows that minority governments tend to be especially common in certain countries, in particular in Scandinavia and Italy. Another pattern that emerges is that, in western though not central and eastern Europe, single-party minority governments are far more common than minority coalitions. This gives some support to the view that many minority governments may be

**TABLE 12.3** Types of government in modern Europe, 1945–2010

| Country | Single-party majority | Minimal winning coalition | Surplus majority coalition | Single-party minority | Minority coalition | Total |
|---|---|---|---|---|---|---|
| *Western Europe* | | | | | | |
| Austria | 4 | 18 | 2 | 1 | | 25 |
| Belgium | 3 | 15 | 16 | 2 | 2 | 38 |
| Denmark | | 4 | | 14 | 17 | 35 |
| Finland | | 7 | 24 | 4 | 6 | 41 |
| France | 1 | 7 | 11 | 5 | 2 | 26 |
| Germany | 1 | 20 | 5 | 3 | | 29 |
| Greece | 11 | 1 | 1 | 1 | | 14 |
| Iceland | | 22 | 4 | 4 | 1 | 31 |
| Ireland | 6 | 8 | | 6 | 5 | 25 |
| Italy | | 4 | 27 | 14 | 9 | 54 |
| Luxembourg | | 18 | 1 | | | 19 |
| Netherlands | | 12 | 10 | | 3 | 25 |
| Norway | 6 | 5 | | 13 | 6 | 30 |
| Portugal | 3 | 5 | 3 | 5 | | 16 |
| Spain | 3 | | | 8 | | 11 |
| Sweden | 2 | 6 | | 18 | 2 | 28 |
| United Kingdom | 22 | 1 | | 1 | | 24 |
| Total | 62 | 153 | 104 | 99 | 53 | 471 |
| Per cent | 13.2 | 32.5 | 22.1 | 21.0 | 11.3 | 100.0 |
| *Central and Eastern Europe* | | | | | | |
| Bulgaria | 2 | 2 | 1 | 2 | 1 | 7 |
| Czech Republic | | 4 | | 2 | 3 | 9 |
| Estonia | | 7 | | 2 | 1 | 10 |
| Hungary | | 4 | 4 | 1 | | 9 |
| Latvia | | 5 | 5 | | 8 | 18 |
| Lithuania | 2 | 3 | 3 | | 3 | 11 |
| Poland | | 7 | 1 | 3 | 5 | 16 |
| Romania | | 1 | 4 | 2 | 6 | 13 |
| Slovakia | | 5 | 1 | 1 | 3 | 10 |
| Slovenia | | 4 | 2 | | 3 | 9 |
| Total | 4 | 42 | 21 | 13 | 33 | 112 |
| Per cent | 3.6 | 37.5 | 18.8 | 11.6 | 29.5 | 100.0 |
| *Europe total* | 66 | 195 | 125 | 112 | 86 | 583 |
| *Europe per cent* | 11.3 | 33.4 | 21.4 | 19.2 | 14.8 | 100.0 |

*Note*: In all cases the number of governments is counted for the period after democratization.

*Source*: Western Europe: Comparative Parliamentary Democracy Archive (www.pol.umu.se/ccpd) assembled for Strøm *et al.* (2008), updated with annual Data Yearbooks of the *European Journal of Political Research,* and authors' calculations. Eastern Europe: Conrad and Golder (2010) and authors' calculations.

formed around particular strong parties with relatively central policy positions, which have the implication that, even though they do not command a majority on their own, they do not need coalition partners in order to be able to form a government.

Table 12.3 shows that surplus majority governments are also very common in modern Europe, east and west, although such governments tend to be concentrated in a small number of countries, notably Finland, France and Italy. Over 20 per cent of cabinets were oversized, containing more members than they need for a majority. Many of the French oversized governments occurred during the French Fourth Republic, when party discipline was notoriously poor, and governments needed a wide margin of legislative safety to be able to govern. Low party discipline may also account for many of the earlier Italian oversized governments, although as we have seen a more recent explanation could well have to do with the incentive under Italy's new electoral system to form pre-electoral cartels of parties that then go into government together as a group.

We can also see that the types of government formed in the eastern European EU accession states following their first open elections conform to broadly the same patterns as their western European neighbours, although conventional single-party or minimal winning cabinets tend to be somewhat rarer (at about 41 per cent) in eastern than in western Europe (about 46 per cent). In general, there are notably fewer single-party governments, and more minority coalitions, in central and eastern Europe. One explanation for this may be that the new eastern European party systems are still in a state of flux – often having a large number of parties with many party splits, fusions and reincarnations, as well as considerable movement of politicians between parties. Perhaps the best-known example of this phenomenon can be seen in the aftermath of the 1991 election in Poland, in which 29 different parties won seats in the 460-seat parliament, with the biggest single party winning no more than 13 per cent of these. Table 12.4 shows the distribution of seats between parties in the Polish parliament after this election, setting what amounted to an almost insoluble puzzle in the parliamentary arithmetic of how to put together a stable government majority. In the event, the government that formed was a minority coalition involving PC, PSL, PL and ZChN – four medium-sized parties from the right of centre – under the premiership of Jan Olszewski from the PC. This survived about six months before being defeated in the legislature. Blondel and Müller-Rommel (2001) provide a series of country reports on government formation in eastern Europe. See also Müller-Rommel et al. (2004) and Conrad and Golder (2010).

Overall, however, Table 12.3 tells a very clear story that, while cabinets do need to win the support of legislative majorities if they are to be able to govern in a parliamentary democracy, the government parties by themselves do not need to control a majority of seats. Both oversized and minority cabinets are clearly quite normal results of government formation in modern Europe.

## 12.5 The allocation of cabinet portfolios

As we saw in Chapter 2, the cabinet is the key organ of government in most European countries, acting both as a committee for making decisions in the name of the entire government and as a collection of individuals with responsibility for making and implementing policy in particular areas. It may come as something of a surprise to people who think of elections and parliaments as being at the heart of representative democracy to find that most important policy decisions do not require the direct assent of the legislature. Rather, it is the provision for legislative votes of no

## BOX 12.1: CABINET TYPES

### Denmark

Denmark is the country with the largest number of minority governments in Europe, about half of these being single-party cabinets. One factor that explains this is the lack of a formal investiture rule, which makes it easier for parties to form minority governments. Furthermore, Denmark's electoral system – proportional representation with a low threshold (2 per cent) – facilitates a large number of parties, which makes it more difficult to form majority coalitions. The Social Democratic Party was, for most of Denmark's recent history, the largest party in parliament. The Social Democrats are also close to the centre of the ideological spectrum, which made it difficult to exclude it from government. In fact, most of Denmark's single-party governments consisted of the Social Democratic Party. This changed after the election of 2001, which began an era lasting to the time of writing during which the Liberal Party became the largest party and formed minority coalitions with the Conservatives.

### France

Government formation in France is to a large extent determined by the powerful role of the president of the republic, both in dissolving the legislature and in nominating potential prime ministers. France was governed by a right-wing coalition from the start of the Fifth Republic in 1958 until 1981. This was sometimes just short of a parliamentary majority, but was able to govern as a result of divisions within the left. Sometimes the government was a minimal winning coalition, and sometimes it controlled a surplus majority (notably after a Gaullist electoral landslide in 1968). Since 1981 French governments have alternated between right-wing coalitions and left-wing socialist administrations. The latter have sometimes been minority cabinets needing support from either communists or centrists. Constitutional changes in 2000 reduced the presidential term of five years, vastly reducing the probability that, following five years in office, a French president might be forced to nominate the prime minister from a rival party that had just won a legislative election, followed by a period of 'cohabitation'.

### Germany

For most of the post-war period German politics revolved around three parties that at some stage formed every possible two-party minimal winning coalition. In the early post-war period the Christian Democrats (CDU/CSU) took other parties into surplus majority governments, despite controlling a legislative majority on their own. There were coalitions between the large CDU/CSU and the much smaller Liberals (FDP) formed between 1957 and 1966, after which a 'grand coalition' of the two big parties – CDU/CSU and Social Democrats (SPD) – formed. This was followed by a coalition between the SPD and FDP. After 1982, a coalition between the FDP and the CDU/CSU remained in place until 1998, surviving the first all-German elections in 1990. In 1998, a 'Red–Green' coalition between the Social Democrats and the Greens replaced what had become one of the most stable party combinations in post-war Europe. However, the more traditional rotation of governments was restored in 2005, with a CDU–SPD grand coalition, followed in 2009 by a CDU–FDP coalition led by Angela Merkel. The overwhelming norm in modern Germany has been minimal winning coalitions.

### Italy

For a long time, one of the most striking features of post-war Italian politics was that the Christian Democrats (DC) were never out of office – always being at the heart of every government and often picking more coalition partners than they needed in order to have a secure parliamentary majority. This was in part a product of a unique and destabilizing system, abolished in 1988, under which parliamentary votes of confidence were by secret ballot and the government could thus not always rely even on its own legislators for support. Surplus majority coalitions were thus quite common.

Having held so much power for such a long period, the DC finally dissolved in the wake of a series of corruption scandals in 1993 that touched the very highest levels of Italian politics. The new electoral system introduced in the wake of these scandals provides strong incentives for coalitions of parties to fight elections as prospective governments, while maintaining their distinct identities. Since 1993 the winning electoral coalition, alternately coming from the centre right or the centre left, has always gone on to form the government, typically comprising more parties than necessary to control a parliamentary majority, and thus generating surplus majority coalitions.

## Netherlands

Superficially, government formation in the Netherlands appears to involve an immense number of possibilities, given the large number of parties in the Dutch legislature, a product of the intensely proportional electoral system. In practice, only a few of these parties have any real bargaining power, and government formation has revolved around four key players: the Labour Party (PvdA), Liberals (VVD), Christian Democrats (CDA) and, since 1994, Democrats 66 (D66). Until 1994, the Christian Democrats were a member of every post-war Dutch government, in alternating partnerships with either the left or the right. They were excluded from office for the first time in 1994 by a 'purple' coalition combining the Labour Party on the left, D66 in the centre, and the right-wing Liberals. Despite appearing to combine quite disparate parties, this combination provided stable government and was re-elected in 1998. Dutch government formation has become increasingly complicated in recent years, as election results have meant that no two parties can form a majority government. Thus, following the November 2006 elections, the eventual coalition that formed in February 2007 combined the PvdA, CDA and the Christian Union. This collapsed in 2010, however, over divisions on the role of the Dutch army in Afghanistan.

## Poland

The process of government formation in Poland has often been difficult because of two major factors: the fragmented nature of the party system, and the role of the Polish president. Up to 1997 there were major internal divisions among the parties, groups and movements that had emerged from Solidarity, the main umbrella organization of pre- and post-independence Poland. That is why it is not surprising that all governments in post-communist Poland should have been coalitions, given the highly fragmented nature of the Polish party system. At times, the role of parties in government formation was much more one of responding than initiating, given the key role the president played in the selection of prime ministers. In the early and mid 1990s President Lech Wałęsa, one of the most prominent figures in Poland's transition to democracy, played a key part in Polish political life, and appointed several prime ministers. The 1997 Polish constitution watered down the role of the president, but remains ambiguous about the extent to which Poland is a semi-presidential system, stating that executive power vests in the president and the Council of Ministers. However, the indications are that the Polish political system has evolved since the late 1990s into one with rather stable and strong cabinet coalitions.

## Spain

Spain since Franco has been very strongly characterized by one-party governments, with or without a parliamentary majority. The first five of these were short-lived one-party minority administrations controlled by the right-wing Union of the Democratic Centre (UCD), which was just short of a parliamentary majority and held office from 1976 to 1982. From 1982, when the Socialist Party (PSOE) won an overall legislative majority, until 1993, Spain was governed by one-party majority socialist

▶ ## BOX 12.1: CONTINUED

cabinets led by Felipe Gonzalez. After the 1993 election, in which the socialists lost their majority, Gonzalez led a minority government. The end of this long era of Socialist one-party government came after the elections of May 1996. The Socialists were defeated and a right-wing minority one-party government formed, led by José Aznar of the Popular Party, which gained a parliamentary majority following in the 2000 election. Spanish politics was rocked by a totally unexpected event on 11 March 2004, with the terrorist bombing of the main Madrid railway station just days before the election. The government, implausibly, insisted the bombing was the work of Basque separatists rather than being a reprisal for the presence of Spanish troops in Iraq as part of the US-led coalition. As a result the socialist opposition, led by José Zapatero, swept to an unexpected victory, formed a one-party cabinet, and immediately announced the withdrawal of Spanish troops from Iraq.

### United Kingdom

The British first-past-the-post electoral system has typically guaranteed one party a parliamentary majority, despite falling far short of a majority of votes. This has led inevitably to a series of one-party governments, which have alternated between Labour and the Conservatives since the Second World War. After the February 1974 election, the only one in the post-war era in which no party won an overall majority, a Labour minority government formed with Liberal support, and lasted until October of the same year. From 1976 to 1979 the Labour cabinet under James Callaghan lost its majority as a result of by-election defeats and continued in office as a minority government, with support first from the Liberals and then from assorted nationalists, before being defeated in 1979. After a very long period of one-party Conservative rule beginning in 1979, the 'New' Labour Party under Tony Blair won landslide victories in the 1997 and 2001 elections, and won again in 2005. The 2010 election result left no party with an overall legislative majority, however, and in a development unprecedented in peacetime politics since the early twentieth century, a minimal winning coalition was formed after a few days of negotiation between the Conservatives and Liberal Democrats, on the basis of a long and detailed joint programme of government and a promise to introduce fixed-term parliaments.

confidence in the executive that gives parliament *indirect* control over the government in all matters. Legislators can in theory instruct the government to act in a particular way, on pain of defeat in a confidence motion. In practice, however, the threat of such a dire sanction constrains executive action only if the issue is of paramount importance, so that the majority of legislators who once supported the government would now be prepared to bring it down. When legislators do not feel this strongly, the technical ability to bring down the government gives legislators a sledgehammer with which to crack a nut. As a result, cabinet ministers in practice have considerable autonomy in relation to most aspects of public policy that fall within their jurisdiction.

We saw earlier in this chapter that the motivations of the politicians who bargain over coalition formation are the key to understanding the party composition of governments in most European states. Some politicians may be driven by the desire to change public policy; others may be more interested in consuming the spoils of office. Whatever their motivations might be, the politicians who bargain over government formation are the very same people who actually consume the spoils of office if they are successful. If they manage to negotiate their party into government, then most of them will also get their feet under the cabinet table, enjoying considerable control over government policy as well as the lifestyles of important public figures. Notwithstanding the control over public policy that can be wielded by cabinet ministers and the

**TABLE 12.4** Parliamentary parties in Poland, 1991

| Party | Seats |
|---|---|
| Democratic Union (UD) | 62 |
| Democratic Left Alliance (SLD) (former Communists) | 60 |
| Catholic Electoral Action (ZChN) | 49 |
| Polish Peasant party (PSL) | 48 |
| Confederation for an Independent Poland (KPN) | 46 |
| Centre Alliance (PC) | 44 |
| Liberal-Democratic Congress (KLD) | 37 |
| Agrarian Alliance (PL) | 28 |
| Independent Trade Union "Solidarity" (S) | 27 |
| Polish Beer-Lovers' Party | 16 |
| German Minority (MN) | 7 |
| Christian Democracy (ChD) | 5 |
| Solidarity of Labour (SP) | 4 |
| Party of Christian Democrats (PChD) | 4 |
| Union of Real Politics/Republic's Rightists (UPR) | 3 |
| Social-Democratic Movement (RDS) | 1 |
| For *Wielkopolska* and Poland (W) | 1 |
| Others | 18 |
| Total | 460 |

evidence that policy is important in government formation, therefore, we should not be too quick to ignore the perks of office. To win a seat at the cabinet table is, after all, the pinnacle of a career in politics for most European politicians. The job brings public recognition, power, patronage, and many other pleasant trappings of success. We should not be surprised to find that many politicians dedicate their political lives single-mindedly to the pursuit of these coveted positions.

This is consistent with a finding by several authors that there is a very strong *proportionality norm*, according to which the allocation of cabinet portfolios between coalition partners closely follows the share of legislative seats controlled by each party (Gamson, 1961; Browne and Franklin, 1973; Browne and Frendreis, 1980; Laver and Schofield, 1998; Warwick and Druckman, 2001, 2006). Analogous findings for central and eastern Europe can be found in Druckman and Roberts (2005, 2008).

This pattern of proportional portfolio allocation can be seen very clearly in Figure 12.3, which plots parties' shares of cabinet portfolios against their shares of the total number of seats controlled by the government, for parties in post-war western European coalition cabinets. The pattern we see in Figure 12.3 is remarkable. The closeness of all plotted observations to the dashed 45 degree line shows that parties' legislative seat shares almost perfectly predict the shares of cabinet portfolios that they receive. There can be little doubt that cabinet portfolios are almost invariably allocated to parties in strict proportion to the shares of legislative seats that they won in the preceding election. We also see a slight tendency for small parties to be 'overpaid', with a higher portfolio share than their seat share indicates; the bottom left of Figure 12.3 shows more observations over the dashed line than under it. There is a compensating tendency for larger parties to be somewhat underpaid, getting a slightly lower portfolio share than their seat share indicates; the top right of Figure 12.3 shows more observations over the dashed line than under it. This may be because of the 'lumpy' nature of cabinet pay-offs, which means that even the smallest cabinet party cannot be given less than one portfolio.

The pattern plotted in Figure 12.3 has been independently reproduced by several authors, and has gone down in the annals of political science as one of strongest and most robust non-trivial empirical relationships that has yet been encountered. The facts suggest unambiguously that European politicians treat the allocation of cabinet portfolios very seriously indeed. This is hardly surprising, because, as we have argued, a cabinet portfolio represents the ultimate ambition for most of them.

### 12.5.1 Proportional cabinet pay-offs in France

As an example of proportional cabinet pay-offs, consider the coalition that formed in France in June 1997, details of which are given in Table 12.5. This cabinet was formed after an early election called by President Jacques Chirac in what some saw as an attempt to pre-empt the possibility of a left-wing victory if the parliament had run its full term. The incumbent right-wing government was, however, defeated at the polls. The Socialist Party and leftist allies made strong gains, but did not win quite enough seats to govern alone. Accordingly, when President Chirac asked Socialist leader Lionel Jospin to form a government, Jospin invited both the Communists and the Greens to join him. As Table 12.5 shows, Jospin formed a surplus majority coalition; only one of the three smaller parties was strictly needed for the government to

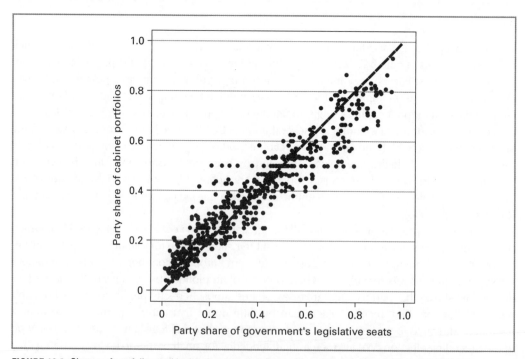

**FIGURE 12.3** Shares of portfolios and legislative seats in western European coalition cabinets, 1945–2002
*Source*: Authors' reanalysis of replication dataset for Ansolabehere *et al.* (2005)

TABLE 12.5 Allocation of cabinet seats in France, June 1997

| Party | Proportionate contribution to | | | Share of cabinet portfolios (%) |
| --- | --- | --- | --- | --- |
| | Number of parliamentary seats[a] | Cabinet's legislative majority (%) | Number of cabinet portfolios | |
| Communist Party | 37 | 12 | 2 | 12 |
| Socialist Party | 246 | 79 | 12 | 71 |
| Movement for Citizens | 7 | 2 | 1 | 6 |
| Left Radicals | 13 | 4 | 1 | 6 |
| Greens | 8 | 3 | 1 | 6 |

[a] Winning threshold: 289 seats.

control a parliamentary majority. Nonetheless, what is striking about the figures in Table 12.5 is the close way in which the allocation of cabinet portfolios matched the proportion of seats that each party contributed towards the government's majority in the legislature. Clearly this situation did not arise by accident. When the government was being formed, it was taken more or less as a given that each party was due a certain number of cabinet portfolios by virtue of the number of seats that it had won in the election. This was despite the fact that some of the parties might well have been able to use their bargaining power to win more portfolios than their 'fair' share.

Bringing any party into the cabinet involves giving it at least one cabinet portfolio; in this case one cabinet portfolio was 6 per cent of the total. Without sawing politicians in half and appointing a half politician from each of two parties to the same portfolio, this was the smallest pay-off that could be given to any government member, despite the fact that each of the three smallest parties contributed only between 2 and 4 per cent of the government's total legislative representation. The largest party underwrote this inevitable 'overpayment' to the small parties, while the medium-sized Communist Party got a precisely proportional pay-off.

## 12.5.2 Qualitative portfolio allocation in Germany

Although the simple arithmetic proportionality of portfolio allocation is very striking, it does not undermine the view that many European politicians participate in politics in order to have an impact on public policy – the interpretation that fits squarely with the facts on the frequency of minority and surplus majority governments. Being in command of a cabinet portfolio, after all, is the best means for a European politician to have an impact on public policy. This means that we must do much more than count portfolios when we analyse coalition outcomes. The allocation of particular portfolios to particular parties is a vitally important matter.

Consider the German example set out in Figure 12.4. This returns to the situation in Germany after the general election of September 2009. It shows the five German parties that won seats in this election, describing them in terms of the number of legislative seats won by each party, out of a total of 622, and their positions on two key dimensions of politics. The horizontal dimension shows party positions on economic policy, seen in terms of the conflict between higher public spending funding higher levels of public service provision, on the left, and lower levels of public service provision enabling lower taxation, on the right. The vertical dimension shows party positions on is immigration policy, which was rated in the Benoit-Laver expert survey as being the second most important policy dimension in Germany at about that time. From left to right on economic policy are the Left Party, the Social Democrats (SPD), the Greens, the Christian Democrats (CDU/CSU) and the Free Democrats (FDP). From liberal (bottom) to conservative (top) on immigration policy are the Greens, Left Party, SPD, FDP and CDU/CSU. From all of this it can be seen that the party at the median position on economic policy was the CDU. Counting from either left or right on economic policy, the CDU's votes turn a minority into a majority. Similarly, the party with the median position on immigration policy was the FDP.

The horizontal and vertical lines in Figure 12.4 form a sort of lattice, and show what each party might be expected to do if put in complete charge of the policy area in question. The solid lines show the policy positions of the median party on each policy dimension. Thus the solid vertical line through the CDU position shows what would happen if the CDU were put in charge of economic policy, by virtue of being allocated the finance portfolio, which gives control over the

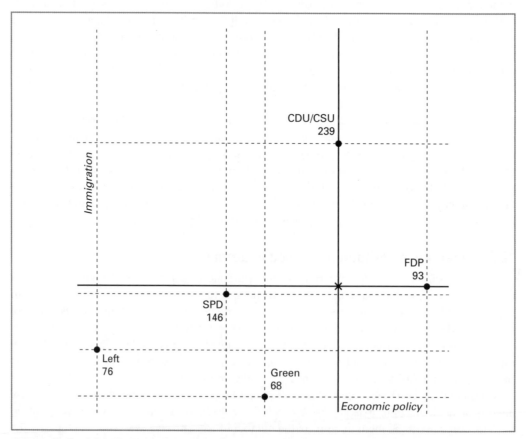

**FIGURE 12.4** Portfolio allocation in Germany, 2009
*Source*: Party positions taken from Benoit and Laver (2006)

Ministry of Finance. We would now know what the government's economic policy is likely to be, although, without knowing who has been given the job of minster of the interior and thereby put in charge of the government department responsible for immigration policy, we could place the government's policy anywhere on this vertical line. In the same way, the solid horizontal line through the FDP position shows what would happen if the FDP were allocated the Interior portfolio and put in charge of immigration policy. Knowing who controls both of these key cabinet portfolios, we can forecast government policy on both policy dimensions. Thus, if the CDU is in charge of economic policy and the FDP is in charge of immigration policy, then we expect government policy to be on both solid lines – at their intersection, marked with a cross in Figure 12.4.

The government that eventually formed after the 2009 election was indeed, as we have seen, a coalition between the CDU/CSU and the FDP. However, because the Christian Democrats were in such a strong bargaining position, able in effect to play off parties of the right against parties of the left, they were what Laver and Shepsle (1996) have called a *strong party*. This means they were able to retain both of these key cabinet portfolios in government formation negotiations, and put their own people into both the Ministry of Finance and the Ministry of the Interior. The CDU/CSU, which came out of the 2009 election in a position of considerable strength, was able to keep control of the cabinet portfolios that set the policy agenda in the two policy areas deemed by experts to be the most important bones of contention.

### 12.5.3 Cabinet portfolios and government policy

Looking more generally at the qualitative allocation of cabinet portfolios, we can see a clear tendency for parties to be rewarded with the ministries that bear directly on the policy areas of special interest to them. There is a strong tendency for agrarian parties to get the agriculture portfolio, for example, and there are weaker but still distinct trends in relation to other portfolios (Budge and Keman, 1990). This means, as we saw in the German case, that the allocation of cabinet portfolios is not simply a matter of handing out of a set of trophies to senior politicians who have managed to take control of the government. It is also an important way in which the policy profile of any new government is defined. Allocating a cabinet portfolio to one senior politician rather than another makes a big difference to the expected policy output of the government. It also means that cabinet reshuffles, which involve redistributing cabinet portfolios between senior politicians, have significant policy implications.

Indeed, one account of government formation sees the allocation of cabinet portfolios as a fundamental defining characteristic of any government, since a cabinet minister is not just a member of the government, but has considerable discretion over government policy in particular areas (Laver and Shepsle, 1996). A minister of health, for example, can have a huge influence over public policy in the area of health; a minister of education can have tremendous power over education policy; and so on. Conversely, changing environmental policy *without* the co-operation of the minister for the environment is a very difficult task indeed. This implies that, if you want to know a government's policy position on any issue, you do not necessarily take official policy statements at face value; these may well be unreliable 'cheap talk'. Rather, you do better to look at the policy preferences of the politicians who have been given the relevant portfolios, as well at what these people actually do when in office. When all is said and done, the preferences and actions of the relevant cabinet ministers are very credible signals about the effective policy positions of any government.

This is illustrated in work by Giannetti and Laver, who looked at the policy impact of cabinet ministers in one Italian cabinet (Giannetti and Laver, 2005). The left–right economic policy positions of individual ministers in the centre-left Ulivo cabinet that held office in Italy between 1996 and 1998 were estimated using computerized analyses of the content of parliamentary speeches made by each minister during 1996. Policy positions of ministers were plotted against changes between 1996 and 1998 in the shares of government spending associated with government departments under their jurisdiction, revealing the pattern shown in Figure 12.5. Looking at the bottom right of the plot, we see that more right-wing ministers tended to preside over departments for which the share of government spending declined; looking at the top left of the plot, we see that more left-wing ministers tended to preside over departments whose share of total government spending increased. In this case, we do indeed see a sharp association between the policy positions of individual cabinet ministers and at least one measure of the policy profile of their department. The policy preferences of ministers do make a difference to government policy outputs in this particular case.

To sum up, the considerable autonomy of cabinet ministers to set public policy in their respective areas of jurisdiction means that the question of who gets into the cabinet is a fundamental driver of party competition in any modern European democracy. In the last analysis, voters choose between alternative sets of politicians, and these politicians bargain over who gets

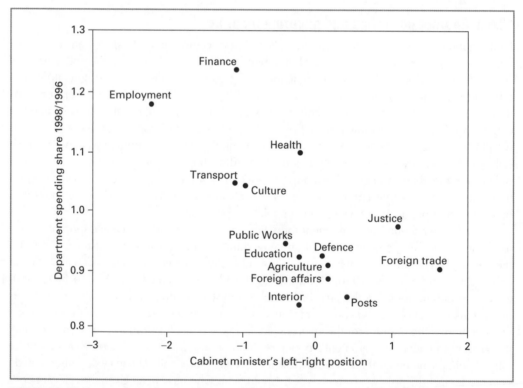

**FIGURE 12.5** The impact of cabinet ministers in Italy, 1996–1998
*Source*: Giannetti and Laver (2005)

what in the cabinet. The ideological complexion of the cabinet that they form represents the most important single way in which party politics in general, and voters in particular, can be said to have an impact on the policy orientations of governments in modern Europe.

## 12.6 The stability of European governments

Some governments last significantly longer than others. At the *stable* end of the spectrum in western Europe we find Luxembourg, Spain, Britain, Ireland and Austria, each of which has governments that tend to last a full parliamentary term. In central and eastern Europe, governments in Hungary, Slovenia and Bulgaria have lasted as long on average as governments anywhere else in Europe (Conrad and Golder, 2010). At the *unstable* end of the spectrum in western Europe, with by far the shortest average cabinet durations, we find Italy and Finland, although cabinets in these countries have become significantly more stable in recent times. Latvia has the least durable governments of those eastern European countries with which we are concerned. To give a sense of the types of duration we are talking about, countries with more stable cabinets have governments that last, on average, about three years. Those with unstable cabinets have governments that tend to last about a year, or even less.

The stability of governments is a self-evidently important matter for all who are interested in politics; considerable intellectual energy has been devoted to understanding it. Before moving on to investigate this, we need to deal with an unexpectedly tricky matter, that of deciding when a government has actually come to an end. Different researchers look at this in different ways. All researchers agree that one government ends and a new government takes office if the party membership of the cabinet changes. Some take this as the only definitive sign that the government has changed. Others regard a new government as having formed after every new election, even if exactly the same parties and the same prime minister resume control. They do this on the grounds that every new parliament represents a new political environment, typically with a host of new faces and a new legislative arithmetic, so that explaining what might appear to some people to be effectively the 'same' government does present a new problem for political analysts.

A further important matter concerns the *turnover* of cabinet ministers from one government to the next. After all, if a government changes its prime minister and even its party composition, but most of the cabinet ministers nonetheless remain the same, then we could argue that not much has changed. This is particularly relevant when we think about the apparent instability of governments in, for example, Italy. While post-war Italian governments have typically been very short-lived on most definitions, there was often a very limited turnover of Italian cabinet ministers from one government to the next. In a comprehensive comparative analysis, Huber and Martinez-Gallardo (2004) show that cabinet stability and cabinet turnover are indeed quite distinct from each other. They confirm the finding that Italy over the post-war period has tended to have short-lived cabinets, but also to have relatively low turnover of cabinet ministers by international standards. Austria, Sweden and Iceland are other countries in which cabinet ministers tend to stay in office for much longer than the average duration of cabinets – implying far less instability of cabinet personnel than might be inferred from simply looking at cabinet durations.

All of this means that the question 'how long did this government last?' is easier asked than answered. The classification of governments reported in Table 12.3 is based on data from

Strøm *et al.* (2008) who have a 'permissive' definition of the end of a government. They see a wide range of factors (elections, new party composition, new prime minister, resignation of incumbent prime minister even if she or he resumes office) as marking the end of a government's life. Obviously, this is likely to show cabinet durations as being shorter than if the sole indicator of the end of a government were a change in its party composition.

Most studies of the duration of European cabinets concentrate on two things. First, cabinets themselves may possess certain *attributes* that lead some to be more durable than others. It is widely believed, for example, that coalition governments are less stable than single-party governments, and that majority governments are more stable than minority governments. Second, there are features of the *political environment* in which a government must survive. If party competition is fragmented between many parties, for example, or if there is a powerful anti-regime party that refuses to take part in any government, then these features of the political system may lead to greater cabinet instability.

### 12.6.1 Cabinet attributes and cabinet stability

Several researchers have confirmed expectations that single-party governments last longer than coalitions, and that majority governments last longer than minority governments. These patterns can be seen by looking at the top part of Table 12.6. On average, across the whole of western Europe, single-party majority governments last noticeably longer than minimal winning coalitions. They last about a year longer than single-party minority governments, and more than twice as long as minority coalitions. Minimal winning governments, in turn, last much longer than minority or surplus majority governments. Overall, minority coalitions are notably the least stable type of government in western Europe.

There is only a short history of parliamentary government in central and eastern Europe from which to draw firm conclusions about government stability. Nonetheless, if we look at the bottom part of Table 12.6, we see emerging trends and what look like interesting differences from the pattern in western Europe. We can draw no conclusion at all about the longevity of single-party majority cabinets in central and eastern Europe, since these exist hardly at all. What is striking, however, is the relative stability of surplus majority governments. This differs from the pattern in western Europe, where governments as a whole tend to last longer, but where surplus majority cabinets are among the *least* durable. This suggests, in the more volatile party systems of central and eastern Europe during the transition era – with parties forming, splitting, fusing and disappearing both between and during election campaigns – that party leaders engaged in government formation had incentives to bolster cabinet stability by including more parties than the bare minimum needed to control parliament at the time the government formed. This lends credibility to the interpretation of surplus majority cabinets as responses to uncertainty and flux in the political environment.

Broad European averages are a crude measure of the durability of different types of government, however, and the body of Table 12.6 shows that the pattern is more complex than it seems at first sight. Some general patterns hold when we compare different types of government within individual countries, but others do not. For example, minority coalitions tend to be less stable than majority coalitions, regardless of country. In most countries, single-party minority governments are less stable than single-party majority governments. Majority status does tend to extend government stability in all political systems. Comparing the stability of minimal winning

**TABLE 12.6** Average durations, in days, of different government types in modern Europe, 1945–2010

| Country | Single-party majority | Minimal winning coalition | Surplus majority coalition | Single-party minority | Minority coalition | Mean duration |
|---|---|---|---|---|---|---|
| *Western Europe 1945–2010* | | | | | | |
| Luxembourg | | 1308 | 472 | | | 1261 |
| Spain | 1315 | | | 1001 | | 1095 |
| United Kingdom | 1054 | | | 200 | | 1017 |
| Ireland | 962 | 1115 | | 825 | 890 | 957 |
| Austria | 1390 | 837 | 696 | 546 | | 905 |
| Greece | 999 | 97 | 136 | 1278 | | 885 |
| Netherlands | | 973 | 916 | | 100 | 840 |
| Sweden | 368 | 704 | | 908 | 785 | 821 |
| Norway | 963 | 1055 | | 759 | 551 | 799 |
| Iceland | | 932 | 769 | 130 | 347 | 784 |
| Germany | 442 | 969 | 491 | 24 | | 764 |
| Portugal | 1551 | 439 | 263 | 869 | | 741 |
| France | 611 | 929 | 744 | 361 | 622 | 704 |
| Denmark | | 794 | | 558 | 744 | 673 |
| Belgium | 464 | 888 | 440 | 71 | 45 | 582 |
| Finland | | 456 | 642 | 457 | 132 | 515 |
| Italy | | 464 | 459 | 223 | 353 | 379 |
| Mean duration | 1017 | 910 | 582 | 608 | 523 | 743 |
| *Eastern Europe 1990–2010* | | | | | | |
| Bulgaria | 1096 | 716 | 1419 | 355 | | 899 |
| Hungary | | 694 | 1063 | 348 | | 835 |
| Slovenia | | 1064 | 592 | | 357 | 681 |
| Czech Republic | | 651 | | 591 | 448 | 570 |
| Lithuania | 660 | 845 | 456 | | 371 | 549 |
| Estonia | | 615 | | 419 | 398 | 547 |
| Slovakia | | 654 | 1422 | 242 | 162 | 530 |
| Romania | | 366 | 342 | 353 | 708 | 498 |
| Poland | | 466 | 500 | 239 | 273 | 359 |
| Latvia | | 298 | 466 | | 263 | 333 |
| Mean duration | 878 | 610 | 659 | 365 | 372 | 533 |

*Note*: Table excludes caretaker and non-partisan cabinets.

*Source*: Western Europe: Comparative Parliamentary Democracy Archive (www.pol.umu.se/ccpd) assembled for Strøm *et al.* (2008), updated with annual Data Yearbooks of the *European Journal of Political Research,* and authors' calculations. Eastern Europe: Conrad and Golder (2010) and authors' calculations.

coalitions with that of single-party majority governments is instructive, however. With the exception of Austria and Portugal, there is no evidence that minimal winning coalitions are less stable. Indeed, in countries that experience both types of government, minimal winning coalitions are likely to be just as stable as single-party majority governments. Europe-wide averages make single-party majority governments look more stable, because these tend to be found more often in countries where the stability of *all* types of government is higher. Put another way, as long as the government has majority status, there is no systematic evidence that coalitions *per se* are less stable than single-party governments.

Moving beyond size, policy differences between members of a coalition cabinet can also have a big impact on government stability. This has been shown most clearly by Warwick (1994), who measures the ideological diversity of coalition cabinets along three important policy dimensions: the traditional left–right dimension; a dimension contrasting pro-clerical and secular ideologies; and a dimension that captures the extent to which party policy is 'anti-system'. Warwick shows that increasing cabinet diversity on any one of these three dimensions reduces the life expectancy of the cabinet, presumably because of the greater possibility for policy disputes.

Not all sources of government instability come from within the cabinet, however. There are large differences between countries in government durability, in both eastern and western Europe, even when we take account of the different types of cabinet that form. Single-party minority governments are much more stable in Greece, Ireland, Sweden and Norway, for example, than in Italy and Belgium. Surplus majority cabinets are much more stable in Hungary than in Latvia. Thus the political system within which a government must survive, as well as the type of government itself, has a systematic impact on government stability.

### 12.6.2 System attributes and cabinet duration

One of the patterns to emerge quite clearly from comparing government stability in different European countries is that countries in which governments are more short-lived tend to be those with relatively large numbers of relatively small parties generating a more complex and unstable parliamentary arithmetic. In Latvia, for example, where the average government duration since independence from the former Soviet Union is less than one year, the 1995 election to the 100-seat parliament generated the parliament described in Table 12.7. There were nine parties, none of which controlled more than 18 per cent of the seats, generating a simply enormous range of coalition possibilities. There was no 'obvious' government emerging from this election result. Furthermore, the Latvian parties were still merging and splitting, while individual legislators were also on occasion shifting parties. Any such change in the party system, however tiny, could change the legislative arithmetic and hence the parliamentary support base of the incumbent government. Clearly this does not seem a political environment conducive, under the rules of parliamentary government, to sustaining stable administrations. In the event, four different coalition cabinets, each comprising six or seven parties, formed and fell in Latvia during the three-year period between the elections of October 1995 and those of October 1998.

In Luxembourg, in contrast, almost no election result that can realistically be forecast is likely to change the power structure in the legislature. After any election, the parliamentary arithmetic almost inevitably reveals that any two of the three largest parties are needed to form a majority administration, and that the large, centrist, Christian Social Party is going to be very difficult to

**TABLE 12.7** Parliamentary parties in Latvia, 1995

| Party | Seats |
| --- | --- |
| DPS (Democratic Party Saimnieks) | 18 |
| LC (Latvia's Way) | 17 |
| TKL (People's Movement) | 16 |
| TB (Fatherland and Freedom) | 14 |
| LPP (Latvia's First Party)/LZS (Latvian Peasants Union) | 8 |
| LVP (Latvian Unity Party) | 8 |
| LNNK (Latvian National Independence Movement) | 8 |
| TSP (People's Harmony Party) | 6 |
| LSP (Latvian Socialist Party) | 5 |
| Total | 100 |

keep out of office. Because the party system in Luxembourg is so stable, there are almost no shocks, surprises or likely changes in the legislative arithmetic that can change the support base of an incumbent government that had demonstrated the support of a parliamentary majority when it took office.

Differences between countries in terms of the complexity of their parliamentary arithmetic, in short, can have a major bearing on government stability. Countries with a record of short-lived cabinets (Belgium, Finland and Latvia for example) all tend to have fragmented party systems in which election results generate a rather large number of rather small parties (see Table 11.5). This yields a large number of coalition possibilities, as in the Latvian case we just looked at, and a consequently high probability that small changes in the political environment might destabilize an incumbent administration. Those with a record of longer-lasting cabinets (Britain, Hungary and Luxembourg for example) all tend to have less fragmented party systems in which elections generate a much simpler parliamentary arithmetic. This may be because one party typically wins a majority, as in Britain. Or it may be because there are just two or three large parties from which a majority coalition in parliament can be formed; this is typically the case in Austria and Luxembourg, and after more recent elections in Hungary. These conclusions are reinforced by extensive cross-national empirical analyses of factors affecting the stability of cabinets (King *et al.*, 1990; Warwick, 1994; Diermeier and Stevenson, 1999, 2000). These show that government duration is significantly affected by two factors that contribute directly to complexity of the political environment within which the government must survive: the fragmentation and the ideological polarization of the party system. The more fragmented the party system, and the greater the ideological polarization of the parties, the less conducive the political environment to durable cabinets.

## 12.6.3 Government stability and political events

The political science account of the stability of European governments that we have just discussed stands in stark contrast to the way that political journalists and practising politicians tend to think about this. Those who are deeply involved in the rough and tumble of day-to-day politics are apt to see the defeat or resignation of any government as the direct product of a particular sequence of events, not some abstract configuration of the party system. Even a government that seemed solid as a rock can be 'ambushed' by events that are largely beyond its control. While we have seen strong general patterns in the stability of European governments, we should not forget that these patterns are no more than trends. In the case of any *particular* government, such trends may inform our views on how stable it is *likely to be*; but how stable it *actually turns out to be* depends to a large extent on the slings and arrow of outrageous fortune.

This alerts us to an important and often neglected distinction between the duration and the durability of governments. The *duration* of any government is a simple observable quantity – the elapsed time between the birth of the government and its replacement by parliament with an alternative. The *durability* of any government is an abstract and unobservable quantity. It refers to how long a government is *likely to last* in a specified range of circumstances, or to how long a past government *might have lasted* if things had been different. There is a big difference between the durability of any particular government and its actual duration. A government that seems on the face of it to be rather durable, perhaps a single-party cabinet with a huge parliamentary majority, can still collapse when people least expect it. There could be a huge political scandal involving the financial affairs of the prime minister, or some pivotal political figure may have a heart attack. Such events can destroy even a durable government in a bolt out of the blue, just days after it looked set fair to govern for several more years. For a discussion of the distinction between the duration and durability of governments, and a more general review of government stability, see Laver (2003).

Thus any government must live its life in a world of *critical events* – of shocks, scandals and other disasters that all test its ability to survive. Any one of these events may be a bullet with the government's name on it. By definition, these events are precisely the things that could not possibly have been foreseen, and thus could not have been taken into account by those who negotiated about the size and shape of the government. The durability of a government, in these terms, can be seen as its ability to withstand critical events. Rather like boxers, durable governments can take a lot of knocks and come back fighting. Less durable governments, in contrast, tend not to survive their first nasty surprise.

Critical events take many different forms. One of the great challenges for political science is that, while it is always easy to be wise after the event, it is much harder to identify *in advance* the type of event that will bring down a given government. For example, an unexpected turnaround in opinion poll ratings may modify the expectations of politicians about the outcome of an upcoming election. This may provoke a reallocation of power within the incumbent government, or may even destabilize a sensitive deal that has been done, and bring the government down (Lupia and Strøm, 1995). More generally, a wide range of different types of political shock may put pressure on the government. As well as public opinion shocks, there may be shocks to the political agenda, arising when unexpected and quite possibly unwelcome issues simply must be decided. Perhaps an oil rig blows up in coastal waters, forcing hard decisions on the trade-off between energy and environmental policies. A major company may go bankrupt, forcing unwelcome decisions on industrial policy. To this can be added unexpected ministerial departures, as a result of deaths, ill-health or scandals. Laver and Shepsle (1998) set out to classify different types of political shock, and explore the types of effect that these might have on government stability.

When we set out to predict the durability of any particular government, therefore, we are talking only about the *probability* that it will last for a specified time. A fuller account of the life cycle of governments must take account not only of the key stability-inducing attributes of cabinet, but also of the possibility that even an apparently stable government can be shot down out of a clear blue sky by an unexpected event. Using appropriate statistical assumptions to model the impact of random events, it is possible to combine both approaches into a single account of government duration in western Europe. Quite a number of political scientists have now done this, using a statistical technique known as *event history modelling* (*King et al.*, 1990; Warwick, 1994; Diermeier and Stevenson, 1999, 2000).These systematic statistical analyses have tended to confirm the more informal judgements we made above about trends in government duration. Longer-lasting governments tend to have majority status; they tend to arise in less fragmented party systems; they tend to arise when there is not a substantial anti-system opposition; they tend to arise when there is a formal parliamentary investiture requirement that tests the government strength before it takes office; and they tend to be less internally divided over policy. Thus if we want to use this work to write down the recipe for an unstable government, it would exist in a party system with a large number of small parties, including at least one anti-system party; it would be a minority coalition of ideologically diverse partners; and it would take office without having to pass an investiture requirement. We would not expect a cabinet with all of these attributes to be able to survive many unwelcome political shocks.

The statistical techniques of event history analysis have also been used in these studies to remove the effect of holding scheduled elections on the lifespan of governments. While many governments never make it to the end of a full parliamentary term, many of the more durable governments might well have been able to survive much longer had it not been for the constitutional need to hold a scheduled election. Thus King *et al.* (1990) found that scheduled elections have little effect on the duration of governments in high-turnover systems such as Finland and Italy. In contrast, if it were not for scheduled elections, governments in Britain would last even longer, on the average, than they do at present. In other words, for the more stable systems, turnover in governments is more a product of the constitutional requirement that elections be held at regular intervals, generating a new parliament, than it is of political forces at work within a particular parliament. In less stable systems, the high turnover of governments seems to arise because governments collapse, even without a constitutional limitation on their tenure, as a result of the forces at work in the very same parliaments that put them in office in the first place.

The same statistical techniques also allow us to estimate whether or not a government faces increasing risks of failure as it goes further into its term of office. Intuitively, this seems plausible. As a new government takes office, it might seem strong and better able to withstand large shocks than it will be after it has been bombarded for a year or two by an endless stream of nasty shocks. The model of cabinet termination put forward by Lupia and Strøm (1995), furthermore, predicted that the risk of termination, the *hazard rate* as it is usually referred to, should rise during the lifetime of a government. This is because, with less time to go before the next constitutionally mandated election, the incentives for coalition partners to renegotiate their deal to keep the government in place in the face of unanticipated political shocks will be less. Indeed, if some surprise event were to ambush a government shortly before an election was due anyway, there might be no point in trying to renegotiate the deal. Diermeier and Stevenson (1999) addressed this problem, distinguishing between cabinet terminations brought about by early dissolutions and those brought about by defeats or resignations of governments between elections. They found that the risk of a government being replaced *between elections* tended to be constant throughout its life – not to increase, as we might have imagined. However, they also found that the risk of a government falling *as the result of an early election* did tend to rise significantly during a government's life.

## BOX 12.2: GOVERNMENT STABILITY

### Denmark

With the largest number of minority governments in Europe, it is not surprising that the duration of Danish governments is below the European average. Almost all cabinets in Denmark relied on support from outside parties, and hence were more prone to lose a vote of confidence in parliament than majority governments. Furthermore, the prime minister in Denmark has the constitutional power to dissolve parliament, which allows for early termination of government for strategic reasons.

### France

The extreme and notorious government instability of the Fourth Republic, with an average government duration of well under one year, was one of the main reasons why the constitution was revised to create the Fifth Republic in 1958. Since then, French cabinets have tended to be rather stable. However, when a president was elected who belonged to a different party from that of the prime minister, this was often followed by an immediate dissolution of the legislature, as the president hoped to be able to nominate a prime minister of the same political complexion.

### Germany

German coalition cabinets are very stable, tending to endure for the natural life of a full parliament. Only twice in recent times, in 1982 and 2005, has a government been brought down between elections. As a result, the average duration of German cabinets, at around three years, is on a par with that to be found in countries, such as Britain, with mainly one-party majority cabinets.

### Italy

Italy is often taken as the classic example of a European coalition system with very unstable cabinets; indeed, the average duration of Italian cabinets used to be the lowest in post-war Europe, at less than one year. Minority governments, in particular, were very short-lived. Quite often, however, the same key people filled the same key portfolios across a series of cabinets, implying quite a lot more underlying stability than might have appeared on the surface. In recent times, however, reforms in the electoral system have encouraged parties to form large pre-election coalitions that have in turn resulted in much longer-lived Italian governments.

This is an interesting finding, which returns our attention to the fact that, as we have seen, many European prime ministers have strategic control over the calling of elections. What seems to be going on is that, as the life of the government progresses, prime ministers typically become more likely to exercise the crucial power to cut and run for an election. This is of course quite understandable, since letting the government run its full constitutional term would leave the prime minister without the option to pick a favourable election date. Once the government is at least a couple of years into its term, then any prime minister worth his or her salt will be keeping an eye on the opinion polls and trying to figure out the best time to call the next election.

A good example can be found in the vigorous speculation about an early election that developed in Britain after the replacement of Tony Blair by Gordon Brown. Figure 12.6 shows a series of opinion poll results for the relative strengths of the two main British parties. The general election of May 2005 had produced a big win for Labour; the left side of Figure 12.6 shows the line plotting Labour support well above the line plotting Conservative support. Tony Blair

## Netherlands

The average duration of Dutch cabinets is towards the top of the range found in continental European coalition systems, excluding short-lived and clearly transitional caretaker cabinets that hold office during the negotiation of more permanent governments. Having typically taken a long time to negotiate, the coalition cabinets that eventually form tend to be quite stable in European terms. This stability is especially striking given the large number of parties represented in the Dutch parliament.

## Poland

Polish politics in the 1990s was often seen in terms of political and ministerial instability, and Poland had six prime ministers and seven cabinets between 1991 and 2000. This seemed to be due to a combination of the fragmented party system in Poland and the often uneasy cohabitation between President Wałęsa and a series of Polish prime ministers. However, since the constitutional reforms of 1997, indications are that both the duration of cabinets and the tenure of ministers in office have tended to increase.

## Spain

A number of rather unstable right-wing minority cabinets formed and fell in the immediate post-Franco period. Since the Socialists gained a single-party legislative majority in 1982, however, Spanish governments have been very durable, typically running for the full inter-electoral period. This stability has carried through into the minority or majority right-wing governments forming after the end of the era of socialist government.

## United Kingdom

Governments in the United Kingdom are among the most durable in western Europe. Single-party majority governments tend to last for a substantial part of the full legal period allowed between elections, although there is a very strong tendency towards the end of this period for governments to watch opinion polls closely and call an election when they hope to maximize their vote. It seems very likely that if it were not for intervening elections, many British governments would have been in a position to last much longer.

became increasingly unpopular as prime minister and Labour's poll lead steadily declined, until the Conservatives pulled ahead of Labour, illustrated in Figure 12.6 when the lines cross over. There was strong internal party pressure on Blair to step down. He did, to be replaced in June 2007 by Gordon Brown, both as Labour leader and as British prime minister. The party's opinion poll fortunes reversed, and a 'Brown bounce' took Labour back ahead of the Conservatives during the summer and autumn of 2007. Brown was urged by party colleagues to hold an early election to take advantage of this opinion poll lead, despite the fact that the next scheduled election was not until May 2010, two and a half years later. Brown held off calling an election, however, only to see Labour's poll figures return to levels well below those of the Conservatives. There may have been a brief strategic window for Brown to call an election, but he chose not to take advantage of this, after which there was a substantial and sustained decline in Brown's popularity. While we shall never know the outcome of the September 1997 election that never happened, the *dénouement* was that Brown stayed in office until the end of his legally mandated

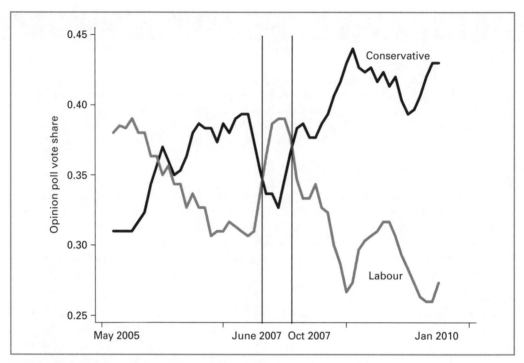

**FIGURE 12.6** Possibilities for strategic election timing in Britain
*Source*: Guardian/ICM opinion polls

term, and then went on to lose power in a May 2010 election. (For an excellent analysis of strategic election timing in Britain, see Smith, 2004.)

The destabilizing effect of anticipated elections is compounded by a crucial feature of *coalition* cabinets; as the next election appears on the horizon, junior coalition partners begin to calculate ways in which they might leave the cabinet and force an election on terms that will put them in the best light possible. Thus coalition partners may begin actually looking for 'deal-breakers' that can form the basis of their next election campaign, thereby destabilizing the government. All in all, as soon as the next scheduled election pops up on the far horizon, the chances increase that some key player is going to cut and run, precipitating an early election. This is why rather few national parliaments in modern Europe run to the very end of their legally mandated term.

## 12.7 Conclusions

First and foremost, the normal situation in modern Europe, given the PR electoral formulae in widespread use, is for no party to have a legislative majority. Given the rules of parliamentary government, this means that *legislative* coalitions will always be needed in such cases if the government is to gain and retain office. But it is by no means necessary that there is an *executive* coalition of parties. If a single-party minority cabinet can find favour with a majority of legislators, then it can build and maintain a viable government. Such minority cabinets are part of the mainstream experience in Europe. Second, the composition of the cabinet is a matter of vital political interest. The proportional allocation of cabinet portfolios among parties is a firmly established norm in most European systems. This does not mean, however, that the allocation takes place according to a sterile political formula. What it means is that the real political action is concerned with which particular politician gets which particular portfolio. The end product of this process determines the fundamental character, and the likely policy outputs, of the government. Third, certain types of political system in which coalition government is the norm do generate more unstable cabinets than others. In countries with stable *coalition* governments, furthermore, these are effectively as stable as one-party governments in Britain, where the stability of one-party majority governments is often put forward as the main advantage of maintaining a non-PR electoral system.

Putting all of this together, the making and breaking of governments in the parliamentary democracies of modern Europe provide the vital link between legislative politics, on which citizens can have at least some small impact when they vote at elections, and the composition of the government, over which voters have at most indirect control. Much of the real political action takes place after the votes have been counted.

## References

**Albert, Max** (2003) 'The voting power approach: measurement without theory', *European Union Politics*, 4 (3), 351–366.

**Almeida, Pedro Tavares de, Antonio Costa Pinto and Nancy Bermeo (eds)** (2003) *Who Governs Southern Europe? Regime Change and Ministerial Recruitment, 1850–2000*, Frank Cass, London.

**Ansolabehere, Stephen, James M. Snyder, Aaron B. Strauss and Michael M. Ting** (2005) 'Voting weights and *formateur* advantages in the formation of coalition governments', *American Journal of Political Science*, 49 (3), 550–563.

**Bagehot, W.** (2000) *The English Constitution*, Adamant Media Corporation, Boston, MA (originally published 1885).

**Baron, David** (1991) 'A spatial bargaining theory of government formation in parliamentary systems', *American Political Science Review*, 85 (1), 137–164.

**Benoit, Kenneth and Michael Laver** (2006) *Party Policy in Modern Democracies*, Routledge, London.

**Blondel, Jean** (1991) 'Cabinet government and cabinet ministers', pp. 5–18 in J. Blondel and J.-L. Thiebault (eds), *The Profession of Government Minister in Western Europe*, Macmillan, London.

**Blondel, Jean and Ferdinand Müller-Rommel (eds)** (2001) *Cabinets in Eastern Europe*, Palgrave, London.

**Browne, Eric and Mark Franklin** (1973) 'Aspects of coalition pay-offs in European parliamentary democracies', *American Political Science Review*, 67 (2), 453–469.

**Browne, Eric and John Frendreis** (1980) 'Allocating coalition pay-offs by conventional norm: an assessment of the evidence from cabinet coalition situations', *American Journal of Political Science*, 24 (4), 753–768.

**Budge, Ian and Hans Keman** (1990) *Parties and Democracy*, Oxford University Press, Oxford.

**Carrubba, Clifford J. and Craig Volden** (2001) 'Coalitional politics and logrolling in legislative institutions', *American Journal of Political Science*, 44 (2), 261–277.

**Conrad, Courtenay Ryals and Sona N. Golder** (2010) 'Measuring government duration and stability in central and eastern European countries', *European Journal of Political Research*, 49 (1), 119–150.

**Diermeier, Daniel and Randy Stevenson** (1999) 'Cabinet survival and competing risks', *American Journal of Political Science* 43 (4), 1051–1068.

**Diermeier, Daniel and Randy Stevenson** (2000) 'Cabinet terminations and critical events', *American Political Science Review*, 94 (3), 627–640.

**Dowding, Keith and Patrick Dumont (eds)** (2009) *The Selection of Ministers in Europe: Hiring and Firing*, Routledge, London.

**Druckman, James and Andrew Roberts** (2005) 'Context and coalition bargaining: comparing portfolio allocation in eastern and western Europe', *Party Politics*, 11 (5), 535–555.

**Druckman, James and Andrew Roberts** (2008) 'Measuring portfolio salience in eastern European parliamentary democracies', *European Journal of Political Research*, 47 (1), 101–134.

**Gamson, William A.** (1961) 'A theory of coalition formation', *American Sociological Review*, 26 (3), 373–382.

**Giannetti, Daniela and Michael Laver** (2005) 'Policy positions and jobs in the government', *European Journal of Political Research*, 44 (1), 91–120.

**Golder, Sona N.** (2005) 'Pre-electoral coalitions in comparative perspective: a test of existing hypotheses', *Electoral Studies*, 24 (4), 643–663.

**Golder, Sona N.** (2006) 'Pre-electoral coalition formation in parliamentary democracies', *British Journal of Political Science*, 36 (2), 193–212.

**Huber, John D.** (1996) *Rationalizing Parliament: Legislative Institutions and Party Politics in France*, Cambridge University Press, Cambridge and New York.

**Huber, John D. and Cecilia Martinez-Gallardo** (2004) 'Cabinet instability and the accumulation of experience: the French Fourth and Fifth Republics in comparative perspective', *British Journal of Political Science*, 34 (1), 27–48.

**Kam, Christopher J.** (2009) *Party Discipline and Parliamentary Politics*, Cambridge University Press, Cambridge.

**Kang, Shin-Goo** (2009) 'The influence of presidential heads of state on government formation in European democracies: empirical evidence', *European Journal of Political Research*, 48 (4), 543–572.

**King, Gary, James E. Alt, Nancy Elizabeth Burns and Michael Laver** (1990) 'A unified model of cabinet dissolution in parliamentary democracies', *American Journal of Political Science*, 34 (3), 872–902.

**Laver, Michael** (1998) 'Models of government formation', *Annual Review of Political Science*, 1, 1–25.

**Laver, M.** (2003) 'Government termination', *Annual Review of Political Science*, 6, 23–40.

**Laver, Michael and Kenneth A. Shepsle** (1994) *Cabinet Ministers and Parliamentary Government*, Cambridge University Press, Cambridge and New York.

**Laver, Michael and Norman Schofield** (1998) *Multiparty Government: The Politics of Coalition in Europe*, Ann Arbor paperback edn, University of Michigan Press, Ann Arbor, MI.

**Laver, Michael and Kenneth A. Shepsle** (1996) *Making and Breaking Governments: Cabinets and Legislatures in Parliamentary Democracies*, Cambridge University Press, New York.

**Laver, Michael and Kenneth A. Shepsle** (1998) 'Events, equilibria, and government survival', *American Journal of Political Science*, 42 (1), 28–54.

**Laver, Michael, Scott de Marchi and Hand Mutlu** (2010) 'Negotiation in legislatures over government formation', *Public Choice*, forthcoming.

**Lupia, Arthur and Kaare Strøm** (1995) 'Coalition termination and the strategic timing of parliamentary elections', *American Political Science Review*, 89 (3), 648–665.

**Martin, Lanny W. and Randolph T. Stevenson** (2001) 'Government formation in parliamentary democracies', *American Journal of Political Science*, 45 (1), 33–50.

**Mishler, William and Richard Rose** (1997) 'Trust, distrust and skepticism: popular evaluations of civil and political institutions in post-Communist societies', *Journal of Politics*, 59 (2), 418–451.

**Müller-Rommel, Ferdinand, Katja Fettelschoss and Philipp Harfst** (2004) 'Party government in central eastern European democracies: a data collection (1990–2003)', *European Journal of Political Research*, 43 (6), 869–894.

**Müller, Wolfgang C. and Kaare Strøm** (1999) *Policy, Office, or Votes? How Political Parties in Western Europe Make Hard Decisions*, Cambridge University Press, Cambridge and New York.

**Roberts, Andrew** (2008) 'Hyperaccountability: economic voting in central and eastern Europe', *Electoral Studies*, 27 (3), 533–546.

**Schofield, Norman** (2008) *The Spatial Model of Politics*, Routledge, London.

**Strøm, Kaare** (1990) *Minority Government and Majority Rule*, Cambridge University Press, New York.

**Strøm, Kaare, Wolfgang C. Müller and Torbjörn Bergman (eds)** (2008) *Cabinets and Coalition Bargaining: The Democratic Life Cycle in Western Europe*, Oxford University Press, Oxford.

**Thies, Michael** (2001) 'Keeping tabs on partners: the logic of delegation in coalition governments', *American Journal of Political Science*, 45 (3), 580–598.

**Volden, Craig and Clifford J. Carrubba** (2004) 'The formation of oversized coalitions in modern parliamentary democracies', *American Journal of Political Science*, 48 (3), 521–537.

**Warwick, Paul** (1994) *Government Survival in Parliamentary Democracies*, Cambridge University Press, New York.

**Warwick, Paul V. and James N. Druckman** (2001) 'Portfolio salience and the proportionality of payoffs in coalition governments', *British Journal of Political Science*, 31 (4), 627–649.

**Warwick, Paul V. and James N. Druckman** (2006) 'The portfolio allocation paradox: an investigation into the nature of a very strong but puzzling relationship', *European Journal of Political Research*, 45 (4), 635–665.

# Politics outside Parliaments

**13**

## 13.1 Introduction

Most of this book deals with the formal politics of representation in modern Europe. This concerns the national politics of choosing a legislature and an executive, the transnational politics of the European Union, and the public policy outputs that emerge from these political processes. While these are all clearly central to politics in any modern European country, they are only part of the story. A large part of representative government in modern Europe takes place outside these formal structures, as different social groups, in what is often described as *civil society*, have impacts on the political process that differ considerably between European countries. There are two quite different models of how this might happen. One model, in which key social groups are closely integrated into the formal political process, is typically described as *corporatist* or *neo-corporatist*. An alternative model, in which groups compete with each other to put pressure on decision-making elites in a political 'marketplace', is typically seen as *pluralist*.

Seeing these distinctions as too stark to capture the complexities of politics in most real countries, many authors now talk in terms of models such as *social partnership*, *tripartism* and *policy networks*, which blend elements of pluralist and corporatist models.

When all is said and done, however, both corporatist and pluralist policymaking styles are symbolic of an 'old' politics that long pre-dates the ongoing revolution in information technology and consequent transformations of the global economy. Even before this revolution took hold, *new social movements* were emerging that brought people together in ways that cut across traditional political alignments. The IT revolution, however, has facilitated radically new channels of communication, radically new forms of social interaction, and radically new types of political organization. While it is still too soon to form a mature judgement about how all of this will play out, in this chapter we pull together some preliminary observations on developments that have the potential to transform the processes of representative government in modern Europe, and take it ever further outside traditional institutional channels.

## 13.2 Corporatism

### 13.2.1 The corporatist model

Corporatism as we know it today has diverse sources in the political thought of the past 100 years or so. One important current that fed into modern theories of corporatist policymaking was the *fascism* of the 1920s and 1930s. Fascist corporatism was a system of totalitarian state control of society based on an intimate interpretation of interest groups and the state. Domination of the major interest groups by the state was one of the main mechanisms of social control by fascist one-party governments, exemplified by Hitler's Germany, Mussolini's Italy and Salazar's Portugal. Obviously, any form of thought even vaguely linked with fascism was totally discredited in Europe after the Second World War. This why post-war theories of corporatism are described as 'neo' or 'liberal' corporatist.

A second intellectual source that flowed into modern corporatism was *Catholic social thought*, especially influential during the early decades of the twentieth century. Catholic church leaders became concerned that the role of the church was being undermined both by the growth of trade unionism and by what they saw as the relentless encroachment of the state into many aspects of social life. They advocated an enhanced role for self-governing interest groups that constituted what they described as the *voluntary* sector. These groups would be intimately involved not only in the *planning* but also in the *provision* of major social services such as health care and education. What lay behind this was that in a predominantly Catholic society these groups would be made up primarily of Catholics, so that public policy would be sensitive to the teachings of the church, despite a formal separation of church and state. These ideas were taken up in the early post-war years by Christian democratic parties (see Chapter 8), whose electoral success gave political impetus to neo-corporatist ideas.

A third factor that contributed to the rise of neo-corporatism was the impulse for *national unity* that followed the destruction and trauma caused by the Second World War in many European countries. As we saw in Chapter 12, a number of states went through the immediate post-war period governed by coalitions of national unity encompassing both the right and the left. A strong feeling that industry and labour needed to work together to rebuild war-torn economies fostered tripartite co-operation in places such as Austria and Germany.

One of the problems with the concept of neo-corporatism is that different people use it in different ways. Some use the term to describe little more than a system of centralized wage bargaining, in which government and the social partners of organized labour and business sit round a table and thrash out a national incomes policy. Others see corporatism as rooted much more deeply in the political system: a set of institutional arrangements that entrenches major social groups in the overall management of the national economy and much more besides. In a comprehensive review of the subject, which also provides an excellent bibliography for interested readers, Siaroff (1999: 180–181) tabulates no less than 24 different working definitions related to corporatism used by authors writing between 1981 and 1997. He also offers the definition he feels best captures the key ideas:

> 66 within an advanced industrial society and democratic polity, the co-ordinated, co-operative, and systematic management of the national economy by the state, centralized unions, and employers (these latter two co-operating directly in industry), presumably to the relative benefit of all three actors.
>
> *(Siaroff, 1999)* 99

See also Lijphart (1999), Beramendi and Reuda (2007) and Rueda (2007).

Working from this general definition, Siaroff breaks down the analysis of corporatist policy-making into four general areas. These are: the *structural* preconditions for corporatism; the *roles* within this structure fulfilled by key actors; the patterns of *behaviour* that result; and the *contextual factors* that make corporatist policymaking more likely to succeed. Structural preconditions for corporatism are typically seen as the following:

- Most workers are organized into a small number of powerful unions.
- The business community is dominated by a small number of powerful firms, organized into a powerful employers' federation.
- Wage bargaining between unions and employers is centralized.
- A powerful state is actively involved in the economy.

Both employers and unions in a successful corporatist system should have a formal institutional role, not only in making policy *but also in implementing it*. This means, for example, that when confederations of unions or employers sign off on wage deals, they must police these by sanctioning members who do not abide by what has been agreed and engage in 'unofficial' action. The types of behaviour by these social partners that are held to make corporatism work include a consensus on broad social values shared by state, unions and employers, and a preference for bargained solutions to problems, rather than solutions that are either imposed from above or the outcomes of industrial conflict.

The contextual factors argued to make corporatism work more smoothly include:

- a long tradition of social democratic rule;
- a small, open economy; and
- high expenditures on social programmes and low expenditures on defence.

The stress on policy *implementation* is what sets corporatism fundamentally apart from other forms of political decision-making that involve different socio-economic groups. For any particular decision-making regime to be seen as corporatist, interest groups must be comprehensive in their representation of particular sectors of society, but must be able to police their members. Siaroff (1999: 198) combined the criteria he extracted from the vast literature on corporatism into a simple additive index, shown in Table 13.1.

**TABLE 13.1** Corporatism scores for European democracies

| | Corporatism score | Social democrat and left % of total cabinet seats 1950–1999 |
|---|---|---|
| Austria | 5.00 | 59.7 |
| Norway | 4.86 | 71.5 |
| Sweden | 4.67 | 77.5 |
| Netherlands | 4.00 | 21.7 |
| Denmark | 3.55 | 53.3 |
| Germany | 3.54 | 24.5 |
| Switzerland | 3.38 | 23.8 |
| Finland | 3.30 | 35.0 |
| Luxembourg | 3.00 | 28.4 |
| Iceland | 3.00 | 31.7 |
| Belgium | 2.84 | 29.5 |
| Ireland | 2.00 | 14.5 |
| France | 1.67 | 24.3 |
| UK | 1.65 | 30.8 |
| Portugal | 1.50 | 30.0 |
| Italy | 1.48 | 15.0 |
| Spain | 1.25 | 57.6 |
| Greece | 1.00 | 19.7 |
| USA | 1.15 | |
| Canada | 1.15 | |

*Sources*: Left cabinet seat shares: western Europe, Swank (2009); eastern Europe, Armingeon *et al.* (2010). Also Siaroff (1999: 198).

Table 13.1 describes the situation in the mid 1990s, and groups countries crisply into three clusters. There were the 'big three' corporatist countries (Austria, Norway and Sweden), rated as clearly more corporatist than the others. After these was a group of countries ranking as moderately corporatist. The Netherlands, Germany, Denmark and Switzerland are at the more corporatist end of this group; Luxembourg, Iceland and Belgium are at the less corporatist end. Finally, there were countries that hardly ranked as corporatist at all, with Britain and Ireland (as well as the USA and Canada) joined by the Mediterranean democracies: Portugal, Spain, Italy, Greece and France. Put crudely, those parts of Europe that are neither Anglophone nor from the Catholic south are likely to be at least somewhat corporatist in their policymaking style.

Table 13.1 also repeats information from Table 14.1 on the extent of left or social democratic control of government over the post-war years, and confirms the view that this is indeed conducive to the development of a more corporatist policymaking regime. Four of the five most corporatist countries – Austria, Norway, Sweden and Denmark – were also those with the most extensive social democratic control of their post-war cabinets. The exception is the Netherlands, in which Christian democratic parties were dominant in the cabinet over much of the post-war era, yet which exhibits strongly corporatist tendencies. In this sense, the Netherlands is more like some members of the group of more moderately corporatist countries, notably including Germany, Switzerland and Belgium. As we can see from Table 13.1, most authors agree that, of all the European countries, Austria exhibits the strongest form of corporatism. By looking in greater detail at the situation in Austria, therefore, we can gain additional insight into what is involved in corporatist policymaking.

## 13.2.2 Corporatism in Austria

Austria has traditionally been seen as the classic example of a political system characterized by corporatist policymaking. More confrontational party politics in recent times, combined with Austrian membership of the European Union, have moved Austria closer to the European mainstream and away from the classic corporatist model, but Austrian politics for most of the post-war period provided one of the main sources of inspiration for scholars writing about corporatism (Crepaz and Lijphart, 1995; Siaroff, 1999; Falkner and Leiber, 2004). Perhaps the most striking and distinctive feature of Austrian politics was the important role of the *chambers*, designed to provide formal representation for the interests of labour, commerce and agriculture. Although chambers (especially chambers of commerce) can be found elsewhere, the Austrian chambers were traditionally much more important, given their statutory position and the vital role that they play in decision-making. They had the formal right to be consulted on and represented in a wide range of matters, as well as to nominate people to other public bodies.

In addition to the statutory chambers, Austria has an extensive system of *voluntary* interest groups. These include a trade union movement organized under the auspices of the 'peak' trade union organization, the ÖGB, and the League of Austrian Industrialists, the VÖI. The ÖGB, in particular, has been a powerful independent actor in Austria, as the main agency engaged in collective bargaining on behalf of its members. The ÖGB is highly centralized: the member unions, legally speaking, are subdivisions of the ÖGB, rather than the ÖGB being a federation of autonomous unions. In addition, the level of trade union affiliation in Austria has traditionally been high, and unions tend to be organized on an industry-by-industry basis.

The three main chambers – the Chambers of Labour, of Commerce and of Agriculture – and. the ÖGB have interacted with one another as the four key players in the process of making and implementing economic policy in Austria, in a system known as *Sozialpartnerschaft,* or social partnership. This system operates in parallel with, rather than in opposition to, the formal parliamentary system. Although the key interest associations are quite distinct from the political parties, the obvious political affiliations of their respective memberships mean that each association tends to be dominated by supporters of one or another of the main parties. This puts interest group leaders in a strong position. As might be expected, the Chamber of Labour and the ÖGB are dominated by the Socialists (SPÖ), and the Chamber of Commerce and Chamber of Agriculture are dominated by the conservative Austrian People's Party (ÖVP). It is important, however, not to see relations between parties and interest groups in Austria as if these were in some sense exclusive entities. On the contrary, there has been an intimate interpenetration of interest groups and parliament, a symbiosis seen by many as one of the strengths of Austrian corporatism.

### 13.2.3 Tripartism and social partners

Fully fledged corporatism reflects a deep-rooted decision-making style that rests on a history and culture of collective accommodation that cannot simply be invented as the need arises. One of the typical institutions of corporatism, the *tripartite* integration in the management of the economy between government and the two key social partners, trade unions and employers' associations, is more commonly encountered across Europe. Successful tripartism of this form depends upon the extent to which social partners can speak and act authoritatively on behalf of those they represent. Two key variables that affect this are the level of trade union membership within the working population and the centralization of wage bargaining – the extent to which national 'peak' organizations for labour and employers are involved in negotiations over wage levels. European trade union membership is densest in Scandinavia, with membership rates at 70 per cent or higher in Denmark, Finland and Sweden, and over 50 per cent in Norway (Visser, 2006). It is much lower than this in France, the Netherlands, Spain and Switzerland. The centralization of wage bargaining is highest in Austria and Scandinavia and much lower in France, Switzerland, Britain and Italy (Wallerstein, 1999; Golden and Londregan, 2006).

Perhaps the most important condition for effective tripartite wage bargaining is that the social partners can rely on strong and effective peak organizations. In Germany, for example, the peak organization for the trade union movement is the German Federation of Trade Unions (DGB), representing over 90 per cent of all unionized workers (Visser, 2006). On the side of business and industry there are three different peak organizations, but these do not compete with one another. The Federation of German Industries (BDI) concentrates on the political representation of business. The Confederation of German Employers' Associations (BDA) deals with social policy and the labour markets, including collective bargaining. The Association of German Chambers of Industry and Commerce (DIHT) represents nearly three million companies, all of which are obliged by law to affiliate, and deals with trade and commerce. Thus the three peak organizations representing the interests of capital co-ordinate their activities, and often function as one. This division of the employers' peak organizations, however, as well as the fact that the DGB can negotiate on general prices and incomes strategy but cannot bind individual member unions in its negotiations, means that Germany is probably better thought of as an example of tripartism rather than of full corporatism.

Successful tripartite negotiations between the social partners can generate a number of the effects attributed to a more comprehensive corporatist policymaking regime. Nonetheless, it is far less deeply rooted than the types of corporatist institutions that are grounded in more fundamental social attitudes about the institutional roles of the key social partners. For a comparative analysis of social partnerships in western Europe, focusing on the Netherlands, Ireland and Austria, see Hamann and Kelly (2007).

### 13.2.4 Tripartism in eastern Europe

While creating a new system of relationships between government, business and trade unions was not the first thing on the agenda for the transition states of eastern Europe, it was nonetheless a crucial matter, and post-communist countries had typically formed their first tripartite institutions by the early 1990s. The perceived achievements of western European neo-corporatism in moderating class antagonisms and co-ordinating the conflicting interests of labour and capital were often used as examples to justify new policies. Eastern European policymakers, by including representatives of labour in negotiations and decision-making, hoped to ease the pains of economic transformation and generate mass support for liberal democracy. Tripartism seemed a stabilizing feature of the social and economic landscape.

Slovenia introduced the most recognizably neo-corporatist arrangements – perhaps not surprising given Slovenia's proximity to and historic ties to the neo-corporatist 'model generator' in Austria (Feldmann, 2006; Vodovnik, 1999). Elsewhere in central and eastern Europe, Hungary formed its first National Interest Reconciliation Council in 1988–1989, and Poland started its Round Table discussions in 1989. Soon, because of dramatic declines in earnings and living standards, these tripartite commissions started focusing on the economic concerns and demands of the general population. The Interest Reconciliation Council (IRC) was formed in Hungary in 1990, and included representatives of several national trade unions and employers' organizations. Critics suggest, however, that this body was largely a remnant of the communist past, and failed to mobilize the working class to fight actively for its interests. They see the origins of tripartism in eastern Europe, not in governments trying to mediate the conflicting interests of labour and capital, but as a way to provide social support for government reform policies (Ost, 2000). Even after the 1994 electoral campaign in Hungary, during which the concept of a social pact dominated almost all parties' electoral platforms, the situation did not radically change. Negotiations on a Social Economic Agreement (SEA) were long, and highly contentious. By 1998 the IRC had been transformed into an informal consultative body, in a context where the government was setting economic policy without much formal input from organized labour.

The Hungarian experience of tripartism was by no means unique across the region. The tripartite commissions in the Czech Republic and Poland were also quite weak in negotiating and implementing agreements, in defending workers' interests, and in negotiating with the employers' associations. Dissatisfaction with what was seen as an essentially symbolic role for tripartism led to union boycotts in Poland, the Czech Republic and Slovakia. In eastern Europe the best that can be said is that tripartism means formal negotiations over very broad issues, with no guarantee that the agreements will become law or be respected by employers (Iankova, 1998; Ost, 2000; Bohle and Greskovits, 2007; Thirkell et al., 2007; Hassel 2009).

### 13.2.5 The decline of corporatism?

Views about the likely spread of corporatism were modified by the 1990s, as the institutions of corporatism appeared to decline in a number of countries during the preceding years of recession. This led to suggestion that corporatism is a 'fair-weather' phenomenon that tends to fall apart when resources become scarce and interest groups must bargain more competitively to divide up a pie that is shrinking or fixed rather than continually expanding. Two further trends may well be leading to a decline in the 'purer' forms of corporatism in modern Europe. The first concerns the ever-expanding role of the European Union in major economic policymaking, particularly after the Maastricht Treaty cemented an agreement to develop a European monetary system and a common European currency, the euro. As we have seen, this forced participating European governments to surrender some of the autonomy they had traditionally employed to manipulate key instruments of macroeconomic policy, such as interest rates, exchange rates and budget deficits. In addition, many other formerly national levers of economic policy have increasingly come under the auspices of the EU, including state supports to industry, competition policy and regional policy.

A second important trend undermining traditional corporatist arrangements concerns the steady shift in the sources of wealth generation in European economies towards the service sector and information technology, with a consequential weakening of the power of the traditional trade union movement. Modern high-tech and service industries have created an increasingly white-collar workforce, a much more rapid turnover in employment histories, and new patterns of work, which have combined to undermine the industrial power of trade unions (Lewin, 1994; Kitschelt *et al.*, 1999; Sano and Williamson, 2008). This transformation of the traditional industrial relations landscape, and the related internationalization of both the economy and economic policymaking, have combined to change in a fundamental way the set of conditions for successful neo-corporatism that we outlined above. This suggests that, over the long term, the traditional corporatist policymaking model, once such an important feature in key regions of modern Europe, will continue to decline in importance.

## 13.3 Pluralism

As with corporatism, pluralism is both a *normative* theory of how politics *ought* to be conducted and a *positive* theory of how groups *actually do* operate. As a normative theory, pluralism is one of the underpinnings of traditional liberal democracy. As a descriptive scheme, pluralism has often been used to characterize interest group activity in countries such as Britain (as well as Canada and the United States). At least in theory, many different social groups influence the policy process in pluralist systems by putting pressure on political elites in a relatively uncoordinated and competitive manner, rather than trying to work collaboratively from inside the system. In contrast to the well-ordered and collusive interaction between groups and elites that is implied by neo-corporatism, the core motif in pluralist systems is a competitive and potentially disorderly market for political influence.

Pluralism can thus be distinguished from corporatism in a number of respects, the most important of which is that pluralist interest groups have no *formal* institutional role in the allocation of resources and the implementation of policy. A second fundamental difference is that interest groups in a pluralist system are assumed to be self-generating and voluntary. This implies the existence of a range of different groups, typically competing with one another to represent the interests of the same classes of people in a given sphere of economic or social activity. A further assumption in much of pluralist theory is that, although not all groups have equal levels of power or resources, it is nonetheless relatively easy for people to form an interest group and thereby gain at least some access to the levers of political power. This suggests that many of the salient social interests in a pluralist system will be represented by the set of competing interest groups. New interests that might emerge, for one reason or another, can be represented in the political system as a result of the capacity of existing groups to adapt, or as a result of the relatively unhindered formation of new groups (Dahl, 1956; Jordan, 1990; Smith, 1990; Michalowitz, 2002).

Clearly, pluralists do not assume that the resources available to different groups are in any sense equal, or that different groups have equal access to key decision-makers. The 'market' in political influence is far from perfect, and key actors have very different capacities to affect important political decisions. Many pluralists accept that business interests are often in a highly privileged position, and that the state is far from neutral. A clear statement of this *neo-pluralist* position can be found in Charles Lindblom's influential book *Politics and Markets*. For Lindblom there are some 'grand' issues that are effectively removed from public debate by the combined power of business interests and the state. The effect of this is that conventional pluralist politics operates most effectively in relation to what can be seen as 'secondary' issues (Lindblom, 1977).

Political pressure can be applied in a number of ways. In the sphere of prices and incomes policy, for example, the process is fairly clear-cut. Policy is set on the basis of bargaining between groups, backed by the threat of the economic sanctions each group has at its disposal. Trade unions get their way in a pluralist system not because they are integrated into the political process, but because they can go on strike and inflict damage on the employers or the government with which they are dealing. Similarly, employers have power because they control the means of production and can inflict pain by engaging in lay-offs, lockouts, outsourcing, and outright plant closures. The most distinctive feature of the pluralist decision-making, therefore, is that it is *characterized by conflict rather than consensus*. Of course, conflict does not always manifest itself in the shape of strikes, lockouts, and the like. It is the *threat* of these sanctions, whether explicit or implicit, that underpins pluralist bargaining. Indeed, if the various actors are rational and equipped with perfect information, they anticipate the outcome of potential conflicts and settle their differences before overt hostilities begin. Manifest conflicts, real-world strikes and lockouts are the product of imperfect information, happening when competing groups test each other's strengths and weaknesses. Taking all of this into account, the outcome of political activity in a pluralist system is assumed to be a product of the balance of forces between the various groups involved. And this balance of forces is determined by the *anticipated* outcomes of head-to-head confrontations over essential conflicts of interest.

Most people put pluralism and corporatism at opposite ends of a spectrum describing different types of group politics. For this reason, studies that describe different countries as being more, or less, corporatist also make judgements about the extent of pluralist decision-making. Thus Table 13.1 is also a ranking of European countries in terms of the extent to which they have a group politics that can be thought of as pluralist. As we have seen, a striking regularity in Table 13.1 is the tight cluster of the Mediterranean and English-speaking European democracies at the pluralist end of this spectrum, all characterized by a more market-oriented style of interaction between the main social partners.

### 13.3.1 Pluralism in Britain

Table 13.1 shows us that Britain is a key member of the pluralist cluster of countries in modern Europe. Notwithstanding the brief existence during the 1970s of a 'social contract' between the then Labour government, the Trades Union Congress (TUC) and the Confederation of British Industry (CBI), the best way of describing interactions between the main social partners during most of the post-war era in Britain is *competitive* rather than *co-operative*. British trade unions have traditionally set great store by their right to *free collective bargaining*, backed up by a right to strike that is regularly exercised. Even more than the unions, British employers have mostly been willing to take their chances in the rough and tumble of the labour market rather than get involved in institutionalized collaboration with the unions.

The fragility of what appeared to be moves towards tripartite decision-making in Britain, with the social contract of the mid 1970s, can be seen clearly from the speed with which confrontational bargaining was restored after the introduction of government-imposed wage ceilings in 1977. Equally striking is the success of the Conservative attack on trade union rights and privileges after Margaret Thatcher's election victory in May 1979. As early as July 1979, the Conservatives proposed a series of restrictions on trade union power. These included: the banning of secondary picketing (that is, picketing away from the main scene of an industrial dispute); the restriction of closed shops (which oblige all who work in a particular employment to join a particular union); and the requirement that unions hold secret ballots of those involved before calling strikes. A series of laws restricting trade union power was passed shortly afterwards. Confrontation between government and unions came to a head in a long and very bruising miners' strike that began in March 1984 and which soured industrial relations in Britain for many years. A strong belief in the effectiveness of the market left no room for tripartite economic planning involving agreements between government, employers and unions. In this regard, not a lot changed after substantial election victories for Labour in 1997, 2001 and 2005. Over three full terms in office from 1997 to 2010 'New' Labour did not seek a dramatic rolling back of Thatcherite trade union legislation, made no conscious attempt to forge a new social contract between the social partners, and gave no real indication that Britain was likely to move away from an essentially pluralist form of interest group representation. There was no sign that the Conservative–Liberal Democrat coalition that came to power in Britain in 2010 would do anything to change this.

### 13.3.2  Pluralism in action: the women's movement

While the corporatist model of interest group politics explicitly refers to management of the economy, and the role of both unions and employers in this, the pluralist model is entirely open as to which particular interests might put pressure on the decision-making system. Indeed, one of the virtues claimed for pluralism by its champions is that a *free market* in influence can adapt to changes in society and allow new groups into the decision-making loop. Whether or not this claim is justified, changes both in the structure of society and in social attitudes do have the potential to change the focus of interest group politics. This can be seen quite clearly in the rise to prominence, towards the end of the twentieth century, of both the women's movement and the environmental movement.

As we saw in Table 11.5, women are systematically under-represented at virtually every level of politics in virtually every European country. This under-representation arises not only within political parties and bureaucracies, but also in the peak organizations of the social partners (there are relatively few women among senior trade unionists or business leaders), and in entrenched economic and professional interest groups such as churches, farmers, lawyers and doctors. The political under-representation of women arises even in Scandinavia, where the women's movement has made more progress than anywhere else. Monique Leyanaar provides a comprehensive overview of the evolution of women's representation in the formal political system (Leyenaar, 2004). While women's issues have been pursued within existing organizations, be they trade unions or political parties, groups promoting women's interests have often been forced to operate outside the formal structure of representative institutions, in single-issue pressure group politics of particular relevance to women, including abortion, divorce, domestic violence, and a range of equal rights causes.

Such activism and 'outside' pressure by women's groups has forced at least the public face of many mainstream decision-making organizations to take women's issues more seriously. More recently, the (almost corporatist) notion of *mainstreaming* gender issues – building gender into the heart of decision-making wherever key decisions might be made – has become central to the debate on the role of gender in the decision-making process. This approach rejects the notion of women as an interest group trying to influence public decision-making from a position that is essentially outside the loop. Rather, women are seen as an integral part of the process. But the very existence and success of mainstreaming policies in a number of countries provides a good example of the way in which issues can be forced up the political agenda by interest group politics (Beveridge *et al.*, 2000; Mazey, 2001).

### 13.3.3 Pluralism in action: the environmental movement

The environmental movement in Europe has for the most part adopted a very different strategy in its attempt to have an impact on public policy, seen in the rise of Green parties, discussed in Chapter 8. Until recently, Green parties tended to look quite unlike traditional political parties, sharing many of the features of new social movements, described in a later section. They promoted views that cut across traditional ideological lines, while having members who had ambivalent attitudes towards the need for strong party leadership. Green parties have increasingly found themselves in a position to bargain their way into government, as they have done on occasion in Belgium, Finland, France, Germany and Ireland, with the most sustained Green government participation in Germany. The main impact of Green parties on mainstream environmental policy across the range of European countries, however, has been indirect – in the 'greening' of their main opponents, many of which have adopted more environmentalist policies once it became clear that Green parties could attract votes.

Notwithstanding the electoral role of the Green parties, there are many other active environmental groups in Europe, most of which use more direct political strategies. Greenpeace, to take the most prominent example, was formed in 1971 to oppose underground nuclear testing by attempting to sail a small ship into a nuclear test zone. Now based in Amsterdam, Greenpeace claims 2.8 million supporters worldwide; it is a major international organization with offices in over 40 countries that employ a substantial number of people. In his introduction to the organization's 2008–2009 annual report, the executive director of Greenpeace begins: 'On my first day as the new Executive Director of Greenpeace, I was arrested.' This sets the tone for the confrontational 'outsider group' style that characterizes the organization. Greenpeace has engaged in a series of headline-grabbing campaigns that have been effective at putting environmental issues on the public agenda, blocking an outfall from the British nuclear reprocessing plant at Sellafield, and placing Greenpeace members in rubber dinghies between whaling ships and whales in the Antarctic, or in the way of ships dumping toxic wastes in the North Sea. One of its most famous campaigns was against French nuclear testing, and culminated in 1985 with the sinking in New Zealand of its boat *The Rainbow Warrior* by the French secret service. Greenpeace now runs a fleet of four boats, spearheading its campaigns to put pressure on national governments. Greenpeace is thus a large and by now long-established example of a classic 'outsider' pressure group with a policy of mass networking and a strategy of confronting policymakers rather than working with them from inside the system.

Most other environmental groups share with Greenpeace the fact that they have almost no institutionalized access to power, and are forced to rely on more direct forms of pressure. When state environmental protection agencies are established, for example, prominent individuals associated with environmental causes may be selected for some role or other, but there are very few examples in Europe of environmentalist groups being given formal policymaking and implementation status, along neo-corporatist lines. In part this may be because the more successful groups, such as Greenpeace, have deliberately distanced themselves from the political establishment and have fostered a counter-cultural appeal. In part it may be because established parties and other organizations have identified the politics of the environment as something that they can profitably annex for themselves. They are therefore unwilling to allow environmental groups to use Green politics to gain any sort of foothold within established political systems (Carter, 2001; Rootes, 2003; Doyle and McEachern, 2008).

## 13.4 Policy networks

Political scientists have come to see pure corporatist and pluralist models of national policy-making as too simplistic to handle the complex patterns of decision-making we find in modern Europe. Two important and related developments, noted in our discussion of the decline of corporatism, derive from the globalization of economic life and the accumulation of functions by the European Union. The net effect is that key decisions are increasingly made, and must therefore be influenced, at a supranational level. The European Union is itself a very distinctive decision-making system, unlike that of any single national government, and blending elements of pluralism and corporatism in its decision-making style. It has become increasingly important for interest groups to influence EU decisions, since these typically bear more upon their interests than decisions taken by national governments. For European farmers, for example, EU agricultural policy has a direct and absolutely vital bearing upon how easy it is for each of them to earn a living (Pappi and Henning, 1999).

These developments have led to a growth in importance of European peak organizations that reflect core economic interests (of farmers, for example, or trade unions) at a supranational level. These peak organizations typically base themselves in Brussels and have direct access to EU decision-making elites. This makes it possible for national interest groups to bypass national governments when they set out to influence EU decision-making. Alternatively, or indeed at the same time, a national interest group may put pressure on its national government in an attempt to influence EU policy via the government's role in the Council of Ministers.

This system of *multilevel governance* creates a complex policymaking environment. Many actors are trying to influence each another, and are exploring different routes through a complicated system of interactions. One way of trying to make sense of such a complex system of links, whether within the EU or elsewhere, is to see them as a network, leading scholars to talk in terms of a *policy network*. The key relationships defining a policy network involve mutual interdependence, and exchanges between key agents in the policymaking system. Since all policy influence involves interaction with others, when some public or private actor interacts over and over again with the same set of other actors, both sides steadily learn about each other and begin to develop well-defined mutual interactions. Thus farmers' organizations deal repeatedly with their national departments of agriculture, with farmers' organizations in other countries, with European peak organizations for farmers, and with particular offices of the European Commission. Each has information the other values. Each may be helpful to the other in some part of the process of either making or implementing policy. In this way, relationships between the various agents involved in the policy process evolve in a manner that is structured by clearly understood informal rules of the game that can be as potent as formal institutions. This set of established interactions can be thought of as a policy network (Pappi and Henning, 1998; Thatcher, 1998; Adams *et al.*, 2005; ). For a sceptical view, see Dowding (1995).

## BOX 13.1: ECONOMIC POLICYMAKING

### Denmark

In terms of standard measures of the extent of corporatist policymaking, Denmark looks quite like Germany and the Netherlands – with strong norms of consensual decision-making that fall short of full neo-corporatism. Union density is high in Denmark, at about 75 per cent. There are national peak organizations for employers, Dansk Arbejdsgiverforening (DA), and unions, Landsorganisationen i Danmark (LO). These tend to operate on the basis of consensual bargaining that leads to national agreements covering a high proportion of the workforce and deal with many aspects of the work environment, over and above wages. The preference of these peak organizations for bipartite consensus solutions has allowed the government to take something of a back seat in this process, and there is no official 'tripartite' bargaining system. This role for government must be seen in the context, however, of welfare state provisions in Denmark that are far more generous that those in many other parts of modern Europe.

### France

The low level of unionization, divisions in the French labour movement, and the fact that the left did not come to power in France until 1981 have led most people to characterize economic policymaking in France as confrontational and pluralist rather than corporatist. A small number of big labour unions have been important, each traditionally associated with a political party rather than with a trade or an industry. Thus political divisions have been reproduced in the union movement, which has rarely been a united, monolithic bloc working against either government or employers. When there have been income policies – for example, in the early 1980s – these have not been based on tripartite agreements between the social partners. Instead, they have been imposed by the government. Both unions and employers are unwilling to sacrifice their autonomy, and even during periods of socialist government, relations between unions and government have not been particularly close. The main areas of conflict between unions, employers and government have been over the shortening of the working week and proposals for funding long-term commitments to pay state pensions.

### Germany

Although the level of unionization is not high, unions are organized on an industry rather than a craft basis, and so all employees at a particular facility belong to the same union. The German Federation of Trade Unions (DGB) represents the vast majority of unionized workers; it deals with union–government relations, while individual unions take care of collective bargaining over wages and conditions. Different employers' federations co-ordinate their actions rather than compete with one another. There have been periods of explicit 'concerted action' when the social partners negotiated an economic programme of prices and incomes that was implemented by the government. In general, the social partners in Germany have been oriented towards negotiation rather than confrontation in economic policymaking.

### Italy

Italy is characterized by a set of labour unions divided on political lines rather than in terms of crafts or industries. Despite the relatively low level of unionization, there are three competing union federations – the CGIL, the CISL and the UIL – confronting a single employers' federation, the Confindustria. There have been brief periods during which social partners attempted to emulate the concerted action arrangements found in northern Europe, notably the period of 'national solidarity' from 1977 to 1979 and the Tripartite Agreement of 1983. Deals such as these did not expand into more broadly based tripartite arrangements, however, and by the early twenty-first century relations between social partners remained essentially market-oriented and pluralistic.

## Netherlands

Economic policymaking in the Netherlands has proved hard for political scientists to classify. The level of unionization is low by European standards, and the major trade union federation does not have a high share of trade union membership. Yet economic policymaking has a broadly co-operative style. Unions have engaged in centralized bargaining with the government, although a strong bureaucratic tradition in the Netherlands has tended to mean that such negotiations are usually dominated by the state. Dutch unions, compared with unions in most other European states, have placed a heavier emphasis in their dealings with government on the development of an extensive system of welfare benefits. In this regard they have been quite successful, and levels of welfare benefits in the Netherlands are among the highest in Europe. The economy of the Netherlands is one of the most open in Europe, with very high levels of foreign investment. This tends to restrict the impact of indigenous employers on the economy, and hence their role as social partners.

## Poland

Since the collapse of communism, in the Polish case closely associated with the activities the trade union movement, Polish governments have been quick to introduce procedures governing industrial relations. The two largest trade unions in Poland are currently the OPZZ (the Polish Alliance of Trade Unions), which sees itself as a partner of the social-democratic groups in Polish politics, and NSZZ (the Solidarity Independent and Self-governing Trade Union), which formed the AWS, a right-wing party that governed Poland from 1997 to 2001. The OPZZ has three million members while Solidarity has 900 000. However, the strength of these and other smaller trade unions has been tempered by very high rates of unemployment in Poland. Furthermore, the political tensions between the OPZZ and Solidarity have ensured that economic bargaining in Poland has retained a pluralist character. Arguably, international organizations such as the EU and IMF have had a far greater impact on Polish economic policy than the domestic social partners.

## Spain

Spain under Franco was a totalitarian state, with government domination of all aspects of economic life over a very long period. In post-Franco Spain, as in France and Italy, unions are organized along political lines, and the level of unionization is relatively low. Nonetheless, there has been a series of pacts between government, the two key peak organizations of unions (the CCOO and the UGT) and a single peak employers' federation (the CEOE), beginning with the Moncloa Pact of 1977. These pacts dealt with wage restraint, on the one hand, and a restrained approach to the problem of rectifying public finances, on the other. Although unions and employers were involved in negotiation of the pacts, which have continued under both bourgeois and socialist governments, they had little formal role in their implementation.

## United Kingdom

Often cited as one of the classic examples of a pluralist rather than a corporatist system, the United Kingdom has a relatively decentralized system of wage bargaining. Wage negotiations are conducted by a large number of trade unions, and are organized on a craft basis rather than on an industry basis, and so many unions may well be involved in simultaneous negotiations with a single

> **BOX 13.1: CONTINUED**

employer – a car manufacturer, for example. Most but not all unions are affiliated with a relatively weak national federation, the Trades Union Congress (TUC), and the proportion of the workforce belonging to a trade union is about average by European standards. For a brief period during the mid 1970s, there was a 'social contract' between unions, employers (represented by the Confederation of British Industry, CBI) and a Labour government. This collapsed after unilateral action by the government, however, and has not since been renewed. Relations between unions and government have been essentially confrontational since then, and a substantial package of anti-union legislation introduced by Margaret Thatcher's Conservative government was left largely unchanged by the Labour government that held power between 1997 and 2010.

### 13.4.1  Policy networks in action: doctors

Physicians are typically organized as members of a self-governing profession. This provides an important basis for the exercise of political power on behalf of sectional interests. The key powers associated with the professional status of physicians derive from the fact that health care is an expert service, one that cannot properly be evaluated by its consumers or even by non-specialist political elites. This gives doctors the more or less unchallenged ability to define and defend professional standards of medical practice, and therefore to control medical training and licensing, and hence access to the profession. This control is typically exercised by a powerful guild-like medical association to which all licensed physicians must belong. The medical association typically also plays a vital policy implementation role, besides controlling professional ethics and standards, and thereby practice, via a system of peer review. Politicians can make all the policies they want on health and medicine, but they cannot implement such policies effectively without the co-operation of the medical profession, organized by the medical association. This gives the medical lobby a very powerful position in the policy process. The control of highly specialized information by the profession, and the need for the co-operation of physicians in the effective implementation of policy, form the basis of an exchange relationship between physicians and decision-making elites that can very usefully be thought of as a policy network. When health policy is made at the national level, medical associations in Europe appear to be able to exploit with potent effect their ability to monopolize the market in expertise, a situation also found in the United States, given the political role of the American Medical Association. And the exercise of this monopoly inevitably gives them both control over vital information and a key role in the implementation, as well as the making, of health care policy. This creates the type of mutual interdependence between decision-makers and interest organizations that can fruitfully be seen as a policy network (Freeman, 2000; Navarro *et al.*, 2006).

### 13.4.2  Policy networks in action: farmers

There is a strong tradition in Europe for farmers' groups to be intimately integrated into the political system, wielding disproportionately more influence over policymakers than other groups with an interest in agriculture – *consumers* of farm products, for example, the unemployed or environmentalists. A succession of wars in Europe led governments to cultivate indigenous food producers very carefully and set up a policymaking regime based upon assumptions of mutual interdependence between decision-makers and interest groups – in other words, to set up agricultural policy networks. As a result, there has been a long tradition of farm support programmes, typically involving government intervention in agricultural markets at guaranteed prices, to protect the interests of farmers. For those countries in what has become the European Union (EU), this tradition was enshrined in the Common Agricultural Policy (CAP), with its system of intervention prices and consequent 'mountains' of stored butter or grain and 'lakes' of surplus wine or milk (see Chapter 5).

The effect of all this was that agricultural policymaking in the European Union for a long time involved a very explicit and effective policy network operating at a supranational level. Farmers' organizations quickly learned that they needed to pile on the pressure in Brussels as well as in their national capitals, and quickly adapted to take account of this. This was made easier because the power of the farmers' lobby is usually exercised, even in pluralist systems such as Britain's, in a very institutionalized way. Farmers' organizations, such as the British National Farmers' Union (NFU), have traditionally had consultative status with ministries of agriculture on many matters. Farmers and civil servants have tended to settle matters between themselves, and to exclude other interest groups if at all possible. It has been quite common, furthermore, for farmers' groups to be involved in policy implementation, especially in relation to the distribution among individual farmers of the official national and regional production quotas for particular agricultural commodities. This close co-operation between the farmers and the civil service might on the face of it look almost corporatist. However, the lack of any formal role in the political equation for any other social partner identifies this type of decision-making arrangement as being more like a closed policy network than an example of full-fledged corporatism.

## 13.5 New social movements

Moving beyond the social partners and traditional economic or vocational interest groups that populate the mainstream policymaking system in modern Europe, we find a cluster of groups and organizations, usually with more loosely defined structures, that have a fair amount in common with one another. As well as women's and environmental movements, it is easy to find active and engaged anti-racist, anti-war, anti-globalization, anti-colonialist or pro-human rights groups, gay rights groups, animal rights and anti-nuclear groups, and groups promoting a range of more or less radical single-issue causes. Many of these share features that, taken together, lead them to be classified as *new social movements* (Kriesi *et al.*, 1992; McAdam *et al.*, 1996), which are seen as *postmaterialist* or *postmodern* alternatives to traditional political parties and entrenched interest organizations.

The membership of a typical new social movement, although this may well not be formally defined, tends to be fluid. People drift in and out of the movement on a rather casual basis, and there may well be no formal membership. The leadership (although some of these groups are actively opposed to any notion of formal leadership) often has an intellectual lineage that can be traced to the period of student radicalism of the late 1960s and early 1970s. The views these movements represent tend to cut across traditional ideological lines. It is fair to say, however, that most of these groups can be seen as aligned more with the left than the right of the traditional ideological spectrum, and that many such movements have emerged as informal activist alternatives to more traditional and formal party political or trade union organizations representing the left.

In terms of internal organization, people supporting new social movements tend to feel strongly in favour of active participation and group democracy, rather than the more passive membership and hierarchical decision-making structures of a traditional political party, trade union, or interest group. Some new social movements, as we have seen, may even refuse to acknowledge that they have any leadership at all. When it comes to intervening in the political process, they tend to work outside traditional institutional channels. Demonstrations, boycotts and other forms of direct action are preferred to lobbying, letter writing, petitions, and more conventional pressure tactics (Dalton, 2002; Pattie and Johnston, 2009). Direct action such as this serves a number of purposes. It mobilizes and engages people who would otherwise be alienated from the political process; it forces new issues onto the political agenda; and it maintains the group's status as a counter-cultural outsider, rather than as a co-opted part of the traditional establishment. Mainstream politicians may fret over declining popular participation in politics, measuring this in terms of steadily declining turnout at local, national and European Parliament elections. At the same time, the success of anti-globalization or anti-war groups in mobilizing people for large popular demonstrations shows that many people may find direct participation in the activities of new social movements more fulfilling, and potentially more effective, than voting for established political parties.

## 13.6 New social networks

One crucial technological change underpinning growing popular participation in various types of less conventional social movement has been explosive growth and penetration of the Internet and World Wide Web. Certainly, as far as modern Europe is concerned, it is now very easy for new movements and organizations to establish a significant presence on the Web, which is growing explosively in importance as a source of information, given the growing power and penetration of Internet search engines. Information on almost any issue is no more than a few mouse clicks away for large numbers of Europe's citizens, especially its younger citizens, and information can be found that is tailored to almost every social and political view (Sunstein, 2002, 2007). Email and social networking sites have made international person-to-person interaction and networking cheap, and effectively instantaneous (Christakis and Fowler, 2009). More importantly, online electronic media have reduced the cost of entry into what we might think of as *cyber activism* to effectively zero.

Perhaps the most active online communities that underlie social movements (at the time of writing though this will surely change) are Facebook and Twitter, both with deep worldwide penetration. While these two popular social networking platforms each do somewhat different things, the ability of both to facilitate social activism is clear. *Facebook* is a robust social networking service that enables users to exchange media content, create special interest pages and, most relevant to this discussion, provide users with the ability to join social activism groups, sign petitions, and connect with local and/or international activists. *Twitter* is a micro-blogging service that enables users to post short messages as frequently as they like. The social networking component is generated by the ability of users to follow each others' posts. This distinguishes Twitter from Facebook, which requires dyadic relationships to exchange information. Twitter is thus inherently public, and its impact on social movements has been largely one of information aggregation and dissemination, rather than collective identification.

A team of computer scientists has studied the structural properties and content of Twitter, only to find that these did not resemble a social network (Kwak *et al.*, 2010). Instead, they found that

Twitter was consistently used as something more like a news service. Users exchanged links to news articles dealing with niche areas of interest, or to disseminate breaking news. A good example of this, outside modern Europe but directly relevant, concerns the use of Twitter during protests following the contested Iranian presidential elections of 2009. Anti-regime groups used Twitter to organize protests and send information about what was going on to an international public, including more traditional media outlets. What was particularly striking about the Iranian case was that this provided a glimpse into political unrest in a country that would otherwise have been an information vacuum.

A primary consequence of these informational and organizational products of new technology is that governments and other 'official' groups find their previously powerful positions in the communications infrastructure greatly undermined. At the same time, forms of political organization that cut radically across traditional social and economic linkages have been greatly facilitated. All of this has had the effect of forcing people to re-evaluate what they have in mind when they think of political participation, political communication and group politics, recent changes in which have the potential to have far-reaching long-term effects (Bimber, 1998, 2003).

While new technologies may have opened new frontiers in social movements, they also have negative consequences for these same movements. First, services like Facebook and Twitter reduce the cost of participation to almost nothing. This means that, while these movements can appear formidable, with huge numbers of 'members', the near-zero cost of membership means that these numbers could well reflect only a tiny group of *active* participants. Having many members in some Facebook group does not make an effective social movement, and casual online behaviour has been referred to as a 'slacktivism' that arises from a general feeling of participating in a social movement, without actually paying a meaningful cost. A second cost arises if the content of exchanges, and the identities and locations of activists, can easily be discovered by state intelligence and security forces. This became readily apparent during the post-election protests in Iran, when the state apparently exploited data available on Twitter to gather intelligence about the protesters and target their activity, even going so far as to establish their own Twitter accounts to post misinformation and disrupt the ongoing protests (Morozov, 2009).

## 13.7 Conclusions

There are enormous and ongoing technology-driven changes in the ways that citizens in every modern European country interact with each other. There is also an undoubted erosion of the classical distinction between the type of corporatist decision-making model we see in Austria and the type of pluralist model we find in France. Nonetheless, we can still distinguish between groups of countries where the general approach to public decision-making on major issues is more corporatist and those where it is more pluralist. At the heart of this distinction is the extent to which major public policy decisions are the outcome of negotiations that take place, away from the public gaze, between established national peak organizations representing fundamental economic and social interests, as happens in the more corporatist decision-making systems. This type of decision-making is inherently consensual, but in effect bypasses the conventional channels of representative government. This contrasts with more pluralist decision-making systems in which there is an underlying acceptance that, at almost any time and in almost any place, groups of interested citizens may band together to put pressure on decision-makers and public representatives in a political arena that is much more openly conflictual.

Everywhere, of course, the only recourse for groups outside the political establishment, the vast majority of groups in any country, is the traditional portfolio of techniques that characterize pressure politics. In most European countries we find groups sharing features of organization, membership and strategy that identify them as new social movements. These groups provide a medium of interest representation that is quite distinct from traditional parties, unions and interest organizations, and they do so in a way that has been significantly enhanced by the development of the Internet and the World Wide Web. In representing interests and opinions in this way, such groups provide an alternative medium for political participation by citizens, and quite possibly counterbalance the long-term trend for declining citizen participation in more traditional forms of public decision-making such as voting in elections. Citizens have never before had so much technology at their disposal to gather their own information, and to communicate and make common cause with like-minded others they have never met.

The other side of this coin is that governments have never before had so much technology at their disposal to gather, analyse and act on information about their citizens, potentially realizing fears expressed in George Orwell's classic dystopian vision, *1984*. We are only at the beginning of this undoubted revolution in the very nature of political interaction, the impact of which will manifest itself on politics that takes place *outside* traditional structures of representative government in modern Europe.

## References

**Adams, James F., Samuel Merrill and Bernard Grofman** (2005) *A Unified Theory of Party Competition: A Cross-National Analysis Integrating Spatial and Behavioral Factors*, Cambridge University Press, Cambridge.

**Armingeon, Klaus, Romana Careja, Sarah Engler, Panajotis Potolidis, Marlène Gerber and Philipp Leimgruber** (2010) *Comparative Political Data Set III 1990–2008*, Institute of Political Science, University of Berne.

**Beramendi, Pablo and David Rueda** (2007) 'Social democracy constrained: indirect taxation in industrialized democracies', *British Journal of Political Science*, 37 (4), 619–641.

**Beveridge, Fiona, Sue Nott and Kylie Stephen** (2000) 'Mainstreaming and the engendering of policy-making: a means to an end?', *Journal of European Public Policy*, 7 (3), 385–405.

**Bimber, Bruce** (1998) 'The Internet and political transformation: populism, community, and accelerated pluralism', *Polity*, 31 (1), 133–160.

**Bimber, Bruce** (2003) *Information and American Democracy: Technology in the Evolution of Political Power*, Cambridge University Press, Cambridge.

**Bohle, Dorothee and Béla Greskovits** (2007) 'Neoliberalism, embedded neoliberalism and neo-corporatism: towards transnational capitalism in Central-Eastern Europe', *West European Politics*, 30 (3), 443–466.

**Carter, Neil** (2001) *The Politics of the Environment: Ideas, Activism, Policy*, Cambridge University Press, Cambridge.

**Christakis, Nicholas A. and James H. Fowler** (2009) *Connected: The Surprising Power of Social Networks and How They Shape Our Lives*, Little, Brown, and Company, New York.

**Crepaz, Markus and Arend Lijphart** (1995) 'Linking and integrating corporatism and consensus democracy: theory, concepts and evidence', *British Journal of Political Science*, 25 (2), 281–288.

**Dahl, Robert A.** (1956) *A Preface to Democratic Theory*, University of Chicago Press, Chicago.

**Dalton, Russell** (2002) *Citizen Politics*, 3rd edn, Chatham House, Chatham, NJ.

**Dowding, Keith** (1995) 'Model or metaphor? A critical review of the policy network approach', *Political Studies*, 43 (1), 136–158.

Doyle, Timothy and Doug McEachern (2008) *Environment and Politics*, 3rd edn, Routledge, New York.

Falkner, Gerda and Simone Leiber (2004) 'Europeanization of social partnership in smaller European democracies?', *European Journal of Industrial Relations*, 10 (3), 245–266.

Feldmann, Magnus (2006) 'Emerging varieties of capitalism in transition countries: industrial relations and wage bargaining in Estonia and Slovenia', *Comparative Political Studies*, 39 (7), 829–854.

Freeman, Richard (2000) *The Politics of Health in Europe*, Manchester University Press, Manchester.

Golden, Miriam A. and John B. Londregan (2006) 'Centralization of bargaining and wage inequality: a correction of Wallerstein', *American Journal of Political Science*, 50 (1), 208–213.

Hamann, Kerstin and John Kelly (2007) 'Party politics and the re-emergence of social pacts in western Europe', *Comparative Political Studies*, 40 (8), 971–994.

Hassel, Anke (2009) 'Policies and politics in social pacts in Europe', *European Journal of Industrial Relations*, 15 (1), 7–26.

Iankova, Elena (1998) 'The transformative corporatism of eastern Europe', *East European Politics and Society*, 12 (2), 222–264.

Jordan, Grant (1990) 'The pluralism of pluralism: an anti-theory?', *Political Studies*, 38 (2), 286–301.

Kitschelt, Herbert, Peter Lange, Gary Marks and John D. Stephens (eds) (1999) *Continuity and Change in Contemporary Capitalism*, Cambridge University Press, Cambridge.

Kriesi, H., R. Koopmans, J.W. Duyvendak and M.G. Giugni (1992) 'New social movements and political opportunities in western Europe', *European Journal of Political Research*, 22 (2), 219–244.

Kwak, Haewoon, Changhyun Lee, Hosung Park and Sue Moon (2010) 'What is Twitter, a social network or a news media?' Paper read at 19th International World Wide Web (WWW) Conference, Raleigh, NC.

Lewin, Leif (1994) 'The rise and decline of corporatism: the case of Sweden', *European Journal of Political Research*, 26 (1), 59–79.

Leyenaar, Monique (2004) *Political Empowerment of Women: The Netherlands and Other Countries*, Martinus Nijhoff, Leiden.

Lijphart, A. (1999) *Patterns of Democracy: Government Forms and Performance in Thirty-Six Countries*. Yale University Press, New Haven, CT.

Lindblom, Charles (1977) *Politics and Markets*, Basic Books, New York.

Mazey, Sonia (2001) *Gender Mainstreaming in the EU: Principles and Practices*, Kogan Page, London.

McAdam, Doug, John D. McCarthy and Mayer N. Zald (eds) (1996) *Comparative Perspectives on Social Movements*, Cambridge University Press, Cambridge.

Michalowitz, Irina (2002) 'Beyond corporatism and pluralism: towards a new theoretical framework', pp. 35–54 in A. Warleigh and J. Fairbass (eds), *Influence and Interests in the European Union: The New Politics of Persuasion and Advocacy*, Europa Publications, London.

Morozov, Evgeny (2009) 'Iran: downside to the "Twitter Revolution"', *Dissent*, 56 (4), 10–14.

Navarro, V., C. Muntaner, C. Borrell, J. Benach, Á. Quiroga, M. Rodríguez-Sanz, N. Vergés and M. Pasarín (2006) 'Politics and health outcomes', *The Lancet*, 368 (9540), 1033–1037.

Ost, David (2000) 'Illusory corporatism in eastern Europe: neoliberal tripartism and postcommunist class identities', *Politics and Society*, 28 (4), 503–530.

Pappi, Franz and Christian Henning (1998) 'Policy networks: more than a metaphor', *Journal of Theoretical Politics*, 10 (4), 553–576.

Pappi, Franz and Christian Henning (1999) 'The organization of influence on the EC's Common Agricultural Policy: a network approach', *European Journal of Political Research*, 36 (2), 257–281.

Pattie, Charles and Ron Johnston (2009) 'Conversation, disagreement and political participation', *Political Behavior*, 31 (2), 261–285.

Rootes, Christopher (ed.) (2003) *Environmental Protest in Western Europe*, Oxford University Press, Oxford.

**Rueda, David** (2007) *Social Democracy Inside Out: Partisanship and Labor Market Policy in Industrialized Democracies*, Oxford University Press, Oxford.

**Sano, Joelle and John Williamson** (2008) 'Factors affecting union decline in 18 OECD countries and their implications for labor movement reform', *International Journal of Comparative Sociology*, 49 (6), 479–500.

**Siaroff, Alan** (1999) 'Corporatism in 24 industrial democracies: meaning and measurement', *European Journal of Political Research*, 36 (2), 175–205.

**Smith, Martin J.** (1990) 'Pluralism, reformed pluralism and neopluralism: the role of pressure groups in policy-making', *Political Studies*, 38 (2), 302–322.

**Sunstein, Cass** (2002) *Republic.com*, Princeton University Press, Princeton, NJ.

**Sunstein, Cass** (2007) *Republic.com 2.0*, Princeton University Press, Princeton, NJ.

**Swank, Duane** (2009) *Electoral, Legislative, and Government Strength of Political Parties by Ideological Group in Capitalist Democracies, 1950–2006: A Database*, Department of Political Science, Marquette University.

**Thatcher, Mark** (1998) 'The development of policy network analysis: from modest origins to overarching frameworks', *Journal of Theoretical Politics*, 10 (4), 389–416.

**Thirkell, John, Richard Scase and Sarah Vickerstaff** (2007) 'Labour relations in transition in Eastern Europe' *Industrial Relations Journal*, 25 (2), 84–95.

**Visser, Jelle** (2006) *Union Membership Statistics in 24 Countries*, United States Department of Labor, Bureau of Labor Statisics.

**Vodovnik, Zvone** (1999) 'Tripartism and industrial relations in Slovenia', pp. 305–318 in G. Casale (ed.), *Social Dialogue in Central and Eastern Europe*, International Labour Organization, Geneva.

**Wallerstein, Michael** (1999) 'Wage-setting institutions and pay inequality in advanced industrial societies', *American Journal of Political Science*, 43 (3), 649–680.

# 14

# Does Representative Government make a Difference?

## 14.1 Introduction

The main reason to be interested in politics is that politics should make a difference. The processes of representative democracy should affect what actually happens. Election results and the formation of governments should affect the public policies that are eventually implemented. If they do not, the whole edifice of representative government is little more than a facade. It sometimes seems, however, that politics at the *national* level is making less and less of a difference in an era of globalization that increasingly constrains the freedom of sovereign governments to implement distinctive policy positions. As we saw when discussing the European Union, furthermore, many aspects of economic policy that were once the exclusive preserve of national governments are now decided at European level.

A major example of this is the creation of a common European currency, the euro. In exchange for the benefits of a common currency, European governments within the Eurozone gave up control over key policy instruments that were previously central to how they ran their economies. To take a key example, Eurozone governments lost the freedom to set interest rates and print money. This means they can no longer try to cool down inflationary booms by raising interest rates or choking off the money supply, or try to stimulate their economies out of recessions by lowering interest rates or allowing their currency to depreciate against the currencies of economic competitors. This loss of national control became critical during the 2010 crisis over the level of public debt in Greece. Finding it increasingly difficult to sell government bonds to finance its debt, the Greek government was unable to use the traditional remedy of printing money and allowing the drachma to depreciate on world markets. What would formerly have been a more isolated national crisis spread quickly to involve the entire Eurozone and thereby the global economy more generally. Moving beyond the economy, freedom to set many aspects of public policy in the central and eastern European states that were candidates for EU membership was significantly affected by the *acquis communautaire*, the body of settled EU law and policy with which candidate states were required to align their national legal and administrative systems (Vachudova, 2005).

In many obvious ways, therefore, national politics has come to make less of a difference for important aspects of policymaking. This comes on top of a general development of the world economy that is characterized by increasingly free and rapid movement of capital, making it ever harder for any national government to buck world economic and financial trends. In the face of all of this, it might well seem that most European governments are far less free these days to do what they want. As a consequence, it might also seem that the scope for politics to make a difference is narrower than it used to be.

These developments must, however, be set in a *social* context where, even in an era of rapidly expanding international travel, most people in most countries are not very mobile. The vast bulk of European populations are born, live, love, work and die in a single country, speak a native language that differs from that of people in other countries, define themselves in large part as German, French, Hungarian, Italian, Greek, and so on, and do not expect things to be different. Land is not mobile. Housing is not mobile. Hospitals, schools, roads, railway lines, airports, police and fire stations are not mobile. For the most part, labour is not very mobile. Social values may be changing, but there are still huge differences between countries in attitudes to matters such as abortion, euthanasia, single-parent families, the role of women in the workplace, and many other matters besides. Even in the realm of socio-economic policy, different core values translate into the very different social welfare systems we find in different European countries. The net result is that, while European governments have surely lost control of some of the key levers of macroeconomic policy, the big public policy differences we still find between states, and the big public policy shifts we sometimes observe within states, imply that representative government at a national level still does make a big difference. This is reflected in the fact that, when most people go to the polls in most elections, they have national issues on their minds – not global or European ones. Most voters *expect* national politics to make a difference (Schmidt, 1996; Garrett, 1998).

An intriguing source of indirect evidence on this matter arises from the fact that people whose financial interests are directly at stake often react strongly to changes in national political environments. Both before and after elections, we routinely read newspaper headlines about how financial markets react to election results and nominations to cabinet positions, showing us that big investors, who are presumably well informed, firmly believe politics makes a difference. There is a growing body of literature that systematically investigates the effects of political change on financial markets, and finds these to be considerable (Bernhard and Leblang, 2006).

We find much more direct evidence of the difference that politics can make in the transitions from communism experienced by central and eastern European states. Indeed, before this process took hold, a truly striking manifestation of how politics makes a difference could be seen crossing Checkpoint Charlie between what where once West and East Berlin, two parts of the same city operating under quite different political regimes. Money had to be changed, passports stamped, and the very look of the two places, one with a huge amount of brash advertising, one with none, was quite different. In a short space of time at the end of the 1980s, as a result of radical political developments in central and eastern European countries formerly under Soviet influence, everything changed. Berlin was reunited, and what had been East Germany joined the Federal Republic of Germany. Estonia, Latvia and Lithuania broke away from the Soviet Union, which itself imploded. The former Yugoslav federation disintegrated, and its constituent parts descended into bitter civil war. Throughout eastern Europe a massive programme of privatizing state assets was set in motion, and the economic environment was radically transformed. We shall return in more detail to some of these developments, but the main point to be made here is that events in eastern Europe have reminded us in no uncertain terms that politics really can make a huge difference when it comes to the big things (Stark and Bruszt, 1998; Orenstein, 2001; Grzymala-Busse and Jones-Luong, 2002).

The short and simple answer to the question 'Does politics make a difference?', therefore, is self-evidently 'Yes, it does!' The longer and more sophisticated answer, however, is surprisingly difficult to find, and presents us with some thorny intellectual puzzles. This is because, before we can assess the impact of any particular government in which we are interested, we need to know *what would have happened in the 'counterfactual' situation in which a different government had been running the same country at the same point in time*. Before we can begin to tackle this problem in a systematic way, we must first think about what senior politicians actually want, and about how these preferences translate into observable differences in public policy outcomes.

As when we considered the making and breaking of governments in Chapter 12, we might assume that politicians are motivated solely by the desire to gain and retain office. One implication of this in the present context is that they have an incentive to stimulate the economy in the run-up to elections, in order to spread wealth among voters and thereby increase their popularity. This pure office-seeking assumption about senior politicians leads us to expect that real economic outcomes such as employment and economic growth should improve before elections, followed by readjustment after the election, creating what has become known as the *political business cycle*. From this perspective, it shouldn't matter which parties are in office, since each would simply be concerned with staying in power. However, we know that different parties are linked historically to different segments of society, so that senior politicians do differ, even if only instrumentally, in their preferences about how, for example, wealth should be redistributed. A growing body of empirical work has found stronger evidence for partisan effects on economic outcomes than for electoral cycles, suggesting that party ideology *does* matter. For an excellent review of electoral and partisan cycles of public policy outcomes see Franzese (2002).

If we assume that party ideology matters, and that different parties would do things differently, the first step is to identify how parties actually differ in their preferred policy positions. This obviously has to be different from observing what parties do once they are in office. We cannot classify, for example, a party as 'right' because it enacted 'rightist' policies when it was in power. Our analysis of whether ideology affects policy outcomes would then be circular. As a second step, we must think about how party preferences translate into government ideology. This is easy when a single party is in power. It is then safe to assume that the party's election manifesto forms its basis for policymaking when in office. When there is a coalition of parties, however, this becomes more complicated, as parties have to compromise on policy decisions. Finally, we have to connect our measure of government ideology with some systematic measure of public policy outcomes. One of the most common measures uses patterns of government spending, data on which can be made comparable across countries and over time, and are usually easy to obtain. Researchers have paid particular attention to spending on all aspects of the welfare state, since this is the largest share of most nations' budgets, while there are sharp differences between parties on the left and parties on the right over preferred levels of welfare state spending.

If, after all these steps, we can show that changes in government ideology are indeed associated with changes in public policy outcomes, we are an important step closer to showing that politics does indeed make a difference. However, we also have to take into account the possibility that changes in real-world policy outcomes simply reflect changes in public opinion. If changes in public policy simply reflect changes in citizens' preferences, then we might conclude that *party* politics does not make a difference, as a different party in the same situation would have acted in exactly the same way. Separating public opinion and partisan effects is very difficult, but there is recent literature that uses carefully designed quasi-experimental research to address this particular question.

In the rest of this chapter we examine in greater detail these different steps that allow us to trace the ways in which representative government might make a measurable difference to real policy outcomes. We begin by motivating our discussions with some very clear-cut cases where, anecdotally at least, politics seems to have made a big difference. We then move on to look at how differences between the policies of different parties lead to differences in the policies of the governments these parties join. Next, we look at how differences in these government policy positions lead to measurable differences in policy outputs. Finally, we try to disentangle public opinion from partisan effects in an effort to form a judgement about whether having a different party in power would have led to different policy outcomes. At the end of it all we still cannot get around the fact that we have no way of knowing what would have happened in a particular country if the particular government for a particular period had been different. But the accumulated weight of evidence we assemble, on the basis of the various approaches we explore, will leave us in little doubt that representative government in modern Europe does make at least some difference to what goes on in the real world.

## 14.2 Clear-cut cases of policy impact

### 14.2.1 Privatization of state assets in Britain and eastern Europe

Massive privatizations of state assets in central and eastern European countries were an integral part of transitions from communist government. The onset of recent large-scale policies of privatizations in Europe, however, can be seen in Britain in the 1980s under the leadership of Margaret Thatcher. This is a clear-cut example of a major discontinuity between policy outputs under one government and those under its predecessor. The Conservative government that took office in 1979 had not fought the election on the basis of an explicit set of commitments on privatization. The privatizing of state assets in Britain started slowly, with denationalization of profitable companies, such as British Aerospace and Britoil, that were easy to sell at discounted flotation prices in a robust bull market. At the same time the Conservative government introduced an ambitious programme of selling a large proportion of the existing stock of rented public housing to its occupants.

The success of early privatizations fed back into Conservative policy and encouraged the party to boost the role given to privatization in the next party manifesto, so the 1983 election was fought and won by the Conservatives on the basis of a much more ambitious privatization programme. Soon afterwards, the victorious Conservative government privatized a series of massive public companies such as British Telecom, British Steel, the British Airports Authority, British Airways, Rolls-Royce and the Rover group. They also sold off enterprises that had previously been thought of as 'untouchable' basic services and natural monopolies: electricity, gas and water services, for example. Within seven years about 50 state corporations, about half the total state sector, had been sold to private investors. The shareholding population in Britain had increased threefold to almost 10 million people. Many billions of pounds sterling had been raised for the government by the sale of state assets. It is estimated that, by 1992, total privatization proceeds in Britain totalled 12 per cent of British GDP (Boix, 1998). On any account, the privatization programmes of successive Conservative governments in Britain involved a massive partisan redirection of public policy that would not have taken place under most conceivable alternative administrations (Feigenbaum et al., 1999). Representative government, without any doubt at all, made a big difference in this case.

If what happened in Britain during the 1980s was big, what happened in central and eastern Europe during the 1990s was an order of magnitude bigger. We obviously do not have space here to do justice to the huge topic of the privatization of state assets during transitions from communism, but some general patterns speak for themselves. What is striking about these huge eastern European privatization programmes is that, while they present complex intellectual challenges, they were all achieved very quickly. In each case, the main political challenges in these countries were to establish stable political institutions. Discussions of the specifics of privatization policy, while obviously central to these transitions from communism, played second fiddle to the main political imperative. As Stark and Bruszt (1998) point out, post-communist privatization policy had to confront three big issues. The first concerned selection and valuation of the state assets to be disposed of. In terms of setting a value on assets selected for privatization, the main choice was between having the assets valued by bureaucrats or letting the market decide. The second issue concerned who would be entitled to acquire these assets. Here, the big decision was between seeing individual citizens as having first call on the assets being disposed of, on the one hand, and private corporations, on the other. The third issue concerned the resources that could be used to acquire these assets. The obvious resource is money, but citizens of the transition states tended to have very little money, and would have been unable to compete against the resources available in international capital markets. One alternative is to give priority to people in particular *positions*, for example workers and managers in the enterprises concerned.

Politicians of different political stripes, in different eastern European countries, came to different conclusions about these important policy dilemmas. In the Czech Republic, for example, a primary objective was to get state enterprises into the hands of private citizens as fast as possible, after which they could be traded, and market forces would determine at least their price, if not their value. All adult citizens were given a fixed set of investment vouchers, for which they had to pay a registration fee, which could then be exchanged for shares in companies being privatized. Risk-averse citizens could put all their vouchers into safe and stable companies, which would command a high price in vouchers, while others might prefer to invest their limited stock of vouchers in more risky companies, offering lower-priced shares with potentially greater returns but a higher risk of failure. Poland also adopted a version of the voucher system, but Hungary took a different route, in general giving much more of a role in the privatization process to the managers and employees of the enterprises concerned. While a massive privatization of state assets that would have been inconceivable under previous political arrangements was a common priority for almost all post-communist regimes, different governments opted for very different types of privatization programme. Politics made a big difference in these cases. For comprehensive overviews of this, see Stark and Bruszt (1998), Roland (2000), Megginson and Netter (2001), Orenstein (2001) and Appel (2004).

## 14.2.2  Withdrawal of Spanish troops from Iraq

Despite the desire of many senior European politicians for a common European foreign policy, and notwithstanding the appointment in December 2009 of an EU High Representative for Foreign Affairs and Security Policy (discussed in Chapter 5), foreign policy remains a key policy area in which individual European governments can make a big difference. This was clearly illustrated in the variegated responses of different European governments in 2003 to the US-led military intervention in Iraq. Some major western European governments – Britain, Spain and Italy, for example – were staunch allies of the US. Others – notably France and Germany – were far more sceptical. There was no common European position on this vital foreign policy issue. But events that unfolded in Spain following 11 March 2004 show that politics can make a big difference to the foreign policy positions of a single state. March 11 was a Thursday, and Spain was in the final stages of an election campaign with voting due at the weekend. That morning, commuter trains pulled into the main Madrid rail station loaded with passengers and carrying bombs hidden by terrorists that were primed to go off, causing maximum damage, when the trains arrived at their platforms. There was a shocking toll of death and serious injury. José Aznar's conservative government, one of US President Bush's strongest European supporters on Iraq, implausibly blamed Basque separatists for the atrocity. This move was widely perceived as an attempt to sway the election in the government's favour, since any implication that the bombing was the act of Islamic terrorists (evidence for which was already in the hands of Spain's security services) could have resulted in voters punishing Aznar for sending a sizeable contingent of Spanish troops to Iraq. The elections were not postponed, and voting went ahead in a hothouse atmosphere. The result was the defeat of the Aznar government and a surprise victory for the socialist opposition, led by José Zapatero. The socialists had campaigned against Spanish intervention in Iraq, and immediately after taking office Zapatero announced that all Spanish troops would be withdrawn as soon as possible from Iraqi soil. They were home in Spain within weeks.

We shall never know for certain whether the Madrid bombing, or Aznar's fumbled attempt to shift the blame for this to the Basques, changed the way people voted in the 2004 election in Spain. What is certain, however, is that Spanish voters did in the event vote to change their government; that they elected a party hostile to the outgoing government's policy of Spanish involvement in Iraq; that Spanish withdrawal from Iraq was announced immediately after the election; and that this withdrawal did actually take place shortly afterwards. In this case, therefore, we see a textbook case of representative government in action.

## 14.3  Party preferences and government policy

### 14.3.1  Party manifestos and government policy programmes

The first step along the rocky road from what is promised at election time to what is actually done by governments in office is to compare parties' election manifestos with the policy positions of the governments they join. The latter are recorded in the official policy programmes typically published by newly formed governments as part of the investiture process, and in the formal statements of official government policy that are typically issued at the beginning of each new session of parliament. A key area of party policy in modern Europe, for example, is the running of the economy. This, of course, generates many policy problems related to unemployment, inflation, exchange rates, investment, government spending, and so on. A group of researchers in the Comparative Manifestos Project (CMP) has systematically analysed party manifestos and government declarations in many countries over the entire post-war period, assessing the relative emphasis that each policy document gives to various aspects of economic policy, as well as to many other themes. For a description of the work of the CMP, and a huge amount of data of party policy positions in many European countries, see Budge *et al.* (1987, 2001) and Klingemann *et al.* (2006). We can compare the policy promises that parties make to voters at election time with what *governments* comprising those same parties propose to do, having won the election and taken power. We do this by conducting a content analysis of party manifestos and comparing this with a content analysis of government policy declarations. Laver and Budge have edited a collection of analyses making precisely these comparisons (Laver and Budge, 1992; see also Debus, 2008).

The general pattern found by Laver and Budge is fairly straightforward. On the one hand, there is a group of countries, for example Norway and Denmark, in which there has typically been clear-cut alternation of power between coalitions or single-party governments of the centre left and coalitions of the centre right. In such countries there is little overlap between the parties who are in cabinets of the centre left and those in cabinets of the centre right. In such countries we do tend to see significant shifts in the ideological complexion of government policy declarations, depending upon which parties are in power. In these cases the acid test is that it is possible to infer the party composition of a government just by looking at the government's published policies. When this happens, the partisan composition of the cabinet has clearly made a difference to government policy. On the other hand, there is a group of countries, such as Italy before 1994 or Germany before 1998, in which a single party was a more or less permanent fixture of government, albeit with a changing set of coalition partners. The alternation of government parties between elections has typically also been only partial in a number of other European countries: the Netherlands, Luxembourg and Austria, for example. Comparing party manifestos with government policy declarations in these cases, we find that the more limited turnover in the partisan composition of the government is much more difficult to track in the changing substance of government policy declarations. Adding or subtracting parties from the cabinet in these cases makes less of a difference to government policy.

Overall, therefore, the limited evidence available suggests that parties do make a difference to the *published policy programmes* of European governments. This is far more clear-cut when the entire party membership of the cabinet is likely to change from one government to the next, and far less obvious when partisan turnover between governments is only partial.

## 14.3.2 Redeeming campaign pledges

It is one thing for a party to announce, when it has just formed a government, that it is going to redeem a particular campaign pledge. It is quite another thing for it actually to do this. The next big step on the path that takes us from the promises made by politicians in an election campaign to what actually happens in the real world is the redeeming of campaign pledges. Before we can get down to the systematic analysis of this matter, however, we must deal with a number of tricky methodological problems.

First, we must decide in a systematic way *what is a genuine pledge to voters and what is a piece of mere campaign rhetoric* that no sensible person would take seriously. This, of course, is a highly subjective matter. It has to do with how specific the promise is, with how literally it is intended to be taken by those who hear it, and with whether a campaign pledge proposes real actions or merely expresses pious hopes and aspirations. Promises to 'make this great country of ours a better place to live in' or to 'banish hunger and poverty from the face of the earth' ought not to be seen as campaign pledges in any real sense of the word. They are either too vague to be taken seriously, or no more than lofty aspirations. In contrast, a promise to 'increase old age pensions by 10 per cent over the next two years' is an explicit statement about something within the competence of any government, for which the person making the pledge can be held to account.

We must also decide *who to blame* when campaign pledges are not redeemed. Has the politician who promised to double the rate of economic growth broken that pledge if he or she has honestly tried as hard as possible but has nonetheless failed to do this? Has that politician broken the pledge if he or she doesn't try at all? Has the pledge been broken if the politician doesn't try very hard? If we are going to excuse pledges that are thwarted for reasons beyond the control of the person who makes them, then someone will have to call the score, pledge by pledge, on who was to blame for the breaking of each.

A third problem relates to the business of giving credit for pledges that do appear to have been redeemed. After all, if some politician promises that 'the sun will rise tomorrow' and the sun does indeed rise the next morning, we shall hardly be inclined to give any credit for this. Finally, there is the problem that many campaign pledges tend to be carried out a little bit; few are enacted in their full splendour. Some limited progress may be made on cutting public spending or reforming the tax system, for example. Unemployment may be reduced somewhat, quite possibly not thanks to the government of the day. To classify these as pledges broken or as pledges fulfilled is a matter of highly subjective judgement, in an environment where the politicians themselves almost invariably claim credit for good outcomes and try to dodge the blame for bad ones.

There are no easy solutions to these problems. The solution adopted by most scholars doing empirical research on the redemption of campaign pledges in Europe is to agonize about the types of problem we have outlined above and then get down to work and do the best they can. Much of the early work on the fulfilment of campaign pledges in Europe related to Britain. The first detailed study was conducted by Richard Rose, who compared the record of redeemed pledges for the 1970–1974 Conservative government with that for the 1974–1979 Labour government. His conclusion, confounding the sceptics, was that manifesto pledges do make a difference, that 'Conservative and Labour governments act consistently with the Manifesto model of governing; in office they do the majority of things to which they pledge themselves' (Rose, 1980: 64). Those same sceptics might retort that this conclusion is a product of an exclusive concentration on manifesto pledges that Rose deems 'doable'. This is compounded by the fact that one reason why the record of these parties seems so good is that they promise to do many things that are straightforward and uncontroversial. Rose finds that about half of all pledges are non-partisan, representing a consensus between the parties. Such pledges are easy to make, and are much easier to carry out than others. Whether we should set much store by them, when trying to decide whether politicians keep their promises, is another matter.

Terry Royed extended this work to a comprehensive comparative evaluation of the role of campaign pledges in Britain and the United States, looking at the relative rates of fulfilment of pledges made by government and opposition parties. Using a more precise definition of a campaign pledge than earlier authors, she found that over 80 per cent of pledges made in Conservative election manifestos were enacted by the Conservative governments of 1979–1983 and 1983–1987 – a significantly higher rate than that found in the US. The high rate of pledge fulfilment by the government party in Britain compares with a much lower rate for the opposition party. (Opposition party pledges may be enacted if these make the same promises as those made by the parties that go on to government.) In fact, when government and opposition disagreed in Britain, Royed found that the opposition had almost zero chance of seeing its pledges enacted (Royed, 1996).

While most of the research on the fulfilment of campaign pledges has been conducted in countries where one-party government is the norm, Thomson investigated the fulfilment of campaign pledges in the Dutch coalition system during the 1980s and 1990s, and this work was subsequently extended to Ireland (Thomson, 2001; Costello and Thomson, 2008). The expectation in a coalition system is that fewer pledges will be fulfilled, because of the policy compromises between parties that must be made in order to form a government. Not only must some pledges be dropped as part of the process of compromise, but the subsequent need to do deals with other parties also provides a ready-made excuse for the non-fulfilment of campaign pledges. Using comparable definitions of pledges in the Netherlands and Britain, Thomson found that rates of pledge fulfilment there were close to 80 per cent in Britain as opposed to about 50 per cent, or even less, in the Netherlands. Pledges made by parties that subsequently join Dutch coalition governments are indeed less likely to be redeemed than pledges made by parties that go on to form single-party governments in Britain.

Coalition systems create a more complex environment for the fulfilment of campaign pledges than that created by single-party governments, and Thomson's work throws useful light on this. He found, for example, that campaign pledges are more likely to be enacted if the party that made them controls the cabinet ministry with jurisdiction over the policy area in question. He found that pledges are more likely to be enacted once they have found their way into the formal agreement signed between the government parties. And he found that pledges are more likely to be enacted if they represent a consensus between the government parties. When a single party controls all cabinet seats, these issues do not arise. When power is shared between parties, Thomson's work suggests that the level of consensus between cabinet partners, the specific policy agreement between them, and the allocation of cabinet portfolios to different parties, all have an impact on the redemption by parties of pledges made during election campaigns.

Summing up the research results we report above, these do suggest that politicians honour more of their campaign pledges than sceptics, rivals and journalists typically give them credit for. This may in part be an artefact of the data, arising because researchers regard as firm pledges only proposals that can be carried out. It may also be a product of real-world party competition, if politicians tend to promise a lot of easy and uncontroversial things precisely so that they can go back to the voters and boast about how they fulfilled most of their promises. Politicians may anticipate all the easy things that they can actually deliver, and make a great song and dance at election time about promising to deliver them. Notwithstanding these reservations, however, the growing body of work on this topic suggests that politicians do redeem campaign pledges to a greater degree than many cynics had previously thought. Representative government does seem to make a difference in this particular sense.

## 14.4 Government policy and changes in public policy outcomes

The next link in the chain of causality that connects the preferences of ordinary citizens to the public policies that are implemented in the real world concerns the relationship between changes in government policies and changes in actual policy outputs. This link has been the subject of extensive research by political scientists. In addition to the tough problem we have already discussed, the problem of establishing, counterfactually, what *would* have happened had a different government been in power, we also encounter tricky measurement problems. How do we measure changes in actual government policy outputs in a systematic and valid way? Crudely, we want to measure 'what actually happens', but so much actually happens that we face a difficult problem of deciding what to measure.

Scholars have used one of three basic approaches to measuring the policy positions of governments. One traditional if fairly crude method is to code cabinets as 'left' or 'right', or 'left-leaning' or 'right-leaning'. This approach is not at all as rough and ready as it might seem at first sight. As we noted in Chapter 2, most elections in parliamentary democracies are essentially fought out between few, typically two, prospective candidates for the position of prime minister. These fights typically resolve into contests between candidate PMs from centre left and centre right. It is easy to see, from day-to-day political discussion and commentary, which candidate PM 'won' the election and went into government. It is precisely these big differences that we expect to have big effects on public policy.

A much more direct way to measure government policy positions makes use of the fact that most governments issue official policy declarations. These often emerge directly out of government formation negotiations between different party leaders. They may also emerge when the government makes an official policy statement to parliament at the beginning of the legislative session. Examples of this are *Queen's speeches* in Britain, when the Queen reads an official statement of government policy, written not by her but by the government. Just as party manifestos can be systematically coded for policy content, the same approach can be applied to official government policy declarations, although this approach suffers from the problem that there is not always an 'official' government policy declaration of this type (Laver and Budge, 1992).

A third way to measure government policy positions is to assume that government policy is some specified combination of the policies of individual government parties. One-party governments are assumed to implement the policies of the party in power. Multiparty coalitions are assumed to implement, for example, some weighted average of the policies of the parties in power – weighting each party by its parliamentary seat share (Kim and Fording, 2002). The is a somewhat ad hoc approach, since it in effect assumes that party seat shares are all that matters in government formation, and not the complex set of factors we reviewed at some length in Chapter 12. Alternatives would be to assume that government policy is the policy of the median party in the coalition on the most important policy dimension, or that the policy in each area is the policy of the minister with jurisdiction over this area (Laver and Shepsle, 1996). Notwithstanding this, the weighted average approach has been used by a number of authors because it is easy to understand and simple to use, given commonly available data.

As we noted above, a trickier problem arises from the need to measure 'what actually happens' in relation to government policy outputs. In what follows, we address this problem in three ways. We first look at the effect of government partisanship at a given time in a given country on the overall level of social spending in that country. This is a crude approach, since many different factors drive patterns of government social spending. In addition to the state of the global economy, these factors include, for example, proportions of citizens who are of elderly and other aspects of the demographic structure. We move on to look at patterns of government spending in more precise areas of public policy, which gives us a better chance of finding out the extent to which government policy outputs are *demand driven* by large-scale demographic factors or *supply driven* by differences in the policy positions of government members. Finally, we look at aspects of government policy that do not have spending implications. At the end of all this, we shall not have found the killer piece of evidence that governments do make a difference, but we shall have assembled a portfolio of small pieces of evidence that all point in this direction.

## 14.4.1 Differences in public spending between and within countries

Whenever public policy has implications for public spending, we have at least one hard indicator of what the government is actually doing. Patterns in the flow of public spending, and links between these patterns and the partisan composition of the government, have been the subject of a large volume of academic research. Basic patterns of public spending in modern western European states can be seen in Table 14.1. The first two columns of data in this table give alternative indicators of the average ideological complexion of European governments. The first column gives average shares of cabinet seats in each country controlled by social democratic and other left-wing parties over the 50-year era from 1950 to 1999. The second column reports an index of the average ideological complexion of governments forming between 1960 and 1999. This index would score 1.0 if a country had been governed by a right-dominated government for the entire period, and 5.0 if it had been governed by a left-dominated government for the entire period. Countries are ranked in the table according to the average ideological complexion of their governments. Ireland experienced the lowest incidence of left-wing parties in government over this post-war era, Norway and Sweden the highest. It is very important to note that we do not use data on the ideological composition of governments from these periods because we do not have more up-to-date information. We do this because we are interested in cause and effect, and therefore want to establish a time sequence. We want to see how the ideological composition of governments over the last half of the twentieth century affects the government policy outputs we can measure in the early part of the twenty-first century.

The third column of data in Table 14.1 therefore shows total public spending in each country, expressed as a percentage of the overall gross domestic product (GDP), averaged over the decade 2000–2009, the decade immediately following the era for which we measure the extent of left-leaning or right-leaning of governments. The top panel of the table shows that government spending as a percentage of GDP does tend to be higher in western European countries, such as Denmark, Austria and Sweden, with a long history of left-wing participation in government. In countries such as Ireland, on the other hand, which experienced extensive right-wing participation in government, the proportion of GDP devoted to public spending tends to be low. There are, however, striking exceptions. France, Belgium and Italy had substantial right-wing participation in government during the second half of the twentieth century, and yet had relatively high levels of public spending in the first decade of the twenty-first century.

**TABLE 14.1** Relationship between long-term ideological complexion of government and government spending

| Country | Social democrat and left % of total cabinet seats 1950–1999 | Mean left score of government 1960–1999 | Total general government expenditure as % of GDP 2000–2009 | Public social expenditure as % of GDP 2000–2009 |
|---|---|---|---|---|
| *Western Europe* | | | | |
| Ireland | 14.5 | 1.5 | 36.0 | 9.9 |
| Italy | 15.0 | 2.3 | 48.3 | 17.1 |
| Netherlands | 21.7 | 1.9 | 46.2 | 11.1 |
| Switzerland | 23.8 | 2.0 | 34.9 | 11.3 |
| France | 24.3 | 2.3 | 52.9 | 17.6 |
| Germany | 24.5 | 2.3 | 46.4 | 18.6 |
| Belgium | 29.5 | 2.3 | 50.2 | 15.8 |
| Portugal | 30.0 | 2.0 | 46.1 | 14.2 |
| UK | 30.8 | 2.3 | 43.7 | 13.0 |
| Finland | 35.0 | 2.6 | 49.7 | 16.3 |
| Denmark | 53.3 | 3.0 | 53.8 | 16.1 |
| Greece | 55.0 | 2.7 | 45.6 | 16.7 |
| Spain | 57.6 | 3.4 | 39.7 | 12.1 |
| Austria | 59.7 | 3.3 | 50.9 | 18.9 |
| Norway | 71.5 | 3.5 | 43.7 | 13.5 |
| Sweden | 77.5 | 4.0 | 54.3 | 16.5 |
| Correlation with left score of government | | | 0.43 | 0.38 |
| *Eastern Europe* | 1990–1999 | 1990–1999 | | |
| Latvia | 16.0 | 2.3 | 36.9 | 9.6 |
| Czech Republic | 19.6 | 1.7 | 44.5 | 12.6 |
| Slovakia | 21.3 | 2.0 | 40.5 | 12.6 |
| Bulgaria | 24.7 | 2.5 | 39.8 | 11.9 |
| Poland | 32.8 | 2.7 | 43.4 | 15.7 |
| Slovenia | 35.4 | 2.6 | 45.9 | 15.7 |
| Hungary | 35.5 | 2.4 | 49.4 | 14.3 |
| Estonia | 44.3 | 2.5 | 36.3 | 9.7 |
| Lithuania | 49.5 | 3.3 | 35.9 | 10.1 |
| Romania | 65.8 | 3.3 | 35.9 | 9.6 |

*Sources*: Left cabinet seat shares: western Europe, Swank (2009); eastern Europe, Armingeon *et al.* (2010). Left score of government: Armingeon *et al.* (2009, 2010). Public spending data: Eurostat (2010).

### 14.4.2 Differences in welfare state effort

The grand total of all public spending, however, covers a multitude of sins. It stretches from welfare to weapons of mass destruction, from old-age pensions to high-security prisons. The final column of data in Table 14.1 therefore shows the level of government *social* expenditure, on matters such as social welfare, pensions, education, housing, and so on. Social expenditure not only constitutes the lion's share of the annual budget, it is also the strongest instrument for redistributive policies, on which left and right most clearly diverge ideologically. The figures show more or less the same pattern as for overall government spending. Countries such as Ireland and Switzerland, which tended to have more right-wing governments, also had distinctly lower levels of public social expenditure. Austria and the Scandinavian countries, which have tended to have more left-wing participation in government, are at the other end of the social expenditure scale. Correlations between measures of public spending and left-wing participation in government are also given in Table 14.1. They show there is a systematic pattern within western Europe, albeit a rather weak one, linking a tradition of left-wing government to higher levels of public spending. In this very general sense, representative government does make some difference.

The bottom panel of Table 14.1 gives the much more limited information available for the central and eastern European countries we consider. The obvious difference is that there has not yet been enough time, following the long post-war era of communist government, to establish long-term trends in the ideological complexion of democratically elected governments in these countries. Therefore we cannot draw reliable conclusions about the relationship between the long-run ideological complexion of the government and patterns of public expenditure. What we do note is that these central and eastern European countries are on a par with their western European neighbours in terms of overall government spending as a proportion of GDP and, perhaps surprisingly, at the low end of the spectrum when it comes to social public expenditure.

One place to look for evidence on whether governments make a difference is to look at whether *changes in the parties of government* in a given country tend to be associated with *changing patterns of public spending*. We must obviously take account of the fact that major patterns of public spending can be shifted only a tiny amount from one year to the next, as well as the fact that many factors other than government policy, from global recessions to environmental disasters, may affect patterns of government spending from year to year. Other factors, including the number of parties in government or the number of spending ministers, can also boost government spending (Perotti and Kontopoulos, 2002; Bawn and Rosenbluth, 2006). Keeping our focus on partisan policy differences, however, governments can in practice have an impact on spending patterns only at the margin, controlling *year-to-year changes in spending flows* much more than they control the overall scale of spending. The actual level of welfare or defence spending, for example, might be much higher in one country than in another, not because of the current political situation but as a result of the interplay of a complex set of historical and structural factors. What an incoming government can do in the short and medium run is to cut or boost welfare or defence spending. But even savage cuts and generous boosts do not, unless they are repeated year after year, have a huge impact on the overall level of spending in these areas.

Schmidt tackled this problem by analysing the year-by-year changes in government spending in a wide range of countries, relating this to the partisan composition of the cabinet, controlling for important economic variables such as the growth rate and changes in the level of unemployment (Schmidt, 1996). He found evidence that having left or centre-right parties in office contributed to annual increases in the level of government spending, while having a right-wing party in government contributed to decreases in this. His conclusion (p. 177) was that 'social democracy and Christian democracy have been major political "engines" in the growth of government ... in contrast to this, conservative parties have been major inhibitors of the growth of government in modern democracies.'

As Margaret Thatcher found in Britain, massive efforts of political will are needed to produce modest effects on public spending. It is not surprising, therefore, that we do not find public spending patterns changing dramatically with every change in government. In general, however, the accumulating evidence does suggest that parties do make a difference to patterns of public spending. The overall effects that we can observe on public spending are small. However, if we focus on particular spending areas, or on the impact of long-serving single-party governments, the impact of parties on public spending becomes easier to see. All of this means that if we look carefully and know what we are looking for, we should indeed be able to detect a change in the party composition of governments by examining patterns of public spending, our acid test of whether representative government does make a difference. For an extended discussion and empirical analyses of this argument, see Garrett (1998), Huber and Stephens (2001), Franzese (2002) and Allan and Scruggs (2004).

### 14.4.3 Beyond public spending

There is much more to public policy than public spending. Even in the realm of economic management, for example, governments have policies on matters such as industrial relations and income inequality. Since governments may try to modify the distribution of both wealth and income using the welfare and tax systems, it is interesting to explore the impact of the partisan composition of the government on income redistribution. This can take place in two quite distinct stages. The first concerns gross income, the aspect of inequality on which trade unions can have the greatest impact. The second concerns net income, which reflects how take-home pay is affected by taxes and by transfer payments in the social welfare system. This is the aspect of inequality on which governments can have the greatest impact. The bigger the change in inequality between gross and net income, the greater the impact of public policy.

Muller conducted an extensive comparative analysis of the impact of politics on income distribution, controlling for a wide range of factors and analysing data from a long list of countries (Muller, 1989). He found that socialist governmental strength depresses the income share going to the richest 20 per cent of the population and narrows the gap between the richest and the poorest 20 per cent. Conservative governmental strength increases the income share going to the richest 20 per cent and widens the income gap between the richest and middle income groups. He found that the negative impact of conservative parties on income equality is greater than the positive impact of socialist parties and concludes, unequivocally (p. 396), that 'most of the cross national variation [in income inequality] is explained by the inegalitarian influence of strong conservative parties.' More recent work on this same topic, however, frames the question in a different way and gets a different answer. Scheve and Stasavage use income tax data to investigate factors affecting the share of income earned by the top 1 and top 10 per cent of the population over the entire twentieth century (Scheve and Stasavage, 2009). Using this tighter definition of income inequality over a much longer time period, they do not find statistically significant partisan effects, and argue that, while *cross country* variations in inequality may be associated with partisan differences, there is much less evidence that, over the long run *within individual countries*, partisan changes affect income inequality.

Focusing more precisely on one specific area of tax policy, taxes on labour, Cusack and Beramendi found significant partisan effects, with left-wing governments more likely to have higher taxes on labour and right-wing governments to have lower ones (Cusack and Beramendi, 2006). Similarly, Allan and Scruggs analysed the relationship between partisan composition of the government and proportions of full-time income replaced by unemployment assistance and sick pay (Allan and Scruggs, 2004). They found quite clear-cut, though time-specific, partisan effects on public policy. Until the 1980s, during the era of welfare state expansion, they found a clear tendency for left-wing governments to increase both unemployment benefits and sick pay in real terms, with no opposing tendency for right-wing governments to reduce this. After the 1980s, during the era of welfare state contraction, they found quite the reverse, with right-wing governments tending to reduce the real value of these welfare benefits, and left-wing governments having no significant effect on this.

Moving beyond economic policy – to environmental or foreign policy, for example, or policy on social and moral issues – we might expect policy to be more responsive to politics, since shifting the dead weight of public finances is not a requirement for policy change. For a number of aspects of social policy, furthermore, particularly those involving the reform of existing social legislation, either action is taken or it is not. Thus either the law on abortion, on divorce, or on capital punishment is reformed, or it is not. Public policy is easy to see in these areas for particular cases – laws on such matters do change following changes in the partisan control of governments – but there is unfortunately little comparative research assessing the impact of parties on them.

However, one recent study did find significant partisan effects on environmental policy outputs (Knill *et al.*, 2010). The authors measured environmental policy outputs using information on a very specific and comparable set of environmental policy measures that might be enacted in any country, dealing with control of air and water pollution, for example, or soil protection (Table 1 of their paper shows these data). They measured party policy stances on the environment using data on coded party manifestos generated by the Comparative Manifestos Project, referred to earlier in this chapter. Their findings are that, controlling for a large number of potentially confounding factors,

> 66 [n]ot only the inclusion of Green parties in a coalition government, but also the extent to which governmental parties stress environmentalism in their election manifestos, have positive and significant impacts on the number of policy adoptions. There is, however, no evidence that governments with a more left-wing ideological 'centre of gravity' or a strong left-wing party positively influence the number of policy adoptions.
>
> *(Knill et al., 2010: 325)* 99

Governments comprising parties that are more concerned to protect the environment do indeed enact more policies designed to protect the environment – although more left-wing governments do not systematically tend to do this.

## 14.5  Conditional partisan effects on public policy

It is of course likely that, while parties do make a difference to public policy outputs, the type of difference they make depends sharply on the political institutions in the country under investigation. We might think of these as *conditional* partisan effects on public policy. For example, Margit Tavits classified countries as having either consensual or majoritarian decision-making institutions – taking into account the proportionality of the electoral system, the prevalence of coalition cabinets, and the degree of corporatist or 'tripartite' decision-making that we discussed in some detail in Chapter 13 (Tavits, 2004). She found partisan effects on public spending similar to those we described above; but she also found that the *interaction* of left-leaning cabinets with strong consensual decision-making institutions leads to disproportionately higher levels of government spending.

In a similar vein, Andre Blais and colleagues found that the majority status of the cabinet has an important effect on the relationship between government partisanship and government policy (Blais *et al.*, 1993). In particular (p. 55), 'parties do not make a difference when the government is a minority one.' As we saw in Chapter 12, minority governments typically remain in place because they are at the centre of the political spectrum, and opposition to them is divided. They can govern quite possibly *because* they do not make a difference by imposing their will over the will of a majority of the legislature. In contrast, Blais *et al.* found that majority governments controlled exclusively by the left did increase overall public spending by a small but statistically significant amount, relative to majority governments controlled exclusively by the right. As might be expected, the difference between left- and right-wing governments is greater for governments that have held office for five years or more. Thus, considering the overall size of the public sector, Blais *et al.* conclude (p. 57) that 'governments of the left spend a little more than governments of the right. Parties do make a difference, but a small one. That difference, moreover, is confined to majority governments and takes time to set in.' For general discussions of ways in which partisan effects on public policy may interact with other institutional factors, see Garrett (1998) and Swank (2002).

## 14.6  Public opinion or partisanship?

Our final problem is to distinguish secular changes in public opinion about desirable public policies from the direct impact of political parties. This is important, because, if both election results and public policy shifts are simply responding to secular changes in public opinion, we cannot say that having different parties in power *in itself* makes a difference to policy outputs in the real world. This brings us back to our original hard question about what would have happened in the *counterfactual* situation in which a government comprising different parties had been running the country.

One recent influential approach has thrown new light on this question, using a methodological device known as a *regression-discontinuity* design. The innovation is to focus on policy outputs in local government – in the case we discuss here, Swedish municipalities (on which, see Chapter 6) – and in particular to compare municipalities in which the electoral margin of victory for one party was tiny, but in which the eventual partisan winner was different (Pettersson-Lidbom, 2008). In these cases we can assume that public opinion in the matching pairs of municipalities is very similar, and that it is 'as if' the election outcome and partisan composition of the local government had been decided randomly. Using this methodological device, we come close to a classical experimental design, with municipalities randomly allocated to left-leaning 'treatment' and right-leaning 'control' groups, providing us with much more leverage over counterfactual questions. This allows for a firm conclusion in the case of Swedish municipalities that

> 66 [the] size of the party effect is quite large. For example, left-wing governments have about 2%–3% higher expenditures as a share of income and about 7% lower unemployment rates than right-wing governments. Left-wing governments also employ about 4% more workers.
>
> *(Pettersson-Lidbom, 2008: 1052)* 99

While of course confined in this particular piece of research to Swedish municipalities, the impressive thing about the regression-discontinuity method behind this conclusion is that it allows us to infer quite directly, more so than in most of the other pieces of empirical research that we report, that it is the *partisanship* of the government that is making a difference.

## 14.7 So, *does* politics make a difference?

The relentless globalization of the world economy has appeared to strip much discretion over the all-important domain of economic policy away from national politicians, at the same time as the EU has taken ever more policy responsibilities from the national governments of member states. This implies that *national* politics, at least, should make less of a difference than it did in the past. To counter this there is strong evidence that, for European voters at least, it is choosing national politicians, rather than MEPs or local councillors, that really matters to them. We can see the self-evident impact made by particular parties on the ambitious privatization programmes of the 1980s and 1990s, both in Britain and in eastern Europe, as well as the dramatic effect on Spanish foreign policy of the 2004 general election there. It is hard to deny that representative government made a big difference in these cases. Looking more closely, we can also see that almost all recent research on the matter concludes that party politics has a measurable impact on policy outputs in the real world, although more years will need to pass before systematic patterns on this can be seen for central and eastern Europe.

Party policies do differ, and it does seem to be the case that government policy programmes tend to reflect the published policies of parties in the government, at least in those countries where there is a clear-cut alternation in the party composition of governments. Promises made to the voters in the heat of an election campaign, even if these promises are carefully selected as 'doable', do seem to be redeemed. It does seem that changes in government spending flows can be partially predicted by major changes in the partisan composition of the government. Spending flows are very sticky, but the evidence suggests that they can, from time to time, be shifted as a result of a major effort of political will. And it does seem to be the case that non-expenditure aspects of policy, whether on the economy or the environment, change according to the partisan composition of the government.

Does all of this add up to mean that representative government makes a difference? The weight of evidence suggests that it does, which gives us all one important reason to get excited about the results of elections.

## References

**Allan, James P. and Lyle Scruggs** (2004) 'Political partisanship and welfare state reform in advanced industrial societies', *American Journal of Political Science*, 48 (3), 496–512.

**Appel, Hilary** (2004) *A New Capitalist Order: Privatization and Ideology in Russia and Eastern Europe*, University of Pittsburgh Press, Pittsburgh, PA.

**Armingeon, Klaus, Panajotis Potolidis, Marlène Gerber and Philipp Leimgruber** (2009) *Comparative Political Data Set 1960–2007*, Institute of Political Science, University of Berne.

**Armingeon, Klaus, Romana Careja, Sarah Engler, Panajotis Potolidis, Marlène Gerber and Philipp Leimgruber** (2010) *Comparative Political Data Set III 1990–2008*, Institute of Political Science, University of Berne.

**Bawn, Kathleen and Frances Rosenbluth** (2006) 'Short versus long coalitions: electoral accountability and the size of the public sector', *American Journal of Political Science*, 50 (2), 251–265.

**Bernhard, William and David Leblang** (2006) *Democratic Processes and Financial Markets: Pricing Politics*, Cambridge University Press, Cambridge.

**Blais, Andre, Donald Blake and Stephane Dion** (1993) 'Do parties make a difference? Parties and the size of government in liberal democracies', *American Journal of Political Science*, 37 (1), 40–62.

**Boix, Carles** (1998) *Political Parties, Growth and Equality: Conservative and Social Democratic Economic Strategies in the World Economy*, Cambridge University Press, Cambridge.

**Budge, Ian, David Robertson and Derek Hearl** (1987) *Ideology, Strategy and Party Change: Spatial Analyses of Post-War Election Programmes in 19 Democracies*, Cambridge University Press, Cambridge.

**Budge, Ian, Hans-Dieter Klingemann, Andrea Volkens, Judith Bara, Eric Tannenbaum, Richard Fording, Derek Hearl, Hee Min Kim, Michael McDonald and Silvia Mendes** (2001) *Mapping Policy Preferences: Parties, Electors and Governments: 1945–1998: Estimates for Parties, Electors and Governments 1945–1998*, Oxford University Press, Oxford.

**Costello, Rory and Robert Thomson** (2008) 'Election pledges and their enactment in coalition governments: a comparative analysis of Ireland', *Journal of Elections, Public Opinion and Parties*, 18 (3), 239–256.

**Cusack, Thomas R. and Pablo Beramendi** (2006) 'Taxing work', *European Journal of Political Research*, 45 (1), 43–73.

**Debus, Marc** (2008) 'Office and policy payoffs in coalition governments', *Party Politics*, 14 (5), 515–538.

**Eurostat** (2010) *Government Finance Statistics 2010*. Available from http://epp.eurostat.ec.europa.eu/portal/page/portal/statistics/themes

**Feigenbaum, Harvey, Jeffrey Henig and Chris Hamnet** (1999) *Shrinking the State: The Political Underpinnings of Privatization*, Cambridge University Press, Cambridge.

**Franzese, Robert** (2002) *Macroeconomic Policies of Developed Democracies*, Cambridge University Press, Cambridge.

**Garrett, Geoffrey** (1998) *Partisan Politics in the Global Economy*, Cambridge University Press, Cambridge.

**Grzymala-Busse, Anna and Pauline Jones-Luong** (2002) 'Reconceptualizing the state: lessons from post-communism', *Politics and Society*, 30 (4), 529–554.

**Huber, Evelyne and John D. Stephens** (2001) *Development and Crisis of the Welfare State: Parties and Policies in Global Markets*, University of Chicago Press, Chicago.

**Kim, Heemin and Richard C. Fording** (2002) 'Government partisanship in Western democracies, 1945–1998', *European Journal of Political Research*, 41 (2), 187–206.

**Klingemann, Hans-Dieter, Andrea Volkens, Judith Bara, Ian Budge and Michael McDonald** (2006) *Mapping Policy Preferences II: Estimates for Parties, Electors, and Governments in Eastern Europe, European Union and OECD 1990–2003*, Oxford University Press, Oxford.

**Knill, Christoph, Marc Debus and Stephan Heichel** (2010) 'Do parties matter in internationalised policy areas? The impact of political parties on environmental policy outputs in 18 OECD countries, 1970–2000', *European Journal of Political Research*, 49 (3), 301–336.

**Laver, Michael and Ian Budge** (1992) *Party Policy and Government Coalitions*, St Martin's Press, New York.

**Laver, Michael and Kenneth A. Shepsle** (1996) *Making and Breaking Governments: Cabinets and Legislatures in Parliamentary Democracies*, Cambridge University Press, New York.

**Megginson, William M. and Jeffry M. Netter** (2001) 'From state to market: a survey of empirical studies of privatization', *Journal of Economic Literature*, 39 (2), 321–389.

**Muller, Edward N.** (1989) 'Distribution of income in advanced capitalist states: political parties, labour unions, and the international economy', *European Journal of Political Research*, 17 (4), 367–400.

**Orenstein, Mitchell A.** (2001) *Out of the Red: Building Capitalism and Democracy in Postcommunist Europe*, University of Michigan Press, Ann Arbor, MI.

**Perotti, Roberto and Yianos Kontopoulos** (2002) 'Fragmented fiscal policy', *Journal of Public Economics*, 86 (2), 191–222.

**Pettersson-Lidbom, Per** (2008) 'Do parties matter for economic outcomes? A regression-discontinuity approach', *Journal of European Economic Association*, 6 (5), 1037–1056.

**Roland, Gerard** (2000) *Transition and Economics: Politics, Markets, and Firms*, MIT Press, Cambridge, MA.

**Rose, Richard** (1980) *Do Parties Make a Difference?*, Chatham House, Chatham, NJ.

**Royed, Terry** (1996) 'Testing the mandate model in Britain and the United States: evidence from the Reagan and Thatcher eras', *British Journal of Political Science*, 26 (1), 45–80.

**Scheve, Kenneth and David Stasavage** (2009) 'Institutions, partisanship, and inequality in the long run', *World Politics*, 61 (2), 215–253.

**Schmidt, Manfred** (1996) 'When parties matter: a review of the possibilities and limits of partisan influence on public policy', *European Journal of Political Research*, 30 (2), 155–183.

**Stark, David and Laszlo Bruszt** (1998) *Postsocialist Pathways: Transforming Politics and Property in East Central Europe*, Cambridge University Press, Cambridge.

**Swank, Duane** (2002) *Global Capital, Political Institutions, and Policy Change in Developed Welfare States*, Cambridge University Press, Cambridge.

**Swank, Duane** (2009) *Electoral, Legislative, and Government Strength of Political Parties by Ideological Group in Capitalist Democracies, 1950–2006: A Database*, Department of Political Science, Marquette University.

**Tavits, Margit** (2004) 'The size of government in majoritarian and consensus democracies', *Comparative Political Studies*, 37 (3), 340–359.

**Thomson, Robert** (2001) 'The programme to policy linkage: the fulfilment of election pledges on socio-economic policy in the Netherlands, 1986–1998', *European Journal of Political Research*, 40 (2), 171–197.

**Vachudova, Milada** (2005) *Europe Undivided: Democracy, Leverage and Integration After Communism*, Oxford University Press, Oxford.

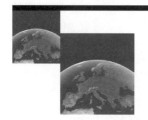

# Index